Get the eBook FREE!

(PDF, ePub, Kindle, and liveBook all included)

We believe that once you buy a book from us, you should be able to read it in any format we have available. To get electronic versions of this book at no additional cost to you, purchase and then register this book at the Manning website.

Go to https://www.manning.com/freebook and follow the instructions to complete your pBook registration.

That's it!
Thanks from Manning!

Self-Sovereign Identity

Self-Sovereign Identity

DECENTRALIZED DIGITAL IDENTITY
AND VERIFIABLE CREDENTIALS

ALEX PREUKSCHAT
DRUMMOND REED

Foreword by DOC SEARLS

MANNING
SHELTER ISLAND

For online information and ordering of this and other Manning books, please visit www.manning.com. The publisher offers discounts on this book when ordered in quantity. For more information, please contact

    Special Sales Department
    Manning Publications Co.
    20 Baldwin Road
    PO Box 761
    Shelter Island, NY 11964
    Email: orders@manning.com

Manning Publications Co.
20 Baldwin Road
PO Box 761
Shelter Island, NY 11964

Development editor:	Toni Arritola
Technical development editor:	Alain Couniot
Review editor:	Aleks Dragosavljević
Production editor:	Lori Weidert
Copy editor:	Tiffany Taylor
Proofreader:	Jason Everett
Typesetter:	Marija Tudor
Cover designer:	Marija Tudor

ISBN 9781617296598
Printed in the United States of America

Thanks to my family, who have always been patient with me as I explore new projects and paths, as in writing this book. Thanks to the identity and blockchain community that helped me discover and learn about many aspects of my true self and where the world might be going with decentralized technologies.
—A.P.

To the love of my life, who has been waiting 33 years since we were married—and 22 years since I went down the digital identity rabbit hole—just to see the one simple thing I promised her—getting rid of those &^%$# passwords!

To my two sons: this is a path to a better world that I've been beating since you were born. I hope you both are able to trod upon it all of your days—and the days of your children's children's children.
—D.R.

brief contents

contents

11 SSI governance frameworks   248
DRUMMOND REED

foreword

Self-Sovereign Identity offers a new perspective on one of the most important challenges of society and computing: safely managing our digital identities. As early adopters and leaders in this area, Drummond Reed and Alex Preukschat are uniquely able to introduce the technology and potential of SSI. In this book, you'll enjoy not just their insights, but also the experiences of many other leading practitioners.

Most of what we call "identity" isn't. It's identifiers. It's how some organization identifies you: as a citizen, a driver, a member, a student. Those organizations may issue you an "ID" in the form of a passport, license, or membership card, but that isn't your identity. It's their identifier. Your identity—how you are known to yourself and to others—is something else: something much more personal and under your control as a self-sovereign human being.

Self-sovereign identity (SSI) gives you control over what others need to verify about you, on a need-to-know basis. Simply put, it replaces identifiers with verifiable credentials. And, in the process, it greatly simplifies and speeds up the way identity works in the digital world for both individuals and organizations.

It's early in the evolution of SSI; but not so early that we can't get answers to the questions of how it's going to work and where it's going. Both of those questions are of massive importance and why this book is essential at this juncture in the history of digital technology. Reading and learning what's being shared here might be the most leveraged thing you do this decade.

But before you start, it should help to visit how identity already works in the natural world where we live and breathe. True, it can get complicated, but it's not broken. For example, if an Inuit family from Qikiqtaaluk wants to name their kid Anuun or Issorartuyok, they do, and the world copes. If the same kid later wants to call himself Steve, he does. Again, the world copes. So does Steve.

Much of that coping is done by Steve *not* identifying himself unless he needs to and then *not* revealing more than what's required. In most cases, Steve isn't accessing a service but merely engaging with other people, in ways so casual that no harm comes if the other person forgets Steve's name or how he introduced himself. In fact, most of what happens in the social realms of the natural world is free of identifiers and free of recollection.

How we create and cope with identity in the natural world has lately come to be called *self-sovereign*, at least among digital identity obsessives such as myself. And there are a lot of us now. (Search for *self+sovereign+identity* and see how many results you get.)

Self-sovereign identity starts by recognizing that the kind of naming we get from our parents, tribes, and selves is at the root level of how identity works in the natural world—and that this is where we need to start in the digital world, as well. In the simplest possible terms, *we need to be in control of it.*

Our main problem with identity in the digital world is that we started with no personal control at all. Everything we did with identity began with organizations' need to put names in databases. This served the administrative convenience of those organizations—and our convenience only to the degree that we are known separately to all the organizations that know us.

If we want to make SSI work on the internet, we have to respect the deeply human need for self-determination. That means we need to provide individuals with new ways to obey Kim Cameron's seven laws of identity (explained in chapter 1), most notably *individual control and consent, minimum disclosure for a constrained use,* and *justifiable parties.*

Put as simply as possible, we need to give administrative systems no more personal information than they require. We call that information *verifiable credentials.* Note that these are still not *identities.* They are nothing more or less than what the other party needs to know.

This book explains how all this works. The authors of those explanations are pioneers and explorers working to make new systems while helping old ones adapt. The main point you need to keep in mind as you read the book is this: *it's personal.*

Self-sovereign identity isn't about administrative systems. It's about you and me and how we selectively disclose personal information to others on a need-to-know basis, and being able to do that at scale. Getting to scale requires lots of help and alignment from the world's incumbent identity systems. But those systems by themselves are not self-sovereign. You and I are. That's the key. And it's the only one that will open the true future of digital identity.

—Doc Searls

preface

On February 4, 2021, the following graphic appeared in the *New York Times*, under the headline "Pack your 'Vaccine Passport'":

The article, written by travel reporter Tariro Mzezewa, starts by explaining this new concept:

> *A vaccination pass or passport is documentation proving that you have been vaccinated against Covid-19. Some versions will also allow people to show that they have tested negative for the virus, and therefore can more easily travel. The versions being worked on now by airlines, industry groups, nonprofits and technology companies will be something you can pull up on your mobile phone as an app or part of your digital wallet.*

The technology described in that paragraph—more formally known as *verifiable credentials*—is precisely the subject of this book. As the article goes on to explain, the worldwide rollout of

Illustration by Lloyd Miller

COVID-19 vaccinations has triggered an avalanche of demand for verifiable digital credentials that will enable individuals to easily, safely, and privately prove they have received a COVID-19 test result or vaccination.

One of the most visible of these initiatives is the World Health Organization (WHO) Smart Vaccination Certificate Working Group (https://www.who.int/groups/smart-vaccination-certificate-working-group). When co-author Drummond Reed was invited in January 2021 to participate in this working group, he was asked if he knew of written materials the working group could read to quickly come up to speed on the open standards, open source code, governance frameworks, and real-world deployments of verifiable credentials.

Given that this book—a product of two years of work by over 45 contributing authors—was just entering the final stages of production, Drummond recommended several of the most relevant chapters. Manning obliged by providing WHO with a digital version of the requested chapters within 24 hours so they could be ready for the first meeting of the working group held February 3–5, 2021.

This anecdote illustrates the extraordinary way in which the COVID-19 pandemic is catapulting verifiable credentials and self-sovereign identity (SSI) technology into the internet mainstream. Just as pharmaceutical manufacturers were called upon to compress the normal four- to five-year vaccination development process into a matter of months, verifiable credential developers and integrators are being asked to compress a typical four- to five-year technology adoption cycle into a matter of months.

It is entirely possible that by the time you read this book, you will have received a "jab" and at the same time—or shortly thereafter—downloaded a digital wallet app, scanned a QR code, and received a verifiable digital credential that you can use to prove the precise vaccination you received.

In short, you will already be using SSI. And so will millions of other people around the world, to help reopen global travel and our economies.

We hope this is just the tip of the iceberg for what SSI can do—for all of us. And that will be just the very beginning of the SSI story.

Of course, we could not have anticipated this when we began work on this book over two years ago. But neither was it a cosmic coincidence. Rather, it was an outcome of the mutual trajectories of our careers. Here is a little about our own stories.

ALEX PREUKSCHAT

In 2014, driven by my interest in cryptocurrencies, I published the world's first graphic novel about Bitcoin, called *Bitcoin: The Hunt for Satoshi Nakamoto*. Over the next several years, it was published in English, Spanish, Russian, Korean, and Brazilian Portuguese. Then, in 2017, I published *Blockchain: The Industrial Revolution of the Internet* (Spanish title: *Blockchain: la revolución industrial de internet*) (Gestión, 2017). This became the reference book about blockchain in the Spanish-speaking world. Shortly after that, inspired by David Birch's book *Identity Is the New Money* (London Publishing Partnership, 2014), I was motivated to begin working in the decentralized digital identity space. I connected with one of the leading companies in that space, where I had the opportunity to begin collaborating with identity evangelist Drummond Reed and cryptographic SSI pioneer Jason Law.

Realizing the enormous potential of this new space being called *self-sovereign identity* or *SSI*, I founded SSIMeetup.org with Drummond's and Jason's support. It was an open community-based platform to share knowledge about SSI with the world. Everything on SSIMeetup is available via a Creative Commons Share-Alike (CC BY SA) license that allows free usage with attribution. I began doing webinars with leaders in the SSI space.

With each webinar I did, and the resulting discussion on social media, I realized the growing role that decentralized digital identity was going to play in the world. It unified everything I had been doing since 2006—understanding money, learning about blockchain, and discovering the power of a new type of digital identity.

That's when I had the inspiration to invite Drummond to join forces to create what we hoped would become the reference book about SSI—one that would explain this fascinating topic not just to developers, but to business people, policymakers, university students, and myriad others who could start to put SSI to work in their everyday lives.

Decentralized digital identity encompasses much more than the word *identity* means by itself. Decentralized digital identity is at the crossroads of the free software / open source world, peer-to-peer technologies, cryptography, and game theory. In the same way that Bitcoin taught us that these disciplines could be recombined to create something new, decentralized digital identity recombines them into something so unique and powerful that some are calling it "the Internet for identity."

While Bitcoin touches on one of the pillars of society—money—identity is even more fundamental. Human lives are too short to fully recognize and appreciate the cycles and changes of mankind, but exponential technologies like blockchain, artificial intelligence, biotech, and many others have accelerated the pace of change much faster than ever before in history. And while we crave change because of the opportunities it provides, we also fear it because of what we might lose in life as we know it.

SSI is one of the expressions of how the world as we know it may be completely reshaped. The outcome of that reshaped world is very hard to predict. It could fulfill the most beautiful of utopian dreams for a better and more balanced society. It could also become a dystopian nightmare.

Of course, the former is my hope for SSI. However, I'm not sure exactly how we will get there and which technologies will create the future "identity stack." What I do know is that it is crucial for as many of us as possible to be involved and understand the opportunities to create that world together. So I have poured my heart and soul into bringing together some of the finest identity evangelists, thinkers, pioneers, and business people I could find, to share their visions of this future.

Each of them speaks in their own voice and shares their own vision—and they are by no means all the same. Much of what you will learn from this book is the different paths and tools they advocate for building that vision. But they share the belief that SSI can become a game-changing tool in your life—personally, professionally, economically, even politically. In short, if you take this path and one day look back at it, I think you'll be glad you did.

DRUMMOND REED

Alex is one persuasive dude. Ever since this technology—nay,—*movement* that we now call SSI started to really take hold in 2018, I have been busier than at any time in my life. And here Alex was asking me to help him put together an entire book on this subject—when I couldn't even find the time to write the papers and blog posts about SSI that were part of my day job at Evernym (and my night job at that time as a trustee of the Sovrin Foundation).

Was he crazy? On the other hand, the webinars I had started giving on his SSI-Meetup.org site were proving to be surprisingly popular, and Alex made a compelling case that *someone* needed to pull together a complete book about SSI to support its growth and transition into the internet mainstream. What finally convinced me was his argument that I would only need to contribute a few chapters about the areas I was most deeply involved with; for the rest of the book, we would curate contributions from other experts across the growing SSI industry and other industries adopting SSI.

We were about a year into that effort—with much of our own content written and many chapters from contributing authors already received—when the COVID-19 pandemic hit. Suddenly our worlds (and everyone else's) were turned upside down. We halted work on the book and, for a time, were not even sure if we would be able to continue. Then, after a few months, we realized that not only was SSI continuing to move ahead in the market, but also the need for verifiable digital credentials as a new tool for dealing with proof of COVID-19 testing—and soon vaccinations—might lead to even greater demand for SSI-based solutions.

Even so, when we restarted work on the book in the late summer of 2020, we had no idea of the tsunami of demand for SSI that was about to be unleashed by the COVID-19 earthquake. Once the arrival of the first vaccinations became imminent in late 2020, the market demand for an easy, fast, hard-to-forge solution for individuals to be able to prove their health status went through the roof. Within weeks, multiple initiatives to issue digital vaccination credentials were announced, including the World Health Organization (WHO) Smart Vaccination Certificate, IATA Travel Pass, Vaccination Credentials Initiative, AOK Pass, and Good Health Pass Collaborative.

Suddenly it was clear to everyone that SSI was about to go mainstream—and that by the end of 2021, verifiable digital credentials would be in the digital wallets of tens of millions of people around the world, being used multiple times every day for travel, work, sports, and other situations where proof of health status was needed for public safety.

Of course, I am heartbroken that a global public health crisis was what catapulted SSI into the limelight. But if SSI can play a part in helping us deal with the tremendous human and economic pain caused by this once-a-century pandemic, then I want to do anything I can to help. And if publishing this book can assist governments, public health authorities, healthcare providers, companies, universities, cities, and other communities around the world in understanding and implementing SSI more quickly, then I am all the more thankful that Alex persuaded me to help write it.

acknowledgments

From the very outset, we envisioned this book as a collaborative effort among many experts in the emerging SSI industry. So we want to begin by thanking each and every one of these contributing authors—this book would have been impossible without them.

A special thanks to several of these authors who did double duty by either contributing to multiple chapters or helping us review and edit multiple chapters. These include some of the best technology writers we know: Daniel Hardman, Markus Sabadello, and Shannon Appelcline.

When Oscar Lage was introduced to Mike Stevens of Manning Publications, that meeting sparked the first conversations in 2018 that kicked off this book. A special thanks to Oscar for that introduction and for co-authoring chapter 19 about the Internet of Things (IoT).

At Manning, we'd like to thank our development editor Toni Arritola for her perseverance as first our workloads and then the pandemic (and then both) stretched the limits of everyone's patience. Her wise words about taking one step at a time paid off in the long run as she promised. Thank you also to our copy editor, Tiffany Taylor, for moving swiftly and surely through a book that was very complicated to edit. And our thanks to Mike Stevens and the rest of the editorial team at Manning for pushing through the extra hardships of the pandemic to get this book to publication.

To all the reviewers: Michele Adduci, Sambasiva Andaluri, Davide Cadamuro, Joe Justesen, Justin Coulston, Konstantin Eremin, Chris Giblin, Milorad Imbra, Michael Jensen, Aidan McCarty, Steven H. McCown, Sanket Naik, Zhu Vlad Navitski, Julien Pohie, Simone Sguazza, Stephen John Warnett, Brian van den Broek, Hilde Van Gysel, Sumit Pal Vincent, Chris Viner, Aleksander Wielgorski, Maura Wilder, and Sander Zegveld, your suggestions helped make this a better book.

We also want to thank our compatriots at Evernym, with whom we have been collectively forging SSI since 2016, especially co-founders Timothy Ruff and Jason Law and the outstanding executive team, board, employees, contractors, and investors. A special mention to Misty Bledsoe, who helped in the early drafting stages of the book.

Thank you also to all the board members, staff, and volunteers of the Sovrin Foundation who helped build the first global public utility for SSI and made it real for the world.

Finally, a shout-out to the co-authors of the Hyperledger Aries RFC that laid the groundwork for the ToIP Foundation: John Jordan, Dan Gisolfi, Darrell O'Donnell, Daniel Hardman, and Matthew Davie.

DRUMMOND REED

I would never have been in a position to write this book without partners and investors who believed in the vision of decentralized data sharing and digital trust infrastructure. This started with my Pattern Language consulting partner, Nick Duckstein, and my Intermind co-founder, Peter Heymann, together with anchor investors Barry Forman and Bill Bauce. It continued with Cordance board chair John Jordan, CEO Vince Calouri, and CFO Lon Weise. And a very special thanks to the executive team at Respect Network—Steve Havas, Les Chasen, and Gary Zimmerman—board chair Gary Rowe, and board members Barry Forman, John Kelly, and Bill Donnelly. I am deeply indebted to all the investors, led by Bill Donnelly and Mike and Trish Peters, whose belief in the Respect Network vision carried us through to the acquisition by Evernym.

I am also very thankful for the unending contributions of the three founders of the Internet Identity Workshop: Kaliya "Identity Woman" Young, Phil Windley, and Doc Searls. You are the moral center of the SSI movement and have kept it on the right path for 15 years. I am also grateful to Joyce Searls for being the ever-steady hand guiding the SSI community with her practical wisdom and effortless clarity every step of the way.

Finally, I want to thank every last member of the global SSI community, so wonderfully described in chapter 16 by Kaliya and Infominer. You have built everything we describe in this book. It is your passion and lifeforce that will "make it so." Keep going!

about this book

Welcome to *Self-Sovereign Identity*! Our goal in this book is to first introduce you to the basic concept of self-sovereign identity (SSI) and give you a solid understanding of why we've reached a watershed in the evolution of internet identity. The rest of the book is designed to help you deepen and broaden that understanding.

We do that not just through our voices, but also through the voices of leading SSI experts from around the world. They share their perspectives on various aspects of SSI: the technology, the business and legal implications, the social impact, and even the philosophy.

We bring you specific examples of how SSI might be used to solve real market problems so you can see how it might be applied in your work, family, company, school, industry, city, or country. We also hope this book will open the discussion for other stakeholders and perspectives from society.

Who should read this book

Our philosophy in composing this book is that successful developers, product managers, and business leaders will benefit from a holistic overview of a foundational new technology in order to see the bigger picture, understand the cross-disciplinary currents, and assimilate upcoming major market shifts into their work. SSI is one of those cases that demands a mix of visions and skill sets to shape it into the future we want for the world.

The target audience of this book is quite varied. We expect all these people to be interested in different parts of the book:

- Architects and developers
- Product managers

- User experience (UX) designers
- Business and government leaders
- Legal professionals
- Privacy, decentralization and blockchain enthusiasts

For this reason, we have structured the book in four major parts:

Part 1 provides an overall introduction to SSI—where it came from, how it works, and its major features and benefits. This should be applicable to all audiences interested in SSI.

Part 2 is specifically designed for technical professionals who want a deeper understanding of the major components and design patterns of SSI architecture without having to go quite all the way down to the code level.

Part 3 goes in the other direction: it focuses on the cultural and philosophical origin story of SSI and what this means about its ultimate impact on the internet and society. This part is especially relevant for readers interested in privacy and those who want to understand the origins of the SSI and decentralization movements.

Part 4 explores what SSI means for business and government through industry experts who convey how it applies to their specific market vertical. This part is especially relevant for architects and product managers who need to convey to their business leaders why SSI matters to their business units—be it opportunity, threat, or disruption.

Chapter 1 introduces the basic concept of SSI and explains how and why it represents the third era of digital identity for the internet. The three remaining chapters in part 1 are as follows:

- *Chapter 2*—Introduces digital credentials, wallets, agents, decentralized identifiers, blockchains, and governance frameworks
- *Chapter 3*—Presents seven examples of how the building blocks can be put together to solve hard problems of digital trust
- *Chapter 4*—Discusses 5 categories summarizing the 25 key benefits of SSI infrastructure

We recommend reading these chapters sequentially as they apply to anyone interested in SSI, regardless of whether your focus is technical, product, business, or policy.

In *part 2*, we dive deeper into SSI technology for those readers who want to seriously understand how it works. While these chapters do not go quite all the way down to the code level (with the exception of some code examples in chapters 7 and 8), they cover all major aspects of SSI architecture and should provide a solid technical introduction for architects, developers, system administrators, and anyone who wants to understand the SSI "stack." The topics are as follows:

- *Chapter 5*—SSI architecture—the big picture
- *Chapter 6*—Basic cryptography for SSI

- *Chapter 7*—Verifiable credentials
- *Chapter 8*—DIDs (decentralized identifiers)
- *Chapter 9*—Digital wallets and digital agents
- *Chapter 10*—Decentralized key management
- *Chapter 11*—SSI governance frameworks

In *part 3*, we broaden the focus to look at SSI as a movement that crosses traditional industry boundaries and encompasses larger technological, legal, social, or political infrastructure. We explore how the decentralization technologies powering SSI are rooted in even larger shifts of philosophy, society, and culture. We discuss the various points of view—historical, political, sociological—on what is and is not considered SSI and why. We hope this part is relevant for all readers, but if your focus is primarily on SSI technology or business solutions you can choose to skip it. Here are the topics:

- *Chapter 12*—Controlling your identity with open source
- *Chapter 13*—Cypherpunks: the origin of decentralization
- *Chapter 14*—Identity for a peaceful society
- *Chapter 15*—Centralization vs decentralization believers
- *Chapter 16*—The evolution of the SSI community
- *Chapter 17*—Identity is money

In *part 4*, we look at how SSI will impact different categories of business, industry, and government—with chapters written by individual experts in each of these verticals. Most chapters end with a SSI Scorecard summary (defined in Chapter 4) assessing the impact of SSI on that particular vertical market:

- *Chapter 18*—Explaining SSI value to business
- *Chapter 19*—The Internet of Things Opportunity
- *Chapter 20*—Animal care and guardianship just became crystal clear
- *Chapter 21*—Open democracy and e-voting
- *Chapter 22*—Supply-chain management powered by SSI in Pharma
- *Chapter 23*—Canada: Enabling Self-Sovereign Identity
- *Chapter 24*—From eIDAS to SSI in the European Union

Finally, we have a set of appendices that provide additional tools and perspectives to help you further explore SSI:

- *Appendix A*—A roster of 11 additional chapters that appear in the liveBook edition of this book to continue the exploration we begin in part 4 of vertical market applications of SSI as explained by experts in each market.
- *Appendix B*—A list of famous essays about SSI, published on the web, that go deep into special topics on SSI and decentralized digital trust infrastructure.
- *Appendix C*—"The Path to Self-Sovereign Identity," by Christopher Allen. This is the original landmark essay about SSI written by the co-author of the SSL protocol that finally standardized encryption on the web.

- *Appendix D*—"Identity in the Ethereum Blockchain Ecosystem," by Fabian Vogelsteller and Oliver Terbu. This is another landmark essay about SSI from one of the best-known developers in the Ethereum ecosystem together and the identity product lead at ConsenSys.
- *Appendix E*—"The Principles of SSI." We conclude the book with a listing of the 12 foundational principles of SSI developed by a global community project hosted by the Sovrin Foundation and published in 15 languages in December 2020.

About the code

The technical chapters of this book are mainly in part 2. Because of the wide-ranging architectural and design choices possible for SSI, the book in general does not go down to the code level. The exception is examples of verifiable credentials in JSON and JSON-LD in chapter 7 and DIDs and DID documents in chapter 8. However we also include numerous references to the major open source projects working on SSI components around the world, most of which are highly accessible.

liveBook discussion forum

Purchase of *Self-Sovereign Identity* includes free access to a private web forum run by Manning Publications where you can make comments about the book, ask technical questions, and receive help from the author and from other users. To access the forum, go to https://livebook.manning.com/#!/book/self-sovereign-identity/discussion. You can also learn more about Manning's forums and the rules of conduct at https://livebook.manning.com/#!/discussion.

Manning's commitment to our readers is to provide a venue where a meaningful dialogue between individual readers and between readers and the authors can take place. It is not a commitment to any specific amount of participation on the part of the authors, whose contribution to the forum remains voluntary (and unpaid). We suggest you try asking the authors some challenging questions lest their interest stray! The forum and the archives of previous discussions will be accessible from the publisher's website as long as the book is in print.

Other online resources

All chapters have references that can be relevant for further reading. We especially recommend the references in chapter 16, which covers the evolution of the internet identity and SSI communities.

Throughout the book, we have included references to SSIMeetup.org webinars whenever there is a webinar with more information about the corresponding chapter. You can also sign up for more updates related to the book at IdentityBook.info.

We especially recommend following these communities to stay current in the SSI space:

- W3C Verifiable Credentials Working Group, https://www.w3.org/groups/wg/vc

- W3C Decentralized Identifier (DID) Working Group, https://www.w3.org/2019/09/did-wg-charter.html
- W3C Credentials Community Group, https://www.w3.org/community/credentials
- Decentralized Identity Foundation, https://identity.foundation
- Sovrin Foundation, https://sovrin.org
- Trust over IP (ToIP) Foundation, https://trustoverip.org
- COVID-19 Credential Initiative, https://www.covidcreds.org

about the authors

ALEX PREUKSCHAT @AlexPreukschat

Alex is passionate about exploring the new horizons that exponential technologies offer for continuous social transformation as a process of self-discovery. He is the co-founder of Blockchain communities BlockchainEspana.com, focused on Spain; AlianzaBlockchain.org of Iberoamerican communities from Argentina, Chile, Colombia, Bolivia, Panama, Guatemala, Costa Rica, Mexico, and Spain; and SSI-Meetup.org which is focused on SSI knowledge sharing. He is the creator of the first Bitcoin graphic novel of the world (BitcoinComic.org) and the Spanish Blockchain bestseller Blockchain: the industrial revolution of the Internet (LibroBlockchain.com). He has also created a cryptocurrency mobile game with MoneyFunGames.com and is a 1729.com enthusiast. Alex was the Global Head of Strategic Blockchain Projects with Evernym and has worked and started a number of Blockchain and Technology ventures in his career. He studied at Universidad Pontificia Comillas-ICADE E-4 in Madrid (Spain) and ESB Reutlingen (Germany).

DRUMMOND REED @drummondreed

Drummond has spent over two decades working in internet identity, security, privacy, and governance. He joined Evernym as chief trust officer after Evernym acquired Respect Network, where he was co-founder and CEO. At the W3C, he is co-editor of the DID (Decentralized Identifiers) specification. At the Trust over IP Foundation, Drummond is a member of the Steering Committee and co-chair of the Governance Stack Working Group and Concepts and Terminology Working Group. At the Sovrin Foundation, he was one of the founding trustees and serves as co-chair of the Sovrin Governance Framework Working Group. For 10 years, he served as co-chair of the OASIS XDI Technical Committee, a semantic data interchange protocol that implements privacy by design. Prior to starting Respect Network, Drummond was executive director of two industry foundations: the Information Card Foundation and the Open Identity Exchange. He has also served as a founding board member of the OpenID Foundation, ISTPA, XDI.org, and Identity Commons. In 2002, he received the Digital Identity Pioneer Award from Digital ID World, and in 2013 he was cited as an OASIS Distinguished Contributor.

about the cover illustration

The figure on the cover of *Self-Sovereign Identity* is captioned "Marguerite of France." The illustration by Rigaud D'Aurellie is taken from a collection of works entitled *Costumes Historiques de la France*, published by the French Administration of Libraries in 1852. The collection includes fine drawings of historical costumes, monuments, statues, tombs, seals, coins, and more. Each illustration is finely drawn and colored by hand and the rich variety of drawings in the collection reminds us vividly of how culturally apart the world's regions, towns, villages, and neighborhoods were just over a century-and-a-half ago. Isolated from each other, people spoke different dialects and languages. In the streets or in the countryside, it was easy to identify where they lived and what their trade or station in life was just by their dress.

Dress codes have changed since then and the diversity by region, so rich at the time, has faded away. It is now hard to tell apart the inhabitants of different continents, let alone different towns or regions. Perhaps we have traded cultural diversity for a more varied personal life—certainly for a more varied and fast-paced technological life.

At a time when it is hard to tell one computer book from another, Manning celebrates the inventiveness and initiative of the computer business with book covers based on the rich diversity of regional life of two centuries ago, brought back to life by pictures from collections such as this one.

Part 1

An introduction to SSI

Although it started in 2015, self-sovereign identity (SSI) as a technology, industry, and movement is still very young. Many people working directly in the digital identity industry are likely to be familiar with it, but to those working in other industries—especially outside of tech—it may be a brand-new concept.

Part 1 gives you everything you need to know to become conversant in SSI, no matter where you are coming from. It is organized into four chapters:

- Chapter 1 begins with the fundamental reasons we need digital identity and why the first two generations of solutions (centralized identity and federated identity) have not solved the problem. It explains the origins of SSI as a new internet identity model based on blockchain, cloud, and mobile computing technology and paints a picture of the impact SSI is already having in e-commerce, finance, healthcare, and travel.
- Chapter 2 introduces the seven basic building blocks of SSI—including digital credentials, digital wallets, digital agents, and blockchains—at a level that should be comfortable for non-technologists.
- Chapter 3 takes the seven building blocks from Chapter 2 and shows how they can be put together to solve different scenarios in digital trust.
- Chapter 4 introduces the *SSI Scorecard* as a tool for systematically evaluating the major features and benefits of SSI (a tool we use again in part 4 to evaluate the impact of SSI on various industries and market verticals).

Why the internet is missing an identity layer—and why SSI can finally provide one

Alex Preukschat and Drummond Reed

Self-sovereign identity—commonly abbreviated SSI—is a new model for digital identity on the internet: i.e., how we prove who we are to the websites, services, and apps with which we need to establish trusted relationships to access or protect private information. Driven by new technologies and standards in cryptography, distributed networks, cloud computing, and smartphones, SSI is a paradigm shift for digital identity similar to other technology paradigm shifts: for example, the shift from keyboard-driven user interfaces (e.g., MS-DOS) to graphical user interfaces (e.g., Windows, Mac, iOS), or the shift from dumb phones to smartphones.

However, the SSI paradigm shift is deeper than just a technology shift—it is a shift in the underlying infrastructure and power dynamics of the internet itself. In this way, it is closer to other infrastructure paradigm shifts such as those in transportation:

- The shift from horse travel to train travel
- The shift from train travel to automobile travel
- The shift from automobile travel to airplanes and jet travel

Each of these shifts in technology resulted in deeper, structural changes to the shape and dynamics of society and commerce. The same is true of the paradigm shift to SSI. While the details are evolving rapidly, the "big picture" of SSI that has already emerged is remarkably coherent and compelling—and this is what is driving adoption.

In this book, we endeavor to explain this SSI paradigm shift in the most approachable way possible. Our motivation is not to impose our vision of the world on you but to humbly convey the technological, business, and social movements that have come together to make SSI possible. Our starting point is this claim:

> *The Internet was built without an identity layer.*
>
> —Kim Cameron, Chief Architecture of Identity, Microsoft [1]

What did Kim Cameron—Microsoft's chief architect for identity from 2004 to 2019—mean by that quote? What is an "identity layer?" Kim gives an answer in his groundbreaking series of essays called "The Laws of Identity," published on his blog over a series of months in 2004 and 2005:

> *The Internet was built without a way to know who and what you are connecting to. This limits what we can do with it and exposes us to growing dangers. If we do nothing, we will face rapidly proliferating episodes of theft and deception that will cumulatively erode public trust in the Internet.*

Kim was saying that when the internet was initially developed in the 1960s and 1970s by the U.S. military (sponsored by the Defense Advanced Research Projects Agency, or DARPA), the problem it was designed to solve was how to interconnect *machines* to share information and resources across multiple networks. The solution—packet-based data exchange and the TCP/IP protocol—was so brilliant that it finally enabled a true "network of networks" [1]. And the rest, as they say, is history.

What Kim was driving at, however, is that with the internet's TCP/IP protocol, you only know the *address of the machine* you are connecting to. That tells you nothing about the *person, organization, or thing* responsible for that machine and communicating with you. (Hackers have demonstrated how to change a computer's hardware [MAC] or IP address before it is sent to remote network devices. This makes it nearly impossible to rely on, or trust, current network-level identifiers.)

This seems like a fairly easy problem to solve—after all, people and organizations built the internet, and we control (or at least we think we do) all the "things" that are using it. So, how hard could it be to design a simple, standard way to identify the person, organization, or thing you are dealing with over the internet?

The answer turns out to be: *very, very hard.*

Why? In a nutshell, the original internet was not very big. The people using the network were mostly academic computer scientists. Most of them knew each other, and they all needed access to expensive machines and sophisticated technical skills to participate. So even though the internet was designed to be decentralized and to have no single points of failure, early on it was effectively a relatively small club.

Needless to say, that has changed completely. There are now billions of people and multiple billions of devices on the internet, and almost all of them are strangers. In this environment, the unfortunate truth is that there are many, many people who want to *deceive you* about who or what you are dealing with over the internet. Identity (or the lack of it) is one of the primary sources of cybercrime.

1.1 How bad has the problem become?

Recall the final sentence of Kim Cameron's 2005 prediction about the internet's missing identity layer: "If we do nothing, we will face rapidly proliferating episodes of theft and deception that will cumulatively erode public trust in the Internet."

Despite all the efforts to solve the internet identity problem, the lack of a breakthrough solution has proved Kim's prognosis true in spades. Never mind that by 2017, the average business user had to keep track of 191 passwords [2] or that username/password management has become the most hated consumer experience on the internet. That's just an inconvenience.

> **WHERE'S THE FOUL?** The deeper damage is in cybercrime, fraud, economic friction, and the ever-growing threats to our online privacy.

The litany of statistics goes on and on:

- IBM President and CEO Ginni Rometty described cybercrime as "the greatest threat to every profession, every industry, every company in the world" [3].
- Global cybercrime damages are predicted to cost $6 trillion annually by 2021 [4].
- Over 90% of American consumers believe they have lost control of how their personal information is collected and used by all kinds of entities [5].
- In 2016, three billion Yahoo accounts were hacked in one of the biggest breaches of all time [6].
- 80% of hacking-related breaches are due to compromised user passwords [7].
- The Equifax breach has cost the company over $4 billion in total [8].
- According to a 2014 study from Ctrl-Shift, the cost of identity-assurance processes exceeds £3.3 billion per annum in the UK alone [9].

Our failure to solve the internet identity problem is reaching the breaking point. Either we fix it, or the very future of the internet is in doubt.

1.2 Enter blockchain technology and decentralization

Like many disruptive innovations, breakthroughs can come from unexpected places. When Satoshi Nakamoto first published *Bitcoin: A Peer-to-Peer Electronic Cash System* in October 2008 [10], no one expected it could also inspire a fundamental transformation in how we think about identity and trust online.

Yet identity and money have been very closely intertwined for centuries—a history explored in rich and entertaining detail in David Birch's 2014 book *Identity is the New Money* [11] (read chapter 17 on money and identity for more details). So it is not surprising that by 2015, when Bitcoin's decentralized blockchain model had started to capture the attention of industry and the world press, it finally came to the internet identity community's attention.

At the Spring 2015 Internet Identity Workshop (IIW), a three-day gathering of internet identity experts that has been held twice a year every year since 2004, several sessions were held on "blockchain identity." That kicked off an informal group to study how best to apply blockchain tech to the challenges of user-centric identity management that IIW had been working on for over a decade. At the Fall 2015 event, that group reported out in a series of sessions that caught fire within the IIW community.

Two months later, the U.S. Department of Homeland Security Science & Technology division published a Small Business Innovation Research (SBIR) grant topic entitled "The Applicability of Blockchain Technology to Privacy Respecting Identity Management" [12]. It said:

> *The potential applicability of blockchain technology goes beyond crypto-currencies (which is simply an application built on top of that technology) to many other uses such as smart contracts, provenance and attribution, distributed validation of information, and more.*
>
> *This SBIR topic is focused on determining and demonstrating if classic information security concepts such as confidentiality, integrity, availability, non-repudiation and provenance as well as privacy concepts such as pseudonymity and selective disclosure of information can be built on top of the blockchain to provide a distributed, scalable approach to privacy respecting identity management.*

Here was a U.S. government agency proposing that the same principles of blockchain technology that power Bitcoin could potentially solve critical problems with the internet's missing identity layer. And it was not alone. The European Union was exploring decentralized digital identity via a number of initiatives (see the International Association for Trusted Blockchain Applications, https://inatba.org; the EU Blockchain Observatory & Forum, https://www.eublockchainforum.eu; and the European SSI Framework [eSSIF], https://ssimeetup.org/understanding-european-self-sovereign-identity-framework-essif-daniel-du-seuil-carlos-pastor-webinar-32), the Chinese government was making Blockchain technologies a national priority [13], and Korea was creating public/private consortia specifically for decentralized identity (http://didalliance.org). And they were all doing this for the same reason: the possibility of moving from centralized to *decentralized* digital identity systems.

But why was decentralization so important?

1.3   *The three models of digital identity*

That question is best answered by the evolutionary progression of internet identity models.

> **NOTE**   This way of describing the evolution of internet identity was first proposed by Timothy Ruff in 2018: "The Three Models of Digital Identity Relationships," Everynym, https://medium.com/evernym/the-three-models-of-digital-identity-relationships-ca0727cb5186.

1.3.1 *The centralized identity model*

The first model is the easiest to explain. It is the model we have long used with almost all identifiers and credentials such as government ID numbers, passports, identity cards, driving licenses, invoices, Facebook logins, Twitter handles, and so on. All of these are issued by centralized governments or service providers like banks or telecom companies. This centralized model is so prevalent in the real world that it can be divided into two types:

- *Scandinavian model*—Private companies (financial and telecom firms) provide a centralized digital identity service to interact with the government (TUPAS in Finland, BankID in Sweden, and so on)
- *Continental model*—In Europe, governments provide digital identity services to companies allowing interaction with their citizens.

NOTE These centralized models are described in the excellent 2016 World Economic Forum report "A Blueprint for Digital Identity" at http://www3.weforum.org/docs/WEF_A_Blueprint_for_Digital_Identity.pdf.

The centralized model is also the original form of internet identity—and the one that, in many cases, we still use today. You establish an identity by registering an *account* (typically a username and password) with a website, service, or application. For this reason, the model is also called *account-based identity*.

In figure 1.1, "You" are a dotted circle because, in the world of centralized identity, the real You doesn't exist without an account in some centralized system. The real You is given permission to plug into a website, service, or application because the Org is lending you credentials *that represent you* with limited controls and permissions. At the end of the day, those credentials belong to the Org. If you delete all your accounts at these centralized providers, your ability to access services will be revoked. The You in figure 1.1 will disap-

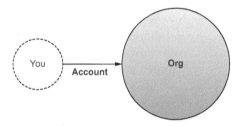

Figure 1.1 The relationship of an individual to a website (or application) under the internet's original centralized, account-based identity model

pear from the internet completely. Yet all the data about you will still belong to the Org, outside of your control.

That is only one of the many problems with centralized identity. Others include the following:

- The burden of remembering and managing all the usernames and passwords (and, in some cases, other multi-factor authentication tools such as one-time codes) falls entirely on *you.*

- Every site enforces its own security and privacy policies, and they are all different (a classic example is the maddingly different rules about passwords: minimum length, special characters allowed, and so on).
- None of your identity data is portable or reusable anywhere (users are warned to never reuse passwords).
- These centralized databases of personal data are giant honeypots that have led to some of the biggest data breaches in history.

1.3.2   The federated identity model

To alleviate some of the pain points of centralized identity, the industry developed a new model called *federated identity*. The basic idea is simple: insert a service provider called an *identity provider* (IDP) in the middle (figure 1.2).

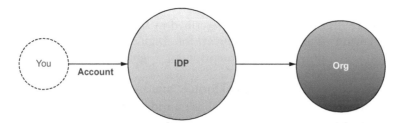

Figure 1.2   The three-way relationship involved in the federated identity model

Now you can just have one identity account with the IDP, and it, in turn, can log you in and share some basic identity data with any site, service, or app that uses that IDP. The collection of all the sites that use the same IDP (or group of IDPs) is called a *federation*. Within a federation, each of the Orgs is often called a *relying party* (RP).

Three generations of federated identity protocols have been developed since 2005—Security Assertion Markup Language (SAML), OAuth, and OpenID Connect—and they have all had some real success. Using these protocols, single sign-on (SSO) is now a standard feature of most corporate intranets and extranets.

Federated identity management (FIM) also started to catch on in the consumer internet, where it began to be called *user-centric identity*. Using protocols like OpenID Connect, *social login* buttons from Facebook, Google, Twitter, LinkedIn, etc. are now a standard feature on many consumer-facing websites (figure 1.3).

Figure 1.3   Examples of the proliferation of social login buttons that try to ease the pain of internet identity for mere mortals

Despite all the work that has gone into federated identity since 2005, it has still failed to provide us with the internet's missing identity layer. There are numerous reasons:

- There isn't one IDP that works with all sites, services, and apps. So users need accounts with multiple IDPs—and pretty soon, they start forgetting which IDP they used with which site, service, or app.
- Because they have to serve so many sites, IDPs must have "lowest common denominator" security and privacy policies.
- Many users—and many sites—are uncomfortable with having a "man in the middle" of all their relationships that can surveil a user's login activity across multiple sites.
- Large IDPs are some of the biggest honeypots for cybercrime.
- IDP accounts are no more portable than centralized identity accounts. If you leave an IDP like Google, Facebook, or Twitter, all those account logins are lost.
- Due to security and privacy concerns, IDPs are not in a position to help users securely share some of their most valuable personal data: passports, government identifiers, health data, financial data, etc.

1.3.3 The decentralized identity model

A new model, inspired by blockchain technology, first surfaced in 2015. (The FIDO [Fast IDenfication Online] Alliance started in 2013; however, it uses a hybrid approach where connections are peer-to-peer but key management is performed centrally by the FIDO Alliance rather than by a blockchain.) This model no longer relied on either centralized or federated identity providers but was fundamentally *decentralized*. It accelerated rapidly, assimilating new developments in cryptography, distributed databases, and decentralized networks. It began spawning new decentralized identity standards such as verifiable credentials (VCs) and decentralized identifiers (DIDs) that we explain in more detail in chapter 2 and part 2 of this book.

However, the most important difference in this model is that *it is no longer account-based*. Instead, it works like identity in the real world: i.e., it is based on a direct relationship between you and another party as *peers* (figure 1.4). Neither of you "provides," "controls," or "owns" the relationship with the other. This is true whether the other party is a person, an organization, or a thing.

In a peer-to-peer relationship, neither of you has an "account" with the other. Rather, you both share a *connection*. Neither of you fully "owns" this connection. It is like a string that you are both holding—if either one of you lets go, the string will drop. But as long as you both want it, the connection will persist.

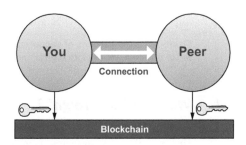

Figure 1.4 The peer-to-peer relationship enabled by the decentralized identity model— returning people to direct, private connections secured by public/private key cryptography

Peer-to-peer connections are inherently decentralized because any peer can connect to any other peer anywhere—exactly how the internet works. But how does this become an identity layer? And why does it need blockchain technology?

The answer lies in *public/private key cryptography*: a way of securing data via mathematical algorithms based on cryptographic keys held by each party. Instead of using blockchain technology for cryptocurrency, identity management uses it for *decentralized public key infrastructure* (DPKI). In the next few chapters, we'll go into this in greater detail. But in essence, blockchain technology and other decentralized network technologies can give us a strong, decentralized solution for

- *Exchanging public keys* directly to form private, secure connections between any two peers
- *Storing some of these public keys* on public blockchains to verify the signatures on *digital identity credentials* (aka *verifiable credentials*) that peers can exchange to provide proof of real-world identity

Ironically, this means the best overall analogy for the decentralized identity model is, in fact, exactly how we prove our identity every day in the real world: by getting out our wallet and showing the credentials we have obtained from other trusted parties. The difference is that with decentralized digital identity, we are doing this with *digital* wallets, *digital* credentials, and *digital* connections (figure 1.5).

Figure 1.5   The essence of decentralized digital identity: turning physical identity credentials in our physical wallets into digital credentials in digital wallets

1.4   Why "self-sovereign"?

As the decentralized digital identity model started to catch on, it quickly developed the moniker *self-sovereign identity* and then the acronym *SSI*. Initially, this term was quite controversial due to its connotations [14]. What made the term so "sticky" [15]—to the point that it is now the standard term for this new identity model used by top industry analyst firms and leading digital identity conferences around the world? (The European Identity Conference, hosted every spring by the EU analyst firm Kuppinger Cole, has a track called "Self-Sovereign Identity.")

Let's start with the word *sovereign*. This is not a word most of us use in everyday speech, so it has some cachet by itself. By definition, it is a powerful word—sometimes used as a direct synonym for *king* or *head of state*, but today also meaning *autonomous* or *independent*. The other frequent connotation is *sovereign nation* or *sovereign state*. The Dictionary.com definition of *sovereignty* is

> *the quality or state of being sovereign, or of having supreme power or authority; the status, dominion, power, or authority of a sovereign; royal rank or position; royalty.*

Add the word *self* in front of it, and suddenly the meaning stands out: "a person who is neither dependent on nor subjected to any other power or state." Given that, what individual would not want to be "self-sovereign"? Conversely, what government might not have serious concerns about its citizens flocking en masse to a new technology called "self-sovereign"?

But of course, the term we are discussing is not *self-sovereign* but *self-sovereign identity*. When you apply that term to a person, following our logic, it literally translates to

> *A person's identity that is neither dependent on nor subjected to any other power or state.*

Aha. Now we can finally understand why the term caught on. When it comes to expressing personal identity, many individuals worldwide will find that definition attractive. And many self-sovereign nations might gladly help endow their citizens with the power of self-sovereign identity—especially because, as we see in chapter 23, *government-issued identity does not compete with self-sovereign identity*. The two are highly complementary.

But we can also see why the term might be controversial—why, despite its power, it sometimes gets in the way of understanding the value of the decentralized identity model. Unfortunately, the term also tends to perpetuate two of the most persistent myths about SSI:

- *Self-sovereign identity is self-asserted identity.* That is, you are the only one who can make identity assertions about yourself. This, of course, is not true, any more than you could be the issuer of all the credentials in your physical wallet today. Most of the information about your identity comes from other trusted sources—that's the reason other parties are willing to rely on it.
- *Self-sovereign identity is just for people.* While the SSI model is very much informed by individuals' needs for security, privacy, and personal data control, the SSI model applies equally for organizations and things. In fact, it applies to *anything* that needs identity on the internet.

Since the acronym SSI is now in such wide use within the internet identity industry, that is the term we use throughout this book. (Co-author Alex Preukschat named his webinar series SSI Meetup for the same reason: https://ssimeetup.org.)

1.5   *Why is SSI so important?*

In many ways, answering this question is the whole point of this book. The chapters in front of you lay out how and why SSI will affect almost everything we do on the internet, day in and day out. Some of these changes may actually be as deep and profound as the internet itself was in the 1980s and 1990s—and the web was after that.

Today, many of us take those two technological advances for granted. Yet if you stop to think about it (if you were even alive back then), the work lives, social lives, and even political lives of billions of people have been radically transformed by the internet and the web. If that seems like an exaggeration, stop to consider that *7 out of the 10 most valuable companies in the world today* would not exist without the internet and the web [16].

> **FORECAST**   We predict that the impact of SSI technology—and the uncounted new patterns of trusted interactions it will enable across all walks of life—will be equally profound.

The fundamental reason is grounded in what we just explained about the term *self-sovereign identity*: it represents a *shift in control*. We started out trying to find a solution to the internet's missing identity layer; we ended up discovering that solving those problems required a shift in control from the *centers of the network*—the many "powers that be"—to the *edges of the network*—where all of us exist and interact as peers. This shift in control is wonderfully captured in figure 1.6 from Tim Bouma, co-author of chapter 23.

In the centralized and federated identity models, the locus of control is with the issuers and verifiers in the network. In the decentralized SSI identity model, the locus of control shifts to the individual user, who can now interact with everyone else as a full peer.

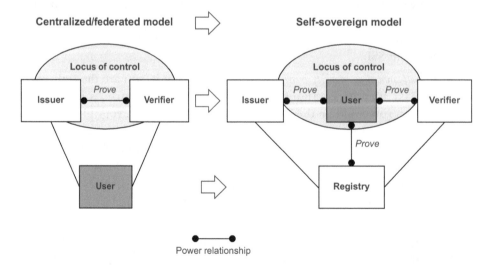

Figure 1.6   The shift in control that happens in the transition from centralized or federated identity models to the self-sovereign model. Only the latter puts the individual at the center.

This is why SSI is about more than technology. It has important business, legal, and social dimensions as well.

Up to this point, we have referred to SSI as if it were a single movement—one driven by communities like IIW (described earlier), Rebooting the Web of Trust (RWOT, www.weboftrust.info), MyData (https://mydata.org), and the W3C Decentralized Identifier (https://www.w3.org/2019/did-wg) and Verifiable Credentials Working Groups (https://www.w3.org/2017/vc/WG). However, as SSI becomes more mainstream, we predict that different flavors and visions of SSI will be implemented. These differences will depend on the needs, wants, and priorities of different communities implementing SSI. The key will be how different SSI architectures become interoperable the same way the internet made different local networks interoperable. Only if this happens will there be one unified SSI infrastructure.

1.6   *Market drivers for SSI*

One way to understand the momentum of SSI—and differences in SSI architectures—is to look at what is driving demand. For the business-minded reader, some of these categories might come across as foreign or ideological, but our aim is to reflect what we observe in the market. The drivers fall into three broad categories:

- *Business efficiency and customer experience*—This market is focused on security, cost savings, and convenience. As we discuss in chapter 4, this is the primary market demand driving SSI in its early stages. Corporations, governments, universities, NGOs—they all want to improve data security, increase compliance with privacy and data-protection regulations, reduce costs by improving workflows, and be more competitive by offering their customers a better user experience.

  These applications of SSI are primarily a disruption to the existing identity and access management (IAM) marketplace. Like most disruptive technologies, they will give rise to new companies, new business models, and new subsegments within the IAM market.

- *Resistance to the surveillance economy*—This is a reaction to the prevailing business model and tactics of some of the most dominant companies on the internet today. As has been widely covered in the media, the web's predominant business model (Web 2.0) is digital advertising. This has led to a worldwide industry that Harvard professor Shoshan Zuboff calls "surveillance capitalism." The backlash to this model has become the market driver for certain governments, privacy-conscious individuals, and a select number of corporations that want to do more than just ride the next wave of technological innovation and growth—they also want to strategically weaken the business model of the global aggregators, resellers, and distributors of personal data.

  Demand in this segment is a mix of ideology (e.g., privacy advocates), consumer sentiment, and strategic positioning. Governments such as the European Union with its General Data Protection Regulation (GDPR) are leading this movement because it puts them on a more level playing field with the internet giants, particularly as exponential technology changes continue to disrupt the "old world."

- *Sovereign individual movement*—This movement is driven by people who want to take back more control over their lives and data. Perhaps the best way to describe this SSI market driver is that *it aims to do for decentralized identity what Bitcoin aims to achieve for decentralized money.* Permissionless cryptocurrency technologies like Bitcoin want to create fully decentralized economies that do not rely on any central parties for their operation. Individuals in this market segment want to apply the same philosophy to digital identity, opting for SSI architectures that maximize decentralization. To understand their motivations, we recommended reading *The Sovereign Individual* by James Dale Davidson and William Rees-Mogg [17]. Ironically, it was published in 1997, well before Bitcoin and decentralization became mainstream subjects. However, the book makes its authors look prescient about the decentralization movement—a subject we explore in greater detail in part 3.

Because the biggest initial driver of SSI adoption is the first category of business efficiency and customer convenience, let's look at a few examples in specific market segments—some of which also shed more light on the other two market drivers.

1.6.1   E-commerce

Figure 1.7 shows the staggering growth of e-commerce. Every e-commerce transaction today involves a digital identity of some kind—either centralized or federated. What happens when consumers are equipped with SSI digital wallets with which they can do all of the following?

- Enjoy passwordless registration and logins at any SSI-enabled website or service
- Automatically receive a warning if the site or service they are connecting to cannot present its own trustworthy digital credentials
- Provide payment directly from their digital wallet without having to fool with "checkout," third-party wallet providers, or external payment gateways

Retail ecommerce sales worldwide
2014 to 2021 by trillions of USD

Figure 1.7   The growth in e-commerce sales over the past decade

- Automatically maintain a private personal log of digital receipts—and provide proof of their purchases to any merchant or recommendation engine of their choice

Not only will the average consumer's experience of e-commerce be transformed, but the additional friction that SSI will wring out of the global digital economy could potentially be measured in hundreds of billions of dollars.

1.6.2 Banking and finance

According to Citi's 2018 Mobile Banking Study, almost one-third of all U.S. adults are now using mobile banking. It's the most popular mobile app after social networking. When it comes to Millennials, the number is almost two-thirds [18].

Nearly all of this mobile banking activity is from dedicated apps provided by banks, credit unions, and other financial institutions directly to their customers. Some of these are award-winning for their usability, security, and privacy features. But most are still dedicated apps with their own logins/passwords that work with a single provider. (Initiatives like Itsme (https://www.itsme.be/en) in Belgium provide a regional solution.)

What happens when individuals gain an SSI digital wallet that does the following?

- Can work with any financial institution that supports SSI, and can access financial services from the entire marketplace of providers without the friction of filling out the same forms over and over
- Can provide digital credentials from trusted third parties that are required to pass KYC (know your customer) and AML (anti-money laundering) checks required of every financial institution
- Can digitally share all the information—digitally signed by trusted issuers—necessary to apply for a loan or mortgage in seconds
- Can do single-party or multi-party digital signatures to authorize important transactions—up to millions of dollars—with cryptographically-protected audit trails

NOTE SSI digital wallets are also being explored as solutions for regulatory-compliant exchange of cryptocurrencies and central bank digital currencies (CBDC).

These breakthrough benefits are not fictional—some of them are being delivered in production. For example, the global credit union industry has formed a consortium to introduce MemberPass™, the world's first global digital credential of credit union membership (www.culedger.com).

1.6.3 Healthcare

Practice Fusion, the largest cloud-based electronic health record (EHR) provider in the United States, provides the following statistic about EHR adoption in 2014:

Less than a decade ago, nine out of ten doctors in the U.S. updated their patients' records by hand and stored them in color-coded files. By the end of 2017, approximately 90% of office-based physicians nationwide will be using electronic health records (EHRs). [19]

Unfortunately, *Healthcare IT News* reports that the average hospital has 16 different EHR vendors in use at affiliated practices [20]. It goes on to sum up the problem this way:

> *Achieving interoperability among different EHR platforms is so difficult, in fact, that the Centers for Medicare and Medicaid Services working with the Office of the National Coordinator for Health IT, the federal agency charged with leading public and private healthcare organizations toward interoperability, essentially retooled the meaningful use EHR incentive program to focus on enabling a more unified view of patient data. Health IT shops across America, meet "promoting interoperability." [20]*

Keep in mind that all this is in the context of healthcare IT systems for doctors, hospitals, and medical institutions. It doesn't even contemplate how the patient could participate in a "unified view" of their own healthcare data. How much easier would the whole EHR portability problem be if patients could use their own SSI digital wallets to do the following?

- Instantly obtain copies (on their phone, or securely stored in a private cloud) of their EHR records immediately after any medical procedure
- Securely and privately share their EHR in seconds with the doctors and nurses of their choice
- Provide secure, legally valid, auditable consent for medical procedures—for themselves, family members, dependents, etc.—directly from their smartphone or other networked device
- Have a lifetime history of vaccinations, allergies, immunities, etc., available in a verifiable electronic record to share in seconds—in person or remotely—with schools, employers, doctors, nurses, or anyone who needs to verify it

Again, this list is not theoretical. The first major network for the patient-centric exchange of SSI digital credentials for healthcare, Lumedic Exchange, was announced in November 2020 and will go into national deployment in the U.S. in 2021 (https://www.lumedic.io/perspectives/introducing-lumedic-connect). This list doesn't even mention how your personal EHR might be used by your own apps on your own devices for your own healthcare, or the impact of being able to securely and anonymously share your medical data with universities and medical researchers who can use it to advance the state of public health for all of us. (Dive into these topics in chapter 22 on health and supply-chain management in the pharmaceutical industry.)

1.6.4 *Travel*

Anyone who has traveled internationally knows the fear in the pit of your stomach when you deplane and take the (often very long) walk to customs. The questions flood your mind: "How long will the line be?" "What if it takes hours?" "Will I miss my connecting flight?"

Governments and airport authorities worldwide have been wracking their brains, trying to figure out how to remove that particular friction from international travel.

Programs like Global Entry and CLEAR in the U.S., Nexus in Canada, Registered Traveller in the UK, and others worldwide are designed to do a deep check of your identity credentials, enroll your biometrics, and thereby give you a fast track through customs. But these programs cost tens of millions of dollars to set up and tens or hundreds of dollars to enroll in and require dedicated facilities and personnel in every airport.

How much simpler will international travel be when you can travel with a smartphone holding an SSI digital wallet that can do the following?

- Produce instant proof of any digital credential you possess in a single QR code on your phone, just like a mobile boarding pass
- At the same time, receive a new credential of having passed through security and/or customs at that particular airport, thereby building a private, verifiable audit trail of your travel that you alone can provide at subsequent checkpoints in your trip
- Do all of this with *privacy by design*—specifically by using cryptographic proofs that disclose only the information required to meet government regulations at each checkpoint
- Have all the travel documents you need—airline tickets, train tickets, hotel reservations, dinner reservations—flow automatically into your digital wallet, so they are always there when you need them

It might sound more like the world of Harry Potter than our world today, but this particular SSI magic carpet ride is the goal of a growing number of airports, travel consortia, and government agencies worldwide. It has been accelerated by the massive impact of the global COVID-19 pandemic—see the November 2020 announcement of the International Air Transport Association (IATA) Travel Pass (https://www.iata.org/en/programs/passenger/travel-pass/). But there are still significant hurdles we need to overcome before a global digital travel credential is a reality.

1.7 Major challenges to SSI adoption

As authors, we believe the SSI paradigm shift is already underway. However, we do not believe it is without significant challenges. At a 2019 event called "The Future of Digital Identity," hosted by Citi Ventures, Vinod Baya, director and head of emerging technology at Citi, pointed out that there are three major challenges to the adoption of SSI [21]:

- Building out the new SSI ecosystem
- Decentralized key management
- Offline access

1.7.1 Building out the new SSI ecosystem

Some of the benefits of SSI (see chapter 4) can be realized by individual companies or communities. However, the full network effects will only be experienced when multiple industries, governments, and other ecosystems start accepting each other's digital credentials. This, in turn, depends on achieving real interoperability between the essential components of SSI, as we discuss in chapter 2 and more deeply in part 2. For example, we will need digital credentials to work across different digital wallets from different vendors—some of which will also integrate digital money (fiat or cryptocurrency, for example). While this infrastructure is underway, it is still not mature, and there is much work to be done before it will be fully ready for internet scale.

1.7.2   Decentralized key management

As we explained earlier, the key to SSI is literally *keys*—cryptographic key pairs where the SSI identity holder holds the private keys in their own digital wallet. Loss of those private keys is tantamount to the complete loss of the holder's digital identity. Key management has always been the Achilles heel of the adoption of cryptography and public key infrastructure (PKI). It has been so difficult that many experts believe it can only be handled by large enterprises and centralized service providers such as banks or government agencies.

The growth of cryptocurrencies has already led to some significant advancements in decentralized key management, and the rise of SSI is leading to much more research in this area. We believe this is one of the primary hurdles to the ultimate market success of SSI, which is why we cover core innovations in decentralized key management in great detail in chapter 10.

1.7.3   Offline access

SSI is based on digital credentials shared over a digital network. Yet there are many situations where we need to be able to prove our identity without having internet access or a digital device. For example, the Canadian Mounted Police might need to verify a driver's license in the far north where internet access is simply not available. So SSI solutions need to be able to work offline or with intermittent or indeterminate connectivity. This is a major engineering challenge being tackled by SSI architects, but it is not yet a solved problem.

Moreover, beyond the technical challenges for the adoption of SSI, there are also risks involved with the adoption of any exponential technology. (See Singularity University's "An Exponential Primer" at https://su.org/concepts.) SSI is not an exception to those challenges. For SSI to deliver its promises and mitigate the risks, the architectural choices made in the early stages of the infrastructure will be critical. This infrastructure is also currently missing the broader expertise needed for a subject as complex as identity. Many of the experts driving SSI have a technical background—and the legal aspects of SSI have attracted some highly internet-proficient lawyers—yet people from all disciplines and spheres of society are needed: sociologists, psychologists, anthropologists, economists, and so on. We hope the involvement of these and others outside the technology community will increase over time.

> ### SSI Resources
>
> For more free content to learn about SSI, please go to IdentityBook.info and SSI Meetup.org/book.

References

1. Cameron, Kim. 2005. "The Laws of Identity." *Kim Cameron's Identity Weblog.* www.identityblog.com/?p=352.
2. Security. 2017. "Average Business User Has 191 Passwords." https://www.securitymagazine.com/articles/88475-average-business-user-has-191-passwords.
3. Morgan, Steve. 2015. "IBM's CEO on Hackers: 'Cyber Crime Is the Greatest Threat to Every Company in the World.'" *Forbes* (November 24). www.forbes.com/sites/stevemorgan/2015/11/24/ibms-ceo-on-hackers-cyber-crime-is-the-greatest-threat-to-every-company-in-the-world.
4. Zaharia, Andra. 2020. "300+ Terrifying Cybercrime and Cybersecurity Statistics & Trends." Comparitech. https://www.comparitech.com/vpn/cybersecurity-cyber-crime-statistics-facts-trends.
5. Rainie, Lee. 2018. "Americans' Complicated Feelings about Social Media in an Era of Privacy Concerns." Pew Research Center. www.pewresearch.org/fact-tank/2018/03/27/americans-complicated-feelings-about-social-media-in-an-era-of-privacy-concerns.
6. Oath. 2017. "Yahoo Provides Notice to Additional Users Affected by Previously Disclosed 2013 Data Theft." Verizon Media. https://www.oath.com/press/yahoo-provides-notice-to-additional-users-affected-by-previously.
7. Neveux, Ellen. 2020. "80% of Hacking-Related Breaches Leverage Compromised Passwords." *SecureLink.* https://www.securelink.com/blog/81-hacking-related-breaches-leverage-compromised-credentials.
8. Lim, Paul J. 2017. "Equifax's Massive Data Breach Has Cost the Company $4 Billion So Far." *Money.* https://money.com/equifaxs-massive-data-breach-has-cost-the-company-4-billion-so-far.
9. Ctrl-Shift. 2011. "Economics of Identity." https://www.ctrl-shift.co.uk/insights/2014/06/09/economics-of-identity.
10. Nakamoto, Satoshi. 2008. "Bitcoin: A Peer-to-Peer Electronic Cash System." https://bitcoin.org/bitcoin.pdf.
11. Birch, David. 2014. *Identity Is the New Money.* London Publishing Partnership. https://www.amazon.com/Identity-Money-Perspectives-David-Birch/dp/1907994122.
12. SBIR. 2015. "Applicability of Blockchain Technology to Privacy Respecting Identity Management." https://www.sbir.gov/sbirsearch/detail/867797.
13. Foxley, William. 2019. "President Xi Says China Should 'Seize Opportunity' to Adopt Blockchain." CoinDesk. https://www.coindesk.com/president-xi-says-china-should-seize-opportunity-to-adopt-blockchain.
14. Cameron, Kim. 2018. "Let's Find a More Accurate Term Than 'Self-Sovereign Identity." *Kim Cameron's Identity Weblog.* https://www.identityblog.com/?p=1693.
15. Heath, Chip and Dan Heath. 2007. *Made to Stick: Why Some Ideas Survive and Others Die.* Random House. https://smile.amazon.com/Made-Stick-Ideas-Survive-Others-dp-1400064287/dp/1400064287.
16. Statista. 2020. "The 100 Largest Companies in the World by Market Capitalization in 2020." https://www.statista.com/statistics/263264/top-companies-in-the-world-by-market-value.
17. Davidson, James Dale and William Rees-Mogg. 1997. *The Sovereign Individual: Mastering the Transition to the Information Age.* Touchstone. https://www.goodreads.com/book/show/82256.The_Sovereign_Individual.

18. Citi. 2018. "Mobile Banking One of Top Three Most Used Apps by Americans, 2018 Citi Mobile Banking Study Reveals." Cision PR Newswire. https://www.prnewswire.com/news-releases/mobile-banking-one-of-top-three-most-used-apps-by-americans-2018-citi-mobile-banking-study-reveals-300636938.html.

19. Vestal, Christine. 2014. "Some States Lag in Using Electronic Health Records." *USA Today* (March 14). www.usatoday.com/story/news/nation/2014/03/19/stateline-electronic-health-records/6600377.

20. Sullivan, Tom. 2018. "Why EHR data interoperability is such a mess in 3 charts." Healthcare IT News. https://www.healthcareitnews.com/news/why-ehr-data-interoperability-such-mess-3-charts.

21. Baya, Vinod. 2019. "Digital Identity: Moving to a Decentralized Future." Citi. https://www.citi.com/ventures/perspectives/opinion/digital-identity.html.

The basic building blocks of SSI

2

Drummond Reed, Rieks Joosten, and Oskar van Deventer

To help describe the core components of SSI architecture, we enlisted two of the leaders in SSI in Europe: Rieks Joosten and Oskar van Deventer of TNO, the Netherlands Organization for Applied Scientific Research. Rieks is a senior scientist focused on business information processes and information security. Oskar is a senior scientist for blockchain networking. Together, they are two of the founders of the European SSI Framework Laboratory (ESSIF-Lab).

As we explained in chapter 1, SSI is relatively new, having only emerged onto the internet stage in 2016. At one level, SSI is a set of principles about how identity and personal data control should work across digital networks. At another level, SSI is a set of technologies that build on core concepts in identity management, distributed computing, blockchain or distributed ledger technology (DLT), and cryptography.

In many cases, these core concepts have been established for decades. What's new is how they are put together to create a new model for digital identity management. The purpose of this chapter is to quickly familiarize you from a conceptual point of view with seven basic building blocks of SSI before we show how they are applied to different example scenarios in chapter 3. These seven building blocks are as follows:

- Verifiable credentials (aka digital credentials)
- The trust triangle: issuers, holders, and verifiers
- Digital wallets
- Digital agents

- Decentralized identifiers (DIDs)
- Blockchains and other verifiable data registries
- Governance frameworks (aka trust frameworks)

Note that we go into much deeper technical detail about most of these building blocks in part 2 of the book. In this chapter, we want to introduce them at a level that anyone with a basic familiarity with digital technology can understand.

2.1   Verifiable credentials

In chapter 1, we summarized the essence of decentralized identity as "to move the utility and portability of physical identity credentials to our digital devices." This is why the concept at the very heart of SSI is *verifiable credentials* (VCs).

First, what exactly do we mean by the term *credential*? It obviously refers to the pieces of paper or plastic (or, in some cases, metal) that you carry around in your wallet to prove your identity: for example, driving licenses, government IDs, employment cards, credit cards, and so on (figure 2.1).

Figure 2.1   Common examples of credentials—not all of which fit in a traditional wallet

But as this figure illustrates, not all credentials fit in your physical wallet. The term *credentials* extends to any (tamper-resistant) set of information that some authority claims to be true about the subject of the credential—and which in turn enables the subject to convince others (who trust that authority) of these truths. For example:

- A birth certificate issued by a hospital or vital statistics agency proves when and where you were born and who your parents were.
- A diploma issued by a university proves you have an educational degree.
- A passport issued by a government of a country proves you are a citizen.
- An official pilot's license proves you are authorized to fly a plane.
- A utility bill proves you are a registered customer of the utility that issued the bill.
- A power of attorney issued by the appropriate authority within a jurisdiction proves that you can legally perform certain actions on behalf of another person.

All of these are examples of credentials about a *human* subject. But VCs are not limited to humans. For example, a veterinarian could issue a VC about the vaccinations for a pet (see chapter 20). A farmer could issue a VC about the feed supply for a head of livestock. Or a manufacturer could issue credentials about an IoT sensor device (see chapter 19).

Every credential contains a set of *claims* about the *subject* of the credential. Those claims are made by a single authority, which in SSI is called the *issuer* of the credential. The entity (person, organization, or thing) to whom the credential is issued, i.e., the one who will keep it in their digital wallet, is called the *holder* of the credential. Note that the subject of the credential is usually the same as the holder, but there are important exceptions to this rule-of-thumb, as discussed in chapter 7.

The claims in a credential can state anything about the subject, such as *attributes* (age, height, weight, etc.), *relationships* (mother, father, employer, citizenship, or others), or *entitlements* (medical benefits, library privileges, membership rewards, legal rights, and so on).

To qualify as a credential, the claims must be *verifiable* in some way. This means a *verifier* must be able to determine the following:

- Who issued the credential
- That it has not been tampered with since it was issued
- That it has not expired or been revoked

With physical credentials, this is typically accomplished through some proof of authenticity embedded directly in the credential (like a watermark, hologram, or other special printing feature) or via a claim stating the expiration date. It can also be done by checking directly with the issuer that the credential is valid, accurate, and current. But this manual verification process can be difficult and time-consuming—a significant reason why there is a worldwide black market in falsified credentials.

This brings us to one of the fundamental advantages of VCs: using cryptography and the internet (and a standard protocol), they can be *digitally verified* in seconds or even milliseconds. This verification process can answer the following four questions:

- Does the credential contain the data the verifier needs in a standard format the verifier expects?
- Does it include a valid digital signature from the issuer (thus establishing its origin and that it has not been tampered with in transit)?
- Is the credential still valid—that is, not expired or revoked?
- If applicable, does the credential (or its signature) provide cryptographic proof that the holder of the credential is the subject of the credential?

NOTE Cryptographic proofs of various kinds—including zero-knowledge proofs (ZKPs)—play a critical role in verifiable credentials. See chapter 6 for details.

Figure 2.2 is based on an illustration from Manu Sporny, co-editor of the W3C Verifiable Credentials Data Model 1.0 specification (https://www.w3.org/TR/vc-data-model), showing how a digital credential can be structured to answer these four questions. The first part of the VC package is a unique identifier for the credential—just like the unique number that appears on your driving license or passport. The second part is metadata describing the credential itself, such as the expiration date for a driving license. The third part is the claims contained in the credential—in figure 2.2, these are all the other items of data (name, date of birth, sex, hair color, eye color, height, weight). The equivalent of the credential subject's signature (the one that appears below the person's picture in the driving license) is a digital signature created using cryptography.

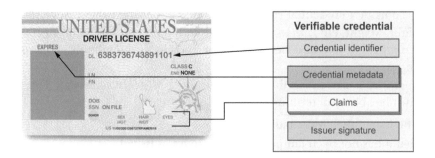

Figure 2.2   A mapping of three of the four core components of a W3C verifiable credential to the physical equivalent. The fourth component—the issuer's digital signature—can only be produced in a physical credential by some form of watermark, hologram, or other hard-to-forge seal.

2.2   *Issuers, holders, and verifiers*

Figure 2.3 illustrates the terminology defined by the W3C Verifiable Claims Working Group for the three primary roles involved with the exchange of VCs (from appendix G of the Sovrin Foundation Glossary V2, https://sovrin.org/library/glossary):

1   *Issuers* are the source of credentials. Every credential has an issuer. Most issuers are organizations such as government agencies (passports), financial institutions (credit cards), universities (degrees), corporations (employment credentials), NGOs (membership cards), churches (awards), etc. However, individuals can also be issuers, and so can things—for example, a properly equipped sensor could issue a digitally signed credential about a sensor reading.

2   *Holders* request VCs from issuers, hold them in the holder's digital wallet (discussed in the next section), and present *proofs* of claims from one or more credentials when requested by verifiers (and approved by the holder). Although we most commonly think of individuals as holder/provers, holders/provers can also be organizations using enterprise wallets or things in the sense of the Internet of Things (IoT).

3 *Verifiers* can be anyone—person, organization, or thing—seeking trust assurance of some kind about the subjects of credentials. Verifiers request proofs from holders/provers of one or more claims from one or more VCs. If the holder agrees (and the holder always has that choice), the holder's agent responds with a proof the verifier can then verify. The critical step in this process is the verification of the issuer's digital signature, typically accomplished using a *DID*, discussed in more detail later in this chapter.

NOTE The working group has the name "W3C Verifiable Claims Working Group" even though the specification it is creating is called "Verifiable Credentials Data Model 1.0." For more details on the terminology and standards for verifiable credentials, see the Verifiable Credentials Primer (https://github.com/WebOfTrustInfo/rwot8-barcelona/blob/master/topics-and-advance-readings/verifiable-credentials-primer.md) and the W3C Verifiable Credentials Data Model 1.0 (https://www.w3.org/TR/verifiable-claims-data-model).

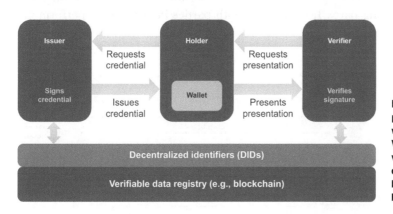

Figure 2.3 The primary roles involved with the exchange of VCs. Digital signature verification is the part of the process enabled by public or private blockchain networks.

The relationship between issuers, holders/provers, and verifiers is often referred to as the *trust triangle* because it is fundamentally how human trust relationships are conveyed over a digital network. Figure 2.4 illustrates how *VCs only convey trust if the verifier trusts the issuer.* This does not mean the verifier must have a direct business or legal relationship with the issuer. It just means the verifier is willing to make a business decision ("Will I accept this credit card?" "Will I board this airline passenger?" "Will I admit this student?") based on the level of trust assurance the verifier has in the issuer.

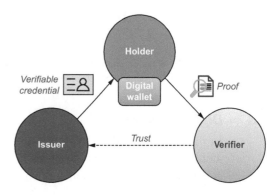

Figure 2.4 The "trust triangle" at the heart of all human trust relationships in the SSI ecosystem

Note that the trust triangle describes only *one side* of a business transaction. In many business transactions, both parties request information from the other. So in a single transaction, both parties play the roles of holder and verifier. Also, many business transactions result in a new credential issued from one party to the other—or even two new credentials, one in each direction.

An example is shown in figure 2.5, which describes the series of steps a consumer goes through when buying an expensive holiday trip from a travel company:

1 The consumer wants to verify that the travel company has insurance against bankruptcy.
2 The travel site wants to verify that the consumer is older than 18.
3 After payment, the travel site sends the tickets to the consumer.
4 After the trip, the consumer confirms that they are a satisfied customer of the travel company.

Each of these pieces of information can be transmitted as a VC with a digital signature from the issuing party. It shows how both parties intermittently perform all roles in the trust triangle.

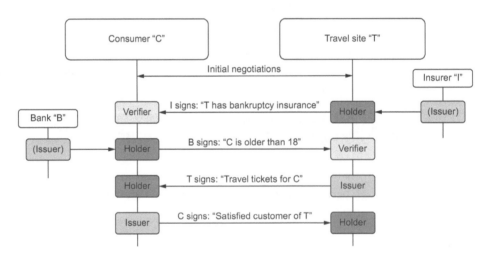

Figure 2.5   A typical multistage transaction where multiple VCs are used and created and both parties play the roles of issuer, holder, and verifier

2.3   *Digital wallets*

In the offline world, we typically store credentials in a physical wallet—it keeps them all in one place, protects them by keeping them close to our body, and makes them easy to carry around and access when we need them. The job of a digital wallet is no different:

- Store your credentials, keys/keycards, bills/receipts, etc.

- Protect them from theft or prying eyes.
- Keep them handy—easily available and portable across all your devices.

Unfortunately, there have been so many attempts at digital wallets over the years that many developers stopped using the term. But two trends have brought the concept back into vogue. The first is *mobile wallets*, particularly those built-in to the operating systems of smartphones to hold credit cards, tickets, boarding passes, and other typical financial or travel credentials (figure 2.6).

Figure 2.6   Two of the most popular smartphone mobile wallets: Apple Wallet and Google Pay. They are widely used because they come built-in to every Apple and Google phone.

The second is *cryptocurrency wallets*. Every purchaser of a cryptocurrency like bitcoin, ether, litecoin, and others needs one of the following:

- A *server-side wallet*, aka *custodial wallet* or *cloud wallet*, in which keys are stored by a broker such as Coinbase
- A *client-side wallet*, aka *non-custodial wallet* or *edge wallet*, which is either a dedicated hardware wallet (figure 2.7) or an app that runs on one or more of the user's devices (smartphone, tablet, laptop, etc.)

Figure 2.7   A typical dedicated hardware wallet for cryptocurrencies. This one, the Ledger Nano S, has its own secure display.

For SSI, any of these general forms of a wallet will work. But there are also some significant differences between cryptocurrency wallets and SSI wallets. In chapter 9, we go deep into these features; but at a high level, these are the two most distinguishing features:

- *An SSI digital wallet should implement open standards* for portable, self-sovereign VCs and other sensitive private data.
- *An SSI wallet works with a digital agent* to form connections and perform credential exchange (discussed in the next section).

Instead of proprietary wallets from different vendors, where each wallet uses that vendor's own APIs and VC designs, for full-fledged SSI, we need general-purpose digital wallets that function much more like the real-world wallets we carry in our pockets or purses. In other words

- *The wallet should accept any standardized VC* just like you can fit any paper or plastic credential of the right size into your physical wallet.
- *You can install the wallet on any device you regularly use,* just like you can put your physical wallet in any pocket or purse you choose. Unlike physical wallets, however, many users will want their digital wallets to automatically stay "in sync" across their different devices the same way many email and messaging apps keep messages in sync across multiple devices today.
- *You can back up and move the contents of your wallet to other digital wallets as needed*—even from different vendors—just like you can move your physical credentials from one physical wallet to another.
- *You should have the same basic experience no matter what wallet you use*—even across different wallets from different vendors—because this is critical to being able to use your wallets safely and securely.

NOTE For more about interoperability and standardization across SSI digital wallets, please see chapter 9. That chapter also answers the other most frequently asked question about digital wallets: "What happens if I lose my phone?" (Without spoiling the punch line, the answer is that by automatically maintaining an encrypted backup, your digital wallet will actually be more secure from loss, theft, or hacking than any physical wallet you carry.)

Equifax VP Identity Adam Gunther, former executive director for Blockchain Trusted Identity at IBM, expresses this last point as, "one wallet, one experience" [1]—one standard way of managing your VCs and trust relationships no matter what wallet or device you are using. Not only will it be the easiest experience for end users, but it will also be the safest approach because it makes it much harder to try to fool or "phish" an identity owner into doing the wrong thing.

Kim Cameron, former chief identity architect at Microsoft, thought this was so important that he made "Consistent Experience across Contexts" the last of his seven

Laws of Identity [2]. He compared it to learning how to drive. The worldwide automotive industry has standardized the controls for driving (e.g., steering wheel, accelerator, brakes, turn signals) across all makes and models of cars to minimize the learning experience and maximize safety for drivers. The reasons are obvious: a car that does not operate the way a driver normally expects could end up killing the driver or others. We need the same level of attention to the safety of our digital lives.

2.4 Digital agents

Another major difference between digital wallets and physical wallets is how they operate. A physical wallet is "operated" directly by a person—the owner. They set it up, add credentials received from issuers, select credentials to be presented to a verifier when a proof is required, and move the wallet from pocket-to-pocket or purse-to-purse as needed.

Because people don't "speak" in binary data, digital wallets require software to operate them. In SSI infrastructure, this software module is called a *digital agent*. As figure 2.8 illustrates, you can think of an agent as a digital guardian that "wraps" around your digital wallet to protect it and makes sure only you, the person responsible for your VCs and cryptographic keys, can use them.

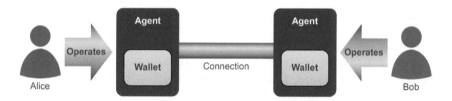

Figure 2.8 In SSI infrastructure, every digital wallet is "wrapped" by a digital agent that acts as a software guardian, making sure only the wallet's controller (typically the identity holder) can access the stored VCs and cryptographic keys.

In SSI infrastructure, an agent has a second job in addition to helping identity owners manage their wallets. Using instructions from their owners, agents "speak" to each other over the internet to *form connections* and *exchange credentials*. They do this via a *decentralized, secure messaging protocol* designed from the ground up for private communication between digital agents. (Read more about this protocol, DIDComm, in chapter 5.)

Figure 2.9 is a high-level overview of how agents and their wallets form connections and communicate in the SSI ecosystem. There are two general categories of agents based on where they are located. *Edge agents* operate at the edge of the network, on an identity holder's local devices. *Cloud agents* operate in the cloud, where they are hosted either by standard cloud computing platform providers or specialized cloud service providers called *agencies*.

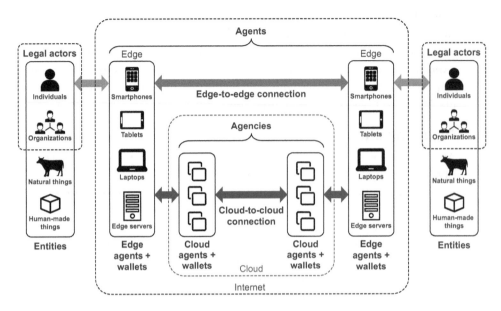

Figure 2.9   An overview diagram of the role of agents and wallets in the SSI ecosystem. Identity owners interact both directly with edge agents operating on local devices and indirectly with cloud agents operating remotely in the cloud. Source: Appendix F of the Sovrin Glossary (https://sovrin.org/wp-content/uploads/Sovrin-Glossary-V3.pdf).

Cloud agents can also be designed to store and synchronize other data on behalf of an identity owner: files, photos, financial records, medical records, asset records, etc. Unlike traditional cloud storage, the data is all encrypted by the identity holder; thus these are called *secure data stores* (SDS; see the Secure Data Storage Working Group at the Decentralized Identity Foundation, https://identity.foundation/working-groups/secure-data-storage.html). Together with digital wallets, SDS can serve as the backbone for digital life management applications and services that process and maintain digital identity data of all kinds for the lifetime of an individual—and beyond: i.e., an SDS can be of great assistance in the management and settlement of a digital estate after its owner has passed away.

So the next question is, how do agents find each other to connect and communicate on behalf of their identity owners?

2.5   *Decentralized identifiers (DIDs)*

What made the internet possible was a new addressing system that allows any device on the internet to connect with and send data packets to any other device on the internet. Figure 2.10 is a diagram of an IP (Internet Protocol) version 4 address.

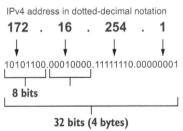

Figure 2.10   Example of an IP address: the addressing format that lets any device on the internet talk to any other device on the internet

As we explained in the opening pages of this book, knowing the IP address of a machine on the internet doesn't tell you anything about *the identity of the person, organization, or thing controlling that machine*. To do that, the controller (the identity holder) needs to be able to provide *proof* about their identity, attributes, relationships, or entitlements. And that proof has to be verifiable in some way.

We've had technology for creating digital proofs for decades now: *public/private key cryptography*. (We explain the basics of public/private key cryptography in chapter 6.) The owner of a private key uses it to sign messages, and anyone else can verify this signature using the owner's corresponding public key. The signature verification shows that the signature was created by the owner of the private key and the message has not been tampered with since.

However, to rely on this verification, the verifier must know the correct public key for the owner. So, for decentralized messaging between digital agents and wallets to be secure—and for agents to be able to send cryptographically verifiable proofs of VCs to each other—we need a strong, secure, scalable way for identity holders and their agents to *prove ownership of their public keys*.

For the past few decades, the solution to that problem has been public key infrastructure (PKI): the system of obtaining public key certificates from a small set of certification authorities (CAs) around the world. However, as chapter 8 explores in depth, conventional PKI is too centralized, too expensive, and too heavyweight to meet the demands of a worldwide SSI infrastructure in which every single participant is managing multiple sets of cryptographic keys.

Just as with the internet's IP addresses, the answer was a new type of identifier. Only this new class of identifiers needed to be designed from the ground up for digital agents and their public keys. And because it had to be extremely secure, these new identifiers required the following four properties:

- *Permanent*—The identifier needs to be able to never change, no matter how often the identity owner moves, uses different service providers, or uses different devices.
- *Resolvable*—The identifier needs to be able to retrieve not just the current public key or keys for the identity owner but also the current addresses to reach the owner's agent or agents.
- *Cryptographically verifiable*—The identity holder needs to be able to prove, using cryptography, that they or it have control of the private key associated with that identifier.
- *Decentralized*—Unlike X.509 certificate trees that rely on centralized registries under the control of single authorities, this new type of identifier must be able to avoid single points of failure by using decentralized networks such as blockchains, distributed ledgers, distributed hash tables, distributed file systems, peer-to-peer networks, etc.

The last of these four properties gave this new address its name: *decentralized identifiers* (DIDs). Given its different purpose, a DID has a much different structure than an IP address. An example DID is shown in figure 2.11.

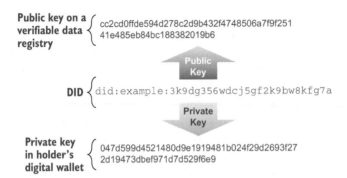

Figure 2.11   An example of a decentralized identifier (DID) and the associated public and private keys. A DID functions as the address of a public key on a blockchain or other decentralized network. In most cases, a DID can also be used to locate an agent for the DID subject (the entity identified by the DID).

Just as the original research for the internet was sponsored by a U.S. government agency (DARPA), the original research and development for the first DID specification was sponsored by a contract with the U.S. Department of Homeland Security (DHS). Published in late 2016, it was subsequently contributed to the W3C Credentials Community Group (CCG) to start the process of becoming an official standard. (See chapter 8 for more about DIDs, DID documents, DID methods, and the DID specification.) That process resulted in the launch of the W3C DID Working Group (https://www.w3.org/2019/did-wg) in September 2019.

DIDs are designed to be able to take advantage of any modern blockchain, DLT, or other decentralized network via a *DID method* that is written specifically for that target system. The DID method defines the following four atomic operations on any DID:

- How to *create* (write) the DID and its accompanying *DID document* (the file containing the public key(s) and other metadata describing the DID subject)
- How to use the DID to *read* (look up) the DID document from the target system
- How to *update* the DID document for a DID, e.g., to rotate a public key
- How to *deactivate* a DID by terminating its usage (usually by updating its DID document to contain no information)

The DID Specification Registry (https://www.w3.org/TR/did-spec-registries) maintained by the W3C DID Working Group includes more than 80 DID methods, including (at the time of publication) three methods for Bitcoin and six for Ethereum. It also includes at least two methods (did:peer and did:git) that do not need a distributed ledger because they work entirely peer-to-peer (https://identity.foundation/peer-did-method-spec/index.html). Just as any two devices with their own IP addresses can use the TCP/IP protocol stack to form a connection and exchange data, any two identity owners with DIDs can use the SSI protocol stack to form a cryptographically secure connection to exchange data. The basic concept of DID-to-DID *connections* (shown in figures 2.8 and 2.9) is not new—it is directly analogous to how connections work in many other networks. But DID-to-DID connections bring five powerful new properties to digital relationships:

- *Permanent*—The connection will never break unless one or both parties want it to.
- *Private*—All communications over the connection can be automatically encrypted and digitally signed.

- *End-to-end*—The secure connection has no intermediaries.
- *Trusted*—The connection supports VC exchange to establish trust to any required level of assurance.
- *Extensible*—The connection can be used for any other application that needs secure, private, reliable digital communications.

2.6 Blockchains and other verifiable data registries

A DID can be registered with any type of decentralized network or *verifiable data registry* (this is the formal term used in the W3C Verifiable Credentials Data Model and Decentralized Identifier specifications)—or even exchanged peer-to-peer. So why would someone choose to register a DID on a blockchain? What do blockchains provide that other types of electronic identifiers and addresses we have been using for decades—telephone numbers, domain names, email addresses—do not?

The answer is deeply rooted in cryptography, databases, and networking. In the standard industry use of the term, a blockchain is a *highly tamper-resistant transactional distributed database that no single party controls.* This means a blockchain can provide an authoritative source of data that many different peers can trust without any single peer being in control (a blockchain must be carefully designed and implemented to resist attacks). Blockchains intentionally trade off many other standard features of distributed transactional databases—performance, efficiency, scalability, searchability, ease of administration—to solve *one* really hard problem: authoritative data that does not need to rely on a central trusted authority. Figure 2.12 illustrates the fundamental design differences in design between traditional databases—whether centralized or distributed—and blockchains.

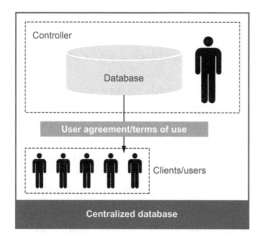
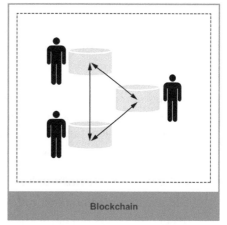

Figure 2.12 The fundamental innovation of a blockchain as a database is that it has no centralized administrator or controller—it uses cryptography to allow many different peers to each control their own transactions, while making it nearly impossible to alter any transaction once it has been written to the blockchain.

It is important to understand how blockchains accomplish the feat of removing the need for a central authority while still maintaining very high trust in the data's integrity. It has been called a *triple play of cryptography*:

1   *Every transaction (the writing of a new record) to a blockchain is digitally signed.* This is how control of the distributed database is spread out across all the peers: each peer manages its private keys and digitally signs its transactions with the blockchain. No new transaction is accepted unless the signature is verified.

2   *Transactions are grouped into* blocks *that are cryptographically hashed and linked to the previous block.* This step creates an immutable *chain* of ordered transactions.

3   *Every new block is cryptographically replicated across all peer nodes on the blockchain network, each of which is run by a different peer.* This step is performed by the *consensus protocol* at the heart of many blockchains. There are many different consensus protocols—some of which (like Bitcoin) involve cryptographic proof-of-work called *mining.* But regardless of the specific protocol, in the end, every peer node in the network ends up with a copy of the latest block, and they all agree on that copy. The fact that each node is run by a different peer—combined in some cases with clever game theory—makes it far less likely that 51% or more of the nodes will collude to try to attack the blockchain (and have some chance of rewriting its history).

This cryptographic triple play is what makes a blockchain so hard to attack. Modifying even a single bit of a single transaction that has already been recorded to the blockchain and replicated to all the peer nodes requires breaking into tens, hundreds, or thousands of machines and changing them all at once.

From the standpoint of SSI—and specifically for registering and resolving the DIDs and public keys that enable digital wallets and digital agents to securely communicate and exchange VCs—the differences between the various types of blockchains (permissionless, permissioned, hybrid, etc.) do not matter much. (We explain more about the differences between blockchains and DLTs in chapter 15.) A DID method can be written to support pretty much any modern blockchain or other decentralized network.

What matters is that blockchains or other verifiable data registries solve a problem that has never had a solution in the history of cryptography: how a globally distributed database can serve as a source of truth for public keys without being subject to single points of failure or attack. This is what provides the strong foundation needed for the ubiquitous adoption of the verifiable digital credentials at the heart of SSI.

2.7   *Governance frameworks*

The ultimate goal of all SSI infrastructure is to achieve a mutually acceptable level of trust between any two parties interacting on the internet—a goal that for many types of transactions is simply not possible today. With SSI, the foundation for this trust layer is first laid by *cryptographic trust*, i.e., by rooting publicly resolvable DIDs and public keys for credential issuers in a decentralized network. This anchors the trust triangle shown in figure 2.4 and again a little later, in figure 2.13, so that verifiers can rely on an issuer's digital signature.

But cryptographic trust is not *human trust.* For example, while Bitcoin uses cryptographic trust and game theory to power its system of value exchange, by itself it does not provide any solution to the challenges of money-transmission regulations such as Know Your Customer (KYC), Anti-Money Laundering (AML), and Anti-Terrorism Financing (ATF). But cryptographic trust in the Bitcoin blockchain network *could* be used to anchor a DID for an issuer of VCs to parties making Bitcoin transactions. Provided the issuer had enough human trust in their authority (for example, a credit union, bank, insurance company, or government agency), those VCs could be used by verifiers to satisfy KYC or AML regulations.

This layering of human trust on top of cryptographic trust is how SSI can deliver the full power of VCs. But trusting in credentials from one issuer at a time doesn't scale. This was the same problem faced in the early days of credit cards in the 1960s. Each major bank tried to issue its own brand of credit card, and merchants were overwhelmed—they couldn't handle hundreds of different credit cards from hundreds of different banks.

Thus credit card adoption didn't take off until banks got together and formed *credit card networks*—Visa and MasterCard being the two best known. These are governed by a set of business, legal, and technical rules known as a *governance framework* (also known in the digital identity industry as a *trust framework*). The entity that creates and administers a governance framework is known as the *governance authority*.

A governance framework creates the second trust triangle shown in the lower half of figure 2.13. This figure shows how a governance framework can make a verifier's job easier: when presented with proof of a credential from an issuer the verifier does not know, the verifier can check to see whether the issuer is authorized under a governance

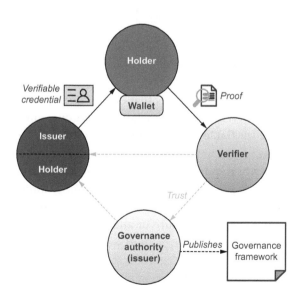

Figure 2.13 Governance authorities and governance frameworks represent a second trust triangle that enables verifiers to determine the authorized issuers for a specific set of VCs.

framework the verifier trusts. This check can take a number of different forms: a simple "whitelist," a lookup from a blockchain or secure directory, or a VC from the governance authority. In all cases, this approach of *recursive trust triangles* can work for any size of trust community—even internet-scale trust communities where verifiers do not directly know all the issuers (e.g., MasterCard and Visa).

Governance frameworks are the flip side of VCs: they specify the policies and procedures issuers must follow to issue a credential. In some cases, they also specify the terms and conditions to which holders must agree to obtain credentials—or to which verifiers must agree to verify credentials. Governance frameworks can also specify business models for credential exchange, such as the "verifier pays issuer" model that works for credit card networks today—including liability policies, insurance, and other legal and business requirements.

Governance frameworks are the secret to how VCs can scale to work in any size of trust community, from a single city to an entire industry, or from one nation-state to the internet as a whole. As we see in the balance of this book, these *digital trust ecosystems* can be as transformative to our digital lives as credit card networks have been to the world of commerce.

2.8   *Summarizing the building blocks*

Although an entire book can (and will) be written on each of these seven fundamental building blocks of SSI, this chapter's goal has been to introduce them so that anyone—technical or non-technical—can understand the basic role they play in SSI infrastructure. We can summarize each building block in a single sentence:

- *Verifiable credentials* are the digital equivalent of the physical credentials we carry in our wallets to prove some aspect of our identities almost every day.
- *Issuers, holders, and verifiers* are the three roles of the trust triangle that make credentials of any kind work: issuing the credential, holding it in a wallet, and verifying it when the holder presents it.
- *Digital wallets* are the digital equivalent of our physical wallets for holding verifiable credentials on any modern computing device—smartphone, table, laptop, and so on.
- *Digital agents* are the apps or software modules that enable us to use our digital wallets to obtain and present credentials, manage connections, and securely communicate and exchange verifiable credentials with other digital agents.
- *Decentralized identifiers* (DIDs) are the new type of digital address powered by modern cryptography so they do not require a centralized registration authority.
- *Blockchains and verifiable data registries* are distributed, cryptographically protected databases that can serve as a source of truth for DIDs and public keys without being subject to single points of failure or attack.
- *Governance frameworks* published by various types and sizes of governance authorities are the set of business, legal, and technical rules for using SSI infrastructure that will enable interoperable digital trust ecosystems of any size and scale.

How do these seven basic building blocks come together to build a coherent overall picture of SSI infrastructure? The answer is the *Trust over IP* (ToIP) *stack*: a four-layer architectural model for SSI-powered digital trust infrastructure now being standardized by the Trust over IP Foundation (https://trustoverip.org, hosted by the Linux Foundation). If you study the picture of the ToIP stack in figure 2.14, you can see where all seven building blocks fit.

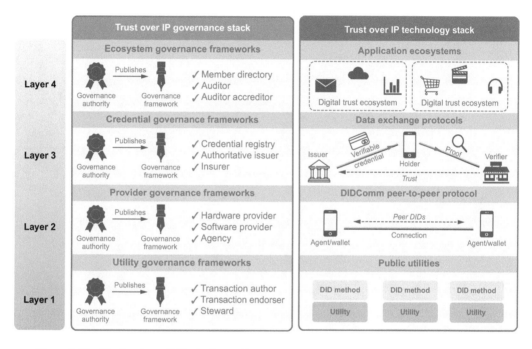

Figure 2.14 The four-layer ToIP stack combines cryptographic trust at the machine-to-machine layers (1 and 2) with human trust at the business, legal, and social layers (3 and 4) to support interoperable digital trust ecosystems. Note that the term *public utilities* is used to refer to blockchains or verifiable data registries for DIDs.

We go much deeper into the ToIP stack and the details of each layer in later chapters of the book, particularly in part 2. But first, in chapter 3, we show how these building blocks can be put together to solve real-world digital identity problems in a series of typical SSI usage scenarios.

SSI Resources

For more free content to learn about SSI, please go to IdentityBook.info and SSI Meetup.org/book.

References

1. IBM Blockchain Pulse. 2019. "Episode 1: The Future of Protecting Your Wallet and Identity." https://www.ibm.com/blogs/blockchain/2019/04/episode-1-the-future-of-protecting-your-wallet -and-identity.
2. Cameron, Kim. 2005. "The Laws of Identity." *Kim Cameron's Identity Weblog.* https://www .identityblog.com/stories/2005/05/13/TheLawsOfIdentity.pdf.

Example scenarios
showing how SSI works

Drummond Reed, Alex Preukschat, and Daniel Hardman

Daniel Hardman, former chief architect and CISO at Evernym and now principal ecosystem engineer at SICPA, has been designing SSI infrastructure since before it was called SSI. He has seen firsthand in the market multiple instances of the basic SSI interaction patterns that we describe in this chapter.

In chapter 2, we examined the core building blocks of self-sovereign identity (SSI). In this chapter, we show you how these building blocks are put together to implement SSI using seven example scenarios that progress from the relatively simple to the reasonably complex. Our objective is to show you how the SSI digital identity model works differently than the centralized or federated digital identity models.

The scenarios we have chosen are as follows:

1 Alice and Bob form a connection after meeting in person at a conference.
2 Alice and Bob form a connection via Alice's blog.
3 Bob logs in to Alice's blog to leave a comment.
4 Alice and Bob form a connection by meeting through an online dating site.
5 Alice applies for a bank account.
6 Alice buys a car.
7 Alice sells the car to Bob.

Our example scenarios use the *Alice* and *Bob* characters that have become so iconic in cryptography and cybersecurity that there is an entire Wikipedia article about them (https://en.wikipedia.org/wiki/Alice_and_Bob). Each scenario illustrates a basic pattern of SSI usage that you will see repeated in the industry-specific SSI scenarios we explore in part 4 of this book.

3.1   *A simple notation for SSI scenario diagrams*

In this chapter, we will use the simple diagramming notation shown in figure 3.1. These 11 icons are all that is needed to show how the concepts of SSI digital credentials can be applied to a myriad of trust problems we encounter as consumers and businesses every day. Most of these icons are self-explanatory, but here is a key:

- *Person*—An individual SSI identity holder (e.g., Alice and Bob)
- *Organization*—An organization or group that holds an SSI identity
- *Thing*—A physical, logical, or natural object with an SSI identity (e.g., a device on the Internet of Things [IoT])
- *Edge agent and wallet*—The device and software used by a person or organization to store, manage, and share their SSI digital credentials (see chapters 2 and 9)
- *Cloud agent and wallet*—The same as an edge agent but operating in the cloud
- *QR code (quick response code)*—A two-dimensional barcode that can be read by the camera on a smartphone, tablet, or other computing device to initiate an interaction
- *Initiation*—The first step in forming a digital identity relationship between any two SSI identity holders (e.g., Alice and Bob)
- *Connection*—A relationship established by consent between two SSI digital identity holders whose agents exchange cryptographic keys with each other to form a secure, private communications channel
- *Credential*—A verifiable digital identity credential (see chapters 2 and 7)
- *Proof*—A digitally signed, cryptographically verifiable proof of specific information from a credential
- *Verification*—The result of an agent successfully verifying a proof

Figure 3.1   The simple set of icons we use for the SSI scenario diagrams in this chapter

In all of these scenarios, we also use the three fundamental roles—issuer, holder, and verifier—from the verifiable credentials trust triangle introduced in chapter 2 (figure 3.2).

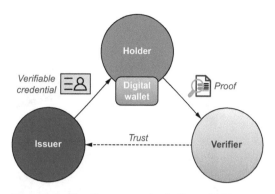

Figure 3.2 The three core roles in the verifiable credential trust triangle

3.2 Scenario 1: Bob meets Alice at a conference

All forms of digital identity exist in the context of a *relationship* of some kind. In typical enterprise identity and access management (IAM) scenarios, this might be the relationship between an employee and a company, or a consumer and a website. Or, in an IoT context, it might be the relationship between an IoT device and its manufacturer or owner.

All of these scenarios are typical *client-server* relationships, where the identity holder is using client software such as a browser to establish an identity with (register) and authenticate to (log in) a server controlled by an enterprise. This classic account-based identity pattern uses either the centralized or federated identity model described in chapter 1.

The SSI identity model is broader. It is based on *peer-to-peer* relationships between any two entities, of which client-server relationships are just one kind. To emphasize this, the first scenario we will run through is one of the most common interactions in business: Alice and Bob meeting each other at a conference and exchanging business cards. In a scenario like this,

- Neither Alice nor Bob is a "client" of the other. They are simply peers.
- Neither Alice nor Bob is running "servers."
- Neither of them is creating an "account" with the other—rather, they are just forming a connection between peers.

In the pre-digital days, this simple peer-to-peer exchange might have looked like figure 3.3.

Figure 3.3 The pre-digital ritual of forming a business connection by exchanging business cards

Figure 3.4 The digital ritual of exchanging business card info using mobile phones and LinkedIn

However, at today's business conferences, the connection is often made digitally, using mobile phones and business networks like LinkedIn. So the ceremony now looks more like figure 3.4.

The digital version of this ritual doesn't just eliminate paper; it puts the contact info directly where it is most useful: on your mobile phone. Even better, if the connection is made through a business network like LinkedIn, the connection will persist even if Alice and Bob change jobs, email addresses, or phone numbers. However, this convenience comes at a cost: sharing all your professional contact information with LinkedIn. For many of us, this is not an issue—the discomfort about privacy is offset by convenience. However, for others whose professional networks are confidential or security-sensitive, using a public social network like LinkedIn, Facebook, or Twitter is not an option.

What if Alice and Bob had an easy, fast way to form their own connection, *directly*, peer-to-peer, without the need for *any* intermediary? What if this connection created a secure private channel that only Alice and Bob could use? And what if this connection could last *forever*—or until either Alice or Bob (or both) decided they did not want it any more?

With the SSI building blocks we introduced in chapter 2, we can build this connection in a fully decentralized manner that does not need to rely on any central party. The actual ceremony depends on the specific capabilities of Alice's and Bob's smartphones and agents. But one popular option—scanning a QR code—is familiar to anyone who has ever used a mobile boarding pass to board a plane (figure 3.5).

Figure 3.5 Forming a new SSI connection can be as easy as scanning a QR code.

Some people are already printing QR codes on their business cards to make it easier to connect with them. But those QR codes usually take you to a centralized service provider like LinkedIn that forms the connection *on the service provider's proprietary network*.

With SSI, you are creating a connection *without using any intermediate service provider or proprietary network.* Alice and Bob are connecting the wallets and agents on their phones directly, cryptographically, so the connection is entirely private to the two of them. It doesn't matter whether Alice scans Bob's QR code or Bob scans Alice's. Either way, once both Alice and Bob approve it, a direct, private, peer-to-peer SSI connection is created between their two agents, as shown in figure 3.6.

Figure 3.6 A simple connection between Alice and Bob, implemented by their respective agents

Using SSI to establish connections without intermediaries has deep implications for the future of communication and trust between people. When an intermediary is no longer needed, all of the terms and conditions and limitations imposed by that intermediary disappear. The two peers are free to structure the relationship, establish trust, and negotiate data exchange any way that works best for them—all of which were goals of the early internet. So in many ways, SSI is just helping us re-establish the original decentralized vision of the internet itself.

Of course, figure 3.6 is an over-simplification. It doesn't show the specific hardware and networks being used or the DIDs and DID documents being exchanged. But conceptually, it is an accurate picture of what exists after Alice and Bob have created their connection.

What's going on under the hood

For more technically minded readers, the following figure takes this scenario down another level of detail. Feel free to skip this sidebar if you don't need the technical minutiae.

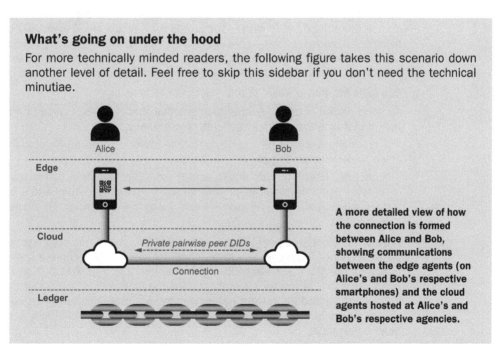

A more detailed view of how the connection is formed between Alice and Bob, showing communications between the edge agents (on Alice's and Bob's respective smartphones) and the cloud agents hosted at Alice's and Bob's respective agencies.

(continued)

First, let's explain how Alice and Bob are each provisioned with the edge agents/wallets and cloud agents shown in the figure. They begin by downloading an SSI mobile wallet app (or using one that comes installed on their smartphone). Just as with browsers and email apps, it should not matter whether Alice and Bob both use the same mobile wallet app, as long as their apps support the open standards for SSI interoperability (see chapter 5).

The first time Alice and Bob open their respective mobile wallet apps, their edge agent software should prompt them to set up a cloud agent. This is similar to setting up your smartphone to use a cloud backup service. Different apps will work with different cloud agent service providers—called *SSI agencies*—who offer the service of hosting cloud agents. This should take less than a minute and only has to be done once. (Once your edge agent is paired with a cloud agent, it should continue to work seamlessly unless you decide to break the connection and pair with a different cloud agent.)

Once Alice and Bob have their mobile wallets, edge agents, and cloud agents set up, this is how the scenario proceeds (assuming that it is Alice who produces a QR code for Bob to scan—the scenario works the same way in reverse if Bob produces the QR code).

1 *Alice produces a QR code.*

   Alice clicks a menu option in her mobile wallet app (edge agent) to cause it to generate a QR code for a new connection called a *connection invitation*. This request includes information about how Bob's agent can reliably contact her over an encrypted channel. The data in this QR code is not secret and does not need strong security guarantees; the encrypted channel adds those guarantees later in the flow.

   Before it generates the QR code, Alice's edge agent generates a *nonce*—a random number used for security—and sends it to Alice's cloud agent to notify it to expect a message associated with that nonce. This nonce is included in the QR code, making the QR code unique to Bob. When Alice forms her next connection with Carol, for example, the QR code will be different.

2 *Bob uses his mobile wallet app to scan the QR code.*

   As soon as Bob's edge agent recognizes that this is a new connection invitation, it instructs the wallet to generate the following:

   – A unique new *public/private key pair* (see chapter 6 for more details about the underlying cryptography).

   – A *peer DID* based on this public/private key pair. This peer DID is a private pairwise pseudonymous identifier that will be used to identify Bob's unique connection to Alice in a privacy-preserving way that only the two of them know about.

   Once the key pair and peer DID are saved in Bob's wallet, his edge agent composes a *connection request* message that includes a DID document (the file of metadata that goes with each DID—see chapters 2 and 8). This DID document is prepared exclusively for Alice: it includes the new peer DID, the corresponding public key, and the private network address of Bob's cloud agent (called a *service endpoint* because that's how other agents can "call" Bob's agent to send a message).

Bob's edge agent sends his connection request message to Bob's cloud agent with instructions to forward it to Alice's cloud agent via the encrypted channel Alice identified in her connection invitation.

3 *The ball is back in Alice's court.*

Alice's cloud agent receives the message from Bob's agent and pushes it to Alice's edge agent, asking if Alice wants to confirm the connection. Alice's edge agent prompts Alice to confirm the connection. Alice clicks Yes, and her edge agent saves Bob's half of the connection information in its wallet.

Now Alice's edge agent does the same thing Bob's did: generates a unique new public/private key pair and a peer DID known only to Bob. It saves these in her wallet and creates a *connection response* that is the mirror image of Bob's connection request: it contains Alice's peer DID, public key, and service endpoints for the connection.

Alice's edge agent can encrypt this message using the public key from Bob's DID document so that only Bob can read it. And it can be sent to the private service endpoint that Bob specified for Alice to use. Best of all, Alice's edge agent can use this message to update the service endpoint and/or keys that Bob originally used for her. This enables the insecure information from the connection invitation to be replaced with new secure information safe from any eavesdropper.

Once it is ready, Alice's edge agent sends her connection response to her cloud agent with instructions to forward it to the private service endpoint that Bob's agent gave Alice.

4 *Bob's agents take the final step to complete the connection.*

Bob's cloud agent forwards the connection response to Bob's edge agent, which saves the DID document describing Alice's half of the peer DID connection information in Bob's wallet. Bob's edge agent notifies Bob that the connection is now complete in both directions.

Now Alice and Bob have a permanent, private connection they can use for cryptographically secure communications of any kind. A few more notes about this:

- *No verifiable credentials had to be exchanged* for Alice and Bob to begin trusting each other because this connection was formed in person. This doesn't mean some type of credential exchange won't be needed in the future—for example, if they are going to do a high-stakes business deal—but right now, they have sufficient trust.
- *No interactions were needed with a public ledger or blockchain.* The whole process took place using peer DIDs and DID documents that were generated and exchanged completely off-chain—good for both privacy and scalability. Public DIDs registered on a public blockchain are generally only needed for issuers of credentials that anyone needs to be able to verify.
- *The connection is completely private and known only to Alice and Bob.* No intermediary service providers were involved except to host cloud agents and deliver encrypted messages. Those cloud agent hosting providers (agencies) only know that there was traffic between two agents. They can't "see" inside the messages

(continued)

> to know who was talking to whom about what. (This can be further privacy-protected by using *onion routing* between agents.)
>
> - *If either Alice or Bob (or both) changes their cloud agent, the connection moves with them.* Their respective agents just send the other an update to their connection information with the new private cloud agent address at the new agency.
> - *This connection invitation flow can work anywhere.* It does not require a pre-established secure channel; nor does the recipient of an invitation need to know anything about SSI, DIDs, or mobile wallets. So it is one way SSI can grow "virally" without any centralized company or network pushing it.

3.3   *Scenario 2: Bob meets Alice through her online blog*

This scenario also results in Alice and Bob forming a connection. But this time they don't meet in person. Rather, Bob discovers Alice's blog about her state-of-the-art website design business. Bob likes the content there and decides he'd like to contact Alice about creating a website for him.

Alice, being a cutting-edge web designer, has SSI-enabled her blog so that it can accept connection requests from visitors who want to connect directly with Alice. To do this, she adds a cloud agent to her blog and connects it to her edge agent (see the following sidebar if you are interested in the details). Because this is Alice's personal blog, this cloud agent acts as another representative of Alice as an individual: it doesn't represent her blog as a separate "thing." This illustrates a key principle of SSI: *Alice can have as many agents as she wants,* on as many devices or web locations as she wants, each of which allows Alice to express her identity and form new relationships in a specific context: in this case, her online presence as a web designer.

> **NOTE**   If she wanted to, Alice could set up her blog to have its own independent SSI identity so that visitors could form connections directly to the blog instead of to Alice the person. See the following sidebar for more information.

Figure 3.7 shows the agents and connections established in this scenario. The numbers indicate the order in which actions are taken.

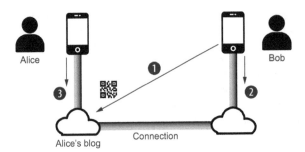

Figure 3.7   The scenario of Bob meeting Alice by first reading her blog and then deciding to request a connection with her by scanning a QR code on her blog

The scenario begins with Bob deciding to request a connection via Alice's blog:

1   *Bob uses his edge agent to scan the QR code for the connection invitation.* This QR code is configured by the SSI plug-in that Alice installed for her blog (see the following sidebar for details).

2   *Bob's edge agent app prompts him to accept the connection invitation.* When Bob presses Yes, his edge agent generates the key pair, peer DID, and DID document for the connection request message as described in the preceding sidebar and sends it to Bob's cloud agent to forward it to Alice's cloud agent to forward to Alice's edge agent.

3   *Alice receives the connection request and approves it.* The rest of this scenario proceeds as in the preceding one: Alice's edge agent generates her key pair, peer DID, and DID document for the connection response message, which is then sent back via the cloud agents to Bob's edge agent, where it is stored to complete the connection.

Note that, as with scenario 1, this scenario does not require any exchange of verifiable credentials. If Alice is willing to accept connection requests from readers of her blog, her agent does not need to ask for any further identity information. But this also exposes Alice to receiving spam connection requests. To guard against these, Alice's edge agent can require proofs of one or more common verifiable credentials that Alice trusts. This is described further in scenario 4.

What's going on under the hood

Alice hosts her blog on WordPress, so we'll assume WordPress has an SSI plug-in. (Such a Wordpress plug-in is under development as this book is being written.) When Alice installs this plug-in, it shows her a QR code needed to set up her cloud agent. Alice uses the edge agent app on her phone to scan the QR code. Her edge agent app then prompts her to approve setting up a cloud agent for her blog.

When Alice says yes, the edge agent sends a message to Alice's existing cloud agent (the figure in the previous sidebar) requesting a) to provision the new blog cloud agent, and b) to form a connection between it and Alice's edge agent. When finished, Alice's existing cloud agent sends a connection response to Alice's edge agent with the peer DID and DID document containing the private network address and public key for encrypted communications with her new blog cloud agent.

Now Alice's blog has a new feature: the ability to display a unique QR code to any reader who wants to request a new connection with Alice.

Note that this process works the same way for any SSI-enabled online resource that Alice might want to have an agent for: her LinkedIn page, her Facebook page, a website she has designed, even the signature on her emails. It can also work for anything offline for which Alice wants to set up an agent, such as her business card or the placard for one of her paintings hanging in a local gallery.

What if Alice wants her blog to have its own set of connections?

(continued)

In the scenario we just described, we assumed Alice wants her blog to act as another of her personal agents. But what if she wanted her blog to stand by itself: for example, as a portfolio of her artwork from which visitors could order prints? In this case, visitors who requested a connection would receive a connection directly to Alice's blog as a "thing" and not to Alice as a person. Alice would still control the cloud agent for this "thing"—which from a legal standpoint might represent her sole proprietorship as an artist—but that cloud agent would be separate from Alice's personal agents that represent her as an individual.

Ideally, an SSI plug-in will give a blog owner the choice of how to configure a cloud agent: to represent a person or to represent a thing.

3.4   Scenario 3: Bob logs in to Alice's blog to leave a comment

Once Bob has a connection with Alice, Bob can use that connection to authenticate himself to Alice at any time. For example, if Bob later returns to Alice's blog and wants

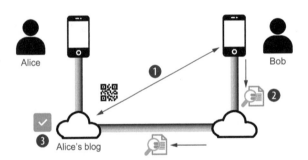

to leave a comment, Bob does not need to create an "account" with Alice's blog. *His connection is the account.* So not only does Bob *not* need to create a new username and password for Alice's blog, *he'll never have to remember them!*

Called *passwordless login* (or *auto-authentication*), this is one of the headline features of SSI (see the complete roster of major SSI features and benefits

Figure 3.8   Bob uses a similar pattern to "log in" whenever he returns to Alice's blog to leave a comment on one of her new posts.

in chapter 4). It works the same way for any SSI-enabled website or application. Figure 3.8 shows the basic sequence:

1. *Alice's blog generates a QR code.* Just as in scenario 2, the first step is for Alice's blog to generate a QR code for a reader to scan if they need to authenticate (e.g., leave a comment or do anything else that requires authorization). This time, when Bob scans the QR code, his edge agent recognizes that Bob already has a connection with Alice. So Bob's edge agent asks Bob to confirm that he wants to authenticate (or, if Bob has told his edge agent to skip those kinds of confirmations, his edge agent will just proceed).

2. *Bob's edge agent generates, signs, and sends a proof.* This proof is signed with the private key in Bob's mobile wallet *for this private peer DID connection only.* The proof is then sent to his cloud agent to forward to the cloud agent for Alice's blog.

3 *Alice's blog cloud agent receives and verifies the proof.* It verifies the signature using the public key it has for her private connection with Bob (shared by Bob when the connection was formed—and updated by Bob whenever his edge agent rotates his encryption keys). If the signature verifies, Bob is "logged in."

What is particularly powerful about auto-authentication is that it can be "tuned" to request the level of authentication a verifier requires for a particular transaction. For example, leaving a comment on a blog is a relatively low-risk activity, so it is enough for Bob to prove he has the private key for the connection (which only Bob knows). But if Bob was asking his credit union to make a $100,000 transaction, the QR code produced by the credit union could request a much stronger proof that this is really Bob.

SSI agents can also produce the authentication tokens needed for other web authentication protocols like OpenID Connect and WebAuthn. For more details, see chapter 5.

3.5 Scenario 4: Bob meets Alice through an online dating site

This scenario will result in Alice and Bob forming a connection just like the one created in scenarios 1 and 2. But this time, the introduction will come via an intermediary matchmaker: an online dating site. Since neither Alice nor Bob has a pre-established trust relationship, this is our first scenario that will require a verifiable credential.

> **IMPORTANT** While the scenarios in this chapter use government-issued ID credentials for illustration purposes, there is no requirement for SSI infrastructure to use government ID credentials—or any other specific type of credential, for that matter. In the end, the verifiers determine what types of credentials they will accept for what purposes. Government-issued ID credentials are simply a widely understood and accepted type of credential.

Figure 3.9 is a diagram of the steps involved:

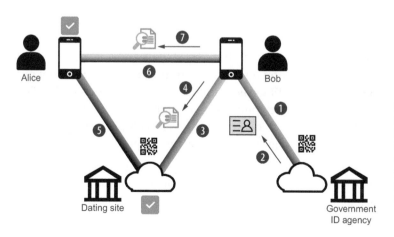

Figure 3.9 The scenario of Alice and Bob meeting through an online dating site, and Bob proving his authenticity to Alice over their newly formed connection.

1   *Bob connects to a Government ID Agency.* Bob knows the Dating Site requires proof of identity from an issuer it trusts, and one option is a government-issued ID credential. So Bob first forms a connection with the Government ID Agency cloud agent by scanning a QR code on its website as described in scenario 2.

2   *Bob requests a Government ID credential.* Bob's edge agent prompts him for the data (or other steps he must take) to prove his identity to the Government ID Agency (which could involve the Agency requesting proofs of other verifiable credentials from Bob). Once Bob meets the Agency's policies for issuing a new Government ID credential, the Agency sends the credential to Bob's edge agent to store in Bob's wallet.

3   *Bob connects to the Dating Site* as per scenario 2.

4   *The Dating Site requests proof of Bob's Government ID credential.* Bob scans a QR code requesting a proof of the Government ID credential. Bob's edge agent prompts Bob to approve sending the proof. Bob agrees, and his edge agent generates the proof, signs it with the private key for this connection, and sends it to the Dating Site's cloud agent. The Dating Site's cloud agent verifies the proof by looking up the DID of the Government ID Agency on a public blockchain such as Bitcoin, Ethereum, or Sovrin to retrieve the DID document with the public key. If the proof verifies, Bob is good to go to use the Dating Site.

5   *Alice joins the Dating Site* by forming a connection the same way. The Dating Site may or may not require Alice to send proof of a credential (not shown in figure 3.9). Alice then shares some profile data (which, if already stored in other credentials she has in her wallet, could be sent in a proof from her edge agent).

6   *Bob requests a connection with Alice.* Bob discovers Alice's profile on the Dating Site and requests a connection by scanning a QR code—just as he would have done via her blog in scenario 2. But this is a different context, so Alice is more cautious. Her edge agent requires Bob to share a proof of his Government ID credential. Note that Alice could rely on the fact that the Dating Site already has a policy requiring a male member to provide proof of a Government ID credential. But with SSI, *Alice can request that proof directly from Bob.* She doesn't have to worry if the Dating Site is not screening members properly.

7   *Bob sends Alice proof of his Government ID credential.* Bob can do this in one click because his edge agent does all the work. Alice's edge agent receives the proof over the private connection it set up with Bob and verifies the proof just like the Dating Site did. If it verifies, Alice accepts the new connection. If it fails, Alice's edge agent can delete the connection immediately *without ever needing to bother Alice.* Her edge agent is effectively serving as Alice's protector to make sure that any suitor meets Alice's minimum verification requirements.

What is even more powerful is that with SSI, *Alice isn't constrained to live with only the filters supported by the Dating Site.* Alice can request whatever proofs she wants from her suitors—and her suitors must supply those proofs before they ever even get to "knock on Alice's door," so to speak. This could significantly change the online dating ecosystem in a way that increases trust for everyone involved.

3.6   Scenario 5: Alice applies for a new bank account

The next scenario is such a clear business case for the value of verifiable credentials that in October 2018, four companies collaborated to demonstrate how it works in a video called "Job-Creds" [1]. The video shows how Alice first obtains a government ID credential from a driving licensing agency and then an employment credential from her employer (IBM) to finally apply for a bank account. Figure 3.10 shows the complete set of connections and interactions:

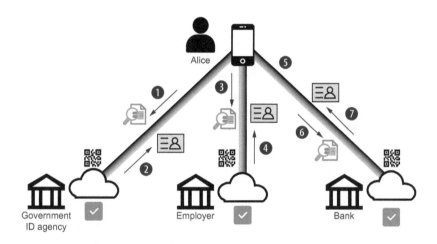

Figure 3.10   The set of proofs Alice is asked to provide in order to be issued the credentials she needs (a Government ID and proof of employment) to qualify for a bank account

  1   *Alice connects with the Government ID Agency, which requests proof of her identity.* This assumes Alice already has a mobile wallet and some credentials the Government ID agency will accept, such as a utility account or a student ID.

  2   *Alice receives her Government ID credential.* Once the Government ID Agency has verified Alice's proofs and validated that they satisfy the Government's policies for issuing an ID credential, the credential is issued to Alice's edge agent.

  3   *Alice connects with her Employer, which requests proof of her Government ID credential.* This step is typically performed as part of onboarding Alice as a new employee (required by law in some jurisdictions). Employers can save money by doing it digitally (see section 4.2).

  4   *Alice receives her Employment credential.* Once the Employer's onboarding policies are satisfied, the Employer issues Alice her new Employment credential.

5   *Alice connects with the Bank where she wants to open a new account.* Note that Alice could do this by scanning a QR code anywhere she might encounter an invitation from the Bank: on a bus, in a subway, in a newspaper advertisement, in an email, on the Bank's website, or others.

It's important to note that in this step, Alice's agent should first request proof of the Bank's credentials. The fact that connections are fundamentally bidirectional is how SSI infrastructure can protect against spoofing and phishing attempts. Once Alice has confirmed this is the real Bank and completes setting up the connection, she will never need to worry about being spoofed or phished over that connection because *only* the Bank will be able to use it to send her messages, and each message will be signed by the Bank's private key which only the Bank controls.

6   *Alice sends a proof of her Government ID credential and her Employment credential to the Bank.* These are the two proofs the Bank requires to open a new account. But for Alice, it is just a single step: when her edge agent prompts Alice for approval, she clicks Send, and her edge agent takes care of the rest.

7   *Alice receives her Bank Account credential.* The Bank's cloud agent verifies both of the proofs sent by Alice's edge agent. If they verify, it completes the all-digital process of provisioning a new account and sends Alice her new Bank Account credential.

Now Alice has a new bank account, and the Bank has a new customer. From the point at which Alice has her Government ID and Employment credentials, this process of onboarding a new bank customer, which normally requires an in-person visit and several person-hours of time, can be performed entirely digitally in under a minute. And the result is more secure than the equivalent offline process, because all the credentials can be immediately verified using strong cryptography instead of bank employees trying to verify paper or plastic credentials that are orders of magnitude easier to fake.

3.7   *Scenario 6: Alice buys a car*

Armed with her new credentials, Alice can now simplify and automate many other kinds of transactions, to the benefit of both herself and the businesses and agencies she interacts with. Figure 3.11 shows the process of Alice buying a new car. In this scenario, we'll assume the following:

- Alice already has connections with her Bank, Auto Dealer, and Licensing Agency.
- She has picked out the car and negotiated the price with the Auto Dealer.
- She has qualified for a car loan from her Bank.

Here are the steps Alice takes:

1   *Alice proves her identity to her Bank to request a loan.* Because this is a major purchase, the Bank requests one or more other credentials (such as her Government ID) to make sure it is really Alice asking for the loan.

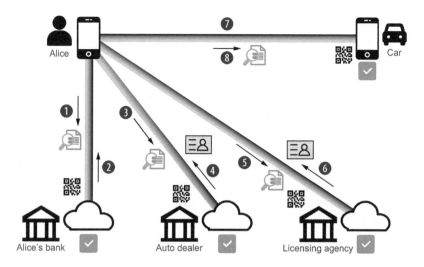

Figure 3.11　Alice buys and registers a car entirely using digital connections and credentials. In the final step, Alice proves her ownership of the car to unlock and drive it away.

2 *Alice receives a Loan credential and Payment Authorization credential from her Bank.* Alice can use the Loan credential to prove she has been authorized to receive the loan; she can use the Payment Authorization credential to pay the Auto Dealer.

3 *Alice completes the purchase of the car from the Auto Dealer.* Alice sends proof of her Payment Authorization credential to the Auto Dealer, which arranges for payment (although not shown in figure 3.11, this process could also use an SSI connection between the Auto Dealer and Alice's Bank).

4 *Alice receives her Purchase Receipt credential from the Auto Dealer.* This is an example of a digital receipt delivered in the form of a verifiable credential: a powerful new tool for both consumers and merchants everywhere (see chapter 4).

5 *Alice applies to the Licensing Agency to register her new car.* Alice presents a proof of her Purchase Receipt credential for the car and a proof of her Loan credential from her Bank. Between them, they contain all the information—including the vehicle identification number (VIN)—that the Licensing Agency needs to issue Alice a Vehicle Registration credential for the car that includes a lien to Alice's Bank.

6 *Alice receives her Vehicle Registration credential.* This goes straight into her digital wallet along with all her other credentials.

7 *Alice forms a connection with her new car.* This is an example of Alice connecting with a thing (as in the Internet of Things) instead of a person or an organization. It works just like our earlier examples, except in this case, Alice scans a QR code on the car (for example, on a window sticker or the car's digital display).

8 *Alice proves her ownership of the car.* The QR code requests proof of a Vehicle Registration credential: not just for any car, but for *that* car, with that specific VIN. That is exactly what Alice was issued by the Licensing Authority, so Alice's edge agent sends it to the car's edge agent (operating as part of the car's onboard computer). Once the car's edge agent verifies the proof, the car unlocks, and Alice can drive it away.

Although that final step might seem like a scene from a sci-fi movie, it is very real. In March 2018, one of the authors of this book gave a demonstration to the R&D division of the U.S. Department of Homeland Security of unlocking a car using a verifiable credential. As we move toward all-electric cars, onboard computers, and autonomous vehicles, the key to your car of the future could well be a verifiable credential on your smartphone. (This would also make it easy to "delegate" car keys to family members, friends, etc. without having to make physical copies. And these digital "keys" can even be time- or usage-restricted: a child could be given a key to take the car for a trip to the movies but not to drive outside of town.)

3.8   *Scenario 7: Alice sells the car to Bob*

In our final example, we pull together all our previous scenarios and show one involving person-to-person, person-to-business, and person-to-thing relationships: Alice selling the car she bought in scenario 6 to Bob (whom she met through scenario 1, 2, or 4). There are enough steps that we'll break this example into two diagrams to make it easier to follow. Part A—the financial arrangements—is shown in figure 3.12. This scenario assumes the following:

- Bob and Alice have already formed a connection and negotiated a price for the car.
- Bob has been approved for a car loan by his Credit Union.
- Bob and Alice both live in a jurisdiction served by the same Licensing Agency.

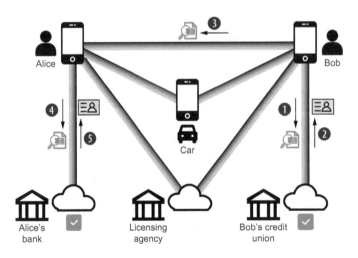

Figure 3.12 Part A of the scenario shows the steps Bob and Alice take to make the financial arrangements for Bob to buy the car.

The steps in part A are as follows:

1 *Bob proves his identity to his Credit Union to request a loan.* This the same first step Alice took in scenario 6.

2 *Bob receives a Loan credential and a Payment Authorization credential from his Credit Union.* Again, this is the mirror of what Alice did in scenario 6.

3 *Bob sends proof of his Payment Authorization to Alice.* Now Alice just needs to complete her side of the deal.

4 *Alice forwards her proof of the Payment Authorization credential to her Bank.* She also sends a proof of the Loan Credential she wants the payment applied to. Alice's Bank uses these proofs to arrange for payment directly from Bob's Bank.

5 *Alice receives an update to her Loan Credential showing that the loan is paid off.* Alice can use this revised credential not just to transfer the car registration in part B, but to prove her credit history to anyone else in the future. Note that *Alice can now do this without needing to rely on a centralized credit rating agency.*

Part B (figure 3.13) shows the remaining steps to transfer the car title and registration:

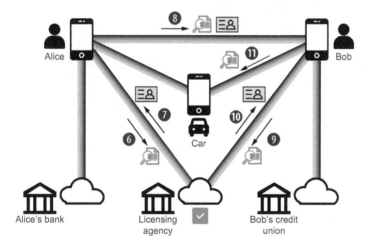

Figure 3.13 **Part B of the scenario shows the steps Alice and Bob need to take to transfer the title and registration for the car.**

6 *Alice sends proof of her updated Loan Credential to the Licensing Agency.* This proves that Alice's Bank has released its lien and Alice is free to sell the car.

7 *Alice receives an updated Vehicle Registration credential from the Licensing Agency.* Now Alice is ready to complete the sale to Bob.

8 *Alice sends Bob a Purchase Receipt and a proof of her updated Vehicle Registration credential.* These are the two digital artifacts Bob needs from Alice to apply for his own new vehicle registration.

9 *Bob applies to the Licensing Agency to register his new car.* Like Alice in scenario 6, Bob sends a proof of his Purchase Receipt and a proof of his Loan credential. Bob also forwards Alice's proof of her Vehicle Registration credential. The Licensing Agency verifies all proofs to confirm that Alice owns the car free and clear, that she has sold it to Bob, and that Bob has a loan from his Credit Union to buy it.

10 *Bob receives his Vehicle Registration credential.* At the same time, the Licensing Agency revokes Alice's Vehicle Registration credential, so her virtual "key" to the car stops working as soon as the car's edge agent detects that Alice's Vehicle Registration Credential has been revoked (for more on how credential revocation works, see chapter 5).

11 *Bob connects to and unlocks his new car.* This is the same step Alice took at the end of scenario 6, only now Bob is the proud new owner.

3.9   *Scenario summary*

This chapter took the SSI building blocks in chapter 2 and put them together to illustrate a variety of common scenarios requiring identity and trust.

- To understand white-collar crime, a detective's mantra is "follow the money." To understand how SSI works, the mantra is "follow the credentials and proofs."
- All that's needed to understand the basic technical flows is to map out the actors that need to establish trust (people, organizations, things), assign them agents (edge and/or cloud), establish the connections between them, and then issue credentials and present proofs to meet all the trust requirements.
- These agent-to-agent exchanges often directly mirror those that take place face-to-face in the physical world. However, they can also mirror how the same exchange would take place on the web today: i.e., via a website representing one party, or via websites or services designed to introduce multiple parties (such as social networks, dating sites, online communities).
- Once established, an SSI connection can also provide passwordless login to any SSI-enabled website or app, can send and receive credentials and proofs in either direction, and can last as long as both parties need it—it does not need to depend on any intermediaries to stay active.
- Entire multi-party workflows, such as applying for a job, buying a car, or one person selling a car to another, can be accomplished by putting together the same basic SSI building blocks.

What may not yet be clear is just how much value can be produced with this new paradigm for achieving digital trust. That is the subject of chapter 4, where we introduce the SSI Scorecard.

SSI Resources

For more free content to learn about SSI, please go to IdentityBook.info and SSIMeetup.org/book.

Reference

1. Gisolfi, Dan. 2018. "Decentralized Identity: An Alternative to Password-Based Authentication." IBM. https://www.ibm.com/blogs/blockchain/2018/10/decentralized-identity-an-alternative-to -password-based-authentication.

SSI Scorecard: Major features and benefits of SSI

Drummond Reed and Alex Preukschat

By now, it should be clear that SSI is not just a point technology, like web shopping carts or mapping apps. It is a fundamental technology shift, akin to the internet or the web itself. As such, it doesn't have just one primary feature or benefit—or even just a small set of them. Rather, it offers an entire spectrum of features and benefits that vary in their impact depending on the particular use cases, application, or industry.

The reason is that the SSI digital identity model solves fundamental problems in digital trust, and it does so at an infrastructure level—much like the internet solves fundamental problems in data sharing at an infrastructure level. So, just like the internet, SSI can eliminate the need for thousands of smaller "bandage" solutions by providing a solid layer of open standard infrastructure.

This approach provides a wide swath of benefits for almost anyone using the internet, and that's what we'll explore in this chapter. To do this, we've developed a tool, the SSI Scorecard, that classifies 25 major features and benefits of SSI into the five categories shown in table 4.1. In part 4 of this book, we use this SSI Scorecard to analyze the impact of SSI across the use cases for a representative set of industry verticals.

The five categories are as follows:

1 *Bottom line*—Features and benefits that deliver directly to a company's bottom line because of cost reduction or new revenue opportunities made possible with SSI.

2 *Business efficiencies*—Features and benefits of SSI that enable the digital transformation of business via business process automation (BPA).

58

3 *User experience and convenience*—The same five features and benefits as the business efficiencies category, but through the lens of how they benefit the end user.

4 *Relationship management*—Features and benefits focused on how SSI will transform aspects of customer relationship management (CRM), digital marketing, and loyalty programs.

5 *Regulatory compliance*—Features and benefits based on how SSI will strengthen cybersecurity and cyberprivacy infrastructure and automated how companies can comply with regulations.

Table 4.1 SSI Scorecard is a tool for analyzing the impact of SSI for any use case, application, industry, or vertical market.

SSI Scorecard	
Category	**Feature/Benefit**
1. Bottom line	Fraud reduction
	Reduced customer onboarding costs
	Improved e-commerce sales
	Reduced customer service costs
	New credential issuer revenue
2. Business efficiencies	Auto-authentication
	Auto-authorization
	Workflow automation
	Delegation and guardianship
	Payment and value exchange
3. User experience and convenience	Auto-authentication
	Auto-authorization
	Workflow automation
	Delegation and guardianship
	Payment and value exchange
4. Relationship management	Mutual authentication
	Permanent connections
	Premium private channels
	Reputation management
	Loyalty and rewards programs

Table 4.1   SSI Scorecard is a tool for analyzing the impact of SSI for any use case, application, industry, or vertical market. *(continued)*

SSI Scorecard	
Category	**Feature/Benefit**
5. Regulatory compliance	Data security
	Data privacy
	Data protection
	Data portability
	RegTech (regulation technology)

4.1   Feature/benefit category 1: Bottom line

This category represents the easiest sale in business: features and benefits that deliver *directly to a company's bottom line*, that is, they either make a company more money or save it money—quickly. Following are five ways SSI can do this.

4.1.1   Fraud reduction

The first and fastest way SSI can help the bottom line is by reducing fraud. Javelin Strategy reported that in 2016, *15.4 million consumers were victims of identity theft or fraud*, costing a total of $16 billion in losses [1]. Javelin also reported that new account fraud—criminals opening up new accounts under victims' names—increased from $3 billion in 2017 to $3.4 billion in 2018 [2].

Although the potential savings from fraud reduction vary by industry segment, it is one of the largest potential sources of savings for some industries. For example, the National Health Care Anti-Fraud Association estimates that in 2017, health care fraud cost the United States about *$68 billion annually*—about 3% of the nation's $2.26 trillion in health care spending.

Bottom line: *even if fraud reduction were the only benefit of SSI*, it would warrant a massive investment by businesses and governments worldwide. Indeed, fraud reduction is one of the primary reasons the global credit union industry is embracing SSI as its first significant use of blockchain technology by introducing the MemberPass digital credential as a standard way for any credit union member to prove their identity (https://www.memberpass.com).

4.1.2   Reduced customer onboarding costs

The cost of customer onboarding varies by industry, but in financial services, in particular, the cost of Know Your Customer (KYC) compliance has gone through the roof. According to Thomson Reuters, out of 92% of the firms it surveyed, *KYC onboarding processes cost an average of $28.5 million* [3]. Ten percent of the world's top financial institutions spend at least $100 million annually on it [4]. And onboarding a new financial services customer takes anywhere from one to three months on average [5].

There is also a steep cost for not being compliant with these regulations. In 2018, Fenergo reported that a staggering *$26 billion in fines* had been imposed on financial institutions worldwide for non-compliance with KYC, Anti-Money Laundering (AML), and sanctions regulations in the last decade [6].

Although SSI in general and verifiable credentials in particular are not a silver bullet for all the complexity of automating customer onboarding and ensuring KYC and AML compliance, they are a major new weapon in this arms race—a weapon that benefits all three sides: customers, financial institutions, and regulators. By securely and privately digitizing the information that companies must gather from their customers under these regulations—and enabling it to be cryptographically verified in real time with a full audit trail—SSI has the potential to save all three groups many billions of dollars annually. And it can reduce customer onboarding time from months to days or even hours.

4.1.3 Improved e-commerce sales

Statista reported that in 2019, an estimated 1.92 billion people purchased goods or services online, and e-retail sales passed $3.5 trillion [7]. Nasdaq predicts that by 2040, *around 95% of all purchases* are expected to be via e-commerce [8].

More than a third of online Black Friday 2018 sales were completed on smartphones [9]. But on average, only 2.58% of e-commerce website visits convert into a purchase [10]. *The global cart abandonment rate for e-commerce is close to 70%.* The Baymard Institute averaged rates from 40 different studies, which give rates from as low as 55% to as high as 81%, to arrive at a global average of 69.89% [11].

When you add the fact that *80% of online shoppers stop doing business with a company because of poor customer experience* [12], the improved convenience (no forms to complete), privacy (minimal disclosure through zero-knowledge proof attestations), and safety (automatic blinding of purchase data) of shopping with an SSI digital wallet means the impact of SSI on improving e-commerce sales is something that no online merchant can afford to ignore.

Of course, SSI technology alone can't make up for poor website design, missing information, or low-quality products. But by removing so much of the friction from the web shopping experience, SSI digital wallets can help level the playing field between smaller e-commerce sites and giants like Amazon and Alibaba.

4.1.4 Reduced customer service costs

Customer service has become one of the primary battlegrounds of modern business. Gartner predicts that *89% of businesses are expected to compete mainly on customer experience* [13].

But it is an expensive proposition. Forbes reports that *in 2018, businesses were losing $75 billion per year through poor customer service*—up $13 billion since 2016 [14]. According to Infosecurity Magazine, just one persistent customer service issue—lost passwords—*costs businesses an average of over $60 per incident* [15].

SSI can have a significant impact on improving the customer experience (CX) and reducing customer-service costs. Passwordless authentication is only the start—the rest of this chapter is filled with examples such as permanent connections (no more losing track of customers), premium private channels, workflow automation, and integrated loyalty management. All of this goes straight to the bottom line—84% of companies that improve their CX report an increase in their revenue [16].

4.1.5 New credential issuer revenue

All of the preceding features and benefits apply to a company's existing lines of business. SSI also opens up new revenue opportunities for a surprisingly wide variety of companies. Any business whose interaction with its customers produces a measure of knowledge about their attributes and interests—or a measure of trust in their behavior—is now in a position to monetize that data in a permissioned and privacy-respecting way: by issuing customers (suppliers, partners, contractors, and others) verifiable credentials that help them use this knowledge. Even better, customers can be the distribution channel for this knowledge to verifiers who need it.

And verifiers will pay for that valuable knowledge for the same reason they pay for customer profile data (from data brokers), credit history (from credit rating agencies), background checks (from background verification companies), and other customer data sources today. SSI can transform this current market much as the web transformed the newspaper classifieds market, the auction market, and the retail market. For example, SSI can provide the following:

- Broader, richer, and more diverse profiles of the customer than those available from third-party sources today
- Fully permissioned and GDPR-compliant data because the customer is the vehicle for sharing the information for their own benefit
- Fresher, richer, and more contextual data about preferences, interests, and relationships
- Selective disclosure of attributes (meaning data owners can choose which pieces of data they want to share)—something that is all but impossible for business-to-business data sharing that takes place behind the customer's back

4.2   Feature/benefit category 2: Business efficiencies

As important as the immediate bottom line is, SSI's larger impact will be in re-engineering business processes—a field known as *business process automation* (BPA) or, more broadly, *digital transformation*. This kind of paradigm shift does not happen very often; it is analogous to the transition businesses underwent from snail mail to email, from phones to fax machines, and from paper to the web.

As we illustrated in chapter 3, these efficiencies are not limited to just one area of business but accumulate across entire workflows and even across entire industries. In this section, we look at five areas where SSI can directly impact business efficiencies.

4.2.1 Auto-authentication

Perhaps no area of web experience is more despised by individuals and companies alike than login. The 2015 TeleSign Consumer Account Security Report said the following [17]:

- 54% of people use 5 or fewer passwords across their entire online life.
- 47% of people use passwords that are at least 5 years old.
- 7 in 10 people no longer trust passwords to protect their online accounts.

In 2019, Auth0 reported that [18]

- The average American email address has 130 accounts registered to it [19].
- The number of accounts per user is doubling every 5 years [20].
- 58% of users admit to forgetting their password frequently [20].
- The average internet user receives roughly 37 "forgot password" emails each year [20].

But besides the sheer hassle, the real impact of username/password-based login is the friction:

- The average person has between 7 and 25 accounts that they log in to every day [21].
- Around 82% of people have forgotten a password used on a website [22].
- Password recovery is the number-one request to help desks for intranets that don't have single sign-on portal capabilities [20].

In short, by moving from conventional login to SSI auto-authentication—using an SSI digital wallet to automatically exchange strong cryptographic proofs instead of a username and password—we can finally "kill the password." (For an example of how this works, see the third scenario in chapter 3. For technical details, see chapters 5 and 7.) It will be like replacing frequent, error-prone toll booths with a wide-open, well-paved highway. Everyone can go about their business faster, more easily, and more safely.

4.2.2 Auto-authorization

Authentication (login) is just the first step in most trusted business processes. It proves that you are the rightful owner of an account. But it does not answer the next questions: What are you authorized to do? What privileges should you be granted? What actions can you take?

In the world of identity and access management (IAM), this is called *authorization*. It is an even more challenging problem than authentication. But this is where verifiable credentials truly shine. To use the analogy illustrated in figure 4.1, if verifiable credentials are a hammer, then authentication is only a thumbtack. Authorization is a full 16-penny nail.

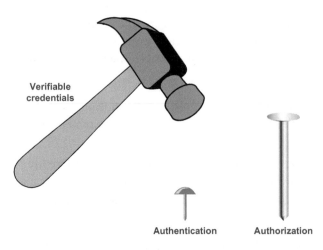

Figure 4.1 While authentication is important, authorization is actually a much bigger nail for the SSI verifiable credentials hammer to hit.

The reason verifiable credentials are such a powerful tool for authorization is that they can solve three hard problems in one stroke:

1 *They can provide exactly the right claims needed for an authorization decision.* These decisions are made by applying the verifier's access control policies. *Attribute-based access control* [23] is based on specific attributes of the identity owner: age, gender, zip code, browser type, and so on. *Role-based access control* is based on the role or roles of the identity owner: employee, contractor, customer, regulator, etc. Either way, verifiable credentials represent the fastest and easiest way for the verifier to request and the holder to supply the precise claims needed. See chapter 7 for details.

2 *They can be cryptographically verified in real time.* To be confident in an authorization decision, a verifier must trust the claims being presented. As explained in chapter 2, the whole point of SSI architecture is to enable a verifier's agent to verify the issuer's signature on the holder's proof in seconds.

3 *They can be bound to the holder of the credential as the authorized party.* One of the greatest sources of fraud is stolen usernames/passwords—they have grown into a $6 billion annual market precisely because they are not verifiable [24]. With verifiable credentials, there are several techniques for proving that the claims they contain were issued to the credential holder. These include sharing proof of a biometric for the holder and cryptographically linking credentials to a holder using zero-knowledge proofs (ZKPs). See chapters 5, 6, and 7 for details.

Using a verifiable-credentials model, a verifier's job can be simplified into three steps:

1 *Determine the set of claims*—attributes describing the subject of a verifiable credential (for example, age, location, employment, education)—that the verifier needs for any particular authorization decision.

2 *Determine the issuers—or governance framework*—that the verifier trusts for those claims. See chapter 11 for details.

3 *Make it easy for users to acquire those credentials* so the user experience is as simple and seamless as possible. See chapter 7.

But the SSI model can go one step further in business efficiency. Once a user has established a connection with a verifier and approved sharing the claims necessary to meet the verifier's policies, *the user can apply their own policies* to this process. For example, the user can instruct their SSI agent (such as a mobile wallet or a cloud agent—see chapter 9) to automatically share the same claims with the verifier when the user needs to repeat a business process in the future (order a supply, approve a budget, publish a web page).

The entire authentication and authorization process for a user—even if quite sophisticated—can be automated to the point it is carried out entirely by the user's and verifier's respective agents, *including the audit trail needed for accountability*. Obviously, this is a big win for users (see section 4.3). However, for verifiers, the benefits of auto-authorization can be on the same order as the benefits of credit cards for merchants: customers can perform an essential exchange of information far more easily and painlessly, accelerating business for everyone.

4.2.3 *Workflow automation*

Every business process has a workflow: the series of steps that must be performed to carry it out end-to-end. Each step that crosses a trust boundary—branch to branch, customer to merchant, supplier to vendor, company to government—typically requires the authentication and authorization processes described previously. So SSI agents can already wring out major inefficiencies just by performing auto-authentication and auto-authorization.

But those same agents can also apply the business logic necessary to orchestrate the steps in the process no matter how many trust boundaries it crosses. This is the heart of business process automation (BPA): designing a business process so humans are doing only the steps that require their expertise, awareness, judgment, and empathy. The rest can be assigned to digital agents (which in some cases may further reassign it to robots). Besides enacting the trust infrastructure necessary to do this work safely, SSI agents are ideal for BPA because they can literally "follow a script"—in this case, JavaScript or a similar programming language that instructs them to apply each step in the flow of a business process. Agents can be pre-programmed with such scripts, or they can download them dynamically via SSI connections with orchestration agents whose job it is to maintain a library of the current scripts required for a specific business process.

SSI is a significant leap forward in BPA because process improvements no longer need to be limited to a single company or a single supply chain. Like the internet and the web, SSI enables BPA workflows to be carried out across any set of trust boundaries, according to any set of policies (governance framework—see chapter 11) agreed to by the participants. It is truly "worldwide BPA."

4.2.4   *Delegation and guardianship*

Digital agents can be given instructions and assigned responsibilities via program code. But most business processes require specific human workers to perform specific functions or make specific decisions as part of the process. How are those humans assigned those responsibilities?

This is the job of a subclass of verifiable credentials called *delegation credentials*. They are how a holder can prove that they have the authority to carry out a specific task or make a specific decision as part of a business process. The following are some common examples in a corporate context:

- *Employees* can be given a delegation credential to send tweets from the company's Twitter account or post new articles to the company's blog.
- *Drivers* can be given a delegation credential to pick up and deliver goods on behalf of the company.
- *Officers* can be given specific delegation credentials authorizing them to execute specific types of contracts on behalf of the company: HR officers to sign an employment contract, procurement officers to sign a purchase order, CFOs to execute a bank order, and so on.
- *Board members* can be given delegation credentials to execute electronic board votes that do not require them to be physically present for a meeting.

There are countless more examples from every context that needs to carry out business processes—governments, schools, non-profits, churches, even households. For example, parents could use delegation credentials to specify how much screen time their children are allowed or what kinds of foods they are permitted to buy for lunch at school.

The parental example brings up another case: taking responsibility for an individual who is not in a position to wield SSI technology on their own. There are many examples besides babies or young children: the elderly, individuals with disabilities, refugees and displaced peoples, and individuals without mobile phones or internet access.

To enjoy the same rights to self-sovereign identity as everyone else, these individuals need *digital guardians*—individuals or organizations who can operate SSI agents and wallets on their behalf. This form of "complete delegation" is carried out using a *guardianship credential.* It acts much like the digital equivalent of a guardianship order from a court (and may be authorized by such an order once court systems begin officially recognizing verifiable credentials). It enables the guardian to set up and operate an SSI agent and wallet on behalf of the dependent and, when necessary, prove that they are acting in the capacity of a guardian. This extends the benefits of SSI to any person regardless of physical, mental, or financial capacity.

> **NOTE**   Official legal recognition of verifiable credentials for guardianship of dementia patients is already being explored in the Province of Ontario, Canada. See https://www.secours.io.

4.2.5   *Payment and value exchange*

Mention the phrase *digital wallet*, and the first thought that comes to many people's minds is payments—because that's the primary task for which we use our physical wallets today (figure 4.2). If digital wallets are the core metaphor for SSI, people will expect them to be used for payment in addition to identity.

Figure 4.2   Digital wallets are the core metaphor for SSI—so it feels natural that they would be applied to payments.

Indeed, since SSI digital wallets incorporate everything necessary for the trusted exchange of digital information—DIDs, private connections, private keys, agent endpoints—extending them to the safe exchange of digital payments is very natural. The good news is

- From the standpoint of SSI agents, payments are just another type of workflow.
- SSI wallets can be designed to work with any type of currency (including cryptocurrencies) as well as with any type of payment system or network (including credit/debit card networks).
- With digital wallets and verifiable credentials, payment can be integrated directly into workflows that require KYC and AML, as discussed earlier.

Even better news: *payments are just one type of value exchange that can be automated using SSI.* The term *payment* usually means a specific type of currency—fiat currencies like dollars, pounds, euros, and yen, or cryptocurrencies like bitcoin and ether. However, there are many additional means of value storage and exchange: points, airline miles, coupons, and other loyalty programs. And SSI digital wallets and agents can be used for all of them as fast as these value-exchange systems can be translated to verifiable credentials and agent-to-agent protocols. (See section 4.4.5.)

This, in turn, means payments can be integrated into almost any business process workflow at almost any level of assurance and regulatory compliance. Payment automation is the frosting on the SSI-enabled BPA cake.

4.3   Feature/benefit category 3: User experience and convenience

This category looks at the same five features and benefits as the last category (business efficiencies), but this time through the lens of how they benefit the end user.

4.3.1   Auto-authentication

How much do users hate passwords? A July 2019 study by MobileIon reported in Security InfoCenter [25] said that when users encounter password troubles,

- 68% feel disrupted.
- 63% feel irritated and frustrated.
- 62% feel they have wasted time.

The same study found that

- IT security leaders felt they could reduce their risk of breach by almost half (43%) by eliminating passwords.
- 86% of those security leaders would do away with passwords if they could.
- 88% of these leaders believed that in the near future, mobile devices will serve as individuals' digital ID to access enterprise services and data.

In February 2019, user-centric biometric authentication leader Veridium published a study of more than 1,000 U.S. adults who have experience with biometrics (such as Apple's TouchID or FaceID) that found 70% wanted to expand their use into everyday login [26]. Speed (35%), security (31%), and not having to remember passwords (33%) were cited as the primary incentives.

On May 1, 2018, Microsoft announced in a blog post that it was "Building a world without passwords" [27]:

Nobody likes passwords. They are inconvenient, insecure, and expensive. In fact, we dislike them so much that we've been busy at work trying to create a world without them— a world without passwords.

This is why Microsoft has been a major supporter of DIDs—the decentralized identifiers at the core of SSI—and is building DID-based passwordless authentication into multiple products (see https://www.microsoft.com/en-us/security/business/identity/own-your-identity).

In short, the age of the password is about to pass, and for users everywhere, it could not come fast enough. There will be rejoicing in the streets.

4.3.2   Auto-authorization

If passwordless auto-authentication replaces the login screen, *auto-authorization will replace many (but not all) web forms.* Can you hear more rejoicing?

Here are some realities about online forms:

- 81% of people have abandoned a form after beginning to fill it out [28].

- 29% of people cite security reasons as one of their main concerns when completing online forms [29].
- More than 67% of site visitors will abandon a form forever if they encounter any complications; only 20% will follow up with the company in some way [29].
- 23% of people will not fill out a checkout form if the company requires them to create a user account [29].
- Better checkout design can reduce form abandonment by as much as 35%, which translates into nearly $260 billion in recovered orders [29].

When you stop to think about it, SSI auto-authorization solves almost every typical complaint about online forms:

- *There is no typing.* All the information being requested by the verifier is transferred from claims to your digital wallet. And even if new self-attested data is requested, your agent can capture it for you so you'll never have to type it again.
- *Your connection is your account.* The whole idea of "click here to automatically create an account with this form data" goes away. You automatically have an "account" anywhere you have a connection.
- *Data verification is built in.* The main point of verifiable credentials is that the issuer has already vetted the claims data.
- *Security is built-in.* All proofs and data sent by your SSI agent automatically use your encrypted private connection with the verifier.
- *Privacy and selective disclosure are built in.* First, verifiers can now ask only for the minimum information they need—reducing their potential liability. Second, the proof your agent sends can be read only by the verifier. If the verifier needs a copy of the underlying data (e.g., asks you to share your actual birth date instead of just proving you are over 18), your agent should be able to automatically warn you if that data will not be covered by a satisfactory privacy policy or governance framework.
- *Auditing is built in.* Your agent can automatically track all the information you share—without requiring you to share that history with anyone else.

In addition, verifiable credentials let you prove many more things about yourself—as an individual, a student, an employee, a volunteer, or in any other role you play—than you could prove via any web form today. With auto-authorization, *your ability to perform tasks online comes much closer to your ability to perform those same tasks in the real world*—i.e., using your physical wallet, paper credentials, and face-to-face verification—but orders of magnitude faster.

4.3.3   *Workflow automation*

From the standpoint of the end user, SSI has the potential to reduce workflow steps that currently can take hours or days to as little as pressing a few buttons on a smartphone. One such scenario—selling a car and transferring the title and registration from one owner to another—was described in detail in chapter 3.

Many more of these scenarios are covered in part 4, where we examine the impact of SSI across different industries and vertical markets. You will see the same patterns repeated over and over: a business process carried out, step by step, by employees, contractors, suppliers, regulators, and other participants exchanging verifiable credentials (or digitally signed messages authorized by these credentials) between their agents and wallets. For every step, all of the following are performed automatically for the user:

1 *Authentication* that the user is the correct party.
2 *Authorization* that the user has the authority.
3 *Verification* that the step is being performed in the right sequence of the business process (and its preconditions have been met).
4 *Validation* that the claims or messages meet the requirements of the business process.
5 *Routing* of the credential or message produced to the next agent or agents needed in the process.
6 *Logging* of the action taken to provide a full digitally signed audit trail (or even automated reporting to regulators—see section 4.5.5).

Perhaps the ultimate example of consumers experiencing the convenience of SSI-enabled workflow automation is the perennial *change-of-address* problem. An individual is moving house and needs to inform dozens if not hundreds of agencies, suppliers, and contacts about the new address. Despite the advent of the internet and the web, this is still an excruciatingly labor-intensive process for the individual. The main reason? *Account takeover.* A fraudulent change of address is the first step in hijacking a bank account, credit card account, company account, or other valuable account to steal from it—or use that account to steal from others. So companies need to add extra hoops for you to jump through to ensure that it's really you requesting a change of address.

With SSI and verifiable credentials, a change of address can be performed in three easy steps:

1 *Obtain a verifiable credential of your new address* from a widely trusted issuer.
2 *Send a proof of that credential over all your connections* who need to know your new address.
3 *Each of their back-end systems can verify the proof* and update their systems with your new address with high confidence that it is valid.

Voilà. Tens of hours of human labor and hundreds of dollars in business savings for every single change-of-address notification. Given that in America alone, an average of 35 million people move house every year [30], this alone adds up to *hundreds of millions of person-hours and hundreds of billions of dollars in savings every year.*

4.3.4 Delegation and guardianship

As we described earlier, delegation credentials enable much of this workflow automation magic. Fortunately, the process of obtaining (or assigning) delegation credentials is just another workflow. The delegator first establishes a connection with the delegate (or vice versa) and then issues a credential granting the necessary authorizations.

As we cover in more technical detail in part 2, delegation credentials can be revised or revoked as conditions and positions change, with both the requirements and the current status being maintained by orchestration agents. All of this can be set forth in one or more governance frameworks that define the legal and business rules applying to the entire business process, whether it is taking place entirely inside one company, across a supply chain, across an entire industry, or in a wide-open process such as international shipping that crosses multiple industries and government jurisdictions. As a general rule, if humans can define the rules of the process, including who can make what decisions when, then SSI agents, wallets, and verifiable credentials can be used to automate the necessary exchanges of data. The end result is that many of today's most difficult user experience challenges—especially entering or interpreting data presented by machines—can be simplified by focusing on the analysis and decisions that humans really need to make.

4.3.5 *Payment and value exchange*

For decades, the challenge of moving money safely has been the focus of entire industries—banking, credit unions, credit cards, and now cryptocurrencies. It is the very heart of human economic activity. And, like the human heart, it is the most vulnerable to attackers. As Willie Sutton famously answered when asked why he robbed banks, "Because that's where the money is."

So there has always been a tension between making it easier to move money and making it safe to do so. Every means of value transfer from Pony Express to PayPal has spawned a new legion of criminals to exploit it. Cryptocurrencies—arguably the most friction-free way to move money ever invented—are no different. CoinDesk reported that in the first nine months of 2018, nearly $1 billion had been stolen from cryptocurrency exchanges and other crypto holders [31]. This shows that the easier it becomes to move money, the easier it can become to steal it unless the proper protections are put in place.

> **NOTE** In 2017, during the CoinDash ICO, a hacker compromised the CoinDash website (Wordpress) to substitute their own crypto wallet address for the legitimate CoinDash wallet address. As a result, customers thinking they were purchasing from CoinDash ended up sending over $7 million to the hacker. If verifiable SSI authentications had been in place, customers would have been immediately warned that the attacker's wallet address didn't authenticate properly, which would have signaled them that they were sending money to the wrong wallet. See Yuval M., 2017, "CoinDash TGE Hack findings report 15.11.17," CoinDash, https://blog.coindash.io/coindash-tge-hack-findings-report-15-11-17-9657465192e1.

While SSI is not a panacea, it does provide a complete infrastructure for trusted information exchange. This includes payments and other forms of value exchange as discussed earlier. With all of the protections that SSI digital agents, wallets, connections, and verifiable credentials provide, SSI could be the infrastructure that finally—from the perspective of end-user experience—makes digital payments one-click easy *and* secure at the same time.

The effect on digital commerce can be profound. Amazon's one-click purchasing capability famously helped vault it to the forefront of e-commerce. With the expiration of Amazon's one-click patent [32] and the arrival of an SSI payments infrastructure, a feature that once exclusively belonged to Amazon could now become "one click everywhere."

4.4   *Feature/benefit category 4: Relationship management*

While saving time and money is important, another category of features and benefits is not purely monetary: those that increase the trust, productivity, and value of relationships. Customer relationship management (CRM) is already a dominant industry in its own right. In January 2019, Forbes reported that [33]

- *CRM now makes up nearly 25% of the entire enterprise software revenue market.*
- Worldwide spending on CRM software grew 15.6% to reach $48.2 billion in 2018.
- Salesforce is the leader, with 19.5% of the CRM market, followed by SAP at 8.3%.

The impact of SSI on CRM has long been anticipated by a movement known as *vendor relationship management* (VRM). Its leader, Doc Searls, who led Project VRM at the Harvard Berkman Center for three years, pithily summarizes VRM as "the inverse of CRM." In other words, VRM is about how customers can control their relationships with companies instead of how companies can control their relationships with customers. Doc wrote the foreword to this book because of how deeply intertwined SSI and VRM have become over the past decade.

This section examines five key ways that SSI will enable better relationship management in *both* directions.

4.4.1   *Mutual authentication*

The first place SSI can improve relationships is right at the very start. This is when the parties are most vulnerable—when they are meeting each other for the first time, especially digitally.

On the web today, this is a struggle from both sides. First, imagine how hard it is for a website to prove that it is authentic when *phishing sites* and *phishing emails* have become so good that even trained professionals can have a hard time spotting them. (During the writing of this book, one of the co-authors received an email from his bank—a household brand—that was so realistic, it took three phone calls to determine it was a phishing attempt.) Verizon's 2018 Data Breach Incident Report said phishing accounted for 93% of all data breaches [34]. Between October 2013 and May 2018, the U.S. Federal Bureau of Investigation (FBI) reported $12.5 billion in company losses due to phishing [35].

Now turn the tables and think about how hard it is for *you*, the end user, to prove to a website that *anything* about yourself is authentic. Most of us have a hard time even proving we are *human*. How many of us have tripped up over something like figure 4.3?

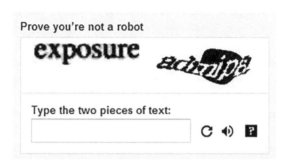

Prove you're not a robot

Type the two pieces of text:

Figure 4.3   A CAPTCHA (completely automated public Turing test to tell computers and humans apart) can often be difficult for even a real human to pass.

If it's that hard to prove you are even human, imagine how hard it is to prove these:

- You are over or under a certain age.
- You live in a certain place.
- You have a certain degree.
- You have a certain job.
- You have a certain income.

Generally, these tasks are impossible over the internet without first proving your real-world identity to the website (somehow) and then having the website independently verify information about you from some authoritative source (like a credit rating agency)—or worse, a data broker that may or may not have accurate information about you (let alone permission from you to share it).

This problem has become acute in both directions—*and SSI can solve it in both directions.* The beauty of SSI auto-authentication (see the earlier sections) is that your agent can share verifiable credentials with a website, and the website's agent can share verifiable credentials with you. Both agents can automatically verify the credentials on behalf of their owners to make sure they meet their respective policies. If so, the relationship can proceed without a hitch. If either agent spots a problem, it can immediately flag its owner—or simply deny the connection, so its owner is never bothered. This is how all our digital relationships should work: mutual auto-authentication on both sides that will put phishers permanently out to sea.

4.4.2   *Permanent connections*

The second major benefit SSI brings to relationship management is a feature no network has ever offered before: *permanent connections.* By *permanent*, we mean a connection that can last *forever* if both parties want it to (the mathematical techniques used to generate DIDs produce numbers so large that, even after thousands of years, the chances of generating the same ones are infinitesimally small).

How can SSI make such a promise? No other digital connection—phone number, email address, Twitter handle, Facebook friend, LinkedIn connection—can make that promise. The reason is that *they all depend on some form of intermediary service provider for the connection to keep working.* And no intermediary service provider can promise to always be in business and always maintain your connections no matter what you do or what your connections do.

Most of them promise you *the exact opposite*: they can terminate your service at any time, for any reason. Just read your terms of service.

With SSI—and the decentralized networks that make it work—*there is no intermediary service provider. Your connections belong to you.* You and the other party are the only ones who can terminate a connection because one or both of you want to end the relationship.

How valuable is this to you—the individual who wants to stay in touch with the people, organizations, and businesses in your life when you move, change jobs, graduate from school, or change service providers? And how valuable is it to all of your contacts and vendors who are trying to keep track of you? Earlier in this chapter, we quantified that simply automating the change-of-address process could save millions of hours and billions of dollars annually. Multiply that by all the other information we'd like to keep in sync with each other over permanent connections, and the total savings could be an order of magnitude greater.

4.4.3 *Premium private channels*

Permanence is not the only benefit of SSI connections. Because they are based on DIDs, DID documents (with public keys), and the DIDComm protocol (see chapter 5), SSI connections natively support *end-to-end secure encrypted communications.*

From a marketing perspective, we can call these *premium private channels*: *premium* because they are exclusive to you and your connection—they are not shared by anyone else; *private* because all your communications are automatically encrypted and decrypted by your respective agents without any effort on your part; and *channels* because you can use them to send and receive any messages or content your respective agents can "speak."

So your connections can be used—without any permission from anyone else—with any SSI-enabled application: messaging apps, voice and video apps, data-sharing apps, social networking apps, productivity apps, payment apps, games, and so on. Every one of these apps can have access to every SSI feature described in this chapter.

Messaging apps have been moving in this direction for some time. Apple iMessage, WhatsApp, Signal, and Telegram all support end-to-end encryption in one form or another. Others, like WeChat and Alipay in China, have also integrated messaging with secure payment and so many other plug-in functions such that many Chinese spend their entire day living and working in these apps [36].

SSI makes premium private channels a universal capability that can be integrated with any app and can work across any trust boundary—just like the internet and the web. You will find multiple examples in parts 3 and 4 of this book. For instance,

CULedger, a global consortium of credit unions developing SSI infrastructure for the credit union industry, plans to use premium private channels to request secure, digitally signed authorizations and consents from credit union members for actions that would otherwise require members to send a fax or make an in-person visit to a credit union office (see https://www.memberpass.com).

4.4.4 Reputation management

Reputation systems have become an essential feature of doing business on the web. For example, a Spiegel Research Center study showed nearly 95% of shoppers read online reviews before making a purchase [37]. A 2016 Harvard Business School study said a one-star increase on Yelp could lead to a 5–9% increase in revenue for a merchant [38].

However, it is precisely because they are so valuable that attacking reputation systems has become big business. A February 2019 study from Fakespot, which analyzes customer reviews, revealed that 30% of reviews on Amazon are fake or unreliable, and a whopping 52% of reviews posted on Walmart.com are inauthentic [39]. Worse, the rise in fake reviews is undermining consumer confidence in reputation systems. A Bright Local 2018 study said 33% of all consumers reported spotting "lots" of fake reviews and that the number went up to 89% for 18-to-34-year-olds who are savvier at detecting the signs of a fake review.

Amazon has long tried to fight this gaming with various protection measures, including its Amazon Verifier Purchase program that is supposed to ensure the reviewer actually bought the product (figure 4.4). However, this works only if a reviewer actually purchased the product at Amazon, and even then, it is relatively easy for a savvy marketing company to subsidize these purchases or find other ways around Amazon's rules. And if Amazon has these issues, imagine the scope of the problem for smaller sites that have only a tiny fraction of Amazon's security budget.

At this point in the book, it should be obvious how SSI can help with this problem. First, reputation systems can require verifiable credentials for reviewers, weeding out the bots. Second, they can require a verifiable credential for a product purchase—a *verifiable receipt*—so programs like Amazon Verified Purchase can work independently of any particular retailer. Third, reviewers can start to build a reliable reputation independent of not just any product vendor but any retailer—so we can start developing

Figure 4.4 An Amazon Verified Purchase mark is supposed to confirm that the reviewer bought the reviewed product—but they are not difficult to work around.

an ecosystem of widely trusted independent reviewers that can become the web equivalent of, say, Walter Mossberg of the *Wall Street Journal* or Jon Udell in his days at *Byte Magazine*.

In short, *reputation management can become an integral part of relationship management*. Any two parties that develop a connection and engage in interactions with each other—purchases, contracts, consulting, or just community engagement—should be able to provide verifiable reputational feedback to each other and the larger community.

The implications extend to any online survey, poll, or vote where it matters that

- Real human beings and not bots are participating.
- Each unique person has only one vote.
- People need to be accountable for voting honestly and not trying to game the system.

Gaming these types of systems with fake votes has become so common that the security community gave it the name *Sybil attack* after the famed case of multiple-personality disorder that was the subject of a 1973 book and a 1976 movie. As fake reviews, fake sites, and fake news multiply like rabbits online, the ability of SSI to counter Sybil attacks and anchor the trustworthiness of reputation systems may become one of its most valuable contributions to the future health of the web.

4.4.5   Loyalty and rewards programs

Every relationship involves an exchange of value of some kind between the two parties—even if it's just an exchange of pleasantries among neighbors. If that exchange is monetary, our earlier discussions of how SSI enables new forms of payment apply. But the stronger a relationship grows, the higher the probability that it involves some form of non-monetary value exchange.

Rewards programs are a perfect example. Whether they involve miles, points, stamps, or some other measure of value, they are an informal, direct, relationship-based way of thanking a customer for past loyalty and incentivizing future loyalty. And they work:

- 69% of consumers say their choice of retailer is influenced by where they can earn customer loyalty/rewards program points [40].
- A 5% increase in customer loyalty increases the average profit per customer by 25–100%.
- 76% of consumers think that loyalty programs are part of their relationship with brands [41].
- The loyalty management market is expected to grow from $1.93 billion in 2016 to $6.95 billion in 2023 [42].

However, for consumers today, managing loyalty programs is anywhere from mildly inconvenient to downright irritating. Imagine if every retailer you dealt with required you to use a different type of money and *a different wallet*—one dedicated to their specific store. That would be ridiculous—and yet that is how loyalty programs work today.

SSI-based relationship management (also called vendor relationship management or VRM, as noted earlier) can turn that on its head. Now every loyalty program can be designed to use its own premium private channel *to the consumer's own SSI digital wallet.* No matter what kind of loyalty currency is involved, they can all be managed securely and privately in one place. Consumers gain dramatically greater convenience and control; retailers gain simpler and more effective loyalty programs that can also take advantage of all the other features of SSI.

4.5 Feature/benefit category 5: Regulatory compliance

Our final category may be the least "sexy" but is still very significant because it covers how SSI can contribute to the strength of our global cybersecurity and cyberprivacy infrastructure. In this section, we cover five major ways SSI can help all actors in the global economy comply with regulations designed to keep us safe while at the same time encouraging greater economic activity through open and fair competition.

4.5.1 Data security

We could begin this section with a shower of statistics about the state of security on the internet, but they are all summed up in this 2015 quote in *Forbes* from Gina Rommety, CEO of IBM, when she addressed the CISOs (chief information security officers), CIOs, and CEOs of 123 companies in 24 industries [43]:

> *We believe that data is the phenomenon of our time. It is the world's new natural resource. It is the new basis of competitive advantage, and it is transforming every profession and industry. If all of this is true—even inevitable—then cyber crime, by definition, is the greatest threat to every profession, every industry, every company in the world.*

That same *Forbes* article said market estimates of the size of the worldwide cybersecurity industry range from \$77 billion in 2015 to \$170 billion by 2020. It is one of the fastest-growing of all enterprise software segments.

By attacking the very root of the problem—digital identity—SSI represents a sea change in cybersecurity. As we explain in great technical detail in part 2, SSI digital wallets and agents will help users generate and manage private keys, automatically negotiate pairwise pseudonymous DIDs, form secure connections, and communicate over premium private channels that provide the data security required by regulations such as the Health Insurance Portability and Accountability Act (HIPAA) in the United States and the General Data Protection Regulation (GDPR) in Europe. This alone will lock down acres of current vulnerabilities—one reason the U.S. Department of Homeland Security funded much of the research into the decentralized identifier and decentralized key management standards that are the foundation of SSI.

NOTE See the SBIR research funding topic "Applicability of Blockchain Technology to Privacy Respecting Identity Management" at https://www.sbir.gov/sbirsearch/detail/867797 and the news release at https://www.dhs.gov/science-and-technology/news/2017/07/20/news-release-dhs-st-awards-749k-evernym-decentralized-key.

SSI can also "detoxify" personal data so it can no longer be used for identity theft and related cybercrimes. Today this personal data is valuable because if a thief has enough of it, they can impersonate you to either break into current accounts or open new accounts in your name. But with verifiable credentials, *your personal data alone can no longer be used to steal your identity.* If the thief does not have your private keys, they cannot produce proofs of your verifiable credentials.

This means *breaches of huge corporate databases containing personal data will become a thing of the past.* Unlike usernames, passwords, and other personal data today, your private keys will never be stored in some centralized corporate database that serves as a giant honeypot for criminals. They are always stored in your local devices, with an encrypted backup copy in the cloud (or wherever you direct it to go). This means to steal an identity, a thief has to break into your personal SSI wallet(s), one at a time.

This is like forcing criminals to eat by catching tiny minnows one at a time instead of spearing a whale (figure 4.5). Give criminals that choice, and they will find another way to eat.

 vs.

Figure 4.5   SSI will force identity thieves to try to steal private keys one wallet at a time (left) vs. break into giant corporate honeypots of personal data (right).

4.5.2   *Data privacy*

Security and privacy go hand in hand, and privacy is every bit as much of a concern on the internet today. In June 2018, *Entrepreneur Magazine* reported that 90% of internet users were "very concerned" about internet privacy [44]. The same article reported that the Cambridge Analytica data scandal so tarnished Facebook's reputation that only 3% of users trust how Facebook is handling their personal data (and only 4% trust Google).

Part of what has pushed internet privacy to this crisis level is the sheer economic value of personal data in today's digital economy. In an April 2019 review of Shoshana Zuboff's book *The Age of Surveillance Capitalism* (https://shoshanazuboff.com/book), *The Nation* magazine said [45]:

> *Zuboff shows that these increasingly frequent invasions of our privacy are neither accidental nor optional; instead, they're a key source of profit for many of the 21st*

century's most successful companies. Thus, these companies have a direct financial stake in the broadening, deepening, and perfecting of the surveillance they already profit from—and in making sure that it remains legal.

Shifting the balance of power in privacy and personal data control will not be easy. However, SSI can help companies comply with applicable privacy legislation in three specific ways:

- *Selective disclosure*—SSI verifiable credential exchange technology, specifically for credentials that use zero-knowledge proof (ZKP) cryptography (see chapter 6), enables companies to request proofs of exactly the personal data they need and no more. For example, a company can request proof that you are over a specific age rather than your actual birthdate.

- *Verifiable consent*—Many consumers have no idea where companies get their personal data. Did it come from online forms they filled out? From marketing partners? From third-party data brokers? With verifiable credentials, there is a clear, verifiable chain of consent to share data that starts with the individual and can easily be traced and audited by the responsible SSI agents.

- *Governance frameworks*—Today, most privacy policies are highly custom documents written by lawyers to protect specific companies—not your privacy. This is why a 2012 study by privacy researchers Lorrie Faith Cranor and Aleecia McDonald estimated that *the average person would require 76 workdays* to read the privacy policies on the websites they visit each year, which for the United States alone would add up to *53.8 billion hours* or *$781 billion in labor costs* [46]. With SSI, company-specific privacy policies could begin to be replaced by governance frameworks that
  - Are uniform across all the sites that adopt them
  - Can be developed in open public forums to represent the best interests of all stakeholders
  - Can be preapproved by regulators to comply with their requirements
  - Can be designed to incorporate the other protections and advantages of SSI

These steps could become the first internet-scale implementation of the principles of *privacy by design* developed and advocated by former Ontario information and privacy commissioner Ann Cavoukian.

4.5.3 Data protection

Although closely related to data privacy, data protection goes beyond privacy controls to enumerate a larger set of specific principles to protect an individual's personal data. Although the European Union's GDPR (https://gdpr.eu) is the best-known data-protection legislation, it is by no means the only one. The California Consumer Privacy Act (CCPA, https://oag.ca.gov/privacy/ccpa) and, more recently, the California Privacy Rights Act are setting new standards for data-protection regulation in the U.S. Many other countries have or are enacting data protection laws along the same lines.

In addition to the data privacy compliance mechanisms listed in the previous section, there are other very specific ways SSI can enable individuals to exercise their rights and companies to comply with their responsibilities under these data protection acts:

- *Pseudonymous identifiers*—GDPR encourages the use of pseudonyms to minimize correlation. SSI connections use pairwise pseudonymous peer DIDs by default.

- *Data minimization*—GDPR requires collecting no more personal data than is necessary for the purpose for which it is being processed. SSI selective disclosure and ZKP credentials are ideal for meeting this requirement.

- *Data accuracy*—GDPR requires that personal data must be accurate and kept up to date. SSI enables data controllers to request personal data supplied by verifiable credentials from reputable issuers—and which can be automatically updated by those issuers when the data changes.

- *Right of erasure* (also known as the *right to be forgotten*)—Enshrined by Article 17 of GDPR, this can be one of the most challenging requirements because it means the data controller (the company) must give the data subject (the individual) a means of confirming what personal data a company holds while at the same time not opening a security hole for attackers. Fortunately, this is precisely the job for which SSI connections and premium private channels were designed. The data subject can use auto-authentication and auto-authorization to request access to the data and, if desired, send a digitally signed request for erasure over the connection. All of these actions can be securely audited for later verification of compliance.

4.5.4   *Data portability*

GDPR enforces one more data-protection right that is deserving of its own discussion: data portability. This is the right that allows data subjects to obtain data that a data controller holds on them and reuse it for their own purposes. In the words of the first paragraph of Article 20 of the GDPR:

> *The data subject shall have the right to receive the personal data concerning him or her, which he or she has provided to a controller, in a structured, commonly used, and machine-readable format and have the right to transmit those data to another controller without hindrance from the controller to which the personal data have been provided …*

The GDPR is only one of many new regulations requiring partial or complete data portability across data controllers. Another EU regulation, the Second Payment Services Directive (PSD2), is designed to drive the adoption of open banking in the EU. In addition, the Fifth Anti-Money Laundering Directive (AML5, https://www.electronicid.eu/aml5-new-anti-money-laundering-directive); the Electronic Identification, Authentication, and Trust Services Regulation (eIDAS); and the Directive on Security of Network and Information Systems (NIS Directive, https://ec.europa.eu/digital-single-market/en/network-and-information-security-nis-directive) all contain data-portability provisions relevant to SSI. All of these were preceded by the requirement for local telephone number portability (LNP) in the U.S. Telecommunications Act of 1996, which in the U.S. also applies to mobile number portability (MNP). MNP is also required to varying degrees by legislation in Africa, Asia, Australia, Latin America, and Canada.

SSI is ideal for data portability because it solves many of the deep security and privacy issues described in the previous sections. The secret is that SSI connections make it easy for the data *to flow in and out of connections with the individual data subject's own agent(s),* where the individual can always exert complete control over the data and the terms and conditions under which they are willing to share it with other parties.

Under this architecture—and especially under governance frameworks designed specifically to work with this architecture—personal data should be able to flow freely between systems while meeting the security, privacy, and control requirements of GDPR and other data protection regulations.

4.5.5 *RegTech (Regulation Technology)*

As substantial as all these breakthroughs are, the one regulators may get most excited about is the ability to connect directly to SSI ecosystems *themselves.* In other words, by deploying their own SSI digital agents and connecting directly to the companies being regulated, *regulators can be directly in the loop of transactions with specific regulatory requirements*—such as KYC requirements for opening a bank account, AML requirements for money transmission, or Anti-Terrorist Finance (ATF) requirements for purchases of certain types of goods.

For example, if a money transmission between two SSI-enabled parties exceeds the threshold over which a financial institution must apply additional AML compliance measures, this can be communicated in real time between the bank's SSI agent and the regulator's SSI agent. This has the potential to change the very nature of regulation enforcement from *an after-the-fact spot-check auditing activity* to a *real-time rules-driven monitoring activity*—decreasing enforcement costs, speeding up enforcement actions, and improving the quality of enforcement data all at the same time—a rare triple win for government regulation.

This is a highly desirable development given the skyrocketing costs of compliance cited earlier in this chapter. It is also consistent with the rapid growth of the global Regulatory Technology (RegTech) market, which Research and Markets expects to grow from $4.3 billion in 2018 to $12.3 billion by 2023, at a compound annual growth rate (CAGR) of 23.5% [47]. With SSI technology's ability to connect secure, private, permissioned SSI agents to any business process requiring regulation, that growth figure could become much higher.

As its name indicates, the SSI Scorecard is a tool for analyzing the impact of SSI on any particular use case, application, industry, or vertical market. We do just that in part 4 of this book, where we examine in-depth use cases for SSI across different vertical markets. Each chapter will wrap up with a scorecard for how much impact SSI is likely to have in that market and why. This should help tie together the building blocks, example scenarios, and features/benefits we have covered in part 1 with the real-world scenarios we look at in part 4.

But first, if you want to dive deeper into the technical aspects of SSI architecture and technology, these are covered by some of the leading experts in these subjects in part 2. If you are more interested in the overall economic, political, and social impacts of SSI, you can skip directly to part 3. Or, if you want to read about example use cases for SSI in specific industries and verticals, you can jump to part 4.

SSI Resources

For more free content to learn about SSI, please go to IdentityBook.info and SSI Meetup.org/book.

References

1. Grant, Kelli B. 2018. "Identity Theft, Fraud Cost Consumers More Than $16 Billion." CNBC. https://www.cnbc.com/2017/02/01/consumers-lost-more-than-16b-to-fraud-and-identity-theft -last-year.html.
2. Marchini, Kyle, and Al Pascual. 2019. "2019 Identity Fraud Study: Fraudsters Seek New Targets and Victims Bear the Brunt." Javelin. https://www.javelinstrategy.com/coverage-area/2019-iden tity-fraud-report-fraudsters-seek-new-targets-and-victims-bear-brunt.
3. FinTech Futures. 2018. "The Future of Client Onboarding." https://www.fintechfutures.com/ 2018/09/the-future-of-client-onboarding.
4. Callahan, John. 2018. "Know Your Customer (KYC) Will Be A Great Thing When It Works." *Forbes.* https://www.forbes.com/sites/forbestechcouncil/2018/07/10/know-your-customer-kyc -will-be-a-great-thing-when-it-works.
5. Dickenson, Kelvin. 2019. "The Future of KYC: How Banks Are Adapting to Regulatory Complexity." Opus. https://www.opus.com/future-of-kyc.
6. Fenergo. 2018. "Global Financial Institutions Fined $26 Billion for AML, Sanctions & KYC Non-Compliance." https://www.fenergo.com/press-releases/global-financial-institutions-fined-$26 -billion-for-aml-kyc.html.
7. Statista Research Department. 2020. "E-Commerce Worldwide—Statistics & Facts." https:// www.statista.com/topics/871/online-shopping.
8. Nasdaq. 2017. "UK Online Shopping and E-Commerce Statistics for 2017." https://www.nasdaq .com/article/uk-online-shopping-and-e-commerce-statistics-for-2017-cm761063.
9. Adobe. 2020. "2020 Holiday Shopping Trends." http://exploreadobe.com/retail-shopping-insights.
10. Khandelwal, Astha. v2020. "eCommerce Conversion Rate Benchmarks—Quick Glance At How They Stack Up." *VWO Blog.* https://vwo.com/blog/ecommerce-conversion-rate.
11. Baymard Institute. 2019. "44 Cart Abandonment Rate Statistics." https://baymard.com/lists/ cart-abandonment-rate.
12. Redbord, Michael. 2018. "The Hard Truth About Acquisition Costs (and How Your Customers Can Save You)." HubSpot. https://research.hubspot.com/customer-acquisition-study.
13. Sorofman, Jake. 2014. "Gartner Surveys Confirm Customer Experience Is the New Battlefield." Gartner. https://blogs.gartner.com/jake-sorofman/gartner-surveys-confirm-customer -experience-new-battlefield.
14. Hyken, Shep. 2018. "Businesses Lose $75 Billion Due to Poor Customer Service." *Forbes.* https:// www.forbes.com/sites/shephyken/2018/05/17/businesses-lose-75-billion-due-to-poor-customer -service.

15. Palfy, Sandor. 2018. "How Much Do Passwords Cost Your Business?" Infosecurity. https://www.infosecurity-magazine.com/opinions/how-much-passwords-cost.

16. Morgan, Blake. 2019. "50 Stats That Prove the Value of Customer Experience." *Forbes* (September 24). https://www.forbes.com/sites/blakemorgan/2019/09/24/50-stats-that-prove-the-value-of-customer-experience.

17. Okyle, Carly. 2015. "Password Statistics: The Bad, the Worse, and the Ugly (Infographic)." *Entrepreneur.* https://www.entrepreneur.com/article/246902.

18. Auth0. n.d. "Password Reset Is Critical for a Good Customer Experience." https://auth0.com/learn/password-reset.

19. Dashlane. 2015. "Online Overload: Worse Than You Thought." http://blog.dashlane.com/wp-content/uploads/2015/07/MailboxSecurity_infographic_EN_final1.jpg.

20. Nielsen Norman Group. n.d. "Intranet Portals: UX Design Experience from Real-Life Projects." www.nngroup.com/reports/intranet/portals.

21. Chisnell, Dana. 2011. "Random Factoids I've Encountered in Authentication User Research So Far." *Authentical.* http://usablyauthentical.blogspot.com/2011/09/random-factoids-ive-encountered-in.html.

22. PasswordResearch.com. 2020. http://passwordresearch.com/stats/statistic97.html.

23. Axiomatics. n.d. "Attribute-Based Access Control—ABAC." https://www.axiomatics.com/attribute-based-access-control.

24. Detrixhe, John. 2018. "Hackers Account for 90% of Login Attempts at Online Retailers." Quartz. https://qz.com/1329961/hackers-account-for-90-of-login-attempts-at-online-retailers.

25. Security. 2019. "8 in 10 IT Leaders Want to Eliminate Passwords." https://www.securitymagazine.com/articles/90530-in-10-it-leaders-want-to-eliminate-passwords.

26. Business Wire. 2019. "Veridium Survey Reveals Strong Consumer Sentiment Toward Biometric Authentication." https://www.businesswire.com/news/home/20190213005176/en/Veridium-Survey-Reveals-Strong-Consumer-Sentiment-Biometric.

27. Microsoft Security Team. 2018. "Building a World Without Passwords." https://cloudblogs.microsoft.com/microsoftsecure/2018/05/01/building-a-world-without-passwords.

28. Delgado, Michelle. 2018. "6 Steps for Avoiding Online Form Abandonment." The Manifest. https://themanifest.com/web-design/6-steps-avoiding-online-form-abandonment.

29. Liedke, Lindsay. 2020. "101 Unbelievable Online Form Statistics & Facts for 2021." *WPForms Blog.* https://wpforms.com/online-form-statistics-facts.

30. Holmes, Colin. 2018. "The State of the American Mover: Stats and Facts." Move.org. https://www.move.org/moving-stats-facts.

31. Khatri, Yogita. 2018. "Nearly $1 Billion Stolen In Crypto Hacks So Far This Year: Research." CoinDesk. https://www.coindesk.com/nearly-1-billion-stolen-in-crypto-hacks-so-far-this-year-research.

32. Pathak, Shareen. 2017. "End of an Era: Amazon's 1-Click Buying Patent Finally Expires." Digiday. https://digiday.com/marketing/end-era-amazons-one-click-buying-patent-finally-expires.

33. Columbus, Louis. 2019. "Salesforce Now Has Over 19% of the CRM Market." *Forbes.* https://www.forbes.com/sites/louiscolumbus/2019/06/22/salesforce-now-has-over-19-of-the-crm-market.

34. Verizon. 2018. "2018 Data Breach Investigations Report." https://enterprise.verizon.com/resources/reports/DBIR_2018_Report.pdf.

35. FBI. 2018. "Business E-mail Compromise: The 12 Billion Dollar Scam." Alert number I-071218-PSA. https://www.ic3.gov/media/2018/180712.aspx.

36. WeChat Mini Programmer. 2018. "Alipay vs. WeChat Pay: An Unbiased Comparison." https://medium.com/@wechatminiprogrammer/alipay-vs-wechat-pay-an-unbiased-comparison-52eafabc7ffe.

37. Spiegel Research Center. 2017. "How Online Reviews Influence Sales." http://spiegel.medill.northwestern.edu/online-reviews.

38. Luca, Michael. 2016. "Reviews, Reputation, and Revenue: The Case of Yelp.com." Harvard Business School. HBS Working Paper Series. https://www.hbs.edu/faculty/Pages/item.aspx?num=41233.

39. Picchi, Aimee. 2019. "Buyer Beware: Scourge of Fake Reviews Hitting Amazon, Walmart and Other Major Retailers." CBS News. https://www.cbsnews.com/news/buyer-beware-a-scourge-of-fake-online-reviews-is-hitting-amazon-walmart-and-other-major-retailers.

40. Maritz Loyalty Marketing. 2013. "Holiday Shoppers' Generosity Extends Beyond Friends and Family to Themselves." Cision. www.prweb.com/releases/2013/11/prweb11372040.htm.

41. Saleh, Khalid. 2020. "The Importance of Customer Loyalty Programs—Statistics and Trends." Invesp. https://www.invespcro.com/blog/customer-loyalty-programs.

42. Sonawane, Kalyani. 2020. "Global Loyalty Management Market Expected to Reach $6,955 Million by 2023." Allied Market Research. https://www.alliedmarketresearch.com/press-release/loyalty-management-market.html.

43. Morgan, Steve. 2015. "IBM's CEO on Hackers: 'Cyber Crime Is the Greatest Threat to Every Company in the World.'" *Forbes.* https://www.forbes.com/sites/stevemorgan/2015/11/24/ibms-ceo-on-hackers-cyber-crime-is-the-greatest-threat-to-every-company-in-the-world.

44. Byer, Brian. 2018. "Internet Users Worry About Online Privacy but Feel Powerless to Do Much About It." *Entrepreneur.* https://www.entrepreneur.com/article/314524.

45. Fitzpatrick, Katie. 2019. "None of Your Business." *The Nation.* https://www.thenation.com/article/shoshana-zuboff-age-of-surveillance-capitalism-book-review.

46. Madrigal, Alexis C. 2012. "Reading the Privacy Policies You Encounter in a Year Would Take 76 Work Days." *The Atlantic.* https://www.theatlantic.com/technology/archive/2012/03/reading-the-privacy-policies-you-encounter-in-a-year-would-take-76-work-days/253851.

47. Research and Markets. 2018. "RegTech Market by Application (Compliance & Risk Management, Identity Management, Regulatory Reporting, Fraud Management, Regulatory Intelligence), Organization Size (SMEs, Large Enterprises), and Region—Global Forecast to 2023." https://www.researchandmarkets.com/research/r8ktnm/global_12_3?w=5.

Part 2

SSI technology

Arthur C. Clarke said, "Any sufficiently advanced technology is indistinguishable from magic." In part 1, we introduced the basic building blocks of SSI at a level comfortable for non-technologists. In part 2, we go behind the curtain to look much more deeply at these building blocks and see how they are assembled to accomplish the "magic" of SSI:

- Chapter 5 gives a big-picture overview of SSI architecture and some of the key design choices facing SSI architects.
- Chapter 6 explains why SSI is "cryptography all the way down" and introduces the innovations in cryptography that make SSI possible.
- Chapter 7 is a mini-textbook on the star of the SSI show: verifiable credentials (VCs). This is the only chapter with code snippets: examples of the JSON and JSON-LD data structures at the heart of the W3C Verifiable Credentials Data Model 1.0 specification.
- Chapter 8 is a deep dive into the other foundational open standard for SSI: the W3C Decentralized Identifiers (DID) Core Specification. It includes an in-depth analysis of how DIDs solve the hardest problem in conventional public key infrastructure (PKI).
- Chapter 9 tackles the two main tools in the hands of SSI users—digital wallets and digital agents—and covers lessons learned from the first generation of implementers.
- Chapter 10 goes even deeper into the very heart of SSI: decentralized cryptographic key management. It includes a full analysis of the most significant innovation in this space: Key Event Receipt Infrastructure (KERI).

- Chapter 11 explains why all of this fabulous new technology will produce real-world benefits only if it is harnessed to a different kind of tool for trust: *governance frameworks* (aka *trust frameworks*) that provide the "glue" to business, legal, and social policies.

SSI architecture: The big picture

Daniel Hardman

The purpose of this chapter is to take the basic building blocks, usage scenarios, features, and benefits of SSI that we introduced in part 1 and place them into an overarching picture of SSI architecture. As we will keep repeating, SSI is young, and many facets are still evolving. Still, the basic layering has emerged, along with several of the key underpinning standards, so the main questions are about how these standards will be implemented and how much interoperability will depend on specific design choices. In this chapter, Daniel Hardman, former chief architect and CISO at Evernym, now principal ecosystem engineer at SICPA—and a contributor to most of the core standards and protocols discussed here—walks you through four layers of SSI architecture, the key components and technologies at each layer, and the critical design decisions facing architects and implementers throughout the stack. This chapter sets the stage for the rest of the chapters in part 2 that dive deeper into specific SSI technologies.

In chapter 2, we discussed the basic building blocks of self-sovereign identity (SSI). Those building blocks represent important commonality—all approaches to the problem agree on them. However, like automobile design in the early 1900s, the young market is producing much innovation and divergence in the details. Some are inventing with two wheels, some with four or three. Some favor steam, while others favor internal combustion engines powered by gasoline or diesel.

In this chapter, we identify important decision points in decentralized digital identity architectures, notable choices for each, and the benefits and challenges they entail.

5.1   The SSI stack

Some types of divergence are irrelevant; others are fundamental. Separating the two is an important topic among identity architects because it affects interoperability. The first attempt to describe all the key choices in SSI stacks was made at the Internet Identity Workshop (IIW) in October 2018 [1]. Conference participants listed 11 layers of technology that are likely to appear in SSI solutions and described their dependencies.

However, subsequent experience has shown this was more granular than necessary to describe the fundamental architectural dependencies in SSI. SSI architects from various backgrounds collaborated under the umbrella of the Hyperledger Aries project in 2019 to produce the four-layer paradigm shown in figure 5.1 that we use throughout this chapter. The bottom layers, while important, are essentially invisible plumbing; the top layers embody concepts visible to ordinary users. They tie directly into business processes, regulatory policies, and legal jurisdictions.

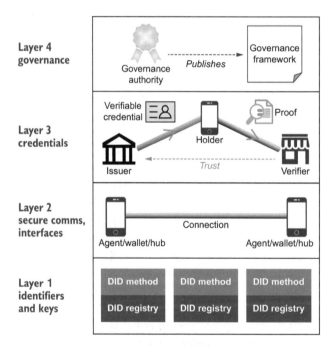

Figure 5.1   **The SSI stack as a four-layer model, where the bottom two layers are primarily about achieving technical trust and the top two layers are about achieving human trust**

Each of these layers embodies key architectural decisions, and each has significant consequences for interoperability. In the balance of this chapter, we discuss the details of each layer, building from the bottom up.

5.2   Layer 1: Identifiers and public keys

Layer 1 is the bottom of the stack, where identifiers and public keys are defined and managed. These are often called *trust roots*, and like real trees, the stronger the roots, the stronger the tree. This layer needs to guarantee that all stakeholders agree to the same truth about what an identifier references and how control of this identifier may be proved using cryptographic keys. It must also allow every party in the ecosystem to read and write data without reliance on or interference from central authorities—a property widely referred to in the blockchain community as *censorship resistance.*

There is broad consensus among the SSI community that the best way to provide these features is to expose a *verifiable data registry* (also called a *DID registry* or *DID network* because it a decentralized source of truth for decentralized identifiers (DIDs, introduced in chapter 2 and described in detail in chapter 8). Each DID registry uses a *DID method* that defines a specific protocol for interacting with that particular type of DID registry. While this standardizes the overall abstraction needed for Layer 1, this approach still allows much to vary in the particulars.

For example:

- What's the best way to implement a decentralized system? Should it be permissioned or permissionless? How should it be governed? How well does it scale?

- How, exactly, should DIDs be registered, looked up, and verified on this decentralized system to ensure they are secure while still protecting privacy?

- What other data needs to be stored on the decentralized system to support the higher layers of the SSI stack?

As chapter 8 discusses, over 80 DID methods are defined in the DID method registry maintained by the W3C DID Working Group (https://www.w3.org/TR/did-spec-registries)—and more are likely in the future. That reflects the great diversity of DID methods developed so far. In this section, we discuss the major architectural categories into which they fall.

5.2.1 Blockchains as DID registries

As noted at the beginning of this book, SSI was born because blockchain technology introduced an exciting new option for implementing a decentralized public key infrastructure (DPKI), explained in more detail in chapter 6. This, in turn, could unlock the power of verifiable credentials (VCs), explained in chapter 7. So naturally, blockchains in their many forms have been the first option for Layer 1. Indeed, as of the writing of this book, more than 90% of the DID methods in the W3C DID specification registry are based on blockchains or distributed ledger technology (DLT).

Besides the well-known public blockchains that support cryptocurrencies (for example, Bitcoin and Ethereum), this family of technologies includes permissioned ledgers (such as Hyperledger Indy), distributed directed acyclic graphs (e.g., IOTA), and distributed hashtables (e.g., IPFS). *Blockchain* has become a general umbrella term for the entire family, although experts argue about exactly how to apply these definitions [2]. In principle, it is expected that, following the architecture choices we outline in this chapter, all of these technologies should be able to achieve the SSI design goals of strong security, censorship resistance, and self-service without central administration.

However, these blockchains also differ in important ways, including

- How much, if at all, they integrate with cryptocurrencies and payment workflows as an identity concern
- Whether identity operations are a first-class feature of the blockchain or a generic feature (for example, smart contracts) that intersects with identity only in certain cases
- How expensive they are to operate and scale
- What latency and throughput they deliver
- How they are permissioned and governed
- How they address regulatory compliance and censorship resistance

In summary, it is best to look at blockchain as one option for meeting the requirements of Layer 1, but not the only option—and not necessarily a good option, depending on the design and implementation of the blockchain and the design and implementation of a specific DID method for using that blockchain. For example:

- A blockchain that's prohibitively expensive to use may put SSI out of reach for many of the world's disadvantaged.
- A blockchain that's too slow may never be adopted.
- A blockchain that is permissioned may not adequately address concerns about censorship resistance.
- A blockchain whose codebase is tightly controlled by a small group may not be considered trustworthy enough for broad adoption.

Since this category is so broad, let's next look specifically at two major subdivisions within it: general-purpose public blockchains and special-purpose SSI blockchains.

5.2.2   *Adapting general-purpose public blockchains for SSI*

Although blockchain technology is less than a decade old, it already has two "granddaddies": Bitcoin and Ethereum. Collectively, their market capitalization at the start of 2021—measured in terms of the total value of their respective cryptocurrencies—is more than four times that of all other cryptocurrencies combined [3]. So they are obviously strong candidates for the stability and broad developer support needed to engender trust in public infrastructure. This explains why some of the first SSI implementations—by Learning Machine (Bitcoin) and uPort (Ethereum)—targeted these blockchains. It also explains why over a dozen of the DID methods registered in the W3C DID Specification Registries are designed to work with either Bitcoin or Ethereum [4].

The common theme among these methods is that they use the cryptographic address of a transaction on the ledger—a *payment address*—as the DID. Payment addresses are already opaque strings, globally unique, and governed by cryptographic keys. Although it predates the W3C standards for verifiable credentials and DIDs, the Blockcerts (https://www.blockcerts.org) standard for educational credentials, championed by Learning Machine, is built on this approach, and credential issuance and verification (Layer 3) work nicely on top of it.

However, payment addresses don't have rich metadata or provide an obvious way to contact the address holder. This limits interactions to a "don't call us, we'll call you" model. Payment addresses are also global correlators, which raises privacy concerns. Law enforcement identified the operators of Silk Road (an online black market and the first modern darknet market, best known as a platform for selling illegal drugs) because payment addresses were traceable. While that case resulted in shutting down a market in illegal goods, the same techniques could be used to harass, find dissidents, or surveil legitimate actors. Some interesting technical solutions have been proposed to mitigate this effect with payment addresses, but implementations are still pending, and more technical and legal measures may be required.

Some blockchains are also designed so that payment addresses are retired as funds move or keys rotate. Without workarounds, this can complicate the stability of reference required by a good user experience (UX) for SSI.

5.2.3 *Special-purpose blockchains designed for SSI*

By 2016, developers were creating the first blockchains designed explicitly to support SSI. The first came from Evernym, which developed an open source codebase for a public permissioned ledger, where all the nodes would be operated by trusted institutions. Evernym helped organize the Sovrin Foundation to become the non-profit governance authority for the blockchain and then contributed the open source code to the Foundation (https://sovrin.org).

The Sovrin Foundation subsequently contributed the open source code to the Hyperledger project hosted by the Linux Foundation, where it became Hyperledger Indy (https://wiki.hyperledger.org/display/indy). It joined other Hyperledger business-oriented blockchain operating systems, including Fabric, Sawtooth, and Iroha. As the only Hyperledger project designed expressly for SSI, the Hyperledger Indy codebase is now being run by other public permissioned SSI networks, including those implemented by Kiva, the non-profit operator of the world's largest microlending platform [5].

The next entrant in purpose-built SSI blockchains was Veres One (https://veres.one), created by Digital Bazaar. It is a public permissionless blockchain optimized to store DIDs and DID documents in JSON-LD, a rich semantic graph format based on the Resource Description Framework (RDF). The Veres One blockchain is being used for multiple SSI pilots involving verifiable credentials for supply chains and provenance [6].

Blockchains that are purpose-built for SSI, such as Veres One and Hyperledger Indy, have transaction and record types that make DID management easy. However, there is more to Layer 1 than just DIDs. In particular, the Hyperledger Indy codebase supports the zero-knowledge proof (ZKP) credential format supported by the W3C Verifiable Credential Data Model 1.0 standard and the Hyperledger Aries open source codebase (discussed in the sections on Layers 2 and 3). ZKP credentials require several other cryptographic primitives at Layer 1 [7]:

- *Schemas*—This is how issuers define the claims (attributes) that they wish to include on a verifiable credential. By putting schema definitions on a public blockchain, they are available for all verifiers to examine to determine semantic interoperability (a critical point for data sharing across silos).
- *Credential definitions*—The difference between a credential definition and a schema is that the credential definition is published on the ledger to declare the specific claims, public key, and other metadata that will be used by a specific issuer for a specific version of a verifiable credential.
- *Revocation registries*—This is a special data structure called a *cryptographic accumulator* used for privacy-respecting revocation of verifiable credentials. See chapter 6 for more details.
- *Agent authorization registries*—This is a different type of cryptographic accumulator used to add additional security to SSI infrastructure. It can authorize and de-authorize specific digital wallets on specific devices—for example, if they are lost, stolen, or hacked.

NOTE *Semantic interoperability* is the ability of computer systems to exchange data with unambiguous, shared meaning. Semantic interoperability is concerned not just with the packaging of data (syntax), but also with the simultaneous transmission of the meaning with the data (semantics). This is accomplished by adding data about the data (metadata), linking each data element to a controlled, shared vocabulary.

Equally important is what does *not* go on the ledger: *any private data*. Although early experiments in blockchain-based identity had the notion of putting an individual's credentials and other personal data directly on the blockchain as encrypted data objects, subsequent research and analysis have concluded that this is a bad idea. First, all encryption has a limited lifespan, so writing private data to an immutable public ledger has the risk that it may eventually be cracked even if the cryptography used for the ledger itself is upgraded. Second, even encrypted data has privacy implications just by watching who writes and reads it. Third, it presents massive issues with the EU General Data Protection Regulation (GDPR) and other data protection regulations worldwide that provide a "right of erasure" to data subjects (see the Sovrin Foundation's white paper on GDPR and SSI for a detailed analysis: https://sovrin.org/data-protection).

5.2.4   *Conventional databases as DID registries*

Although it may seem antithetical to a decentralized approach, the user databases of internet giants have shown that modern web-ready database technologies can achieve the robustness, global scale, and geographical dispersion needed by a DID registry. Some have even proposed that a massive social network database like Facebook's, or a comprehensive government identity database like India's Aadhaar, could be the basis for rapid adoption of DIDs—citing broad coverage, proven ease-of-use, and existing adoption as a rationale.

However, such databases are neither self-service nor censorship-resistant. Trust in these databases is rooted in centralized administrators whose interests may not align with those of the individuals they identify. Privacy is questionable when a third party mediates every login or interaction. This is true whether the organization that runs them is a government, a private enterprise, or even a charity. Such centralization undermines one of the most important design goals of SSI (and also of the internet): eliminating single points of control and failure. For this reason, most practitioners of SSI discount traditional databases as a viable implementation path for Layer 1.

5.2.5   *Peer-to-peer protocols as DID registries*

As DID methods have matured, SSI architects have realized that there is an entire category of DIDs that do not need to be registered in a backend blockchain or database. Rather, these DIDs and DID documents can be generated and exchanged *directly between the peers that need them* to identify and authenticate each other.

The "DID registry" in this case is the digital wallet of each of the peers—each is the "root of trust" for the other—along with trust in the protocol used to exchange these *peer DIDs*. Not only does this approach have massively better scalability and performance than blockchain- or database-based DID methods, but it also means the DIDs, public keys, and service endpoints are completely private—they never need to be shared with any external party, let alone on a public blockchain.

The primary peer-to-peer DID method, called `did:peer:`, was developed under the auspices of the Hyperledger Aries project and then moved to the sponsorship of the Decentralized Identity Foundation. It is defined in the *Peer DID Method Specification* (https://identity.foundation/peer-did-method-spec). Peer DIDs are generated directly in the digital wallets of the two peers involved and exchanged using their digital agents, so in reality, Peer DID is a Layer 1 solution that's implemented entirely at Layer 2 of the SSI stack. However, the Peer DID method is developing fallback solutions for situations where one or both of the peers (such as two people represented by their mobile phones) move to new service endpoints (such as new mobile phone carriers) and lose touch with one another. Some of these require clever triangulation against a public blockchain at Layer 1.

Triple-Signed Receipts is an example of another protocol that also solves this problem without any blockchain. It was originally described as an evolution to standard double-entry accounting but can also be used to solve double-spend problems in identity (for example, claiming to one party that a key is authorized while claiming to another party that a key is not). Each party in the protocol signs a transaction description that includes not just the inputs but also the outputs (resulting balance). An external auditor signs as well. Once all three signatures have accumulated, there is no question about the truth of a transaction—and because the signed data *includes the resulting balance* in addition to the inputs, no previous transactions need be consulted to know the effect of the transaction.

Key Event Receipt Infrastructure (KERI) is a complete architecture for portable DIDs developed around the concept of self-certifying identifiers at the heart of peer DIDs. KERI goes further to define a corresponding decentralized key management architecture. For details, see chapter 10.

Given the rich possibilities, we anticipate that additional peer-based protocol solutions to Layer 1 functionality will be developed over the coming years, all of which will add to the overall strength of this foundational layer of the SSI stack.

5.3   *Layer 2: Secure communication and interfaces*

If Layer 1 is about establishing decentralized trust roots—either publicly verifiable or peer-to-peer—then Layer 2 is about establishing trusted communications between the peers relying on those trust roots. This is the layer where the digital agents, wallets, and encrypted data stores we introduced in chapter 2 live and where their secure DID-to-DID connections are formed.

Even though actors of all kinds—people, organizations, and things—are represented by these digital agents and wallets at Layer 2, the trust established between those actors at this layer is still only *cryptographic trust*—in other words, trust that

- A DID is controlled by another peer.
- A DID-to-DID connection is secure.
- A message sent over a connection is authentic and has not been tampered with.

These are all conditions that are *necessary but not sufficient* to establish human trust because they don't yet establish anything about the person, organization, or thing identified by the DID. For example, a DID-to-DID connection doesn't care whether a remote party is ethical or honest or qualified—only whether talking back and forth can be done in a way that's tamper-proof and confidential. For that, we have to move up to Layers 3 and 4.

The architectural issues at this layer fall into two main categories: protocol design and interface design. This section discusses the two main protocol design options and then the three main interface design options.

5.3.1   *Protocol design options*

Of course, protocols are the heart of the internet itself—the TCP/IP protocol stack is what made the internet possible, and the HTTP and HTTPS protocols are what made the web possible. With SSI, protocol design is critical because it defines the rules by which agents, wallets, and hubs communicate.

Two main protocol design architectures are being pursued in the SSI community:

- *Web-based protocol design* follows the same basic HTTP protocol patterns detailed in the W3C's classic "Architecture of the World Wide Web" document (widely considered the "bible" of web architecture; https://www.w3.org/TR/webarch). This approach has a special reliance on the Transport Layer Security (TLS) standard used in the HTTPS protocol.

- *Message-based protocol design* uses the DIDComm protocol for peer-to-peer communications between agents—an architectural approach more similar to email.

5.3.2 *Web-based protocol design using TLS*

The first approach is rooted in a simple observation: we already have a ubiquitous, robust mechanism for secure web communication in the form of Transport Layer Security (TLS). Why reinvent the wheel?

Proponents of this view are building systems where parties talk to one another by making RESTful web service calls (representational state transfer [REST] is a software architectural style that defines a set of constraints to be used for creating web services). The tooling and libraries for such mechanisms are well understood, and millions of developers are comfortable with them. Progress is relatively easy.

However, challenges exist:

- Although TLS can be applied to other protocols, its primary adoption success has been with HTTP. This means TLS is only an immediate answer when at least one of the parties runs a web server.
- It is inherently two-party (client and server).
- It requires a relatively direct request-response interaction, with both parties being online at the same time.
- The server is passive; it reacts when called and can trigger webhooks or callback URLs—but it can't reach out to the other party on its own unless the other party is also running a web server.
- The security model for TLS is asymmetric: servers use X.509 digital certificates (introduced in chapter 2 and discussed in more detail in chapter 8); clients use passwords, API keys, or OAuth tokens. This tends to perpetuate a *power imbalance*, where organizations having high-reputation server certificates dictate the behavior of low-reputation clients. It is antithetical to the peer-to-peer philosophy of decentralization in SSI. It also makes the control of DIDs and their cryptographic keys a secondary (or even redundant) concern.
- Its privacy and security guarantees are imperfect. *SSL visibility appliances* are well-known hacking tools that insert a man-in-the-middle for each TLS session that runs through an institutional LAN. X.509 certificate authorities are operated by humans and can be gamed. And TLS has no story for securing communications data at rest or outside the secured channel.

For all these reasons, although there is a great deal of SSI code development following the conventional web architecture path of using HTTPS, at least as much, if not more, development effort is going into a more inclusive approach.

5.3.3 *Message-based protocol design using DIDComm*

This second approach is called *DID communication* (*DIDComm* for short). It conceives of Layer 2 as message-oriented, transport-agnostic, and rooted in interactions among peers. In this paradigm, communications between agents are similar in concept to email: it is inherently asynchronous, it may involve broadcasting to multiple parties at the same time, delivery is best-effort, and replies may arrive over different channels or not at all.

> **NOTE**   From an architectural perspective, DIDComm has much in common with proprietary protocols used by many secure messaging apps today. It even supports analogous grouping constructs. However, it also differs in important ways. Its DID foundation lets it work peer-to-peer rather than needing all traffic to route through centralized servers. It focuses on the delivery of machine-readable rather than human-readable messages; this makes its problem domain far broader than just secure chat. Software uses DIDComm messages to facilitate interactions of every conceivable kind between institutions and IoT devices as well as people. This means some users of DIDComm may not perceive the interactions to resemble conventional secure messaging apps.

However, DIDComm differs from SMTP email in that

- Recipients are identified by a DID rather than an email address.
- All communication is secured (either encrypted, signed, or both) by the keys associated with DIDs. This is true even of data at rest.
- Messages may be delivered over any transport: HTTP, Bluetooth, ZMQ, file system/sneakernet, AMQP, mobile push notifications, QR codes, sockets, FTP, SMTP, snail mail, etc.
- Security and privacy guarantees are the same regardless of transport. A single route may use more than one of these transports.
- Because of the transport independence, security is also portable. That is, two parties may interact partly over email using proprietary tools from vendors A and B, partly over social-media-based chat controlled by vendor C, and partly over SMS that uses multiple mobile providers. However, only two sets of keys (the keys for each party's DID) are needed to secure all of these contexts, and the interaction history is tied to the DIDs, not the channels. Vendors that own channels cannot force lock-in by owning the security.
- Routing is adapted for privacy; it is designed so no intermediary knows a message's ultimate origin or its final destination—only the next hop. This allows for (but does not require) the use of mixed networks and similar privacy tools.

DIDComm can easily use HTTP or HTTPS in a request-response paradigm, so this approach to protocol design is a superset of the web-based approach. However, DIDComm provides flexibility for other situations, including those where a party is connected only occasionally or channels contain many untrusted intermediaries.

DIDComm's most important technical weakness is its novelty. Although tools used by the world's web developers (CURL, Wireshark, Chrome's Developer Tools, Swagger, etc.) are relevant and somewhat helpful with DIDComm, tools that understand DIDComm natively are immature. This makes DIDComm a more expensive choice in the early days of the SSI ecosystem.

Nevertheless, DIDComm is gaining momentum rapidly. Although it was originally incubated within the Hyperledger developer community (Indy and Aries; https:// github.com/hyperledger/aries-rfcs/tree/master/concepts/0005-didcomm), in December 2019, the growing interest beyond Hyperledger led to the formation of the DIDComm Working Group at the Decentralized Identity Foundation (DIF) [8]. Already there are roughly a dozen implementations of various parts of DIDComm for different programming languages (https://github.com/hyperledger/aries).

5.3.4 *Interface design options*

From an architectural standpoint, interface design is about how SSI infrastructure becomes available for programmatic use by developers who want to solve real-world problems for individuals and institutions. The approaches here depend to some degree on protocol design. For web-based client/server protocols, Swagger-style API interfaces are a natural complement; with DIDComm, peer-to-peer protocols are a more natural model. However, both underlying protocols can be paired with either style of interface, so the question is somewhat orthogonal.

SSI solutions tend to emphasize one of these three answers to the interface question:

- *API-oriented interface* design favors using decentralized web or mobile wallet decentralized apps (Dapps) with APIs.
- *Data-oriented interface* design uses encrypted data stores to discover, share, and manage access to identity data.
- *Message-oriented interface* design uses digital agents (edge-based or cloud-based) that route the messages and interactions they share.

However, these answers are not mutually exclusive; all approaches overlap. What differs is the focus [9].

5.3.5 *API-oriented interface design using wallet Dapps*

The API-based approach stems from the philosophy that SSI features are best exposed through decentralized web and mobile apps (Dapps) and associated Web 2.0 or Web 3.0 APIs on complementary server-side components. Here, the prototypical SSI Dapp for an individual is a mobile wallet that holds all cryptographic material and provides a simple UX for requesting and providing credential-based proof about identity. This wallet also interfaces directly or indirectly with a blockchain to verify data.

The Blockcerts app and the uPort app are examples of this model. These apps interface with Learning Machine's server-side Issuing System or with uPort's Ethereum-based backend, respectively. Programmers are encouraged to write their own apps or automation to call these backend APIs and use the identity ecosystem. Because the approach is conceptually straightforward, the learning curve is not steep, aiding adoption.

This paradigm works well for SSI use cases where individuals want to prove things to institutions because individuals carry mobile devices and institutions operate servers with APIs. However, when individuals are the receivers rather than the givers of proof, and when identity owners are IoT devices or institutions instead of people, there is some impedance with the overall model. How can an IoT device hold a wallet and control a Dapp, for example? Perhaps we will see clever extensions of this model in the future.

5.3.6   *Data-oriented interface design using identity hubs (encrypted data vaults)*

Digital Bazaar, Microsoft, and various other players in the Decentralized Identity Foundation (DIF) and W3C CCG communities have championed a data-centric view of identity. In this paradigm, the primary task of actors using SSI infrastructure is to discover, share, and manage access to identity data.

In this view, management's focus is an *identity hub* (or, in W3C parlance, an *encrypted data vault*)—a cloud-based point of presence through which a web API accesses identity data. Hubs are services configured and controlled by an identity controller. In the case of individuals, they are usually imagined to be sold as a SaaS subscription, providing a sort of *personal API*. Institutions or devices can also use hubs. Importantly, hubs are not necessarily conceived of as directly representing a particular identity controller; they can be independent services that manage data on behalf of any number of identity controllers, as directed by each individual controller. Figure 5.2 illustrates the role an identity hub plays in the SSI ecosystem envisioned by the DIF.

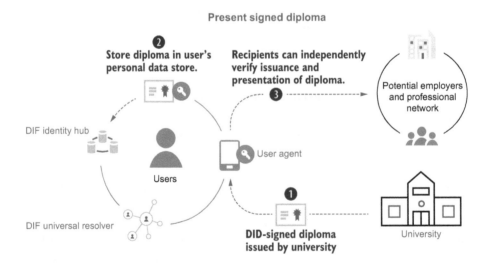

Figure 5.2   An identity hub shown as part of the SSI ecosystem envisioned by DIF

Although hubs, in theory, can execute code on a schedule or trigger, most design documents focus on the hub as a passive responder to external clients. Most examples assume they are always online to provide a stable portal for interaction and behave like a specialized web server. Thus, they were originally imagined as HTTP-oriented and RESTful, with service endpoints defined in a DID document (https://github.com/decentralized-identity/identity-hub/blob/master/explainer.md). However, as DIDComm has evolved, some hub APIs have been recast as message-based and capable of using Bluetooth, NFC, message queues, or other transport mechanisms besides HTTP. Still, the architectural center of hub design remains fundamentally rooted in data sharing.

Security for hubs is provided by encryption of messages, using keys declared in a DID document. Early discussions of encryption approaches centered on the JSON Web Token (JWT) format, part of the JavaScript Object Signing and Encryption (JOSE) stack, but the particulars are still in development. As of early 2021, the DIF's Secure Data Storage Working Group is busy unifying the various efforts to specify interoperable identity hubs and encrypted data vaults (https://identity.foundation/working-groups/secure-data-storage.html).

The data hub model is attractive for companies that want to sell hosting services to consumers and enterprises. It is also convenient for institutions that want to contract with consumers to generate value from their data. On the plus side, programming against hubs is likely to be very easy for developers. On the minus side, it is not clear whether consumers want to manage their identity as a service in the cloud. There are also privacy, security, and regulatory issues with hosting providers that need to be explored. This is one area where market validation is particularly needed.

5.3.7 *Message-oriented interface design using agents*

The Hyperledger Aries project and the Sovrin community have championed an SSI interface paradigm that focuses most heavily on active *agents* and the messages and interactions they share. Agents are direct representatives of identity, rather than being indirect or external representatives like hubs. When you interact with an agent, you interact as directly as possible with the entity whose identity the agent represents.

As introduced in chapter 2 and explored in depth in chapter 9, an SSI digital agent can be hosted anywhere: on mobile devices, IoT devices, laptops, servers, or anywhere in the cloud. Architectural diagrams for agent ecosystems don't put a blockchain at the center, and words like *client* and *API* are generally absent. The mental model might be best visualized as shown in figure 5.3.

Here, a loose collection of agents—the circular nodes—is interconnected in various ways. The dotted lines between the agent nodes are connections: Alice to Acme as an employee, Faber College to Bob as school, Alice to Bob as an acquaintance. Some agents have many of these connections; others have few. Some agents

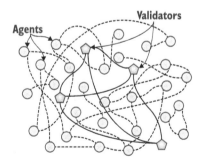

Figure 5.3 An example of a Layer 2 Hyperledger Aries ecosystem: a loose mesh of peer agents interspersed with some acting as validator nodes for DIDs at Layer 1

may even connect to the same peer more than once (Alice to Carol as coworker, Alice to Carol as ham radio buddy).

Connections are constantly forming, and new agent nodes are constantly appearing. Each connection requires a private, pairwise peer DID for each party. As explained earlier in this chapter, these DIDs and their DID documents are not written to any blockchain but are stored in each agent's wallet. The entire mesh is fluid and fully decentralized; connections are direct between peers, not filtered through any interposed authority.

The mesh of nodes is horizontally scalable, and its performance is a function of the nodes' collective capacity to interact and store data. Thus it scales and performs in the same way the internet does. The overwhelming majority of protocol exchanges and meaningful interactions that produce business or social value take place directly between the agent nodes. Once a peer DID connection is formed through an exchange of DIDs and DID documents, the resulting channel (the dotted and solid lines in figure 5.3) can be used for anything the respective agents need: issuing credentials, presenting/proving credentials, exchanging data, securely messaging between humans, and so on.

Mingled with the circular agent nodes in figure 5.3 are a few five-sided shapes. These are validator nodes that provide public blockchain services as a utility to the rest of the ecosystem. They maintain connections with one another to facilitate consensus as the blockchain is updated. Any agent node can reach out to the blockchain to test a community truth (such as check the current value of a public key in a DID document). They can also write to the blockchain (for example, create a schema against which credentials can be issued). Because most DIDs and DID documents are not public in this ecosystem, the bulk of traffic between agent nodes doesn't need to involve the blockchain, thus avoiding attendant scalability, privacy, and cost issues. However, blockchains are still very useful for establishing public trust roots—for example, the DIDs and public keys for institutions that issue (and revoke) credentials that can be broadly trusted.

The interface to this world is *decentralized n-party protocols*. These are recipes for sequences of stateful interactions (a core concept of REST—*representational state transfer*—architecture) representing the business problems solved by applications. Because agents are not assumed to be steadily connected like servers, and because data sharing is only one of an agent's concerns, protocols unfold as encrypted JSON messages that are exchanged, not as APIs that are called (although underlying APIs may be called to trigger specific messages).

To support these protocols, a developer just has to produce and consume JSON over whichever set of transports the target population of agents support. Specific protocols are in various stages of standardization and implementation for many popular interaction patterns, including the verifiable credential exchange protocols we discuss in the next section.

In conclusion, agent-oriented architecture (AOA) is designed to model the variety and flexibility of interactions in the real world while still providing the security, privacy, and trust guarantees necessary to perform transactions that otherwise require direct human intervention at an order of magnitude higher cost and slower speed. On the downside, since the AOA model focuses on loosely coordinated actors with behavior guided by convention, it is more complicated than alternative approaches, more sensitive to network effects, and harder to build and debug. It is also more emergent and, therefore, harder to characterize with confidence. So only time will tell whether AOA will be successful in the market.

5.4 Layer 3: Credentials

If Layers 1 and 2 are where *cryptographic trust*—trust between *machines*—is established, Layers 3 and 4 are where *human trust* enters the picture. Specifically, Layer 3 is the home of the verifiable credential trust triangle introduced in chapter 2. For convenience, we reproduce it in figure 5.4.

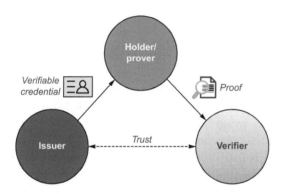

Figure 5.4 The verifiable credential trust triangle that is at the heart of all credential exchange (physical or digital)

This trust triangle is where humans can answer questions like these:

- Is the party asking for my phone number really my bank?
- Is the person digitally signing this contract really an employee of X company?
- Does the person applying for this job really have Y degree?
- Is the seller of the product I want to buy really based in Z country?
- Does the person who wants to buy my car hold a valid passport?
- Is the device I am plugging into my wall socket really approved by Underwriter Laboratories?
- Is the coffee in this bag really sustainably grown in Nicaragua?

Of course, questions like these are endless—they encompass everything we as humans need to know to make trust decisions, whether in our personal capacity, our business capacity, our governmental/citizen capacity, or our social capacity. The goal of Layer 3 is to support interoperable verifiable credentials that can be used in all of these capacities—from any issuer, for any holder, to any verifier.

Given all the capabilities we have described at Layers 1 and 2, interoperability at Layer 3 comes down to two straightforward questions:

- What format of verifiable credential will the parties exchange?
- What protocol will the parties use to exchange it?

Unfortunately, the answers to these questions are anything but straightforward. The SSI community has significant divergence on the answers, meaning Layer 3 is at risk of not being interoperable.

In this section, we dive into the details of the different answers—first concerning credential formats (what credentials look like on the wire and on disk) and then with regard to the protocols used to exchange them. We cover the three main credential formats:

- JSON Web Token (JWT)
- Blockcerts
- W3C Verifiable Credentials

5.4.1   JSON Web Token (JWT) format

One approach to a credential format is to use the well-established JWT specification (RFC 7519, https://tools.ietf.org/html/rfc7519). JWTs (often pronounced "jots") were designed as a carrier of authentication and authorization grants; they are used extensively in OAuth, Open ID Connect, and other modern web login technology. JWTs have good support in various programming languages (search for "JOSE JWT library"). For example, the uPort SSI ecosystem is JWT-centric.

One challenge of JWT tooling is that it provides no help for interpreting the rich metadata that is desirable in a credential. A JWT library can confirm that a college transcript is signed—but it has no idea what a college transcript is or how to interpret it. Thus, a JWT solution to credentials must add additional layers of semantic processing, or it must defer all such work to proprietary, non-interoperable software or human judgment.

Another drawback of using JWT for verifiable credentials is that it reveals everything in the signed document. There is no option for selective disclosure—the credential holder's ability to only reveal certain claims on the credential or to prove facts about those claims without revealing the claim value (such as proving "I am over 21" without revealing my birthdate).

> **NOTE**   The term *selective disclosure* is used in both the privacy community and the financial community. In the privacy community, it has the positive meaning discussed in this section. See https://www.privacypatterns.org/patterns/Support-Selective-Disclosure. In the financial community, it has a negative meaning (a publicly traded company disclosing important information to a single person or a group instead of all investors).

JWTs were originally conceived as short-lived tokens to authenticate or authorize moments after creation. Using them as long-lived credentials is possible, but without any predefined mechanism for credential revocation, it is not obvious how to test the validity of a JWT driver's license months after issuance. It is possible to build such revocation mechanisms—perhaps with revocation lists, for example—but currently, there is no standard for this and thus no tooling to support it.

5.4.2 Blockcerts format

Blockcerts is an open source proposed standard for machine-friendly credentials and the mechanisms that allow those credentials to be verified. It can use multiple blockchains—notably Bitcoin and Ethereum—as an anchor for credentials. Blockcerts was designed and is championed by Learning Machine. (In 2020, Learning Machine was acquired by Hyland and is now Hyland Credentials: https://www.hylandcredentials .com.)

Blockcerts are digitally signed JSON documents that encode the attributes describing the credential holder. They are issued to a payment address that must be controlled by the holder, and the payment address is embedded in the signed JSON. The holder can then prove that the credential belongs to them by demonstrating that they control the private key for the payment address. Work to adapt blockcerts to use DIDs is underway but has no announced schedule.

Blockcerts are typically issued in batches. Each blockcert is hashed, and hashes of all the certificates in the batch are then combined in a Merkle tree, with the root hash of the batch recorded on a blockchain as shown in figure 5.5. Merkle trees are explained in more detail in chapter 6.

> **DEFINITION** A *Merkle tree* is a data structure that holds hashes of data, then hashes of those child hashes, then hashes of those parent hashes, and so forth. These hashes enable efficient proofs that data has not been modified.

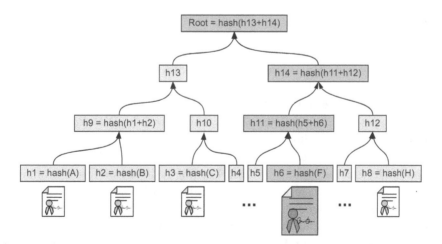

Figure 5.5 A Merkle tree of blockcert hashes, where the root hash is anchored to a public blockchain such as Bitcoin or Ethereum

Verifying a blockcert proves the following for a credential:

- It has not been modified since issuance.
- It is signed by the correct issuer.
- It has not been revoked.

Verification involves evaluating a Merkle proof, which means the hash of the credential is shown to map to a chain of hashes that ends with the hash stored on the ledger. The hash stored on the ledger must be a transaction recorded by the issuer (meaning digitally signed by a key that's also claimed by the issuer) at a uniform resource identifier (URI) that is also embedded in the credential. *Revocation* is tested by calling the issuer at another URI where revocation lists are stored. (A smart-contract-based revocation feature that improves privacy has been described but is not yet in production [10].)

5.4.3   *W3C verifiable credential formats*

The need to establish a worldwide standard for interoperability of verifiable credentials was one of the primary reasons for the formation first of the Verifiable Claims Task Force and then the Credentials Community Group at the W3C (https://www.w3.org/community/credentials). The incubation work resulted in the formation of the Verifiable Claims Working Group in 2017 and, finally, the publication of the Verifiable Credentials Data Model 1.0 as a full W3C Recommendation (official standard) in November 2019 (https://www.w3.org/TR/vc-data-model).

Verifiable credentials are so central to SSI infrastructure that they are covered in their own chapter (chapter 7). For our purposes in this chapter, we can summarize that the Verifiable Credentials Data Model is an abstract data model that uses JavaScript Object Notation for Linked Data (JSON-LD—another W3C standard, http://www.w3.org/TR/json-ld) to describe credentials that can have different schemas and digital signature formats. Two general styles of W3C verifiable credential usage are contemplated: one that focuses on simple credential sharing and one that uses specialized cryptographic signatures to facilitate zero-knowledge proofs.

In the *simple credential-sharing model*, advocated by uPort, Digital Bazaar, Microsoft, and others, credentials contain the DID of the holder (e.g., the person to whom they are issued). When the credential is presented, the holder reveals the whole credential, including this DID. The holder can then prove that the credential belongs to them because they possess the cryptographic keys that control this DID. Revocation for such credentials uses *revocation lists*.

One challenge with the simple credential-sharing model is that it is inherently non-repudiable. Once shared, a credential can be reshared without the holder's permission to any number of parties. Perhaps legislation will clarify how consent for such resharing could be managed.

Another challenge is that revealing a credential in its entirety, including either the hash of the credential or the DID in the credential, provides an extremely easy and strong way to correlate the holder across all verifiers with whom the credential is shared. The extensive privacy risks of this approach are noted in the Verifiable

Credentials Data Model specification (https://www.w3.org/TR/vc-data-model/#privacy-considerations). Advocates of simple credential sharing point out that these privacy concerns do not, in general, apply to credentials for businesses or business assets (like IoT devices). While this is true, privacy engineers have very serious concerns that if the simple credential model is extended to people, it will become the strongest correlation technology in history. So it's fair to say that this is one of the most vigorous debates in all of SSI architecture.

The *zero-knowledge proof* (ZKP) *model* seeks to address these privacy concerns. The best-known implementation of the ZKP model for VCs is in the Hyperledger Indy project. Microsoft has recently announced plans for a ZKP model of its own, and work has also begun on a JSON-LD-ZKP hybrid approach that Hyperledger Aries and Hyperledger Indy may end up sharing.

ZKP-oriented credentials are not presented directly to a verifier. Instead, they are used to generate ZKP of whatever data a verifier needs to be proved—no more, no less. (ZKP technology is explained in more detail in chapter 6.) A *proof* is essentially a derived credential that exactly matches the proof criteria. The proof is generated just in time, only when a verifier requests it. Furthermore, a unique proof is generated each time proof is requested—and the resharability of the proof can be controlled by the holder's cryptography. Because each presentation of a proof is unique, trivial correlation from using the same credential is avoided.

For example, suppose Alice lives in a city that provides free electric car-charging services to its residents. Alice could prove her residency to the charging station day after day, for years, without the station being able to track Alice's movements through the city's charging stations. Each presentation of proof is different and discloses nothing correlatable.

It is important to note that this technique does not eliminate correlation in all cases. For example, if the verifier requires Alice to disclose her real name or mobile phone number in the proof, it will become easy to correlate her. However, Alice's agent can warn her if a proof is asking for highly correlatable personal data so she can make an informed decision.

ZKP-oriented credentials can also take a unique approach to revocation. Instead of revocation lists, they can use privacy-preserving cryptographic accumulators or Merkle proofs rooted on a blockchain. (See chapter 6 for more details.) This allows any verifier to check in real-time for the validity of a credential while not being able to look up a specific credential hash or identifier in a way that leads to correlation.

The primary criticism of ZKP models is the complexity of implementation. ZKPs are an advanced area of cryptography and are not as widely understood as more conventional encryption and digital signature technologies. However, ZKP adoption is gaining ground rapidly as its advantages are being recognized across many different technical fields. A number of newer blockchains, including ZCash and Monero, are based on ZKP technology. ZKP support is also being built into the next generation of Ethereum [11]. ZKP support is built into the core of Hyperledger Ursa (https://wiki.hyperledger.org/display/ursa), an industrial-strength crypto library that is now the standard for all Hyperledger projects. Just as support for the then-new TCP/IP protocol was hampered until hardened libraries became available to developers, the same will be true of ZKPs.

5.4.4   Credential exchange protocols

Regardless of the format of a verifiable credential, interoperability still depends on how that credential is exchanged. This involves any number of complex protocol questions. For example:

- Should potential verifiers reach out to holders proactively, or should they wait to challenge them when holders attempt to access protected resources?
- How do verifiers ask for claims that may be in different credentials?
- Can verifiers add filters or qualifications to their proof requests, such as only accepting claims from specific issuers or only if a credential was issued before or after a specific date?
- Can verifiers contact a party other than the holder to get credential data?

This is where Layer 3 has a direct dependency on Layer 2. For example, if you think of credentials primarily as inert data and believe the best way to distribute identity data is through hubs, then a natural way to exchange that data might be to call a web API and ask that the data be served to you. A credential holder could leave the credential on the hub, with a policy that tells the hub what criteria must be met before serving it to anyone who asks. This is the general paradigm embodied in the approach taken by credential-serving APIs being incubated for DIF identity hubs (https://identity.foun dation/hub-sdk-js).

On the other hand, if you place a higher emphasis on disintermediation and privacy, and you want proofs of credential data to be generated dynamically in the context of a specific connection, a more natural answer would be to use a peer-to-peer credential exchange protocol using agents and DIDComm. This has been the approach of the Hyperledger Indy, Hyperledger Aries, and Sovrin communities. (The protocols are specified in Aries RFC 0036: Issue Credential Protocol 1.0, and Aries RFC 0037: Present Protocol Proof 1.0. Multiple implementations of these protocols are already in production.)

Again, this is the layer where, as of the writing of this book, there is the most divergence in architectures and protocol philosophies. Standardization efforts are active, but so far, consensus is elusive. However, from the "glass half-full" perspective, this is also the area where real-world adoption drives convergence most quickly, as happened with earlier "protocol wars" such as the OSI-vs.-TCP/IP struggle that eventually birthed the internet. An encouraging example of this is DIF's Presentation Exchange spec (https://identity.foundation/presentation-exchange), which describes how verifiers can ask for credential-based proof regardless of which credential technologies are in play.

5.5   *Layer 4: Governance frameworks*

Layer 4 is not just the top of the stack; it is also where the emphasis moves almost entirely from machines and technology to humans and *policy*. When we introduced governance frameworks in chapter 2, we used the diagram shown in figure 5.6 because it shows how directly governance frameworks build on verifiable credentials.

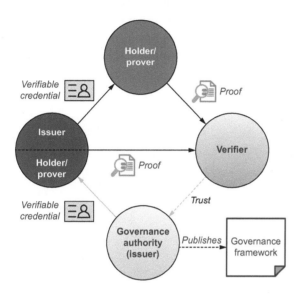

Figure 5.6   Governance frameworks are another trust triangle and solve specification, adoption, and scalability challenges of verifiable credentials.

Governance frameworks enable verifiers to answer an entirely different—but equally relevant—set of questions about verifiable credentials. For example:

- How do I know this driving license was issued by a real government agency?
- How do I know the claims on this credit card came from a real bank or credit union?
- How do I know this diploma was issued by a Canadian university?
- How do I discover what types of credentials are issued by high schools in Austria?
- Was KYC required by the Brazilian lender that issued this mortgage credential?
- Can I rely on a proof based on the birthdate in a Japanese health insurance credential?

Governance frameworks are such a core component of many SSI solutions that we devote an entire chapter to them (chapter 11). Because they are also among the SSI stack's newer components, not many SSI-specific governance frameworks have been created yet. This is in contrast to *trust frameworks* designed for federated identity systems, of which there are quite a few around the world (https://openidentityexchange.org).

However, early work on SSI governance frameworks has convinced many SSI architects that these frameworks will be essential to broad adoption of SSI because they are where the rubber meets the road. In other words, they are the bridge between the technical implementations of the SSI stack and the real-world business, legal, and social requirements of SSI solutions. Furthermore, these architects realized governance frameworks apply at all four levels of the SSI stack. John Jordan, executive director of emerging digital initiatives at the Province of British Columbia in Canada, christened this combination of technology and governance the *Trust over IP* (ToIP) *stack*. The full ToIP stack, shown in figure 5.7, is a "dual stack" where the right side represents technology layers and the left side represents governance layers. See chapter 10 for more details.

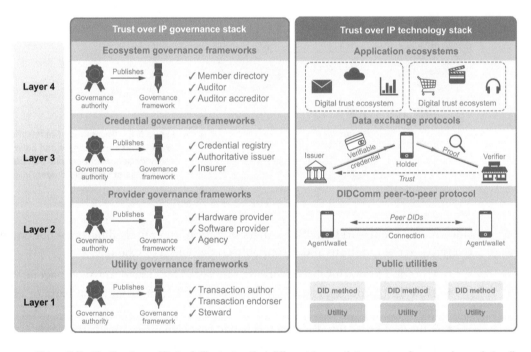

Figure 5.7   The Trust over IP stack illustrates that different types of governance frameworks apply to all four levels of the SSI stack.

During the writing of this book, support for the ToIP stack gained enough momentum that the Linux Foundation launched a new project called the ToIP Foundation (https://trustoverip.org) as a sister project to Hyperledger and the Decentralized Identity Foundation. It grew from 27 founding member organizations in May 2020 to over 140 members by the end of 2020. It now has seven working groups actively working on fully defining, hardening, and promoting the ToIP stack as a model for decentralized digital trust infrastructure.

Despite the fact that governance is where different trust networks and ecosystems within the SSI universe are likely to vary most significantly, the promise of the ToIP stack is that they can use an interoperable metamodel to define those governance frameworks. This can enable both humans and digital agents to much more easily make *transitive trust* decisions across different trust communities, such as many of the questions listed at the start of this section.

As of the writing of this book, work is very actively going on by governance authorities of all kinds around the world to produce ToIP-compliant governance frameworks at all four levels. These are discussed in greater detail in chapter 11.

5.6 Potential for convergence

The field of SSI is young enough that the market is generating many variations in architecture. In this chapter, we have tried to provide a big-picture overview of where the market stands as of the writing of this book. We have been realistic that there are many areas of divergence. This is true at all four levels: different DID methods at Layer 1, different protocols and interfaces at Layer 2, different credential formats and protocols at Layer 3, and different approaches to governance and digital trust ecosystems at Layer 4.

However, at each level, there is also the potential for convergence. The good news is that *this is what market forces want*. With automobiles in the early 1900s, market forces drove the industry to standardize on four wheels and internal combustion engines. With the internet, they drove us to standardize on the TCP/IP stack. With the web, they drove us to standardize on HTTP-based browsers and web servers.

We are hopeful the same market forces will drive convergence in SSI so that it, too, can rise to ubiquitous adoption. However, it also seems likely that more surprises await us. Digital identity architecture is likely to remain a fertile field for innovation for a long time to come.

In the next chapter, we provide some baseline cryptographic knowledge that will help with understanding the rest of the chapters in part 2, especially VCs and DIDs. If you already have a deep cryptographic understanding, you can skip chapter 6 or just skim through it to learn how these cryptographic techniques are applied in SSI.

SSI Resources

For more free content to learn about SSI, please go to IdentityBook.info and SSI Meetup.org/book.

References

1. Terbu, Oliver. 2019. "The Self-sovereign Identity Stack." Decentralized Identity Foundation. https://medium.com/decentralized-identity/the-self-sovereign-identity-stack-8a2cc95f2d45.
2. Voshmgir, Shermin. 2019. "Blockchains & Distributed Ledger Technologies." https://blockchainhub.net/blockchains-and-distributed-ledger-technologies-in-general.

3. CoinMarketCap. 2021. "Today's Cryptocurrency Prices by Market Cap." https://coinmarketcap .com (as of 02 January 2021).

4. W3C. 2020. "DID Methods." https://w3c.github.io/did-spec-registries/#did-methods (as of 19 January 2021).

5. Krassowski, Alan. 2019. "Kiva Protocol: Building the Credit Bureau of the Future Using SSI." SSI Meetup. https://www.slideshare.net/SSIMeetup/kiva-protocol-building-the-credit-bureau-of-the -future-using-ssi.

6. Annunziato, Vincent. n.d. "Blockchain: A US Customs and Border Protection Perspective. *Enterprise Security.* https://blockchain.enterprisesecuritymag.com/cxoinsight/blockchain-a-us-cus toms-and-border-protection-perspective-nid-1055-cid-56.html.

7. Tobin, Andrew. 2017. "Sovrin: What Goes on the Ledger?" Evernym. https://sovrin.org/wp-con tent/uploads/2017/04/What-Goes-On-The-Ledger.pdf.

8. Terbu, Oliver. 2020. "DIF starts DIDComm Working Group." Medium. https://medium.com/ decentralized-identity/dif-starts-didcomm-working-group-9c114d9308dc.

9. Hardman, Daniel. 2019. "Rhythm and Melody: How Hubs and Agents Rock Together." Hyperledger. https://www.hyperledger.org/blog/2019/07/23/rhythm-and-melody-how-hubs-and -agents-rock-together.

10. Santos, João and Kim Hamilton Duffy. 2018. "A Decentralized Approach to Blockcerts Credential Revocation." Rebooting Web of Trust 5. http://mng.bz/w9Ga.

11. Morris, Nicky. 2019. "EY Solution: Private Transactions on Public Ethereum." Ledger Insights. https://www.ledgerinsights.com/ey-blockchain-private-transactions-ethereum.

Basic cryptography
techniques for SSI

Brent Zundel and Sajida Zouarhi

Cryptography is the fuel that powers all of self-sovereign identity (SSI). The goal of this chapter is to help you be conversant in the basic building blocks of cryptography: hash functions, encryption, digital signatures, verifiable data structures, and proofs, as well as common patterns for how they are combined to create the cryptographic magic SSI delivers. Cryptography as a topic is too broad and complex to summarize in a few pages. We intend this chapter to be a reference and a refresher for those readers who understand the basic cryptographic techniques explained here and an index of what may be studied in more depth for those who have had less exposure to cryptography. Your guides will be two technical cryptographers with direct experience in the SSI space: Brent Zundel, senior cryptography engineer at Evernym, and Sajida Zouarhi, engineer and researcher with ConsenSys. Brent also serves as co-chair of the W3C Decentralized Identifier Working Group that is producing the DID standard (the subject of chapter 8).

To paraphrase the famous philosophical observation, "It is turtles all the way down," many SSI architects have said, "It is cryptography all the way down." Modern cryptography uses techniques from mathematics and computer science to secure and authenticate digital communications around the world. Encryption, digital signatures, and hashing are just some of the uses of cryptography that help make SSI possible—and also what make blockchains and distributed ledgers possible. The SSI building blocks introduced in chapter 2 and covered in more detail in the coming chapters, including verifiable credentials (VCs), decentralized identifi-

111

ers (DIDs), digital wallets and agents, and decentralized key management, rely on these cryptographic techniques.

This chapter is intended to give you a basic understanding of the cryptographic techniques used in SSI infrastructure. While understanding these techniques is not essential to exploring SSI, it will make you more confident in some of the SSI "magic." The cryptography underlying SSI infrastructure is constructed from five basic building blocks:

- Hash functions
- Encryption
- Digital signatures
- Verifiable data structures
- Proofs

6.1   Hash functions

A *cryptographic hash* is like a unique digital fingerprint of a digital message or document. It is a fixed-length character sequence produced by running the input through a *hashing function*. Every input document produces a different output hash. If the same hashing function is applied to the same input data, the resulting hash will always be the same. A change of even a single bit of the input data will cause the resulting hash to be different. Table 6.1 shows some examples of hashes using the SHA-256 hash function. (You can try this online using this website or other online resources: https://www.xorbin.com/tools/sha256-hash-calculator.)

Table 6.1   **Examples of hashes that use the SHA-256 hash function**

Message (input)	Hash result in hexadecimal (output or digest)
"identity"	689f6a627384c7dcb2dcc1487e540223e77bdf9dcd0d8be8a326eda65b0ce9a4
"Self-sovereign identity"	d44aa82c3fbeb2325226755df6566851c959259d42d1259bebdcd4d59c44e201
"self-sovereign identity"	3b151979d1e61f1e390fe7533b057d13ba7b871b4ee9a2441e31b8da1b49b999

The purpose of a hash is not to encode or hide a message, but to verify a message's integrity. If a document has not been tampered with, its hash will stay the same. For example, hashes are used by software companies when they publish software programs with a corresponding hash. When users download the software, they can verify the integrity of the files by comparing the hash of the software downloaded with the hash provided by the company. If the hashes are the same, the users know that the files have not been tampered with or corrupted—the file received by the user is an exact copy of the file published by the company.

6.1.1   Types of hash functions

Hash functions are an example of a *unidirectional function* (also called a *one-way function*). A unidirectional function is a mathematical function that provides a quick and efficient method to perform a calculation, with no known method to reverse the calculation in a reasonable amount of time.

There are many different hash functions, such as MD5 and SHA-256. Hash functions differentiate themselves by some basic characteristics:

- *Efficiency*—How fast you can generate a hash, and what the computational cost is.
- *Resistance to preimage*—The input of a hash function is called the *preimage*. Resistance to preimage means that for a given hash, it is very difficult to discover the input. The output of a preimage-resistant hash function appears random and cannot be predicted unless calculated. For example, if given the hash value `689f6a627384c7dcb2dcc1487e540223e77bdf9dcd0d8be8a326eda65b0c e9a4`, it would be computationally infeasible to determine that the input was the word "identity."
- *Resistance to second preimage or collision*—Resistance to second preimage means for a given hash, there will be only one preimage. In other words, two different inputs will not produce the same hash. If two inputs produce the same hash, this is known as a *collision*. A hash function that has resistance to second preimage is also called *collision-resistant*. For example, a collision-resistant hash function that produces `689f6a627384c7dcb2dcc1487e540223e77bdf9dcd0d8be8a326 eda65b0ce9a4` as the hash of "identity" will not produce the same output for any other input.

> **NOTE**   There are many types of unidirectional functions. A well-known example is the product of two prime integers. Multiplying two large prime numbers is quick and efficient, but reversing that calculation and using the product to find the two input prime numbers is very difficult. This problem is called *integer factorization*.

Some hash functions, such as MD5 and SHA-1, are no longer considered cryptographically secure. Cryptanalysts have found good attack vectors for these.

SHA-256 (SHA stands for Secure Hash Algorithm) belongs to the family of SHA-2 functions designed by the National Security Agency (NSA) and recognized by the National Institute of Standards and Technology (NIST) in the USA.

6.1.2   Using hash functions in SSI

Hash functions are used as a building block for verifiable data structures and as part of digital signature algorithms, both of which enable necessary components for self-sovereign identity. Blockchains and distributed ledgers, verifiable credentials, and DIDs all rely on cryptographically secure hash functions.

6.2   *Encryption*

Encryption is a way to hide the content of messages or documents so they can only be read by someone who knows a secret. Early examples of encryption consisted primarily of substitution ciphers and other methods of shuffling text. The secret messages usually relied on some secret method for their security. If an adversary knew the secret method, they could read the secret message. The secret message is also called the *ciphertext.*

Modern encryption methods no longer rely on keeping the encryption method secret. Instead, the encryption methods are public and well-studied, and the security of the encryption methods is based on the difficulty in solving some underlying problem. This difficulty is known as *computational hardness.* The secrecy of the ciphertext relies on secret keys. If the encryption methods are computationally hard, and the key is kept secret, the ciphertext will be unreadable for anyone who doesn't know the secret key.

Cryptography is divided into two families: *symmetric-key* and *asymmetric-key.* In symmetric-key cryptography, the secret key used to encrypt messages is the same as the one that is used to decrypt ciphertexts. Symmetric-key cryptography may also be called *secret-key encryption.*

In asymmetric-key cryptography, there are two keys, one for encrypting messages and the other for decrypting secret messages. Asymmetric-key cryptography has also been called *public-key encryption* because the key used for encrypting messages is called the *public key.* The key used for decrypting ciphertexts is called the secret key or *private key.*

NOTE   The intimate relationship of public and private keys to DIDs is explored in great detail in chapter 8.

6.2.1   *Symmetric-key cryptography*

In symmetric-key cryptography, where the same key is used to encrypt and decrypt, one of the challenges is safely sharing the secret key with the recipient to enable them to decrypt the ciphertext. It follows that some of the most convenient uses of symmetric-key cryptography are when there is no need to share the secret key. For example, if you want to encrypt your hard drive, you can encrypt and decrypt it with the same key.

One other advantage of symmetric-key cryptography is that it is more efficient than public-key cryptography; it provides the same levels of security but uses much smaller keys and much faster computations. One of the best-known algorithms for symmetric-key cryptography is Advanced Encryption Standard (AES). AES uses secret keys of up to 256 bits.[1] This is 256 zeros and ones in a random sequence, as in this example:

```
01110101001010111010111101001010110100100001011010101001001110101111010001
01001001010111010010011010000110110010010010111001101111110011101110110010
10111000010100110110011011111011001100111001110100001110000001101010001111
0001111010101000010010010011111
```

---

[1] This means 2^256 possible combinations of zeros and ones. The number of possible 256-bit keys is 115,792,089,237,316,195,423,570,985,008,687,907,853,269,984,665,640,564,039,457,584,007,913,129,639,936.

The size of secret keys is a critical element in determining the security of a cipher. The greater the number of possible keys, the more difficult it is for a computer to discover the valid key through a *brute-force attack* (an attack based on trying one possible secret key at a time).

6.2.2 *Asymmetric-key cryptography*

Asymmetric-key cryptography, also known as *public-key cryptography*, uses a pair of keys, one public, and one secret, as shown in figure 6.1. The keys are related mathematically and are always used in pairs. If one key is used to alter a message, only the other key can change the message back.

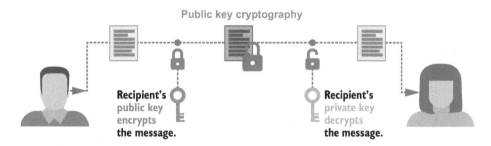

Public key cryptography

Recipient's public key encrypts **the message.**

Recipient's private key decrypts **the message.**

Figure 6.1 In this example, Bob uses Alice's public key to encrypt a message that only Alice will be able to decrypt with her private key.

A secret key must be kept private, but the public key can be shared with the world. Anyone can use a public key to encrypt a message that only someone with the secret key will be able to decrypt. The secret key may also be called the private key.

In many public-key cryptosystems, you use the private key to calculate the public key, but the private key cannot be derived from the public key. The function to derive a public key is another type of unidirectional function.

The private key may be nothing more than a large random number. This secret number is so big that it is nearly impossible to discover with a brute-force attack. Some public-key cryptographic systems include algorithms such as Rivest–Shamir–Adleman (RSA).

To encrypt a message using public-key cryptography, it is necessary to know the recipient's public key. The public key is used to transform the message into a ciphertext. The ciphertext can only be decrypted back into the message using the associated private key.

DIDs make use of asymmetric-key cryptography. Following the same principle, a DID holder stores private keys for DIDs in their digital wallet, while the public keys for DIDs may be publicly discoverable. Figure 6.2 is an example of the public and private keys that correspond to a DID that uses the Sovrin DID method. (See chapter 8 for more about DIDs.)

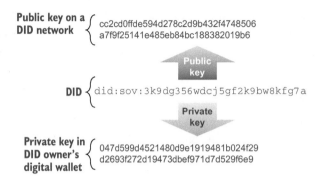

Public key on a DID network { cc2cd0ffde594d278c2d9b432f4748506 a7f9f25141e485eb84bc188382019b6

Public key ↓

DID { did:sov:3k9dg356wdcj5gf2k9bw8kfg7a

Private key ↓

Private key in DID owner's digital wallet { 047d599d4521480d9e1919481b024f29 d2693f272d19473dbef971d7d529f6e9

Figure 6.2   An example of a DID on the Sovrin DID network. A DID functions as the identifier of a public key on a blockchain or other decentralized network. In most cases, it can also be used to locate an agent for interacting with the entity identified by the DID.

NOTE   As of early 2021, the Sovrin DID method is evolving to become one of the Indy DID methods, so the DID prefix will become did:indy:sov.

6.3   *Digital signatures*

Written or "wet ink" signatures are used every day to verify the authenticity of documents, indicate the signer's consent, or both. Digital signatures use cryptographic functions to accomplish the same goals. Signing a message means transforming it in some verifiable way using a private key. The transformed message is called a *signature*. The message is then sent along with the signature to a recipient. The recipient can check the validity of a signature to verify that only the one who knew the private key could have created the signature from the message.

Digital signatures rely on public-key cryptography as described previously. A digital signature is created using the private key of a key pair, and the signature can be verified using the associated public key. The larger the random number used to generate the private key, the harder it is to discover with a brute-force attack. Some public-key cryptographic systems include specific algorithms for digital signatures, such as Elliptic Curve Digital Signature Algorithm (ECDSA).

Digital signatures are used everywhere in SSI infrastructure—across all four layers of the SSI stack described in chapter 5. For example:

- In Layer 1, they are used for every transaction with a blockchain.
- In Layer 2, they are used to form DID-to-DID connections and sign every DID-Comm message.
- In Layer 3, they are used to sign every verifiable credential (some VCs contain digital signatures over each individual claim in the credential).
- In Layer 4, they are used to sign governance framework documents to ensure that they are authentic and to sign VCs issued for assigned roles within a governance framework.

6.4   *Verifiable data structures*

Cryptography can also be used to create data structures that have specific useful properties for data verification.

6.4.1 Cryptographic accumulators

An *accumulator* is a single number that represents the result of some computation on a large set of numbers. Someone who knows one of the accumulated values can prove their number is a member of the set or, alternatively, prove their number is not contained in the set. Some accumulators are based on a set of prime numbers, while others are based on a set of elliptic curve points. The benefit of using a cryptographic accumulator is the minimal size of the accumulated value, but there are drawbacks in the size of the data that must be used to generate proofs against the accumulated value.

6.4.2 Merkle trees

One of the most interesting cryptographic data structures was invented by Ralph Merkle in the early days of public-key cryptography. Called a *Merkle tree*, it provides a very compact and computation-efficient way to verify the integrity of even very large data sets. (Merkle first described the Merkle tree in his 1979 paper "A Certified Digital Signature" and subsequently patented it.) Merkle trees are now a core component of many blockchain and decentralized computing technologies—starting with the Bitcoin protocol based on the blockchain architecture originally described by Satoshi Nakamoto in 2008.

The basic idea of a Merkle tree (also known as a *hash tree*) is that it can provide proof that a specific item of data—such as a blockchain transaction—exists somewhere within a very large amount of information (for example, the history of all bitcoin transactions) using a mathematical process that results in a single hash called the *Merkle root*.

BUILDING A MERKLE TREE

To show how a Merkle tree is built, let's start with a formal definition:

> *A Merkle tree is a tamper-resistant data structure that allows a large amount of data to be compressed into a single hash and can be queried for the presence of specific elements in the data with a proof constructed in logarithmic space. [1]*

This means even though a Merkle tree may contain 1 million pieces of data, proving that any single piece of data is in the tree takes only around 20 calculations.

To build a Merkle tree, a computer will gather the hashes of all the inputs and then group them in pairs—an operation called a *concatenation*. For example, if you start with 20 inputs, after the first round of concatenation, you will have 10 hashes. Once you repeat the operation, you will have five hashes, then three, then two, and then one.[2] This final hash is called the Merkle root. This overall structure is shown in figure 6.3.

---

[2] Since 5 is an odd number, the fifth element is duplicated (we now have six elements) and grouped with itself; hence the resulting three hashes in the next round. The same process repeats with the third element in this round. It is duplicated (we now have four elements) and grouped with itself to result in two hashes in the next round.

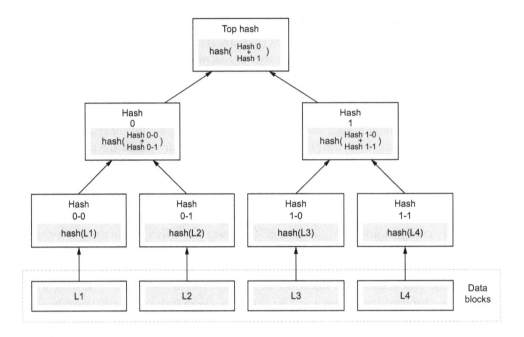

Figure 6.3   In a Merkle tree, different transactions are hashed until a unique hash is created for all the transactions included in the tree.

The goal of a structure like this is not to store or transfer the exhaustive set of input data but to save a proof of their existence in a format small enough that it can be easily stored and exchanged between computers.

SEARCHING A MERKLE TREE

A computer (such as a *node* on a blockchain like Bitcoin, which has a local copy of the Merkle tree of all the transactions in a block) can quickly verify that a specific piece of information (for example, a bitcoin transaction) exists within the Merkle tree. To do so, the computer only needs the following *proof information*:

- The *leaf* hash, which is the hash of the piece of information (such as a transaction hash).
- The *Merkle root* hash.
- The hashes along the root *path*. The root path is the path from leaf to the root—it consists of the sibling hashes needed to compute the hashes on the path all the way from the leaf to the Merkle root.

Instead of having to verify the whole set of transactions, a computer can quickly and efficiently verify just that a certain hash exists in the Merkle tree. This can help ensure data integrity and can also be used in consensus algorithms to reveal if a computer is trying to lie about transactions to its peers.

Merkle trees are used mainly for the following:

- *Storage optimization*—For a large volume of information, there's no need to store the complete data set.
- *Verification speed*—Only a few data points are needed for verification, rather than the whole data set.

The key concept that makes the Merkle tree tamper-proof is the hash function's resistance to a *preimage attack*: an attack that tries to find the message that has a specific hash value. To put it simply, we can easily verify that a value belongs in a Merkle tree by computing the resulting hash for each level in the path all the way down to the Merkle root. However, we cannot find the inputs that were used to generate a specific hash. Hashing is a unidirectional function, which means it is computationally infeasible to retrieve the original inputs from a hash.

6.4.3 *Patricia tries*

We have seen the value of Merkle trees for protocols (e.g., the Bitcoin protocol). Building on this concept, we now focus on another interesting cryptographic data structure called a *Patricia trie*. (The word *trie* comes from *reTRIEval*.) Instead of hashes, these tries are constituted of regular alphanumeric strings. But first, what is a trie, and why do we need tries in SSI?

A *radix trie* (or *compact prefix trie*) is a data structure that looks like a hierarchical tree structure with a root value and subtrees of children with a parent node, represented as a set of linked nodes. The subtlety of radix tries is that the nodes don't store any information; they are only there to indicate a location in the trie where there is a split in the string of characters. Because it knows the key, an algorithm knows how to reassemble the previous prefixes (*edge labels*), leading to that position in the trie. Figure 6.4 shows an example using a set of dictionary words.

The acronym PATRICIA stands for "Practical Algorithm To Retrieve Information Coded In Alphanumeric." (Donald

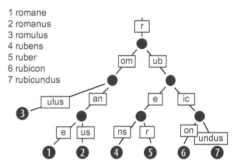

```
1 romane
2 romanus
3 romulus
4 rubens
5 ruber
6 rubicon
7 rubicundus
```

Figure 6.4 In a radix trie, nodes don't store any information; they are indicators of a location in a trie. The algorithm goes through the trie and walks a path called the *key* to find the word. If we take the node in position 6 as the key and run through the trie as the algorithm would (from top to bottom), we reconstitute the word "rubicon."

R. Morrison first described what he called *Patricia trees* in 1968.) A Patricia trie is a variant of the trie we just saw; however, instead of explicitly storing every bit of every key, the nodes store only the position of the first bit, which differentiates two subtrees. This makes a Patricia trie more compact than a standard binary trie and thus faster at finding common prefixes and lighter in terms of storage.

6.4.4 *Merkle-Patricia trie: A hybrid approach*

Merkle trees and Patricia tries can be used in combination to create data structures in different ways depending on the aspect a protocol needs to optimize, such as speed, memory efficiency, or code simplicity. A particularly interesting combination example is the modified Merkle Patricia trie (MPT) [2] found in the Ethereum protocol (https://ethereum.github.io/yellowpaper/paper.pdf#appendix.D). MPT also forms the basis of the architecture for the Hyperledger Indy distributed ledger discussed in chapter 5—a codebase designed for use in SSI infrastructure.

All MPT nodes have a hash value called a key. Key-values are paths on the MPT, just as we saw with the radix trie in figure 6.4.

MPT offers a *cryptographically authenticated data structure* that can be used to store key-value bindings in a fully deterministic way. This means when you are provided with the same starting information, you will get the same trie with a $O(\log(n))$ efficiency.

6.5   *Proofs*

A *proof* is a way of using cryptography to demonstrate that a computational fact is true. For example, Patricia tries let you *prove* that a large set of data is correct without storing the entire set. They are very useful for blockchains because instead of storing past transactions for 24 hours, for example, you only need to store new "proof information" *on-chain*. The rest of the data can be securely stored *off-chain*. No one can tamper with the data without it being evident to the rest of the network.

> **NOTE**   *On-chain* transactions are reflected on a public ledger and are visible to all participants on the blockchain network. *Off-chain* transactions are transfer agreements between two or more parties.

Hybrid systems that combine on-chain and off-chain capabilities are used to overcome some blockchain limitations (e.g., scalability, privacy). This is particularly useful for applications such as SSI, where there is frequently the need to protect private information by keeping it off-chain. Hybrid systems enable software architects to have the best of both worlds.

A digital signature, as discussed previously, is also a form of proof. Anyone with knowledge of the public key but no knowledge of the private key can prove that a specific signature was indeed generated by someone having prior knowledge of the corresponding private key. The *prover*, who signs, can prove to the *verifier* possession of knowledge of information (the private key) without revealing any information about the key: only the message and the signature.

6.5.1 *Zero-knowledge proofs*

Now imagine if it were possible to also keep the signature and parts of the signed message secret. The only thing revealed would be the parts of the message that were disclosed and that the prover *knew* the signature. This is the goal of *zero-knowledge proof* (ZKP) cryptography.

A ZKP needs to have the following three properties [3]:

1 *Completeness*—"If the statement is really true and both users follow the rules properly, then the verifier would be convinced without any artificial help."

2 *Soundness*—"In case of the statement being false, the verifier would not be convinced in any scenario." (The method is probabilistically checked to ensure that the probability of falsehood is equal to zero.)

3 *Zero-knowledge*—"The verifier in every case would not know any more information."

Properties 1 and 2 are needed for all interactive proof systems, such as digital signature proofs. Property 3 is what makes the proof "zero-knowledge."

As explained in chapter 5 and in much more detail in chapter 8, zero-knowledge digital signatures are used with some verifiable credential systems. Other ZKPs that have emerged are the *zk-S*ARK* family of arithmetic-circuit based proof systems:

1 *zk-SNARK (optimized for privacy and consensus)*—This is a zero-knowledge succinct non-interactive argument of knowledge. It is used in blockchain protocols such as Zcash to hide the information relative to the sender and recipient of a transaction and the amount of the transaction itself, while at the same time allowing this transaction to be verified by the network and confirmed to the blockchain.

2 *zk-STARK (optimized for scalability and transparency)*—This form of ZKP, introduced by Eli Ben-Sasson, provides proofs that can be verified much faster by scaling exponentially relative to the data set they are representing.

6.5.2 *ZKP applications for SSI*

ZKPs can be very useful to prove information regarding an individual's credentials without having to fully disclose other sensitive personal identity information. Every scenario where we need to prove that a person has the right to access a service without disclosing more personal data than necessary is a potential application for a ZKP. In the following sections, we will look at a number of specific examples in SSI.

PRIVACY AND PERSONAL CONTROL

Concerns about privacy are driving significant changes in the way data is gathered, stored, and used. News coverage of continual data breaches has led to growing public unease about the lack of security around personal information, while political controversy has triggered alarm about the collection and sale of personal information without full and clear individual consent.

If personal data is less generally available, identity theft and fraud can be reduced. The best way to do this is if people—"data subjects" in terms of data-protection regulations like the EU General Data Protection Regulation (GDPR)—have an easy, practical way to exercise personal control over what information they need to reveal to access online resources.

SIGNATURE BLINDING

With conventional public/private key cryptography, a digital signature is every bit as correlatable as a public key. Zero-knowledge cryptographic methods *do not reveal the actual signature.* Instead, they only reveal a cryptographic proof of a valid signature. Only the holder of the signature has the information needed to present the credential to a verifier. This means ZKP signatures do not increase correlation risk for the signer and automatically protect the signer from impersonation.

SELECTIVE DISCLOSURE

Selective disclosure means you don't have to reveal all of the attributes (*claims*) contained in a credential. For example, if you only need to prove your name, you should not need to disclose your address or telephone number. Similarly, verifiers shouldn't have to collect more data than is necessary to complete a transaction. Selective disclosure is not just a privacy boon for individuals; it also reduces a verifier's liability for handling or holding personal data they do not need.

> **NOTE** The term *selective disclosure* is used in both the privacy community and the financial community. In the privacy community, it has the positive meaning discussed in this section. See https://www.privacypatterns.org/patterns/Support-Selective-Disclosure. In the financial community, it has a negative meaning: a publicly traded company disclosing material information to a single person or a limited group of people or investors, as opposed to disclosing the information to all investors at the same time.

Zero-knowledge cryptography allows a credential holder to choose which attributes to reveal and which attributes to withhold on a case-by-case basis—*without the need to involve the issuer of the credential in any way.* Furthermore, for every attribute in a credential, ZKP gives you two selective disclosure options:

- Prove that the attribute exists in the credential, but do not reveal its value.
- Reveal the value of an attribute without revealing any other attributes.

PREDICATE PROOFS

A *predicate proof* is a proof that answers a true-or-false question about the value of an attribute. For example, if a car rental company requires proof that you are old enough to rent a car, it doesn't need to know your exact birthdate. It just needs a verifiable answer to the question, "Are you over the age of 18?"

Using zero-knowledge methods, predicate proofs are generated by the credential holder at the time of presentation to a verifier and *without the issuer's involvement.* For example, a credential with the attributes `name`, `birthdate`, and `address` can be used in a presentation to reveal your name and prove you are over the age of 18 while withholding everything else. The same credential could then be used in a different presentation to reveal just your address and proof that you are over the age of 25 while never revealing your birthdate.

MULTI-CREDENTIAL PROOFS

Another benefit of ZKP-based verifiable credentials is that proofs can be produced across any set of credentials in a holder's wallet. The verifier does not need to ask for a specific attribute in the context of a specific credential from a specific issuer. However, the verifier can still do that if they need to—in other words, specify that an attribute must be from a specific credential and/or issuer. The ability to simply ask for proof of a set of attributes across all ZKP-based credentials in a holder's wallet makes life much easier for verifiers and also significantly promotes selective disclosure.

REVOCATION

There are many reasons a credential may need to be revoked by the issuer: the data has changed, the holder no longer qualifies, the credential has been misused, or the credential was mis-issued. Regardless of the reason, if a credential is revocable, verifiers need to be able to determine the credential's current revocation status.

As explained earlier in this chapter, zero-knowledge methods such as cryptographic accumulators enable the verifier to confirm that a credential is not revoked without revealing the list of revoked credentials (which could have serious privacy implications). The holder can produce a proof of non-revocation, and the verifier can check this proof against the revocation registry on a public ledger. If the credential is *not* revoked, the proof will validate. If the credential is revoked, the proof will fail. But the verifier is never able to determine any other information from the cryptographic accumulator. This reduces the ability of network monitors to correlate a holder's credential presentations.

ANTI-CORRELATION

Correlation is the ability to link data from multiple interactions to a single user. Correlation can be performed by a verifier, by issuers and verifiers working together, or by a third party observing interactions on the network. *Unauthorized correlation* is when a party collects data about a user without the user's consent or knowledge. This includes a party who deanonymizes private transactions. For example, say a person uses a credential to prove their legal identity so they are authorized to vote in an election. The person then submits a secret ballot that is supposed to be anonymized. If it is possible to deanonymize the voting data and correlate the person's credential with the secret ballot, the vote could be linked to a specific voter. This is a clear violation of the democratic process as it could enable retaliation and other negative consequences.

One way to reduce correlation is through *data minimization*: sharing only the information required to complete a transaction, as discussed earlier in the "Selective disclosure" and "Predicate proofs" sections.

A second way to reduce correlation is to avoid using the same globally unique identifiers across multiple transactions. Globally unique identifiers such as government ID numbers, mobile phone numbers, and reusable public keys make it easy for an observer to link multiple interactions to a single user. ZKPs avoid this linkability by producing unique proofs for every transaction.

Correlation can never be eliminated completely—and *intentional correlation* is sometimes a business requirement (such as when searching criminal records). The goal of zero-knowledge methods is to reduce the probability of *unintentional correlation* and put control over the level of correlation into the credential holder's hands.

6.5.3   *A final note about proofs and veracity*

As previously discussed, a verifiable credential is "verifiable" because it contains one or more cryptographic proofs that can be verified as being true. Some VC proofs are composed of many different smaller proofs. For example, if I wanted to prove the value of my first name based on a claim on a digital birth certificate signed by the government, I would also need to prove the following:

- The birth certificate was issued *to* me.
- The birth certificate was issued *about* me.
- The government is actually the one that issued the birth certificate.
- The birth certificate wasn't tampered with.

Even with these proofs, the verifier still needs to determine whether they trust that the government didn't make a mistake. In other words, even after I've proven the *integrity* of the credential (i.e., that it hasn't changed, is about me, and was issued by the government to me), the verifier still has no guarantees about the *veracity* of the data in the credential (i.e., whether it is true—some also use the term *validity*), beyond the level of their trust in the issuer (this is another place where governance frameworks come into play; see chapter 11).

This applies throughout all uses of cryptography. For example, if the information sent to a blockchain network is not verified prior to its storage, then false information is being stored in an immutable blockchain ("garbage in, garbage out"). The presumption that information is correct simply because it is encrypted is dangerous, particularly if it is fed to other cryptographic components, such as smart contracts, without raising an error in the system.

The point is that the cryptographic properties used in blockchain technology can't help the system know what is true and what is false, only what is stored and when. Cryptography is fundamental to SSI because it enables data to be verified for *integrity* or *traceability*, but not *veracity* or *validity*. Regardless of how cutting-edge or complicated a cryptographic proof may be, it can still only prove a computational fact about data. It cannot prove facts about the real world—only humans can do that (at least, until we start to have very advanced artificial intelligence).

However, cryptographic proofs *can* help humans make some decisions about veracity and validity. For example, certain kinds of proofs can enable *non-repudiation*—the property that when someone performs a cryptographically verifiable operation, they can't afterward claim that they did not make that operation, some other entity did. Non-repudiation also prevents someone from adding or deleting information about someone else without their permission. So non-repudiable proofs help increase the accountability of humans for their digital interactions.

In this chapter, we have shown that blockchain technology was the dawn of SSI because it proved that cryptography could be deployed at scale in highly decentralized systems with extremely strong security properties. SSI takes the next step in harnessing that cryptography to prove digital facts about the identities and attributes of the participants in an SSI ecosystem. Every layer of the SSI architecture described in chapter 5 uses the cryptographic structures—hash functions, encryption, digital signatures, verifiable data structures, and proofs—described in this chapter.

In the next chapter, we will dive into the core data structure enabled by all this cryptography—the "carrier of trust" across the trust triangle—verifiable credentials.

> ### SSI Resources
>
> To learn more about cryptography as it is used in SSI, please check out https://ssimeetup.org/zero-knowledge-proofs-zkp-privacy-preserving-digital-identity-clare-nelson-webinar-14.

References

1. Hackage. 2018. "Merkle-Tree: An Implementation of a Merkle Tree and Merkle Tree Proofs of Inclusion." http://hackage.haskell.org/package/merkle-tree.
2. Kim, Kiyun. 2018. "Modified Merkle Patricia Trie—How Ethereum Saves a State." CodeChain. https://medium.com/codechain/modified-merkle-patricia-trie-how-ethereum-saves-a-state-e6d7555078dd.
3. Goldwasser, S., S. Micali, and C. Rackoff. 2018. "The Knowledge Complexity of Interactive Proof Systems." *SIAM Journal of Computing* 18 (1), 186–208. https://dl.acm.org/citation.cfm?id=63434.

Verifiable credentials

David W. Chadwick and Daniel C. Burnett

Verifiable credentials (VCs) are the very heart of SSI architecture. In this chapter, you learn how VCs evolved, what they look like as data structures, what different formats and digital signature options are supported, and how VCs have been standardized at World Wide Web Consortium (W3C). Your guides are two of the primary authors of the W3C Verifiable Credentials Data Model 1.0 standard: David Chadwick, professor of information systems security at the University of Kent, and Daniel Burnett, executive director of the Enterprise Ethereum Alliance and former blockchain standards architect at ConsenSys. Daniel also served as co-chair of the W3C Verifiable Claims Working Group that created the VC standard.

We all use the physical version of verifiable credentials (VCs) many times each day (even though you may not realize it). Examples include plastic credit cards, driver's licenses, passports, membership cards, bus passes, and more. We can't live without them because they provide us with many benefits. In fact, we wouldn't possess them if they didn't provide us with those benefits. There would be no point.

Unfortunately, you can lose or misplace plastic cards and paper certificates or have them stolen. Worse still, they can be copied or cloned without you knowing about it. But most importantly, you can't use them online—not unless you type all of their details into a web form, which is time-consuming, error-prone, and privacy-invasive. VCs, which are now a full World Wide Web Consortium (W3C) open standard (https://www.w3.org/TR/vc-data-model), will allow issuers to convert the physical VCs they produce today into digital VCs so that you can carry them around in your mobile phone, tablet, laptop, and other devices and use them online by simply pointing and clicking the screen.

Coupled with this ease of use advantage, you also gain other benefits with digital VCs:

- They cannot be copied or cloned.
- They are extremely hard to steal (an attacker would need to steal your electronic device and the method you use to authenticate to the device).
- They are more privacy-protecting since they support *selective disclosure* (disclosing only part of some verifiable data).
- They are more secure because they support *least privileges* (also known as *least authority*: having permission to do only the required tasks and nothing more).
- They cost virtually nothing to issue.
- They are not bulky to carry around like plastic cards.
- You can delegate them to other people to use (providing that the issuer allows this).

7.1 Example uses of VCs

While VCs can be used for all the same things we use physical credentials for nearly every day, VCs can be used for much more because they are digital. Here are some typical usage scenarios.

7.1.1 Opening a bank account

Imagine that you want to open a bank account at BigBank. You visit the local branch of BigBank, and the assistant asks you to provide two official forms of identification—the so-called Know Your Customer (KYC) check. You have a passport and various utility bills that qualify, but unfortunately, you left them at home. Fortunately, the bank supports the use of W3C VCs, and you always carry your mobile phone around with you—on which you've stored several dozen VCs.

You select your government-issued passport VC, which confirms your nationality, name, and age; and your health insurance VC, which confirms your current residential address. Both also contain a digital image of your face. Because the bank trusts the government and the insurance company, it is willing to accept these VCs as proof of your name and address and that the person making the application is really you. This allows the bank to open your bank account and be confident of your identity.

Consequently, the bank issues you a new VC that provides your bank account details, and you add this to your set of VCs on your mobile phone. You can use this new VC in a variety of ways. You can add these bank account details to your online auction, payments, and shopping accounts, give them to your employer for your monthly salary payments, or use them when opening a new high-interest savings account with another bank.

7.1.2 Receiving a free local access pass

You're a pensioner (or a member of the FitSports sports club). You have a VC issued by the local senior citizen center (or FitSports) that says you are entitled to free travel on buses in the local metropolitan area (or entry into all leisure centers operated by FitSports). Whenever you enter a local bus (or a FitSports venue), you simply place your mobile phone on the NFC proximity reader, and it transfers a copy of your bus pass (or FitSports membership) VC to the operator, who then grants you free unrestricted access to the bus (or venue).

Periodically you need to renew this VC by applying online and paying the fee. The website does not need a username or password to authenticate you. Instead, you simply present your existing VC together with your credit card VC (for payment). A replacement VC is issued with a new expiry date; it automatically replaces the old VC on your mobile phone.

7.1.3   *Using an electronic prescription*

You are ill. You visit the doctor, who diagnoses an infection, for which she prescribes penicillin. The prescription is written in the form of a VC, where you are the subject, the doctor is the issuer, and the contents are the drugs that have been prescribed to you.

You don't feel well enough to go to the pharmacy yourself to pick up your prescription, so you ask your wife to go in your place. You transfer the prescription VC to her mobile phone and issue a relationship VC for your wife, with her as the subject, you as the issuer, and an attribute or property that says she is your wife.

> **NOTE** Some identity management systems talk about a subject's *attributes* or *identity attributes,* others about a subject's *personal information* (PII). The VC specification talks about a subject's *properties.* We use the term *property* throughout this chapter, with the understanding that it is synonymous with *attribute, identity attribute,* or *PII.*

Your wife goes to the pharmacy and presents the prescription VC and relationship VC. The pharmacist checks who issued the prescription, and because he knows the doctor who signed it and has previously validated her medical practitioner VC, he's happy to give the prescribed drugs to your wife. The pharmacist records all this information in his audit log for future inspection.

These scenarios are just a few examples of how VCs can greatly simplify your life, both online and in the physical world. VCs were created for the following two purposes:

- To provide a digital version of the credentials we carry in our digital wallets today.
- To allow us to prove our identities "bottom-up"—with a set of claims about an identifier—rather than "top-down" by trying to define an identity and then attach information to it.

In the rest of this chapter, we explain these points and delve more into the technical details of VCs.

7.2   *The VC ecosystem*

As you can see from the previous examples, a number of entities and roles are involved in the VC ecosystem. These entities and roles are shown in figure 7.1.

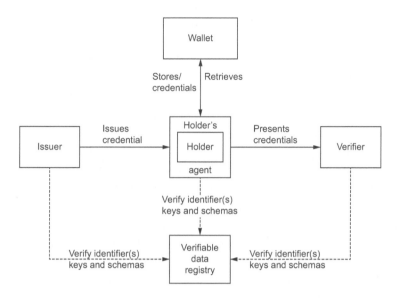

Figure 7.1 The overall architecture of VCs, in which the holder sits at the center—the essence of user-centric design.

NOTE To help familiarize you, in this section, the specific roles defined in the official W3C VC specification have Uppercase First Letters. In subsequent sections, they appear as standard generic nouns.

The components of the VC architecture are as follows:

- *Issuer*—The entity that issues VCs to users. In most cases, the user is the Subject, but in some cases, it may not be; for example, if the Subject is a pet cat and the VC is a vaccination certificate, then the Issuer will issue the VC to the cat's owner.
- *Subject*—The entity whose properties are stored in the VC. A Subject can be anything with an identity: a person, organization, human-made thing, natural thing, logical thing, and so on.
- *Holder*—The entity that is currently holding the VC and presents it to the Verifier. In most cases, the Subject and the Holder are the same entity; but as you saw in the previous prescription and cat examples, this is not always the case.
- *Verifier*—The entity that receives the VCs from the Holder and provides benefits in return.
- *Wallet*—The entity that holds the VCs for the Holder. In many cases, the Wallet is integral to the Holder's Agent, but the model allows for a remote wallet to exist, such as a cloud storage wallet.
- *Holder's Agent*—The software that interacts with the VC ecosystem on behalf of the Holder. This could be an app that you load onto your mobile phone or a program you run on your laptop.

- *Verifiable Data Registry*—Conceptually, an internet-accessible registry that holds all the essential data and metadata that enables the VC ecosystem to operate. Examples of the types of data and metadata that can be stored in this registry are the following:
  - The public keys of Issuers
  - The schema or ontology for all the properties that the VCs may contain; revocation lists of revoked VCs
  - The subject properties that Issuers say they are authoritative for (for example, a national government may list Social Security numbers and passport details; a university may list its degrees and transcripts)

In practice, we envisage that many different Verifiable Data Registry components will exist initially because currently, there are no standards for them. VCs have become popularized due to the potential for blockchains and distributed ledgers to serve as decentralized, Verifiable Data Registries. However, blockchains are by no means the only option. Some Verifiable Data Registries may be centralized, others widely distributed but based on different technologies, and still others virtual and preconfigured into holders' software agents. This may change in the long term as standards evolve, but for now, this entity is a placeholder to indicate that such a registry or registries are essential for any practical VC ecosystem to operate effectively and efficiently.

The VC ecosystem will consist of many Issuers, Verifiers, Holders, and registry services working together in *ecosystems* or *trust networks*. A typical arrangement might operate as follows:

1 A Verifier defines its policies for accepting VCs from Holders for its supported services. One notable feature of the VC ecosystem is that a Verifier may offer a range of services, and each service may have a different policy. This helps to provide the *least-privileges* feature because the Verifier needs to request only those subject properties that are necessary for the requested service. Each policy says which Issuers the Verifier trusts to issue which VCs for this service; for example, a pizza website might have a policy that says to place an online order for a pizza, the user should present a credit card VC issued by Visa or Mastercard (for payment), and optionally either a preferred customer VC issued by itself or a student VC issued by the National Students Association (to claim a 10% discount on the order).

2 Either before or after or simultaneously with step 1, the various Issuers issue their VCs to their Subjects, who store them in their digital wallets. In some instances, the VC is issued to a Holder who is not the Subject (e.g., pet vaccination VC) or multiple Subjects (e.g., marriage certificate VC).

3 When allowed by Issuers, some Subjects may pass on their VCs to other Holders.

4 The ultimate Holder requests a particular service from a Verifier.

5 The Verifier returns its policy to the Holder's Agent, which checks whether the Holder has the necessary set of VCs in its Wallet. If so, the policy can be fulfilled.

6 The Holder presents the requested set of VCs to the Verifier, optionally inside a Verifiable Presentation (VP), which is a packaging mechanism to cryptographically prove that the Holder is sending the VCs, along with any conditions they may be placing on the Verifier.

7 The Verifier verifies that:

– The presented VCs and VP (if present) have authentic digital signatures.

– The VCs match its policy.

– The Holder is entitled to hold them.

– The Verifier will conform to any conditions the Holder may have placed in the VP.

8 If all is good, the Verifier performs the requested service for the Holder; if not, it returns an error message.

One caveat: as noted in chapter 5, the standards for Verifiers' policies and the protocols between the various entities are still evolving in the marketplace. It is also worth noting that using VCs does not require DIDs, just as DIDs do not require VCs to take advantage of using distributed ledger services for identification. However, combining VCs and DIDs brings many advantages to both technologies. VCs can use distributed ledgers to implement components of the Verifiable Data Registry, and distributed ledgers can use VCs to gain access to their services (as outlined previously).

7.3 *The VC trust model*

The *verifiable* in *verifiable credentials* means the credential can be digitally signed and the digital signature can be cryptographically verified, as described in chapter 6. But that is not the only factor in determining whether a verifier can trust a particular VC. In this section, we discuss the complete VC trust model.

7.3.1 *Federated identity management vs. VCs*

For those familiar with today's federated identity management (FIM) systems (described in chapter 1), you see that the VC architecture is quite different from FIM architecture.

> **DEFINITION** The *FIM architecture* comprises the user, identity provider (IDP), and service provider (SP). At first sight, this appears very similar to the holder, issuer, and verifier roles in VC architecture. But the way the various parties interact is fundamentally different. In the FIM architecture, the user first contacts the SP and is then redirected to the IDP, where they log in and are then redirected back to the SP, providing the latter with the user's identity attributes that the IDP is willing to release. In VC architecture, there is none of this web-based redirection within a defined "federation"—the user as holder obtains VCs from issuers and uses them independently at any verifier that will accept them.

The FIM architecture places the *IDP at the center of the ecosystem*, whereas the VC architecture places the *holder at the center of the ecosystem*. This is fundamental to understanding the VC philosophy: *users are paramount, and they decide whom to give their VCs to.* This compares drastically with the FIM philosophy: *IDPs are paramount, and they decide who can receive the user's identity attributes.*

One of the world's largest FIM infrastructures is eduGAIN, comprising thousands of university IDPs from all over the world, along with numerous academic service providers. This community directly recognizes this key deficiency of FIM [1]:

> *Insufficient attribute release by IDPs is considered by user communities as the major problem today in the eduGAIN space.*

The FIM architecture has this requirement because IDPs must trust SPs to maintain the privacy and confidentiality of the user's attributes that they send to the SP. In the VC ecosystem, this connection is broken. Issuers send the user's identity attributes to the user as properties in VCs, and the user decides what to do with them, just as they would with a physical credential issued to the user's physical wallet. The issuer doesn't know which verifiers the user is giving their VCs to (unless the user or the verifier tells the issuer). So the issuer no longer needs to trust the verifier. This is a fundamental difference between the trust models of conventional FIM systems and the VC system.

7.3.2 *Specific trust relationships in the VC trust model*

The differences between the FIM trust model and the VC trust model are apparent from figure 7.2. Here we see the three major actors—issuers, holders, and verifiers—and their relationships to the three technical components: the holder's agent, the wallet, and the verifiable data registry. Trust relationships are shown with arrows.

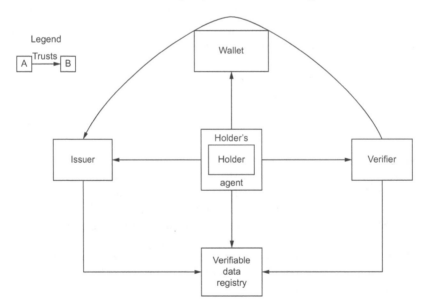

Figure 7.2   The VC trust model, where holders are at the center, and verifiers only need to trust issuers (and the verifiable data registry trusted by all parties)

Let's delve more deeply into each of the trust relationships depicted here:

- *The verifier must trust the issuer to be authoritative for the subject's properties that are contained in a VC that it receives.* For example, a verifier would usually trust a national government to be authoritative for a subject's nationality property but would not necessarily trust the government to be authoritative for a university degree property. Conversely, a verifier would usually trust a university to be authoritative for a subject's degree qualification property, but not necessarily for the subject's golf club membership property. *Each verifier determines its own trust rules.* There is no compulsion for any verifier to trust any VC or any issuer. The verifier determines which VCs from which issuers to trust according to its risk profile. However, to help verifiers make their trust decisions, a verifiable data registry (or a governance authority that publishes a governance framework—see chapter 11) will often contain a list of known issuers and the properties for which they state they are authoritative. Verifiers can then determine who and what to trust from this list.

- Consequently, *all participants trust the verifiable data registry* to be tamper-evident and to be an accurate and up-to-date record of which data is controlled by which entities. Note that we say *tamper-evident* and not tamper-proof. No system on earth can stop determined attackers from tampering with it, but the verifiable data registry should allow its users to detect whether it has been tampered with.

- *Both the subject/holder and the verifier must trust the issuer to issue true VCs.* An issuer that lies cannot be trusted by anyone.

- *Both the subject/holder and the verifier must trust the issuer to revoke VCs that have been compromised or are no longer true,* in a timely manner. This policy is determined by the issuer. The best practice is for issuers to publish the revocation timeframes under which they operate because this is fundamental to the risk-mitigation strategies of the verifiers. In certain circumstances, a subject may know that an issuer holds out-of-date information and that the corresponding VC is incorrect, but the subject finds it very difficult to get the issuer to update its database and reissue the VC. For this reason, there is a dispute procedure that is discussed further in section 7.8.2.

- *The holder trusts their wallet to store VCs securely,* not release them to anyone other than the holder, and not allow them to be corrupted or lost while in its storage.

As you can see, this is a relatively simple trust model that corresponds almost exactly to the trust model for the physical credentials we have been using for decades. This is one of the major strengths of the VC ecosystem for the simple reason that it *works the same way trust in the real world does*—there is no artificial insertion of an identity provider into all of a user's relationships.

7.3.3 *Bottom-up trust*

Credentialing systems often begin with a notion of first "securing one's identity," as in the PKI world. However, these top-down approaches to trust lead to centralization of information and control, dominance by small numbers of commercial entities, and loss of individual privacy. The bottom-up approach to trust taken with VCs seeks to avoid these pitfalls.

One of the biggest challenges to adoption so far has been the simplicity of the VC trust model. The current dominance of the internet giants that operate the largest FIM systems globally (the "Login with _____" buttons you see on websites everywhere) has trained internet users to believe they are the only sources of truth that verifiers will trust. But in the offline world, there are millions of issuers of credentials and millions of verifiers of those credentials, and the entire system is decentralized. Trust relationships are established peer-to-peer, "pairwise," directly between holders and verifiers. This is sometimes called the *web of trust* model, and it is the bottoms-up trust model that VCs emulate. There are numerous examples of how this will work in parts 3 and 4 of this book.

7.4   *W3C and the VC standardization process*

The work on what we now call verifiable credentials began as an offshoot of the Web Payments Interest Group at the World Wide Web Consortium (W3C). The W3C is the standards body that defines the HTML web programming language and the other key standards for the interoperability of the web. The Web Payments Interest Group's job was to standardize how to make payments on the web: in other words, how to pay directly from your web browser.

This required a way to authenticate individuals. So the Web Payments Interest Group started up the Verifiable Claims Task Force (VCTF, https://w3c.github.io/vctf) to explore whether the W3C could productively work in this area. This new non-standards-track group consisted mostly of members from both the Web Payments Interest Group and the W3C Credentials Community Group (another non-standards track group that is incubating all things related to digital credentials).

The VCTF developed an initial specification from which the group concluded that, indeed, W3C could productively help in this area. The VCTF wrapped up in May 2017 and transferred its specification to the newly created W3C standards-track Verifiable Claims Working Group (VCWG). At first, the specification was named the Verifiable Claims Data Model and Syntaxes specification, but after a year's worth of work, the VCWG changed the name to Verifiable Credentials Data Model 1.0.

At this point, you may be wondering why the group was named Verifiable Claims while the specification name talks about Verifiable Credentials. The working group's initial proponents very much believed—and still do—that the work is about creating verifiable credentials, where each credential can contain one or more claims from the same issuer. As the standards-track Working Group was being created, some parties at W3C objected to using the term *credentials* out of a concern that in the web security community, the word *credentials* meant only a username and password. Once the VCWG was underway and more people joined the effort, that concern diminished—especially as it became clear that *credential* really was the appropriate word.

In summary, the W3C Verifiable *Credentials* Data Model 1.0 specification (which we will refer to as the VC Data Model spec; https://www.w3.org/TR/vc-data-model) was created in the W3C Verifiable *Claims* Working Group.

The specification defines more than just a data model for VCs, however. It includes:

- A data model for VCs, the credentials that an issuer provides to a holder
- A data model for verifiable presentations (VPs), the collection of credentials that a holder may present to a verifier
- A way to represent (or express) that data model using JSON Linked Data (JSON-LD) syntax
- A way to represent (or express) that data model using JSON Web Tokens (JWT) syntax.

We refer to the latter two items as *syntactic representations* of the data model. The difference between a data model and a syntactic representation (also sometimes referred to as a *serialization*) is that a data model describes relationships of one entity to another: for example, *I am a son to my father* or *he is a father to me*. We could represent that with a diagram, but diagrams are not convenient for computers to work with. Alternatively, we could represent those relationships using a written format or *syntax* that is readable to computers, humans, or both. Both of the syntactic representations for VCs that we cover are readable by both computers and humans.

7.5 Syntactic representations

Although it might seem logical to describe the general data model before delving into how that data model is expressed in a concrete syntax, the data model is much easier to explain using concrete examples. So, in this section, we present concrete representations defined by the specification. These support the examples we show later. For now, do not be concerned with the various properties or attributes you see in these examples; definitions will come later in section 7.6. First, some background.

7.5.1 JSON

The two syntactic representations defined by the VC data model 1.0 specification are based on *JavaScript Object Notation* (JSON), which is a simplification of the syntax used to represent collections of data items in the JavaScript programming language. This subsection summarizes JSON; the following subsections summarize the two syntactic representations defined in the VC data model specification based on JSON.

> **NOTE** Although these two syntactic representations, the *JSON-LD representation* and the *JWT representation*, are the only ones defined in the 1.0 specification, it is expected that others will be defined in the future.

A JavaScript object consists of an outer pair of curly braces that contain zero or more key-value pairs separated by commas, where each key-value pair is a key string, a colon, and a value. Between any two of those parts, white space is ignored. The key is referred to as a property of the object, and the value is the property's value. Here are some examples:

```
{height:5, width:7}
{"my height":75, "your height": 63}
{direction:"left",
 coordinates1: {up:7, down:2},
 coordinates2: {up:3, down:5},
 magnitude: -6.73986
}
```

In the first example, the first key string is `height`, and its value is 5; the second key string is `width`, and its value is 7.

Notice that by default, a key is a sequence of alphanumeric characters (beginning with a letter) without spaces but that spaces can be introduced by quoting the string. The value can be a string, an integer, a floating-point value, or another object. Some unquoted strings have particular meanings when used in JavaScript. Examples include `true`, `false`, and `null`.

7.5.2 *Beyond JSON: Adding standardized properties*

JSON allows for direct representation of any tree-structured data, but there is no standard set of properties for JSON objects. By standardizing a set of properties for VCs, it becomes possible to automate the creation and use of those credentials. The next two subsections describe how to represent VC data with standardized properties using two different syntactic representations: JSON-LD and JWT. The properties in each that are critical to the data model are mappable one-to-one between the two formats.

7.5.3 *JSON-LD*

JSON Linked Data makes it easy to incorporate properties defined in structured templates called *schemas*. As an example, https://schema.org/Person defines a set of properties for a person. JSON-LD processors know how to automatically use these schemas to see what types of values the schema's properties expect.

In JSON-LD, the desired schema locations are listed in the `@context` property's value. Then the `type` property specifies which particular schemas from those locations are being used. Those, in turn, define the allowed properties.

Here is an example where we are using properties from the `Verifiable-Credential` schema at https://www.w3.org/2018/credentials/v1 and the `alumniOf` property from the `Person` schema at https://schema.org:

```
{
  "@context": [
    "https://www.w3.org/2018/credentials/v1",
    "https://schema.org",
  ],
  "id": "http://example.edu/credentials/58473",
  "type": ["VerifiableCredential", "Person"],
```

```
  "credentialSubject": {
    "id": "did:example:ebfeb1f712ebc6f1c276e12ec21",
    "alumniOf": "Example University"
  },
  "proof": { ... }
}
```

This approach to naming is incredibly flexible since anyone can create a new schema (called a *context*), post it at a stable URL on the internet, and then reference its properties in the VC. Since the previous example only cares about the alumniOf property, we can create a new, more specific JSON-LD context called AlumniCredential that contains only one property, alumniOf. Assuming the new context is stored at https://mysite.example.com/mycredentialschemas, the example now looks like this:

```
{
  "@context": [
    "https://www.w3.org/2018/credentials/v1",
    "https://mysite.example.com/mycredentialschemas",
  ],
  "id": "http://example.edu/credentials/58473",
  "type": ["VerifiableCredential", "AlumniCredential"],
  "credentialSubject": {
    "id": "did:example:ebfeb1f712ebc6f1c276e12ec21",
    "alumniOf": "Example University"
  },
  "proof": { ... }
}
```

An essential aspect of JSON-LD contexts is that the URLs and schema definitions *must* be stable and unchanging. This allows the context and schema definitions to be looked up only once (either automatically or manually) and used from then on without any risk of them changing. It is very important to note that the JSON-LD syntax for VCs can be used *without any dynamic fetching of context information.* Essentially, these contexts can be thought of as defining separate namespaces, so one person's definition of alumniOf does not have to be the same as someone else's. When the contexts are different, you know that they are not intended to be the same thing. This feature of JSON-LD is very helpful in VCs since the VC data model is purposefully an *open-world* data model, where user-defined properties may be added at any time.

As in the Verifiable Credentials Data Model specification, this chapter uses JSON-LD as the default syntax for most of the examples. (If you're interested in learning more, we recommend https://json-ld.org/primer/latest.)

7.5.4 *JWT*

JSON Web Tokens (RFC7519), pronounced either "J W Ts" or "Jots," are a previously standardized way to represent signable claims, or *attestations*, using JSON. The syntax is convenient for converting into binary representations that are precise in using white space and easily compacted to reduce storage and transmission costs. Given the breadth of the JWT-based ecosystem, it made sense to find a way to represent VCs and VPs in JWTs.

JWTs have three parts: a *header*, a *payload*, and an optional *signature* (of the payload). For our purposes, the *header* and its property values are not particularly relevant but are outlined in the VC Data Model specification. Since the JWT *payload* is essentially a restructuring of a JSON-LD VC, the easiest way to understand the JWT syntax for VCs is to first generate the JSON-LD syntax and then convert it. The most common properties are mapped as follows:

- Replace the `id` property with `jti`.
- Replace the `issuer` property with `iss`.
- Replace `issuanceDate` with `iat`, and change the date format to a UNIX timestamp (`NumericDate`).
- Replace `expirationDate` with `exp`, and change the date format to a UNIX timestamp (`NumericDate`).
- Remove the `credentialSubject.id` property, and create a `sub` property with the same value.

A similar process is used to convert VPs to a JWT payload, with details explained in the specification. If a JSON Web Signature (JWS) is provided in a VC, it proves the issuer of the VC; and in a VP, it proves the holder of the VP. The VC `proof` property may still be provided if other proof information is used: for example, zero-knowledge-based approaches.

After the previous conversions, any other remaining properties (including `proof`, if present) are moved into a new JSON object under the new JWT custom claim `vc` (or `vp` for a presentation).

As an example, let's look at a JSON-LD VC (minus the proof):

```
{
  "@context": [
    "https://www.w3.org/2018/credentials/v1",
    "https://schema.org"
  ],
  "id": "http://example.edu/credentials/3732",
  "type": ["VerifiableCredential", "Course"],
  "credentialSubject": {
    "id": "did:example:ebfeb1f712ebc6f1c276e12ec21",
    "educationalCredentialAwarded":
      "Bachelor of Science in Mechanical Engineering"
  },
  "issuer": "did:example:abfe13f712120431c276e12ecab",
  "issuanceDate": "2019-03-09T13:25:51Z",
  "expirationDate": "2019-03-09T14:04:07Z"
}
```

After converting to a JWT payload, the same VC looks like this (note that the cryptographic nonce—an arbitrary number that can be used just once in a cryptographic communication—is a feature of JWTs not derived from the original JSON-LD VC):

```
{
  "sub": "did:example:ebfeb1f712ebc6f1c276e12ec21",
  "jti": "http://example.edu/credentials/3732",
```

```
    "iss": "did:example:abfe13f712120431c276e12ecab",
    "iat": "1541493724",
    "exp": "1573029723",
    "nonce": "660!6345FSer",
    "vc": {
      "@context": [
        "https://www.w3.org/2018/credentials/v1",
        "https://schema.org"
      ],
      "type": ["VerifiableCredential", "Course"],
      "credentialSubject": {
        "educationalCredentialAwarded":
          "Bachelor of Science in Mechanical Engineering"
      }
    }
}
```

This description was designed to give experienced users of JWTs a rough idea of how this conversion process works and let others know that the JWT syntax exists. The entire JWT-based syntactic framework is fairly extensive, and there are subtleties in how the pieces work together for VCs and VPs. These are best answered by reading the VC Data Model spec.

7.6 Basic VC properties

Now that we've covered the syntactic representations, we can explain the properties defined by the data model. The most basic VC needs to hold only six pieces of information (encoded as JSON properties), as shown in figure 7.3.

The contents of each of these JSON properties are described next:

- @context—When people communicate, they need to know what language and vocabulary to use. While the default encoding language used for VCs is JSON-LD, that does not tell us what JSON properties a VC might contain. The @context property tells us which sets of vocabularies were used to construct this VC. Syntactically, @context comprises a sequence of one or more uniform resource identifiers (URIs). Ideally, each URI should point to a machine-readable document containing a vocabulary that a verifier can automatically download and configure. Because many implementations may not be that sophisticated, the URI may alternately point to a human-readable specification that allows an administrator

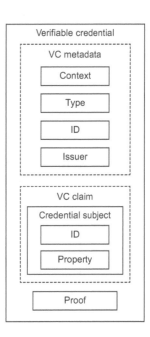

Figure 7.3 The structure of a basic VC, showing the metadata component, the claim component, and the proof component

to configure the verifier software with the necessary vocabulary. Note that `@context` on its own may provide more information (vocabulary) than a verifier wishes to use. Therefore, the VC also contains a `type` property.

- `type`—The `type` property contains a list of URIs that assert what type of VC this is. The first type must always be `https://www.w3.org/2018/credentials/v1`, which can be abbreviated to `VerifiableCredential` using the JSON-LD `@context` mechanism. Verifiers can read the list of types and quickly determine if they can understand and process this VC. If the VC is a type the verifier does not recognize, the verifier can immediately reject it without further processing.

- `id`—The `id` property is the unique identifier of this VC, created by the issuer. It consists of a single URI. This allows any entity to unambiguously reference this VC.

- `issuer`—The `issuer` property uniquely identifies the issuer. It is a URI. This URI can point to a document that fully describes the issuer—for example, a DID that points to a DID document—or it can contain the DNS name of the issuer, and the verifiable data registry can contain further details about the issuer, such as its X.509 public-key certificate.

- `credentialSubject`—This property contains the claims the issuer is making about the subject. It consists of the ID of the subject and the set of properties the issuer is asserting about the subject. In some cases, the ID may be missing: for example, if this is a bearer VC (such as a concert ticket) that can belong to anyone. Since VCs are designed to preserve a subject's privacy, the ID is a pseudonym for the subject in the form of a URI. A subject can have countless pseudonyms, and each VC can contain a different ID. In this way, without additional information, a verifier cannot know that two VCs with different subject IDs belong to the same individual.

NOTE *Selective disclosure* is another privacy feature that VCs can support. There are two recommended ways to achieve this: by including the absolute minimum number of properties (preferably one) in a single VC (a so-called *atomic VC*), or by using zero-knowledge proof (ZKP) VCs (discussed in section 7.10). In the former case, an issuer, instead of issuing a complex VC containing multiple properties, may issue a set of atomic VCs. For example, a full driving license VC may contain the following four properties: name, address, date of birth, and vehicle classes, whereas the alternative is four atomic VCs, each containing one property and a link ID (to link them all together). The holder can then selectively disclose individual properties from his or her driving license.

- `proof`—For a credential to be verifiable, it needs a signature, referred to more generally in the VC Data Model spec as a *proof*. This cryptographically proves that the issuer issued this VC and that it has not been tampered with since issuance. Every VC must contain either the `proof` property or, if using JWT syntax, a JSON Web Signature. There is no single standard for the proof property's contents since several different types of proof are envisaged (see section 7.10). If this property is used, the one common property that all proofs must contain is the type property, which asserts the type of the proof.

Other basic properties that are optional but generally very useful include the following:

- issuanceDate—The combined date and time, in ISO 8601 format, after which the VC is valid. Note that it is not necessarily the actual date the VC was issued, as an issuer may issue a VC before or after this date, but it is the date *before* which the VC is invalid.

- expirationDate—The combined date and time, in ISO 8601 format, after which the VC is invalid.

- credentialStatus—Provides the verifier with details of the VC's current status: whether it has been revoked, suspended, superseded, or otherwise changed since its issuance date. This is a particularly useful property for a long-lived VC but less so for a short-lived VC, i.e., one where it is expected that the VC will not change its status before its expiration date. (Whether a VC is short-lived or long-lived depends on the application using the VC and the risk profile of the verifier. For a stock market transaction, long-lived might be greater than a few seconds; for a national passport, short-lived might be 24 hours.) There is no standard format for the credentialStatus property, but every status must contain an id and type property. The id property is the unique URL for this credential status instance—it is where the verifier can get the status information for this VC. The type property states the type of credential status, which in turn dictates what other properties the status property should contain.

Here is a VC, encoded in JSON-LD, that contains all these basic properties:

```
{
 "@context": [
    "https://www.w3.org/2018/credentials/v1",
    "https://example.com/examples/v1"
 ],
 "id": "http://example.edu/credentials/3732",
 "type": ["VerifiableCredential", "UniversityDegreeCredential"],
 "issuer": "https://example.edu/issuers/14",
 "issuanceDate": "2010-01-01T19:23:24Z",
 "expirationDate": "2020-01-01T19:23:24Z",
 "credentialSubject": {
    "id": "did:example:ebfeb1f712ebc6f1c276e12ec21",
    "degree": {
       "type": "BachelorDegree",
       "name": "Bachelor of Science in Mechanical Engineering"
    }
 },
 "credentialStatus": {
    "id": "https://example.edu/status/24",
    "type": "CredentialStatusList2017"
 },
```

```
"proof": {
  "type": "RsaSignature2018",
  "created": "2018-06-18T21:19:10Z",
  "verificationMethod": "https://example.com/jdoe/keys/1",
  "nonce": "c0ae1c8e-c7e7-469f-b252-86e6a0e7387e",
  "signatureValue": "BavEll0/I1zpYw8XNi1bgVg/sCneO4Jugez8RwDg/+
    MCRVpjOboDoe4SxxKjkCOvKiCHGDvc4krqi6Z1n0UfqzxGfmatCuFibcClwps
    PRdW+gGsutPTLzvueMWmFhwYmfIFpbBu95t501+rSLHIEuujM/+PXr9Cky6Ed
    +W3JT24="
  }
}
```

While this example describes the basic properties of a VC, also note the following:

- A VC can contain multiple claims, where each claim is about a different credential subject. For example, a marriage certificate VC could contain one claim about subject ID x and another claim about subject ID y. The property of the first claim could be "married to subject ID y" and of the second claim "married to subject ID x."
- A VC can contain multiple proofs; for example, a highly confidential or valuable VC might require two directors of the issuing company to sign it.
- VCs can optionally be wrapped in a VP by the holder.

7.7   *Verifiable presentations*

A VP is one way a holder may combine several VCs to send to a verifier. It is very similar to a VC in that it contains metadata about the presentation plus a proof signed by the holder. However, the contents are now a set of VCs rather than a set of claims (see figure 7.4).

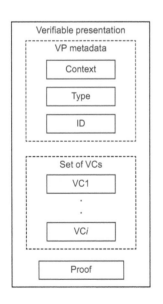

One notable difference between a VC and a VP is that the `issuer` property is missing. If present, it would have contained the holder's ID, and indeed, a draft version of the specification did contain just that. When it was present, if the VP issuer's ID equaled the ID of the credential subject, it was very easy for the verifier to determine that the holder was the subject of the encapsulated VC. However, this property was removed in order for ZKP implementations not to be forced to reveal the ID of the holder (see section 7.10 for a fuller explanation). For non-ZKP VCs, it is expected that the verifier can determine the holder either from the protocol exchange before the VP is sent or from the `proof` property of the VP (which can contain an identifier for the signer).

Another difference between a VP and a VC is that the `id` property is optional. It needs to be present only if the holder wants to uniquely refer to this VP on a subsequent occasion.

Figure 7.4 A basic VP that contains a group of VCs plus metadata about them

Similar to VCs, a VP may contain multiple proofs. For example, say a holder has several VCs, each with a different credential subject ID that identifies the holder, implying a different asymmetric key pair for each VC. Then the holder can send a VP to a verifier containing this set of VCs and a set of proofs, each created by one of the key pairs.

Although usually clear from the context, it is common for users of VCs and VPs to refer to both generically as VCs unless they are specifically talking about a VP.

7.8 More advanced VC properties

VCs were developed using an open-world model, meaning anyone can add any property to a VC that is suitable for their application needs. Nevertheless, there are several properties that VCWG thought would be generally useful for a range of applications. These are described in this section. The following section describes the rules the VCWG recommends application designers follow if they wish to extend their VCs, remain conformant to the W3C specification, and interoperate with others. (Of course, anyone can extend a VC in any way they wish, but in that case, they should not expect other implementations to interoperate with theirs.)

7.8.1 Refresh service

VCs are designed to have a limited lifetime for several reasons. First, cryptography grows weaker over time, so enhanced proof mechanisms need to be put in place. Second, people's circumstances and credentials change with time. A good example is a VC based on age-related properties or a student ID for a specific grade level.

The `refreshService` property allows an issuer to control and provide details about how the current VC can be refreshed or updated. If the issuer wants the verifier to know how to refresh the VC, the issuer can insert the `refreshService` property into the VC. If the issuer only wants the holder to know how to refresh the VC, the `refreshService` property should *not* be inserted into the VC, but rather into the VP that encapsulates the VC the issuer sends to the holder, since this VP is retained by the holder and is not forwarded to anyone else.

The `refreshService` property contains two mandatory properties:

- `id`—URL where the enquirer can obtain the refreshed VC
- `type`—Says what type of refresh service this is, and controls what other properties the `refreshService` property should contain

If a verifier wants to know whether the presented VC contains the very latest information about the subject, it can use the refresh service to find out. However, there are several caveats to doing so. First, this can breach the subject's privacy because the issuer now learns that the subject's VC has been presented to a particular verifier. Second, the verifier will need to be authorized to access the issuer's refresh service (because the issuer is unlikely to issue a subject's VCs to anyone who asks for it). Yet if the verifier is already authorized, it will already know the refresh service details and won't need to consult the `refreshService` property. Consequently, the practice of inserting the `refreshService` property into a VC generally is not recommended.

Conversely, if a subject/holder knows that a VC is about to expire or that a property (claim) in their VC is out of date (and the issuer knows the new property value), then using the `refreshService` property in a VP is an easy way for the holder to obtain an updated VC (and for the issuer to simultaneously revoke the old VC).

An example of a VC containing the `refreshService` property is given in listing 7.1 in section 7.8.4.

7.8.2   Disputes

Sometimes an issuer holds out-of-date information about a subject—but the subject cannot compel the issuer to update its database and issue a revised VC. Other times, a person is the victim of identity theft, and an attacker masquerades as them by using falsely obtained VCs. In both these cases, the VCs that exist are false, and the rightful subject wants them to be revoked. If the issuer is slow to act in these circumstances, what should the rightful subject do? The answer is a `DisputeCredential`. This differs from a normal VC in that

- The issuer is set to the URI of the rightful subject.
- It is signed by the rightful subject and not the original issuer.
- The `credentialSubject` property ID contains the ID of the disputed VC.
- The `credentialSubject` property should also contain the following:
  - A `currentStatus` property with the value set to `Disputed`.
  - A `statusReason` property with the value set to the reason for the dispute. This is currently a free-form string rather than an encoded value, but standardized reason codes are anticipated in the future.
  - If only part of the disputed VC is wrong, and some of its claims are correct (i.e., it is not an atomic VC), then the `credentialSubject` property can also contain a reference to the disputed claim.

In the case of an out-of-date or incorrect VC held by the rightful subject, both the disputed VC and the `DisputeCredential` can be sent to the verifier. The verifier can then validate that the subject is the same in both VCs and determine the disputed property(ies).

If a criminal is performing identity theft on a rightful subject, or if a denial-of-service attacker is trying to cause a verifier to doubt a valid VC, the subject in the disputed VC is different from the subject who signed the `DisputeCredential`. In this case, the verifier should ignore the `DisputeCredential` unless the verifier has some out-of-band means of assessing its validity. Verifiers must establish their own policies for how to handle these cases.

Here is an example of a `DisputeCredential`:

```
{
    "@context": [
        "https://www.w3.org/2018/credentials/v1",
        "https://www.w3.org/2018/credentials/examples/v1"
    ],
```

```
            "id": "http://example.com/credentials/123",
            "type": ["VerifiableCredential", "DisputeCredential"],
            "credentialSubject": {
                  "id": "http://example.com/credentials/245",
                  "currentStatus": "Disputed",
                  "statusReason": "Address is out of date"
            },
            "issuer": "https://example.com/people#me",
            "issuanceDate": "2017-12-05T14:27:42Z",
            "proof": {
                  "type": "RsaSignature2018",
                  "created": "2018-06-17T10:03:48Z",
                  "verificationMethod": "did:example:ebfeb1f712ebc
                  6f1c276e12ec21/keys/234",
                  "nonce": "d61c4599-0cc2-4479-9efc-c63add3a43b2",
                  "signatureValue": "pYw8XNi1..Cky6Ed="
            }
      }
}
```

7.8.3 Terms of use

Most physical VCs today are governed by terms of use. Some are stated on a plastic card, while others are published on a website, with the plastic card containing the URL of the web page. Examples of terms of use printed on physical cards include "Not Transferable" and "Only the authorized signatory may use this card." Examples of referring to a website include "Go to <URL> for full details of membership" or "Refer to <URL> for conditions of use."

The standard way of adding terms of use to a VC (or a VP) is via the `termsOfUse` property. Terms specified by the issuer—that apply to both the holder and any verifier—are typically inside the VC. Terms specified by the holder—which apply only to the verifier—are inside the VP. Like all extensions to the basic VC (or VP), the `termsOfUse` property must contain its `type`, as this governs its contents. The `id` property is optional, but if present, it should point to a web page where the terms of use for this VC (or VP) can be obtained.

It is recommended that the terms of use should specify actions that the verifier, if it is to accept the VC (and or VP) from the holder,

- Must perform (an obligation)
- Must not perform (a prohibition)
- May perform (a permission)

More sophisticated terms of use may specify *when* these actions should take place: "Notify the subject *upon accepting* this VC," "delete this information *after 2 weeks*," "archive this VC *for up to one year,*" and so on. An example `termsOfUse` property is shown in listing 7.1.

7.8.4 Evidence

The VC ecosystem is based on trust. However, trust is rarely binary (on or off). It is usually qualified. I may trust you with $50 but not with $5,000. Similarly, a verifier may trust a VC issuer, but the level of trust that the verifier places in the issuer and the issued VC may be qualified depending on the procedures undertaken by the issuer, the strength of the cryptographic algorithms it used, the evidence it gathered, what service the holder wishes to perform, and so on. The evidence property is designed for the issuer to help the verifier determine the level of confidence it can have in the claims inside the VC.

Authentication systems have the concept of *level of assurance* (LOA). As defined by the widely followed original NIST standard [2], this is a four-level metric informing recipients about the level of confidence they can have in the strength of authentication of the remote party. This has since been superseded by a more sophisticated LOA matrix from NIST [3] because experience showed that a simple 1-to-4 LOA is insufficient to convey the inherent complexity of user authentication.

VCs are just as complex as authentication tokens, if not more so. Consequently, rather than inserting a simple fixed metric into a VC, similar to an authentication LOA, the VCWG adopted an open-ended approach using the evidence property. This allows the issuer to insert whatever information it wishes into a VC to assist the verifier in determining the level of confidence it can have in the VC's claims. It also provides future-proofing: as VCs gain more traction and user experience, usage of the evidence property is bound to become more sophisticated.

As always, every evidence property must contain its type since this determines what type of evidence it is and what other properties the evidence must contain. The id is an optional field that should point to where more information about this evidence instance can be found. The following listing includes an example of the evidence property.

> **Listing 7.1   Complex VC containing several advanced properties**

```
{
    "@context": [
        "https://www.w3.org/2018/credentials/v1",
        "https://example.org/examples/v1"
    ],
    "id": "http://example.edu/credentials/3732",
    "type": ["VerifiableCredential", "UniversityDegreeCredential"],
    "issuer": "https://example.edu/issuers/14",
    "issuanceDate": "2010-01-01T19:23:24Z",
    "credentialSubject": {
        "id": "did:example:ebfeb1f712ebc6f1c276e12ec21",
        "degree": {
            "type": "BachelorDegree",
            "name": "Bachelor of Science in Mechanical Engineering"
        }
    },
    "credentialSchema": {
        "id": "https://example.org/examples/degree.json",
        "type": "JsonSchemaValidator2018"
    },
```

```
"termsOfUse": {
        "type": "IssuerPolicy",
        "id": "http://example.com/policies/credential/4",
        "profile": "http://example.com/profiles/credential",
        "prohibition": [{
                "assigner": "https://example.edu/issuers/14",
                "assignee": "AllVerifiers",
                "target": "http://example.edu/credentials/3732",
                "action": ["Archival"]
        }]
},
"evidence": [{
        "id": "https://example.edu/evidence/f2aeec97-fc0d-42bf-
        8ca7-0548192d4231",
        "type": ["DocumentVerification"],
        "verifier": "https://example.edu/issuers/14",
        "evidenceDocument": "DriversLicense",
        "subjectPresence": "Physical",
        "documentPresence": "Physical"
}, {
        "id": "https://example.edu/evidence/f2aeec97-fc0d-42bf-
        8ca7-0548192dxyzab",
        "type": ["SupportingActivity"],
        "verifier": "https://example.edu/issuers/14",
        "evidenceDocument": "Fluid Dynamics Focus",
        "subjectPresence": "Digital",
        "documentPresence": "Digital"
}],
"refreshService": {
        "id": "https://example.edu/refresh/3732",
        "type": "ManualRefreshService2018"
},
"proof": {
        "type": "RsaSignature2018",
        "created": "2018-06-18T21:19:10Z",
        "verificationMethod": "https://example.com/jdoe/keys/1",
        "nonce": "c0ae1c8e-c7e7-469f-b252-86e6a0e7387e",
        "signatureValue": "BavEll0/I1zpYw8XNi1bgVg/s...W3JT24 = "
    }
}
```

7.8.5 *When the holder is not the subject*

In many VC uses, the subject and the holder are the same entity. The verifier can determine this simply by ensuring that the credentialSubject ID inside the VC equals the identity of the holder who signed the VP. But what about those cases where the holder and the subject are different? We have already cited several examples, such as when the subject is a pet, an IoT device, or a relative of the holder. How is the verifier to know the difference between a rightful holder, who obtained the VC with the full permission of both the subject and the issuer, and an attacker who stole the VC from the rightful holder? (For security purposes, both the subject and the issuer should give their permission for the VC to be transferred. The VCWG is standardizing a way for the issuer to mandate that the VC must not be transferred.) For example, say

I steal your prescription VC and take it to the pharmacy so that I can obtain your drugs. How is the pharmacist to know the difference between your friend, whom you want to collect your prescription, and myself, who claims to be your friend?

The VC Data Model spec contains the following four suggested ways to do this. However, none of them were standardized in version 1.0 because it was deemed too early to determine which of these will become the preferred method(s):

- The issuer issues the VC to the subject, who passes it to a holder; then the subject issues a new, very similar VC to the holder. This new VC contains the same `credentialSubject` property value as the original VC, but now the holder is the subject, and the original subject is the issuer of the new VC. An example of this "passing on" is provided in listing 7.2.
- The issuer issues the VC to the subject, who passes it to a holder; then the subject issues a *relationship VC* to the holder, indicating the relationship between them. An example of a relationship VC is given in listing 7.3.
- The issuer issues the VC directly to the holder (who is not the subject), and then *the issuer also issues a relationship VC* to the holder, indicating the relationship between the subject and the holder.
- The issuer issues the VC to the subject with a *relationship claim* that asserts the relationship between the subject and a third party. Now the subject can pass the VC to the third party to become the holder, either immediately or later. For example, a VC could be issued to a child that contains a relationship claim to the ID of the child's parent. An example of this is given in listing 7.4.

Listing 7.2   VP containing a VC passed to the holder with confirmation

```
{
        "id": "did:example:76e12ec21ebhyu1f712ebc6f1z2,'
        "type": ["VerifiablePresentation"],
        "credential": [{
                    "id": "http://example.gov/credentials/3732",
                    "type": ["VerifiableCredential",
                        "PrescriptionCredential"],
                    "issuer": "https://example.edu",
                    "issuanceDate": "2010-01-01",
                    "credentialSubject": {
                            "id":
    "did:example:ebfeb1f712ebc6f1c276e12ec21",
                            "prescription": {
                                    "drug1": "val1"
                            }
                    },
                    "revocation": {
                            "id": "http://example.gov/revocations/738",
                            "type": "SimpleRevocationList2017"
                    },
                    "proof": {
                            "type": "RsaSignature2018",
                            "created": "2018-06-17T10:03:48Z",
```

```
                             "verificationMethod":
                              "did:example:ebfeb1f712ebc6f1c276e12ec21/
                              keys/234",
                             "nonce": "d61c4599-0cc2-4479-9efc-
c63add3a43b2",
                             "signatureValue": "pky6Ed..CYw8XNi1="
                     }
             },
             {
                     "id": "https://example.com/VC/123456789",
                     "type": ["VerifiableCredential",
                         "PrescriptionCredential"],
                     "issuer": "did:example:ebfeb1f712ebc6f1c276e12ec21",
                     "issuanceDate": "2010-01-03",
                     "credentialSubject": {
                             "id":
"did:example:76e12ec21ebhyu1f712ebc6f1z2",
                             "prescription": {
                                     "drug1": "val1"
                             }
                     },
                     "proof": {
                             "type": "RsaSignature2018",
                             "created": "2018-06-17T10:03:48Z",
                             "verificationMethod":
                              "did:example:ebfeb1f712ebc6f1c276e12ec21/
                              keys/234",
                             "nonce": "d61c4599-0cc2-4479-9efc-
c63add3a43b2",
                             "signatureValue": "pYw8XNi1..Cky6Ed="
                     }
             }
     ],
     "proof": {
             "type": "RsaSignature2018",
             "created": "2018-06-18T21:19:10Z",
             "verificationMethod":
                 "did:example:76e12ec21ebhyu1f712ebc6f1z2/keys/2",
             "nonce": "c0ae1c8e-c7e7-469f-b252-86e6a0e7387e",
             "signatureValue": "BavEll0/I1..W3JT24="
     }
}
```

Listing 7.3 Relationship VC issued to a parent that identifies the child

```
{
     "id": "http://example.edu/credentials/3732",
     "type": ["VerifiableCredential", "RelationshipCredential"],
     "issuer": "https://example.edu/issuers/14",
     "issuanceDate": "2010-01-01T19:23:24Z",
     "credentialSubject": {
         "id": "did:example:ebfeb1c276e12ec211f712ebc6f",
         "child": {
             "id": "did:example:ebfeb1f712ebc6f1c276e12ec21",
             "type": "Child"
```

```
                }
        },
        "proof": {
                "type": "RsaSignature2018",
                "created": "2018-06-18T21:19:10Z",
                "verificationMethod":
                        "did:example:76e12ec21...12ebc6f1z2/keys/2",
                "nonce": "c0ae1c8e-c7e7-469f-b252-86ijh767387e",
                "signatureValue": "BavEll0/I1..W3JT24="
        }
}
```

Listing 7.4   Child's VC containing the identification of the mother

```
{
        "id": "http://example.edu/credentials/3732",
        "type": ["VerifiableCredential", "AgeCredential",
                "RelationshipCredential"],
        "issuer": "https://example.edu/issuers/14",
        "issuanceDate": "2010-01-01T19:23:24Z",
        "credentialSubject": {
                "id": "did:example:ebfeb1f712ebc6f1c276e12ec21",
                "ageUnder": 16,
                "parent": {
                        "id": "did:example:ebfeb1c276e12ec211f712ebc6f",
                        "type": "Mother"
                }
        },
        "proof": {
                "type": "RsaSignature2018",
                "created": "2018-06-18T21:19:10Z",
                "verificationMethod":
                        "did:example:76e12ec21ebhyu1f712ebc6f1z2/keys/2",
                "nonce": "c0ae1c8e-c7e7-469f-b252-86e6a0e7387e",
                "signatureValue": "BavEll0/I1..W3JT24="
        }
}
```

7.9   *Extensibility and schemas*

As mentioned earlier, VCs are built on an open-world model, meaning anyone is free to extend VCs any way they want to—"permissionless innovation" is the phrase used in the VC Data Model spec. Open extensibility maximizes the applicability of VCs since all application developers can extend VCs to satisfy their application's requirements. But if this extensibility is not properly controlled, it will lead to a lack of interoperability, as software A will not be able to understand a VC transmitted by software B.

This is not a new problem. X.509 certificates had the same issue. They solved it by allowing the content of certificates to be extended—in any way that anyone wanted—by requiring every extension to be labeled with a globally unique object identifier (OID). (OIDs form a hierarchical tree of numbers where the control of nodes is delegated downward. You can think of this as the DNS in numerical form.) The flaw in this solution was that there was no global OID registry, so it was impossible for software A to find out what an extension used by software B meant. This led to the IETF PKIX group standardizing dozens of extensions and publishing their OIDs so that everyone could know what they meant. But this was a cumbersome and time-consuming mechanism. Something better was needed.

VCs have a new way of solving the extensibility problem by using the internet to publish all the extensions that application developers invent and mandating that VCs include the following in their encoding:

- *The* `@context` *for this VC*—As we saw earlier, this allows the issuer, holder, and verifier to establish the right context, in terms of VC vocabularies (properties and alias names), for understanding the contents of the VC. One disadvantage of the `@context` property, for non-JSON-LD users, is that contexts can be (and often are) nested, so several levels may need to be plumbed to discover the complete set of definitions.

- *What type of VC this is*—As we saw earlier, this allows a verifier to very quickly check if it supports this type of VC and, if not, to quickly reject it without the need for further processing.

- *What schemas this VC uses*—Different types of VCs contain different properties, and both the `@context` and `credentialSchema` properties say where the definitions of these new properties can be found on the internet. An example of the `credentialSchema` property was given in listing 7.1. It is perhaps easier for non-JSON-LD users to understand and use than the `@context` property.

The preferred way of extending VCs is by using the JSON-LD syntax and its built-in `@context` extension mechanisms since these already define how to extend objects in a way that maximizes interoperability. However, using JSON-LD is not strictly necessary as pure JSON can be used, providing the `@context` feature of JSON-LD is supported as a JSON property. Remember that the `@context` property provides short-form aliases for URIs so that they can be more easily referenced in the VC. It also says where the definitions of the core properties of VCs can be located on the internet.

Diagrams of the VC ecosystem, such as figure 7.1, often show a verifiable data registry where this extensibility data resides. In practice, there does not need to be a single place for this data; it may be implemented as one or more decentralized blockchains or as standard web pages accessible via HTTPS. However, it is important that the system serving as the verifiable data registry be designed to persist at least as long as the expiration of any VC issued that references it.

7.10 Zero-knowledge proofs

As explained in chapter 6, the term *zero-knowledge proof* (ZKP) refers to a class of cryptographic algorithms or protocols intended to allow for proof of the knowledge of a specific secret value, such as a password, without revealing the secret. Algorithms that fall under this category include *ZK-Snarks, ZK-Starks, bullet proofs*, and *ring signatures*.

Many tutorials explain what such proofs are and how they work, but for our purposes, it is enough to understand that they can do one or more of the following:

- Provide verification of claims in a VC without the issuer being involved or knowing who the verifier is (in other words, digital signatures)
- Provide verification of claims in a VC while protecting the privacy of the holder
- Allow for selective disclosure of a subset of the claims in a VC without revealing the contents, or even existence, of the other claims
- Allow for derived claims to be presented to a verifier (e.g., over 18) rather than providing the full claim (e.g., date of birth)

These properties are extremely helpful when VCs are used in strong privacy-preserving contexts or ecosystems. In particular, the approach taken in the VC Data Model spec focuses on preserving the privacy of the holder. In the many cases where the holder is also the subject, this preserves the subject's privacy.

In the VC Data Model spec, the use of ZKPs involves three stages:

1 One or more *base* VCs are created by issuers using any proof (signature) approach. Additionally, the `credentialSchema` property in each contains a DID that identifies that base credential and `type` indicating the ZKP system that will be used. One such system is the *Camenisch-Lysyanskaya ZKP* system (https://eprint.iacr.org/2001/019.pdf), also known as *CL Signatures.*

2 For each VC the holder wishes to present to a verifier, the holder creates a *derived* VC. In this derived VC, `credentialSchema` has the exact same contents as in the original base credential, which is how you know they are linked. However, the `proof` section contains a CL proof that enables the holder to prove knowledge of a signature from the issuer over the credential *without revealing that signature.* This means only the holder can prove the signature, yet the proof does not reveal who the holder is to anyone else who might intercept the credential. Additionally, this derived credential can support *selective disclosure* by presenting only a subset of the base VC's claims.

3 The derived VCs are placed inside a VP issued by the holder to the verifier. The VP's `proof` section contains a CL proof with the following properties: the verifier can prove knowledge of a proof that all of the derived credentials were issued to that specific holder without revealing the latter proof. This means only the verifier—and no one else—can verify this proof (the verifier cannot share it with anyone else), yet the VP's proof still does not reveal who the holder is to anyone else who might intercept the VP.

Many of the details here are glossed over in the VC Data Model spec, largely because of the huge variability in ZKP systems. However, the data model and syntax of VCs and VPs should be sufficient to accommodate a variety of ZKP-based proof types. (For examples of ZKP-type implementations, see the Hyperledger Indy [https://wiki.hyperledger.org/display/indy] and Hyperledger Aries [https://wiki.hyperledger.org/display/aries] projects.)

7.11 Protocols and deployments

The VC Data Model 1.0 specification defines the format and contents of a VC and a VP that can be used to transfer a set of VCs from the issuer to the holder and transfer a set of VCs from the holder to a verifier. However, it does not define protocols for transferring and using VCs. That was deliberately put out of scope to keep the work of creating the 1.0 spec manageable. Obviously, these are needed before a VC identity ecosystem can become operational.

Communities of SSI implementers have been experimenting with different ways of transferring VCs. Several of these protocols are discussed in detail in chapter 5. In this section, we discuss some additional considerations. Earlier, we outlined the most likely steps involved in an operational VC ecosystem. Most of these steps still need to be standardized:

- How does a verifier describe its policy (or requirements) for access to its resources and transfer this to the holder?
- How does a holder request a VC from an issuer?
- How does an issuer inform the holder which VCs it is capable of issuing?

The first demonstration of VCs was by Digital Bazaar in its Credential Handler API (CHAPI) for websites (https://w3c-ccg.github.io/credential-handler-api). (A video demo of this process is available at https://www.youtube.com/watch?v=bm3XBPB 4cFY) It is a common problem on the web that login pages for websites have a list of potential ways to log in: for example, using your Facebook account, Google account, LinkedIn account, etc. This has been referred to as the "NASCAR problem" because of the growing list of logos that websites need to display to accommodate all these identity providers. When using CHAPI, the web browser acts as a mediator for the user, presenting them with choices in a standardized way to simplify the user experience. Different websites can be VC storage/holders (wallets), VC issuers, VC verifiers, or any combination of these.

The process begins when a user visits a credential storage site to get a new wallet. The site uses CHAPI to set up handlers for both `CredentialStoreEvents` and `CredentialRequestEvents`. The browser agent saves the service address for this site and records that this site is a credential repository. The user then visits a credential-issuing site.

When the site calls the credential management `store()` method, the browser presents the user with the credential to be stored and the user's list of wallets into which the credential can be stored. When the user selects a wallet, the browser sends a `CredentialStoreEvent` to the wallet provider's service address, at which point the credential is sent from the issuer to the wallet, where it is stored (and a "hint" for the credential is saved by the browser).

Similarly, when the user visits a credential-requesting site (a verifier), and the site calls the credential management `get()` method with a requested type of credential, the browser presents the user with hints for the list of available credentials of the requested type. When the user selects the credential, the browser sends a `CredentialRequestEvent` to the wallet provider's service address, at which point the wallet sends the credential to the requester. Note that wallet and credential options are only presented to the user via the browser agent and that credentials are directly transported between wallet and issuer/verifier.

One of the earliest VC ecosystems was defined in 2015 by co-author David Chadwick. Built in 2016, it was presented at the European Identity Conference in 2017 (https://www.kuppingercole.com/speakers/405). It was based on enhancements to the (at that time) new FIDO specifications. In this ecosystem, VCs are held on the user's mobile phone and tied to the FIDO keys used for pairwise authentication with verifiers.

The system uses a hybrid model of centralized and decentralized identity models discussed in chapter 1. The holders, issuers, and verifiers are peers of the distributed model that communicate via connections established with FIDO keys. The blockchain component is replaced with the FIDO Alliances' centralized schema and key management services. When the user contacts an issuer, the issuer says which identity attributes it can issue as VCs, and the user decides which ones they want. This provides the issuer with consent, an important requirement of GDPR.

Each verifier is assumed to provide a range of services, and each service has its own authorization policy: i.e., its VC requirements for access to the particular resource. After the user has browsed the verifier's services and decided which one they want to access, the verifier sends its specific policy to the user's device. The agent on the user's device searches the VCs that are obtainable from the various issuers to decide whether the policy can be fulfilled. If it can, then VCs are requested from each issuer to be bound to the FIDO public key for the verifier. These are then packaged together into a VP and signed by the user (using the private key paired to the verifier).

In this way, the verifier receives a set of VCs, each bound to the same public key ID, which the user has proved ownership of by signing the VP. The system was tested with university students and a small sample of British National Health Service patients, who unanimously found it easy to use and much preferable to usernames and passwords.

There are already a number of other deployments of VCs. For example, the government of the Province of British Columbia, Canada, has developed the Verifiable Organizations Network to serve as a public holder of business credentials (https://vonx.io). OrgBookBC (https://orgbook.gov.bc.ca/en/home) contains a searchable registry of publicly available licenses and permits granted to businesses in the province. Although the digital credentials will eventually be given directly to the subject organizations, publishing the credentials to the OrgBook makes the same information publicly available (and cryptographically verifiable). This simplifies the process of identifying which businesses comply with relevant laws or, more critically, suggested but not mandated guidelines. It also serves as a convenient way for business owners, once they acquire a VC wallet, to obtain the relevant VCs for their business.

7.12 *Security and privacy evaluation*

The Security Considerations (https://www.w3.org/TR/vc-data-model/#security-con siderations) and Privacy Considerations (https://www.w3.org/TR/vc-data-model/ #privacy-considerations) sections of the VC Data Model spec run tens of pages each. In this section, we summarize the major points made in those sections:

- VCs are integrity protected end to end—from the issuer to the verifier through any intermediate storage wallet—because they have a `proof` property (or a JWT signature) inserted by the issuer that cryptographically provides tamper detection.
- VCs should be confidentially protected during transfer by transferring them only via encrypted communications links such as TLS.
- VCs have high availability if they are stored on the holder's device since they do not require any communications with the issuer or any other third party to be transferred to the verifier.
- VCs facilitate the security property of *least privileges* by allowing the verifier to only request those subject properties (or attributes) essential for providing its service.
- VCs provide privacy protection through *selective disclosure* by the issuer issuing either a ZKP VC or a set of atomic VCs, which allow the holder to only disclose those attributes that the verifier needs and nothing more.
- VCs provide privacy protection to subjects by identifying them via pseudony-mous IDs rather than their names of other identities. If these IDs are pairwise between subjects and verifiers, then no globally unique correlating handles are created.
- VCs support flexible role-based and attribute-based access controls because the verifier only needs to specify which roles or attributes are needed to access its services and not the identities of the users who can access its services.

Of course, the ultimate security and privacy of any operational system depend on the quality of the implementation and its correct use. If a holder provides their unique email address and telephone number to a verifier, then the use of pseudonymous IDs will not protect them from releasing globally unique correlating handles. Similarly, if the user stores their VCs on an unprotected device, which is stolen, the thief will be able to masquerade as the user.

7.13 *Hurdles to adoption*

Physical VCs, such as plastic cards and passports, are indispensable in today's society. It is high time we moved these credentials into the electronic world so that we can carry them around on our mobile devices and have them with us all the time. But as we have seen, there are technical, security, and privacy hurdles that must be overcome before electronic plastic cards become ubiquitous. And of course, there is also the question of the business models needed to give issuers the incentive to adapt or adopt this new model.

As we explained in the first part of this chapter, today's federated identity management infrastructures give issuers (IDPs) great power because they are at the center of the ecosystem. VCs turn this model on its head and place users at the center. So, issuers will need to see some financial benefit before they are willing to move. Many of the compelling benefits are discussed in chapter 4, and others are discussed in part 4 of the book.

As they say in the movies, VCs are the hero of the SSI show. They are the most visible icon of SSI infrastructure since they will sit directly in the digital wallets of individuals (and organizations) and be presented to verifiers digitally the same way we present physical credentials to verifiers today (such as to airport security agents when we want to board a plane).

But in the move from physical credentials made of paper and plastic (and even metal, for some of the latest premium credit cards) to digital credentials, every last bit matters—literally. Since all the security and privacy properties of VCs depend on cryptography, the data structures and rules for composing and verifying VCs must be locked down to the last detail. That's what this chapter has walked through, from the supported syntaxes to the required and optional properties to the different signature mechanisms and extensibility options.

In the next chapter, we dive one level deeper: into the special new form of cryptographically verifiable identifiers designed explicitly to support VCs and now being standardized in its own W3C Working Group: decentralized identifiers (DIDs).

SSI Resources

For more free content to learn about SSI, please go to IdentityBook.info and SSI Meetup.org/book.

References

1. Mantovani, Maria Laura, Marco Malavolti, and Simona Venuti. 2016. EU AARC Project Deliverable DNA2.4: "Training Material Targeted at Identity Providers." AARC. https://aarc-project.eu/wp-content/uploads/2016/07/AARC-DNA2.4.pdf.
2. Burr, William, et al. 2013. NIST Special Publication (SP) 800-63-2: "Electronic Authentication Guideline." https://nvlpubs.nist.gov/nistpubs/specialpublications/nist.sp.800-63-2.pdf.
3. Grassi, Paul A., Michael E. Garcia, and James L. Fenton. 2017. NIST Special Publication (SP) 800-63-3: "Digital Identity Guidelines." https://nvlpubs.nist.gov/nistpubs/specialpublications/nist.sp.800-63-3.pdf.

Decentralized identifiers

8

Drummond Reed and Markus Sabadello

Decentralized identifiers (DIDs) are the cryptographic counterpart to verifiable credentials (VCs). Together these are the "twin pillars" of SSI standardization. In this chapter, you learn how DIDs evolved from the work started with VCs, how they are related to URLs and URNs, why a new type of cryptographically verifiable identifier is needed for SSI, and how DIDs are being standardized at World Wide Web Consortium (W3C). Your guides are two of the editors of the W3C Decentralized Identifier 1.0 specification: Markus Sabadello, founder and CEO of Danube Tech, and Drummond Reed, chief trust officer at Evernym.

At the most basic level, a *decentralized identifier* (DID) is simply a new type of globally unique identifier—not that different from the URLs you see in your browser's address bar. But at a deeper level, DIDs are the atomic building block of a new layer of decentralized digital identity and public key infrastructure (PKI) for the internet. This *decentralized public key infrastructure* (DPKI, https://github.com/WebOf TrustInfo/rebooting-the-web-of-trust/blob/master/final-documents/dpki.pdf) could eventually have as much impact on global cybersecurity and cyberprivacy as the development of the SSL/TLS protocol for encrypted web traffic (currently the largest PKI in the world).

This means you can understand DIDs at four progressively deeper levels (figure 8.1). In this chapter, we travel all the way down through these four levels to provide a much deeper understanding of DIDs.

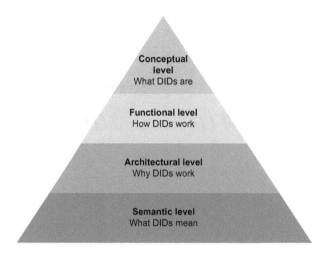

Figure 8.1   The progression of four levels at which we can understand DIDs—from a basic definition to a deep understanding of how and why they work and what they mean for the future of the internet and the web

8.1   *The conceptual level: What is a DID?*

As defined by the W3C DID Core 1.0 specification (https://www.w3.org/TR/did-core) published by the W3C DID Working Group (https://www.w3.org/2019/did-wg), a DID is a new type of *globally unique identifier*: a string of characters that identifies a *resource*.

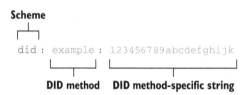

Figure 8.2   The general format of a DID: the scheme name followed by a DID method name followed by the method-specific string, the syntax for which is defined by the DID method

(*Resource* is the term used by the W3C across all web standards. The digital identity community generally uses the term *entity*. For the purposes of this book, the two terms can be considered equivalent.) A resource is *anything that can be identified*, from a web page to a person to a planet. This string of characters (figure 8.2) looks very much like any other web address, except instead of http: or https:, it begins with did.

8.1.1   *URIs*

In terms of technical standards, a DID is a type of Uniform Resource Identifier (URI). URIs are an IETF standard (RFC 3986, https://tools.ietf.org/html/rfc3986) adopted by the W3C to identify any type of resource on the World Wide Web. A URI is a string of characters in a specific format that makes the string globally unique—in other words, no other resource has that same identifier. Of course, this is very different from human names where many people can have exactly the same name.

8.1.2   *URLs*

A Uniform Resource Locator (URL) is a URI that can be used to *locate* a *representation* of that resource on the web. A representation is anything that describes the resource.

For example, for a website URL, the resource is a specific page on that site. But if the resource is a person, they obviously can't be "on the web" directly. So the representation needs to be something describing that person, such as a résumé, blog, or Linked-In profile.

Every resource representation available on the web has a URL—web page, file, image, video, database record, and so on. It's not "on the web" if it doesn't have a URL. The addresses that appear in your browser's address bar are generally URLs; figure 8.3 is an example of the URL for this book on the Manning website.

Figure 8.3   An example of a browser address bar displaying the URL for the web page about this book

Why do we need the distinction between URIs and URLs if everything on the web has a URL? Because we also need to identify resources that are *not* on the web: people, places, planets—all the things we had names for long before the internet even existed. All of these are resources that we often need to *refer to* on the web without the resource actually being *represented on* the web. A URI that is not a URL is often called an *abstract identifier*.

> **NOTE**   The question of whether a DID by itself serves as a URL—while sounding trivial—is actually quite deep. We will have to go all the way down to the semantic layer before we can answer it completely.

8.1.3   URNs

If URLs are the subclass of URIs that point to *the location of a representation of a resource* of the network—which can always change—then what about the subclass of URIs that *identify the abstract resource itself* and thus are designed never to change? It turns out there are many uses for this kind of *persistent identifier* (also called a *permanent identifier*). This is exactly what you want when you need to be able to refer to the resource:

- Independent of any particular representation
- Independent of any particular location
- Independent of any particular human language or name
- In a way that will not change over time

In web architecture, the subclass of URIs reserved for persistent identifiers are called *Uniform Resource Names* (URNs). They are defined by RFC 8141 (https://tools.ietf.org/html/rfc8141), which goes into great detail about both the syntax and the policies necessary to manage namespaces for identifiers that are meant never to change. (Think about how complex it would get if every phone number, email address, and human name could be assigned only once and never reused for another person ever again for the rest of time.) Figure 8.4 shows how URLs and URNs are both subclasses of URIs.

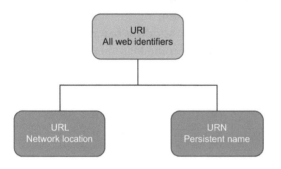

Figure 8.4   URLs and URNs are subclasses of URIs. URLs always point to representations of resources on the web, whereas URNs are persistent names for any resource, on or off the web.

8.1.4   DIDs

Having described URIs, URLs, and URNs, we can now be more precise about the definition of a DID. A DID is a URI that can be *either* a URL or a URN and that can be looked up (resolved) to get a standardized set of information (metadata) about the resource identified by the DID (as described in the next section). If the identified resource has one or more representations on the web, the metadata can include one or more of those URLs.

The four core properties of a DID:
1. A permanent (persistent) identifier
     It never needs to change.
2. A resolvable identifier
     You can look it up to discover metadata.
3. A cryptographically verifiable identifier
     You can prove control using cryptography.
4. A decentralized identifier
     No centralized registration authority is required.

Figure 8.5   A summary of the four core properties of a DID presented at the first meeting of the W3C DID Working Group

But that definition captures only two of the four properties of a DID: *persistence* and *resolvability*. The other two properties—cryptographic verifiability and decentralization—most strongly distinguish a DID from other URIs or any other globally unique identifiers. At the first meeting of the W3C DID Working Group in September 2019 at Fukuoka, Japan, one presenter summarized the four properties as shown in figure 8.5.

What is special about the third and fourth properties is that they both depend on cryptography (chapter 6). In the first case—cryptographic verifiability—cryptography is used to generate the DID. Since the DID is now associated with exactly one public/private key pair, the controller of the private key can prove that they are also the controller of the DID. (See section 8.3 for more details.)

In the second case—decentralized registration—cryptography eliminates the need for centralized registration authorities—the kind needed for almost every other globally unique identifier we use, from postal addresses to telephone numbers to domain names. The centralized registries run by these authorities can determine if a particular identifier is unique—and allow it to be registered only if it is.

By contrast, cryptographic algorithms for public/private key pairs are based on random number generators, large prime numbers, elliptic curves, or other cryptographic techniques for producing globally unique values that do not require a central registry to effectively guarantee uniqueness. We say "effectively guarantee" because there is an infinitesimally small chance of a collision with someone else using the same algorithm. But this chance of collision is mathematically so small that for all practical purposes, it can be ignored.

As a result, anyone with the proper software can generate a DID according to a particular DID method (discussed in the following sections) and begin using it immediately without requiring the authorization or involvement of any centralized registration authority. This is the same process used to create public addresses on the Bitcoin or Ethereum (or other popular) blockchains—it is the essence of what makes a DID *decentralized.*

8.2 The functional level: How DIDs work

We now go down to the second level of detail to explain how DIDs function.

8.2.1 DID documents

Identifiers can, of course, be useful by themselves, as strings of text characters that can be used to refer to a resource. This string can be stored in a database or a document, attached to an email, or printed on a t-shirt or business card. But for digital identifiers, the usefulness comes not just from the identifier but also from how it can be used by applications designed to consume that particular type of identifier. For example, a typical web address that starts with http or https is not very interesting as a string by itself. It only becomes useful once you type it into a web browser or click a hyperlink to access a representation of the resource behind the identifier (such as a web page).

This is similar with DIDs: although it is not yet possible to type a DID into a web browser and have it do anything meaningful, you can give it to a specialized piece of software (or hardware) called a *DID resolver* that will use it to retrieve a standardized data structure called a *DID document.* This data structure is not like a web page or an image file—it is not designed to be viewed directly by end users in a web browser or similar software. (In the future, "DID navigators" may be able to let you travel across a "trust web," but most likely this will be done using conventional web pages associated with DIDs.) Instead, it is a machine-readable document designed to be consumed by digital identity applications or services such as digital wallets, agents, or encrypted data stores, all of which use DIDs as fundamental building blocks.

Every DID has exactly one associated DID document. The DID document contains metadata about the *DID subject,* which is the term for the resource *identified by* the DID and *described by* the DID document. For example, a DID for a person (the DID subject) has an associated DID document that typically contains cryptographic keys, authentication methods, and other metadata describing how to engage in trusted interactions

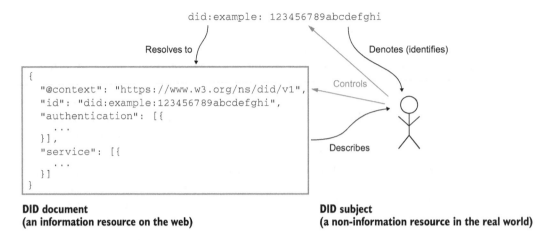

DID document
(an information resource on the web)

DID subject
(a non-information resource in the real world)

Figure 8.6   Relationships between the DID, DID document, and DID subject (in the case where the DID subject is also the DID controller)

with that person. The entity that controls the DID and its associated DID document is called the *DID controller*. In many cases, the DID controller is the same as the DID subject (figure 8.6), but they can also be different entities. An example is when a parent controls a DID that identifies their child—the DID subject is the child, but the DID controller (at least, until the child comes of age) is the parent.

Theoretically, a DID document can contain any arbitrary information about the DID subject, even personal attributes such as a name or an email address. In practice, however, this is problematic for privacy reasons. Instead, the recommended best practice is for a DID document to contain only the minimum amount of machine-readable metadata required to enable *trustable interaction* with the DID subject. Typically, this includes the following:

- One or more *public keys* (or other verification methods) that can be used to authenticate the DID subject during an interaction. This is what makes interactions involving DIDs trustable, and this is also the essence of the DPKI enabled by DIDs.
- One or more *services* associated with the DID subject that can be used for concrete interaction via protocols supported by those services. This can include a wide range of protocols from instant messaging and social networking to dedicated identity protocols such as OpenID Connect (OIDC), DIDComm, and others. See chapter 5 for more details about these protocols.
- Certain additional metadata such as *timestamps, digital signatures,* and other *cryptographic proofs,* or metadata related to *delegation and authorization.*

The following is an example of a very simple DID document using a JSON-LD representation. The first line is the JSON-LD *context statement*, required in JSON-LD documents (but not in other DID document representations). The second line is the DID being described. The authentication block includes a public key for authenticating the DID subject. The final block is a service endpoint for exchanging verifiable credentials.

Listing 8.1 DID document with one public key for authentication, and one service

```
{
  "@context": "https://www.w3.org/ns/did/v1",
  "id": "did:example:123456789abcdefghi",
  "authentication": [{
    "id": "did:example:123456789abcdefghi#keys-1",
    "type": "Ed25519VerificationKey2018",
    "controller": "did:example:123456789abcdefghi",
    "publicKeyBase58" : "H3C2AVvLMv6gmMNam3uVAjZpfkcJCwDwnZn6z3wXmqPV"
  }],
  "service": [{
    "id":"did:example:123456789abcdefghi#vcs",
    "type": "VerifiableCredentialService",
    "serviceEndpoint": "https://example.com/vc/"
  }]
}
```

This metadata associated with every DID, especially public keys and services, is the technical basis for all interaction between different actors in an SSI ecosystem.

8.2.2   DID methods

As we explained in the previous sections, DIDs are not created and maintained in a single type of database or network like many other types of URIs. There is no authoritative centralized registry—or a hierarchy of federated registries like DNS—where all DIDs are written and read. Many different types of DIDs exist in today's SSI community—see section 8.2.7. They all support the same basic functionality, but they differ in how that functionality is implemented, e.g. how exactly a DID is created or where and how a DID's associated DID document is stored and retrieved.

These different types of DIDs are known as *DID methods.* The second part of the DID identifier format—between the first and second colons—is called the *DID method name.* Figure 8.7 shows examples of DIDs created using five different DID methods: sov (Sovrin), btcr (Bitcoin), v1 (Veres One), ethr (Ethereum), and jolo (Jolocom).

```
did:sov:WRfXPg8dantKVubE3HX8pw

did:btcr:xz35-jzv2-qqs2-9wjt

did:v1:test:nym:3AEJTDMSxDDQpyUftjuoeZ2Bazp4Bswj1ce7FJGybCUu

did:ethr:0xE6Fe788d8ca214A080b0f6aC7F48480b2AEfa9a6

did:jolo:1fb352353ff51248c5104b407f9c04c3666627fcf5a167d693c9fc84b75964e2
```

Figure 8.7   Example DIDs generated using five different DID methods

NOTE   In 2021, the Sovrin DID method is planned to evolve into the Indy DID method, and the prefix will become `did:indy:sov:`. See https://wiki.hyperledger.org/display/indy/Indy+DID+Method+Specification.

As of early 2021, more than 80 DID method names have been registered in the DID Specification Registries (https://www.w3.org/TR/did-spec-registries) maintained by the W3C DID Working Group (https://www.w3.org/2019/did-wg). Each DID method is required to have its own technical specification, which must define the following aspects of the DID method:

- The syntax that follows the second colon of a DID. This is called the *method-specific identifier*. It is typically a long string generated using random numbers and cryptographic functions. It is always guaranteed to be unique within the DID method namespace (and is recommended to be globally unique all by itself).
- The four basic "CRUD" operations that can be executed on a DID:
    - *Create*—How can a DID and its associated DID document be created?
    - *Read*—How can the associated DID document be retrieved?
    - *Update*—How can the contents of the DID document be changed?
    - *Deactivate*—How can a DID be deactivated so it can no longer be used?
- Security and privacy considerations specific to the DID method.

It is difficult to make generic statements about the four DID operations since DID methods can be designed in very different ways. For example, some DID methods are based on blockchains or other distributed ledgers. In this case, creating or updating a DID typically involves writing a transaction to that ledger. Other DID methods do not use a blockchain; they implement the four DID operations in other ways (see section 8.2.7).

One consequence of the technological variety of DID methods is that some may be better suited for certain use cases than others. DID methods may differ in how "decentralized" or "trusted" they are, as well as in factors of scalability, performance, or cost of the underlying technical infrastructure. The W3C DID Working Group charter includes a deliverable called a "rubric" document whose purpose is to help adopters evaluate how well a particular DID method will meet the needs of a particular user community (https://w3c.github.io/did-rubric).

8.2.3 *DID resolution*

The process of obtaining the DID document associated with a DID is called *DID resolution*. This process allows DID-enabled applications and services to discover the machine-readable metadata about the DID subject expressed by the DID document. This metadata can be used for further interaction with the DID subject, such as the following:

- To look up a public key to verify a digital signature from the issuer of a verifiable credential
- To authenticate the DID controller when the controller needs to log in to a website or app

- To discover and access a well-known service associated with the DID controller, such as a website, social network, or licensing authority
- To request a DID-to-DID connection with the DID controller

The first three of these scenarios are illustrated in figure 8.8.

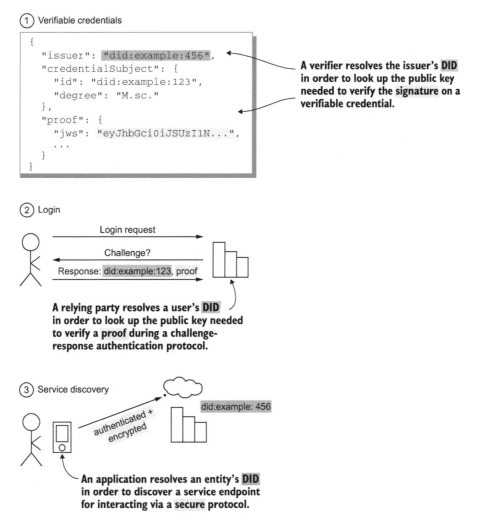

Figure 8.8 Common scenarios requiring DID resolution. The first is using a DID to identify the issuer of a verifiable credential, the second to log in to a website, and the third to discover a service associated with the DID.

The DID-resolution process is based on the Read operation defined by the applicable DID method. As we have noted, this can vary considerably depending on how the DID method is designed. This means DID resolution is not confined to a single protocol in the same way as DNS (the protocol for resolving domain names to IP addresses) or HTTP (the protocol for retrieving representations of resources from web servers).

For example, no assumption should be made that a blockchain, distributed ledger, or database (centralized or decentralized) is used for resolving DIDs—or even that interaction with a remote network is required during the DID-resolution process. Furthermore, a DID document is not necessarily stored in plain text in a database or for download from a server. Although some DID methods may work like this, others may define more complex DID-resolution processes that involve on-the-fly construction of virtual DID documents. Therefore, rather than thinking of DID resolution as a concrete protocol, it should be considered an abstract function or algorithm that takes a DID (plus optional additional parameters) as its input and returns the DID document (plus optional additional metadata) as its result.

DID resolvers can come in several architectural forms. They can be implemented as a native library included in an application or even an operating system—the same way as DNS resolvers are included in all modern operating systems. Alternatively, a third party can provide a DID resolver as a hosted service, responding to DID resolution requests via HTTP or other protocols (called *bindings*). Hybrid forms are also possible—for example, a local DID resolver could delegate part or all of the DID-resolution process to a preconfigured, remotely hosted DID resolver (figure 8.9). This is similar to how DNS resolvers in our local operating systems typically query a remote DNS resolver hosted by an internet service provider (ISP) to perform the actual DNS resolution work.

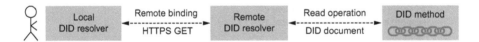

Figure 8.9   An example of a local DID resolver querying a remote DID resolver, which then retrieves the DID document according to the applicable DID method

Of course, reliance on an intermediary service during the DID-resolution process introduces potential security risks and potential elements of centralization, each of which can impact the security and trust properties of other layers in the SSI stack that rely on DIDs. Therefore, whenever possible, DID resolution should be integrated directly into a DID-enabled application in such a way that the application can independently verify that the DID-resolution result is correct (in other words, the correct DID document has been returned).

8.2.4   *DID URLs*

DIDs are powerful identifiers by themselves, but they can also be used as the basis for constructing more advanced URLs rooted on a DID. This is similar to the http: and https: URLs used on the web: they can consist not only of a domain name but also of other syntactic components appended to the domain name, such as an optional path, optional query string, and optional fragment, as shown in figure 8.10.

Figure 8.10   DIDs and DID URLs

With web URLs, these other syntactic components enable identifying arbitrary resources under the domain name's authority. The same is true for DIDs. So even though the primary function of a DID is to resolve to a DID document, it can also serve as a root authority of a set of *DID URLs* that enable an *identifier space* for additional resources associated with the DID.

DID URLs can be used for many different purposes. Some will be well-known and standardized, whereas others will depend on the DID method or application. See table 8.1 for examples of DID URLs and their meanings:

Table 8.1   Example DID URLs and their meanings

did:example:1234#keys-1
DID URL with a fragment. Identifies a specific public key inside the DID's associated DID document. This is similar to how an http: or https: URL with a fragment can point to a specific bookmark within an HTML web page.

did:example:1234;version-id=4
DID URL with a DID parameter (`version-id`). Identifies a previous version of the DID's associated DID document, as opposed to the latest version. This is useful when the contents of a DID document have been updated but a stable reference to a specific version is needed.

did:example:1234;version-id=4#keys-1
This DID URL is a combination of the previous two examples. It identifies a specific public key inside a specific previous version of the DID's associated DID document.

did:example:1234/my/path?query#fragment
DID URL with a path, query string, and fragment. The meaning and processing rules of this DID URL are not defined by the core DID standard but are dependent on the DID method and/or the application that consumes the DID URL.

did:example:1234;service=hub/my/path?query#fragment
DID URL with a DID parameter (`service`). Identifies a specific service inside the DID's associated DID document (in this case, the `hub` service). The meaning and processing rules of the remaining syntactic components (path, query string, fragment) are not defined by the core DID standard but are specific to the `hub` service.

Processing a DID URL involves two stages. The first stage is *DID resolution*: calling a DID resolver to retrieve the DID document. The second stage is *DID dereferencing*. Whereas resolution only returns the DID document, in the dereferencing stage, the DID document is further processed to access or retrieve the resource identified by the DID URL—which can be either a subset of the DID document itself (such as the public key example given earlier) or a separate resource identified by the DID URL, such as a web page. These two terms—*resolution* and *dereferencing*—are defined by the URI standard

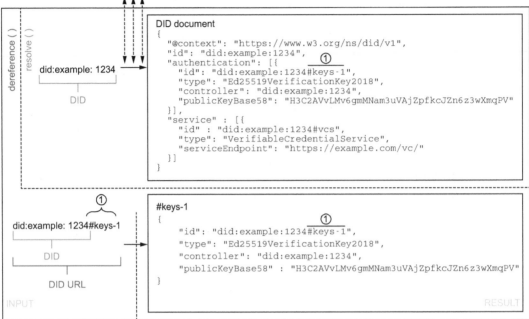

Figure 8.11 **The process of first resolving a DID and then dereferencing a DID URL containing a fragment. The result is a specific public key inside the DID document.**

(RFC 3986), and they apply not only to DIDs but to all types of URIs and the resources they identify. Figure 8.11 is an example of how these two processing stages differ.

8.2.5   *Comparison with the Domain Name System (DNS)*

We have already used domain names and the Domain Name System (DNS) as an analogy when explaining certain aspects of DIDs and how they are different from other identifiers. Table 8.2 summarizes the similarities and differences between DIDs and domain names.

Table 8.2 **Comparison of DIDs and domain names**

Decentralized identifiers (DIDs)	Domain names (DNS)
Globally unique	Globally unique
Persistent or reassignable (depends on the DID method and DID controller)	Reassignable
Machine-friendly identifiers (i.e., long character strings based on random numbers and cryptography)	Human-readable names

Table 8.2   Comparison of DIDs and domain names *(continued)*

Decentralized identifiers (DIDs)	Domain names (DNS)
Resolvable using different mechanisms defined by the applicable DID method	Resolvable using the standard DNS protocol
Associated data is expressed in DID documents	Associated data is expressed in DNS zone files
Fully decentralized namespace without delegation	Hierarchical, delegatable namespaces based on centralized root registries with top-level domain names (TLDs)
Secured by DID method-specific processes and infrastructure (e.g., blockchains)	Secured by trusted root registries and traditional PKI (DNSSEC)
Cryptographically verifiable	Verifiable using DNS security extensions (DNSSEC)
Used as an authority component in DID URLs	Used as an authority component in http: and https: web addresses as well as email addresses and other identifiers
Governed by the authority for each DID method (anyone can create a DID method)	Governed by the Internet Corporation for Assigned Names and Numbers (ICANN)
Fully under the control of the DID controller	Ultimately controlled by ICANN and the registry operator for each DNS TLD

8.2.6   *Comparison with URNs and other persistent Identifiers*

As we explained previously, DIDs can meet the functional requirements of URNs: they have the capability of being used as persistent identifiers that always identify the same entity and are never reassigned. There are many other types of persistent identifiers that differ from DIDs in ways that make them generally less suitable for SSI applications. Table 8.3 lists other types of persistent identifiers and how they compare to DIDs.

Table 8.3   Comparison of DIDs with other types of persistent identifiers

Universally unique identifiers (UUIDs, also called globally unique identifiers or GUIDs)	Not resolvable Not cryptographically verifiable
Persistent URLs (PURLs) Handle System (HDLs) Digital Object Identifiers (DOIs) Archival Resource Keys (ARKs) Open Researcher and Contributor ID (ORCID)	Not decentralized; creating and using these identifiers depends on a central or hierarchical authority Not cryptographically verifiable
Other URNs	Either not resolvable, or the resolution process and metadata vary with each type Not cryptographically verifiable

Figure 8.12 is a visual way of depicting how most of the other URIs in use today compare to DIDs. Note that it does not include a circle for *cryptographic verifiability* because DIDs are the only identifiers that offer that property. However, it does include a circle for one property DIDs do *not* explicitly have: *delegatability*—the ability for one identifier authority to delegate a sub-namespace to another identifier authority. An example is a domain name like maps.google.com, where the .com registry delegates to Google, and Google delegates to its maps service.

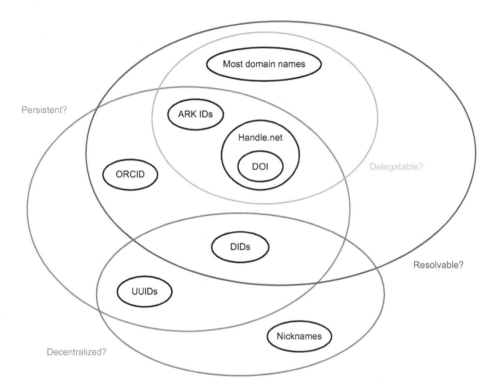

Figure 8.12   Compared to other identifiers, DIDs are persistent, resolvable, and decentralized (cryptographic verifiability is not shown since it does not apply to any of the other identifiers).

8.2.7   *Types of DIDs*

Since their invention, interest in DIDs has grown exponentially (see the next section). Although the first DID methods were closely tied to blockchains and distributed ledgers, as DIDs started evolving, many more types of DIDs have been developed. At the first meeting of the W3C DID Working Group in September 2019 in Fukuoka, Japan, a set of presentations described the various DID methods developed to that point as falling into the broad categories in table 8.4.

Table 8.4 The broad categories of DID methods developed as of August 2020

Category	Description and examples

Ledger-based DIDs	The original category of DID methods involves a blockchain or other distributed ledger technology (DLT), which serves the purpose of a registry that is not controlled by a single authority. This registry is typically public and globally accessible. A DID is created/updated/ deactivated by writing a transaction to the ledger, which is signed with the DID controller's private key:
	
	`did:sov:WRfXPg8dantKVubE3HX8pw`
	`did:btcr:xz35-jzv2-qqs2-9wjt`
	`did:ethr:0xE6Fe788d8ca214A080b0f6aC7F48480b2AEfa9a6`
	`did:v1:test:nym:3AEJTDMSxDDQpyUftjuoeZ2Bazp4Bswj1ce7FJGybCUu`

Ledger middleware (Layer 2) DIDs	An improvement to classic ledger-based DID methods, this category adds an additional storage layer such as a distributed hash table (DHT) or traditional replicated database system on top of the base layer blockchain. DIDs can be created/updated/deactivated at this second layer without requiring a base layer ledger transaction every time. Instead, multiple DID operations are batched into a single ledger transaction, increasing performance and decreasing cost:
	
	`did:ion:test:EiDk2RpPVuC4wNANUTn_4YXJczjzi10zLG1XE4AjkcGOLA`
	`did:elem:EiB9htZdL3stukrklAnJ0hrWuCdXwR27TNDO7Fh9HGWDGg`

Peer DIDs	This special category of DID method does not require a globally shared registration layer such as a blockchain. Instead, a DID is created and subsequently shared with only one other peer (or a relatively small group of peers). The DIDs that are part of the relationship are exchanged via a peer-to-peer protocol, resulting in private connections between the participants (see https://identity.foundation/peer-did-method-spec/index.html): `did:peer:1zQmZMygzYqNwU6Uhmewx5Xepf2VLp5S4HLSwwgf2aiKZuwa`
Static DIDs	There is a category of DID methods that are "static", i.e. they enable a DID to be created and resolved, but not updated or deactivated. Such DID methods tend to not require complex protocols or storage infrastructure. For example, a DID may simply be a "wrapped" public key, from which an entire DID document can be resolved algorithmically, without requiring any data other than the DID itself: `did:key:z6Mkfriq1MqLBoPWecGoDLjguo1sB9brj6wT3qZ5BxkKpuP6`

Alternative DIDs	A number of other innovative DID methods have been developed that do not fall into any of the previous categories. They demonstrate that DID identification architecture is flexible enough to be layered on top of existing internet protocols, such as Git, the Interplanetary File System (IPFS), or even the web itself:
	
	`did:git:625557b5a9cdf399205820a2a716da897e2f9657`
	`did:ipid:QmYA7p467t4BGgBL4NmyHtsXMoPrYH9b3kSG6dbgFYskJm`
	`did:web:uport.me`

8.3   *The architectural level: Why DIDs work*

Having explained what DIDs are and how they work, let's now go a step deeper into *why* they work. Why is there so much interest in this new type of identifier? To answer this, we must delve more deeply into the core problems they solve, which are less problems of identity and more problems of *cryptography*.

8.3.1 The core problem of Public Key Infrastructure (PKI)

Since it was first conceived, PKI has had one hard problem at its very core. It is not a problem with cryptography per se, i.e., with the math involved with public/private keys or encryption/decryption algorithms. Rather, it is a problem with *cryptographic infrastructure*: how we can make public/private key cryptography easy and safe for people and organizations to use at scale.

This is not an easy problem. It has vexed PKI ever since the term was invented. The reason lies in the very nature of how public/private key cryptography works. To

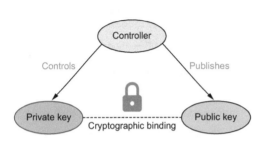

understand this, let's take a look at the basic PKI trust triangle (figure 8.13). It shows that it's not enough to think about public/private key pairs. You have to see each key pair in relation to its controlling authority (controller), be that a person, an organization, or even a thing (if the thing has the capacity to generate key pairs and store them in a digital wallet).

Figure 8.13   The basic trust triangle at the heart of all public/private key cryptography

Public and private keys are bound to each other mathematically such that neither can be forged—each can be used only for a specific set of functions defined by a specific cryptographic algorithm. But *both* types of keys are intrinsically related to the controller. Regardless of the algorithm, these two fundamental roles are highlighted in figure 8.14. The private key must be reserved for the controller's exclusive use (or its delegates) and must never be revealed to anyone else. By contrast, the public key is just the opposite: it *must* be shared with any party that wishes to communicate with the controller securely. It is the only way to encrypt messages to—or verify messages from—that controller.

Although the task of keeping a private key private is not trivial by any means, that is not the hard problem at the heart of PKI. Rather, the hard problem is on the *other* side of the PKI trust triangle, as shown in figure 8.15.

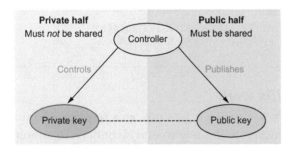

Figure 8.14   The fundamental roles of public keys vs. private keys in PKI

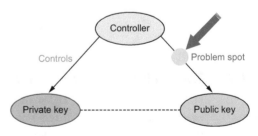

Figure 8.15   The core problem at the heart of PKI: how do you bind a public key to its controller?

The problem is simply this: *how do you strongly bind a public key to its controller* so that any party relying on that public key (the *relying party*) can be sure they are dealing with the real controller? After all, if you can fool a relying party into accepting the public key for controller B when the relying party thinks it is the public key for controller A, then for all intents and purposes, controller B can fully impersonate controller A. The cryptography will work perfectly, and the relying party will never know the difference—until they become the victim of whatever cybercrime controller B is perpetrating.

Therefore, as a relying party, it is essential to know *you have the correct public key at the correct point in time* for any controller you are dealing with. That is indeed a challenging problem because whereas public keys are purely digital entities whose cryptographic validity can be verified in milliseconds, controllers are *not.* They are real people, organizations, or things that exist in the real world. So the only way to digitally bind a public key to a controller is to add one more piece of the puzzle: a digital identifier for the controller.

This means the *real* PKI trust triangle is the triangle shown in figure 8.16. The additional piece of the puzzle is an identifier for the controller that can be bound to the public key in such a way that relying parties can be confident the public key belongs to the controller and nobody else.

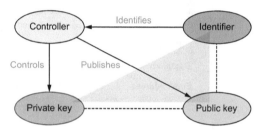

Figure 8.16 The *real* PKI trust triangle includes a digital identifier for the controller.

What figure 8.16 reveals is that this identifier-binding problem has two parts:

- How do you strongly bind the identifier to the controller?
- How do you strongly bind the public key to the identifier?

These two problem spots are called out in figure 8.17.

These are the two problem areas that PKI has struggled with since it was born in the 1970s. In the balance of this section, we'll look at four different solutions to these two problems:

1 The conventional PKI model
2 The web-of-trust model
3 Public key-based identifiers
4 DIDs and DID documents

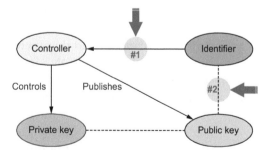

Figure 8.17 The two problem spots when it comes to strongly binding an identifier to a controller

8.3.2   *Solution 1: The conventional PKI model*

The first solution is the conventional PKI model for issuing *digital certificates* (certs). This is the predominant model that has evolved over the last 40 years. Probably the best-known example is the SSL/TLS PKI, which uses X.509 certs to provide secure connections in browsers using the HTTPS protocol (the lock you see in your browser address bar).

The conventional PKI solution to the first problem—identifier-to-controller binding—is to use one of the most suitable existing identifiers and then follow industry best practices to strongly bind this identifier to the controller. Figure 8.18 summarizes the potential choices of identifiers for conventional PKI and highlights the ones used most often in X.509 certificates.

Identifier	Challenges with strong binding
Phone number	Reassignable, limited #, hard to register
IP address	Reassignable, hard to register
Domain name	Reassignable, spoofable, DNS poisoning
Email address	Reassignable, spoofable, weak security
URL	Depends on a domain name or IP address
X.500 dist. name	Hard to register

X.509 certs

Figure 8.18   The different identifier choices for conventional PKI. The highlighted choices are those typically used in X.509 digital certificates.

The primary advantage of a URL (based on a domain name or IP address) is that automated tests can be performed to ensure that the public key controller also controls the URL. However, these tests cannot detect homographic attacks (using look-alike names or look-alike characters from different international alphabets) or DNS poisoning.

The primary advantage of an X.500 distinguished name (DN) is that it can be administratively verified to belong to the controller. However, this verification must be performed manually and thus is always subject to human error. Furthermore, it is not easy to register an X.500 DN—it is certainly not something the average internet user can be expected to undertake.

The conventional PKI approach to the second problem—public-key-to-identifier binding—seems obvious in the context of cryptography: *digitally sign a document containing both the public key and the identifier*. That is the origin of the *public key certificate* (a specific kind of digital certificate). This solution is illustrated in figure 8.19.

The question, of course, is *who digitally signs this digital certificate?* This introduces the whole notion of a *trusted third party* (TTP)—someone the relying party must trust to sign the digital certificate, or else the whole idea of PKI falls apart. The conventional PKI answer is a *certificate authority* (CA)—a service provider whose entire job is

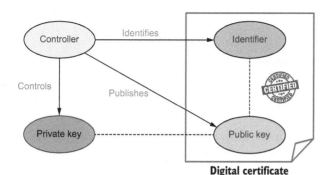

Figure 8.19 Conventional PKI solves the public-key-to-identifier binding problem using digital certificates signed by some type of certificate authority.

to follow a specified set of practices and procedures to confirm the identity of a controller and the authenticity of its public key before issuing a digital certificate that binds the two of them and signing it with the CA's private key.

Different PKI systems use different certification programs for CAs; one of the best known is the *WebTrust* program originally developed by the American Institute of Certified Public Accountants and now run by the Chartered Professional Accountants of Canada (https://www.cpacanada.ca/en/business-and-accounting-resources/audit-and-assurance/overview-of-webtrust-services). WebTrust is the certification program used for the SSL/TLS certificates that indicate a secure connection in your browser. Certification is obviously critical for CAs because acting as a TTP is inherently a human process—it cannot be automated (if it could, a TTP would not be needed). And unfortunately, humans make mistakes.

But being human is only one issue with TTPs. Table 8.5 lists the other drawbacks.

Table 8.5 The drawbacks of using the TTPs required in conventional PKI to solve the identifier binding problem

Drawbacks of TTPs	Description
Cost	Inserting a TTP (that must perform work only humans can do) into trust relationships adds costs that someone must pay.
Friction	Introducing a TTP requires additional work on the part of all the parties to a trust relationship.
Single point of failure	Each TTP becomes an attack point because a single breach can compromise all of its digital certificates.
Identifiers changing	If an identifier changes, the old digital certificate must be revoked and a new one issued.
Public keys changing	When a public key is rotated (as most security policies require periodically), the old digital certificate must be revoked and a new one issued.

Despite all these drawbacks, conventional PKI has so far been the only commercially viable solution to the identifier binding problem. But as the internet has climbed in usage and commercial value—and cybercrime rates have climbed with it—so has the demand for a better solution.

8.3.3   Solution 2: The web-of-trust model

One alternative to the conventional PKI model was formulated by one of the pioneers in public/private key cryptography, Phillip Zimmermann, inventor of Pretty Good Privacy (PGP). He coined the term *web of trust* for this model because it didn't rely on centralized CAs, but rather on individuals who knew each other directly and therefore could individually sign each other's public keys—effectively creating *peer-to-peer digital certificates*. Figure 8.20 is a visual depiction of how the web-of-trust model works.

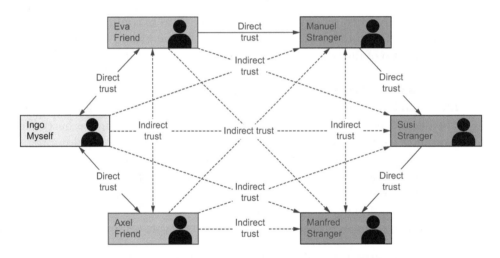

Figure 8.20   **A diagram of how a web of trust can be constructed**

Since the original formulation, hundreds of academic papers have been written exposing issues with and proposing improvements for the web-of-trust model. However, the primary challenge is that the only thing it really changes in the conventional PKI model is *who* signs the digital certificate. It turns the problem of "Who do you trust?" (the TTP problem) into the problem of "Who do you trust who knows someone else you can trust?" That is, how do you discover a "trusted path" to the digital certificate you want to verify? So far, no one has developed a reasonably secure, scalable, adoptable solution to this problem.

8.3.4   Solution 3: Public key-based identifiers

The drawbacks of both the conventional and web-of-trust PKI models ultimately led to a very different approach: removing the need for a TTP by replacing it with yet another clever use of cryptography. In other words, rather than trying to reuse an existing identifier for the controller (e.g., domain name, URL, X.500 DN) and then binding it to the public key, reverse the whole process and *generate an identifier for the controller based on the public key* (either directly or via a transaction with a blockchain, distributed ledger, or similar system). This new approach to constructing the PKI trust triangle is illustrated in figure 8.21.

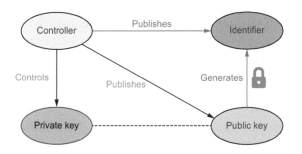

Figure 8.21 **Public key-based identifiers take a completely different approach to the identifier binding problem by generating the identifier for the controller from the public key.**

There are two basic approaches to generating a globally unique identifier from a public key:

- With the *transactional* approach, the controller uses the public/private key combination to perform a transaction with a blockchain, distributed ledger, or other algorithmically controlled system to generate a transaction address (such as a Bitcoin or Ethereum address). This transaction address becomes the identifier because it is globally unique and provably controlled by the controller.
- With the *self-certifying* approach, the controller performs a cryptographic operation, such as a one-way hash function, on the public key (and potentially other metadata) to produce a globally unique value that, by definition, only the controller can prove they control.

The significant difference between the two approaches is whether they require an external system. Transaction addresses require an external system such as a blockchain, distributed ledger, distributed file system, and so on. This external system essentially replaces a TTP run by humans (the CA required with conventional PKI) with a TTP run by machines. The argument is that the latter is more secure (no humans in the loop), is more decentralized (depending on the design and implementation of the blockchain), and has a dramatically lower cost.

Self-certifying identifiers have the advantage of not requiring any external system—they can be verified by anyone in milliseconds using cryptography alone. This also should make them the most decentralized and lowest cost of all options. See chapter 10—in particular, section 10.8 on Key Event Receipt Infrastructure (KERI)—for much more about this approach.

Regardless of the specific architecture, there are two obvious benefits of using public key-based identifiers to solve the public-key-to-identifier binding problem. First, they remove humans from the loop. Second, they also solve the identifier-to-controller binding problem because *only the private key controller can prove control of the identifier.* In other words, with public key-based identifiers, *the controller controls all three points of the real PKI trust triangle* because all three values are generated cryptographically using key material that only the controller possesses.

As powerful as public key-based identifiers appear, by themselves they have one major Achilles heel: the controller's identifier changes every time the public key is rotated. As we explain further in chapter 10, key rotation—switching from one public/private key pair to a different one—is a fundamental security best practice in all types of PKI. Thus the inability for public key-based identifiers alone to support key rotation has effectively prevented their adoption as an alternative to conventional PKI.

8.3.5 *Solution 4: DIDs and DID documents*

What if there was a way to generate a public key-based identifier once and then be able to continue to verify it after every key rotation? Enter the DID and DID document.

First, the controller generates the original public key-based identifier—the DID—once, based on the genesis public/private key pair, as shown in figure 8.21. Next, the controller publishes the original DID document containing the DID and the public key, as shown in figure 8.22.

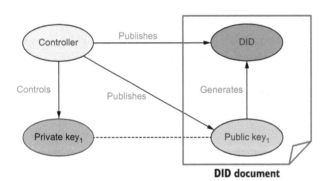

Figure 8.22 The controller publishes the DID and the original public key in the original DID document.

At this point, anyone with access to the DID document can cryptographically verify the binding between the DID and the associated public key—either by verifying the transaction address or by verifying the self-certifying identifier.

Now, when the controller needs to rotate the key pair, the controller creates an *updated DID document* and signs it with the *previous private key,* as shown in figure 8.23. Note that if a transactional DID method is used, the controller has to make a new transaction with an external system (such as a blockchain) to register the updated DID document. But there is no human in this loop—the controller can perform this transaction at any time, provided the controller controls the associated private key.

This chain of trust between DID documents can be traced back through any number of updates to the original DID document with the original public key-based

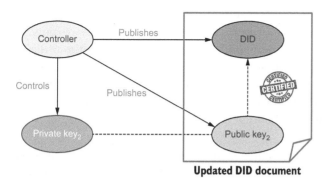

Figure 8.23 The controller publishes an updated DID document containing the original DID and the new public key and then digitally signs it with the original private key, creating a chain of trust between the DID documents.

identifier. Essentially each DID document serves as a new digital certificate for the new public key as shown—but without the need for a CA or any other human-based TTP to certify it.

8.4   *Four benefits of DIDs that go beyond PKI*

So DIDs allow us to finally achieve broad adoption of public key-based identifiers and still enjoy key rotation and other essential features of conventional PKI—without the drawbacks. But the benefits of DIDs do not stop there. In this section, we cover four benefits of DIDs that go *beyond* what is offered by PKI as we know it today.

8.4.1   *Beyond PKI benefit 1: Guardianship and controllership*

DIDs provide a clean way to identify entities *other* than the DID controller. Conventional PKI generally assumes the registrant of the digital certificate (the controller of the private key) is the party identified by the digital certificate. However, there are many situations where this is not the case. Take a newborn baby. If the baby were to need a DID—for example, to be the subject of a birth certificate issued as a verifiable credential—the newborn is in no position to have a digital wallet. The baby would need a parent (or another guardian) to issue this DID on their behalf. In this case, the entity identified by the DID—the DID subject—is explicitly *not* the controller, as shown in figure 8.24.

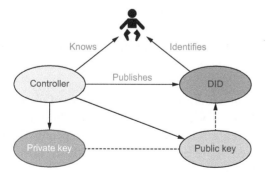

Figure 8.24   An example of a DID used to identify a DID subject (a newborn baby) that is *not* the controller of the DID

Of course, newborns are just one example of when a DID subject cannot be its own controller. There are dozens more just among humans: elderly parents, dementia patients, refugees, people experiencing homelessness, anyone without digital access. All of these need the concept of *digital guardianship* (https://sovrin.org/guardian ship/)—a third party who accepts the legal and social responsibility to manage a digital wallet on behalf of a DID subject called the *dependent.* SSI digital guardianship is a very broad, deep, and rich subject that is explored separately in chapter 11 on governance frameworks.

Digital guardianship only applies to humans, however. What about all the non-human entities in the world? The vast majority are not in a position to issue DIDs either. For example:

- *Organizations of all kinds*—Every legal entity in the world that's not an individual human needs some form of identifier to operate within the law. Today they have business registration numbers, tax ID numbers, domain names, and URLs. Tomorrow they will have DIDs.
- *Human-made things*—Virtually everything in the Internet of Things (IoT) can benefit from having one or more DIDs, but relatively few connected things (e.g., smart cars, smart drones) will be smart enough to have their own digital agents and wallets generating their own DIDs (and even then, they will still be controlled by humans). So these human-made entities will have "digital twins" that can be the subject of verifiable credentials. Goods moving through supply chains—especially across borders—are already being assigned verifiable credentials. (See the discussion of VCs in supply chains at https://www.cyber forge.com/attestation-patterns/.)
- *Natural things*—Animals, pets, livestock, rivers, lakes, geological formations: not only do these have identities, but in many jurisdictions, they also have at least a limited set of legal rights. So they too can benefit from DIDs.

These represent categories of entities that need *third-party controllers*—a relationship that has been called *controllership* to differentiate it from the guardianship of a human being. With guardianship and controllership, we can now extend the benefits of SSI and DPKI to every entity that can be identified.

8.4.2   *Beyond PKI benefit 2: Service endpoint discovery*

The second added benefit of DIDs is their capacity to enable *discovery:* i.e., to determine how to interact with a DID subject. To do this, the DID controller publishes one or more service endpoint URLs in a DID document (see listing 8.1 for an example). This three-way binding is shown in figure 8.25.

While this makes DID documents generally useful for many types of discovery, it is essential for discovering the *agent endpoints* necessary to remotely establish DID-to-DID connections (discussed next) and communicate via the DIDComm protocol (chapter 5). We could say that DID-based discovery of agent endpoint URLs is as essential to SSI as DNS-based discovery of IP addresses is to the web.

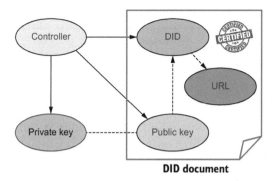

DID document

Figure 8.25 The three-way binding between DIDs, public keys, and service endpoint URLs

8.4.3 Beyond PKI benefit 3: DID-to-DID connections

SSL/TLS is the largest PKI in the world because the public key in an X.509 digital certificate can be used to secure an HTTPS connection between a web server and a browser. In other words, demand for secure e-commerce, e-banking, e-health, and other online transactions drove the growth of the SSL/TLS PKI.

The same will be true for SSI. Because DID documents can include both public keys and service endpoint URLs, every DID represents the opportunity for its controller to create an instant, secure, private, peer-to-peer connection with any other DID controller. Even better, unlike static public key certificates that must be obtained in advance from a CA, DIDs can be generated immediately, locally, on-the-fly as they are needed for new connections. In fact, in table 8.4, we cited one DID method—peer DIDs—created exclusively for this purpose (https://identity.foundation/peer-did-method-spec/index.html).

Originally developed by Daniel Hardman and the Hyperledger Aries community—and now being standardized by a working group at the Decentralized Identity Foundation (https://identity.foundation/working-groups/identifiers-discovery.html)—peer DIDs do not need a blockchain, a distributed ledger, or any other external database. They are generated locally in the DID controller's digital wallet and exchanged directly, peer-to-peer, using a protocol based on Diffie-Hellman key exchange. This creates a connection between the two parties that is not like any other connection in traditional network architecture. Table 8.6 highlights the five special properties of DID-to-DID connections.

Table 8.6 The five special properties of DID-to-DID connections

Property	Description
Permanent	The connection will *never break* unless one or both parties want it to.
Private	All communications over the connection can be automatically encrypted and digitally signed by the private keys for the DIDs.
End-to-end	The connection has no intermediaries—it is secure from "DID to DID."
Trusted	The connection supports verifiable credential exchange to establish higher trust in any relevant context to any level of assurance.

Table 8.6 The five special properties of DID-to-DID connections *(continued)*

Property	Description
Extensible	The connection can be used for any application that needs secure, private, reliable digital communications via the DIDComm protocol or any other protocol supported by both agents.

Whether between peer DIDs (the default) or public DIDs, DID-to-DID connections are the centerpiece of Layer 2 of the Trust over IP stack described in chapter 5. Agents at this layer communicate using the secure DIDComm protocol in much the same way web browsers and web servers communicate over the secure HTTPS protocol. DIDs "democratize" the SSL/TLS PKI plumbing, so now secure connections can be available to anyone, anytime, anywhere.

8.4.4   *Beyond PKI benefit 4: Privacy by design at scale*

At this point, it should be obvious how much DIDs can help increase security on the internet. But while security is necessary for privacy, it is not sufficient. Privacy is more than just preventing private information from being snooped or stolen. It ensures that parties with whom you choose to share your private information (doctors, lawyers, teachers, governments, companies from whom you buy products and services) protect that information and do not use or sell it without your permission. So how can DIDs help with *that?*

The answer may surprise you. Conventional identifiers for people are assigned one time by third parties: government ID numbers, health ID numbers, driving license numbers, mobile phone numbers. When you share these as part of your personal data, they make it easy for you to be tracked and correlated across many different relying parties. They also make it easy for those parties to share information and compile digital dossiers about you.

DIDs turn that whole equation upside down. Rather than you sharing the same ID number with many different relying parties, you can generate and share your own peer DID each time you form a relationship with a new relying party. That relying party will be the only one in the world that knows that DID (and its public key and service endpoint URL). And that relying party will do the same for you.

So rather than you having a single DID, similar to a government-issued ID number, you will have *thousands of DIDs*—one per relationship. Each pairwise-unique peer DID gives you and your relying party your own *permanent private channel* connecting the two of you—just as originally envisioned by Philip Zimmermann with PGP. The first advantage of this channel is that you can authenticate each other automatically—in both directions—just by exchanging messages signed by each of your private keys. Spoofing or phishing a relying party with whom you already have a connection becomes next to impossible.

The second significant advantage is that peer DIDs and private channels give you one simple, standard, verifiable way to share *signed personal data*—personal data for which you have granted specific permissions data to the relying party. On your side, the benefit is convenience and control—at a glance, you can see what you shared with whom and why. On the relying party side, the benefit is fresh, first-person data with cryptographically verifiable, GDPR-auditable consent—plus an easy, secure way to support all the other GDPR-mandated personal data rights (access, rectification, erasure, objection).

The third major benefit is that, with signed data, we can finally protect both individuals and relying on parties from the damage caused by the massive data breaches we read about almost daily (Target, Equifax, Sony, Yahoo, Capital One). What motivates criminals to break into those data silos is the value of that personal data—primarily because the criminals can use it to break into accounts all over the internet.

As those accounts convert to using pairwise peer DIDs and signed personal data, the value of that personal data *to anyone but the relying party who has explicit signed permission* disappears. If you cannot cryptographically prove you have permission to use the data, then not only does the data become worthless—it becomes *toxic*. Mere possession of unsigned personal data could become illegal. Like toxic waste, it will be something companies, organizations, and even governments will want to get rid of as quickly as possible.

So now you see why many in the SSI community consider the arrival of DIDs, verifiable credentials, and the Trust over IP stack to be a sea change in privacy on the internet. While we are still in the early stages of implementing this new approach, it can finally give individuals badly needed new tools for controlling the use of their personal data. And this control, when bundled with the rest of the tools in the Trust over IP stack for building and maintaining digital trust, might be a path to putting the privacy genie back in the bottle—a feat that many have believed was impossible.

8.5 The semantic level: What DIDs mean

Having explained how and why DIDs work, we now turn to the lowest level of understanding DIDs: exploring what they mean for the future of SSI and the internet.

8.5.1 The meaning of an address

Addresses do not exist on their own. They only exist in the context of a network that uses them. Whenever we have a new type of address, it is because we have a *new type of network* that needs this new address to do something that could not be done before. Table 8.7 shows this progression over the past few hundred years.

Table 8.7 An historical perspective on the evolution of addresses for different types of networks

Origin	Address type	Network
Pre-history	Human name	Human networks (family, clan, tribe, etc.)
~1750	Postal address	Postal mail network
1879	Telephone number	Telephone network
1950	Credit card number	Payment network
1964	Fax number	Fax (facsimile) network
1971	Email address	Email network

Table 8.7   An historical perspective on the evolution of addresses for different types of networks

Origin	Address type	Network
1974	IP address	Internet (machine-friendly)
1983	Domain name	Internet (human-friendly)
1994	Persistent address (URN)	World Wide Web (machine-friendly)
1994	Web address (URL)	World Wide Web (human-friendly)
2003	Social network address	Social network
2009	Blockchain address	Blockchain or distributed ledger network
2016	DID	DID network

So the real meaning of a DID comes down to what can be done with it on a *DID network*.

8.5.2   *DID networks and digital trust ecosystems*

Just as everything on the internet has an IP address—and everything on the web has a URL—everything on a DID network has a DID. But that begs the question: *Why* does everything on a DID network need a DID? What new communications network functionality do DIDs enable that could not be done before?

The short answer is that DIDs were invented to support both the *cryptographic trust* and the *human trust* required for any *digital trust ecosystem* based on the *Trust over IP stack* introduced in chapter 5 and shown again in figure 8.26.

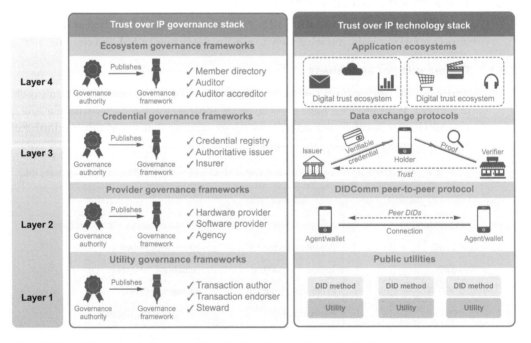

Figure 8.26   DIDs are foundational to all four levels of the Trust over IP stack.

DIDs are essential to each layer of the stack as follows:

1 *Layer 1: Public DID utilities*—DIDs published on public blockchains like Bitcoin and Ethereum; distributed ledgers like Sovrin, ION, Element, and Veres One; or distributed file systems like IPFS can serve as publicly verifiable trust roots for participants at all higher layers. They literally form the foundation of a trust layer for the internet.

2 *Layer 2: DIDComm*—By definition, DIDComm is a P2P protocol between agents identified by DIDs. By default, these are pairwise pseudonymous peer DIDs issued and exchanged following the Peer DID specification, so they exist only at Layer 2. However, DIDComm can also use public DIDs from Layer 1.

3 *Layer 3: Credential exchange*—As covered in chapter 7, DIDs are integral to the process of issuing and verifying digitally signed verifiable credentials as well as to the discovery of service endpoint URLs for credential exchange protocols.

4 *Layer 4: Digital trust ecosystems*—As we will cover in chapter 11, DIDs are the anchor points for discovery and verification of the governance authorities (as legal entities) and governance frameworks (as legal documents) for digital trust ecosystems of all sizes and shapes (as well as for the participants they specify). DIDs also enable verifiable credentials to persistently reference the governance frameworks under which they are issued—and for governance frameworks to reference each other for interoperability.

In short, DIDs are the first widely available, fully standardized identifiers designed explicitly for building and maintaining digital trust networks that are protected by cryptography "all the way down."

8.5.3   Why isn't a DID human-meaningful?

Many people have asked, if DIDs are the latest and greatest identifier for the cutting edge of communications on the internet, why aren't they more human-friendly? The answer lies in a conundrum called *Zooko's triangle,* named after Zooko Wilcox-O'Hearn, who coined the term in 2001. (Zooko worked in the 1990s with famous cryptographer David Chaum developing DigiCash and also founded Zcash, a cryptocurrency aimed at using cryptography to provide enhanced privacy for its users.) It is the trilemma illustrated in figure 8.27, which states that an identifier system can achieve at most two of the following three properties:

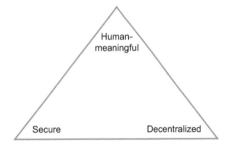

Figure 8.27   Zooko's triangle is a trilemma that proposes an identifier system can have at most two of these three properties

- *Human-meaningful*—Identifiers are semantic names from ordinary human language (and therefore low-entropy by definition).
- *Secure*—Identifiers are guaranteed to be unique: each identifier is bound to only one specific entity and cannot easily be spoofed or impersonated.

- *Decentralized*—Identifiers can be generated and correctly resolved to the identified entities without using a central authority or service.

Although some believe Zooko's triangle can be solved, most internet architects agree it
is far easier to achieve two of these three properties than all three. As this chapter makes
clear, with DIDs, the two properties chosen were *secure* and *decentralized* (the latter being
built right into the acronym "DID"). What was given up—due to the cryptographic algorithms used to generate DIDs—was any attempt at being human-meaningful.

But while the SSI community realized that while DIDs alone could not solve the
human-meaningful naming problem, they could in fact anchor a promising new solution. The trick was not to do it at the public DID utility layer (Layer 1 of the ToIP
stack)—or at the peer DID layer (Layer 2)—but *at the verifiable credentials layer* (Layer
3). In other words, a specific class of verifiable credentials could assert one or more
verifiable names for a DID subject. By creating searchable *credential registries* for the
names in these credentials, we could collectively build a naming layer that is semanti-
cally richer, fairer, more trusted, and more distributed than the current DNS naming
layer. This is shown in figure 8.28.

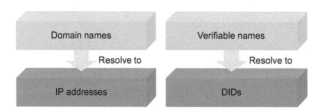

**Figure 8.28   Verifiable credentials
for the human-meaningful names of
DID subjects can be layered over
machine-friendly DIDs the same
way human-meaningful DNS names
were layered over machine-friendly
IP addresses.**

This *verifiable naming layer* would no longer need to be arbitrarily divided into top-level
domain (TLD) name registries but could capture the full richness of human name(s)
in any language for any kind of DID subject: person, organization, product, concept,
and so on. Furthermore, the authenticity of names—for people, companies, products—could be attested to in a decentralized way by issuers of all kinds, so spoofing or
phishing would become an order of magnitude harder than it is in today's internet
Wild West.

8.5.4   *What does a DID identify?*

We saved this question for last because, from a semantic standpoint, it is the deepest.
The easy answer is exactly what it says in the W3C DID Core specification (https://
www.w3.org/TR/did-core/): "A DID identifies the DID subject." And that is completely true, no matter what that subject is: a person, organization, department, physical object, digital object, concept, software program—anything that has identity.

Where confusion may arise is with the DID document that a DID resolves to. Does
the DID identify the DID document as a resource?

After much debate, the answer from the W3C DID Working Group was "No." As an appendix to the DID Core Specification states:

> *To be very precise, the DID identifies the DID subject and resolves to the DID document (by following the protocol specified by the DID method). The DID document is not a separate resource from the DID subject and does not have a URI separate from the DID. Rather the DID document is an artifact of DID resolution controlled by the DID controller to describe the DID subject.*

The same appendix includes figure 8.29 as a visual illustration of this conclusion.

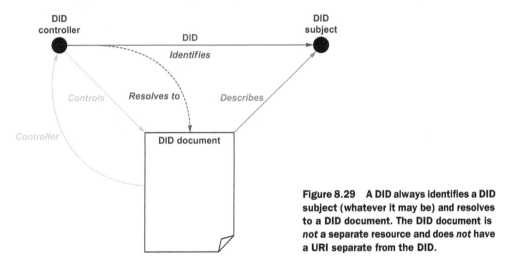

Figure 8.29 A DID always identifies a DID subject (whatever it may be) and resolves to a DID document. The DID document is *not* a separate resource and does *not* have a URI separate from the DID.

Note that in figure 8.29, the DID controller and DID subject are shown as separate entities, which may be the case when digital guardianship or controllership is required, as discussed earlier in this chapter. The common case where the DID controller and DID subject are the same entity is shown in figure 8.30.

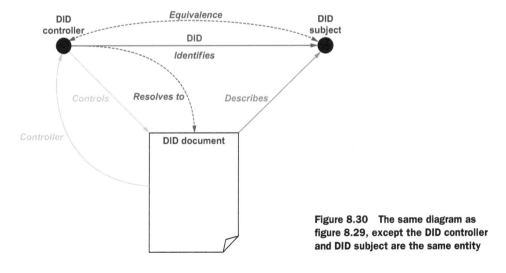

Figure 8.30 The same diagram as figure 8.29, except the DID controller and DID subject are the same entity

This final point about the semantics of what a DID actually identifies matters because it highlights another key feature of DID identification: DIDs can be used to identify any resource of any kind—*whether that resource is on or off the web*—and yet always produce the same kind of description of that resource: a DID document. This provides a universal means of cryptographically verifiable resource identification that does not need to rely on any centralized authorities.

Although this is one of the longest chapters in this book, if you've read it this far, you now have a much deeper understanding of why we call DIDs "the atomic building block of decentralized digital trust infrastructure." They are far more than just a new type of globally unique identifier. By relying on cryptography for both generation and verification, DIDs change the internet's fundamental power dynamics. Instead of scale laws pulling everything into the gravity well of the internet giants at the center, DIDs push power to the very edges—to the individual digital agents and wallets where DIDs are born and DID-to-DID connections are made. This Copernican inversion creates the new spacetime of decentralization: a universe where entities of all kinds can be self-sovereign and interact as peers using all four layers of the Trust over IP stack.

This is why in the next chapter, we move up to Layer 2 of the stack to understand the digital wallets and digital agents required to generate DIDs, form DID-to-DID connections, exchange verifiable credentials, and handle decentralized key management.

SSI Resources

To learn more about DIDs, check out https://ssimeetup.org/decentralized-identifiers -dids-fundamentals-identitybook-info-drummond-reed-markus-sabadello-webinar-46.

Digital wallets and digital agents

Darrell O'Donnell

We introduced digital wallets and agents in chapter 2 as two of the basic building blocks of self-sovereign identity (SSI). While the basic concepts are relatively straightforward, the details could easily fill an entire book. This chapter is based on Darrell O'Donnell's continuously updated report on the state of digital wallets that he began writing in the winter of 2019. Digital wallet and agent technology has been advancing so fast that Darrell has been speaking globally about the evolving industry since then. Darrell is uniquely suited to write on this subject because he advises and works with many startups, large corporations, and governments that are down in the trenches of SSI, establishing the basic and advanced capabilities required. He is an entrepreneur, investor, and technologist implementing and supporting SSI, digital wallets, and agents.

> *If I look in my wallet, most of the stuff in there is nothing to do with payments. If Apple or Google want to replace my wallet, that means that they have to replace my driving licence, my loyalty cards, my rail discount pass, my travel insurance, my health insurance document, my blood donor card, my AA membership... well, you get the point... But in the long term, it's much more valuable.*
>
> —Dave Birch, *Forbes* [1]

Digital wallets and agents are to SSI what browsers and servers are to the web: the basic tools we need to make the whole infrastructure work. While browsers and servers exchange *web pages*, digital wallets and agents exchange *verifiable digital cre-*

dentials (VCs). (Digital wallets and agents can also use the DIDComm protocol to exchange any other form of cryptographically verifiable data. See chapter 5.)

As simple as the concept of a digital wallet sounds, when you add up all the requirements for security, privacy, cryptography, functionality, portability, and usability, it becomes a real feat of engineering. Building a full-featured SSI wallet is a design and development effort similar in scope to building a full-featured browser. Since the space is evolving so fast, for a list of current SSI digital wallet projects, see the Wikipedia page on SSI.

In this chapter, we cover the following:

- What is a digital wallet, and what does it typically contain?
- What is a digital agent, and how does it typically work with a digital wallet?
- An example usage scenario.
- Design principles for digital wallets and agents.
- Basic anatomy of a digital wallet and agent.
- Standard features of end-user digital wallets and agents.
- Backup and recovery.
- Advanced features of wallets and agents.
- Enterprise wallets and agents.
- Special features for guardianship and delegation.
- The "wallet wars"—the coming battle between open source, open standard, and proprietary digital wallets and agents.

Note that one topic closely associated with digital wallets—*key management*—is deep enough that we cover it separately in the next chapter.

Topics we will *not* cover in this chapter, except for brief mentions, include the following:

- Cryptocurrency wallets
- Payments and value exchange
- Personal data stores (PDS) and secure data storage (SDS) (aka identity hubs and encrypted data vaults)

9.1   *What is a digital wallet, and what does it typically contain?*

We should say right up front that there is not yet a universally accepted definition of the term *digital wallet*. There are at least half a dozen definitions, depending on the particular segment of the SSI community you talk to. The one overarching theme everyone seems to agree on is this:

> *A digital wallet consists of software (and optionally hardware) that enables the wallet's controller to generate, store, manage, and protect cryptographic keys, secrets, and other sensitive private data.*

In other words, a digital wallet (and the digital agent used with it—see the next section) is the *nexus of control* for every individual, organization, and thing participating in SSI.

Interestingly, what falls under the heading of "other sensitive private data" that might be stored in a digital wallet is as varied as what people might choose to put in their physical wallets or purses. Some current or planned SSI digital wallet implementations include these:

- Decentralized identifiers (DIDs: peer DIDs, contextual DIDs, public DIDs for any of your relationships)
- Verifiable credentials for which you are the holder
- Digital copies (e.g., PDFs) of physical credentials such as passports, driver's licenses, birth certificates, diplomas, and other credentials that have not yet been converted into verifiable credentials
- Business cards and other personal contact information
- Personal data of all kinds
- Resumes, CVs, and other biographical information
- Usernames, passwords, and other data typically maintained in a password manager

Again, this list does not include data related to cryptocurrencies, digital tokens, or other forms of value exchange, as those are currently the domains of more specialized cryptocurrency wallets. However, many believe that SSI wallets and cryptocurrency wallets are on a collision course and will become one and the same in the future. See chapter 17 for more.

9.2 What is a digital agent, and how does it typically work with a digital wallet?

In chapter 2, we compared physical wallets with digital wallets and used the analogy that a physical wallet doesn't do anything by itself; rather, it is always a person—the owner—who puts credentials into the wallet and takes them out to show proof of the owner's identity. With a digital wallet, the owner needs software to manage those interactions. This software module is known as a *digital agent.*

SSI community terminology around the term *agent* is still fuzzy. For example,

- Some SSI vendors do not differentiate between digital wallet and agent functionality and simply call their entire application a *digital wallet* or *mobile wallet.* In this case, you can consider the agent functionality built-into the wallet.
- Other SSI vendors take the opposite approach and consider their digital agent to be the primary offering. In this case, the wallet functionality is treated as a feature of the agent.
- To top it off, the term *agent* has myriad uses and meanings in the world of software and networking. For example, both web browsers and email clients are technically called *user agents. Intelligent agents* are another computer science category that can cover anything from a digital thermostat to an autonomous drone. Entire populations of agents can be combined into *complex adaptive systems* whose emergent behavior is more than the sum of the parts, as described in chapter 19.

For this chapter, we use the following definition:

> A digital agent *is to a digital wallet what an operating system is to a computer or smartphone. It is the software that enables a person to take actions, perform communications, store information, and track usage of the digital wallet.*

This means a digital agent typically performs the following functions on behalf of the person or organization in control (whom we call the *controller*):

- Request the generation of cryptographic key pairs and DIDs from the wallet.
- Initiate and negotiate DID-to-DID connections to form new relationships.
- Request the issuance of a verifiable credential, accept the issued credential, and store it in the wallet.
- Receive a request from a verifier for proof of one or more claims from a credential, ask the controller for consent to release the proof, calculate the required proof (including any necessary digital signature), and deliver the proof to the verifier.
- Accept notification messages received over a connection, apply the controller's filtering rules, and, if necessary, notify the controller and process any resulting action.
- Send digitally signed messages from the controller to one or more of the controller's connections.
- Apply digital signatures to documents or artifacts at the controller's request.

9.3   *An example scenario*

To ground our discussion of the various functions of digital wallets and agents, let's take a real-world scenario where we make frequent use of our physical wallets: a business trip. From start to finish, these are the times on a business trip when you usually need to share information from your physical wallet:

1. Making plane, car rental, and hotel reservations
2. Passing through airport security
3. Presenting your boarding pass for the plane
4. Car rental, hotel, and conference check-ins
5. Business card exchange

It's easy to envision the all-digital version of this scenario if you see your agent as your surrogate, doing most of the work, and your digital wallet as a replacement for your physical wallet. Assuming that you have an agent and wallet installed on your smartphone, here are the digital versions of each step:

1. *Making plane, car rental, and hotel reservations*—At each website, you use your phone to scan a QR code. Your agent prompts you for permission to establish a private, peer-to-peer connection. (After associating this new connection with your existing website account, you should be able to "log in" to the website using your digital agent and wallet without any username or password.) When

you are finished making your reservation, your agent prompts you to accept a digital credential for your reservation. When you click Yes, your agent stores the reservation credential directly in your digital wallet, ready for your trip.

2 *Passing through airport security*—You tap your phone on an NFC device, and your agent prompts you to share the required information from an acceptable government ID credential. You click Yes, the security agent verifies your picture, and you are good to go.

3 *Presenting your boarding pass for the plane*—Your phone connects with a Bluetooth Low Energy (BLE) device when you are three feet from the gate as you get in line to board the plane. Your digital agent (not the gate agent) prompts you to share your plane reservation credential. You click Yes. A facial recognition scanner compares your face with your plane reservation. If everything matches, the light turns green, and you board the plane.

4 *Car rental, hotel, and conference check-ins*—Each of these is essentially the same ceremony: you scan a QR code, are prompted by your agent to share the necessary credential proofs, click Yes, wait for the proofs to be verified and your biometrics (such as your picture) to be matched, and then are finished.

5 *Business card exchange*—When you meet someone at a conference with whom you want to exchange business cards, one of the two of you opens your digital wallet app and clicks the menu to display a QR code. The other one scans it. (This ceremony can also work via Bluetooth, NFC, and other edge networking protocols.) The two agents instantly negotiate a private DID-to-DID connection. Then each agent prompts its controller for the business card(s) to share over this new connection. Choose the card(s), and you're finished. You both now have a direct personal connection—with no intermediary—that will last as long as you both want it. (We walk through this person-to-person connection scenario in greater detail in chapter 3.)

NOTE In the context of the COVID-19 crisis and potential similar future situations, *100% of the transactions just described can be touchless.* The ability to carry on business as usual without direct physical contact becomes a real advantage of SSI.

9.4 Design principles for SSI digital wallets and agents

This new breed of digital wallets and agents designed for SSI is unlike any attempt at digital wallets before (and there have been many). The main reason is that to be compatible with the philosophy of SSI discussed throughout this book, SSI wallets and agents need to follow the design principles in this section.

9.4.1 Portable and Open-By-Default

As we explained in chapter 2, almost every smartphone today comes with a digital wallet built in. Although vendors like Apple and Google allow third parties to design credentials to be used with their wallets, they are still proprietary wallet APIs controlled by single vendors—and the credentials they contain are not portable to other digital wallets.

From an SSI perspective, that makes about as much sense as buying a physical wallet that came with rules restricting what you can and cannot put in the wallet. Of course, you would never tolerate that.

So the number-one design criteria for SSI-compatible digital wallets is that they must implement *open standards* for DIDs, cryptographic keys, verifiable credentials, and any other user-controlled contents. This enables the controller to enjoy true *data portability*: i.e., the ability at any point in time to move all of the contents of their wallet to a different wallet from a different vendor—or even to build their own.

This also means multiple digital wallets and agents from different vendors should be able to fully interoperate on behalf of the same controller—whether that controller is a person with multiple devices (e.g., smartphone, tablet, laptop) or an organization with different operating systems and applications from multiple vendors (not to mention different employees using different devices and operating systems).

While the requirement in some digital trust ecosystems to use only certified and accredited devices may limit portability (see more about that topic in chapter 11), these limitations will likely only apply to very high-assurance situations (e.g., approving large money transfers; signing legal documents for a corporation).

9.4.2   *Consent-driven*

A second core design principle is that, given the sensitive nature and value of a digital wallet's contents, *a digital agent should never take an action that has not been authorized by its controller.* This doesn't mean an agent must interrupt its controller for consent every single time any transaction is made. Agents can be designed to remember the policies and preferences of their controllers and automatically take certain actions with the controller's consent. A common example, already widely implemented in banking, is auto-payment of recurring bills. The account owner sets up the rules, and the bank's backend systems automatically pay certain bills every month.

Digital agents can do the same thing for many routine transactions. However, for anything that is not routine, such as forming a new relationship or performing a new type of transaction, the agent must request explicit consent from the controller. One of the SSI infrastructure's best features is that digital agents and wallets can produce an auditable log of controller consent actions *for both parties for every transaction.* Thus in business-to-consumer (B2C) transactions, both the business and the consumer can have their own cryptographically verifiable event logs. This enables businesses to comply with data protection regulations such as General Data Protection Regulation (GDPR) while enabling consumers to track down when and where they shared sensitive personal data (and thus to more easily monitor, update, or delete it as desired).

9.4.3   *Privacy by design*

The previous design principles already address some of the principles of privacy by design as originally defined by Ann Cavoukian during her tenure as Ontario information and privacy commissioner (and adopted by the International Assembly of Privacy Commissioners and Data Protection Authorities in 2010). Given that a digital wallet and its accompanying agent should be among the most trusted tools we have for navigating the wild and woolly World Wide Web, it is highly recommended that implementers follow all seven principles:

1 Proactive, not reactive; preventive, not remedial
2 Privacy as the default setting
3 Privacy embedded into the design
4 Full functionality—positive-sum, not zero-sum
5 End-to-end security—full life-cycle protection
6 Visibility and transparency—keep it open
7 Respect for user privacy—keep it user-centric

As we discussed in chapter 5, the overall architecture of SSI makes it possible to implement privacy by design on a scale that has not been possible before. Specifically, SSI can offer the following:

1 *Cryptographically protected private storage*—Although some of us use password managers today, many others do not have any place to safely store and guard the personal data they share on the web. That is why merely having (or stealing) access to that data can be used to impersonate someone for the purpose of identity theft. SSI digital wallets finally give us a standard place to safely lock up private personal data so it is used only with our consent.
2 *Privacy-protected connections*—Digital agents can form private peer-to-peer connections by exchanging peer DIDs and DID documents so we do not have to rely on intermediaries to maintain and monitor our communications relationships.
3 *End-to-end encryption*—Messages and data exchanges can be encrypted from wallet to wallet (or DID to DID) so they can be viewed only by the authorized parties.
4 *Watermarked personal data*—Data shared using verifiable credentials has cryptographically verifiable proof of the associated consent. This turns the tables on data brokers and others so that anyone using unmarked personal data—data without the associated consent—will have to prove they have a legitimate reason.
5 *Shared governance frameworks*—Today's privacy policies exist primarily to protect the rights of businesses to use personal data as they define it. Because the power relationship is so asymmetric, consumers are essentially unable to say no if they need the product or service the business provides. SSI governance frameworks, discussed in detail in chapter 11, provide a new tool to establish much broader privacy and data protection norms—and, consequently, bring much more public and regulatory pressure to bear on businesses to "do the right thing" with their privacy and data protection practices.

9.4.4 Security by design

If there is one thing every digital wallet must do very well, it is to securely store and safeguard its contents. Those contents are the keys to the (digital) kingdom. If an attacker can break into or steal the contents of a digital wallet, they can do very serious damage.

Fortunately, we can make this a very uneven playing field—tilted in favor of the good guys—by using the following security-by-design features of SSI architecture:

- *Secure hardware*—Designers and developers of digital wallets can take advantage of specialized hardware components (secure enclaves in smartphones, trusted execution environments in computers, hardware security modules in servers) designed explicitly for secure storage and protection of digital keys and other sensitive data.

- *SSI decentralization by design*—As a rule, digital wallets will be spread out all over the edges of the network, where they are hardest to attack. Furthermore, breaking into a single digital wallet will net the attacker only a limited set of keys and secrets with which to compromise a single controller—not a giant honeypot of personal data that, once penetrated, can be used to impersonate millions of people.

- *Private DID-to-DID connections*—These are individually authorized, verified as authentic using an exchange of digital credentials, and end-to-end message-encrypted by default. This means attackers have far fewer entry points with which to try to launch an attack (especially compared to the wide-open email addresses used for all manner of social engineering attacks today).

- *Using well-designed governance frameworks*—SSI can use well-designed governance frameworks to propagate and enforce best-of-breed security practices across all members of a digital trust ecosystem—vendors, issuers, holders, verifiers, auditors, and so on.

- *Digital agents as their own monitors*—Every digital agent can serve as its own monitor of local security-related activities and watch for possible signs of a breach, applying the security principle of "many eyes" to detect attacks and coordinate responses across entire digital trust ecosystems.

9.5 *Basic anatomy of an SSI digital wallet and agent*

Figure 9.1 shows the conceptual architecture of a typical SSI wallet and agent. The top box shows the primary agent functions, and the bottom box shows the primary wallet functions called by the agent.

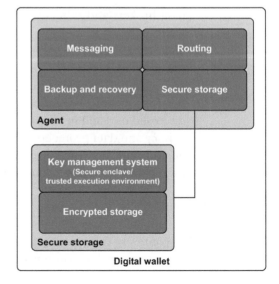

Figure 9.1 Conceptual architecture of a typical SSI digital wallet and agent

Although specific wallet/agent implementations may differ in how they divide up these functions, broadly speaking, they will cover the areas in Table 9.1.

Table 9.1   Core functions of SSI digital wallets and agents

Component	Function
Agent	*Messaging*—In some ways, an agent functions like a specialized email or chat application: it sends and receives data, structured messages, and push notifications on behalf of the controller. This can be any combination of tightly defined protocol messages (such as those used for peer DID or verifiable credential exchange), structured messages defined by either party, and general-purpose secure messages.
	Routing—Some agents, particularly those representing enterprises or agencies, serve as intermediaries for routing other agent-to-agent messages using protocols like DIDComm, designed for multi-agent routing. DIDComm originated in the Hyperledger Aries project and is being standardized by the DIDComm Working Group at the Decentralized Identity Foundation (https://identity.foundation/working-groups/did-comm.html). It has explicit support for the "Russian doll" nesting of encrypted messages to support privacy-respecting multi-agent routing.
	Backup and recovery—Given the value and sensitivity of the data stored in a digital wallet, in almost every case, the wallet must support robust backup and recovery options in case of loss, corruption, or hacking of the wallet/agent software and/or hardware. See section 9.7.
	Secure storage—This component of an agent calls the wallet's services, typically via a secure API provided by the wallet.
Wallet	*Key management system*—The heart of every digital wallet is how it handles the generation, rotation, revocation, storage, signing, and protection of cryptographic keys and associated secrets such as the link secrets used in zero-knowledge proofs. You can read more about this in chapter 10.
	Encrypted storage—The other primary wallet function is the protected storage of the keys, secrets, and other private data that the controller elects to store in the wallet. Depending on the size and type of wallet, this may take many forms, e.g., secure enclaves on mobile phones, secure storage governed by trusted execution environments (TEEs), or hardware security modules (HSMs) on servers and cloud-hosted wallets.

For another perspective on what should be standard in an SSI digital wallet, see the draft Universal Wallet specification submitted to the W3C Credentials Community Group in August 2020 by Orie Steele of Transmute (https://w3c-ccg.github.io/universal-wallet-interop-spec).

9.6   Standard features of end-user digital wallets and agents

In addition to the basic features and functions covered in table 9.1, this section lists other features commonly provided by commercial-grade digital wallets intended for personal use.

9.6.1 Notifications and user experience

Whether the application is called a digital wallet or a digital agent or both, there is universal agreement that it is *the* critical component in managing the user experience (UX) of SSI. This is where the rubber meets the road as to whether self-sovereign identity actually looks and feels "self-sovereign." For example, does the end user

- Feel fully informed about what is happening with their credentials and the sensitive personal data those credentials may contain (identity data, health data, financial data, family data, travel data)?
- Trust the providers of the wallet and agent software and hardware?
- Trust the credential issuers?
- Trust the credential verifiers?
- Trust the governance frameworks and trust marks under which providers, issuers, and/or verifiers are operating?
- Trust the peer-to-peer connections they are making?
- Feel fully in control of the whole experience, such that the user's confidence in their use of the internet, their digital identity, and the privacy, security, and protection of their personal data is significantly (or dramatically) better?

Of course, part of this is also the end user's feeling of satisfaction with the behavior of the wallet and agent application, particularly with regard to the following:

- How easy and intuitive is it to use?
- How carefully does it balance between security, privacy, and ease of use?
- How often and accurately does it notify the user—and how appropriate are the interrupts when it needs to "steal the user's attention"?

This last question is particularly important when it comes to a highly secure application like a digital wallet. Mobile and desktop operating systems such as iOS, Android, macOS, and Microsoft Windows already have sophisticated notification systems that notify the user only when it's necessary or relevant. (Microsoft learned the hard way when it added so many new security notifications in Windows 10 that users either ignored them or turned off all notifications.) But even those can be challenging to configure or tune. If a digital wallet and agent app is to earn the user's respect and trust, it must be very sensitive to providing only notifications the user *must* see (for legal reasons, like GDPR), *should* see (for security reasons, such as authentication), and/or *wants* to see (for an exchange of value, or to better control their personal information).

9.6.2 Connecting: Establishing new digital trust relationships

SSI architecture pairs a digital agent with a digital wallet because the cryptographic keys, secrets, and credentials stored in the wallet don't do anything by themselves. Their entire purpose is for building and maintaining *digital trust relationships* on behalf of their controller.

One of the most frequent actions the controller will take is scanning a QR code, tapping a Near-Field Communication (NFC) or BLE device, clicking a link, or otherwise activating their agent to form a new DID-to-DID connection with a person, an organization, or a thing. For example, in our scenario of an all-digital business trip, each step in the journey involved creating a new connection (if one did not already exist) with an airline, car rental company, hotel, conference registrar, and so on.

Fortunately a digital agent makes this a simple, standard action requiring no knowledge of cryptography, key management, or any of the underlying complexity—just scan a QR code or click a link, approve the new connection, and decide what credentials to exchange in that particular interaction. Both parties to the connection enjoy these benefits:

- *Your agent and wallet will automatically remember the connection.* It's like having an assistant automatically add each new person you meet to your address book.
- *The connection will last as long as you need it.* There is no reason for it to break because the other party moves, changes address, or somehow loses touch. SSI connections only need to end when one or both parties no longer want them.
- *The connection has no intermediary.* There is no social network, email provider, or telco between the connected parties.
- *All messages are encrypted end-to-end.* This new communication channel is completely secure and private to the connected parties.
- *You can use the connection for anything you want.* There are no third-party terms of service for an SSI connection. It belongs entirely to the connected parties, who can use it for any application they want.

9.6.3 Receiving, offering, and presenting digital credentials

Once a connection is established, the typical next step is for the parties to exchange credentials in one or both directions—either to issue new credentials (the left leg of the trust triangle in figure 9.2) or to verify issued credentials (the right leg of figure 9.2).

Both processes are carefully orchestrated dances between the agents for the two parties—and these dances can vary depending on the credential format being used. In general, the credential-issuance process proceeds along these lines:

1 The issuer requests whatever authentication is necessary for the holder to qualify for a new credential.

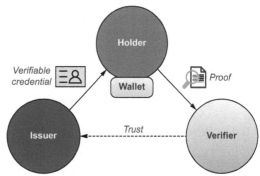

Figure 9.2 The verifiable credential trust triangle

2 Once authenticated, either the holder requests a new credential *or* the issuer offers a new credential.

3 Either way, the issuer agrees to issue the credential, and the holder consents to accept it.

4 The issuer's agent and the holder's agent follow the specific protocol steps for issuing a credential in the desired format.

5 At the conclusion of the protocol, the issued credential is downloaded into the holder's wallet.

The credential-verification process proceeds with these general steps:

1 The holder requests some interaction with a verifier that requires verification (such as requesting access to a non-public web page).

2 The verifier presents a proof request to the holder (such as displaying a QR code that the holder can scan with a smartphone).

3 The holder's agent processes the proof request and determines whether the holder's wallet contains the credentials and/or claims necessary to satisfy it. If so, it prompts the holder to share a proof.

4 The holder consents to share the proof.

5 The holder's agent prepares the proof presentation and sends it to the verifier's agent.

6 The verifier's agent uses the issuer's DID in the proof response together with the credential definition (and any other information needed from the associated verifiable data registry) to verify the proof.

7 If the proof verifies, the holder is granted access.

One significant variation in this process is when the credential uses zero-knowledge proof (ZKP) cryptography. In this case, the holder's agent and wallet can support sophisticated selective disclosure features (see https://www.privacypatterns.org/patterns/Support-Selective-Disclosure). This means the verifier sees only the exact information required by the proof request. For example, if the verifier only needs to know the holder is over 21, the holder can prove that fact without revealing the holder's actual age or birthdate.

Support for ZKP-based verifiable credentials, which are explicitly supported in the W3C Verifiable Credentials Data Model standard, is one of the key differentiating features of SSI agents and wallets. The earliest work on this feature started in the Hyperledger Indy and Aries open source projects in 2018, but it is now spreading to other SSI digital wallet and VC projects.

9.6.4 Revoking and expiring digital credentials

Once a physical credential has been issued to a person and stored in their wallet, the only practical way to revoke it is to give it an expiration date. If the credential needs to be revoked before the expiration date—such as a driver's license being revoked due to traffic offenses or a passport being revoked due to a change in citizenship—the only way a verifier can check the revocation status is to contact the issuer.

With digital credentials, agents, and wallets, we can do better. In order of increasing preference:

- Verifiers can check with issuers via an online API. This is the least desirable option because it still requires verifiers to integrate with issuers, and it requires issuers to host a high-availability evocation API.

- Issuers can maintain a revocation registry using a Layer 1 verifiable data registry (VDR) such as a blockchain or distributed ledger. This solves the problem of verifiers needing to integrate with issuers—a verifier only needs to integrate with the VDR—and also of issuers needing to host their own revocation API. However, a conventional revocation registry can leak privacy information about revoked credentials.

- The most privacy-preserving solution is to maintain a revocation registry on a VDR that uses ZKP cryptography. This enables verifiers to check on the revocation status of a credential in near-real time but *only when a holder presents a proof.* Otherwise, the revocation registry does not reveal any information about what credentials have been revoked.

Again, all the complexity (and work) of updating and verifying a credential's revocation status is handled automatically by agents for the issuer, holder, and verifier.

9.6.5   *Authenticating: Logging you in*

Usernames and passwords are the banes of our online existence. Some of us maintain long lists in spreadsheets or word processors. Others use password managers like Apple Keychain, 1Password, LastPass, and Dashlane. Regardless of the solution, the problem is a universal headache—and with over 3 billion people online, that's a pretty big headache. It is also one of the weakest points of our cybersecurity infrastructure.

As chapter 4 explained, *auto-authentication* is one of the headline benefits of SSI. From what we've covered in this chapter so far, it should be easy to understand how your agent and wallet can finally relieve you of the burden of usernames and passwords—essentially eliminating the need for you to "log in" at all.

They simply do the job for you. The peer DID your agent negotiates when it first creates a new connection becomes your "username," and your digital signature on a message sent over the connection becomes your "password."

NOTE   Cryptographically, your digital signature, produced using the private key associated with your peer DID, is much stronger than any password.

This is already considered multi-factor authentication (MFA) because it requires both your digital wallet and at least a PIN or passcode to unlock it. A verifier that needs an even higher level of assurance that it's really you can request the following:

- A biometric (e.g., fingerprint, facial scan) to open your digital wallet
- A proof of one or more verifiable credentials in your wallet
- A *liveness check* (such as recording a short video) to prove that you—the person holding the wallet—are the holder to whom the credentials were issued

All of these are well-known MFA techniques that have been incorporated into federated identity standards like OpenID Connect and Fast IDentification Online (FIDO). SSI wallets and agents standardize and automate MFA in much the same way smartphones have automated the process of remembering and dialing phone numbers. As SSI adoption spreads, the process of manually entering a username and password to log in to a website will start to seem as antiquated as dialing a rotary telephone (digit … by … digit … by … digit).

9.6.6 Applying digital signatures

Just as your agent and wallet can digitally sign a message to authenticate you, they can sign almost any other digital object requiring your signature. The basic steps are as follows:

1. You establish a connection with the party requesting the signature (the verifier).
2. The verifier uses the connection to send you the object requiring your signature (e.g., a structured message, a PDF document, a JSON file). (Depending on the digital object, you can sign it directly or sign a hash of the object after your agent and wallet verify the hash. See chapter 6.)
3. Your agent prompts you to approve the signature request.
4. Your agent calls your digital wallet to generate the signature based on the appropriate DID and private key.
5. Your wallet returns the signature to the agent.
6. Your agent returns the signature to the verifier.

Note that this digital signature process is an order of magnitude stronger than most "electronic signature" services such as DocuSign, HelloSign, and PandaDoc. As a rule, those services do not apply cryptographically generated digital signatures; rather, they apply digital facsimiles of handwritten signatures. The latter are legally accepted in most jurisdictions, but they are not cryptographically bound to the underlying digital document.

9.7 Backup and recovery

At this point, it should be clear that a well-used digital wallet will rapidly become as valuable—if not more valuable—than a physical wallet. So what if you lose it or it is stolen, hacked, or corrupted?

Ironically, a well designed and engineered digital wallet should be *safer and better protected from loss* than a physical wallet—but *only if the owner takes the necessary recovery preparation steps*. This section explains why.

9.7.1 Automatic encrypted backup

Any commercial-grade SSI wallet should come with an automatic encrypted backup feature. After an initial setup step to establish your *recovery keys*, your agent will automatically and continuously maintain an encrypted backup copy of your wallet in the location of your choice. Usually, that means in the cloud—either on a generic cloud-based storage service like Dropbox or Google Drive or on a specialized encrypted backup service from your wallet/agent vendor.

> **NOTE** Unlike many crypto wallets, an SSI wallet requires a backup file *and* recovery keys. The backup file is needed because the wallet may be the only place where certain data exists.

This way, if anything happens to your wallet—e.g., your device is lost, stolen, corrupted, or broken—you can recover the contents of your digital wallet right up to the most recent actions you took with it. Recovery is typically performed using one of the options discussed next.

9.7.2 Offline recovery

The first option is to simply store a copy of your recovery keys in a safe location offline (*cold storage*) where you can find them when you need to recover (figure 9.3). This is not as easy as it sounds. To begin with, you have to hide your recovery keys in a safe place where only you or your trusted delegates can access them (otherwise, they could be used to steal your digital wallet without your permission).

Second, you need to be able to locate your recovery keys many years or even decades after you first store them. (Even safe deposit boxes in banks can be difficult to access after long periods of inactivity.)

Third, you need to make sure your recovery keys stay fully intact. For example, if you store them on a cold-storage device, such as a USB key, it better not suffer a hardware failure. If you store them on paper, such as a printed QR code or written passphrase, you must guard against the print fading over time or being incinerated in a fire. This is why some experts recommend etching recovery keys in titanium or another fireproof metal. (The Blockchain Commons Smart Custody Project has much more information about key backup and recovery options: https://www.smartcustody.com.)

Figure 9.3 Typical offline recovery techniques: QR codes and hardware cold-storage devices

Keep in mind that if your recovery key is lost or corrupted, *there is no other way to recover your digital wallet.* With SSI, there is no "password reset service" you can call and no higher authority to appeal too. If there were, it would not be self-sovereign—someone else would ultimately be in control.

9.7.3   *Social recovery*

A second option is called *social recovery* because it relies on one or more of your trusted connections to assist you in recovery. In this approach, rather than printing or saving your recovery key offline (or in addition to doing that), your agent and wallet use a cryptographic technique called *key sharding* to break your recovery key into several fragments. At least M of N of these fragments (for example, two out of three) must be brought back together to reproduce the original recovery key. Your agent then encrypts and shares a shard over the connection you have with each of your chosen *trustees*—the people or institutions you trust to safeguard the shard and return it to you (and only you) if you ever need to recover. This is illustrated in figure 9.4.

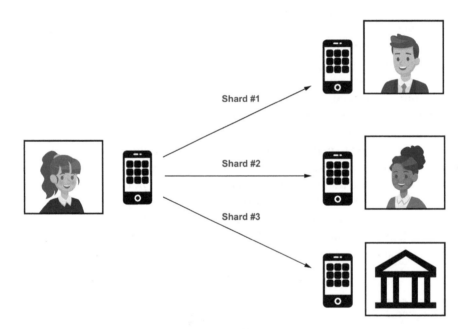

Figure 9.4   Sharing a sharded recovery key using social recovery

The primary advantages of social recovery are as follows:

- *It doesn't require storing or remembering the location* of an offline recovery key.
- *The recovery process can be performed entirely online,* provided you can contact a sufficient number of your trustees (and convince them it is really you).
- *You can periodically adjust your trustees* so they represent the connections you trust the most at any particular time.
- *Your agent can periodically remind you of your trustees* (and them of you) to make it easier to recover if you need to.

The downsides of social recovery are these:

- *A sufficient number of your trustees must be available* to decrypt and share back their shards when you need to recover.
- *Your trustees are potentially subject to a social engineering attack* by a determined adversary who wants to trick them into sharing enough shards to assemble your recovery key and steal your encrypted backup.

9.7.4 Multi-device recovery

A third option for recovery—and usually the easiest—is available if you have a digital wallet installed on more than one device. This option is essentially self-recovery because it works just like social recovery but is performed with your own family of devices. If one of your devices becomes lost, damaged, or corrupted, you use your other devices to share back shards of your recovery key to a new device. See section 9.8.1.

9.8 Advanced features of wallets and agents

This section covers more sophisticated capabilities that we expect to see on the market within a few years of this book's publication.

9.8.1 Multiple-device support and wallet synchronization

Multi-device support is a standard feature of many modern apps (e.g., Slack, Facebook, iMessage) and even operating systems (Apple Keychain, iCloud) because they want to provide a consistent user experience across all your devices. Generally, they do this by synchronizing each instance of the app via a cloud service.

Like these apps, your digital wallet will be immensely more useful if it can operate seamlessly across all your devices. However, synchronizing it is much more challenging due to the security requirements. Complete synchronization is often impossible because private keys simply cannot be copied out of secure enclaves or other hardware security modules, for good security reasons. And some high-assurance credentials may require binding the wallet to a particular device, requiring the credential to be re-issued to move it to a different wallet.

Open source projects and wallet/agent vendors are currently working on cross-wallet synchronization protocols that will address these challenges—while at the same time enabling digital wallet portability and interoperability. Early architectural work in this area began with the Decentralized Key Management System (DKMS) project contributed to Hyperledger Indy (http://mng.bz/5jP8) and continues in the DIDComm Working Group at the Decentralized Identity Foundation (https://identity.foundation/working-groups/did-comm.html).

9.8.2 Offline operations

Today, if you were driving too fast in the remote reaches of Canada and a Royal Canadian Mounted Police (RCMP) officer pulled you over and asked to see your driver's license, you would simply reach into your wallet and hand it over. Internet connectivity would not be a factor.

But if all you had was your digital wallet—and the only way you could show your driver's license was if you had an internet connection—that would be a problem. If you are in a no-coverage area—or if your data plan doesn't work in Canada—how can the officer verify your digital driver's license?

This is not a hypothetical situation. Governmental agencies in multiple countries and several U.S. states have already published requests for proposals (RFPs) for digital driver's licenses that require that they be verifiable without an internet connection. Many edge networking protocols such as Bluetooth and NFC enable this, so the only real obstacle is standardization and interoperability testing.

9.8.3   *Verifying the verifier*

Any new technology that offers significant new benefits also entails new risks. As SSI gains traction in the market, one risk that regulatory authorities like the European Commission are concerned about is *coercion*: verifiers abusing the power of SSI digital wallets and agents to make information quickly and easily available by coercing holders to share certain credentials or claims as a requirement of receiving service.

The Request for Comments (RFC) for the Trust over IP stack stated the risk of coercion this way:

> *The concept of "self-sovereign" identity presumes that parties are free to enter a transaction, to share personal and confidential information, and to walk away when requests by the other party are deemed unreasonable or even unlawful. In practice, this is often not the case… A point in case are the infamous cookie walls, where a visitor of a website get the choice between "accept all cookies or go into the maze-without-exit."*

NOTE See https://github.com/hyperledger/aries-rfcs/tree/master/concepts/0289-toip-stack#countermeasures-against-coercion. The section on anti-coercion was contributed by Oskar van Deventer of TNO in the Netherlands.

The RFC goes on to explain the basic strategy for protecting against such coercion:

> *Governance frameworks may be certified to implement one or more potential countermeasures against different types of coercion. In case of a machine readable governance framework, some such countermeasures may be automatically enforced, safeguarding the user from being coerced into action against their own interest.*

The number-one countermeasure recommended by this RFC has become known as *verifying the verifier*. It is a governance framework policy that requires a verifier to be authorized under the governance framework to make a particular proof request. The holder's agent can verify this authorization—typically by checking that the verifier's public DID is included in a verifiable data registry maintained by governance authority—before the agent even asks the holder for consent to share the proof. If the "verifying the verifier" check fails, the agent can not only refuse to proceed but can warn the holder of a possible scam—and even automatically report a possible violation to the governance authority.

This technique is not entirely new. Similar protections exist on global credit card networks today: for example, only an authorized Mastercard merchant network can request payment using a Mastercard. But with SSI, this kind of protection can be extended to any type of verifiable data exchange. And it can directly support data-protection regulations in various jurisdictions.

9.8.4   Compliance and monitoring

Verifying the verifier is just one type of regulatory or governance compliance for which an agent can monitor. As a trusted digital assistant (assuming the controller does trust the agent), an agent can watch for other behaviors, conditions, and actions:

- *Applicable governance frameworks*—Is a credential being issued under a governance framework that the controller trusts? If it is new, can the agent verify the bona fides of the governance authority? Who else is using or endorses the governance framework?
- *Sensitive data*—Is a verifier asking for especially sensitive data, and if so, why? See section 9.8.6 for how agents can recognize such requests.
- *Receipt tracking*—Agents can automatically categorize, store, and monitor your transaction receipts to help you analyze your activities. Personal finance software like Quicken and Mint already do this. So do personal health monitors like Apple Health and CommonHealth (https://www.commonhealth.org). Enterprise agents can monitor to be sure a transaction taken by an employee or contractor falls within the policies applicable to their role, e.g., buying authority, purchase categories, and spending limits.

Agents and wallets can also maintain *cryptographically verifiable audit logs* to enable forensic analysis if issues or problems arise. In some cases, particularly in an enterprise context, an agent may maintain a connection with and send regular reporting transactions to an independent *auditing agent*—one that may be hosted directly by a regulatory authority.

9.8.5   Secure data storage (vault) support

Just as your real-world wallet (or your pocket or purse) has a physical limit on how much it can carry, digital wallets are designed to store and protect a relatively limited amount of sensitive data. They are not generally designed to store your entire lifetime of financial records, tax records, health records (X-rays, CAT scans), educational records, portfolios, journals, files, and so on.

But you should have the capability to store any and all of these records under digital lock and key just as you would keep such documents safely in a fireproof file cabinet, home safe, or safe deposit box at a bank. Such a secure data store (SDS) has many names in the SSI community, including these:

- Personal data store (PDS)
- Personal cloud

- Hub (or identity hub)
- Vault (or encrypted data vault)

Regardless of the name, these all refer to the same basic design: electronic file storage (typically in the cloud) accessible only to the controller because the contents are encrypted with private keys from the controller's digital wallet. The Secure Data Storage Working Group is developing standards and open source implementations for interoperable SDSs at the Decentralized Identity Foundation (https://identity .foundation/working-groups/secure-data-storage.html).

9.8.6   *Schemas and overlays*

The credentials stored in a digital wallet are based on underlying schemas that define the semantics and data type for each claim (attribute) in the credential. However, data semantics can be extremely rich and complex. Take just one dimension: the name of a claim. What language is it in? Can you describe the name in different languages? How do you add that description without making the basic schema definition very complex?

The answer is an architecture called *schema overlays*. As shown in figure 9.5, schema overlays are descriptions of a base schema that can add rich descriptive and contextual metadata without complicating the base schema.

The Inputs and Semantics Working Group is standardizing this overlay-capture architecture (OCA) at the Trust over IP Foundation (https://wiki.trustoverip.org/ display/HOME/Inputs+and+Semantics+Working+Group). Digital wallets and agents that support schema overlays will make it easier for issuers, holders, and verifiers to

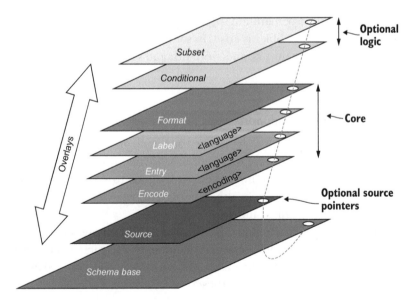

Figure 9.5   Different producers and consumers of data can develop multiple schema overlays to provide rich metadata describing a single set of data.

identify, describe, and manage the credentials and claims they need. To cite an example from earlier in this chapter, a regulatory agency or an industry watchdog organization can publish a schema overlay describing the degree of privacy sensitivity of the data contained in specific credentials. Agents and wallets can use this overlay to warn verifiers about requesting and holders about sharing such highly privacy-sensitive data.

9.8.7 Emergencies

Government agencies and medical authorities publish guidelines about what information people should make easily available in their physical wallets in case of a medical emergency such as an accident, a heart attack, or an allergic reaction. The same applies to our digital wallets—if not even more so, for these reasons:

- If first responders can access emergency information in a digital wallet, it will make such data easier and faster to obtain.
- The information available can be much richer and more current than the data typically available in a physical wallet.
- The digital wallet can be configured to enable first responders to access other medical records for the holder that may be even more helpful.
- The digital wallet can allow first responders to quickly reach emergency contacts while still respecting their privacy.

For all these reasons, proprietary smartphone wallets such as Apple Wallet already support an emergency mode. For example, the author of this chapter provides information about a peanut allergy that anyone can use if they have access to his phone.

However, the information is very limited, and there is no restriction on who can access the device. By contrast, if a bona fide first responder can prove that fact (e.g., using a standard First Responder credential that the agent can verify), the agent can release much more information.

9.8.8 Insurance

Where there is risk, there is insurance. With digital wallets, agents, and credentials, there are these risks:

- The vendor of the wallet or agent software is negligent or malicious.
- The issuer of a digital credential makes an error, or their system gets hacked.
- A holder of a digital wallet has it hacked or stolen, and as a result, crimes are committed, or their credit score is ruined.

All three of these risks can be mitigated with different forms of insurance:

- Wallet and agent software vendors can be insured against product liabilities.
- Issuers can insure against mistakes in issued credentials or compromises in the issuer's systems.
- Holders can insure against theft or loss of their digital wallet and the attendant damages.

Of course, the application for and issuance of an insurance policy for these types of coverage can be handled via—what else?—digital credentials. Having a cryptographically verifiable audit history of purchases by an insured party—such as a homeowner or business owner—can be extremely helpful in the unhappy situation of needing to file a claim due to loss from fire, theft, natural disaster, and so on.

9.9   *Enterprise wallets*

While the term *wallet* makes us think primarily about personal use, every entity participating in SSI needs a digital wallet. Even though organizations are run by people, jurisprudence requires that their legal identity (and thus their digital identity) *must* be separate from an individual. Even a sole proprietorship (a business operated by a single individual) is legally separate from the proprietor's personal identity.

So every organization, no matter what the size, should have its own separate *enterprise wallet*. While enterprise wallets need all the standard features we have discussed, they also require the special features covered in this section.

9.9.1   *Delegation (rights, roles, permissions)*

In the context of SSI, *delegation* refers to one identity controller giving permission to another to perform certain actions on the first controller's behalf. For example, an elderly parent might delegate to an adult child the authority to manage the parent's bank account. With verifiable credentials, this is accomplished using a *delegation credential*. See section 9.10 for more.

While individuals may or may not need delegation for their personal agents and wallets, organizations have no choice. Enterprise wallets must be able to delegate authority for specific transactions to specific individuals acting in specific roles within the organization. These types of functions are often managed by directory systems and identity and access management (IAM) systems within many enterprises, adapted to work with SSI and digital credentials.

Besides the other advantages of SSI, the use of digital credentials for delegation will make it easier to orchestrate and digitally execute legally binding transactions across companies and borders. Some verifiable credential ecosystems are being developed explicitly to support this capability. The Global Legal Entity Identifier Foundation (GLEIF, https://www.gleif.org) is developing the vLEI, a verifiable credential version of the Legal Entity Identifier (LEI); see https://www.gleif.org/en/newsroom/blog/advancing-a-global-standard-in-digital-trust-with-the-trust-over-ip-foundation).

Organizations of any kind can be issued a digital LEI to verify their legal status. An organization can issue delegation credentials to its employees, directors, and contractors so they can provide proof of the specific roles in which they are authorized to act and digitally sign documents on behalf of the organization in a specific capacity.

9.9.2   *Scale*

While millions or billions of personal wallets and agents may be active at the same time, each is running on its own computing device at the edge of the network, so questions of throughput and scale are no different from those that the internet and cloud computing face today. However, enterprise wallets and agents are a different question. Here, instead of a single person performing authentication or exchanging credentials, you may have hundreds of thousands of employees actively authenticating or presenting enterprise credentials at the same time. So the underlying wallets, agents, and agencies need to function at that kind of scale. See chapter 10, especially section 10.8, for more on this topic.

9.9.3 Specialized wallets and agents

Individuals are likely served by a single wallet and agent per device, even though the agent may apply specialized behaviors for specific types of connections or credential exchanges. But enterprises may require specialized wallets and agents optimized for specific groups of tasks. For example:

- *Accounting and Finance*—Management of purchasing, invoicing, receipts, and expense tracking will likely create its own mini-industry of specialized agents. For example, every employee's agent will probably have a connection to a Corporate Expense agent for automated expense tracking, reporting, and reimbursement.
- *Operations*—As covered in chapter 4, SSI will be a boon to business process automation. Many business processes can be orchestrated and automated by connecting employee and contractor agents to Business Process agents that apply the necessary business logic and help manage costly exceptions.
- *Compliance*—Recording and monitoring transactions for compliance with regulatory requirements can be simplified, and some cases can be automated, using Auditing and Reporting agents.
- *News*—Organizations thrive when different parts of the organization can share relevant and trusted information more quickly. As wallets and agents evolve, key events in which they participate (e.g., "contract signed," "purchase order received") can be shared instantly with looser integration than traditional systems integration requires.

9.9.4 Credential revocation

One of the classic challenges of IAM systems is managing hundreds of permissions across thousands of systems for millions of employees—and then updating them quickly when an employee's or contractor's status changes. With SSI, this complexity can be significantly reduced. The enterprise can issue revocable verifiable credentials, and every system or application can rely on them as a verifier. When an employee's or contractor's status changes, the relevant credentials can be revoked in near-real time without needing to know anything about what verifiers are relying on them.

9.9.5 Special security considerations

If personal wallets contain the keys to an individual's kingdom, imagine the potential damage if an enterprise wallet suffers a major breach of security. Corporate assets worth millions or billions of dollars could be at stake—not to mention corporate reputation.

The good news is that, like a bank vault, an enterprise wallet is built from the ground up to support the levels of security necessary to protect such valuable assets:

- *Multi-signature authorization policies*—Depending on the level of sensitivity of a particular transaction, it may require multiple digital signatures from different employees, officers, or directors.
- *Trust assurance frameworks*—Most enterprises will operate enterprise wallets and agents under the provisions of one or more governance frameworks. These will commonly include a trust assurance framework that will require many industry-standard security practices, such as ISO 27001 certification (https://www.iso.org/isoiec-27001-information-security.html), together with period testing and recertification.
- *Penetration testing*—Rather than wait for problems to surface, enterprises can pay white-hat professionals to find and fix vulnerabilities.
- *Automated monitoring and self-auditing*—Enterprise agents can use their own sophisticated monitoring and self-inspection tools that employ artificial intelligence (AI) and machine learning to detect anomalies and predict problems.
- *Device certification*—Some enterprise use cases will support only certain devices or digital wallets that have been certified to meet specific security/privacy standards or governance frameworks, particularly for high-assurance use cases.

9.10 Guardianship and delegation

As we said at the beginning of this chapter, a digital wallet is the nexus of control for every participant in the SSI infrastructure. As powerful as this tool is, it limits the direct use of SSI to individuals who have digital access and the legal capacity to use the technology. For SSI to work for everyone, it must work for individuals who do not have digital access or do not have the appropriate physical, mental, or economic capacity to use a digital wallet and agent. These individuals require another person or organization to serve as their *digital guardian.*

Digital guardianship is first and foremost a legal and regulatory construct, so it is covered in more detail in chapter 11. However, we cover two technical aspects of digital guardianship in this section.

9.10.1 Guardian wallets

For most intents and purposes, a digital wallet under guardianship is functionally identical to a conventional SSI digital wallet. The difference is that the wallet's controller is the guardian, not the individual who is the subject of the credentials in the wallet, who is called the *dependent.* When the guardian requests credentials on behalf of the dependent, or when the credentials are presented to a verifier on behalf of the dependent, it is the guardian who is asserting the dependent's rights to self-sovereign identity.

There are countless cases where this pattern is needed: parents acting on behalf of babies or young children; adult children acting on behalf of aging parents;

guardians acting on behalf of patients suffering from dementia or other physical or mental ailments; NGOs acting on behalf of refugees, homeless, or displaced populations; and so on.

The following distinguish guardian wallets:

- *They are typically hosted in the cloud.* This makes it easier for guardian delegates to access them using guardian credentials (see the next section). A service specializing in hosting guardian wallets is called a *guardian agency*.
- *They use biometrics to authenticate the presence of the dependent.* This is a safeguard against abuse that also provides a strong binding of the wallet and its contents to a specific human being. However, it is of paramount importance that any such biometrics be stored and managed following privacy-by-design principles that prevent the biometric from being stolen or weaponized against the dependent.
- *They are typically controlled using guardian credentials* (see the next section). This allows specifically authorized guardian delegates, such as members of a family or employees of an NGO, to take actions on behalf of a dependent but only after strongly authenticating themselves using their own SSI wallet and agent.
- *They usually operate under strict governance frameworks* that include special security, privacy, portability, and auditing requirements to prevent impersonation and abuse.

Ironically, a well-designed guardian wallet shares many features in common with an enterprise wallet because the set of directors, employees, or partners who control the enterprise wallet are essentially acting as "guardian delegates," just in a different legal capacity than an actual guardian.

9.10.2 *Guardian delegates and guardian credentials*

Guardians can be either individuals, such as parents for their children, or organizations, such as NGOs helping refugees or homeless persons. In the case of individuals, the guardian may or may not have a *guardianship credential*—a credential issued by a legal authority, such as a government agency that officially appoints the individual as a guardian. In the case of an organization, a guardianship credential is often a prerequisite for digital guardianship because it is required under a guardianship governance framework of some kind (see section 11.7 and the white paper "On Guardianship and Self-Sovereign Identity," Sovrin Guardianship Task Force, 2019, https://sovrin.org/wp-content/uploads/Guardianship-Whitepaper2.pdf).

When an organization is serving as a guardian, the actual actions taken on behalf of the dependent are taken by individuals acting as delegates of the organization. The best way to authorize these *guardian delegates* is using delegation credentials, covered earlier in this chapter. This way, each action taken on behalf of a dependent can be cryptographically verified as being taken by an authorized delegate on behalf of an authorized guardian organization.

9.11   Certification and accreditation

How will you know that you can trust a particular digital wallet or digital agent application? Given the highly personal and private data these applications will be storing and exchanging—and its high value to everyone from marketers to criminals—users will want some surety that the design and engineering are safe and their information isn't being leaked or shared inappropriately.

The standard solution for this kind of requirement is certification and accreditation programs such as those that exist for other categories of secure hardware and software like smartcards and hardware security modules. For particularly sensitive applications, such as banking or healthcare, you may have no choice but to use certified wallets and agents for your own safety.

However, this raises serious questions about user choice, self-sovereignty, and fair competition. Who gets to set the certification standards? (These are often tilted in favor of large industry players.) Who is going to accredit the accreditors? (Too often, these programs become slow and bureaucratic.) How much review is needed? (Having a trusted third party review an application for security or privacy flaws can be very expensive.)

Most of all, is it fair to ask Bubba, the masterful developer of Bubba's Wallet, to pay a third party $5,000 to certify his application? What if the amount is $50,000? $250,000? Higher? Will the cost of certification be so high that it stifles the innovation needed in the SSI digital wallet community?

And finally, who gets to provide the digital "seal of approval" that end users can trust to know that the hardware and/or software for a digital wallet and agent has been certified successfully and has not been tampered with since then? These questions are the perfect lead-in to the Wallet Wars.

9.12   The Wallet Wars: The evolving digital wallet/agent marketplace

> *Apple has recently registered a number of patent claims across the general field of "verified claims of identity" which have quite rightly attracted some attention... I think these applications are really important and that the fact that Apple wants to control means of presenting and verifying "identity" through devices, including iPhones, is a signal to the industry that the wallet wars are about to heat up.*
>
> —Dave Birch, *Forbes*, 29 August 2020 [1]

In the early days of the modern (post-web) internet, there were two distinct periods: the two Browser Wars. 1995–2001 saw the shift from Netscape to Internet Explorer (IE). Antitrust cases didn't save Netscape, and IE ended up dominating. In 2008, the introduction of Google's Chrome changed the field again. As of early 2019, Chrome and its Chromium engine-based brethren make up more than 70% of web browser activities—no other major browser exceeds 10% usage. Even Microsoft threw in the towel on its engine, adopting Chromium for its Edge browser in 2020.

Very little revenue has ever been claimed for the sale of web browsers. However, billions have been spent on R&D to create baseline capabilities to support browsing—and the underlying monetization regime that supports the commercial internet. The reason is simple: web browsers are a required internet tool, and having your eyeballs on a vendor's browser gives the vendor enormous power in the market.

A similar war is brewing over digital wallets—one that may eclipse the competitive landscape of web browsers. We will quickly explore three dimensions of these upcoming Wallet Wars:

- *Who* are the players that will attempt to influence or control your wallet (and agent)?
- *What* aspects of your wallet are they trying to influence and control?
- *How* they will exert this control and influence?

9.12.1 Who

In any large-scale shift, one of the most important things to understand is who the main players are and what they are attempting to accomplish. In the Wallet Wars, the players are diverse:

- *Governments and nation-states*—Regardless of the level of freedom a nation-state provides, it will want to control and influence some key aspects of the digital wallets used by its citizens.
- *Big tech*—The vast majority of big tech is heavily reliant on targeted advertising while espousing that they support privacy for all. As we adopt digital wallets and agents for more of our daily activity on the web, big tech may lose the ability to apply surveillance techniques to target us. They will adapt, but they will want to shape the battleground in their favor.
- *Telcos*—As the telecommunication business becomes more and more commoditized and telcos become pure data-pipe providers, they too are looking for a competitive advantage. And they have the benefit of already having a direct billing relationship with us.
- *Equipment and OS manufacturers*—Apple, Android, Samsung, Huawei, and others who build our devices (and the operating systems that run them) stand to be in a strong position of control. They have access to the lowest-level control points, starting with the specialized hardware (secure enclave; trusted execution environment) needed to support encryption, key management, and data availability. They also provide the layers of APIs that apps need to access these capabilities.
- *Financial institutions and payment networks*—Our current physical wallets and the early proprietary digital wallets (Apple Wallet, Google Pay, etc.) are centered around making payments easier while also capturing valuable intelligence about where we spend our money. This incentive will only increase as SSI-enabled digital wallets become a constant tool in all our digital relationships

and communications—which may give these players an even bigger role in our increasingly digital lives.

9.12.2 What

This chapter has provided a long list of the capabilities that digital wallets and agents provide. The Wallet Wars will likely focus on certain extra-strategic capabilities:

- *Security and encryption*—The underlying hardware (secure enclaves; trusted execution environments) and OS will be critical. Defining the highest levels of security will likely require a small set of hardware components that are certified and accredited for certain uses (e.g., digital passports, payment tokens).

- *Third-party insertion*—Many services from digital wallets and agents can be performed peer-to-peer without any intermediary or third party required. However, there are many cases where third parties can add value or can be inserted to help even if they are not strictly needed. They are points of control and influence.

- *Payments*—Payments are already a ripe area for consolidation. "Old tech" payment providers (Mastercard, Visa, Amex, China UnionPay) and "new tech" (Stripe, Square, PayPal, Apple Pay, AliPay, WeChat Pay) are all vying for a "top of wallet" position. This will intensify in our digital wallets.

- *Certification and accreditation*—As discussed in the previous section, knowing whether we can trust "Bubba's wallet" will become a key consideration of many governance frameworks (see chapter 11). As the industry matures, we may have no choice but to use an accredited wallet and agent for certain highly secure connections, credentials, and transactions, e.g., obtaining a digital version of our passport or making high-value payments.

- *Integration*—Many of us choose smartphones today because of how seamlessly they are integrated with many other aspects of our digital lives (laptops, smartwatches, cloud storage, email, calendaring, contacts, intelligent assistants, and so on). The same may apply to choosing a digital wallet and agent.

- *Portability and self-sovereignty*—This is a fascinating dimension of the competition between digital wallets and agents. As repeated multiple times in this book, "If it's not portable, it's not self-sovereign." As much as digital wallet vendors will want to add special features that entice us to use their wallet, if they try to lock us into those features, they lose out on this feature.

9.12.3 How

Like the Browser Wars, the strategies and tactics of the Wallet Wars are likely to be manifold. Some chess moves will be obvious, while others will happen in the background and won't be understood until much later. A few of the chess pieces are as follows:

- *Standards*—Anyone who has worked on them knows how open standards can easily be weaponized. There are many tactics for doing this: rushing standards to market, slowing them to a snail's pace, watering down features to such a low common denominator that they aren't useful, and so on. Even if the standards effort is well-intentioned, premature standardization can be a problem, especially for a technology as young as SSI. As shown in figure 9.6, standards and protocols take time to evolve. (For a full treatment of this topic, see Darrell O'Donnell, "Protocol Evolution," Continuum Loop, 2018, https://www .continuumloop.com/protocol-evolution.)

- *Regulation*—Identity and money are two facets of our lives in which governments have been involved since the dawn of civilization. This probably will not change with digital wallets. Some role may be justified—at times. The hard part will be setting the boundaries for what is appropriate versus what is overreach.

- *Open source projects*—As open source becomes more prevalent, players are beginning to create new projects or shift existing projects to meet their goals. Altruism is great, but this is one gift horse you should look in the mouth. Examine the incentives of the sponsors and contributors. Are they all contributing to the good of the internet? What are their other objectives, and do they align with yours?

- *"Freeware" and limiting functionality*—Free tools have become the norm on the internet, but, as we know, nothing is ever truly free. We pay with our attention, our data, or both. With digital wallets and agents, the bargain is different than with websites and digital advertising. It will be fascinating to see what new bargains digital wallet/agent vendors will offer in the land of SSI.

- *Convenience and usability*—Ultimately, the best UX that provides the most value from digital wallets and agents is likely to win. Who will drive that UX? Will it be the same for everybody, or will it have many different niches and flavors? This is likely where the Wallet Wars will be won.

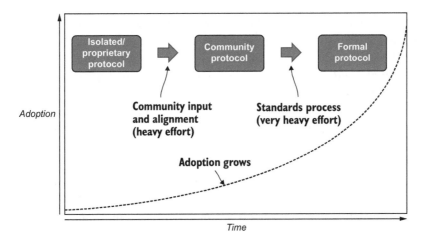

Figure 9.6 Protocols and standards often take years to evolve in order to reach broad adoption.

This chapter has covered an enormous amount of ground on the subject of digital wallets and agents. These are the key takeaways:

- SSI digital wallets are conceptually very similar to physical wallets except for the credentials they hold, and the functions they can perform will be much smarter.
- Every digital wallet is paired with a digital agent: the software module that mediates all interactions between the wallet, the user, and other agents.
- SSI digital wallets differ from previous generations of digital wallets because they follow different design principles, including being portable and open by default, being consent-driven, using privacy by design, and using security by design.
- An SSI digital wallet's basic anatomy includes four primary agent functions (messaging, routing, backup and recovery, and secure storage) and two secure storage functions (encrypted storage and a key management system).
- Standard features of most SSI digital wallets include notification and user experience; receiving, offering, and presenting digital credentials; revoking and expiring credentials; authentication (login); applying digital signatures; and handling backup and recovery.
- Backup and recovery are critically important for SSI digital wallets because there is no higher authority to fall back on. They must include an automatic encrypted backup function and multiple options for recovering a lost, stolen, damaged, or hacked wallet, such as offline recovery methods (e.g., QR codes or cold storage devices); social recovery methods, where your recovery key is cryptographically broken into pieces and shared with trusted connections; or multi-device recovery methods.
- The SSI digital wallet space is evolving *very* rapidly, and advanced features that we see coming include multi-device support, multi-language support, offline operations, anti-coercion and data safety, compliance monitoring, secure data storage support, emergency data access, and insurance options.
- Digital guardianship requires special guardian wallets that can be hosted in the cloud and include special features such as biometric verification, delegation credentials, and automated enforcement of guardianship governance policies to prevent abuse.
- Certification and accreditation programs for digital wallets and agents will be inevitable given the highly sensitive data they handle and the potential for hacking or abuse. The big question is whether these programs will evolve in a way that is compatible with an open, fair, competitive market.
- In the next evolutionary stage of the internet, SSI digital wallets are expected to be as strategic as browsers. This means the Wallet Wars will see many of the same competitors and tactics—if not more so. Pay attention: self-sovereignty is what is ultimately at stake.

The function at the very core of digital wallets—key management—is so important that we made it the subject of the next chapter.

SSI Resources

We invite you to learn more about the evolution of digital wallets at https://ssi meetup.org/state-digital-identity-crypto-wallets-darrell-odonnell-webinar-22.

Reference

1. Birch, David G.W. "Apple Pay Was Not Disruptive, but Apple ID Will Be." *Forbes*. https://www.forbes.com/sites/davidbirch/2020/08/29/apple-pay-was-not-disruptive-but-apple-id-will-be/#52310fb44d0f.

Decentralized key management

Dr. Sam Smith

Chapter 9 covered the overall topic of SSI digital wallets and agents. However, the function at the very core of digital wallets—cryptographic key management—is deep enough to merit its own chapter. Although thousands of papers and dozens of books have been written on the subject of key management, for this chapter on decentralized key management, we called on Dr. Sam Smith, who is not only one of the most prolific thinkers and authors in SSI but the inventor of Key Event Receipt Infrastructure (KERI), covered in the final section of this chapter. Sam received his PhD in electrical and computer engineering from Brigham Young University in 1991; spent 10 years at Florida Atlantic University, reaching full professor status; and then retired to become a full-time entrepreneur and strategic consultant. He has over 100 refereed publications in the areas of machine learning, AI, autonomous vehicle systems, automated reasoning, blockchains, and decentralized systems.

Chapter 9 began with this overarching definition of digital wallets:

> *A digital wallet consists of software (and optionally hardware) that enables the wallet's controller to generate, store, manage, and protect cryptographic keys, secrets, and other sensitive private data.*

We followed that by saying that a digital wallet is the *nexus of control* for every actor in SSI. The essence of that control is *key management*: everything involved with the generation, exchange, storage, use, termination/destruction, and rotation/replacement of cryptographic keys. It includes design of cryptographic protocols, key servers, and secure storage modules. Key management also encompasses human processes such as organizational policies, user training, certification, and auditing.

In this chapter, we cover the following:

- Why any form of digital key management is hard
- Standards and best practices for conventional key management
- The starting point for key management architectures: roots of trust
- The special challenges of *decentralized* key management
- The new tools that verifiable credentials (VCs), decentralized identifiers (DIDs), and self-sovereign identity (SSI) bring to decentralized key management
- Key management for ledger-based DID methods
- Key management for peer-based DID methods
- Fully autonomous decentralized key management with Key Event Receipt Infrastructure (KERI)

The final section on KERI is a special feature of this book as it summarizes the technical architecture of KERI, one of the most comprehensive solutions for decentralized cryptographic key management available at the time of publication.

10.1 *Why any form of digital key management is hard*

People new to cryptography and public/private key infrastructure often wonder why there is so much fuss about keys. Isn't managing digital keys similar to managing physical keys, where we usually have a small set that we keep on a key ring or fob?

While there is clearly an analogy between physical and digital keys, in reality the differences are dramatic:

- *Digital keys can be stolen remotely.* Stealing a physical key requires having physical access to where the key is stored—or to the person who is carrying it. Digital keys that are not properly protected can be stolen remotely over a network. Even when they are well-guarded, digital keys can still be stolen using side-channel attacks (but those are very hard to pull off).
- *You may not be able to tell if a digital key has been stolen.* A stolen physical key is easy to spot (unless the thief can quickly copy and replace it—a real challenge). But if an attacker can gain access to a digital key, they can copy it in milliseconds without you ever even knowing.
- *Digital locks are much harder to pick.* The alternative to stealing a physical key is breaking the lock. For many real-world assets, like a car or a home, that is entirely feasible. Breaking a digital lock protected with strong encryption is nearly impossible.
- *The value that digital keys can unlock may be vastly greater than in the physical world.* Most assets protected by a physical key—a car, a house, a bank vault—have a value proportional to the strength of the physical security provided for the asset. But with digital assets, a single key can potentially unlock billions of dollars of value in the form of cryptocurrencies, digital fiat currencies, or some other form of digital asset.

NOTE   Anyone protecting high-value digital assets should be using multisignature (*multisig*) because its security scales much faster than the size of the digital asset. For example, there are no reported cases of exploiting the Gnosis multisig Ethereum wallet (https://gnosis-safe.io) despite some of those wallets holding billions in assets.

- *If lost or stolen, digital keys can be irreplaceable.* This is the real kicker. It is nearly impossible to protect a physical asset with enough physical security that it cannot be broken given enough time and money. But digital assets can be protected with encryption so strong (even quantum-proof) that, in theory, it can withstand all the computing power in the universe for the rest of time (or at least the next few millennia). So digital keys can be almost immeasurably more valuable than physical keys. In 2019, the *Wall Street Journal* estimated that one-fifth of all bitcoin is missing because the private keys have been irretrievably lost [1]. At the time we are writing these lines, that lost bitcoin is worth well over $100 *billion.*

- *With SSI, your digital keys will become the "keys to your digital life."* It is hard to say that about your physical keys. Yes, they are important; they unlock your car, house, mailbox, office, and safe deposit box. But if you lost the whole set, it would only take you a few days or weeks to replace all of them. If you lost all the keys in a mature SSI digital wallet (and did not have a recovery method), it could put your digital life on hold for months.

The bottom line: control over your digital keys—as well as the rest of the contents of your digital wallet—is probably the single most critical element of the SSI architecture.

10.2   *Standards and best practices for conventional key management*

Fortunately, digital key management is not new—we have decades of experience deploying it with conventional PKI and, more recently, with cryptocurrency keys and wallets. Moreover, since key management is fundamental to cybersecurity infrastructure, research bodies like the U.S. National Institute of Standards and Technology (NIST) have published extensive recommendations on the subject. Several of the best known from NIST are as follows:

- *NIST Special Publication 800-130: A Framework for Designing Cryptographic Key Management Systems (CKMS)*—A 112-page publication that provides a comprehensive guide to every topic in key management (https://nvlpubs.nist.gov/nistpubs/SpecialPublications/NIST.SP.800-130.pdf)
- *NIST Special Publication 800-57: Recommendation for Key Management*—A three-part series that NIST is constantly updating (https://csrc.nist.gov/projects/key-management/key-management-guidelines):
    - Part 1—General
    - Part 2—Best Practices for Key Management Organizations
    - Part 3—Application Specific Key Management Guidance

Following is an example of some of the guidelines from section 2 of NIST 800-57 Part 2 (https://nvlpubs.nist.gov/nistpubs/SpecialPublications/NIST.SP.800-57pt2r1.pdf):

> *Because the compromise of a cryptographic key compromises all of the information and processes protected by that key, it is essential that client nodes be able to trust that keys and/or key components come from a trusted source, and that their confidentiality (if required) and integrity have been protected both in storage and in transit.*

> *In the case of secret keys, the exposure of a key by any member of a communicating group or on any link between any pair in that group compromises all of the information that was shared by the group using that key. As a result, it is important to avoid using a key from an unauthenticated source, to protect all keys and key components in transit, and to protect stored keys for as long as any information protected under those keys requires protection.*

Section 2.3.9 of the latest version of NIST 800-57 Part 2 includes this guidance about centralized vs. decentralized key management:

> *A CKMS can be either centralized or decentralized in nature. For a PKI, the public key does not require protection, so decentralized key management can work efficiently for both large-scale and small-scale cases. The management of symmetric keys, particularly for large-scale operations, often employs a centralized structure.*

As you might expect, many standards and protocols have been developed for different aspects of key management. For example, section 2.3.10 of NIST 800-57 Part 2 (https://nvlpubs.nist.gov/nistpubs/SpecialPublications/NIST.SP.800-57pt2r1.pdf) includes a list of 14 Requests for Comments (RFCs) for key management from the Internet Engineering Task Force (IETF). NIST Special Publication 800-152 (https://doi.org/10.6028/NIST.SP.800-152) contains requirements for the design, implementation, or procurement of a CKMS meeting the standards of the U.S. Federal Government.

Another example is the Key Management Interoperability Protocol (KMIP) that has been developed at the Organization for Structured Information Standards (OASIS) since 2010. It has become the industry standard for interoperability of centralized key management servers, which are typically deployed by an enterprise to standardize and automate key management across a large number of applications and services.

10.3 The starting point for key management architecture: Roots of trust

Whether a key management architecture is centralized, federated, or decentralized, it all begins with a *root of trust* (aka *trust root* or *trust anchor*). The root of trust is the starting point in a *chain of trust* because it is the only point in the chain where trust does not need to be *derived* (meaning verified by some means). Instead, trust is *assumed* in the root of trust, i.e., verifiers simply accept axiomatically that the root of trust can be trusted.

In conventional PKI architecture such as the X.509 standards, the root of trust is represented by a special digital certificate called the *root certificate*. A relying party (also called the *trusting party*) must have a copy of the root certificate already in its possession before it can do any further validation of a trust chain. This is why most computer and mobile operating systems provide built-in lists of root certificates. So do browsers like Firefox and Chrome. This means the user is implicitly trusting the software or browser manufacturer and also the certification authority (CA) that issued the root certificate.

The reason SSI represents such a sea change in key management is that it starts with a different set of assumptions about roots of trust, as illustrated in figure 10.1:

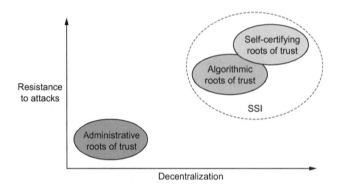

Figure 10.1 **SSI starts with different assumptions about a root of trust—rather than administrative roots, SSI uses algorithmic or self-certifying roots.**

- *Administrative roots of trust* are used in conventional PKI: certificate authorities (CAs) staffed by humans who follow rigorous procedures (Certification Practice Statements) to ensure the quality and integrity of the digital certificates they issue. Assumed trust in administrative roots of trust is based on the service provider's reputation as attested by industry certifications and accreditations.

- *Algorithmic roots of trust* (also called *transactional roots of trust*) are based on computer algorithms designed to create secure systems where no single party is in control yet all parties can agree on a shared source of truth. Blockchains, distributed ledgers, and distributed file systems like InterPlanetary File System (IPFS) are all examples of algorithmic roots of trust. (See chapter 5 for a complete description of how different SSI architectures use various algorithmic roots of trust.) Although all algorithmic roots of trust are based on cryptography, assumed trust requires more than that—it is based on the reputation of the system as a whole, e.g., the number and size of participants, the history of the project, how long the ledger has been running, whether there have been any security issues, and the prospect (or history) of forking. However, as we explain in chapter 15, there are plenty of disagreements about which of these approaches is most trustworthy.

- *Self-certifying roots of trust* (also known as *autonomic roots of trust*) are based solely on secure random number generation and cryptography. In the case of SSI, this means DIDs that can be generated using only a digital wallet. The most secure self-certifying roots of trust use special hardware such as a secure enclave or a trusted processing module (TPM) to generate and key pairs and store private keys. Assumed trust in self-certifying roots of trust is based on the specifications, testing, certification, and reputation of the hardware and software.

The reasons these distinctions are so important are summarized in table 10.1.

Table 10.1   Summary of the differences among the three types of roots of trust

Property	Administrative root of trust	Algorithmic root of trust	Self-certifying root of trust
Centralized / single point of failure	Yes	No	No
Requires human involvement in validation	Yes	No	No
Requires the involvement of external parties	Yes	Yes	No

In short, the paradigm shift to SSI and decentralized key management is the shift from *administrative* roots of trust—which are inherently centralized and subject to human fallibility—to *algorithmic* and *self-certifying* roots of trust, which can be partially or fully automated and decentralized. The only difference between algorithmic and self-certifying roots of trust is the role of any third party (discussed later in this chapter).

10.4   The special challenges of decentralized key management

While decades of work have gone into centralized key management practices, decentralized key management is a much newer topic. It barely existed until the first version of the DID (see chapter 8) was published as a community specification in December 2016. Since DIDs are both decentralized and cryptographically verifiable, they demanded a decentralized solution for managing the associated public/private keys. The growing interest in DIDs led the U.S. Department of Homeland Security (DHS) to award a research contract on decentralized key management to SSI vendor Evernym in 2017 [2]. As the announcement summarized:

> *Through a project titled "Applicability of Blockchain Technology to Privacy Respecting Identity Management," Evernym is developing a DKMS—a cryptographic key management approach used with blockchain and other distributed-ledger technologies—to boost online authentication and verification. Within a DKMS, the initial "root of trust" for all participants is a distributed ledger that supports a decentralized identifier—a new form of root identity record.*

DKMS stands for *decentralized key management system* (in contrast to CKMS, *cryptographic key management system*). In the two-year research project, Evernym assembled a group of cryptographic engineers and key management experts to produce a document called "DKMS Design and Architecture" that was published as part of the Hyperledger Indy project at the Linux Foundation (http://mng.bz/5jP8). The introduction states:

> *DKMS (Decentralized Key Management System) is a new approach to cryptographic key management intended for use with blockchain and distributed ledger technologies (DLTs) where there are no centralized authorities. DKMS inverts a core assumption of conventional PKI (public key infrastructure) architecture, namely that public key certificates will be issued by centralized or federated certificate authorities (CAs).*

As stated in section 1.3 of this document, DKMS is designed to provide the following major benefits:

- *No single point of failure*—Since DKMS uses either algorithmic or self-certifying roots of trust, there is no reliance on a central CA or other registration authority whose failure can jeopardize large swaths of users.
- *Interoperability*—DKMS enables any two identity owners and their applications to perform key exchange and create encrypted peer-to-peer (P2P) connections without reliance on proprietary software, service providers, or federations.
- *Portability*—With DKMS, users can avoid being locked into any specific implementation of a DKMS-compatible wallet, agent, or agency. Users should—with the appropriate security safeguards—be able to use the DKMS protocol to move the contents of their wallet (although not necessarily the actual cryptographic keys) between compliant DKMS implementations.
- *Resilient trust infrastructure*—DKMS incorporates all the advantages of distributed ledger technology for decentralized access to cryptographically verifiable data. It then adds on top of it a distributed web of trust where any peer can exchange keys, form connections, and issue/accept verifiable credentials from any other peer. (*DKMS Design and Architecture* was published before the invention of KERI. However, it is compatible with KERI's fully decentralized key management architecture. See the final sections of this chapter.)
- *Key recovery*—Rather than app-specific or domain-specific key-recovery solutions, with DKMS, robust key recovery should be built directly into the infrastructure, including agent-automated encrypted backup, DKMS key escrow services, and social recovery of keys—for example, by backing up or sharding keys across trusted DKMS connections and agents. (See chapter 9 for more about the role of SSI digital wallets and agents in key recovery.)

To provide these benefits, however, DKMS needs to address the following challenges:

- *There cannot be any "higher authority" to fall back on.* It is surprising how much simpler you can make a system if you know you can ultimately fall back on a centralized authority. But with DKMS, there is no "password reset" option. If there is an outside authority to whom you can turn to replace your keys, then that authority can always take away your keys—or their systems can be compromised to break into your keys. So a DKMS system must be designed to be failsafe for the key holders from the start.
- *DKMS cannot come from a single company—or even a single consortium.* It must be based entirely on open standards that any open source project or commercial vendor can implement—much like the W3C Verifiable Credentials and Decentralized Identifier standards that are already foundational for SSI. This eliminates the proprietary approaches of some of the popular secure chat products today, e.g., Apple iMessage and Facebook Messenger.
- *DKMS cannot dictate a single cryptographic algorithm or cipher suite that everyone must use.* Many problems can be solved by everyone agreeing on the same

cryptography. But there are simply too many options—and the field is advancing too fast—for DKMS to lock into a single type of cryptography. DKMS must be able to accommodate the evolutionary advancement of cryptographic algorithms and protocols.

- *DKMS key and wallet data must be portable across different technical implementations from different vendors.* As often said in SSI circles, "If it's not portable, it's not self-sovereign." Furthermore, portability must be proven against formal interoperability testing, not just marketing slogans.
- *DKMS cannot assume any specialized knowledge or skills on behalf of end users.* DKMS-enabled digital wallets and agents must be as easy—or easier—to use as modern browsers and email clients. Most of all, they cannot require end users to understand anything about cryptography, blockchains, SSI, or even the concept of public/private keys. It just needs to work—*and* be secure.

Some developers reading these requirements might throw up their hands and say it cannot be done. However, a growing community of architects, cryptographers, and usability experts are intent not just on doing it, but on baking the solution deep into the infrastructure of the internet so it is available to everyone, just as email and the web are today.

10.5 The new tools that VCs, DIDs, and SSI bring to decentralized key management

SSI depends on decentralized key management, but it also brings new tools to the table to enable it. In this section, we list the specific contributions from VCs (chapter 7), DIDs (chapter 8), and digital wallets and agents (chapter 9).

10.5.1 Separating identity verification from public key verification

In addition to decentralized roots of trust, the primary innovation enabling DKMS is the ability of DIDs to separate the verification of the public key of a DID controller from verification of other identity attributes such as the controller's legal name, URL, address, government ID number, and so on. With conventional PKI, these two steps are bound together in the issuance of an X.509 digital certificate by a certificate authority (CA). This is shown in figure 10.2 (taken from the in-depth explanation of how DIDs work in chapter 8).

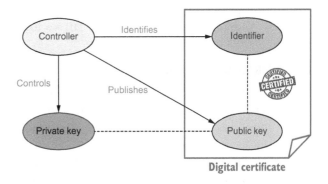

Figure 10.2   How conventional PKI-based digital certificates bind together identification of an entity with verification of the entity's public key

With SSI, a DID is generated from a public/private key pair using either an algorithmic root of trust or a self-certifying root of trust. This means the DID controller can always provide proof of control of their DID by using their own private key to digitally sign their own DID document, as shown in figure 10.3 (also taken from chapter 8).

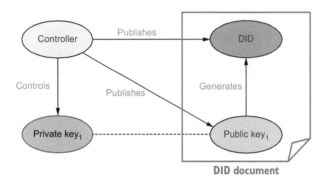

Figure 10.3   DIDs enable identity controllers to prove their own public keys without an intermediary by digitally signing their own DID documents.

If the DID method uses a self-certifying root of trust, the key-generation and -rotation operations may take place entirely under the aegis of the DID controller—in their digital wallet or some other key-generation and -signing system they control. If the DID method uses an algorithmic root of trust, a second step is needed: a transaction with an external verifiable data registry (VDR) such as a blockchain. However, in both cases, these steps can be performed automatically by the DID controller's agent without human intervention. Eliminating the need for a human in the loop provides two other major benefits: the cost of these steps can drop to nearly zero, and the scale at which DIDs can be generated and used increases dramatically. The combination removes any barrier to DID controllers having as many DIDs as they need.

> **NOTE** See chapter 8 for more about how random-number generation and cryptographic algorithms enable the creation of an almost infinite number of public/private key pairs and DIDs without collusion. This is the essence of what enables decentralization.

10.5.2 *Using VCs for proof of identity*

If DIDs and DID documents can handle the challenge of key verification, that leaves VCs to do what they do best: convey third-party attestations of the real-world identity attributes of the DID controller. This is what a verifier needs to establish real-world business or social trust.

Furthermore, by separating identity verification from public-key verification, the number and diversity of issuers for identity verification attributes should grow much larger. This gives both DID controllers and verifiers a wider range of choices and lowers the cost for everyone.

10.5.3 *Automatic key rotation*

Another core key-management problem that DIDs help solve—also explained in depth in chapter 8—is automated key rotation. Because the DID is an immutable identifier, all DID methods (except a special category called *static*) define how the DID controller can change the public/private key pair(s) associated with the DID by publishing an update to the associated DID document. The specifics of how this is done vary with different DID methods, but they all follow the same principle: the DID controller can accomplish key rotation without the need to rely on any external administrator.

10.5.4 *Automatic encrypted backup with both offline and social recovery methods*

The fact that SSI digital wallets cannot appeal to a higher authority to reset the password or replace the keys means backup and recovery must be built directly into the infrastructure. This can be accomplished by building backup and recovery functions directly into digital wallets and agents, as described in chapter 9, or by using special key-recovery capabilities designed into specific DID methods—or both. See section 10.8 for more about the sophisticated decentralized key-recovery architecture built into KERI.

10.5.5 *Digital guardianship*

With centralized key-management systems, key servers operated by corporations or governments can serve a wide population of users with different levels of capabilities. With decentralized key management, a solution needs to cover individuals who lack the physical, mental, or economic capability to operate their own devices and manage their own keys. This critical aspect of SSI infrastructure is referred to as *digital guardianship*, a topic covered in more detail in chapter 11.

Ironically, from a high level, digital guardians can look very much like centralized key-management systems. Under the hood, however, they are very different. Guardians typically host individual cloud wallets for each person depending on them, called the *dependent*. Guardians are usually issued *guardianship credentials* by an official authority to authorize their guardianship role; they in turn issue *delegation credentials* to staff people or contractors to authorize their actions. Finally, digital guardians usually operate under a governance framework that places strict legal requirements on their roles as information fiduciaries. (See "Information Fiduciaries and the First Amendment" by Jack M. Balkin: https://lawreview.law.ucdavis.edu/issues/49/4/Lecture/49-4_Balkin.pdf.) Since any person or organization can operate as a digital guardian—and digital guardianship uses the same open standards and infrastructure as the rest of SSI—it extends the ability to control and manage digital keys to those who could not do it on their own.

10.6   *Key management with ledger-based DID methods (algorithmic roots of trust)*

All DID methods rely on a root of trust, as shown in figure 10.1—a starting point for proving the chain of trust based on a public/private key pair. Although the key pair is usually generated in secure hardware using a long random number (see https://tools.ietf.org/html/rfc4086 for how to do this securely), most DID methods do not rely on this root of trust alone (i.e., they are not *self-certifying*). They require a second step: using the private key to digitally sign a transaction in a distributed ledger or blockchain to "record" the DID and the initial associated public key. Once that record is created, the ledger becomes the *algorithmic* root of trust for the DID.

This means verifiers must check with the ledger to verify the current public key and any other contents of the DID document associated with the DID. In other words, verifiers must trust:

- The consensus algorithm and the operation of the particular ledger: i.e., its ability to withstand a 51% attack or any other form of corruption or attack
- The security of the resolver used to access records on the ledger
- The genesis records used by the resolver (or the verifier) to verify resolution results

Given the success of large, well-established public blockchains like Bitcoin and Ethereum, together with the well-known mechanisms for verifying lookups from those ledgers, these are widely considered to be strong algorithmic roots of trust. In addition, for many DIDs, it is desirable for them to be publicly resolvable and verifiable. Thus it is no surprise that, as of early 2021, 95% of the over 80 DID methods registered in the W3C DID Specification Registry (https://www.w3.org/TR/did-spec-registries) use DID methods based on an algorithmic root of trust.

But ledger-based DID methods also have several downsides:

- *Dependency on another party or network*—Although the ultimate root of trust is still the key pair used to generate the DID and update the DID document on the ledger, a ledger-based DID method requires a DID controller to depend on a distributed ledger and its associated governance mechanisms to be trustworthy. To the extent a DID controller can count on the ledger to be incorruptible and always available, that risk may be small, but it is still non-zero. For example, all distributed ledgers are subject to 51% attacks, forking, and changes in their governance or regulatory status.
- *Non-portability ("ledger lock")*—Ledger-based DIDs are "locked" to a specific ledger and cannot be moved if problems develop with the ledger or its governance—or if the DID controller desires to use other DID methods.
- *Potential conflicts with the GDPR "right to be forgotten"*—While not an issue with DIDs meant for use by organizations (or things), DIDs and public keys for personal use are considered "personal data" under the EU General Data Protection Regulation (GDPR) and thus subject to the *right of erasure*, popularly known

as "the right to be forgotten." This can be a serious issue for immutable public ledgers. Because these ledgers co-mingle transactions from all users, transactions for a given DID may not be removable without destroying the integrity of the ledger for all the other users.

NOTE For an in-depth discussion of this problem, see the Sovrin Foundation white paper "Innovation Meets Compliance: Data Privacy Regulation and Distributed Ledger Technology": https://sovrin.org/data-protection.

10.7 Key management with peer-based DID methods (self-certifying roots of trust)

Once DIDs and DKMS started to catch on, it was not long until some security architects realized that, while ledger-based DIDs have many advantages, the use of a ledger is not technically required to gain the benefits of DIDs. Given that the ultimate root of trust is the long random number on which a public/private key pair is based—and that this root of trust exists only in the DID controller's digital wallet—these architects saw that for many scenarios, DIDs and DID documents that were *self-certifying* could be generated entirely within a digital wallet and exchanged directly—peer-to-peer. (Self-certifying identifiers [SCIDs] are explained further in the following section.)

This led to the development of the `did:peer:` method defined by the Peer DID Method Specification (https://identity.foundation/peer-did-method-spec), first published by Daniel Hardman in 2018. As of August 2020, this specification had 15 contributing authors and had moved to the Identifier and Discovery Working Group at the Decentralized Identity Foundation for further standardization (https://identity .foundation/working-groups/identifiers-discovery.html). To quote from the overview:

> *Most documentation about decentralized identifiers (DIDs) describes them as identifiers that are rooted in a public source of truth like a blockchain, a database, a distributed filesystem, or similar. This publicness lets arbitrary parties resolve the DIDs to an endpoint and keys. It is an important feature for many use cases. However, the vast majority of relationships between people, organizations, and things have simpler requirements. When Alice (Corp|Device) and Bob want to interact, there are exactly and only 2 parties in the world who should care: Alice and Bob. Instead of arbitrary parties needing to resolve their DIDs, only Alice and Bob do. Peer DIDs are perfect in these cases.*

In many ways, peer DIDs are to public, blockchain-based DIDs what Ethereum Plasma state channels are to on-chain smart contracts—or what Bitcoin's Lightning Network is to on-chain cryptocurrency transactions. The Peer DID Method *specification* goes on to list these benefits of peer DIDs:

- They have no transaction costs, making them essentially free to create, store, and maintain.
- They scale and perform entirely as a function of participants, not based on any central system's capacity.
- Because they are not persisted in any central system, there is no trove to protect.

- Because only the parties to a given relationship know them, concerns about personal data and privacy regulations due to third-party data controllers or processors are much reduced.
- Because they are not beholden to any particular blockchain, they have minimal political or technical baggage.
- They can be mapped into the namespaces of other DID ecosystems, allowing a peer DID to have predictable meaning in one or more other blockchains. This creates an interoperability bridge and solves a problem with blockchain forks fighting over the ownership of a DID.
- Because they avoid a dependence on a central source of truth, peer DIDs free themselves from the often-online requirement that typifies most other DID methods and are thus well suited to use cases that need a decentralized peer-oriented architecture. Peer DIDs can be created and maintained for an entire lifecycle without any reliance on the internet, with no degradation of trust. They thus align closely with the ethos and the architectural mindset of the local-first (https://www.inkandswitch.com/local-first.html) and offline-first (http://offlinefirst.org) software movements.

Key rotation and key recovery with peer DIDs are a matter of each peer, as the controller of their own peer DID, communicating updates to their peer DID document to the other peer. This is the purpose of the *peer DID protocol* defined in section 4 of the Peer DID Method Specification. It defines the standard for the DID CRUD (create, read, update, and deactivate) operations peers must perform:

1 *Create/register* peer DIDs and DID documents with each other.
2 *Read/resolve* peer DIDs.
3 *Update* peer DID documents for key rotation, service endpoint migration, or other changes.
4 *Deactivate* a peer DID to end a peer relationship.

Peer DIDs bypass the need for an algorithmic root of trust because they are based directly on the self-certifying root of trust used to generate the initial key pair without having to rely on a network. Since any well-designed SSI digital wallet can provide this function—and protect the resulting private key—peer DIDs eliminate the need for any external dependencies. They are fully "portable" and can be as decentralized and scalable as the internet itself (if not more so). This design also favors censorship resistance, an attribute highly valued by many in the decentralized technology community.

> **NOTE** The internet's TCP/IP still relies on federated identifiers (IP addresses) and routing tables that ultimately have a centralized root managed by ICANN. Peer DIDs have no central root.

The only downside is that peer DIDs are not publicly discoverable and resolvable. What if there were a DID method that relied only on a self-certifying root of trust, yet provided the best of both worlds: publicly discoverable/resolvable DIDs *and* peer DIDs?

10.8   *Fully autonomous decentralized key management with Key Event Receipt Infrastructure (KERI)*

As figure 10.1 illustrates, the ideal root of trust from a security point of view—superior to both administrative and algorithmic—is a *self-certifying* root of trust that does not have to rely on a network. Properly implemented, it is both the most decentralized and the most resistant to attack. Every DID controller's wallet can serve as their own self-certifying root of trust, and these wallets can live anywhere on the network—ideally on edge devices, where they are hardest to attack remotely.

The peer DID method (discussed in the previous section) applies this architecture by using a simple type of *self-certifying identifier* (SCID). A SCID is derived from a public/private key pair using one or more applications of cryptographic one-way functions (see chapter 6). The SCID is now bound to that key pair, and only the holder of the private key can prove control of the SCID.

Many other blockchains use this same concept of a public key-based identifier—for example, this is how a Bitcoin user proves control of a Bitcoin address. The difference is that SCIDs do not require a blockchain—or any other infrastructure—to verify the binding with the public key. Anyone with the SCID and the public key can verify the binding using cryptography alone. This is what is meant by *self-certifying.*

The next step is to *make the entire DID method self-certifying,* i.e., not just the initial SCID, but all key rotations after that. That was the inspiration for *Key Event Receipt Infrastructure* (KERI). In KERI architecture, *the history of all uses or changes to the public/ private key pair can be compiled* to enable universal self-certifying proofs of the binding between the SCID and the associated public/private key pairs. With KERI architecture, the SCID is agnostic about where it is registered or discovered—it is completely portable and can form the root of a namespace for other SCIDs from the same controller. (See the following sections for details of how this works.)

As far as the authors, KERI is the first identifier and key management system to propose completely autonomous, portable, cryptographically verifiable identifiers that can be as public or private as required. While this might sound similar to the original vision for Pretty Good Privacy (PGP), PGP key sharing infrastructure needed to be manually set up and maintained by humans via key signing parties. Key rotation was a manual, laborious (and error-prone) process as well [3]. With KERI, we can finally—25 years later—achieve Phil Zimmermann's vision by using the distributed computing infrastructure and blockchain-inspired cryptographic engineering. KERI aims to be the first decentralized key management architecture that can be adapted to any underlying digital wallet or key management server and can be interoperable across all of them. A DID method based on KERI inherits all these features. So from the standpoint of SSI, KERI is positioned to deliver the greatest degree of self-sovereignty of all of the options for DIDs and DKMS, including anything rooted on shared ledgers.

In this section we will explain the basics of KERI architecture by way of summarizing its seven major benefits. KERI is defined in a 140-page technical white paper that is being standardized by the Identifier and Discovery Working Group at the Decentralized Identity Foundation; for full technical information, see https://keri.one.

10.8.1 *Self-certifying identifiers as a root of trust*

As previously explained, the starting point for KERI architecture is *self-certifying identifiers* (SCIDs). SCIDs were introduced in chapter 8 because they are the subclass of DIDs that depend exclusively on a self-certifying root of trust—they do not require an administrative or algorithmic root of trust. The basic concept is illustrated in figure 10.4 (repeated from chapter 8).

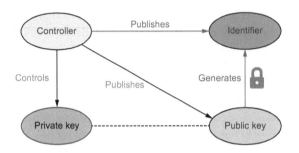

Figure 10.4 Self-certifying identifiers (SCIDs) generate the identifier for the controller directly from the public/private key pair without the need for any external administrator or algorithmic root of trust.

The identifier is self-certifying because, given the associated public key, anyone can instantly verify that the identifier was generated from the public/private key pair using a one-way function such as a hash function. The diagram on the left side of figure 10.5 shows how the controller starts the process by instructing the digital wallet to generate a large random number (using a secure source of entropy as described in IETF RFC 4086; see https://tools.ietf.org/html/rfc4086 for how to do this securely). Then the digital wallet generates a cryptographic key pair. Finally, the digital wallet derives the identifier (SCID) from the key pair. The result is a SCID whose binding with the public key can be verified instantly using cryptography alone—no need for a ledger, an administrator, or any other external source of truth.

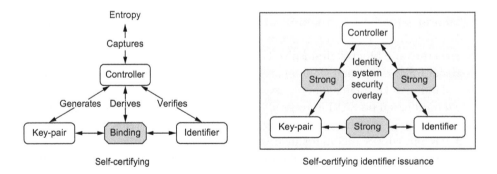

Figure 10.5 (Left) The process for generating a SCID. (Right) The resulting bindings between the controller, the cryptographic key pair, and the SCID.

SCIDs are 100% portable identifiers because the controller can "take them anywhere" and prove control without a verifier needing to trust anything but the cryptography and the security of the controller's digital wallet. (Peer DIDs are a subclass of SCIDs that share this same benefit of full portability.)

Because all other capabilities in KERI depend on the integrity and strength of SCIDs, the KERI technical paper defines several specific subtypes of SCIDs (basic, self-addressing, multisig self-addressing, delegated self-addressing, and self-signing) together with their syntactic structure, derivation code, inception statements, and generation algorithms inside a self-certifying root of trust.

10.8.2 Self-certifying key event logs

KERI takes its name not from the SCIDs at the heart of the architecture but from how it handles one of the hardest problems in decentralized key management: key rotation and recovery. This approach is summarized on page 32 of the KERI technical paper:

> *[KERI] leverages the fact that only the controller of the private key may create and order events that perform verifiable operations on the keys. As long as one complete verifiable copy of the event history is preserved, the provenance of control authority may be established.*

With KERI, every rotation to the key pair associated with a SCID generates a new *key event*. The KERI protocol dictates the exact structure of a *key event message*. Every key event message includes a sequence number. Every key event message except the very first one (the *inception event*) also includes a digest (hash) of the previous key event message. The controller then digitally signs the new key event message with the new private key, producing a *key event receipt*.

The result is an ordered sequence (chain) of key event receipts called a *key event log* that anyone can verify in much the same way they verify the sequence of transactions on a blockchain—but without needing an algorithmic root of trust. Figure 10.6 illustrates a sequence of key event messages in a key event log.

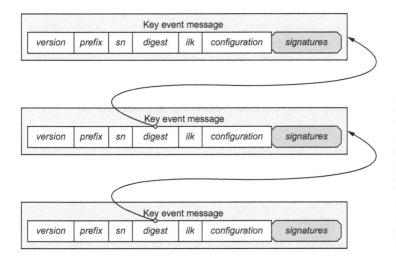

Figure 10.6   Each key event message in a key event log (except the first one) includes a sequence number and a digest of the previous key event message, creating a tamper-proof, ordered sequence similar to a blockchain but without needing an algorithmic root of trust.

10.8.3 Witnesses for key event logs

One of KERI's primary innovations is that *parties other than the controller can also digitally sign key event messages.* These parties are called *witnesses* because they are "witnessing" the controller's digital signature on a key event message, just as they would witness a person's physical signature on a paper document (as is often legally required for high-value documents like wills and mortgages).

As shown in figure 10.7, the KERI protocol standardizes how witnesses can receive key event messages from the controller. If the witness can verify the key event message, the witness can then add their own signature to create their own independent copy of the key event log.

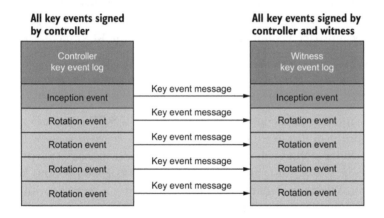

Figure 10.7 Witnesses increase the trustworthiness of a KERI key event log by adding their own digital signature to each event and maintaining their own independent copy of the log.

Each witness becomes a *secondary root of trust* to the controller's primary self-certifying root of trust. To the extent a witness is trusted by a verifier to serve as an independent source of truth about key event messages, each additional witness increases the trustworthiness of the key event log. Again, this works just like human witnesses to the "wet ink" signing of a physical document. If you have the signature of one witness attesting when and where they saw the signer sign the document, that's good. If you have the signature of four witnesses saying when and where they saw the signer sign the document, that's better.

10.8.4 Pre-rotation as simple, safe, scalable protection against key compromise

The challenge that all key-management systems must answer is not just how to rotate keys, but how to protect against the compromise of a private key via any of the myriad ways that can happen:

- Lost or stolen device
- Security flaw in the self-certifying root of trust (digital wallet)
- Side-channel attack on the self-certifying root of trust

- Social engineering attack on the controller
- Extortion attack on the controller (*rubber-hose cryptanalysis*)[1]

Private key compromise is even more dangerous in decentralized key management because there is no authority higher than the controller of the keys. So losing control of a private key is tantamount to handing over control of all DIDs or SCIDs that depend on the private key.

For this reason, KERI builds protection against compromised private keys right into the heart of the architecture using a technique called *pre-rotation*. In short, starting with the inception event and continuing in every key-rotation event, the controller publishes not only the new public key but a *cryptographic commitment to the next public key* (called the *pre-rotated public key*). This commitment is in the form of a digest (cryptographic hash function—see chapter 6) of the pre-rotated public key. This digest is included in the key event message establishing the new current public key, as shown in figure 10.8.

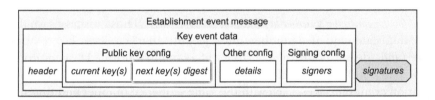

Figure 10.8   KERI uses pre-rotation of key pairs to protect against the compromise of private keys.

Pre-rotation enables the controller to pre-establish an entirely new and different public/private key pair for the next key rotation event. This means an attacker who compromises the current private key will not be able to take over the SCID by rotating to a new public key because the next public key has already been committed to.

The only way the attacker can take over the SCID is *to steal the pre-rotated private key.* But a number of factors make this extremely difficult:

- *The attacker does not know what the pre-rotated public key is* because all that has been published is its digest.
- *The pre-rotated key pair does not need to be exposed in any signing operations* until the next key rotation event.
- *The pre-rotated key pair can be safely stored offline* (air-gapped) *under very high security* because it is not needed until it is placed into active service after the next key rotation event.

---

[1] Although the origin of this term is tongue-in-cheek, this attack vector is deadly serious because in most cryptosystems, the human user is the weakest link.

- *Each pre-rotated key pair can be used to safely generate the next one* prior to going into active service.
- *Pre-rotation can even be quantum secure* as long as the digest function uses a quantum-secure cryptographic hash function.

Section 9.3.1 of the KERI technical paper summarizes why this pre-rotation architecture is so secure:

> *For many exploits, the likelihood of success is a function of exposure to continued monitoring or probing. Narrowly restricting the exposure opportunities for exploits in terms of time, place, and method, especially if the time and place happens only once, makes exploits extremely difficult. The exploiter has to either predict the one time and place of that exposure or has to have continuous universal monitoring of all exposures. By declaring the very first pre-rotation in the inception event, the window for its exploit is as narrow as possible.*

But if an attacker compromised an existing private key, couldn't they immediately publish their own conflicting key event message asserting a new pre-rotated key pair for which the attacker controls the private key? *Not if the controller already had one or more witnesses for the controller's earlier key rotation event message.* Those witnesses would recognize the duplicate sequence number and reject the attacker's later key rotation event message (and, ideally, notify the controller of a potential private key compromise).

What if the controller was malicious? Couldn't the controller publish two conflicting key rotation event messages, each with the same sequence number and timestamp but with two different pre-rotated key pair digests? Again, the witnesses (or any verifiers) could see these duplicitous events and flag the SCID as no longer being trustworthy.

The power of pre-rotation may be better understood after contrasting it with the use of hierarchically-derived keys. Many cryptocurrency wallets begin with the generation of a random seed. This seed is then used to derive all of the public/private keys pairs controlled by the wallet, and the value of the seed grows as more keys are derived from it. The seed must be stored securely, since compromise of the seed also results in compromise of every derived key pair. KERI inverts this process with pre-rotation. Instead of storing the root seed and needing to protect it forever, pre-rotation creates the next key pair, which must be stored securely only until it is time to use it.

Pre-rotation is a powerful key management security technique. For a deeper explanation, see section 9 of the KERI technical paper.

10.8.5 *System-independent validation (ambient verifiability)*

DID methods that rely on an algorithmic root of trust, such as a distributed ledger, produce DIDs that can only be verified by reference to that root of trust. The KERI technical paper refers to this dependency as *ledger lock*. Such DIDs are not portable to another source of verification, i.e., a different distributed ledger, a distributed file system, a centralized registry, a peer-to-peer protocol, or any other potential source of truth.

By contrast, KERI depends exclusively on a *self-certifying root of trust*—the controller's digital wallet. So KERI SCIDs and key event logs are self-verifying. All that is required is a copy of the complete key event log from *any* potential source—the controller itself, or any witness to whom a verifier has access. As stated on page 13 of the KERI technical paper:

> *[The key event log] is end verifiable. This means the log may be verified by any end user that receives a copy. No trust in intervening infrastructure is needed to verify the log and validate the chain of transfers and thereby establish the current control authority. Because any copy of the record or log of transfer statements is sufficient, any infrastructure providing a copy is replaceable by any other infrastructure that provides a copy.*

This results in a very robust, flexible, decentralized infrastructure where every controller can choose the witnesses they feel are needed to provide the level of assurance required by verifiers in any particular context. It not only frees DID methods based on KERI SCIDs and key event logs from ledger lock but also frees issuers and verifiers from needing to agree on the governance of a verifiable data registry (VDR) such as a blockchain or distributed ledger. The KERI technical paper summarizes this "separation of control" on page 86:

> *... the design principle of separating the loci-of-control between controllers and validators removes one of the major drawbacks of total ordered distributed consensus algorithms, that is, shared governance over the pool of nodes that provide the consensus algorithm. Removing the constraint of forced shared governance allows each party, controller and validator, to select the level of security, availability, performance specific to their needs.*

From the standpoint of the Trust over IP (ToIP) four-layer architecture introduced in chapter 2, this means both governance and technology for Layer 1 public utilities can be simpler, faster, less expensive, and more general-purpose.

The KERI technical paper goes into great depth on the protocol, configuration, and operation of KERI ambient verifiability infrastructure. See section 10 on protocol operational modes, section 11 on the KERI Agreement Algorithm for Control Establishment, and section 12 on event semantics and syntax.

10.8.6 Delegated self-certifying identifiers for enterprise-class key management

For personal use, an individual should be able to generate and manage as many SCIDs as needed in their digital wallet. But when we graduate to enterprise usage, the scale and complexity of key management increases dramatically. As discussed throughout this book, enterprises need to be able to easily yet safely delegate use of DIDs, VCs, and the attendant key management to directors, officers, employees, contractors, and anyone else taking actions on behalf of the organization.

This *delegated key management* enables the organization to "tree out" from its own self-certifying root of trust to establish subroots for delegates, where each serves as its own self-certifying root of trust. To quote from page 48 of the KERI technical paper:

> *A common use case would be to delegate signing authority to a new identifier. The signing authority may be exercised by a sequence of revocable signing keys distinct from the*

keys used for the root identifier. This enables horizontal scalability of signing operations. The delegation operation may also authorize the delegated identifier to make delegations of its own. This enables a hierarchy of delegated identifiers that may provide a generic architecture for decentralized key management infrastructure (DKMI).

In the KERI protocol, delegation may be performed using a *key interaction event*, so-named because it does not involve the inception or rotation of the primary SCID but rather is used to perform operations that do not affect the establishment of control authority of the primary SCID. In this case, a key interaction event is used to authorize the inception or rotation of a delegated SCID. Figure 10.9 depicts a key interaction event message containing the delegation seal for a new delegated SCID.

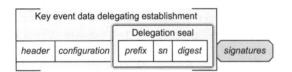

Figure 10.9   KERI key events can include delegation events, where one SCID delegates to another SCID to produce a delegation tree.

In addition to delegation, key interaction events (and their logs) can be used for tracking and verifying other operations with a key pair, such as generating a digital signature for an electronic document. Figure 10.10 shows a series of key interaction events from one delegate controller (Delegator C) to another (Delegate D).

Delegated SCIDs can use whatever delegated self-certifying root of trust provides the appropriate level of security. Some may need to be delegated to hardware security modules (HSMs) or trusted platform modules (TPMs); others can be hosted on servers locally or in the cloud; still others may be safe enough on edge devices that use secure enclaves.

Delegated SCIDs can also have witnesses—either witnesses shared across the entire enterprise or dedicated witnesses for special types of keys or functions. Section 9.5 of the KERI technical paper covers the different delegation modes and deployment architectures—including univalent, bivalent, and multivalent—that should be robust enough to serve even large multinational enterprises.

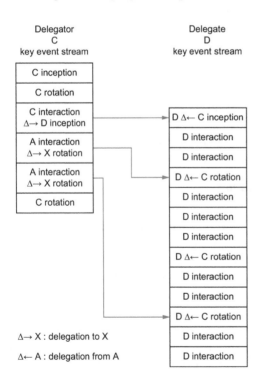

Figure 10.10   A series of key interaction events to perform the inception followed by the rotation of a delegated SCID

10.8.7 Compatibility with the GDPR "right to be forgotten"

KERI also provides a solution to the longstanding dichotomy in SSI between: immutable public blockchains where data lives forever and an individual's right to be forgotten—the right granted under the EU GDPR and other data-protection regulations for individuals to have their personal data deleted from any system where it is no longer legally required to be stored.

Since a DID that identifies an individual (regardless of the DID method) and its associated public key are both considered personal data under GDPR—*even if the DID is pseudonymous*—then writing that DID and its DID document to an immutable public ledger where it cannot be deleted appears to create an irreconcilable conflict. The Sovrin Governance Framework Working Group spent most of 2019 working with Sovrin stewards (organizations that run nodes of the Sovrin public permissioned blockchain), legal counsel, and GDPR experts trying to solve this problem. The result was a 35-page paper proposing how and why an individual's right to assert a self-sovereign identity should not be in conflict with that same individual's right to use an immutable public blockchain to secure that self-sovereign identity ("Innovation Meets Compliance: Data Protection Regulation and Distributed Ledger Technology"; Sovrin Foundation, 2019, https://sovrin.org/data-protection).

However, because the EU Commission and other data-protection regulators have yet to rule directly on the matter, this remains an area of regulatory uncertainty (and a potential inhibitor to SSI adoption). Thus a clear-cut alternative would be very welcome.

KERI provides that alternative. As we have emphasized throughout the preceding sections, the primary root of trust for a KERI SCID and key event log is *not* a blockchain or distributed ledger. Rather, it is a self-certifying root of trust—the digital wallet alone. If an algorithmic root of trust like a blockchain is used as a KERI witness, it serves only as an *optional* secondary root of trust.

Such a secondary root of trust is fine if the key event log is for a public organization where there are no GDPR issues (GDPR applies only to the personal data of individuals). However, if the controller is an *individual*—and therefore the SCID and key event log are considered *personal data*—then the obvious solution is, *do not use an immutable public ledger as a witness.*

Instead use any of the myriad other options for witnesses: a distributed database, a replicated directory system, a cloud storage service with automated failover—or all of them. These systems permit the deletion of stored data. And since KERI allows the key event log for one SCID to be deleted without affecting any other SCID, it becomes easy for a witness to comply with the right to be forgotten. And *the process can be fully automated* because the controller can issue a single KERI protocol command instructing all witnesses to perform the deletion. In short, KERI can eliminate the tension between GDPR and SSI so both can meet their intended goals.

10.8.8 *KERI standardization and the KERI DID method*

As should be clear at this point, KERI is broader than DIDs. KERI can be used with any type of SCID. And the KERI protocol specifies all the key event message types necessary to support KERI's decentralized key-management architecture. This is why standardization of KERI is underway in a working group at the Decentralized Identity Foundation (DIF, https://identity.foundation/working-groups).

However, KERI is fundamentally compatible with DID architecture and thus can also be implemented either as its own DID method or as an option within other DID methods. Defining a KERI DID method is one of the action items for the DIF IDWG. The current plan is to use the following DID method name:

```
did:keri:
```

KERI support is also planned to be included in the DID method for Hyperledger Indy-based public permissioned blockchains. In this case, KERI-based SCIDs will be a sub-namespace that can be supported on any Indy blockchain using the following syntax:

```
did:indy:[network]:[method-specific-id]
did:indy:[network]:keri:[scid]
```

where [network] is the identifier of a specific Hyperledger Indy-based ledger, [method-specific-id] is the identifier of a *non-KERI* DID, and [scid] is a KERI-based self-certifying identifier.

This forwards-compatible approach allows any Indy network to incorporate KERI SCIDs that return DID documents containing KERI key event receipts. Other DID methods can also include forwards-compatibility with KERI by taking the same approach of reserving a sub-namespace exclusively for KERI SCIDs.

10.8.9 *A trust-spanning layer for the internet*

This quote from the KERI technical paper summarizes its trust architecture:

> *Because at issuance self-certifying identifiers make a universally unique cryptographically strong binding between the identifier and a key-pair, there may be no other verifiable source-of-truth besides the controller who created the key-pair and thereby holds the private key.*

This is why KERI is a significant contribution to decentralized key management: it enables every digital wallet used by every controller everywhere to serve as its own self-certifying root of trust. And since KERI does not impose any special requirements on any device, system, database, network, or ledger to serve as a KERI witness, all of these can be *secondary* roots of trust.

The ability of KERI to provide universally portable, interoperable, and verifiable SCIDs and key event logs means the KERI protocol can enable a *trust spanning layer* for the internet the same way the Internet Protocol (IP) created a *data spanning layer* for the internet. This is a profound concept. It takes all of section 5 of the KERI technical paper. However, the essence of the idea can be conveyed in a few diagrams. Figure 10.11 shows how the dependencies between the various protocols in the internet protocol suite form an hourglass shape. Figure 10.12 simplifies figure 10.11 to make the hourglass shape more apparent.

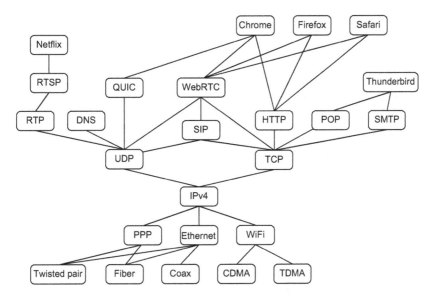

Figure 10.11   The internet protocol suite forms a natural hourglass shape with IP as the "waist" in the middle.

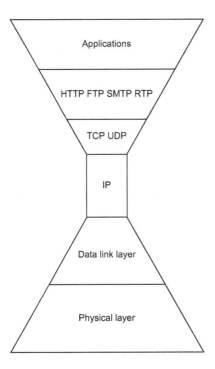

Figure 10.12   A more abstract version of figure 10.11 that shows how IP is at the middle of the hourglass formed by the supporting protocols below it and the supported protocols above it

The "hourglass theorem" of protocol stack design is wonderfully articulated in a 2019 ACM paper by Micah Beck [4]. He summarizes the theorem this way:

> *The shape suggested by the hourglass model expresses the goal that the spanning layer should support various applications and be implementable using many possible support-ing layers. Referring to the hourglass as a design tool also expresses the intuition that restricting the functionality of the spanning layer is instrumental in achieving these goals. The elements of the model are combined visually in the form of an hourglass shape, with the "thin waist" of the hourglass representing the restricted spanning layer, and its large upper and lower bells representing the multiplicity of applications and supporting layers, respectively.*

Figure 10.13 illustrates how a spanning layer should be designed to be as thin, weak, or restricted as possible and still support the applications above it.

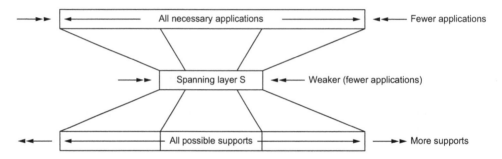

Figure 10.13   A spanning layer is the weakest (simplest) possible layer that still supports the necessary applications above it.

Beck's paper goes on to define a formal model to explain why the hourglass theorem works. The paper also provides several examples of where the hourglass theorem has been applied in multicasting, internet address translation, and the Unix operating system.

Section 5 of the KERI technical paper builds on this foundation by proposing another application of the hourglass theorem to a different kind of spanning layer—a *trust spanning layer*. We cannot fix the missing security in IP directly—at the level of the existing data-spanning layer—because that ship sailed over 40 years ago. However, we *can* fix it now by adding a second, higher-level spanning layer. From the paper,

> *Because a [trust spanning layer] necessarily uses protocols above the IP layer, it cannot span the internet at the IP layer but must span somewhere above it. This gives rise to a "double waisted" or "waist and neck" shape where the [trust spanning layer] is the neck.*

Figure 10.14 is a diagram of this double-hourglass shape showing both the IP span-ning layer and the trust spanning layer.

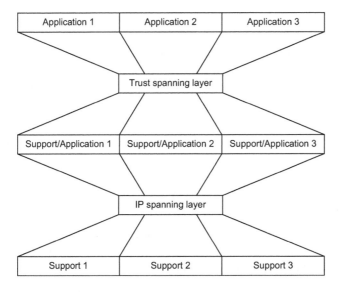

Figure 10.14 **With KERI, we can have a double hourglass—a trust spanning layer on top of the applications supported by the IP spanning layer.**

This prospect—of an interoperable trust spanning layer that works everywhere across the internet, allowing any two peers to connect and establish mutual, cryptographically verifiable trust—is enormously exciting. It aligns perfectly with the goals of the ToIP stack, shown again in figure 10.15 with a highlight over Layers 1 and 2 where

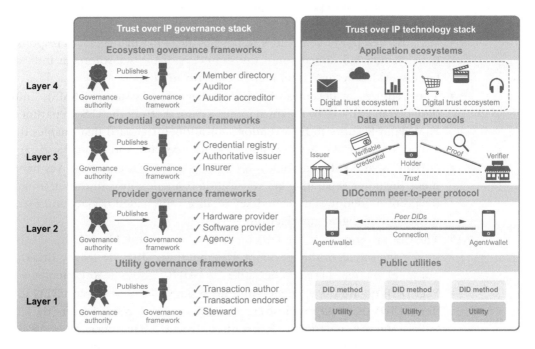

Figure 10.15 **KERI fits perfectly into the ToIP stack, with its self-certifying roots of trust living in digital wallets at Layer 2 and public utilities serving as KERI witnesses at Layer 1.**

KERI can be implemented in digital wallets at Layer 2 and with public utilities serving as KERI witnesses at Layer 1.

Most importantly, KERI gives us a consistent way to implement decentralized key management that can be integrated across all the devices, systems, networks, and applications we use every day. To be sure, the development, battle-testing, deployment, and integration of KERI infrastructure will take time—just as the adoption of the internet took time. But if KERI can deliver a trust spanning layer for the internet, its adoption will become as inevitable as the adoption of the internet was 40 years ago.

10.9   *Key takeaways*

This chapter provided in-depth coverage of the deepest topic in SSI: decentralized key management. The key takeaways are as follows:

- All forms of cryptographic key management are hard because digital keys are just strings of bits that must be very carefully guarded. If they are lost, stolen, or corrupted, they can be literally irreplaceable.
- Standards and protocols for conventional key management are well established, including major publications from NIST and the Key Management Interoperability Protocol (KMIP) from OASIS.
- The paradigm shift to decentralized key management is the migration from *administrative* roots of trust to *algorithmic* or *self-certifying roots of trust*. Both of the latter eliminate a dependency on trust in humans or organizational assertions of new or rotated keys.
- With this new power comes new responsibilities—key management responsibilities that now fall directly onto the shoulders of the self-sovereign individuals because with SSI, there is no higher authority to turn to.
- This requires a decentralized key management system (DKMS), initially designed in 2018–19 by Evernym under a contract from the U.S. Department of Homeland Security to be a vendor-neutral open standard that enables digital wallets to be portable across vendors, devices, systems, and networks.
- DIDs, VCs, and SSI bring new tools to help enable decentralized key management, including separating key verification from identity verification, using VCs for proof of identity, automated key rotation, automated backup and recovery methods, and digital guardianship.
- The vast majority (95%) of DID methods currently use blockchains or distributed ledgers as algorithmic root of trust, but these DIDs are ledger-locked (not portable) and may have conflicts with the GDPR right to be forgotten.
- Peer DIDs do not use a ledger—they use a simple form of self-certifying identifier (SCID) that relies exclusively on a self-certifying root of trust (the digital wallet) and are shared directly peer-to-peer where each peer can verify them. They are also highly scalable and privacy-preserving. The only downside is that they are not publicly discoverable.

- KERI (Key Event Receipt Infrastructure) uses a generalized approach to SCIDs that provides a complete decentralized key management infrastructure for any application—a solution even more generalized than DIDs. The KERI section of the chapter covers all seven of the major features and benefits of KERI.
- The ability of KERI to provide universally portable, interoperable, and verifiable SCIDs and key event logs means the KERI protocol can enable a *trust spanning layer* for the internet the same way the Internet Protocol (IP) created a *data spanning layer* for the internet. This fits perfectly with Layers 1 and 2 of the ToIP stack.

Having covered one of the deepest technical topics in this book, we now need just one more chapter to complete our deep dive into SSI technology. Ironically this final chapter in part 2 is not about technology—it is about a different kind of "code" we need alongside technology to address the human side of digital trust: *governance frameworks*.

SSI Resources

To learn more about KERI as it is used in SSI, please check out https://ssimeetup.org/key-event-receipt-infrastructure-keri-secure-identifier-overlay-internet-sam-smith-webinar-58.

References

1. Krause, Elliott. 2018. "A Fifth of All Bitcoin Is Missing. These Crypto Hunters Can Help." *Wall Street Journal*. https://www.wsj.com/articles/a-fifth-of-all-bitcoin-is-missing-these-crypto-hunters-can-help-1530798731.
2. Department of Homeland Security. 2017. "DHS S&T Awards $749K to Evernym for Decentralized Key Management Research and Development." https://www.dhs.gov/science-and-technology/news/2017/07/20/news-release-dhs-st-awards-749k-evernym-decentralized-key.
3. Franceschi-Bicchierai, Lorenzo. 2015. "Even the Inventor of PGP Doesn't Use PGP." *Vice*. https://www.vice.com/en_us/article/vvbw9a/even-the-inventor-of-pgp-doesnt-use-pgp.
4. Beck, Micah. 2019. "On the Hourglass Model." *Communications of the ACM* 62 (7): 48–57, https://cacm.acm.org/magazines/2019/7/237714-on-the-hourglass-model/fulltext.

SSI governance
frameworks

Drummond Reed

In chapter 2, we introduced the basic concept of the *governance framework* as a core building block of SSI architecture. In this chapter, we go much deeper into the special role governance frameworks play in fusing SSI technology with the realities of business, law, and society. As you read this chapter, keep in mind that SSI is a cutting-edge technology movement, and SSI governance frameworks are at the cutting edge of SSI. As a result, there are still relatively few governance frameworks in production as examples to which we can point. However, many in the SSI community believe they will be a crucial part of SSI's success. In particular, the ToIP Foundation is the first industry body to explicitly focus on the role of governance frameworks in decentralized digital trust infrastructure. This chapter will use the ToIP stack and other initiatives in the space to explain how different governance frameworks are relevant to each layer of SSI architecture. This subject will undoubtedly evolve quickly over the next few years; our goal is for this chapter to be a starting point for anyone who wants to explore and/or contribute to this area.

11.1 Governance frameworks and trust frameworks: Some background

Governance is as old as human society. In today's world, it is the job of governments, companies, and any other human organization. But the concept of a *governance framework* is newer. From the perspective of technology infrastructure, the ISO/IEC 38500 standard defines governance as "a system by which the current and future use of information technology (IT) is directed and controlled." More specifically, within the digital identity industry, this can be specialized as an *identity governance framework*.

248

In identity policy circles, this is also called a *trust framework*—a term often used interchangeably with *governance framework.*

Nacho Alamillo, chief trust officer of the Alastria Blockchain Ecosystem and leader of the ISO/WD TR 23644 on "Blockchain and Distributed Ledger Technologies— Overview of Trust Anchors for DLT-based Identity Management (TADIM, https://www.iso.org/standard/81773.html), defines a trust framework this way:

> *Trust frameworks exist to describe the policies, procedures and mechanisms for the operation of digital trust across a community of trust, whether that exists in a legally binding agreement or whether it is mandatory across the nation or jurisdiction under the rule of law. In almost all cases, the start point for a trust framework is the legal baseline upon which the Common Policy framework is built, which forms the core of the trust framework.*

Trust frameworks were originally applied to public key infrastructures (PKI), particularly in support of cross-certification and certificate authority (CA) bridge models. The use of trust frameworks grew with the emergence of federated identity systems (chapter 1) where the organizers needed to agree on the rules under which the federation members (especially the identity providers) would operate. These rules naturally fell into three buckets:

- *Business rules* governing who could join the federation, membership costs, operating costs, business models, and so on
- *Legal rules* governing jurisdiction, membership, liability, insurance, and so on
- *Technical rules* for what standards, systems, and protocols were required for interoperability

Dazza Greenwood, an attorney, digital identity consultant, and lecturer at MIT Media Lab, coined the term *BLT sandwich* for this "stack" of policies, as shown in figure 11.1.

By the late 2000s, federated identity systems had grown to the point where there was a need to start standardizing and promoting them. In 2009, when the Obama administration came to power in the United States, it proposed to work with private industry to build a trust framework under which U.S. government agencies could begin accepting federated identities from

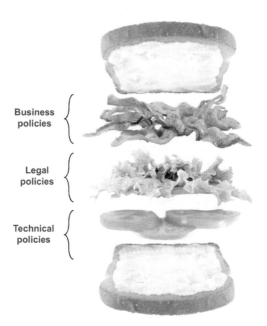

Business policies

Legal policies

Technical policies

Figure 11.1 The BLT sandwich metaphor for the general three-part structure of governance frameworks

private identity providers like banks, social networks, insurance companies, and healthcare providers. Since no existing industry association was designed for that purpose, the OpenID Foundation and the Information Card Foundation got together and created a new international non-profit organization called the Open Identity Exchange (OIX, https://openidentityexchange.org).

For the next decade, OIX hosted the development of a number of trust frameworks across both government and industry, including telecom, healthcare, and travel. The common theme was defining the set of rules under which a specific federated identity and data sharing network could operate. But starting in 2015, the identity community was inspired by a new type of network that roared onto the global stage: the blockchain network. As we explained in chapter 1, some digital identity architects began to see how blockchains could enable the next step beyond federation: a decentralized approach to digital identity infrastructure that no longer needed to rely on centralized identity providers. Thus SSI was born.

However, decentralization does not necessarily mean *less* governance. Although this view is not shared by everyone in the SSI movement (see chapter 15), in a February 2018 blog post, Phil Windley, founding chairperson of the Sovrin Foundation, framed the argument this way [1]:

> *One of the ironies of decentralized systems is that they require better governance than most centralized systems. Centralized systems are often governed in an ad hoc way because the central point of control can easily tell all participants what to do. Decentralized systems, on the other hand, must coordinate across multiple parties, all acting independently in their own self-interest. This means that the rules of engagement and interaction must be spelled out and agreed to ahead of time, with incentives, disincentives, consequences, processes, and procedures made clear.*

That, in a nutshell, is a governance framework. The term itself is rooted in blockchain technology: as blockchain networks evolved, governance models became one of the major differentiating features among different blockchain projects. Thus when the first blockchain networks appeared that were expressly designed to support decentralized identifiers (DIDs), the SSI community was more comfortable with the term *governance framework* than *trust framework*. One of the reasons is how well the governance trust triangle fits with the verifiable credential trust triangle.

11.2   *The governance trust triangle*

In chapter 2, we introduced the basic trust triangle for verifiable credentials (the top half of figure 11.2). We then added the governance trust triangle (the bottom half of figure 11.2) to show how trust networks based on verifiable credentials can scale to any size.

Although the concept of a governance trust triangle might seem new, it is precisely the same structure used by several of the world's largest trust networks. This becomes clear when we fill in the names for one of these networks in figure 11.3.

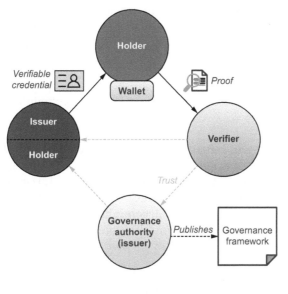

Figure 11.2 The governance trust triangle (bottom half) multiplies the use of the verifiable credential trust triangle (top half).

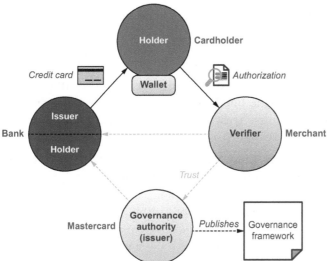

Figure 11.3 Global credit card networks like Mastercard and Visa are good present-day examples of how governance frameworks enable trust networks to scale globally.

Here's how the two trust triangles work together in the Mastercard network example:

- *Mastercard* is the *governance authority*. It establishes the rules and policies governing the issuance and acceptance of credit cards, debit cards, and other credentials on the Mastercard network, including onboarding, payment authorization, chargebacks, liability, and so on. It also sets the requirements for security, privacy, data protection, and other regulatory compliance policies. Finally, it specifies the technology, testing, and certifications necessary to operate on the network.

- *Banks*, credit unions, and other financial institutions are the *issuers* of credentials on the network.
- *Cardholders* are the credential *holders*.
- *Merchants* are the *verifiers* of the credentials—in this case, to obtain a payment authorization.

NOTE   Dee Hock, the founder and initial CEO of Visa, is the author of *One From Many* (Berrett-Koehler, 2005; originally called *Birth of the Chaordic Age*), one of the breakthrough books to argue that our current organizational structures are failing the world and how "chaordic" organizations (chaos + order) could be the way forward as part of a decentralized world. Many of Hock's ideas are closely related to the decentralization movement in the blockchain ecosystem that we explain in detail in chapter 15.

While credit card networks are good general examples of governance frameworks from the current business world, in SSI, governance frameworks can become more specialized. We will illustrate this by showing how they can apply to each layer of the ToIP stack.

11.3   *The Trust over IP governance stack*

At the end of chapter 2, we introduced the four-layer Trust over IP (ToIP) stack (figure 11.4) to show how the basic building blocks of SSI can be assembled into the architecture for a comprehensive trust layer for the internet. With regard to governance, there are three key takeaways from this diagram:

- *Governance is half the stack.* Most stacks, such as the TCP/IP stack that is the basis for the internet, consist entirely of technology components: protocols and APIs. While the ToIP stack includes a technology stack, it is only half the picture. When it comes to establishing trust both within and across the boundaries of trust communities worldwide, *governance* is equally important—many would argue it is *more important*. (This final point was a primary rationale for the establishment of the ToIP Governance Stack Working Group at the ToIP Foundation. Its job is to define standard models and templates for governance frameworks at all four layers of the stack.)
- *Technical trust is separated from human trust.* Governing how machines and protocols must be designed and deployed to be trusted by humans is very different from governing what people and organizations must do to be trusted by one another. The first two layers of the stack use cryptography, distributing networking, and secure computing to lay a solid foundation for technical trust. The top two layers add the components that only humans can judge: verifiable credentials (VC) about real-world attributes and applications that produce and consume VCs to power digital trust ecosystems.

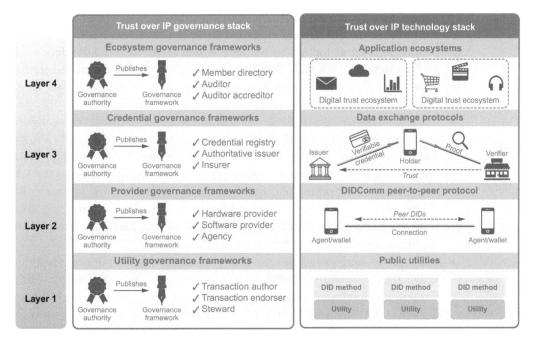

Figure 11.4   The Trust over IP stack includes both a governance stack and a technology stack.

- *Each of the four layers requires a different type of governance framework.* This was a critical learning of the SSI community—that governance frameworks are not "one size fits all." Each of the four layers has structural roles and processes that require policies tailored for that layer.

The following sections explain the special governance challenges at each layer.

11.3.1   Layer 1: Utility governance frameworks

At this lowest layer of the stack, governance applies to the operation of a public utility that provides the verifiable data registry (VDR) services on which higher layers need to rely. You can think of the VDR as a decentralized datastore that can take many different forms depending on the technology architecture being used—blockchain, distributed ledger, distributed file system, distributed directory system, or peer-to-peer protocols.

The roles and processes necessary for the governance of a Layer 1 public utility depend on the architecture of that VDR. For example:

- *Public permissionless proof-of-work blockchains* such as Bitcoin do not have any formal governance; they rely on the meritocracy of an open source project and the "vote with your feet" power of the miners who operate Bitcoin nodes and effectively govern the network by choosing what version of the open source codebase to run. For many of the most traditional participants of the Bitcoin community, the concept of having centralized organizations define rules for the network goes against all principles that the blockchain movement stands for. However, while Bitcoin was designed to be a peer-to-peer cash system, some people argue that today's technology is not ready to run fully decentralized identity networks but that decentralization will be good enough to start with. This is a subject that creates heated debates and that we cover extensively in chapter 15.

- *Public permissionless proof-of-stake blockchains* are governed by a voting algorithm programmed into the blockchain code that ties voting power to the size of the voter's holdings of the associated token. (Examples include Stellar, Cosmos, and Neo. Ethereum also has a stated goal of moving to proof-of-stake.) However, projects built on top of these blockchains, such as the EU European Blockchain Services Infrastructure (EBSI), are building formal governance frameworks based on EU legal instruments such as Electronic Identification, Authentication, and Trust Services (eIDAS).

- *Public permissioned blockchains* such as Sovrin and others based on Hyperledger Indy (https://wiki.hyperledger.org/display/indy) use formal governance frameworks developed under an open public process. An example is the Sovrin Governance Framework, first published in June 2017 and now in its third generation of development (https://sovrin.org/governance-framework).

- *Hybrid blockchains* such as Veres One and Hedera combine aspects of permissioned and permissionless models. For example, on Veres One, anyone can run a blockchain node, but changes to the network and business model are governed by a community group and a board of governors (https://veres.one/net work/governance).

- *Private blockchains* such as Quorum are operated by their members for their own usage. Their governance frameworks may or may not be public.

Keep in mind that *blockchains and distributed ledgers are not the only options for providing a VDR* at Layer 1. Other options include distributed file systems like InterPlanetary File System (IPFS), key event logs like those used by Key Event Receipt Infrastructure (KERI), and distributed hash tables (DHTs).

> **NOTE** Not all VDRs need to be decentralized. For some trust communities, it is acceptable to rely on *centralized registries*, *directory systems*, or *certificate authorities*.

Purist permissionless network proponents will argue that a real decentralized network does not need a governance framework since mathematics and cryptography ensure that proper governance is in place. Again, in chapter 15, we expand on many of these philosophical architecture choices and how they express themselves in the SSI market.

Depending on the governance model, standard governance roles at Layer 1 can include

- *Maintainers*—Developers of the blockchain code
- *Miners*—Operators of a permissionless blockchain node

- *Stewards*—Operators of a permissioned blockchain node
- *Transaction authors*—Anyone initiating a transaction with a blockchain
- *Transaction endorsers*—Parties who can authorize transactions to a permissioned blockchain

The draft ISO 23257 standard, Blockchain and Distributed Ledger Technologies—Reference Architecture (https://www.iso.org/standard/75093.html), describes the role of a blockchain governance authority at this level as a *DLT governor*:

> *Given that DLT systems are inherently distributed, with multiple nodes typically owned and operated by multiple organizations, there is a need for a role which governs the DLT systems as a whole and keeps the DLT systems able to execute the tasks for which they were established.*

The draft standard goes on to list the following typical activities of a DLT governor:

- Developing DLT policy considering applicable laws and regulations
- Communicating the policy with stakeholders
- Resolving conflicts and managing changes
- Defining polices for consensus mechanisms
- Defining policies for nodes that can participate in the DLT networks, including the minimum security requirements
- Working with DLT providers
- Working with DLT node operators to ensure that monitoring and governance are enforced

11.3.2 *Layer 2: Provider governance frameworks*

Layer 2 governance is a different beast from Layer 1 because what is being governed is not a public utility but the capabilities of digital wallets, agents, and agencies (see chapter 9). The need is primarily to establish baseline security, privacy, and data-protection requirements, plus interoperability testing and certification programs, for the following roles:

- *Hardware developers* who provide compliant hardware, e.g., secure enclaves, trusted execution environments, and hardware security modules (HSMs)
- *Software developers* who provide compliant wallets, agents, secure data stores, etc.
- *Agencies* who host cloud wallets and agents for individuals, organizations, and guardians

Hardware and software security requirements are relatively well understood (if not always well-implemented) and can be subject to rigorous conformance testing. But hosting digital wallets and agents in the cloud requires a new type of service provider—an *agency*—that has not existed before. Strictly speaking, an agency is not required—agents can connect directly peer-to-peer, as shown in figure 11.5. However, whenever that is not practical, agencies can provide agent-to-agent message routing and queuing and wallet backup, synchronization, and recovery services.

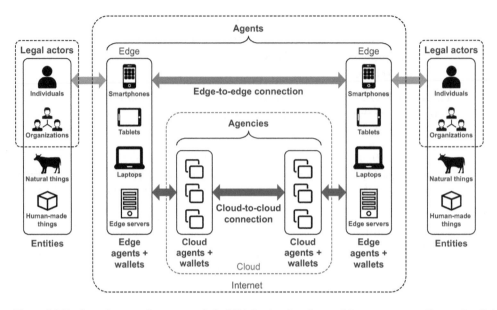

Figure 11.5 Agencies can play a core role in SSI infrastructure by providing message routing and wallet backup, synchronization, and recovery services.

Since all of these services are closely tied to the wallet holder's activity, Layer 2 governance frameworks are expected to cover agencies' security, privacy, and data-protection requirements. Furthermore, specialized agency services are necessary to support the services of *digital guardianship*, covered in chapter 9. The guardian—be it a person or an organization—needs to be able to host and manage a cloud wallet on behalf of the *dependent*—anyone not in a position to manage their own digital wallet or agent at all (e.g., refugees, people experiencing homelessness, the infirm, young children). Since a guardian is acting as an information fiduciary on behalf of the dependent, a digital guardian's legal duties and responsibilities need to be spelled out in a Layer 2 governance framework.

11.3.3 *Layer 3: Credential governance frameworks*

Layer 3 is where we transition from technical trust to human trust, so governance frameworks at this layer will start to look more familiar. The reason is simply that the credential trust triangle and governance trust triangle (shown earlier in this chapter) for digital credentials are very similar to those for physical credentials. Many of the policy frameworks we have for governing physical credentials today—credit cards, driver's licenses, passports, health insurance cards—can be adapted with relatively little modification to the digital version. See Table 11.1 for standard roles and policy types at this layer.

The roles of issuers, holders, and verifiers are discussed at length in chapter 7. But the concept of a *credential registry* was not part of the W3C Verifiable Credentials Data

Table 11.1 Standard roles and types of policies for Layer 3 governance frameworks

Role	Policy types
Issuers	Qualification and enrollment Security, privacy, data protection Credentials and claims qualified to issue Identity and attribute verification procedures Level of assurance Credential revocation requirements and time limits Business rules Technical requirements
Holders	Qualification and enrollment Wallet and agent certification Anti-fraud and anti-abuse
Verifiers	Security, privacy, data protection Proof request limitations (anti-coercion) Data usage limitations Business rules
Credential registries	Security, privacy, data protection Acceptance Retention Deletion Availability Disaster recover
Insurers	Insurance policy types Qualifications Coverage limits Rates Business rules

Model specification. Rather, it is a new Layer 3 role conceived by the digital identity team at the Province of British Columbia in Canada. They realized that the cryptographic architecture of the W3C Verifiable Credentials Data Model could enable a powerful new component of decentralized digital trust infrastructure, as shown in figure 11.6.

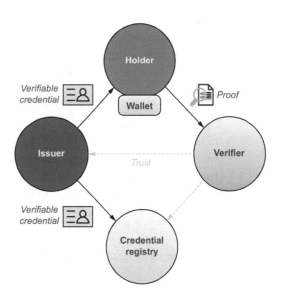

Figure 11.6 Credential registries are a powerful new component in decentralized digital trust infrastructure because they can serve as verifiable directories of VCs.

You may be wondering what the difference is between the VC issued to the holder at the top of figure 11.6 and the VC issued to the credential registry at the bottom. The answer is, *it is the same VC issued to two different holders.*

In other words, the data in the claims in the credential describing the credential subject—whomever or whatever that is—is *identical.* The only difference is the holder to whom the VC is issued. At the top of the figure, the holder is the credential subject (or a guardian or delegate). At the bottom of the figure, the holder is a credential registry whose job is to *publish the credential so it can be searched, discovered, and verified by any qualified verifier.*

Obviously, credential registries are not for all types of credentials—you would not use them for driver's licenses, passports, or other sensitive personal information. But for public information—for example, business registrations and licenses that are *required* by legislation to be published publicly in most jurisdictions—a credential registry is an excellent way to provide that service. For example, the BC government's credential registry service, called the OrgBook (https://vonx.io), publishes the business registrations and licenses of every single business registered in the Province of British Columbia.

The secret of credential registries is that the DIDs (or link secrets for ZKP credentials) are different for the VC issued to the real holder and the VC issued to the credential registry. This is why the credential registry cannot impersonate the real holder. However, the credential registry *can* produce a cryptographic proof that it is *also* an authentic holder of the credential for purposes of discovery and verification. And this cryptographic proof cannot be tampered with by an attacker either outside or inside the credential registry provider—a very desirable security property, especially in a decentralized system.

Another standard Layer 3 role in some governance frameworks is *insurers.* Any time there is risk, there is insurance. The higher the VC's value, the greater the liability if an issuer makes a mistake or its system is hacked. Some issuers will offset that risk with insurance, ostensibly making their VCs more attractive to verifiers who know there is a recourse in case they rely on a falsified, hacked, or erroneous credential.

11.3.4 Layer 4: Ecosystem governance frameworks

The top layer of the ToIP stack is the application layer. The purpose of governance frameworks at this layer is to lay the groundwork for entire *digital trust ecosystems*—for countries, industries (finance, healthcare, education, manufacturing, travel), or other trust communities of any type or size. The ToIP Foundation defines a digital trust ecosystem as follows (https://wiki.trustoverip.org/display/HOME/EFWG+Concepts +and+Workflow):

> *The set of all parties who have rights and responsibilities under a governance framework for applications at Layer Four of the ToIP stack.*

A Layer 4 ecosystem governance framework is the broadest in scope. This means

- *It may specify requirements that apply to every other layer of the stack*—for example, security and privacy requirements that apply to Layer 3 credentials, Layer 2 wallets and agents, and Layer 1 utilities that want to operate within that ecosystem.

- *It may span multiple governance authorities.* Digital ecosystems, like real-world ecosystems, are usually built up from constituent trust communities, each of which has its own governance authorities and governance frameworks. So an ecosystem governance framework represents a level of cooperation across all of these other governance authorities and frameworks.

- *It may span other ToIP Layer 4 ecosystems.* Ecosystems can contain ecosystems. For example, a Canadian national ecosystem defined by a governance framework (such as the *Pan-Canadian Trust Framework*; see section 11.9) can define policies that apply to provincial ecosystems. And those, in turn, can define policies that apply to ecosystems at the city or county level.

Because they operate at the application layer, ecosystem governance frameworks govern the elements that most directly touch humans—the people and organizations that operate within those ecosystems. The ultimate purpose of SSI and the entire ToIP stack is to enable these humans to easily form digital trust relationships and confidently make trust decisions online. So ecosystem governance frameworks tackle areas such as the following:

- *Interoperability*—The first goal of every digital trust ecosystem is to enable the applications within it to talk to each other and safely share the data that users want them to. For years, we have been focused on how to enable this technically. But as we solve those technical challenges, the remaining issues are the legal, business, and social barriers. This is where ecosystem governance frameworks can shine.

- *Delegation and guardianship*—Many of us don't want to manage our data ourselves, even if we can. That's why we hire professionals and service providers to do it—bankers, lawyers, doctors, accountants. Others are not able to wield SSI digital wallets and agents directly—they lack the physical, mental, economic, or legal capacity. For both cases, we need to establish legal, technical, and business rules for how we can easily, efficiently, and safely delegate responsibilities to others we trust to manage them for us.

- *Transitive trust*—With SSI technology and governance frameworks, we unlock the ability for trust developed in one context to be recognized and applied in another context. This happens every day with physical credentials—for example, when a car rental company decides to rent you a car because you have a driver's license and two major credit cards. Until SSI, this has been nearly impossible to do online. Digital trust ecosystems will change all that—they will make it easy to establish transitive trust between applications and websites within the ecosystem: for example, a travel network or school system.

- *Usability*—All of SSI will be for naught if it is not easy to use and safe for anyone to use without specialized knowledge about how it works. Ecosystem governance frameworks can define usability guidelines, mandate or provide incentives for their use, and offer certification programs for verifying compliance.

- *Trust marks*—In the real world, people associate trust with brands represented by trust marks. This is the reason global trust networks like Mastercard and Visa pour billions of dollars into advertising campaigns for their names and logos. The same is true for thousands of other major brands around the world. So one of the most visible functions of ecosystem governance frameworks will be defining their trust mark(s) and the rules for earning and using them. Their goal should be to wrap together everything a person needs to make a digital trust decision.

For ecosystem governance frameworks, the standard roles are more general than the lower layers. They can include the following:

- *Member directories (also called trust registries or trust lists)*—To establish transitive trust across members of an ecosystem, one of the most vital functions is confirming a particular entity is a member of the ecosystem—and thus bound by the terms and accountability requirements of its governance framework. Member directory services fulfill this role. They can be implemented in many ways, from traditional centralized directory services to federated registries to fully decentralized ledgers. And all of them can function as credential registries as defined in the previous section.

- *Certification authorities*—If trust marks are a meaningful tool for an ecosystem governance framework, they must have some teeth. One way to do that is for the governance framework to define the criteria for an entity to be certified for any particular role. Certification authorities then oversee this assessment and publish the results (using a VC, of course).

- *Auditors*—Reviewing the policies, practices, and procedures implemented by a particular entity to determine if they meet the requirements of a governance framework and qualify for certification is the job of a professional auditor.

- *Auditor accreditors*—This role approves the auditors. The job could be performed directly by the governance authority, but the larger an ecosystem needs to scale, the greater the need to outsource that function to an auditor accreditor organization. This is a role that WebTrust (https://www.cpacanada.ca/en/business-and-accounting-resources/audit-and-assurance/overview-of-webtrust-services) plays for the X.509 digital certificates used by SSL/TLS protocol (the lock in your browser) and organizations like the Kantara Initiative (https://kantarainitiative.org) play for other digital trust frameworks.

11.4   *The role of the governance authority*

There is one standard role in all governance frameworks: the *governance authority* that develops, maintains, and enforces it. Who can be a governance authority?

- *Governments at all levels*—Laws and regulations are already a governance framework, so producing SSI governance frameworks is a natural extension of the governmental function at any level—international, national, regional, state, district, local. All of these are nested Layer 4 ecosystems with natural Layer 3 credentials.

- *Industry consortia*—These exist in many industries to solve problems that no single member of the industry can solve alone. Industry-wide governance frameworks, especially at the ecosystem level, are a perfect example.

- *NGOs*—Non-profit organizations often play a special role in establishing trust by removing the profit incentive. This definitely applies to governance frameworks.

- *Corporations and enterprises*—A company and its employees, customers, partners, suppliers, and shareholders form a natural trust community—and a natural home for a governance framework.

- *Universities and school systems*—Educational institutions of all kinds—and the networks they form together—are natural SSI governance authorities because one of the primary outcomes of learning systems is credentials that the learner can use throughout the rest of their lives. (The Internet of Education Task Force was formed under the ToIP Ecosystem Foundry Working Group in July 2020: https://wiki.trustoverip.org/pages/viewpage.action?pageId=66102.)

- *Religious organizations*—Some of the world's strongest trust networks are based on religious affiliations, and these can be extended to digital governance frameworks.

- *Online communities*—Governance authorities do not necessarily need to be formal legal entities—or bound to specific jurisdictions. New types of virtual organizations and communities are forming online, and these can define their own governance frameworks.

The key point is that with SSI governance frameworks, governance to facilitate digital trust is now a tool available to anyone in any community of any size in any jurisdiction.

Who governs the governance authority? That is a classic question of all governance systems, and the answer is: "Whatever works for that trust community." There is no fixed answer, only a growing number of best practices based on experience with similar initiatives. (Establishing best practices for SSI governance authorities is a key deliverable of the ToIP Governance Stack Working Group: https://wiki.trustoverip.org/display/HOME/Governance+Stack+Working+Group.) However, one best practice is clear from the outset: the governance authority's own governance structure and policies should be published transparently as part of its governance framework (see section 11.6.1).

11.5   What specific problems can governance frameworks solve?

Governance frameworks are not abstract documents about intentions—they are sets of rules, policies, and specifications designed to help solve a specific set of problems for a trust community.

11.5.1 *Discovery of authoritative issuers and verified members*

The first question most audiences ask when they learn about digital credentials is, "How do I know I can trust the issuer of the credential?" This one of the primary purposes of Layer 3 and 4 governance frameworks.

Let's take an example. Say you are an employer, and you want to hire an employee with a college degree in a specific field. An applicant presents you with a proof of a VC of her diploma. Your digital agent verifies that the digital signature on the VC is valid from the DID of the issuer. But how do you know that the issuer DID is a real, accredited university? No employer knows all the accredited universities in the world, let alone all their DIDs.

The answer is that the VC also contains *the DID of the governance framework* (GF DID) under which the VC was issued. The employer's digital agent can now use the GF DID to answer two questions:

1 Is the GF DID from a governance authority the employer trusts for educational credentials? (See figure 11.3.)
2 If so, can the agent verify that the member directory for that governance framework includes the issuer DID?

If the answer to both questions is "Yes," the employer is satisfied. If the answer to the first question is "No," the employer's digital agent can try to answer a third question:

3 Is the GF DID included in the member directory of *another* governance framework the employer trusts for educational credentials?

This question is very important because it illustrates exactly how *transitive trust* works. Two different digital trust ecosystems for educational credentials—say, one for Australia and one for New Zealand—could decide to *cross-certify*: i.e., each recognizes the other's authority to specify the accredited educational institutions in its jurisdiction. Each ecosystem appears as a member of the other in its member directory. Now, if the employer is in New Zealand and trusts the New Zealand educational governance authority, but the applicant has a degree from a university in Australia, the employer will still get a thumbs-up from the employer's digital agent because of the transitive trust between the New Zealand and Australian educational governance frameworks.

With DIDs, this discovery can work in both directions. If you have a DID, you can resolve it and ask its agent what governance frameworks it is a member of. You can also start with the member directory for a governance framework and discover the DIDs of verified members.

11.5.2 Anti-coercion

The basic principles of SSI presume that parties are free to enter a transaction, share personal and confidential information, and walk away when requests from the other party are deemed unreasonable or even unlawful. In practice, this is often not the case. As Oskar van Deventer of TNO says in "SSI: The Good, the Bad, and the Ugly" [2], it's like the old joke:

> *"What do you give an 800-pound gorilla?"*
>
> *"Anything it asks for."*

Examples of such 800-pound gorillas are big tech providers, immigration offices, and uniformed individuals alleging to represent law enforcement. The typical client-server nature of web transactions reinforces this power imbalance, where the human party behind the browser (client) feels coerced into surrendering personal data to a server because otherwise they are denied access to a product, service, or location. A point in case is the infamous *cookie wall*, where a visitor to a website gets the choice between "accept all cookies" or "go into the maze-without-an-exit."

Governance frameworks can implement countermeasures against different types of coercion. For example:

- *Require verifiers to be verified members of an ecosystem.* This holds the verifiers accountable for abiding by the privacy and anti-coercion policies of the governance framework.
- *Require proof requests to have a non-repudiable digital signature from the verifier.* That way, a holder can prove a verifier's behavior in court.
- *Require an anonymous complaint mechanism or ombudsman.* If a governance framework builds in a service that holder agents can use to report bad behavior of a verifier, this "thousand eyes" approach can be a strong deterrent to such behavior.

In the case of a machine-readable governance framework, some of these countermeasures could be automatically enforced by the user's digital agent, safeguarding the user from being coerced into action against their own interest. Different governance frameworks may choose different balances between full self-sovereignty and tight control, depending on the interests at play and applicable legislation.

11.5.3 Certification, accreditation, and trust assurance

Another frequent question about the various players in a governance framework is, "How do I know they are playing by the rules?" In other words, no matter how well-designed or complete the governance framework is, how do you know the actors playing each role are complying with the policies specified for that role?

As explained in the next section, most governance frameworks include a key component for this purpose: a *trust assurance framework*. It is a separate document that establishes the policies under which actors in each role can be audited, monitored, and certified for compliance. It also specifies the rules for selecting, accrediting, and monitoring auditors or auditor accreditors. Since this answers the question "Who watches the watchers?" it can be one of the most important elements of a governance framework.

11.5.4 *Levels of assurance (LOAs)*

Identity and other trust decisions often are not binary. They are judgment calls. Any time judgment is not a simple "Yes/No" answer, you have the option for *levels of assurance* (LOAs).

LOAs are most often used to represent the degree of an issuer's confidence that one or more claims in a credential are true and belong to the intended subject. For example, a bank may be 99% sure that there is more than $10,000 in an account holder's account but only 80% sure that it has the account holder's current mailing address.

LOA is a very deep topic in digital identity and thus can be a significant factor in both credential and ecosystem governance frameworks. This is where the LOA criteria can be established for a single VC, for a family of VCs, or across an entire digital trust ecosystem. (For more about LOAs in digital identity, see the U.S. National Institute of Standards and Technology [NIST] Special Publication 800-63-3: Digital Identity Guidelines, https://pages.nist.gov/800-63-3/sp800-63-3.html.)

11.5.5 *Business rules*

The next most frequent question is, "How do I make money?" For any governance framework to be effective, the members need incentives to develop, implement, operate, and abide by it. In some cases, those incentives might be entirely external, such as regulatory compliance or humanitarian goals. But even then, the governance authority and members will want costs and burdens to be allocated fairly. Of course, commercially oriented governance frameworks need clear business motivations aligned with market forces.

As a result, *business rules* are a critical part of governance frameworks, such as the following:

- Who is going to pay the shared costs of the infrastructure? How and when?
- What are the available sources of revenue within the framework? Who can charge for what, and when?
- Are revenues split? How?
- How is pricing set?
- Are there penalties or fines for noncompliance?
- How is the governance authority sustainable? Do members pay a membership fee? Licensing fee? Revenue share? Tax?

As a rule, the earlier a governance authority tackles these questions, the more successful the governance framework.

11.5.6 *Liability and insurance*

One more question always comes to light: "What happens if something goes wrong? Who can get sued? For how much?" This question is essential for any collaborative endeavor to produce something of value. And trust has real value—just look at the "Goodwill" line item on many corporate balance sheets.

So, another standard feature of governance frameworks is policies about liability limits and allocation. Depending on the framework, this can also be coupled with requirements for members to have insurance coverage adequate for their roles.

11.6 What are the typical elements of a governance framework?

Although there are many approaches to crafting a governance framework, the ToIP Governance Stack Working Group has developed a metamodel for ToIP-compatible governance frameworks (https://wiki.trustoverip.org/display/HOME/ToIP+Gover nance+Metamodel+Specification) that consists of the modules outlined in figure 11.7.

• Master document
    • Introduction
    • Purpose
    • Scope
    • Principles
    • Core policies
    • Revisions
    • Extensions
    • Schedule of controlled documents
• Controlled documents
    • Glossary
    • Risk assessment, trust assurance, and certification
    • Governance rules
    • Business rules
    • Technical rules
    • Information trust rules
    • Inclusion, equitability, and accessibility rules
    • Legal agreements

Figure 11.7   The metamodel for governance frameworks developed by the Governance Stack Working Group at the ToIP Foundation

Organizing a governance framework into these modules does the following:

- *Makes it easier for stakeholders to focus* on specific policies of interest or relevance to them
- *Enables governance of each policy module to be delegated* to specific committees, working groups, or task forces within the governance authority who have the relevant subject matter expertise
- *Allows policy modules to be versioned independently* without requiring a "forklift upgrade" of the entire governance framework

Although their contents may vary considerably, these modules are the same for governance frameworks at all four layers of the ToIP stack.

11.6.1 Master document

If you think of a governance framework like a website (indeed, most human-readable governance frameworks are published on the web), the master document is the "home page." It is the starting point for navigating all the components of the framework. In the ToIP metamodel, master documents contain the standard sections listed in table 11.2.

Table 11.2   **Standard sections of the master document of a governance framework**

Section	Purpose
Introduction	Overall background, context, and motivations
Purpose	Mission statement(s)—typically just a few sentences
Principles	High-level guidelines against which specific policies can be evaluated to ensure that they are aligned
Core policies	Policies that generally apply to the whole of the governance framework (specialized policies go in policy modules)
Revisions	Policies governing how the governance framework itself can be revised or amended
Extensions	Policies governing how other governance frameworks (at the same ToIP layer or other layers) may be incorporated as extensions
Schedule of controlled documents	A listing of all the controlled documents in the governance framework and the status, version, and location of each

11.6.2 *Glossary*

Digital identity can be challenging to describe with great precision because the concepts can be fuzzy, confusing, and even language-dependent (for example, in Russian, there is no good term for the concept of "self-sovereignty"). So both technical specifications and governance frameworks for digital identity benefit greatly from well-researched and documented glossaries. For examples, see the Decentralized Identity Foundation Glossary Project (https://identity.foundation/open-groups/glossary .html), the Sovrin Glossary (https://sovrin.org/wp-content/uploads/Sovrin-Glossary-V3.pdf), and the ToIP Concepts and Terminology Working Group (https://wiki .trustoverip.org/pages/viewpage.action?pageId=65700).

The good news is that once a term is defined in a glossary with the precision required for technical, legal, and policy interpretations, it can be shared across all the documents in the governance framework that need to reference it. Even better, once a term is well defined in one governance framework, it can be reused in other governance frameworks by reference using a permalink to the original source.

11.6.3 *Risk assessment, trust assurance, and certification*

This category of modules includes policies for assessing and managing risk, including how parties can be certified against the governance framework. Controlled documents in this category should include

- A risk assessment
- A risk treatment plan
- A trust assurance framework (TAF)

As defined earlier in this chapter, a TAF is a module that specifies how members of the trust community can be audited, monitored, and certified for compliance. The TAF is used by auditors to perform the formal assessments that the governance framework may require for qualification, certification (or recertification), and accreditation of different members in different roles. For an example of a TAF developed as a component of the Sovrin Governance Framework, see the *Sovrin Trust Assurance Framework*: https://sovrin.org/wp-content/uploads/Sovrin-Trust-Assurance-Framework-V1.pdf.

(To learn more about the entire subject of TAFs for SSI, see the "Trust Assurance Development Kit" white paper by Scott Perry, co-chair of the ToIP Governance Stack Working Group: http://mng.bz/6gdG.)

11.6.4 Governance rules

These module(s) are devoted to the governance of the governance authority itself. This can vary greatly depending on the legal form of the governance authority and the nature of the governance framework (algorithmic, human-administered, hybrid). The governance rules are often embodied in the charter, bylaws, and operational policies of a non-profit organization or consortium.

This component is critical because trust in a governance framework can be no stronger than trust in the responsible governance authority. Pay particular attention to the rules governing changes to the governance framework itself (i.e., the amendment or revision process). They dictate how easy, fair, and equitable it is (or is not) to evolve the governance framework to reflect the changing stakeholders, needs, and values of the trust community.

11.6.5 Business rules

Infrastructure of any kind at any layer costs real money to develop, govern, and maintain. As pointed out in chapter 15, this is one reason virtually every blockchain project in the world uses some form of cryptocurrency or digital token to provide incentives for members. The same is true of SSI infrastructure. A standard component of any governance framework is the business rules governing who pays what to whom to provide incentives for all members/participants to engage and sustain the governance authority so it can continue to maintain and improve the infrastructure.

11.6.6 Technical rules

On the subject of technical specifications, the ToIP Foundation recommends that governance authorities refrain from "rolling their own" technology because that approach is usually anathema to interoperability (imagine if every website told you "its way" to build a web browser). Rather, that is the purpose of the ToIP Foundation, the Decentralized Identity Foundation, the W3C Credentials Community Group, the MyData Consortium, and other industry consortia: developing open standard specifications and vendor-neutral technology components from which governance authorities can choose what is needed to meet the requirements of their trust community. This maximizes interoperability and transitive trust while minimizing the potential for vendor lock-in.

In particular, the goal of the ToIP technology stack (the right half of figure 11.4; https://wiki.trustoverip.org/display/HOME/Technology+Stack+Working+Group) is to standardize the choices that governance authorities need to make to implement their policies in a manner that maximizes interoperability with other ToIP-compliant governance frameworks. Ideally, the technical policies are simply profiles of the required and optional ToIP standard specifications (TSSs) needed for that governance framework.

11.6.7 Information trust rules

These are the policies governing information security, privacy, availability, confidentiality, and processing integrity as these terms are defined by the AICPA for service organizations (https://www.aicpa.org/content/dam/aicpa/interestareas/frc/assuranceadvisoryservices/downloadabledocuments/trust-services-criteria.pdf). Controlled documents in this category typically include the following:

- Security and access control
- Privacy and data protection
- Information availability and robustness
- Information confidentiality
- Information processing integrity
- Trust marks and publicity rules
- Dispute resolution

For some industries, many of these requirements are already specified by regulations or covered by industry-standard compliance certification programs such as ISO/EIC 27001 or SOC-2.

11.6.8 Inclusion, equitability, and accessibility rules

These are policies governing how the framework does not discriminate among eligible participants and provides equitable access for all, including capabilities specifically aimed at digital accessibility, such as the W3C Web Accessibility Guidelines (https://www.w3.org/WAI/standards-guidelines). To the extent it is relevant, these policies should also address digital guardianship and controllership (covered later in this chapter).

11.6.9 Legal agreements

Not all governance frameworks require legal agreements. It depends on the framework's design and legal architecture and the governance authority (see section 11.8). However, if the framework defines clear rights and obligations of members in specific roles, then it is natural for the framework to include standard legal agreements for this purpose. Another common reason to include legal agreements is to assist with regulatory compliance, especially in the areas of security, privacy, data protection, and inclusion.

Typically, such agreements are in the form of contracts between the member and the governance authority. They include the rights and obligations of both parties. The overall structure of the governance framework can often simplify these agreements because many of the standard components of a legal contract—the "whereas" clauses, definitions of terms, and relevant business rules—are defined in other parts of the framework and can be included by reference. A typical operational requirement of a governance authority is executing, filing, monitoring, and, when necessary, terminating these agreements with participating members.

11.7 Digital guardianship

Several times in this chapter, we have touched on the special importance of digital guardianship. Although there are certainly technical aspects of implementing guardianship, those pale in comparison to the governance aspects: i.e., the legal, business, and social policies that apply to digital guardians and their duties to dependents. The reasons should be apparent from the following definition of *guardianship* taken from section 2 of the Sovrin Governance Framework (https://sovrin.org/wp-content/uploads/Sovrin-Governance-Framework-V2-Master-Document-V2.pdf):

> *Guardianship*
>
> *An Individual who does not have the capability to directly control that Individual's Identity Data (a Dependent) shall have the right to appoint another Identity Controller who has that capability (an Independent or an Organization) to serve as that Dependent's Guardian. If a Dependent does not have the capability to directly appoint a Guardian, the Dependent shall still have the right to have a Guardian appointed to act on the Dependent's behalf. A Dependent has the right to become an Independent by claiming full control of the Dependent's Identity Data. A Guardian has the obligation to promptly assist in this process provided the Dependent can demonstrate that the Dependent has the necessary capabilities. Guardianship shall not be confused with Delegation or Impersonation. Guardianship under the Sovrin Governance Framework should be mapped in the proper contexts to various legal constructs, including legal guardianship, power of attorney, conservatorship, living trusts, and so on.*

In short, with guardianship, there is ultimately no technical mechanism to prevent the dependent from being taken advantage of or impersonated by the guardian. It is a reflection of the same level of vulnerability in real-world guardianship.

NOTE As discussed in the previous section, governance frameworks designed for digital guardianship are in a special class because they define the obligations of guardians as information fiduciaries. This is a new and rapidly expanding area of the law. For more information, we recommend the Electronic Freedom Foundation (EFF) page on the topic and the foundational 2015 paper "Information Fiduciaries and the First Amendment" by Jack M. Balkin, Knight professor of constitutional law and the First Amendment at Yale Law School (https://lawreview.law.ucdavis.edu/issues/49/4/Lecture/49-4_Balkin.pdf).

This is why guardianship is a special case when it comes to governance frameworks—and likely will lead to governance frameworks specialized for this purpose. Some may be directly from governments, others from international NGOs like the Red Cross or the World Bank ID4D project, and still others from specialized NGOs devoted to problems like refugees, human trafficking, homeless, dementia, and so on. (For more on this topic, see the Sovrin Foundation white paper "On Guardianship in Self-Sovereign Identity" from the Guardianship Working Group: https://sovrin.org/guardianship.)

11.8   Legal enforcement

Another frequent question about SSI governance frameworks is, "Are they legally enforceable? Or are they just statements about the good intentions of the members of a trust community that have no actual teeth if their policies are violated?"

As we indicated earlier in this chapter, the answer depends on the needs of the trust community and the design of the governance framework. Certainly, if a governance framework specifies legal agreements that create specific contractual obligations for members performing specific roles, it is legally enforceable under contract law just like any other contract. For example, the Sovrin Governance Framework (discussed in the next section) includes legal agreements for three roles:

- *Stewards* who operate nodes of the Sovrin ledger (https://sovrin.org/wp-content/uploads/Sovrin-Steward-Agreement-V2.pdf)
- *Transaction authors* who write transactions to the ledger (https://sovrin.org/wp-content/uploads/Transaction-Author-Agreement-V2.pdf)
- *Transaction endorsers* who digitally sign transactions to authorize them (https://sovrin.org/wp-content/uploads/Transaction-Endorser-Agreement-V2.pdf)

After the activation of the EU General Data Protection Regulation (GDPR) in 2018, all three of these agreements had to be carefully revised to account for the regulatory obligations of all three parties as *data controllers* or *data processors*. As a result, two more legal agreements were added in the second generation of the Sovrin Governance Framework. (For more information, see the white paper on this topic published by the Sovrin Governance Framework Working Group: https://sovrin.org/data-protection.)

However, whenever it comes to legal enforcement of digital rights, asymmetry of power is a real issue. Between individuals who need to defend their rights and corporations or governments who have transgressed them, who has the greater legal expertise and resources? It's not a fair fight. In fact, in most cases, it's not even a fight—because the individual cannot afford to (or is afraid to) enter the ring.

SSI governance frameworks bring new tools to help level this playing field and encourage everyone in the trust community to do the right thing:

- *Transparent, community-wide policies*—One of the reasons privacy policies have been so ineffective at delivering real privacy is that every site has its own such policy. A 2008 paper by privacy experts Aleecia M. McDonald and Lorrie Faith Cranor estimated it would take the average American internet user over 200 hours to read the privacy policies of all the websites they use—and would cost the U.S. economy $781 billion in lost productivity annually if everyone did so [3]. Well-designed governance frameworks can establish uniform baselines for privacy, security, data protection, and other digital trust policies that apply to all members—increasing confidence across the entire trust community.

- *Community monitoring and reputational incentives*—For all its flaws, social media has created powerful new incentives for players to maintain good reputations in the market. Well-designed governance frameworks and community-based monitoring and reporting mechanisms can tap this same incentive to motivate their members to play by the rules.

- *Collective action*—When the first two tools are not enough, governance frameworks can incorporate specific legal support for members taking collective action against violators. As long as the design includes the appropriate safeguards against abuse, this can be an extremely effective disincentive to break the rules.

Some SSI experts believe that the groundwork SSI lays for sharing cryptographically verifiable assertions across trust boundaries will enable so much more effective and scalable reputation systems that legal enforcement of governance frameworks will rarely be needed. We will see if this prediction proves to be true.

11.9 Examples

SSI governance frameworks are at the cutting edge of SSI, so there are not yet many production examples to point to. Table 11.3 summarizes some of the earliest market entrants.

Table 11.3 Examples of SSI-compatible governance frameworks

Example	Description
Sovrin Governance Framework (SGF, https://sovrin.org/governance-framework)	Mentioned several times already in this chapter, this is the most mature governance framework designed explicitly for SSI. The first version was published by the Sovrin Foundation in June 2017, SGF V2 was published in December 2019, and the third generation is now under development by the Sovrin Governance Framework Working Group. It will split the SGF into two ToIP-compatible governance frameworks: the Sovrin Utility Governance Framework and the Sovrin Ecosystem Governance Framework. The SGF is licensed under Creative Commons, so the trust community can use it as the basis for its own governance framework.
Veres One Governance (https://veres.one/network/governance)	Veres One is a hybrid blockchain network that has both permissionless and permissioned aspects. It is governed by a five-party system: the Veres One community group, the board of governors, advisory committees, nodes, and the maintainer.
CCI Governance Framework (https://www.covidcreds.com)	This is a deliverable of the Rules Task Force of the COVID-19 Credential Initiative. The first version was delivered in June 2020, and the second version is currently in development.

Table 11.3   Examples of SSI-compatible governance frameworks *(continued)*

Example	Description
Lumedic Health Network Governance Framework (https://www.lumedic.io/perspectives/introducing-lumedic-connect)	This is the first SSI governance framework designed exclusively for the exchange of VCs for patient-centric healthcare. Announced in November 2020, the first version will be published in Q1 2021.
Pan-Canadian Trust Framework	While not specific to SSI, this is the most mature national governance framework globally, and the latest version was revised specifically to incorporate the key architectural design principles of SSI. For the full story, see chapter 23.

We expect the number of SSI governance frameworks to begin growing rapidly in 2021. A selection of efforts underway that are known to the authors of this book include the following (the ToIP Governance Stack Working Group maintains a list of SSI- and ToIP-based governance frameworks as they come onto the market):

- ToIP Layer 1 networks in Finland (https://www.findy.fi), Germany (https://www.snet.tu-berlin.de/menue/projects/ssi4de), and Canada (https://canacred.ca)
- National SSI governance frameworks underway in the EU—the Europe Self-Sovereign Identity Framework (https://www.eesc.europa.eu/sites/default/files/files/1._panel_-_daniel_du_seuil.pdf) and eSSIF-Lab (https://essif-lab.eu) and New Zealand (https://www.digital.govt.nz/digital-government/programmes-and-projects/digital-identity-programme/digital-identity-trust-framework/)
- Ecosystem governance frameworks are under development by the Global Legal Entity Identifier Foundation (GLEIF, https://wiki.trustoverip.org/download/attachments/66630/Accelerating-Digital-Identity-with-the%20LEI_ToIP-Ecosystem-Foundry_WG_v1.0_final%20.pdf) for organizational identity and by GS1 for global supply chain

Note that many other blockchain-related projects have governance frameworks that are also looking to incorporate SSI. Examples include the Enterprise Ethereum Alliance (EEA, https://entethalliance.org) and the Corda Network (https://corda.network/governance/governance-guidelines).

There are only a few good examples of SSI governance frameworks as of the publication of this book, but many more are on the way.

SSI Resources

For more free content to learn about SSI, please go to IdentityBook.info and SSI Meetup.org/book.

References

1. Windley, Phil. 2018. "Decentralized Governance in Sovrin." *Technometria.* https://www.windley .com/archives/2018/02/decentralized_governance_in_sovrin.shtml.
2. Van Deventer, Oskar. 2019. "Self-Sovereign Identity - The Good, the Bad and the Ugly." TNO. https://blockchain.tno.nl/blog/self-sovereign-identity-the-good-the-bad-and-the-ugly.
3. McDonald, Aleecia M. and Lorrie Faith Cranor. 2008. *I/S: A Journal of Law and Policy for the Information Society* 4 (3): 543–568. https://kb.osu.edu/handle/1811/72839.

Part 3

Decentralization as a model for life

Like most other exponential technology stacks, SSI stands on the shoulders of giants. In chapters 12 and 13, we explain how SSI is built on two fundamental pillars:

- The open source and free software movements
- The *cypherpunk* movement, fueled by the liberating power of cryptography, which led to the development of blockchain technology

Having laid this foundation, in chapters 14–17, we explore what this means for other aspects of modern society both within and beyond technology, including the following:

- The global peace movement
- Technical and social trends to decentralization and the belief systems in which these trends are rooted
- The evolution of the global SSI community (which is larger than you think)
- The intersection of identity and money (which is also larger than you think)

How open source software helps you control your self-sovereign identity

Richard Esplin

All internet infrastructure depends to a great degree on open source software, simply because this foundational layer must be, in the words of Doc Searls and David Weinberger, "NEA: No one owns it; Everyone can use it; Anyone can improve it." But with SSI, open source plays an even more important role. To explain this, we have tapped Richard Esplin, who for eight years held roles in sales, marketing, and product management at Alfresco, the largest open source content management system (CMS) company (acquired in 2020 by Hyland Software), and more recently director of product management at Evernym.

In 1984, the technology journalist Steven Levy published his first major book, *Hackers: Heroes of the Computer Revolution* [1]. Using the original meaning of the term *hacker*, he celebrated those pioneers in technology whose ingenuity and intellectual playfulness exemplified the positive impact of engineering. (As we explain in more detail in chapter 13, these hackers are offended when their label is applied to those who maliciously break into computer systems; hackers call them *crackers* [2].) At the conference to launch the book, the attendees debated the future of software technology. Stewart Brand is reported to have said the following [3]:

> *On the one hand information wants to be expensive, because it's so valuable. The right information in the right place just changes your life. On the other hand,*

information wants to be free, because the cost of getting it out is getting lower and lower all the time. So you have these two fighting against each other.[1]

This tension has always existed in technology and has serious implications for our digital identities. The software industry has a strong motivation to commercialize the information that makes up our digital identities and has reaped large rewards in the process. This drive for profit meets resistance from a subset of activists and civic technologists who follow the mantra that "Information wants to be free." They believe that society is harmed by the restriction of information, especially scientific and technical knowledge, and so encourage sharing the source code necessary to modify their software so that users have visibility into the way the software operates and can exercise control.

This approach to software development goes by different names depending on the motivation of the speaker. Those who believe sharing source code is an ethical duty because it contributes to people's freedom call it *free software* or *libre software*. The term *libre* is intended to highlight the freedom of usage and the openness of engineering and is often contrasted with the term *gratis* to say that the movement is about more than just saving money. Free software helps democratize access to technology, increases the accountability of technology vendors, and ensures users' freedom to control the digital tools they use. Those who use the term *open source* generally focus on the engineering benefits that come with providing access to the source code: faster innovation, higher quality, wider collaboration, and improved competitiveness in the marketplace.

To fully understand the world of self-sovereign identity (SSI) and the impact it can have on society, you need to know about the importance of the free software and open source movements. If you are already familiar with these concepts, you can skip to the next chapter to continue digging deeper on how decentralization shapes the SSI world.

12.1 The origin of free software

The attitude that software should be shared dates to the dawn of computing. Computational theory was conceived as a branch of mathematics in the early 20th century, and digital computation technology was developed by governmental and academic researchers who were accustomed to publishing their results. By the 1950s, it was possible to buy general-purpose computer hardware,[2] but the software was not seen as an independent product, and users commonly exchanged code the same as they exchanged other technical information about their machines [4].

Technology user groups developed along with the industry, such as SHARE (https://www.share.org), which was founded by IBM users in 1955. It was in this environment that the seminal operating system Unix was created at AT&T Bell Labs,

---

[1] Joshua Gans corrects the quote using a recording of the event (https://digitopoly.org/2015/10/25/informa tion-wants-to-be-free-the-history-of-that-quote), but I use Levy's misquote because of how it impacted the industry.

[2] The Manchester Ferranti Mark I was delivered February 1951, and is considered the first commercially available general-purpose computer by the Computer History Museum, https://www.computerhistory.org/time line/1951.

which distributed it along with the source code to academic institutions due to an antitrust settlement with the United States government that prevented AT&T from commercializing the product [5]. The adoption and broad influence of Unix were fueled by this culture of investigating, modifying, and sharing enhancements to the operating system. This eventually resulted in a free distribution of Unix (BSD) from the University of California at Berkeley that included the source code.

As the industry matured, hobbyists started experimenting with software tools outside of work. The Homebrew Computer Club nurtured great Silicon Valley entrepreneurs like Steve Jobs and Steve Wozniak as they developed the ideas that would later become Apple Software [6]. These computer clubs were also famous places to share software, which in 1975 prompted a young Bill Gates, the founder of "Micro-Soft," to publish an "Open Letter to Hobbyists" in which he argued that what the hobbyists called "sharing" was actually stealing and would prevent a commercial software industry from being successful [7]. From that time on, most of the software industry has worked to boost the value of software by limiting its distribution and restricting access to the source code.

Some responded to the push for restrictions by increasing their efforts to share. While working as a graduate student at the Massachusetts Institute of Technology, a talented software engineer named Richard Stallman was frustrated when his co-workers in the AI lab were hired away by a company that refused to allow them to continue collaborating with him. He saw this lack of cooperation as offensive and unethical. In response, he focused on independently replicating the company's product and releasing it as a free clone. When he proved successful at matching the work of that team of engineers, he broadened his ambition and in 1983 announced his plan to create a freely available replica of all of Unix, named GNU (a self-referential acronym for GNU's Not Unix) [8].

Achieving Stallman's goal of a free Unix-compatible operating system that would encourage sharing and cooperation would require innovations beyond software. In 1985, Stallman founded the Free Software Foundation (https://www.fsf.org) to collect donations, coordinate governance, and sponsor advocacy for free software projects. Working through the Foundation, Stallman identified four essential freedoms that a program's users must have (numbered from zero "for historical reasons") [9]:

0   The freedom to run the program as you wish, for any purpose.
1   The freedom to study how the program works and change it so it does your computing as you wish. Access to the source code is a precondition for this.
2   The freedom to redistribute copies so you can help others.
3   The freedom to distribute copies of your modified versions to others. By doing this, you can give the whole community a chance to benefit from your changes. Access to the source code is a precondition for this.

Stallman wanted to guarantee these freedoms to users of free software even when the software was received through intermediaries. In 1989, he devised a legal tool that would protect user freedom by cunningly employing copyright law and software licenses—the same techniques that others use to prevent software sharing. Copyright restricts the copying of software without permission from the author, and that permission often comes in the form of a software license that dictates the terms of use. Stallman's software license, the GNU General Public License (GPL), requires that the source code be included with any copy of the software. Further, if a developer chooses to include that code in another program, then the combined work can only legally be distributed under the terms of the GPL. Stallman branded this clever use of copyright to require sharing *copyleft*.

By 1991, the GNU project contained most of the components for a functional operating system, but it still lacked a *kernel*, which is the part that interfaces with the hardware and orchestrates all the programs. That year, a University of Helsinki student named Linus Torvalds bought a new Intel 386 PC and wrote a kernel as a learning exercise. By combining his kernel with the GNU tools, it was possible to assemble a functional Unix-compatible operating system for personal computers. Torvalds shared his kernel on the pre-web internet to see if it would be useful to anyone who might contribute improvements. He was surprised that people around the world used his work and suggested improvements.

This new operating system was soon called Linux, even though calling it GNU/Linux would have been more correct (as free software advocates like to emphasize). To manage the many contributions, and because he benefited from GNU tools during development, Torvalds changed the license to the GNU GPL near the first anniversary of development. Over time, Torvalds has been clear that he chose that license not as a political statement about the ethics of free software, but because sharing source code is a better approach to engineering [10].

12.2 Wooing businesses with open source

To explain why sharing source code results in better products, early Linux contributor and self-styled hacker anthropologist Eric Raymond drew a distinction between the top-down development of a cathedral and the competing agendas of a bazaar. Both can produce economic value, but as each person in the bazaar "scratches their own itch," the bazaar benefits from the competition of ideas and adapts to the participants' needs. The project also benefits from the differing perspectives of a large group of developers, as what is complex to one might be simple to another—or, as Raymond says, "Given enough eyeballs, all bugs are shallow" [11]. Aside from these pragmatic benefits, many developers see the bazaar's individually driven collaborative development model as more fun than cathedral-style engineering.

Linux wasn't the only software project to benefit from an open development model. The National Center for Supercomputing Applications (NCSA) at the University of Illinois at Urbana-Champaign released a free program that would allow people to publish information on the brand new World Wide Web. NCSA wasn't interested in continuing development, but the code was available, and other developers were motivated to improve it. They self-organized as the Apache Group, and within a few years, the Apache HTTP Server was the most popular web server on the internet.

By the mid-1990s, new companies like Red Hat and SUSE were attempting to commercialize the thriving ecosystem of free software. These young businesses found it challenging to explain their emerging business models because of the countercultural style of development. Business leaders often assumed that free software could not be sold—that "free" referred to price instead of legal rights and freedoms. The ethical stance taken by Stallman and the Free Software Foundation was seen as a distraction from the commercial conversation about the benefits of collaborative development.

Regardless, the free software movement started to get significant commercial attention in 1998. First, Netscape announced it would release the source code for its web browser, which would eventually evolve into Mozilla Firefox. Next, IBM announced it would be contributing to the Apache HTTP Server. And finally, Oracle announced it would port its flagship database to Linux. These announcements pushed free software into the mainstream, and the question of how to make the free software brand palatable to businesses became a common topic at free software conferences.

By the end of 1998, most developers were using the term *open source*, as coined by Christine Peterson, the founder of the Foresight Institute [12]. The Open Source Initiative (https://opensource.org) was established as a legal entity to hold the trademark and arbitrate which software licenses would qualify as providing sufficient protection for user freedom. The Open Source Initiative approved a wider range of licenses than the Free Software Foundation, accommodating various commercial models; however, businesses and consumers could still have confidence that software distributed under an approved open source license would protect the four essential freedoms described by Stallman.

Although many developers immediately embraced the *open source* brand, Richard Stallman represents a significant faction who refuse to use the term because it doesn't sufficiently emphasize freedom. In his words, "While a free program by any other name would give you the same freedom today, establishing freedom in a lasting way depends above all on teaching people to value freedom" [13]. As the many points of view in this book illustrate, these kinds of disagreements happen in all communities—which is why governance systems must be carefully designed (see chapter 11).

12.3 How open source works in practice

The Voyager 1 spacecraft was launched in September 1977 and exited the solar envelope on August 25, 2012. Although the probe completed its primary mission in November 1980 with a flyby of Saturn, it is expected to continue transmitting data until 2025 [14]. For NASA to keep receiving data from the spacecraft, the probe's antenna has to stay pointed at Earth. Because the attitude control thrusters had degraded, in November 2017, the team decided to use the trajectory correction maneuver thrusters for the first time in nearly 40 years and differently than for what they had been designed.

To achieve this task, the engineers had to study the original source code. To everyone's relief, the maneuver was successful, which will allow NASA to continue receiving data from the probe for a few years longer than previously expected [15]. NASA's control over the software in the spacecraft yielded two important benefits: first, NASA could study the software to better understand it. And second, NASA could modify it to meet a different use case than the one for which it had originally been designed.

NASA applied these lessons while designing missions to visit Europa. It selected an open source content management system to model the relationships between the components on the craft (https://github.com/Open-MBEE). The system designers had not envisioned this use case, but they recognized that it took advantage of the system's strengths. In addition to the benefits of being able to study and modify the code, NASA wanted others to collaborate in developing the solution [16]. It seemed unlikely that NASA would find external contributors for such a niche need, but within a year, the organization was contacted by a major aerospace company that wanted to work together [17]. Another win for open source!

This example highlights some of the reasons why many modern enterprise technology companies market open source solutions. Buyers have a perception that open source solutions will prevent vendor lock-in, be available at a lower cost, receive faster innovation, and be more secure. These benefits become possible when software freedom is respected, determined by the license under which the software is distributed.

As mentioned earlier, Linux is distributed under the GNU GPL, which was authored by Richard Stallman. This software license protects the four essential freedoms of downstream users by restricting developers who choose to use GPL code. If a developer chooses to redistribute a program that benefits from GPL software, the developer cannot select the resulting program's license—it must be redistributed under the GPL, and the source code of any original intellectual property must also be shared. This "viral" nature is why in 2001, the CEO of Microsoft called Linux "a cancer," as it spreads to downstream products [18]. However, it is important to recognize that individuals and organizations that adopt GPL products for their own use are not redistributing the software. In this case, the GPL has no impact on other intellectual property.

The Apache Group chose a different approach when it adapted the license used by Berkeley's Unix distribution. The Apache License allows recipients to do whatever they want with the source code, including incorporating the software into a proprietary product that does not grant downstream users freedom. It is similar to the American concept of dedicating software to the public domain, but with consistent protections for authors and users across legal jurisdictions. This unrestricted usage allows commercial interests to participate in collaborative development without giving up control of their business models.

Bruce Perens, the creator of the Open Source Definition, summarized the three basic approaches to open source licensing that will meet most goals [19]:

1 A *gift* license, like the Apache license, which promotes spreading standards through widespread adoption.
2 A *sharing with rules* license, like the GPL, which ensures that people share under the same terms as they receive.

3 An *in-between* license, like the GNU Lesser General Public License (LGPL), which requires people to share their modifications to a program but not to release the larger work that incorporates it. This allows inclusion in proprietary programs but still encourages some sharing.

Perens later recognized an additional model: a *time-based* license, such as the Business Source License (BSL, https://mariadb.com/bsl11), which is a restrictive license that converts to an open source license at some point in the future—four years at most. This allows commercial developers to recoup their development costs while still providing the guarantees of open source to users [20].

While an open source license enables software freedom, most of the benefits of open source require community development. As important as the Apache HTTP Server is to the history of technology, the Apache Group's biggest innovation was the democratic process it adopted to develop software collaboratively. As the Apache Group matured into the Apache Software Foundation (http://apache.org), its governance model matured to allow contributors from all backgrounds to collaborate without a single entity taking control of the software project, even when participants have competing commercial interests. This is important for avoiding vendor lock-in to the technology and insuring the project against the risk of a participant ceasing to contribute.

In chapter 11, you can see that SSI solutions add layers of governance on top of the models adopted by open source communities. These governance frameworks use many of the same practices to establish trust, align incentives, and resolve conflict. This is starting to be called *open governance*.

Finally, the benefits of open source also depend on the adoption of open standards. These standards allow users to migrate between software packages as their needs change over time and interoperate with users who select other software packages. Most developers of SSI solutions are already basing their work on two open standards from the World Wide Web Consortium (W3C): the Verifiable Credentials Data Model 1.0 standard (https://w3c.github.io/vc-data-model) for how to format and digitally sign interoperable verifiable credentials (chapter 7) and the DID Core Specification (https://w3c-ccg.github.io/did-spec) for how to create, read, update, and delete a decentralized identifier (DID) and its associated DID document (chapter 8).

12.4 Open source and digital identities

The fundamental goal of digital identity solutions is to establish trust between individuals and organizations. Noted security researcher and public-interest technologist Bruce Scheier identifies four methods that society uses to enforce trustworthy behavior: morals, reputation, laws, and technical systems [21]. Professor of constitutional law Lawrence Lessig points out that as our society's dependence on information technology increases—as code becomes a regulator of behavior—technical systems become more central to our experience in a democracy. To preserve our rights, we need the ability to analyze the code and algorithms used in those systems [22].

While the rights protected by open source software are important for operating systems, web browsers, and spacecraft, *they are far more important for our digital identities.* As our world becomes more connected, our identity systems become increasingly "mission-critical" for our lives. Governments, businesses, and charities push for the adoption of digital identity systems to reduce the cost of completing their missions. Too often, these systems are designed to protect corporations' interests, not the rights of users as individuals. Source code secrecy encourages such abuse.

Real-world examples of such problems are easy to come by. Mark Zuckerberg, the founder of Facebook, announced in 2019 that "the future is private" [23]. This apparent change in policy was a response to widespread outcry from the public learning how Facebook's proprietary algorithms were used. Among other transgressions, people criticized how Facebook's system

- Manipulated user emotions without consent [24]
- Shared user data with Cambridge Analytica for political use [25]
- Stole email contact data [26]

Similarly, the American consumer credit reporting agency Equifax has suffered from a series of data breaches culminating in the 2017 exposure of 143 million Americans' private information (for a detailed list compiled by technology journalist and security researcher Brian Krebs, see https://krebsonsecurity.com/tag/equifax [27]). Equifax's lack of transparency prevented the public from understanding what information was being collected on individuals, who that information was being shared with, and how poor their security systems were.

Government programs are similarly vulnerable to abuse when systems are built with proprietary source code, secret algorithms, and unknowable security. India's Aadhaar program to create a centralized database of biometric and identity information has been criticized for

- Not reducing corruption [28]
- Excluding vulnerable members of society [29]
- Being required in inappropriate contexts [30]
- Being accessed improperly [31]

All of these results contradict the noble goals of the program.

One more example: China's emerging social credit system, although intended to increase the trust necessary to do business [32], is being used to prevent people from complaining about local authorities even before its nationwide rollout [33].

Contrast these identity failures with the system that humanitarian NGO iRespond deployed among the Myanmar refugees in Thailand. As documented in *Newsweek*, the system is designed to put each individual in control of their data [34]. Although individual refugees might not have the skills necessary to examine the system's open source components, they benefit from the analysis of many researchers who have made suggestions for improvements. The open standards used to implement the system are intended to allow the refugees to take their digital identities with them when they leave the camp [35].

This chapter demonstrates why it is imperative that *identity solutions that claim to be self-sovereign need to be open source*. Each identity holder must have the legal right to examine the software that provides their digital identity and collaborate with a community that can modify that software for as long as it is useful. As these systems use open standards, the identity owner's scope for autonomy further increases. The ability to exercise our rights as individuals and citizens is no accident; to enjoy our rights, we as citizens and consumers must hold governments and vendors accountable for providing digital systems we can control.

The movement to promote software freedom with open source development contributed to the emergence and evolution of self-sovereign identity. In the next chapter, we explore how the cypherpunks built on that foundation as they created Bitcoin and other blockchain technologies that early SSI solutions use. As with free software, the philosophy behind their work is as important as their technical innovations.

SSI Resources

To learn more about how open source makes SSI possible, please check out https://ssimeetup.org/self-sovereign-identity-ssi-open-source-richard-esplin-webinar-16.

References

1. Levy, Steven. 1984. *Hackers: Heroes of the Computer Revolution*. Anchor Press/Doubleday.
2. Raymond, Eric S. "Hacker." 2004. The Jargon File v4.4.8 www.catb.org/jargon/html/H/hacker.html.
3. Levy, Steven. 2014. "'Hackers' and 'Information Wants to Be Free.'" *Backchannel*. https://medium.com/backchannel/the-definitive-story-of-information-wants-to-be-free-a8d95427641c.
4. Grad, Burton. 2015. "Software Industry." Engineering and Technology History Wiki. https://ethw.org/Software_Industry.
5. Toomey, Warren. 2011. "The Strange Birth and Long Life of Unix." IEEE Spectrum. https://spectrum.ieee.org/computing/software/the-strange-birth-and-long-life-of-unix.
6. Levy, Steven. 2010. *Hackers: Heroes of the Computer Revolution, 25th Anniversary Edition*. O'Reilly Media, Inc.
7. Gates, William Henry III, 1976. "An Open Letter to Hobbyists." *Homebrew Computer Club Newsletter* 2 (1). www.digibarn.com/collections/newsletters/homebrew/V2_01/gatesletter.html.
8. Williams, Sam. 2002. *Free as in Freedom: Richard Stallman's Crusade for Free Software*. O'Reilly Media, Inc. Available online at Project Gutenberg: www.gutenberg.org/ebooks/5768. An updated version with changes by Richard Stallman was produced in 2010: https://www.fsf.org/faif.
9. Stallman, Richard. 2001. "What Is free software?" https://www.gnu.org/philosophy/free-sw.en.html.
10. Torvalds, Linus and David Diamond. 2001. *Just for Fun: The Story of an Accidental Revolutionary*. Harper Collins.
11. Raymond, Eric S. 2001. *The Cathedral & the Bazaar: Musings on Linux and Open Source by an Accidental Revolutionary*. O'Reilly Media, Inc.
12. Moody, Glyn. 2001. *Rebel Code: Inside Linux and the Open Source Revolution*. Perseus Publishing.
13. Stallman, Richard. 2007. "Why Open Source Misses the Point of Free Software." https://www.gnu.org/philosophy/open-source-misses-the-point.html.
14. NASA JPL. n.d. https://voyager.jpl.nasa.gov/frequently-asked-questions.
15. NASA, JPL. n.d. https://voyager.jpl.nasa.gov/news/details.php?article_id=108.

16. Esplin, Richard. 2014, "Alfresco Tech Talk Live 81: Alfresco as a Model-Based Engineering Environment." https://www.youtube.com/watch?v=SD1PFNLoc14.

17. Personal experience of the author.

18. Newbart, Dave. 2001. "Microsoft CEO Takes Launch Break with the Sun-Times." *Chicago Sun-Times* (June 1).

19. Perens, Bruce. 2009. "How Many Open Source Licenses Do You Need?" Datamation. https://www.datamation.com/osrc/article.php/3803101/Bruce-Perens-How-Many-Open-Source-Licenses-Do-You-Need.htm.

20. Perens, Bruce. 2017. "MariaDB Fixes Its Business Source License With My Help, Releases MaxScale 2.1 Database Routing Proxy." https://perens.com/2017/02/14/bsl-1-1.

21. Schneier, Bruce. 2012. *Liars and Outliers: Enabling the Trust that Society Needs to Thrive.* Wiley.

22. Lessig, Lawrence. 2006. *Code: Version 2.0.* Basic Books.

23. Kleinman, Zoe. 2019. "Facebook Boss Reveals Changes in Response to Criticism." BBC News. https://www.bbc.com/news/technology-48107268.

24. BBC News. 2014. "Facebook Emotion Experiment Sparks Criticism." https://www.bbc.com/news/technology-28051930.

25. BBC News. 2018. "Facebook Appeals Against Cambridge Analytica Fine." https://www.bbc.com/news/technology-46292818.

26. BBC News. 2019. "Facebook copied email contacts of 1.5 million users." https://www.bbc.com/news/technology-47974574.

27. Gressin, Seena. 2017. "The Equifax Data Breach: What to Do." Federal Trade Commission. https://www.consumer.ftc.gov/blog/2017/09/equifax-data-breach-what-do.

28. Khera, Reetika. 2017. "Impact of Aadhaar in Welfare Programmes." SSRN. https://papers.ssrn.com/sol3/papers.cfm?abstract_id=3045235.

29. Sinha, Dipa. 2018. "Aadhaar—A Tool for Exclusion." *Swarajya.* https://swarajyamag.com/magazine/aadhaar—a-tool-for-exclusion.

30. Dixit, Pranav. 2017. "Amazon Is Asking Indians to Hand Over Their Aadhaar, India's Controversial Biometric ID, to Track Lost Packages." BuzzFeed News. https://www.buzzfeednews.com/article/pranavdixit/amazon-is-asking-indians-to-hand-over-their-aadhaar-indias.

31. Khaira, Rachna. 2018. "Rs 500, 10 Minutes, and You Have Access to Billion Aadhaar Details." *The Tribune.* https://www.tribuneindia.com/news/nation/rs-500-10-minutes-and-you-have-access-to-billion-aadhaar-details/523361.html.

32. Pak, Jennifer. 2018. "Inside China's 'Social Credit' System, Which Blacklists Citizens." *Marketplace.* https://www.marketplace.org/2018/02/13/world/social-credit-score-china-blacklisted.

33. Mistreanu, Simina. 2019. "Fears About China's Social-Credit System Are Probably Overblown, but It Will Still Be Chilling." *The Washington Post.* https://www.washingtonpost.com/opinions/2019/03/08/fears-about-chinas-social-credit-system-are-probably-overblown-it-will-still-be-chilling.

34. Piore, Adam. 2019. "Can Blockchain Finally Give Us the Digital Privacy We Deserve?" *Newsweek.* https://www.newsweek.com/2019/03/08/can-blockchain-finally-give-us-digital-privacy-we-deserve-1340689.html.

35. Sovrin. 2019. "Use Case Spotlight: iRespond, Using Sovrin to Provide NGOs with Trusted Digital Identity Systems." https://sovrin.org/use-case-spotlight-irespond-using-sovrin-to-provide-ngos-with-trusted-digital-identity-systems.

Cypherpunks: The origin of decentralization

Daniel Paramo and Alex Preukschat

Daniel Paramo is an experienced account and business development executive, data scientist, and engineer. A former account executive at Learning Machine and a former business development manager at Bell Helicopter, Daniel has founded several startups in blockchain technology and the sharing economy. He holds a master's degree in aerospace engineering from the University of Texas at Arlington.

In the previous chapter, we presented how the free software and open source communities influenced the emergence of self-sovereign identity (SSI). In this chapter, we explain how SSI also stands on the shoulders of cryptography giants. These cryptography pioneers of the 1970s inspired a movement known as the *cypherpunks*, which subsequently inspired the Bitcoin and cryptocurrency movement based on blockchain and distributed ledger technologies (DLTs). Understanding the cypherpunks—and their unique motivations—sheds light on the larger trend to decentralization, Web 3.0, and SSI.

13.1 The origins of modern cryptography

In his landmark 2001 book *Crypto*, Steven Levy explains how cryptography in the United States of America evolved over 50 years [1]. What began as a "monopoly" controlled by the National Security Agency (NSA) ended with the progressive dismemberment of that monopoly, led by the academic community—a community in which many of the Bitcoin, cryptocurrency, and blockchain pioneers were involved.

NOTE   *Crypto* has been cited as a key influence by both the main authors of this book as well as many of the contributing authors. The first chapter is available for free in the *New York Times* archives: https://archive.nytimes.com/www.nytimes.com/books/first/l/levy-crypto.html.

One of the central protagonists of Levy's story is Bailey Whitfield "Whit" Diffie. When Diffie became interested in cryptography, he quickly realized that the NSA had a monopoly on knowledge about the most advanced cryptography techniques and that only very basic techniques were studied at universities. Levy tells the story of a conversation Diffie had with his boss, a mathematician named Roland Silver, when both of them worked at the Mitre Corporation in Boston in the mid-1960s [1]:

> *One day, walking with Silver along Mass Avenue near the railroad tracks, he [Diffie] spilled his concerns. Cryptography is vital to human privacy! he railed.*

So Diffie decided to look for information across the country to learn more about cryptography. He used a 1967 book called *The Codebreakers* by David Kahn as his guidebook. It was one of the very few sources available then—even the NSA had tried to block its publication. To quote chapter 1 of Steven Levy's book [1]:

> *By the time Whitfield Diffie finished The Codebreakers, he was no longer depending on others to tackle the great problems of cryptography. He was personally, passionately engaged in them himself. They consumed his waking dreams. They were now his obsession.*

After several years of research, Diffie eventually met Martin Hellman at Stanford. The two decided to work together to create better cryptographic algorithms. Between them, they developed the core concepts of *public-key cryptography* in the early 1970s. As chapter 6 explains in more detail, this is the cryptography at the heart of all modern digital security infrastructure. It is what you are using under the hood every time you see the lock in the address bar of your browser—your web session is being secured using the public/private key cryptography in the SSL/TLS standard (the HTTPS protocol).

NOTE   The co-author of the SSL 1.0 standard, Christopher Allen, is one of the pioneers of SSI and wrote the groundbreaking essay "The Path to Self-Sovereign Identity." See www.lifewithalacrity.com/2016/04/the-path-to-self-soverereign-identity.html.

Shortly after reading the report on public-key cryptography by Diffie and Hellman, Ralph Merkle contacted them. Based on their conversations, Merkle conceived of one of the first public/private key exchange protocols, which he named *Diffie-Hellman key exchange*. As you may have guessed, this is the same Merkle who invented the Merkle tree used in the Bitcoin blockchain structure and other public blockchains (see chapter 6 for more).

Diffie-Hellman inspired three MIT professors—Ron Rivest, Adi Shamir, and Leonard Adleman—to create the first implementation of public-key cryptography.

They invented a practical way (based on prime number factorization) to create the one-way function envisioned by Diffie and Hellman. In April 1977, they published "A Method for Obtaining Digital Signatures and Public-Key Cryptosystems" (https://people.csail.mit.edu/rivest/Rsapaper.pdf). After applying for a U.S. patent, the three professors co-founded RSA Security in 1982. Later known simply as RSA, it became the most successful security company globally, eventually selling to EMC Corporation in 2006 for $2.1 billion.

While developing Simple Public Key Infrastructure (SPKI) in the 1990s, Ron Rivest realized that cryptographic credentials could be used as authorization tokens, allowing their bearers to securely access services. Now authorization systems could focus on *what you can do* instead of *who you are*. This seed would later grow into the cryptographically verifiable credentials at the heart of SSI—especially those that enabled holders to share identity data selectively instead of having to disclose all data in a credential. (See chapter 7 for more about verifiable credentials and zero-knowledge proofs.)

Inspired by the MIT team and frustrated by the lack of free, open source encryption software, Phil Zimmermann created the first version of Pretty Good Privacy (PGP) in 1991. He released it onto the internet as open source code and a book that could be exported anywhere in the world. PGP gained a considerable following and was a major step toward democratizing cryptography so it could be used by the masses.

13.2 The birth of the cypherpunk movement

Bruce Bethke coined the term *cyberpunk* in 1980 for his short story of the same name published in 1983. Arguably the most famous writer connected with this term is William Gibson due to his famous 1984 novel, *Neuromancer.* Cyberpunks were primarily a literary movement—a genre that had the character of a quasi-counterculture in the 1980s. A cyberpunk was an individual who defended—in an exaggerated way— freedom of expression, freedom of information, and communications privacy.

But the literary genre crossed over into the real world—or at least the *cyber* world— when, in 1992, a group of people interested in building tools to protect their freedom and privacy started communicating via an electronic mailing list. In their first meeting, they decided to call themselves the *cypherpunks.* Wikipedia defines the term as "any individual advocating widespread use of strong cryptography and privacy-enhancing technologies as a route to social and political change."

The origins of the cypherpunks goes back further than 1992. In 1986, Loyd Blankenship, aka "The Mentor," wrote a manifesto called "The Conscience of a Hacker" (www.phrack.org/archives/issues/7/3.txt) by hand from a prison cell in the United States. Also known as "The Hacker's Manifesto," this essay became legendary as the first clear articulation of the motivations of "hackers" and "hacktivism." It is a reproach to society for criminalizing hackers without stopping to understand their motivations— and a clear vindication of their actions. In the words of Blankenship, "Yes, I am a criminal. My crime is curiosity." (Years later, Blankenship also created a role-playing game called *GURPS Cyberpunk,* which was seized by the U.S. Secret Service.)

Blankenship was part of the group of hackers who considered the "profession" worthy, almost humanistic. It was an activity that combined craftsmanship and intelligence and never accepted violence. In the purest sense of the word, hackers are enthusiastic about the creation and development of the most sophisticated machines in the world. They firmly believe that technology has a duty to "do something": to contribute something. For this reason, they share and exchange ideas, codes, and advice that they use to improve and discover solutions to technical problems.

This movement grew through the Cypherpunk mailing list, which by 1997 had over 2,000 subscribers. It was one of the most active and authoritative forums anywhere for technical discussions of mathematics, cryptography, computer science, and politics involving privacy and encryption. In 1993, Steven Levy wrote a *Wired* article titled "Crypto Rebels" about the cypherpunk movement that captured its essence [2]:

> *The people in this room hope for a world where an individual's informational footprints can be traced only if the individual involved chooses to reveal them. There is only one way this vision will materialize, and that is by widespread use of cryptography. The obstacles are political —some of the most powerful forces in government are devoted to the control of these tools. In short, there is a war going on between those who would liberate crypto and those who would suppress it.*

One of the Cypherpunk mailing list founders, John Gilmore, went on to become a founder of the Electronic Frontier Foundation (EFF), one of the best-known nonprofit organizations fighting to defend privacy and personal freedom in the digital world.

13.3 Digital freedom, digital cash, and decentralization

The core ideas the cypherpunks explored for the defense of digital privacy and freedom led some of them into the realm of digital money. Famous cypherpunks like Wei Dai, Nick Szabo, and Hal Finney later inspired the creator of Bitcoin, Satoshi Nakamoto.

> **NOTE** Wei Dai is the creator of b-money, Nick Szabo of bit gold, and Hal Finney of Reusable Proof-of-Work (RPOW). Satoshi Nakamoto's white paper refers to Wei Dai. Hal Finney did the first-ever bitcoin transaction with Satoshi Nakamoto. In chapter 17, we explore the overlap of cypherpunks, identity, and money.

They also influenced David Chaum, a legendary cryptographer, who had worked since 1981 on trustworthy voting systems inspired by the creators of public-key cryptography. David later became famous for his work on *digital anonymous cash*, the digital equivalent of physical cash. He wanted digital money to be anonymous—just like fiat money could be—but without physical barriers. He created a company, DigiCash, as part of his quest to provide a digital currency to the internet. (For more about the relationship of digital identity, money, and SSI, see chapter 17.)

All of these solutions for the exchange of digital value depended on cryptography not just for security but also for decentralized control. Whit Diffie recognized the inherent link between privacy and decentralization very early on, when he was still at MIT. The main MIT computer system, called Compatible Time-Sharing System (CTSS), was one of the first to use time-sharing, a way to enable multiple users to work on the machine simultaneously. This required some way to protect the privacy of each person's information. CTSS performed this by assigning a password to each user; this was their "key" to unlocking their own files. As Steven Levy tells the story in *Crypto* [1]:

> *Passwords were distributed and maintained by a human being, the system operator. This central authority figure, in essence, controlled the privacy of every user. Even if he or she were scrupulously honest about protecting the passwords, the very fact that they existed within a centralized system provided an opportunity for compromise. Outside authorities had a clear shot at that information: simply present the system operator with a subpoena. "That person would sell you out," says Diffie, "because he had no interest in defying the order and going to jail to protect your data."*
>
> *Diffie believed in what he called "a decentralized view of authority."*
>
> *By creating the proper cryptographic tools, he felt, you could solve the problem—by transferring the data protection from a disinterested third party to the actual user, the one whose privacy was actually at risk.*

What Whit Diffie had envisioned sounds just like what is now being implemented with SSI: decentralized digital wallets where each of us can control our cryptographic keys to our own identity, our data, our relationships, and eventually our own money.

13.4 From cryptography to cryptocurrency to credentials

In this chapter, we have shown that the common thread from the creation of public-key cryptography, to the academic entrepreneur cryptographers, to the cypherpunks, to the cryptocurrency pioneers, to the SSI community is to *provide people with more privacy-preserving tools for communication in the digital age.*

The influence of the cypherpunk movement is still very present, not just for Bitcoin, but also for blockchain ecosystems like Ethereum—co-founded by leaders like Vitalik Buterin who often refer to themselves as cypherpunks. And these "modern cypherpunks" in the Bitcoin, Ethereum, and other blockchain communities all recognize the fundamental need for SSI as part of their vision to build a decentralized economy.

In the next chapter, we explore how these principles express themselves in another key subject for humanity: peace through digital identity.

SSI Resources

To learn more about the ideological inspiration for SSI, check out https://ssi meetup.org/self-sovereign-identity-why-we-here-christopher-allen-webinar-51.

References

1. Levy, Steven. 2001. *Crypto: How the Code Rebels Beat the Government—Saving Privacy in the Digital Age.* Viking.
2. Levy, Steven. 1993. "Crypto Rebels." *Wired.* http://archive.wired.com/wired/archive/1.02/crypto.rebels.html.

14

Decentralized identity for a peaceful society

Markus Sabadello

The first two chapters in part 3 have looked backward at how SSI has roots in open source technology, cryptography, and the cypherpunk movement. In this chapter, we look forward at one of the key potential implications for SSI: that it may make a significant contribution to world peace. Our guide in this chapter, Markus Sabadello, is deeply qualified to write about this subject in two respects. First, he is one of the foremost technical experts on the subject— co-editor of the W3C DID Core Specification (and co-author of chapter 8 of this book), co-chair of the Identifiers & Discovery Working Group at the Decentralized Identity Foundation (DIF), and a founding member of the Technical Governance Board at the Sovrin Foundation. At the same time, Markus is a graduate of the European Peace University, where he has an MA in Peace and Conflict Studies.

In our efforts to implement decentralized identity technologies, we are trying to build better tools for individuals and organizations, and many of us also aspire to create something beneficial to humanity as a whole. In this chapter, we specifically explore how the self-sovereign identity (SSI) paradigm can serve the ideal of peace, which we understand not only in the sense of *negative peace* (the absence of physical violence) but also as *positive peace* (a state in which all people are content and their needs are served).

Considering that today, digital applications and services affect all parts of our lives and digital identity is a prerequisite for any kind of online transaction or interaction, it is not an exaggeration to state that the nature of the infrastructure for digital identity directly affects human well-being and society as a whole. If this infrastructure does not work in the best interest of individuals, then the loss of control or misuse of digital identity—and the consequences in the real world—can threaten human rights, violate the ideals of both negative peace and positive peace, and lead to "structural violence": the impairment of fundamental human needs.

In 2009, an online initiative successfully campaigned to nominate the internet for the Nobel Peace Prize [1]. The initiative argued that the internet is a "web of people" rather than a "network of computers"; that it has laid the foundations for a new kind of society that is advancing dialogue, debate, and consensus through communication; that contact with others has always been the most effective antidote to hatred and conflict; and that therefore the internet is a tool for peace and nonviolence.

During the opening ceremony of the World Summit on the Information Society's second phase in 2005 in Tunis (http://www.itu.int/net/wsis/docs2/tunis/off/6rev1 .html), then-Secretary General of the United Nations Kofi Annan articulated the desire to use digital technologies for working toward the ideal of peace. He declared:

> *While most other conferences focus on global threats, this one will tell us how to best use a new global asset.*

One of the outcome documents of this summit recognized in 2005 that the Information Society and its technical infrastructure should be "people-centered." In other words, it should not be architected around powerful, central authorities.

14.1 Technology and society

> *A community will evolve only when a people control their own communication.*
>
> —Frantz Fanon

Those of us who work on decentralized digital identity have always understood that our work is about more than creating more privacy, security, trust, transparency, or economic value. Ultimately, our goal is to transport into the digital world how individual identity and social structures function in the real world. We are attempting to create digital data formats and protocols to model real-world concepts. We feel that today's dominant centralized digital identity systems are misaligned with how individuals and their relationships function in the real world and that we are essentially trying to fix this misalignment.

We like to use metaphors such as "digital slavery" and "digital enlightenment" to express our conviction that current centralized identity systems do not reflect values such as freedom and human rights, which many of us take for granted in the real world. This misalignment also explains why we often speak not only of *decentralization* but also of *re-decentralization* to emphasize that we are simply building digital infrastructure the way it was meant to be in the first place.

Of course, our real-world understanding of human nature and social structures is not constant. It varies across cultures. For example, when we explain the need for decentralized identity technologies in the Western world, we often quote the philosopher René Descartes, who said, "I think, therefore I am," arguing that the basis for one's identity is something that should be self-determined rather than assigned by an authority to an individual. However, this concept of individual sovereignty is less central in Eastern cultures that put a stronger emphasis on communal governance than on individual control. And in the South African context, the Nguni Bantu term *Ubuntu* is often translated as "I am who I am because of who we all are"—in other words, there can be no individual identity without a collective identity. So if we want to design digital identity systems that benefit all people, we must take such cultural differences into account.

Understanding of human identity also changes over time. In today's world shaped by global connectivity, affordable long-distance travel, and migration, some traditional aspects of our identities (such as being citizens of nation-states) become less important, while others may become more dominant. Attempts to define human identity can therefore never be universalized or taken as constant, and any technology we build to model such identity will always have to evolve along with our changing society.

We are also aware that not only do real-world ideas influence the identity technologies we create, but also the other way round. Technology affects political and social realities. Often, when evaluating the positive and negative effects of a particular technology, it is argued that "technology is neutral." It is tempting to say that everything depends solely on the humans who decide to use technology for good or evil—that this has nothing to do with technology itself.

However, this point of view contrasts with the more contemporary position that says technology always has built-in values and inherent biases. Therefore, it is not neutral but rather built with certain assumptions and intentions that favor and incentivize certain uses and behaviors. As leaders and engineers who are defining the current movement to digital decentralization, we decide to a large extent whether the technology we build will work for or against users. We have power over those individuals who are going to use our technologies. So, we have an enormous responsibility and obligation to "do it right"—to design technology in a way that serves the interests of all people.

14.2 A global civil society

> We are tied together in the single garment of destiny, caught in an inescapable network of mutuality. And whatever affects one directly affects all indirectly.
>
> —Martin Luther King, Jr., *"Remaining Awake Through a Great Revolution"*

Bearing in mind the strong mutual interdependence between digital infrastructure and real-world society, we should try to learn from those human forms of organization and interaction that are well suited to promote the ideal of peace. They will enable us to design identity technologies in a way that is simultaneously based in such forms of organization while at the same time supporting them in the digital world. When looking for such inherently peaceful human structures, we quickly arrive at the concept of *civil society*, which is characterized by direct, dynamic, and fundamentally decentralized human relationships and interactions.

Civil society is sometimes described as a *third system* in addition to the state (organized in a centralized way) and the economy (organized like a market). This third system does not seek governmental or economic power, but rather autonomous power vis-à-vis both the state and the economy [2]. The emergence of civil society is rooted in the desire to establish a context of autonomy and a private sphere beyond the reach of overly powerful authorities.

Civil society has always been linked to peace [3]—a "societas civilis," a zone of civility in which violence has been minimized—in contrast to nation-states, which historically have often had a war-making function. In this sense, civil society may not directly be a recipe for peace, but it certainly offers mechanisms for debating and addressing issues leading to conflicts. For Hegel, civil society was the "achievement of the modern age"; for Marx, it was the "theatre of history"; and for Vaclav Havel, it was the "universality of human rights to allow us to fulfill our potential in all our roles."

Taking a closer look, it becomes evident that the core properties of civil society are the same as the properties of the decentralized identity systems we are now creating. These shared properties include

- Self-organization
- Self-determination
- Spontaneity
- Dynamic adaptation to changes
- Pluralism
- Independence from but interaction with actors of the state and economy
- Aspiration to freedom and independence
- A public sphere in which interactions take place

DIDs, verifiable credentials, digital agents and wallets, and other technical building blocks of SSI that we introduce in chapter 2 (and dive deeply into in part 2) are expressions of principles in the digital world that mirror the foundations on which a civil society can flourish in the real world.

Today, civil society is no longer confined to the territorial state. The *global civil society* that is emerging reflects a new reality enabled by the fusion of the terms *globalization* and *civil society*. It is accompanied by a *global public sphere*, which is both an outcome and an agent of global interconnectedness. Individuals and groups of individuals communicate across borders, and the strongest concepts that define them (their identity) are often no longer the nation-state but transnational values and causes they share and care about. A global civil society promises to apply a global, holistic approach to global challenges, unlike nation-states, which are mostly concerned with their own spheres of influence.

NOTE This process is known as *deterritorialization*, which means that location, distance, and borders no longer have a determining influence. While globality has not taken over territoriality, territoriality no longer has the monopoly on social geography. See F. Miszlivetz and J. Jensen, 2006, "Global Civil

Society: From Dissident Discourse to World Bank Parlance," in P. Wagner (ed.), *The Languages of Civil Society*, 177–205, Berghahn Books.

For those of us working on SSI, the responsibility lies in developing the technological basis in a way that reflects the organizational form of the global civil society it enables. This means an open, decentralized, and dynamic network structure where identity and communication flow directly between individuals—and where network connections adapt dynamically according to the actual communication processes they are serving. For a global civil society to truly work, both the architectural structure and the governance mechanisms of its communication channels must be based on civil society principles. If we keep this in mind, we will have the opportunity to support a well-functioning global civil society—a global public sphere that can effectively host the discourses needed to approach and solve the big global problems of our time.

14.3 Identity as a source of conflict

> *Cultural and religious identities are major sources for conflict.*
>
> —Samuel P. Huntington, *The Clash of Civilizations and the Remaking of World Order* (Simon & Schuster, 1996)

> *Culture is more often a source of conflict than of synergy.*
>
> —Geert Hofstede, *Culture's Consequences: Comparing Values, Behaviors, Institutions* (SAGE Publications, 2001)

Throughout history, the identities of individuals and groups have always played a key role in conflicts and wars. Identity is required for a conflict to develop; after all, it is impossible to designate an enemy unless you have a notion of "us" versus "them." But identity issues can also themselves lead to competition and conflict.

In his book *Identity: The Demand for Dignity and the Politics of Resentment* [4], Francis Fukuyama argues that identity fuels much of today's world politics. As humans, we have a natural desire for recognition and respect for our identity—who we are as individuals, and what cultures, nations, religions, tribes, or other groups we feel like we belong to. Unfortunately, this desire for identity sometimes is not directed toward a shared and universal understanding of human dignity but instead is misdirected toward restriction and a sense that the identity of others is threatening our own identity. In this way of thinking, identity is not only what defines us as individuals or groups but also a description of what separates one individual or group from another.

Leaders of populist political movements often use this exclusionary approach to identity politics. They claim that they are the only ones who understand and represent "the people"—where this term sounds very broad but is actually meant to designate a narrow "in group" that excludes large parts of a population. Consequently, such identity politics may lead to misunderstandings, social injustices, conflicts, and violence. Incarnations of such adversarial identity politics include extreme anti-immigrant parties, "Islamist" political groups, apartheids, white supremacism, and many other problematic political movements.

So we can say that notions of identity are both a prerequisite and fuel for human conflict. Going one step further, it turns out that historically, the worst atrocities have always been committed in conflicts that have identity issues as a central factor—or a root cause of the conflict. Identity is used as a direct justification for conflict and violence. All instances of genocide throughout history have followed a sequence of stages that includes a process of dehumanization: completely denying groups of individuals their humanity. This was the case in the Rwandan genocide, where the Tutsi people were called *inyenzi* (cockroaches), and in the Holocaust, where terms such as *untermenschen* (subhumans) were used. (This complete denying of someone's identity as a human being can be considered a violation of article 6 of the Universal Declaration of Human Rights: "Everyone has the right to recognition everywhere as a person before the law"; see https://www.un.org/en/universal-declaration-human-rights.) The lessons for our work on building decentralized digital identity systems are that no actor should be able to have authority to define the identity of "the people" and that individual identities should not be defined in a way that puts them in opposition to one another.

14.4   Identity as a source of peace

> *War is not inherent in human beings. We learn war and we learn peace. The culture of peace is something which is learned, just as violence is learned and war culture is learned.*
>
> —Elise Boulding, keynote, *"Cultures of Peace"* conference, 5 February 1999

Identities can be a source of conflict but also a source of peace. Mutual understanding, recognition of and respect for the "other," appreciation of what we have in common and what distinguishes us—these are the foundations for being able to engage in dialogue, to learn from one another and about each other, and to engage in intercultural dialogue and overcome cultural differences which so often lead to conflict and war. If we know enough about each other—if we realize that diversity of identity is as important to humanity as biodiversity is to nature—then we will be less likely to adopt an "us" versus "them" mindset or rhetoric. We will be more likely to understand, respect, and perhaps even enjoy each other's identity, and less likely to engage in conflict and violence against each other. And if we recognize each other as equal human beings instead of engaging in adversarial identity politics and processes of dehumanization, we will be able to solve conflicts before they unfold their destructive character.

The United Nations Educational, Scientific, and Cultural Organization (UNESCO) is tasked with preventing causes for war by promoting intercultural dialogue and mutual understanding. Its Universal Declaration on Cultural Diversity (http://unesdoc.unesco.org/images/0012/001271/127160m.pdf) was adopted soon after the September 11, 2001 terrorist attacks. It states:

> *Affirming that respect for the diversity of cultures, tolerance, dialogue and cooperation, in a climate of mutual trust and understanding are among the best guarantees of international peace and security.*

Culture is our way of looking at the world. Cultural identity is the distinct set of behaviors, habits, rules, traditions, customs, attitudes, values, and beliefs of an individual or a group of individuals. This definition can also include language, history, religion, ideology, cosmology, art, and our overall way of life. Elements of culture that are not so visible at first sight, but unfold only after interaction, are sometimes referred to as *deep culture* [5]. This cultural identity that we embody within ourselves and share with others to various degrees can be defined by ourselves, and others can observe it.

For us as technologists, this means that in designing decentralized identity infrastructure, we must not only consider simple attributes such as name, date of birth, or whether we have a driver's license but also model all other aspects of human identity that unite and separate us, including deep cultural identity. Decentralized identity technologies can create the conditions for mutual understanding, a global civil society, and renewed dialogue among cultures and civilizations, thereby preventing causes of war.

In building this technology, it will be interesting to observe that whereas technical developments like DIDs and verifiable credentials will be most effective when they are standardized and uniform, *the actual content of digital identity credentials for humans will be most valuable when it is varied and unique.* The low-level identity infrastructure should strive to be globally interoperable and culture-neutral, but identity itself is most powerful when it is shaped by all forms of human diversity.

SSI Resources

For more free content to learn about SSI, please go to IdentityBook.info and SSI Meetup.org/book.

References

1. Wallace, Lewis. 2009. "Wired Backs Internet for Nobel Peace Prize." *Wired.* https://www.wired.com/2009/11/internet-for-peace-nobel.
2. Nerfin, Marc. 1987. "Neither Prince Nor Merchant: Citizen—An Introduction to the Third System. Development Dialogue," IFDA dossier 56: 3–28.
3. Kaldor, Mary. 2003. *Global Civil Society. An Answer to War.* Blackwell.
4. Fukuyama, Francis. 2018. *Identity: The Demand for Dignity and the Politics of Resentment.* Profile Books.
5. Shaules, Joseph. 2007. Deep Culture: The Hidden Challenges of Global Living. Multilingual Matters Ltd.

Belief systems as drivers for technology choices in decentralization

Alex Preukschat

In this chapter, we continue the theme of part 3, exploring the historical origins and movements that led to SSI and the social, political, and philosophical implications going forward. This chapter goes directly to the heart of the matter: belief systems, the overarching mental and value paradigms that define everything we do in our lives—including our technology choices and architectures. Note that this chapter lays the groundwork for understanding chapter 16, which explains the evolution of the SSI community.

15.1 What is a belief system?

Many books have been written and will be written about what belief systems are, but let us try to present a short and (hopefully) generally acceptable definition:

> *The belief system of a person or society is the set of beliefs they have about what is right and wrong and what is true and false.*

Belief systems answer all kinds of minor and major questions of life—and thus can be quite controversial. Such questions include, "Is party A or party B good or bad for the country?" "Are you in favor of the death penalty or against it?" "Do my children need a religious education?" "Is capitalism the source of the wealth gap?"

On almost any issue, the position we take depends on our belief system. This might happen with or without evidence—either way, our belief systems will guide us, even if it consists only of educated guesses or the sum of our life experiences.

Belief systems affect everything from the most challenging political, wealth, family, and religious questions to the smallest questions about life.

If we look at SSI from this perspective, it should come as no surprise that some discrepancies exist about what might be considered SSI. For example, one reference point within the SSI community for defining what is considered SSI is based on the 10 principles of SSI defined by Christopher Allen in his 2016 essay "The Path to Self-Sovereign Identity" [1]. One of these is that SSI architecture needs decentralization to be *censorship-resistant.* Censorship resistance is a key concept of the decentralization community. People in the open source, blockchain, and SSI communities believe centralization needs to be avoided because if any single party has full control, in the long run, that control will be most certainly abused. You may or may not agree with this idea, but in the end, it is your belief system that is guiding you in accepting or rejecting it.

In the early days of SSI technology, many SSI projects chose a blockchain or distributed ledger technology (DLT) to act as a decentralized, verifiable data registry (see chapter 2). Decentralized technologies used for SSI might change in the future, but in this chapter, we explain the differences between first-generation blockchain and DLT technologies to exemplify how nuanced, ideological, and passionate the discussion around decentralization technology can become.

NOTE There is no agreement on the market definition of the terms *blockchain* and *DLT.* We are using and explaining them in this chapter to highlight the ideological difference between blockchain and DLT. However, other people claim that blockchain is a subcategory of DLTs. In this chapter, we claim that Bitcoin started the blockchain technology and that DLTs are a separate technology.

We claim that the technology choices made for blockchain or DLT are reflections of belief systems about ownership and governance and highlight how this is relevant for SSI—and probably for anything else in life. The lesson we aim to convey is that keeping an open mind—and remembering that worldviews influence everything we hear and say—will help us to have empathy for people who might make different choices.

15.2 *Blockchain and DLT as belief systems*

The blockchain ecosystem started with the launch of the Bitcoin network on January 3, 2009, by Satoshi Nakamoto. As we detailed in chapter 13, Satoshi created Bitcoin to act as a peer-to-peer cash system without intermediaries or human authorities issuing currency. Instead, the network issued and registered all transactions in an architecture built on peer-to-peer technology, using monetary incentives based on game theory.

The early adopters of Bitcoin were often interested in cryptography, finance, decentralized systems, libertarian ideology, and the Austrian school of economics, among other things. The years after the launch of the Bitcoin network gave rise to different cryptocurrency-inspired speculation bubbles. The cryptocurrency bull market of 2013 that drove the bitcoin price to $1,200, a historic high at the time, was followed by a bear market that drove the price all the way down to $200 in the following two years.

NOTE   Capital *B* (Bitcoin) refers to the Bitcoin protocol and lowercase *b* (bitcoin) to the token or cryptocurrency of the Bitcoin protocol.

During this period, a new line of thinking developed that insisted on the virtues of blockchain as an architecture for consensus-driven data, yet without making cryptocurrency tokens the central function of the system. Some of these projects used so-called *non-monetary tokens* for internal governance functions but limited their transferability or currency-like properties, while others did away with the mechanisms of token economics.

NOTE   In the computer security and cryptocurrency industry, the term *token* generally refers to a cryptographic string of numbers and letters that contains no real data but relates back to real data. One bitcoin is an example of such a cryptographic string, as explained in chapter 6.

This line of thinking initially was called *DLT* to emphasize the role of the ledger over the token. Different technology players started creating decentralized data systems for the corporate world with a wider range of governance options, including highly centralized ones. This period is relevant to SSI because the worlds of blockchain, SSI, and DLT started cross-pollinating, exchanging ideological approaches and technical architectures.

Blockchains, DLTs, and P2P

Blockchain and DLTs are peer-to-peer (P2P) networks run by many interconnected computers, such as BitTorrent. You have to install on your computer the corresponding software that allows you to become part of a P2P network and communicate with other computers. When you download that software to your computer, your machine becomes a node of a decentralized network.

Bitcoin, Ethereum, and others are also called *permissionless systems* because anyone with an internet connection can participate. In this chapter, we call them *blockchain* technologies. DLTs are often called *permissioned systems* because you usually need permission to participate as a node. Examples of DLTs are Hyperledger projects like Fabric, Sawtooth, and Indy. To make this even more confusing, DLT projects often define themselves as blockchains in general, but blockchain projects don't usually use the term *DLT* to define themselves.

To highlight how SSI relates to those blockchain and DLT technologies, we think that exploring the underlying belief systems can illuminate the sometimes abstract debates around technology choices. While they may become outdated over time, the core idea is to understand that even technology choices are influenced by belief systems. Note that neither of the two examples we use has to represent reality—they are just illustrations.

15.2.1 Blockchain "believers"

Adherents to early blockchain projects like Bitcoin and Ethereum tend to distrust traditional centralized institutions, even claiming this distrust as a core motivation to invest in decentralization projects. They often believe that, over the long run, centralized institutions will side with the strong or the large against the small, weak, or independent actors in an economy or society. As such, individuals need tools to protect themselves against the dominance of these centralized institutions of commerce, information, and law.

For cypherpunks (chapter 13), the key to a healthy system lies in decentralizing power. Because their trust in institutions is low, blockchain believers want governance systems that are as decentralized as possible. Many lobby for mechanisms to block or disincentivize re-centralization, such as incenting anyone to run an infrastructural *node* in order to have as many different node operators as possible—which also helps ensure censorship resistance. (A *node* is a computer or server running specific software that can connect with other nodes to run a peer-to-peer network.) In many of these systems, a unique token also plays a central and structural role. This is why blockchain discourse often focuses on disruptive change of economic and social power structures, often modeled on the classic Silicon Valley trajectory from startup to transnational corporation.

15.2.2 DLT "believers"

DLT believers tend to trust some centralized institutions more than others. They often see in decentralized technologies an opportunity to optimize current business and compliance processes—or discover new business opportunities in transparency and cooperation. For a DLT believer, some centralized institutions can work well, particularly if they incentivize a common architecture across industries, limiting competition to the services offered on top of a shared infrastructure.

For many, their distrust of tokens is rooted in legal, transparency, and regulatory concerns. Others fear that tokens could create new forms of monopoly or centralization. In both cases, DLTs are generally designed less to disrupt industries than to make industries more stable, compliant, and efficient. DLT believers strive to shift the terms of cooperation and competition in ways that create new business models.

15.3 How are blockchains and DLTs relevant to SSI?

If the main differences between blockchain and DLT believers are their attitudes toward economic and social central authorities, SSI complicates this further by focusing on a wider problem space. For example, the SSI ecosystem is motivated to help people and companies protect their privacy (from both the state and other people and companies) through decentralization. Many (not all) governments are generally comfortable with this approach because it does not undermine their authority. They know people are increasingly concerned about the prying eyes of big tech companies. Some governments actively encourage market solutions to privacy concerns, especially if those solutions can relieve them of the onerous task of enforcing citizens' privacy.

In that sense, the SSI community—as you can read in more detail in chapter 16—is less rebellious or anarchistic than some of the blockchain early adopters. As an overall community, it wants to use decentralization to fulfill its vision of creating identity systems that enable trust and defend privacy without having to rely on a central party.

However, the challenge is that decentralization isn't black and white but comes in various shades. Achieving decentralization is a fundamental and ongoing design challenge: depending on the use case, different levels of decentralization might be possible or necessary. To understand this, let's explore some specific characteristics of blockchain and DLT systems.

15.4 Characterizing differences between blockchain and DLT

Between the two extremes of blockchain and DLT believers, there are many shades of gray. We can simplify somewhat by creating two general classifications:

- Blockchains are trustless or permissionless systems: i.e., they are more open to new participants without permission from a centralized authority.
- DLTs are trust-based or permissioned systems that generally require permission for future unknown participants to join.

Figure 15.1 illustrates the spectrum of possibilities between these two approaches. It is important to note that, while blockchain and DLT architectures have been driving SSI in its early days, new approaches to decentralized architectures such as pure peer-to-peer (P2P) networks are also emerging. So, there may be other ways to fulfill the decentralization and openness requirements of the SSI principles without depending on either blockchains or DLTs.

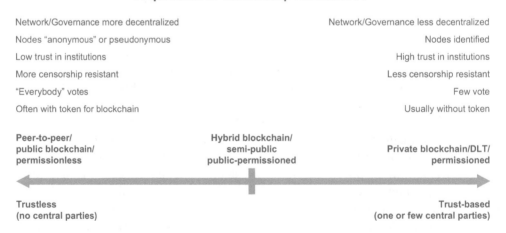

**Trustless vs. trust-based solutions:
A question of censorship resistance?**

Network/Governance more decentralized	Network/Governance less decentralized
Nodes "anonymous" or pseudonymous	Nodes identified
Low trust in institutions	High trust in institutions
More censorship resistant	Less censorship resistant
"Everybody" votes	Few vote
Often with token for blockchain	Usually without token

Peer-to-peer/ public blockchain/ permissionless	Hybrid blockchain/ semi-public public-permissioned	Private blockchain/DLT/ permissioned

| Trustless (no central parties) | | Trust-based (one or few central parties) |

Figure 15.1 **Trustless systems are more open and internally governed, usually using token-based systems, while trust-based systems tend to delegate governance and gatekeeping to trusted authorities.**

Starting with network governance, we can explore how blockchains, hybrid blockchains, and DLTs differ with regard to decentralization.

15.4.1 *Governance: How open is the network to open participation?*

The governance of a blockchain or DLT is defined by how open it is to participation. The more decentralized and open to participation it is, the more challenging it usually is to create a system that is resistant to new forms of attack:

- *Blockchain*—Governance in a blockchain like Bitcoin is decentralized through the global distribution of all nodes, each node containing all the blockchain data. This is enabled by free open source software that allows anyone to participate in Bitcoin. It also enables the relative decentralization of mining (which has become more centralized over time) [2] to reach a consensus on the truth in that blockchain. In Bitcoin and similar blockchain efforts, every effort is taken to maximize and protect decentralization according to the consensus around how that might be best achieved.
- *Hybrid blockchain*—Governance in a semi-public or public permissioned blockchain is often defined by the validator nodes that are identified. These are usually controlled by public institutions like government agencies, consortia, educational institutions, and corporations. However, read access to the ledger is open to everyone, which is different from DLTs, which limit read access as well.
- *DLT*—Governance in DLTs is mostly centralized in one or a few validator nodes that are identified and other nodes that might have read access with the permission of the validator nodes. Governance is closed: the network is made up of nodes by permission, and new nodes can only join with permission from the current validator nodes and/or external authorities.

15.4.2 *Censorship resistance: How centralized is trust?*

Censorship resistance [3] is often related to the level of decentralization of a blockchain or DLT. The fewer parties control a system, the less censorship-resistant it is because those few parties can influence censor transactions:

- *Blockchain*—Censorship resistance in Bitcoin was envisioned as very strong by decentralizing the verification of transactions in many computers. However, the progressive concentration of mining that has come with increased hashing power (the total computational power behind a network) is a specter that may threaten Bitcoin's censorship-resistance. This is a constant source of discussion in systems like Bitcoin.
- *Hybrid blockchain*—Trust in a hybrid blockchain is lower than in a private permissioned DLT, but that trust is delegated to publicly identified nodes. Censorship resistance in this model depends on the nodes' geographic and participant distribution, the level of transparency of their selection and expansion, and the risk of active attacks against the identified nodes. For example, if you run a

network in Japan and all your nodes are Japanese, in the end, the Japanese government will most likely have the final say in architecture and governance.

- *DLT*—Trust in the participating nodes in this model is high and can make sense when a corporation wants to organize its own internal network or when an industry or government wants to organize a consortium where all participants trust each other. Censorship resistance in this model is low, but that is rarely a key requirement since permissions and access are already in centralized hands. The more trust people have in the public or private institutions administering the DLT, the less need there is for more decentralization.

15.4.3 *Openness: Who can run a node?*

Blockchains and DLTs are composed of multiple computers or servers (nodes) interconnected in a peer-to-peer network. The easier it is for someone to operate a node, the more decentralized the network can be, although this can be complicated by tiered systems where nodes hold different privileges and responsibilities:

- *Blockchain*—The ability to run a node is open to everyone, in principle, but the example of Bitcoin has shown that running a full node has become more difficult and costly over time due to scaling issues with the protocol. The token, or unit of account, is a fundamental aspect of the game theory model of a permissionless blockchain. For example, if an individual user runs a node that is not part of a professional mining pool, it is unlikely they will solve the cryptographic puzzle needed to mine a new block. However, they can still participate in decentralization by running a full node that verifies and relays transactions and verifies new blocks just for the sake of it. Some scalability research points to the importance of these nodes, but this too is a significant point of controversy.
- *Hybrid blockchain*—Participation in a hybrid blockchain is usually open to all nodes, but they must fulfill predetermined requirements, usually involving setup, testing, node operation costs, and public or semi-public identification.
- *DLT*—Only select, invited, identified nodes in a DLT can validate transactions. Because that process happens externally, a DLT usually does not need tokens except as an anti-spam mechanism.

15.5 *Why "believers" and not "proponents" or "partisans"?*

There are many different ways to achieve decentralization. Blockchain, DLTs, and pure P2P systems are just three of the possible approaches to SSI technology, and more are likely to appear. What is most beneficial is learning from each other and finding the best technology to improve life for everyone.

In addition, after the "blockchain hype cycle" [4], the keywords *blockchain* and *DLT* have lost a great deal of their meaning. We need to look beyond the labels and focus on how decentralization can be achieved for different solutions and use cases. Time might show that some solutions will need permissioned or hybrid models—because governments and institutions will require that from their citizens and companies—while other models might become completely permissionless—because the technology is good enough to eliminate the need for external management by traditional institutions. And sometimes centralized solutions might still be good enough.

We hope these examples convey how belief systems drive technology choices. Let's explore now how these choices can be expressed in the decentralization community.

15.5.1 How do we measure decentralization?

From a computer science point of view, Satoshi Nakamoto created one possible solution to the long researched *double spending problem* that had limited the development of digital cash protocols or peer-to-peer electronic cash systems [5]. Satoshi's proof-of-work (PoW) algorithm, a combination of technology and game theory, also provided a possible solution to the *Byzantine Generals Problem* [6], a computer science challenge for reaching consensus when communication channels are not safe and cannot be trusted. Much of the technical excitement around blockchain protocol design stems from these new solutions to decentralization obstacles.

In his 2017 reference article, influential Ethereum co-founder Vitalik Buterin [7] laid out his three-part criterion for decentralization. He theorized that centralization could creep back into systems designed to be decentralized if their architecture, logic, and political governance were not designed to maintain decentralization into the future. Of course, this whole discussion is relevant only if you strongly believe that decentralization is essential.

Architectural decentralization is ensured in a P2P network by distributing nodes across various subnetworks; these usually communicate in the traditional TCP/IP addressing structure of the mainstream internet. The portion of nodes that can fail at a given time without bringing down the entire network is a key criterion for this kind of decentralization, as is the portion of nodes owned or controlled by any one entity. In some cases, the portion of nodes located in any one jurisdiction or nation-state may be important, or the portion of nodes reliant on any one manufacturer of hardware, software, or infrastructure.

Logical decentralization means making all core code open source (transparent to independent development teams) and making all data readable across different implementations of a given protocol. Along these lines, important questions include the following:

- Are the interfaces and data structures one discrete unit or a swarm of many distinct interacting units?
- What would happen if we cut the system in half, between users and suppliers?
- Would the two new units continue operating as independent entities if, for instance, half the nodes forked to a different implementation of the protocol?

Political governance decentralization is when a separation of powers between codebase maintenance and operation of the network—in combination with incentive structures informed by game theory—prevents any single stakeholder group (developers, miners, investors, markets, users, and so on) from pushing through changes to the protocol without the collaboration of the majority. On this dimension, the core questions are explicitly political:

- How many individuals, contracts, or computers are needed to change the protocol?
- What protects the minority from abuse at the hands of a majority of stakeholders?
- What incentives do minorities have to stay in the system if their interests diverge from the majority's?

This last concept of political decentralization is maybe the most ideologically charged and controversial of the three—and the most useful in identifying differences between decentralized systems. Some analysts propose that since blockchain data systems operate as infrastructure for both economic and non-economic systems, the separation-of-powers model of their internal governance should be more explicitly— and more carefully—modeled on the separation of powers in real-world political systems, particularly in modern liberal democracies.

Because of all this, designating a project as "decentralized" is not meaningful unless you consider all aspects of a system and its governance—and specifically how much sustained decentralization is core to its design. Bitcoin has achieved a high level of decentralization largely because of its global scale and the number of stakeholders maintaining equilibrium. But that status was not easily achieved. Building for decentralization is a significant challenge, particularly in smaller and privately controlled protocols. What's more, the benefits of decentralization are not easily transferable to all use cases; and adequate decentralization is not guaranteed by anchoring data to a highly decentralized protocol or building on top of it.

15.6 Technical advantages of decentralization

From Buterin's technical point of view, a decentralized system has to be fault-tolerant, attack-resistant, and collision-resistant. These traits often have significant positive side effects for the resilience and durability of a data system that offset the cost of blockchain development:

- *Fault tolerance* means decentralized systems can continue working properly even when parts of the network are disconnected by fault or malfeasance, because the network is composed of many parts that can continue operating independently from each other. When they are connected again, even if transactions have been lost, the parts will synchronize based on the incentives in place. Fault tolerance is a fundamental aspect of any decentralized system.
- *Attack resistance* for a decentralized system means redundancies make it exponentially more expensive to attack, destroy, or manipulate many nodes simultaneously, as opposed to centralized systems where only one central codebase or database needs to be attacked. Decentralization requires such an attack to be scaled up in proportion to the overall size of the system.

- *Collusion resistance* in a decentralized system means it has been designed to prevent or at least disincentivize groups of participants colluding to take advantage of (or force the behavior of) other participants.

The diversity of a decentralized ecosystem is often one of the key elements to make it resistant to all three types of attacks. All these elements need to be assessed and weighed against each other to decide whether a decentralized system is resilient and decentralized enough for a given set of use cases and/or the values of its stakeholders.

While this last criterion of aligning with values is important, building consensus between shareholders can be a slow and costly process. Furthermore, creating decentralized systems can be exceedingly complicated and often expensive—making consensus even more elusive when such systems have no clear revenue model. In such situations, many "shareholders" will rightly question how much decentralization they can afford to pay for beyond the needs dictated by their use case.

The original cypherpunk dream (chapter 13) promises to empower individuals, leading to the belief that decentralized technologies can create a better, utopian world. However, there is also a risk that these technologies could backfire, creating a more dystopian world. Assessing the opportunities and risks requires us to be explicit and deliberate about our beliefs and the governance models encoded in them. It is not always an easy conversation to have, but with our planet's global infrastructure at stake, the long-term consequences justify the discomfort and friction of some frank talk about politics and values.

SSI Resources

For more free content to learn about SSI, please go to IdentityBook.info and SSI Meetup.org/book.

References

1. Allen, Christopher. "The Path to Self-Sovereign Identity." *Life with Alacrity.* http://www.lifewith alacrity.com/2016/04/the-path-to-self-soverereign-identity.html.
2. Kharif, Olga. 2020. "Bitcoin's Network Operations Are Controlled by Five Companies." *Bloomberg.* https://www.bloomberg.com/news/articles/2020-01-31/bitcoin-s-network-operations -are-controlled-by-five-companies.
3. Andrew, Paul. 2018. "Bitcoin Censorship Resistance Explained. CoinCentral. https://coincen tral.com/bitcoin-censorship-resistance.
4. Litan, Avivah and Adrian Leow. 2020. "Hype Cycle for Blockchain Technologies, 2020." Gartner Research. https://www.gartner.com/en/documents/3987450/hype-cycle-for-blockchain-tech nologies-2020.
5. Nakamoto, Satoshi. 2008. "Bitcoin: A Peer-to-Peer Electronic Cash System." https://bitcoin.org/ bitcoin.pdf.
6. Stevens, Anthony. 2018. "Understanding the Byzantine Generals' Problem (and How It Affects You)." Coinmonks. https://medium.com/coinmonks/a-note-from-anthony-if-you-havent -already-please-read-the-article-gaining-clarity-on-key-787989107969.
7. Buterin, Vitalik. 2017. "The Meaning of Decentralization." https://medium.com/@Vitalik Buterin/the-meaning-of-decentralization-a0c92b76a274.

The origins of the SSI community

Infominer and Kaliya "Identity Woman" Young

Self-sovereign identity grew out of a decade-long movement widely known as user-centric identity, *of which Kaliya "Identity Woman" Young is one of the most distinguished pioneers. Kaliya started the Internet Identity Workshop (IIW) in 2005 with Doc Searls and Phil Windley. Held twice every year since then, IIW has been the birthplace of almost every major innovation in decentralized digital identity. As SSI has grown, it has attracted newcomers such as Infominer, a prolific (and anonymous) SSI writer and curator, coached by Kaliya (who has always supported bringing more talent into the community). Together, they have co-founded Identosphere.net. In this chapter, the two of them describe the fascinating evolution of the SSI community from its origins to the present. Obviously, this will need to be updated over time, but we hope this chapter gives you a broad perspective on where the SSI movement has come from and why it has gained so much attention.*

The term *self-sovereign identity* (SSI) grew from a 2012 blog post by Devon Lofretto to the VRM (vendor relationship management) mailing list. The post was titled "Sovereign Source Authority" [1]. Since then, SSI has grown into the banner of an ecosystem of communities, organizations, tools, and specifications aiming to put users in control over their digital identifiers and personal information. The quest for SSI is a journey of community awareness and organization—of building and promoting the use of tools and frameworks that empower users—and the gradual warming of the world to a cause that, ironically, embraces some of the same core values that led to the development of the internet itself.

310

16.1 *The birth of the internet*

From the very beginning, the system underlying the internet has relied on a centralized Internet Assigned Numbers Authority (IANA) for the assignment of identifiers used in the operation of the internet. IANA has handed down authority to other central authorities, such as the Internet Corporation for Assigned Names and Numbers (ICAAN) and certificate authorities (CAs).

> **NOTE** See the 1990 RFC "IAB Recommended Policy on Distributing Internet Identifier Assignment and IAB Recommended Policy Change to Internet 'Connected' Status," https://tools.ietf.org/html/rfc1174.

From 1972 until 1989, "Jake" Elizabeth Feinler [2] was the director of the Network Information Systems Center at the Stanford Research Institute. Her group ran the Network Information Center (NIC) for the ARPANET as it became the Defense Data Network (DDN) and later the internet.

> *Jake was a volunteer at the Computer History Museum, where the Internet Identity Workshop (IIW) began meeting in 2006. Seeing the agenda at one of our first meetings there, she asked if it was an ICANN meeting and stayed to share about her team creating the first namespace system convention.*
>
> —Kaliya "Identity Woman" Young

At first, centralized agencies were required to manage the assignment of identifiers online. They have continued to operate in such a fashion, in part because once empowered, organizations are reluctant to relinquish that power—and in part due to the many other challenges of creating widely accepted and interoperable decentralized solutions. But the internet was always designed to be decentralized, and now pioneers in cryptography have opened the way for it to become even more so (see chapter 13 for more about this).

16.2 *Losing control over our personal information*

The inventor of blind signatures and "Father of digital currency," David Chaum, was among the first to discuss how individuals were losing control over the way our personal information is used. Chaum's proposed solution involved creating a unique digital pseudonym with each party we transact. As he described it [3]:

> *Large-scale automated transaction systems of the near future can be designed to protect the privacy and maintain the security of both individuals and organizations.*

Chaum made it clear that such a system would put users in control over their identity—as opposed to using a token created by a third party, whom users then had no choice but to entrust with the management of their personal information.

Chaum might well be thought of as the "grandfather of SSI." (He can also be designated the grandfather, among others, of digital cash, blockchain, and cryptocurrency technologies, as described in chapters 13 and 17.) His work inspired a generation about the potential to create novel cryptographic systems and privacy-preserving applications.

Soon after Chaum came Roger Clarke, who introduced the term *dataveillance*. In 1988, he defined it as follows [4]:

> *The systematic monitoring of people's actions or communications through the application of information technology.*

Clarke expresses the need for laws to safeguard personal privacy and states that IT professionals must strive to create applications that preserve their users' privacy.

16.3 Pretty Good Privacy

After World War II, many government agencies prohibited the distribution of secure encryption schemes. For example, in the United States, encryption was treated as a munition, and exporting it was illegal. As a result, businesses were required to use weak encryption for international products, which for practical business reasons meant they often had to use the same weak encryption for their domestic products.

In response to the growing danger of losing our right to personal privacy, Phil Zimmerman created *Pretty Good Privacy* (PGP) in 1991 [5]. His thought was that if strong encryption became widespread, it would be difficult for the government to criminalize.

The release of PGP marked the first time in history that strong encryption became available to the general public. PGP's public key cryptography, and Zimmerman's concept of the *web-of-trust* [6] provided an early foundation for self-sovereign identity. Unfortunately, PGP had a reputation of being difficult to use, and thus it failed to achieve wide adoption for the encryption of personal communications. However, the early popularity of PGP demonstrated that the same values that inspired the academic world of cryptography and computer science in the early 1970s were still alive and well and leading to innovative new technologies and events.

16.4 International Planetwork Conference

In May 2000, the first International Planetwork Conference (https://planetwork.net/about.html) was held in San Francisco, with the theme of Global Ecology and Information Technology. This conference (held again in 2003 and 2004; see https://web.archive.org/web/20060714223112/http://www.planetwork.net/2004conf)   and the community that developed around it planted the seeds of much that followed. The conversation that began at that first conference continued informally through 2001, when it became known as LinkTank (https://planetwork.net/linktank.html), a group seeking to create and maintain "a digital communications platform, operated as a public interest utility."

The XNS Public Trust Organization (XNS.org) was founded in July 2000, shortly after Planetwork, to promote individual ownership of digital identity and personal data based on Extensible Resource Identifier (XRI) and Extensible Data Interchange (XDI), open standards contributed to OASIS by OneName Corporation. (See https://web.archive.org/web/20011101021136/http://www.onename.com [unrelated to Blockstack\Onename].)

In 2001, the Identity Commons, led by Owen Davis and Andrew Nelson, joined forces with XNS.org to promote XRI and XDI as the basis of an identity layer of the internet. They worked with Cordance and Neustar to create Extensible Name Services (https://icannwiki.org/XDI.org), which sought to instill an element of trust between people and the new data-sharing networks. It had a centralized global registry for human-readable names, iNames, that would be paired with a namespace of never-recycled identifiers called iNumbers.

NOTE Cordance (https://web.archive.org/web/20120117204002/http://www.cordance.net) created the technology under the development of the XRI and XDI Oasis Technical Committees. Neustar (https://www.home.neustar) is a telecommunications company originally charged with maintaining the system of directories and databases for telephone area codes and prefixes in North America.

16.5 *Augmented Social Network and Identity Commons*

In 2003, Ken Jordan, Jan Hauser, and Steven Foster published *The Augmented Social Network: Building Identity and Trust into the Next-Generation Internet* [7], born from ideas developed through Planetwork and LinkTank. *The Augmented Social Network* (ASN) sought to build a persistent online identity into the architecture of the internet—giving users complete control over their identity.

Following the June 2004 Planetwork conference, Kaliya Young began working as an evangelist and community builder with Identity Commons. She collaborated with Doc Searls and Phil Windley of the Social Physics team, led by Paul Trevithick and Mary Ruddy, to weave together a community of like-minded individuals scattered across the country.

This community, focused on user-centric identity, first came together at the Digital Identity World conference in the fall of 2004. That meeting resulted in the creation of a mailing list (https://lists.idcommons.net/lists/info/community); and that December, over the holidays, Doc Searls invited a number of identity leaders to appear together on the *Gilmore Gang* podcast. That's where the name *Identity Gang* was coined; and with the encouragement of Doc Searls, a number of people began blogging about *user-centric identity*.

16.6 *The Laws of Identity*

Among those bloggers was Kim Cameron, chief architect of identity at Microsoft, who published the *Laws of Identity* [8]. He implored us to build systems where users were in full control over how their personal information was exposed, for that exposure to be minimal, and for it to be shared only with parties having a justifiable need for it. He also postulated that individuals should be difficult to correlate across services, while at the same time identity technologies should be interoperable between identity providers.

Between Kim's blog, other blogs, and the community mailing list, there was a robust sharing of ideas and technical paths toward achieving them. Among all these quite different leaders, Paul Trevithick took the lead in creating the Identity Gang Lexicon (see https://web.archive.org/web/20080916112039/wiki.idcommons.net/Lexicon).

16.7 Internet Identity Workshop

In the fall of 2005, the mailing list organized a community gathering in the Bay Area at the Hillside Club in Berkeley. It was called the Internet Identity Workshop (IIW, https://web.archive.org/web/20060720180524/http://www.socialtext.net:80/iiw2005 /index.cgi?internet_identity_workshop_2005), and it was co-produced by Kaliya Young, Doc Searls, and Phil Windley.

The first day was a regular-style conference, with each of the eight different user-centric ID systems/paradigms presenting. On the second day, Kaliya facilitated an *unconference* (http://unconference.net) supporting the co-creation of its agenda by attendees. That was where Yadis (Yet Another Digital Identity Interoperability System) was born [9]. Led by Johannes Ernst [10], Yadis was a decentralized system to enable interoperability between dominant identity schemes of the time.

16.8 Increasing support of user control

Over the years that followed, IIW facilitated the creation of technologies that increasingly supported user control of our identities, starting with OpenID, OAuth, System for Cross-domain Identity Management (SCIM), Information Cards, and later Fast IDentity Online (FIDO), User-Managed Access (UMA), and OpenID Connect. In 2010, Markus Sabadello began Project Danube (https://web.archive.org/web/ 20101221105543/http://projectdanube.org) to work on the creation of an XDI-based personal data store that always remains under the control of its users. From that point on, an array of emerging companies began to work on personal data stores, user-centric identity, and other tools to manage personal data and identifiers. In 2011, Kaliya founded the Personal Data Ecosystem Consortium (http://pde.cc/) to connect them.

Respect Network was founded around the same time; its architects included Drummond Reed, Markus Sabadello, and Les Chasen. Their goal was to create a cloud environment for the secure management of personal data. Members of the Respect Network were governed by the five principles of the award-winning Respect Trust Framework (https://respectnetwork.wordpress.com/respect-trust-framework):

> *These five principles can be summed up by "the 5 p's" in one sentence: A promise of permission, protection, portability, and proof.*

16.9 Rebooting the Web of Trust

In 2014, Manu Sporny of Digital Bazaar proposed the formation of a Credentials Community Group at the W3C (https://www.w3.org/community/credentials/) to explore the creation of common standards for a decentralized system of credentials. This marked the beginning of a new era for decentralized identity.

In the fall of 2015, Christopher Allen announced a new type of event—a "design workshop"—devoted to the topic of how blockchain technology could enable the long-sought goals of user-centric identity. The first event was called the *Rebooting the Web of Trust* (RWoT). These design workshops support small groups working together intensively for a few days to produce key pieces of collaborative work.

RWoT participants work on white papers, specifications, pieces of code—all around creating next-gen, decentralized, web-of-trust based identity systems. The first RWoT workshop [11] facilitated nearly 50 topic papers and advance readings contributed by its participants and produced five completed white papers, including the following:

- "Opportunities Created by the Web of Trust for Controlling and Leveraging Personal Data" by du5t, Kaliya "Identity Woman" Young, John Edge, Drummond Reed, and Noah Thorp (https://github.com/WebOfTrustInfo/reboot ing-the-web-of-trust/blob/master/final-documents/satisfying-real-world-use-cases.pdf). This seminal paper began with the following paragraph:

  Today, decentralized Webs of Trust remain as important as ever. Now is the time to extend them to be usable by everyone who has access to digital networks ... from marginalized persons like stateless refugees and victims of human trafficking to members of the informal or unregulated economy—urgently need to participate in otherwise privileged economic and political fora, but they face technical, economic, and political barriers to entry.

- "Decentralized Public Key Infrastructure" by Christopher Allen, Arthur Brock, Vitalik Buterin, Jon Callas, Duke Dorje, Christian Lundkvist, Pavel Kravchenko, Jude Nelson, Drummond Reed, Markus Sabadello, Greg Slepak, Noah Thorp, and Harlan T Wood (https://github.com/WebOfTrustInfo/rwot1-sf/blob/mas ter/final-documents/dpki.pdf). This paper put a stake in the ground for what is turning out to be one of the most important uses of blockchain technology, as described in the opening paragraph:

  Today's Internet places control of online identities into the hands of third-parties. ... This paper describes a possible alternate approach called decentralized public key infrastructure (DPKI), which returns control of online identities to the entities they belong to.

By this point, ConsenSys had begun working on uPort, an Ethereum- and IPFS-based solution for self-sovereign identity, which was initially described at DEVCON1 by Christian Lundkvist (November, 2015) [12].

16.10 *Agenda for Sustainable Development and ID2020*

The United Nations Agenda for Sustainable Development was published toward the end of 2015 and included 19 sustainable development goals (SDGs). SDG 16.9 was "To provide legal identity for all by 2030." To this end, the World Bank founded Digital IDs for Development (ID4D, http://www.worldbank.org/en/events/2015/06/23/digital-ids-for-development) to work "leveraging digital identities (IDs) as part of a unified system to better deliver services and benefits to people, especially the poor and the disadvantaged." The early work of ID4D was largely aligned with centralized identity management paradigms and vendors who provide tools to nation-states.

After learning that "one of the biggest problems in protecting children who are at risk of sexual violence is a lack of birth certificates or identity" [13], John Edge was inspired by the possibility of using blockchain to issue self-sovereign identities to those with no official capacity to acquire one. John helped to found the first ID2020 Summit, an event aligned with SDG 16.9 "legal identity for all," held at UN headquarters in New York. ID2020 is a nonprofit public-private partnership that seeks solutions for the 1.1 billion people without any officially recognized identification (see https:// datacatalog.worldbank.org/dataset/identification-development-global-dataset).

Christopher Allen, who was part of the team organizing ID2020, published "The Path to Self Sovereign Identity" [14], outlining the Principles of Identity (see https:// github.com/WebOfTrustInfo/self-sovereign-identity/blob/master/self-sovereign-identity-principles.md) building from Cameron's Laws of Identity, the Respect Trust Framework, and the Verifiable Claims Working Group (http://w3c.github.io/webpayments-ig/VCTF/charter/faq.html).

The Second Rebooting Web of Trust workshop was held in conjunction with ID2020 and was hosted by Microsoft and facilitated by Kaliya Young. This was the workshop where the initial decentralized identifier (DID) white paper was completed. Notable output from this workshop included the following:

- "Requirements for DIDs" by Drummond Reed and Les Chasen (Respect Network; https://github.com/WebOfTrustInfo/rwot2-id2020/blob/master/final -documents/requirements-for-dids.pdf). DIDs are a common standard for self-controlled, privacy-respecting identifiers that enable individuals and organizations across the globe to connect and communicate securely (see chapter 8). This document was inspired by the principles of the XDI.org Registry Working Group to seek maximum interoperability, decentralization, neutrality, and sovereign identity. It was the first in a series about producing a concrete DID system aligned with the goals of the W3C Credentials Community Group.
- "Identity System Essentials" by Samuel Smith and Dmitry Khovratovich (https:// github.com/WebOfTrustInfo/rwot2-id2020/blob/master/topics-and-advance -readings/Identity-System-Essentials.pdf). This was the initial white paper from Evernym, a startup focused entirely on self-sovereign identity.

In addition to their paper discussing the needs of an identity system, Evernym had begun working on a public-permissioned blockchain for self-sovereign identity that later would become the Sovrin ledger.

16.11 *Early state interest*

In the spring of 2016, the U.S. Department of Homeland Security (DHS) awarded $100,000 Small Business Innovation Research contracts to four companies focused on the "Applicability of Blockchain Technology to Identity Management and Privacy

Protection." These contracts included one to Digital Bazaar to study the feasibility of developing a flexible standard for distributed ledgers to support DIDs and verifiable credentials to fulfill the needs of DHS use cases (https://www.sbir.gov/sbirsearch/detail/1241085) and one to Respect Network to "research and develop a decentralized registry and discovery service for Decentralized Identifiers (DIDs) to integrate with the public blockchain" (https://www.sbir.gov/sbirsearch/detail/1241097)

In August 2016, the Digital Identity and Authentication Council of Canada (DIACC) published the "Pan-Canadian Trust Framework Overview" (described in detail in chapter 23; https://diacc.ca/wp-content/uploads/2016/08/PCTF-Overview-FINAL.pdf), a collaborative approach to defining interoperable digital identity that would work across all of Canada's provinces and beyond. It said,

> *A trust framework consists of a set of agreed definitions, requirements, standards, specifications, processes and criteria. The set of agreed details enable identity management process and authorization decisions carried out by other organizations and jurisdictions to be relied on with a standardised level of confidence.*

16.12 *MyData and Learning Machine*

MyData (http://mydata2016.org) was founded in August 2016 to provide a legal structure for an international movement promoting the rights of individuals to control our personal information. In September 2016 [15], Phil Windley announced the formation of the Sovrin Foundation to promote the creation of a decentralized identity layer for the internet using the codebase for a public-permissioned ledger developed by Evernym. Soon after, Evernym's acquisition of Respect Network (see https://pitchbook.com/profiles/company/53867-44) heralded what has proved to be a powerful joining of forces.

By this point, Learning Machine had been working with MIT for about a year to develop an open standard for blockchain credentials. Led by Chris Jagers, Kim Hamilton Duffy, and John Papinchak, their Blockcerts prototype was released in October [16].

Joe Andrieu continued the discussion of self-sovereign identity principles in "A Technology-Free Definition of Self Sovereign Identity" [17] submitted to the third RWoT Workshop in San Francisco. As this paper put it,

> *To fund, co-develop and eventually deploy a global self-sovereign solution to UN Sustainable Development Goal 16.9, it would be prudent to begin with an explicit requirements process independent of any specific technology.*

In light of UN SDG 16.9, Andrieu detailed three core characteristics for SSI:

1 Users should have control over their identity information.
2 The credentials should be accepted as widely as possible.
3 Their cost should be as low as possible.

16.13 *Verifiable Claims Working Group, Decentralized Identity Foundation, and Hyperledger Indy*

In April 2017, the charter for the Verifiable Claims Working Group was approved at the W3C [18]. Chaired by Daniel Burnett of ConsenSys and digital identity expert Matt Stone, its purpose was to develop a standard for machine-readable personal information that would be verified by a third party on the web. Verifiable credentials could include any form of digitally signed data including banking information, educational records, healthcare data, and other forms of personally identifiable machine-readable data.

At Consensus 2017, a leading global blockchain conference, Microsoft, uPort, Gem, Evernym, Blockstack, and Tierion announced the formation of the Decentralized Identity Foundation (DIF, http://identity.foundation). DIF's goal was to collaboratively develop the foundational components of an open, standards-based, decentralized identity ecosystem for people, organizations, apps, and devices.

In May 2017, the Hyperledger initiative at the Linux Foundation announced the introduction of the Sovrin codebase into its family of open source tools and frameworks for blockchain technology. This new project was given the name *Hyperledger Indy* [19]. Finally, in July 2017, Digital Bazaar began working to create Veres One (https://github.com/veres-one), a public permissionless blockchain fit for purpose to support a decentralized identity network.

16.14 *Increasing state support for SSI*

In July 2017, as a result of work accomplished by Respect Network and Digital Bazaar since their preliminary funding, the DHS SBIR awarded each company an additional $749,000 for Phase 2 contracts:

- Evernym's contract was "to design and implement a decentralized key management system (DKMS) for blockchain technologies based on National Institute of Standards and Technology Special Publication 800-130, A Framework for Designing Key Management Systems" [20].
- Digital Bazaar's contract was "to develop a flexible software ecosystem that combines fit-for-purpose distributed ledger technology, digital credentials and digital wallets to address a wide variety of identity management and online access use cases for the Homeland Security Enterprise (HSE)" [21].

In 2013, the Canadian Province of British Columbia, which has a long history of digital identity innovation, launched a citizen services card with a triple-blind backend database. In September 2017, it announced detailed plans to build tools to support the creation of publicly verifiable credentials for businesses in the province via the *Verifiable Organizations Network* (VON; see https://archive.org/details/TBSIdentityPolicyWorkshop).

16.15 *Ethereum identity*

Jolocom originally began in 2002 as a project to help companies communicate and share information among themselves. In August 2017, Jolocom announced its efforts to create an Ethereum-based SSI application and smart wallet [22].

In October 2017, Fabian Vogelsteller began work on *ERC 725*, describing proxy smart contracts that can be controlled by multiple keys and other smart contracts (https://github.com/ethereum/eips/issues/725). ERC 735 is an associated standard to add claims to and remove them from an ERC 725 identity smart contract. These identity smart contracts can describe humans, groups, objects, and machines.

16.16 *World Economic Forum reports*

At the start of 2018, the World Economic Forum (WEF) published "The Known Traveller—Unlocking the Potential of Digital Identity for Secure and Seamless Travel" [23], which promoted the use of a distributed ledger, with no central authority, for digital identity. It also highlighted Sovrin, uPort, and Blockcerts as examples of self-sovereign identity technologies that are vendor-agnostic and support user control.

On May 25, 2018, the General Data Protection Regulation (GDPR) was enacted into law across the European Union. In development since 2015, this legislation shifts ownership of customer data from organizations to individuals and applies to anyone doing business with European citizens. To remain compliant, an identity system must support *privacy by design* and *privacy by default*. The GDPR represents the first time there has been data protection legislation so strongly aligned with SSI principles.

In September 2018, the WEF published "Identity in a Digital World: A New Chapter in the Social Contract" [24]:

> *It outlines what we've learned to date on what user-centricity means and how to uphold it in practice. It attempts to offer a shared working agenda for leaders: an initial list of immediate-term priority actions that demand cooperation.*

16.17 *First production government demo of an SSI-supporting ledger*

On September 3, 2018, the ERC 725 Alliance formed to promote the development of Ethereum standards supporting SSI [25]. A few days later, on September 10, the Government of British Columbia's Verifiable Organization Network went into production [26]. VON makes it easier for public organizations to apply for credentials, simplifies issuance, and "makes verifying credentials more standard, trustworthy, and transparent—anywhere in the world."

Also in September 2018, Microsoft unveiled "Decentralized Identity: Own and Control Your Identity," a white paper about joining a diverse community to build an open and interoperable, standards-based DID solution for individuals and organizations [27].

16.18 SSI Meetup

In early 2018, Alex Preukschat, with initial support from Evernym, created SSI Meetup (https://ssimeetup.org) to be an open, independent, collaborative community to help SSI evangelists worldwide. SSI Meetup hosts regular webinars that are shipped with extensive infographics—pre-labeled with a Creative Commons license for ease of sharing. SSI Meetup has become a widely shared educational resource for the SSI community.

16.19 Official W3C standards

One of the most significant milestones in the evolution of SSI was the final approval, in September 2019, of the *W3C Verifiable Credentials Data Model* 1.0 specification. For the SSI community, this heralded the official beginning of the world's recognition of SSI as a new model for digital identity on the internet. Not coincidentally, the same month marked the official announcement of the establishment of the W3C Decentralized Identifier (DID) Working Group with a two-year charter to take DIDs to the same level of official W3C standard. DIDs are the first identifier to enter the full Working Group standardization process at the W3C since the adoption of the HTTP and HTTPS URLs at the dawn of the web.

16.20 Only the beginning

Those in the SSI community feel that the tide has truly turned for those seeking to create an internet-wide identity layer. In addition to regulatory support from the GDPR, systems for decentralized identity are now being developed to meet the needs of the U.S. Department of Homeland Security, Canadian governments (both federal and provincial), a public/private partnership called Findy in Finland (https://www.findy.fi), a similar national project in Germany called SSI4DE (https://www.snet.tu-berlin.de/menue/projects/ssi4de), and the UN SDGs. Corporations such as Microsoft, IBM, Mastercard, Cisco, and Accenture have joined forces with blockchain consortia such as Ethereum Enterprise Alliance, Hyperledger, and the Sovrin Foundation to create SSI networks that can serve people, organizations, and things worldwide.

Our community is in active evolution. The best way to dive into our diverse community and learn more is to attend one of the workshop events where these systems are actively being co-created. The IIW continues every six months in Mountain View, California (www.internetidentityworkshop.com); and RWoT continues worldwide twice a year (www.weboftrust.info).

There are several other regular conferences where SSI is a major topic, including these:

- *MyData*—Building a global community of people who want control of their data along with the companies working on making it happen (https://mydata.org)
- *ID2020*—Helping bring sustainable digital identity to the 1.1 billion people in the world without a legal identity (https://id2020.org)

- *Identity North*—A series of events for individuals and organizations interested in Canadian digital identity and the digital economy (https://www.identitynorth.ca)
- *The European Identity Conference*—Europe's oldest and most respected digital identity conference (https://www.kuppingercole.com/events/eic2021)

SSI Resources

For more free content to learn about SSI, please go to IdentityBook.info and SSI Meetup.org/book.

References

1. Lofretto, Devon. 2012. "What Is "Sovereign Source Authority?" *The Moxy Tongue.* https://www .moxytongue.com/2012/02/what-is-sovereign-source-authority.html.
2. Weber, Marc. 2009. Interview: "Oral History of Elizabeth (Jake) Feinler." Computer History Museum. https://web.archive.org/web/20110811175249/http://archive.computerhistory.org/ resources/access/text/Oral_History/102702199.05.01.acc.pdf.
3. Chaum, David. 1985. "Security Without Identification: Transaction Systems to Make Big Brother Obsolete." *Communications of the ACM* 28 (10): 1030. https://www.cs.ru.nl/~jhh/pub/secsem/ chaum1985bigbrother.pdf.
4. Clarke, Roger. 1988. "Information Technology and Dataveillance." *Communications of the ACM* 31 (5): 498–512, www.rogerclarke.com/DV/CACM88.html.
5. Zimmerman, Philip. 1991. "Why I Wrote PGP." https://www.philzimmermann.com/EN/essays/ WhyIWrotePGP.html.
6. Ryabitsev, Konstantin. 2014. "PGP Web of Trust: Core Concepts Behind Trusted Communication." https://www.linux.com/learn/pgp-web-trust-core-concepts-behind-trusted-communication.
7. Jordan, Ken, Jan Hauser, and Steven Foster. 2003. "The Augmented Social Network: Building Identity and Trust into the Next-Generation Internet." *First Monday* 8 (8). https://firstmonday .org/ojs/index.php/fm/article/view/1068.
8. Cameron, Kim. 2009. "7 Laws of Identity." *Kim Cameron's Identity Weblog.* https://www.identityblog .com/?p=1065.
9. Windley, Phil. 2005. "Yet Another Decentralized Identity Interoperability System." *Technometria.* http://www.windley.com/archives/2005/10/yet_another_dec.shtml.
10. Ernst, Johannes. 2009. "From 1 to a billion in 5 years. What a little URL can do." *Upon 2020.* https://upon2020.com/blog/2009/12/from-1-to-a-billion-in-5-years-what-a-little-url-can-do.
11. Galt, Juan. 2015. "Andreas Antonopoulos: The Case Against Reputation and Identity Systems." Bitcoin.com. https://news.bitcoin.com/andreas-antonopoulos-case-reputation-identity-systems.
12. ConsenSys. 2015. "The Identity Crisis." https://medium.com/@ConsenSys/identity-is-defined- in-merriam-s-dictionary-as-who-someone-is-a3d6a69f5fa4.
13. Jordan, Gina. 2016. "Projects Aim for Legal Identity for Everyone." SecureIDNews. https:// www.secureidnews.com/news-item/projects-aims-for-legal-identity-for-everyone.
14. Allen, Christopher. 2016. "The Path to Self-Sovereign Identity." *Life with Alacrity.* http://www .lifewithalacrity.com/2016/04/the-path-to-self-soverereign-identity.html.
15. Windley, Phil. 2016. "Announcing the Sovrin Foundation." Technometria. http://www.windley .com/archives/2016/09/announcing_the_sovrin_foundation.shtml.
16. Jagers, Chris. 2016. "Verifiable Credentials on the Blockchain." *Learning Machine.* https:// medium.com/learning-machine-blog/blockchain-credentials-b4cf5d02bbb7.
17. Andrieu, Joe. 2016. "A Technology-Free Definition of Self Sovereign Identity." https://github .com/WebOfTrustInfo/rwot3-sf/blob/master/topics-and-advance-readings/a-technology-free -definition-of-self-sovereign-identity.pdf.

18. Jia, Xueyuan. 2017. "Verifiable Claims Working Group Charter Approved; join the Verifiable Claims Working Group (Call for Participation)." W3C. https://lists.w3.org/Archives/Public/public-vc-wg/2017Apr/0000.html.

19. Sovrin Foundation. 2017. "Announcing Hyperledger Indy." https://www.cuinsight.com/press-release/announcing-hyperledger-indy-purpose-built-decentralized-independent-identity-individuals-enterprise.

20. Department of Homeland Security. 2017. "DHS S&T Awards $749K to Evernym for Decentralized Key Management Research and Development." https://www.dhs.gov/science-and-technology/news/2017/07/20/news-release-dhs-st-awards-749k-evernym-decentralized-key.

21. Department of Homeland Security. 2017. "DHS S&T Awards $750K to Virginia Tech Company for Blockchain Identity Management Research and Development." https://www.dhs.gov/science-and-technology/news/2017/09/25/news-release-dhs-st-awards-750k-virginia-tech-company.

22. Lohkamp, Joachim.2017. "Jolocom: Who Owns and Controls Your Data?" https://stories.jolocom.com/jolocom-who-owns-and-controls-your-data-effc7bc02ee8.

23. World Economic Forum. 2018. "The Known Traveller—Unlocking the Potential of Digital Identity for Secure and Seamless Travel." http://www3.weforum.org/docs/WEF_The_Known_Traveller_Digital_Identity_Concept.pdf.

24. World Economic Forum. 2018. "Identity in a Digital World: A New Chapter in the Social Contract." https://www.weforum.org/reports/identity-in-a-digital-world-a-new-chapter-in-the-social-contract.

25. Bennett, George. 2018. "Introducing the ERC-725 Alliance." https://medium.com/erc725alliance/introducing-the-erc725-alliance-2fe0682e3515.

26. Jordan, John, and Stephen Curran. 2018. "A Production Government Deployment of Hyperledger Indy." Decentralized Identity. https://decentralized-id.com/government/canada/bcgov/von/hgf-2018-production-government-deployment-hyperledger-indy/.

27. Microsoft. 2018. "Decentralized Identity: Own and Control Your Identity." https://query.prod.cms.rt.microsoft.com/cms/api/am/binary/RE2DjfY.

Identity is money 17

Alex Preukschat

If you've made it this far into the book—to the last chapter in part 3—it is likely you have concluded that the self-sovereign identity (SSI) technology and philosophy play at the edges of possibility about how the world can be organized. Bitcoin and the blockchain movement have opened up the discussion about what money is beyond its traditional boundaries; SSI is doing the same for identity. Our aim in part 3 has been to introduce these movements' inner workings and how they inspire each other. One of the identity pioneers who has pushed the boundaries of what is possible even further is David Birch, a world-renowned expert in both digital identity and payments and author of the book *Identity Is the New Money* (http://www .dgwbirch.com/words/books/identity-is-the-new-money.html; see also his more recent book, *Before Babylon, Beyond Bitcoin:* https://beforebabylonbeyondbitcoin .com). David inspired us to share with you how the combination of these two fundamental tools of social organization can be combined in this accelerating process of technological change to disrupt the way we think about these concepts.

17.1 Going back to the starting point

Digital trust is a fundamental requirement in a digital economy, where money is intangible and purely *fiat*: in other words, not backed by a physical asset or precious metal. In this context, the conjoining of identity and trust becomes key. In the same way the internet disrupted the sharing of information worldwide, SSI might disrupt the concept of money [1]. To explore this, we need to go back in time to the origins of the decentralized internet and decentralized money.

NOTE   *Fiat money* is a government-issued currency that is not backed by a commodity such as gold and therefore relies entirely on trust in the issuing government. Fiat money enables central banks to have greater influence over the economy because they can control how much money is printed. The majority of modern paper currencies, such as the U.S. dollar, are fiat currencies.

Internet money was a major theme for the internet in the 1990s. Those pursuing decentralized money included groups like the cypherpunks (chapter 13), David Chaum and Nick Szabo at DigiCash, Wei Dai, and Hal Finney. It was also being discussed by well-known companies and recognized economists like Milton Friedman, who said the following [2]:

> *The one thing that's missing, but that will soon be developed, is a reliable e-cash, a method whereby on the Internet you can transfer funds from A to B, without A knowing B or B knowing A.*

In chapter 1, we explained how Kim Cameron, chief architect of identity at Microsoft, said in 2004 that we were missing an identity layer for the internet. Following the same line of thinking, in 2015, Dan Morehead from Pantera Capital explained that money happens to be one of the missing pieces to complete the internet. He shared a metaphorical illustration (left half of figure 17.1) showing how Bitcoin—while not being fiat money—is the missing piece of the internet protocol puzzle. (One of the key phrases used in the 1977 paper by Ron Rivest, Adi Shamir, and Leonard Adleman was "electronic funds transfer," which Satoshi Nakamoto made a reality in 2009 by brilliantly combining different well-known cryptography techniques like public key cryptography and Merkle trees.) Following the same rationale, we can include decentralized digital identity in that puzzle (right half of figure 17.1) by integrating the two core W3C open standards: verifiable credentials (VCs, chapter 7) and decentralized identifiers (DIDs, chapter 8).

As with many other aspects of the early internet era, these technology visionaries were already foreseeing how future use cases and applications were coming together to re-create the concept of money with decentralized digital identity.

The final piece of the protocol puzzle with BTC		
TCP	IP	FTP
SMTP	HTTP	UDP
DNS	TLS/SSL	BTC

The final piece of the protocol puzzle with BTC and identity		
TCP/IP	VC/DID	FTP
SMTP	HTTP	UDP
DNS	TLS/SSL	BTC

Figure 17.1   (Left) The final piece of the protocol puzzle is a metaphor showing how Bitcoin or other cryptocurrency-based systems could be the internet's missing payment layer. Source: Dan Morehead. (Right) We have expanded this metaphorical model to include decentralized digital identity with verifiable credentials (VCs) and decentralized identifiers (DIDs).

17.2 Identity as the source of relationships and value

As we know it today, identity in the industrial society is often related to *administrative* or *bureaucratic identity*, which is defined by our passport or any other government-issued identity documents. Before the Industrial Revolution, identity was often defined by family, religion, and clan.

If we try to visualize the times of the hunter-gatherers—when people lived in small groups and everyone knew each other intimately—identity was individual to each person. The sum of the individual identities defined the identity of the group. To exchange value, these small groups did not need money. Rather, they *generalized reciprocity*—usually regulated through kinship—as the main conduit for collaboration [3]. People living in those cultures would not understand money at all. (We make a distinction in this chapter between modern vs. pre-industrial societies, referring to pre-agricultural societies with ancient Neolithic economies. To avoid misunderstandings, money was "invented" and very much in use before the Industrial Revolution.)

> **CONSIDER** In these hunter-gatherer groups, exchange of value was accounted for using a subjective *mental ledger* that each person carried. It could also be called an *IOU ledger* (abbreviated from the phrase "I owe you") because it accounts for what you owed and what others in your group owed you. Individual contributions, depending on roles, were registered in these IOU ledgers. This went for hunting, helping, creating goods, healing, and more. Money, as we know it, had no place.

It was easy for each person to maintain their own mental IOU ledger when the group was relatively small. But as groups grew larger and more trade started happening between groups, the IOUs became more complex. The evolution of money reflected the needs of a highly complex society where people didn't know each other, and trust had to be established with intermediary tools and technologies like money to create a common medium for exchange.

17.3 The properties of money

As technology advanced, the forms of money evolved. Gradually, humans began to understand the set of properties required for "good" money—money that worked well for tracking all these IOUs. Many monetary economists have described these properties—here is a basic summary:

- *Limited supply*—For money to maintain its value, it must be in limited supply. Excess supply erodes purchasing power. A historical example is cattle: as a measure of wealth, they were in limited supply and high demand—and therefore useful as money.
- *Durability*—To hold value, money must not wear out or be easily destroyed. For example, cattle are relatively durable and very difficult to fake.
- *Uniformity*—For money to be fungible, it needs to be uniform so that any unit can be exchanged for any other unit. This can be a challenge with cattle

because they are not very uniform—you need to be an expert to assess each animal's value.

- *Divisibility*—Money needs to be divisible so that different needs and wants can be measured in the corresponding unit. Cattle are not ideal in this respect: they are not divisible (at least until the time of consumption), which made commerce very complicated outside of barter—and even that required a double coincidence of wants, i.e., two transacting parties who wanted something similar in value at the same time.

- *Portability*—To be useful in commerce, money needs to be easy and safe to transport. Compare cattle to cash: which is easier to put in your wallet and carry around?

- *Storability*—Money needs to be storable so we can save it to use in the future or leave it for future generations. While cattle have a good lifespan, they still age in a way that money should not.

NOTE   Accounting started in the first states, where temple officials needed to count the amount of taxes collected. Taxes were at first in species (raw goods) and finally collected through money, as an indirect unit of account. Debt issuance in those states began the first financial operations of humankind. Thanks to Álvaro Rodríguez for this and other contributions to this chapter. For more detailed reading, see "Palatial Credit: Origins of Money and Interest" by Michael Hudson, https://michael-hudson.com/2018/04/palatial-credit -origins-of-money-and-interest.

17.4 *The three functions of money*

Money that has the properties we have defined can serve three functions:

- *Store of value*—Money can hold value over time because it's durable, difficult to fake, scarce (limited supply), and storable. Many other stores of value exist, such as land, art, precious gems, and other durable assets. As we typically use it, money may not be the best store of value, but it is more liquid than most other assets.

- *Medium of exchange*—If it is uniform, divisible, and portable—and trusted— money can be used as a medium of exchange to facilitate transactions in commerce.

- *Unit of account*—By combining the two previous functions, money can serve as a unit of accounting—a common measure of the value of goods and services being exchanged.

When you isolate these specific functions of money, you begin to see it is not just a tool for communicating and exchanging value, but a *technology*. In a society where most of us do not stop to think about how money works, it can be startling to think of money as a technology. But as a tool for solving a specific set of common problems, money is indeed a technology much like plumbing (for moving water), electricity (for powering lights, heat, and motors), and networks (for sharing information). Like these other technologies, money can be subject to new technological discoveries that, if they meet all the required properties, can improve on previous monetary technologies in significant ways.

And like other technological innovations, these improvements often end up changing the shape and form of the human systems that created them. Decentralized digital identity is just such an innovation. Like other exponential technologies, it might just be a new step in the evolution of money as a technology.

17.5 *The tokenization of value with identity*

The next evolutionary step for identity and money could be defined again by our social graphs—just as it was as at the times of the hunter-gatherers—because it takes us back to the concept of identity of the pre-industrial era, only now in a digital context. *Crypto tokens*, units of account governed by cryptography in a decentralized transaction database, can fulfill all the properties of money discussed earlier. These include serving as a store of value for the long term (some would claim Bitcoin is already serving this purpose) [4]. In a decentralized economy, a cryptocurrency like bitcoin could become the *Internet of Money* if the right use cases provide the underlying crypto assets with a base value.

Today, our fiat currency is generally accepted as money mainly for two reasons. First, it is *legal tender*—the currency we are obliged to use as the money of the jurisdiction where we operate. For example, if you want to pay for a drink in a bar in the United States, in most cases, you can pay only with US dollars and not with other currencies. The other important reason is that to *pay taxes* in a jurisdiction, you must pay with legal tender. Since taxes are usually a significant portion of an economy, this creates a large demand for fiat money in any jurisdiction. In addition, our current nation-states' capacity to impose law and order through their "monopoly on violence" is a key element enabling this very delicate system of trust to work.

> **CONSIDER** *Legal tender* is anything recognized by law as a means to settle a public or private debt or meet a financial obligation, including tax payments, contracts, and legal fines or damages. A creditor is legally obligated to accept legal tender toward repayment of a debt. Bitcoin and other cryptocurrencies are *not* legal tender and currently do not have the support of any government. The communities of usage that have developed around these cryptocurrencies provide value to the tokens. The larger these communities grow, the more value the tokens have.

Since the value of a currency—any form of money—ultimately depends on the trust that people have in that particular store of value, medium of exchange, or unit of account, the connection between SSI as a model for decentralized digital trust infrastructure and cryptocurrencies as decentralized, permissionless monetary systems starts to become obvious. You can see why Dave Birch proclaimed "Identity is the new money" (the title of his 2014 book) and how Dan Morehead envisioned a future decentralized digital trust economy that combined the Internet of Money with the Internet of Identity (figure 17.1).

After all, when you use a physical wallet today, what do you use it for? Identity or money? For 99.9% of us, the answer is *both*. The two are inextricably linked. And that's Dave Birch's and Dan Morehead's point: the SSI digital wallet of the future *could* be both how you prove your identity (in a highly contextualized and privacy-preserving way) and how you exchange value (in a highly contextualized and privacy-preserving way). The key to both will *literally* be the cryptographic keys you generate, store, and manage in that wallet.

This will be a profound shift—in many ways, as profound as the internet itself. For humans, the challenge is that our lives are short, and it is difficult for us to recognize how such profound shifts fit into the flows and cycles of evolution. We're also often naturally resistant to change because change creates uncertainty. But if the almost 8 billion people living on this planet could be represented as a massive peer-to-peer (P2P) network that encompassed the social graph of all true human relationships (and not just artificial social networks like Facebook), then putting humans at the center, interconnected with the rest of the world in a privacy-preserving and empowering way, suggests how perhaps the nature of money could change, too. Maybe, in the kind of decentralized P2P economy powered by attention and relationships envisioned by Doc Searls (who wrote the foreword for this book) in *The Intention Economy* (Harvard Business Review Press, 2012), the Internet of Money and the Internet of Identity could come together into the *Internet of Humans*.

> **NOTE** The use of multiple private currencies has been tried before and failed, as in the U.S. Free Banking Era. See "The Crazy Story of the Time When Almost Anyone in America Could Issue Their Own Currency," by Rob Wile: https://www.businessinsider.com/history-of-the-free-bank-era-2013-2. SSI technology might change that.

We are made to trust each other, and decentralization could provide a platform to make trust scalable. Dee Hock (the founder of Visa, who is responsible for effectively creating payment networks as we know them today) best summarizes this in his book *One from Many* (Berrett-Koehler, 2005):

> *The essence of community, its heart and soul, is the non-monetary exchange of value, things we do and share because we care for others and the good of the place.*

As we said at the outset, this chapter plays at the very fringes of where human institutions operate today and may evolve in the future. Many more books and articles will be written about these fascinating new ways human interaction will be organized. As we transition now to part 4 of this book, we come back down to earth to explore use cases that might change life and industry for people today or in the very short term. John Philipps opens part 4 with a chapter suggesting how to explain SSI to people in your organization and others you want to influence to adopt it.

> **SSI Resources**
>
> For more free content to learn about SSI, please go to IdentityBook.info and SSI Meetup.org/book.

References

1. Capie, Forrest, Geoffrey Wood, and Juan Castañeda. 2016. "Central Bank Independence in Small Open Economies," in *Central Banks at a Crossroads*. Cambridge Press. https://www.cambridge.org/core/books/central-banks-at-a-crossroads/central-bank-independence-in-small-open-economies/F3071D7C34896E6DF08CC1335B3E6683.
2. Cawrey, Daniel. 2014. "How Economist Milton Friedman Predicted Bitcoin." CoinDesk. https://www.coindesk.com/economist-milton-friedman-predicted-bitcoin.
3. Morehead, Dan. 2015. "Money - Past, Present, Future." Bitcoin.net. https://www.youtube.com/watch?v=iL7CM3bL4bc.
4. Sahlins, Marshall. 2017. *Stone Age Economics* (Routledge).

Part 4

How SSI will change your business

Having explored SSI from a historical, technological, and sociological point of view, in part 4, we get down to business. We begin with chapter 18, written by an experienced SSI practitioner who offers lessons learned about how best to explain (and sell) SSI to business decision-makers.

Chapters 19–22 were written by industry experts who give specific examples of how SSI is already penetrating, transforming, and benefiting their market segments:

- Internet of Things
- Animal care and guardianship
- Open democracy and voting
- Healthcare and pharmaceutical supply chains

Finally, we conclude with chapters 23 and 24, by several of the world's leading experts in digital identity for government. They explain how SSI is transforming identity infrastructure for both citizens and businesses in Canada (with the Pan-Canadian Trust Framework) and the European Union (with eIDAS and the EU SSI Framework).

Explaining the value of SSI to business

John Phillips

To realize the true potential of Self-Sovereign Identity (SSI), we need to be able to explain the value that SSI represents to organizations and people. We need to provide a compelling, understandable, and truthful account of what SSI can mean, so our audience sees the value in it for themselves. This is as essential to SSI's success as the technology that underpins it. We selected this as the first chapter in part 4 because it provides guidance on how best to communicate the value of SSI to business leaders. It is also important for technologists, who can use these ideas to better understand business goals. The author, John Phillips (of 460degrees, based in Australia), speaks from experience—he is one of the world's leading communicators about the value of SSI. Lucky enough to start his career working with international space agencies and living in a number of countries, John is now directing his efforts and passion toward better digital trust for all.

One of the key pivot points that helped our understanding of how to explain SSI occurred while working with a group of undergraduate students at Swinburne University of Technology in Melbourne, Australia. We had given the final-year design class a challenge for their capstone project (the last major project of their degree): how to design an approach to SSI and digital wallets for the people of Melbourne. The project ran for most of the second semester, with the students working in groups on the challenge. By the end of the project, the students had come up with brilliant ideas, and we learned at least as much from the experience as they did.

During an early discussion, one of the students shared the challenge she'd had at home during the week when trying to explain SSI to her father, a 50-something Australian who had worked on the land for most of his life. "He just didn't get it! How can you explain this stuff to someone like my dad?"

We left that meeting wondering how best to answer that question. We experimented with ways to explain SSI (not our first visit to this challenge) and started to look through the items we had in the innovation/design thinking craft drawer in the office. We used a familiar use-case story (renting a property) and animated it using foam figures, hand-written cards, envelopes, and popsicle sticks.

For the next few days, we carried this kit with us wherever we went and tried it out on every person we had coffee with or met in a meeting. We got better at telling the story as we practiced. We found that despite (or perhaps because of) the "craft kit" qualities, the approach worked well—people got it. The conversation would become animated, and people picked up the items and moved them around as they asked questions. At our next meeting with the students, we excitedly showed them our new way of explaining SSI—an approach that could even work with a retired sheep shearer (we hoped).

The experience of working with these students, the challenges and questions they raised, and our own experiences working with the business community made us realize that we needed a way to explain SSI that was simpler, more compelling, and able to reach diverse audiences. This is an essential problem for the SSI community to solve. No matter how much technical elegance it has, SSI will be successful only if we can convince people and organizations to use it—and if we can convince organizations to, quite literally, buy into it.

As the Swinburne students observed, understanding SSI is no easy matter. The technology and underlying philosophy are rich and complex. Understanding why it was designed this way, how it works, and what it can and can't do takes time. We can't expect everyone to dive deep enough to understand all the technical facets of SSI, nor should we.

So how, then, can we motivate the very adoption we need for SSI to be successful? The answer to this challenge is understanding what SSI can mean for organizations and people in the context of their own lives and markets—the value of SSI to *them*.

The next few sections explain how we learned, through a series of experiments, what works and what doesn't work when explaining SSI. The chapter concludes with recommendations about how to explain SSI in any given situation.

18.1 How might we best explain SSI to people and organizations?

Let's explain the technology. After all, it is pretty damn cool when you get to understand it—and surely everyone else will see it that way if we can just explain it well enough.

18.1.1 Failed experiment 1: Leading with the technology

Most SSI converts start by exploring the technology, often because that is their core expertise. We explain the math, the software, the standards, and all the bits that make SSI work. This explanation is impenetrable to most people in a short meeting and also fails to clarify the "why" of SSI for them: how it can make their lives and/or businesses better.

At best, a technology-first approach will work in only a few instances with a handful of people. Of course, it is essential that the technology works—and that there is proof that others can peer review. However, when we want to discuss the *opportunity* SSI presents with people and organizations, most of the time they don't have the time or technical background to understand the underlying technology.

> **NOTE** For those already steeped in SSI: you would do well to remember how long it took you to first understand the technology. I doubt it was a one-hour meeting.

Here are two key reasons why leading with the tech is not the best approach:

- *It's overwhelming.* Explaining SSI by explaining the technology is like trying to explain the internet by describing the Request for Comments (RFC) documents that define the standards in the TCP/IP suite. Most people just want to know what using a browser can let them do, not how RFC 2616 works (the RFC for the HTTP protocol).

    A lot of work has been done by many very good engineers over several years to develop the SSI framework—and that work continues. You can't expect your audience to "get it" in the few minutes you have to explain the value of SSI.

- *It's irrelevant.* Consider your audience. Organizations exploring SSI typically have a mix of people, interests, and experience in the room—technologists, marketers, product owners, and business executives. Each of them has a personal and professional mental model of digital identity and digital trust—and the technical and commercial environments in which those things exist. In addition, they have a collective view built around their own way of handling digital identity and trust in their organization.

For the majority of the audience, the technology part is a distraction at best. They expect the tech to work—otherwise, they wouldn't take the time to look into it—but they are far more interested in the problems it will solve for *them*.

18.1.2 Failed experiment 2: Leading with the philosophy

Rather than leading with the tech, we could start by explaining the principles and philosophy of *self-sovereign identity*. After all, that's what many of us personally find so attractive. We might feel it is important to share the underlying principles and history since they are so rich and interesting and deeply woven into the authentic fabric of SSI. It really matters that we believe SSI can make the world a better place, protect privacy, strengthen democracies, and protect us against the evils of surveillance capitalism.

What we've found when embarking on these discussions is that the words *self*, *sovereign*, and *identity* come loaded with personal meaning and interpretations—some of which are quite often radically different for each individual in the room. Each of these terms could be the subject of an entire philosophy or humanities course. (Many SSI adherents have spent considerable time seeking alternative terms that better describe the essence of SSI without such strong connotations—or at least with less risk of distraction or misinterpretation.)

Our experience is that, with almost all organizations, the philosophy of SSI is interesting but almost certainly irrelevant to their main interest, which is the benefits SSI brings to their organization. Concentrate on that first before making any attempt to explain why SSI can be a force for global good. Attempting to explain the philosophy behind SSI and the meaning of the terms in the context of a short meeting risks delay and derailing the conversation that will lead to adoption.

> **NOTE** There is a secondary risk, too. Many of us who are drawn to SSI are passionate about this work and the meaning it gives to our lives. If we spend too much time focusing on this message, we risk being seen as idealists and perfectionists rather than pragmatic and focused on business value.

So if we want SSI to be as successful as we believe it can be, we need to focus on the benefit to each adoptee while remaining true to the principles and philosophy of SSI.

18.1.3 *Failed experiment 3: Explaining by demonstrating the tech*

This approach is attractive since we're "proving" that what we're talking about exists and works. Except we're not, really.

Demonstrating working technology is an expected part of any process of convincing someone that something is real and worth having/using. It will be important at some point in their discovery process. However, if they are truly skeptical, they'll know you can give whiz-bang demos that can make almost anything look good. After all, nowadays, it's easy to make a presentation deck behave like a web application.

In addition, all demonstrations are by necessity simplifications. They must use stub websites or mock interactions. So skeptics often remain unconvinced because you haven't done the hard part of making the technology work in production.

The other, perhaps more curious, reason that showing the technology doesn't impress as much as we'd hope is that people *expect* the tech to work. Hence it's not a surprise when it does. After all, we wouldn't be showing it to them if it didn't work, would we?

Furthermore, part of the power of SSI is that *the magic happens invisibly in the math and communication protocols that underpin it*. That's the beauty of it—and what makes it usable. Surfacing that magic by instrumenting the code and showing what is (and isn't) being read and written on the ledger, for example, risks making the technology look complex.

Bottom line: demos have a role to play at some point, but first your audience needs to be motivated by the benefits. Then they need to know where to look for the magic when you demonstrate, so you have to narrate the parts they can't actually see.

18.1.4 Failed experiment 4: Explaining the (world's) problems

It is an accepted truth among SSI practitioners that the digital world we all live in has serious and growing problems with privacy and trust. The concepts of identity theft, honey-pots for hackers, toxic stores of personal identifying information, privacy erosion, and surveillance capitalism are increasingly common in the mainstream media [1]. These issues are some of the drivers for the development of SSI.

We might expect that the people and organizations we talk to about SSI understand these issues, at least to some extent, and we can certainly increase their awareness during our discussion. However, to put it bluntly, this is most likely irrelevant to the current conversation. While we would like to help achieve a peaceful, safe, and privacy-enabled future, this isn't on the strategic goals list of many organizations (unless you're talking to people like the UN).

There are, of course, ways to make this element meaningful to the audience. For example, we can focus on the organization's use of customer data and its honey-pots for hackers. We can talk about how SSI can enhance the digital trust between the business and its customers and partners. We can talk about risk reduction and how the company can reduce its compliance burden or become compliant. But these are the *business's* problems; and if they also happen to reflect the world's problems, so much the better if the business can solve them in its own domain.

18.2 Learning from other domains

Fortunately, we can take ideas from many other domains to help us explain the value of SSI to people and organizations. Some of the key sources are the following:

- *Teaching*—Clearly, what we are aiming to do has an element of teaching, and there is a wealth of research and materials to lean on.
- *Human-centered design*—Many resources are available on this topic from universities and organizations like IDEO.
- *(Professional) story telling*—Human beings are wired to understand and remember using stories or anecdotes. Explaining through a story structure means the subject will be easier for the audience to understand and remember.
- *Pitch decks*—Another easily accessible wealth of advice and templates centers on how to explain (that is, sell) your new, wonderful (possibly patented) idea to an audience to try to convince them to invest.
- *Consulting processes*—All consulting companies have processes of one form or another that describe how they explain the results of their work to the client that paid for them. The details vary, but the intent is much the same: explain an issue, and present a course of action to be taken. A classic example is *The Pyramid Principle: Logic in Writing and Thinking* (Barbara Minto; Prentice Hall, 2008).

- *Behavioral economics*—A growing body of work and practitioners are looking at why people make the decisions they do and what influences those decisions. Daniel Kahneman, Amos Tversky, Richard Thaler, Dan Ariely, and others have developed models of understanding around how we are all "predictably irrational" (to use Ariely's phrase).

- *Professional sales processes*—We should not be shy about the fact that we are selling the idea of SSI. High-value, high-stakes sales professionals follow a framework for "honorable" selling, where trusted relationships are established and maintained and selling isn't a once-and-done (or once-and-run) activity. This means taking the time to explore whether what we have to offer (SSI) is good for the organization or person we are talking to and sincerely digging into learning how that person or organization might best go about adopting SSI.

18.3   *So how should we best explain the value of SSI?*

The lessons we learned from trying each of the approaches discussed earlier—in person, in writing, in presentations, and in demonstrations—helped us better understand how to explain SSI in a business context. Ultimately, the design students at Swinburne helped us to think of this challenge as a *design problem*. In other words, think of "designing" your explanation of SSI for the business you want to talk to.

Using a design framework, we can identify the key elements that we need to focus on:

1 *Empathize.* Understand your audience: their market, their business, and the people in the organization. Whom are you seeing? What is their professional and personal interest likely to be? What sorts of issues/opportunities are they likely to be troubled by and interested in?

2 *Define the problem(s).* Select the issues you think they can solve with SSI and the opportunities they can realize. Define these in simple terms that will resonate with your audience. Use the design thinking "How might we …" structure.

3 *Ideate.* Develop your idea about how to solve the problem(s) you identify. Test these for their practicality and relevance. Do they make business sense? Do they solve a problem worth solving or deliver an outcome worth having? Does the investment look reasonable against the return?

4 *Select.* Choose the ideas that make the most sense, ideally by pre-testing them with people from the company you are selling to (or someone who knows the organization well).

5 *Prototype. Select materials*, and build the elements you need. These might be presentation decks, craft supplies, software, videos, or other ways you can explain the ideas.

6 *Test.* Try the approach with people in your organization, learn from their reactions, and revisit earlier stages.

7 *Launch.* Share with the business you want to talk to (and learn from this step, too!).

The lessons learned at each of these stages might require revisiting earlier assumptions. Developing the best approach to explain how SSI can add value to a specific business is an iterative process—you are very unlikely to get it right the first time.

18.4 *The power of stories*

In our experience, there is one consistent approach for explaining the value of SSI to professionals and businesses: tell stories. By this, I mean having a planned narrative, using anecdotes that people can associate with professionally and personally, and making the journey personal, relatable, and meaningful to their business.

Why stories? Because most of us are pre-conditioned to listen to stories. They are part of being human—part of our upbringing and background. For most of us, stories are far easier to remember than lists of facts or take-home points.

We recommend that you use a story architecture even for business stories. Stories typically have an arc like this:

1 [At a point in time] this was the case …
2 … then this happened …
3 … so now we have this challenge/opportunity …
4 … and if we take these steps …
5 … we can reach this destination/goal.

Gifted storytellers can change the order of these points, hint at future reveals, provide unexpected twists, and give the punchline before the background; but for most of us, it is easiest to stick to this order.

Note that I'm saying *story*, not *use case*. Yes, a use case can be a story (and most would be better if they were told as stories to give them context and meaning). However, most use cases are dry, depersonalized affairs, devoid of interest for anyone except their narrator. Having a "persona" does not make your use case a story. Give your persona(s) a back story and context, give your use case a plot and a moral, and now you've got a story.

18.5 *Jackie's SSI story*

Here's the example we developed when working with the Swinburne University students. This became the story we captured on video for mostly internal purposes (and which eventually caught the attention of the editors of this book).

The story has three parts:

1 The current world of physical documentation (to get on the same page as everyone in the audience through a shared experience)
2 The future, better, world made possible by SSI
3 The current world of our digital lives—full of hidden, and not-so-hidden, problems

We normally tell this in person using props, but since this is a book, we'll use a cartoon storyboard version of the story.

18.5.1 *Part 1: The current physical world*

Our story introduces Jackie, a fictional character living in Melbourne, Australia, who has just started her career. Recently she got a new job nearer the city. She's currently living in a shared apartment where she pays some of the bills, but she wants to move closer to the city to be nearer her new job.

Jackie has found a great apartment that she wants to rent, offered by Highly Rated Rentals.

Highly Rated Rentals tells Jackie that she'll need to complete a tenancy application and provide proof of identity. Jackie reads the application and sees that she'll need to complete a *100-point check*—an Australian government standard for ID checks.

Jackie heads back to her current place to get her documents.

Jackie is lucky: she has a driver's license and her birth certificate. She keeps the birth certificate in a drawer at home and her driver's license in her wallet.

Jackie can share these documents with whomever she chooses, when she chooses, without the issuer ever needing to know. Each document says who issued it, who it was issued to (Jackie, in this case), and what it verifies about the holder.

Jackie decides to use her driver's license, her birth certificate, and an employment pay slip for her 100-point check.

Jackie asks her new employer for a pay slip as she doesn't have a copy.

When she gets the pay slip, she scans it with her other documents and sends the copies by email to Highly Rated Rentals.

Highly Rated Rentals stores a copy of Jackie's documents and starts to verify them.

Hang on: that part is a little scary.

Not only has Jackie sent sensitive documents by email, but how secure is Highly Rated Rentals? Highly Rated Rentals has a *lot* of sensitive information about a lot of people, not just Jackie. Is that information safe, now and for the foreseeable future?

It takes a few days for the document verification process to complete. Finally, Highly Rated Rentals call Jackie to tell her the check is finished, her application has been accepted, and she can rent the apartment.

At the office of Highly Rated Rentals, Jackie pays the damage deposit (also called a bond), gives her bank account details for a direct debit, and signs the rental agreement.

In return, Highly Rated Rentals gives Jackie a copy of the agreement and hands her the key to her new apartment.

That's the end of part 1.

18.5.2 *Part 2: The SSI world—like the current physical world, but better*

In part 1, we saw Jackie lease her new apartment using documents she owns to prove her identity. That's the world many of us live in right now. In part 2, we're going to see how this process works in an SSI-enabled world. Spoiler alert: it will be like the current world, but better.

To keep the story simple and get to the moral faster, we'll show what Jackie experiences if she already has an SSI digital wallet with a couple of credentials loaded. (The origin story will come later. Doesn't it always?)

Each digital credential that Jackie has is much like the physical version she had in part 1. The credential says who issued it, whom it was issued to (Jackie, in this case), and what attributes the issuer verifies about Jackie.

She keeps these credentials in the digital wallet of her choice and can show them to whom she wants, when she wants. She can share the whole credential or just the relevant parts. And she can even prove that she has the credential without sharing any details. That's very cool!

To start with, we'll give her a birth certificate and a driver's license in her wallet.

This time, the Highly Rated Rentals website tells Jackie that she can apply online and receive confirmation in minutes, not days. She'll still need to complete a 100-point check, though (SSI doesn't change the laws, nor does it need to).

Using the Highly Rated Rentals website, Jackie creates a unique, secure SSI connection and starts the application process.

Her wallet receives a *proof request* from Highly Rated Rentals and tells her that she has two of the three things she needs. But she still needs the third: proof of her employment.

Jackie contacts her new employer and asks them to send her an SSI verifiable credential (yes, that could have happened when she got her job, but we're showing how Jackie can get new VCs when she needs them).

Once she gets the employment credential from her employer, she has all she needs to respond to the Highly Rated Rentals proof request. She responds to the proof request using her wallet and confirms the three VCs she wants to use.

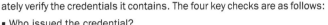

Highly Rated Rentals receive Jackie's proof response and can immediately verify the credentials it contains. The four key checks are as follows:

- Who issued the credential?
- Was it issued to Jackie?
- Has Jackie changed it?
- Has the issuer revoked it?

Note that we're showing people in the process, because stories need characters! And people were certainly needed to issue Jackie's credentials—that's what makes them trustworthy.

However, we can, and should, use software to automate the verification process. We don't need people to do boring, repetitive tasks that require sustained attention to detail. People would rather do tasks that add value for them and others around them (but that's a whole other story).

And Highly Rated Rentals has confirmation that Jackie accepted the agreement and the other exchanges the company has had with Jackie.

Jackie's private SSI connection with Highly Rated Rentals offers a secure, trustworthy communication channel for all of this—and for anything else they need to exchange for as long as they both want the relationship.

Within seconds of Highly Rated Rentals sending the response, Jackie receives an offer for the rental agreement on her wallet.

After viewing the offer, she accepts it. This sends a confirmation back to Highly Rated Rentals.

Jackie now has a secure, verifiable history of everything she has sent to and received from Highly Rated Rentals, including the verified rental agreement.

Jackie still needs to set up the payment details. (There's some really interesting stuff here that SSI can improve on.) And she needs to pick up the key for the flat. But at least she can do that over a great cup of Melbourne coffee.

That's the end of part 2.

18.5.3 Part 3: Introducing the Sparkly Ball[1]—or, what's wrong with many current digital identity models

In part 1, we saw Jackie lease her new apartment using documents she owns to prove her identity. In part 2, we showed how SSI can enable a familiar but better version of this process for Jackie and Highly Rated Rentals. In part 3, we talk about the problem with many current digital identity models.

At the moment, in most countries in the world, the primary documents we use for identification are physical. For most of us, items like passports, driver's licenses, education and training certificates, vaccination records, and other identity-related records are physical documents we store in wallets, drawers, and filing cabinets. Increasingly, however, we need to access services and products online, and for that, we need some form of digital identity.

Let's say Jackie needs a digital identity to access services online from a number of organizations. To get a digital identity, she needs to find an *identity service provider* of some kind—an organization that can issue a digital identity. While any online organization can create an online identity, to be useful, this identity needs to be recognized and trusted by other organizations.

The degree of trust depends on the provider's reputation, the processes they use, and the legal and social licenses they hold. Digital identity service providers can be government agencies, commercial companies, or non-profit organizations. In Australia, these providers are governmental (such as MyGovID), commercial entities recognized by the government (such as AusPost Digital ID), and social/commercial entities like financial institutions and technology companies (Apple, Google, Facebook, Amazon, Microsoft, and so on).

The basic process is that you provide the identity service provider (*issuer*) with a bunch of information about you, and, depending on the checks the provider needs to do, it issues a digital identity for you. Sometimes the checks are quite demanding (proof of citizenship, birth, bank accounts, and so on), and sometimes you just need to prove that you control an email address or a mobile phone number.

The level of proof demanded and verified is one of the factors that determines how strongly that digital identity is linked to you and thus how much trust it conveys when you use it. Once you have the digital identity from the provider, you can use it with other organizations that accept it as proof of identity.

Now, if this were the SSI model, the identity service provider would give you a verifiable credential with a bunch of verified data in it that you could store in a digital wallet of your choice. You could use this when you chose, with whom you chose, showing as much or as little as you chose without the issuer needing to know you're using the credential.

But it's not SSI. It's a legacy digital identity containing a legacy identifier for you.

---

[1] One of our explainer videos uses a Sparkly Ball (from our box of craft supplies) to represent the third-party identity provider: https://www.youtube.com/watch?v=81GkdBRmsbE&feature=emb_logo.

These legacy systems—whether centralized or federated—give you an identifier and a way for you to prove that identifier was given to you. This proof can be a password or, ideally, a combination of several things (multi-factor). Each time you use the identifier, the receiving organization (*verifier*) asks the identity service provider to verify it.

Therein lies the privacy issue. Now the identifier you are using is known to both the issuer and the verifier. Using the same identifier across multiple spaces introduces a correlation risk, just like today's problem with tracking cookies on the web.

Once the identifier is authenticated, the receiving organization looks you up in its databases to see what services and resources your identifier can access. The verifier needs to remember all this information about you because it has no other way to know what you are and are not allowed access to on its system. That's a bureaucratic burden for the verifier—and a risk for both of you since if that personal data is hacked, it can be used to impersonate you for identity theft.

Ethical identity service providers try to not watch or learn about what you're doing. They digitally "cover their eyes" (deliberately forgetting connection details) and promise to forget everything they learned within a short period (say, every 30 days). Others might not be so inclined, for the simple reason that their business model motivates them to gather data about you so that they can sell it to others.

But good intentions or no, the problem with identity service providers is that they can't help being in the loop. So whether they are actively authenticating or passively linking your data trail, your privacy is at serious risk.

That's why we don't like "shared identity" models of any kind, whether centralized, federated, or hybrid. Only by moving to the SSI model where the only party in the loop at all times is you, the individual, can we finally have both strong security and strong privacy.

18.6 SSI Scorecard for apartment leasing

The SSI Scorecard is color-coded as follows:

Transformative	Positive	Neutral	Negative

In each of the chapters in part 4 of this book, we use the SSI Scorecard we developed in chapter 4. For each of the five categories in the Scorecard (Bottom Line, Business Efficiencies, User Experience & Convenience, Relationship Management, and Regulatory Compliance), the chapter author(s) evaluate whether the impact of SSI is Transformative, Positive, Neutral, or Negative.

For this chapter, we use the story of Jackie leasing an apartment. We evaluated that SSI will be Transformative for User Experience & Convenience and Regulatory Compliance. It will also have clear positive effects for the Bottom Line, Business Efficiencies, and Relationship Management categories (table 18.1).

Table 18.1 SSI Scorecard: apartment leasing

Category	Key benefits
Bottom Line	The common practice of taking whole copies (electronic or paper) of valuable identity documents as part of establishing a leasing agreement presents a risk for the renter and a bureaucratic burden for the rental agency. SSI can minimize this risk and maximize trust.
Business Efficiencies	Minimal, secure, verifiable information exchange enables a rental agreement to be reached much more quickly and efficiently, reducing cost and effort for both the renter and landlord.
User Experience & Convenience	For renters in a competitive market, being able to apply and have an application processed for a rental property in real time can be the difference between getting the apartment they really want and missing out.
Relationship Management	Each party in a rental transaction needs to trust the others over an extended period. So it helps to have a secure private channel that isn't dependent on email addresses, phone numbers, or any other contact data that may change over time. In addition, all correspondence between the parties is secure and provides a verifiable trail.
Regulatory Compliance	In some jurisdictions, the SSI model may require changes to regulations so that verifiable credentials can be recognized as legal documents, and digital document exchange is allowed as an alternative to physical documents. But overall, the impact of SSI will be a boon for helping landlords and tenants prove compliance to regulations—and for regulators to validate this compliance.

SSI Resources

To learn more about how to think about the conceptualization of SSI use cases, check out https://ssimeetup.org/explaining-ssi-c-suite-executives-anyone-else-john-phillips-webinar-48.

Reference

1. Zuboff, Shoshana, 2019. *The Age of Surveillance Capitalism: The Fight for a Human Future at the New Frontier of Power.* PublicAffairs.

The Internet of Things opportunity

19

Oscar Lage, Santiago de Diego, and Michael Shea

The world of the Internet of Things (IoT) has the same challenge as the rest of the internet with the lack of verifiable identity of what is being connected to whom. This creates significant security and privacy risks for both the operators of IoT devices and the public at large. Although the number of IoT devices continues to multiply, the value they bring to business and society will be seriously compromised unless security and privacy issues related to the identity of these devices are addressed. This chapter outlines how the application of the self-sovereign identity (SSI) paradigm in the IoT space can close some of these security gaps and provide a resilient identity layer for IoT. Our guides include three active contributors to SSI and IoT infrastructure: Oscar Lage, global head of cybersecurity at Tecnalia; Santiago de Diego, cybersecurity researcher at Tecnalia Research; and Michael Shea, managing director, The Dingle Group.

19.1 IoT: Connecting everything safely

The IoT landscape is one of immense diversity. Loosely, the IoT includes any device that can connect to a network (over any transport), stream data, and receive commands from afar. IoT covers industrial systems, building automation, home automation, healthcare, agriculture, mining, mobility, and wearables, just to name a few segments. Very few areas of our modern life are not touched by the IoT.

In structure, an IoT system consists of a *hub* (or controller) and *devices*. Devices can be sensors (e.g., temperature, CCTV) or actuators (e.g., lights, door locks). A typical IoT network may contain multiple hubs (or controllers) and hundreds (or thousands) of devices. Hubs/controllers, in most cases, are hosted in a cloud environment (e.g., Amazon Web Services, Microsoft's Azure); however, they can be on-premises as well.

From a security and privacy viewpoint, in our highly connected world, it is best to assume that all networks are constantly under attack. IoT systems, especially, with their poor security reputation, have become entry points for targeting critical infrastructure. In 2019, cyberattacks on IoT devices increased by 300%. In the first half of 2019, the number of attacks surpassed the billion mark for the first time, reaching 2.9 billion attacks, a 3.5× increase compared to the second half of 2018 [1].

In June 2020, the JSOF research lab announced that it had discovered a number of zero-day vulnerabilities in a widely used low-level TCP/IP software library developed by Treck, Inc. [2]. The 19 vulnerabilities, given the name Ripple20, affect millions of IoT devices and include multiple remote-code-execution vulnerabilities. The vulnerable software library was integrated into IoT devices for Caterpillar, Cisco, HP (Hewlett-Packard), HPE (Hewlett-Packard Enterprise), Intel, Rockwell, Schneider Electric, Digi, and more. All these companies' devices are potentially vulnerable to remote hacks by cybercriminals.

> **NOTE** A *zero-day vulnerability* is a computer-software vulnerability that is unknown to, or unaddressed by, those who should be interested in mitigating the vulnerability (including the vendor of the target software) and that is being actively exploited in the wild.

When the number of devices in a network is numbered in the hundreds or thousands—and every device on the network is a potential attack vector—keeping all devices identified and up to date is an enormous task. For network administrators to have any chance of keeping up with the attackers, automation is critical for provisioning, key rotation, and revocation of rights to devices to keep networks safe, as explained in chapter 10.

The research company IDC estimated in 2019 that the global spend on IoT-related devices and services was $745 billion and forecasted a 17.8% compound annual growth rate (CAGR) over the next five years [3]. While this information is very positive for those participating in the IoT sector, the report also mentions that the industry has failed to reach the forecasted growth rates for the past several years. IDC believes there are two main reasons for this repeated underachievement:

- Continued concern around security and IoT
- Difficulty in establishing the return on investment (ROI) required to make the transition

We believe that SSI could become one of the driving forces to catapult the IoT industry to reach its full potential.

19.2   *How does SSI help IoT?*

SSI cannot solve all of the security and privacy challenges within the IoT sector. However, the integration of SSI into the IoT ecosystem can address the following:

- Robust and interoperable identity and authentication
- Privacy and information confidentiality
- Data provenance and integrity

The first significant contributions from SSI are decentralized identifiers (DIDs) and DID documents (chapter 8). These can provide the following:

- *Identifiers and identity verification mechanisms* needed to establish trusted connections with IoT devices
- *A verifiable list of the services* offered by the device in a standardized way
- *Secure, private connections* over which to exchange digitally signed information between devices and controllers (or other peer devices)

The second key contribution is from verifiable credentials (VCs, chapter 7). These provide:

- *A standard authorization mechanism* by which any device can assert the provenance of data from sensors or processing of commands to actuators
- *A much richer data model* for handling and disclosing attributes
- *The ability to do selective disclosure* through zero-knowledge proofs or semantic schemas for data model extensibility, neither of which are available with traditional X.509 certificates [4]

The combination of DIDs and VCs can bring *high-assurance identity*—the missing element of IoT. With high assurance identity,

- *Data streaming* from IoT sensors can be traced back to a verifiable source, enabling organizations to prove provenance and maintain reliable data supply chains.
- *Remote devices* will know with confidence where their commands are coming from.
- *Firmware updates* can be easily validated for their source and trustworthiness.

19.3 *The business perspective for SSI and IoT*

SSI is an important new development in technology; however, it is frequently sold on its technological merits without connecting it to the business problems it solves. (See chapter 18 for more guidance on how to explain SSI to businesses.) For adoption of SSI in IoT, we should stress these business benefits:

- *SSI allows owners and users of IoT devices to become their own root of trust*, eliminating dependencies, vulnerabilities, and costs associated with third parties.
- *The cost to identify devices or rotate keys can drop to fractions of a cent*, and devices can be added or removed with very low risk.
- *SSI high-assurance identity means fewer concerns, interruptions, or delays* caused by security issues within an IoT network.
- *Secure DID-to-DID connections and verifiable credential exchange* mean assured provenance of data, which means better results from machine learning algorithms processing that data.

As SSI gains traction in the IoT market, we expect to see hard data backing up these promises.

19.4   *An SSI-based IoT architecture*

To help you visualize what this might mean, we have created a basic SSI reference architecture for IoT. It begins with the actors and their digital agents involved in an SSI-based IoT ecosystem:

- *Manufacturer:* Produces IoT devices
- *Certification Body:* The entity that issues a VC to a Manufacturer
- *Verifier:* The person, device, or entity who verifies a VC
- *Verifiable Data Registry:* A trusted Layer 1 registry accessible to everyone (see chapter 2)

The first step, initialization, is where the IoT device connects with both the Manufacturer and the Certification Body. All communications during these steps use secure channels (Transport Layer Security [TLS], DTLS [Datagram Transport Layer Security], DIDComm). This is shown in figure 19.1:

1 The device generates its key pair, DID, and DID document. Note that the device needs a secure element or trust execution environment (TEE) to protect its own keys.
2 A one-time token is issued by the Manufacturer and incorporated into the device in the manufacturing process to enable the device to authenticate with the Manufacturer.
3 The device forms a connection and shares its self-generated DID with the Manufacturer using the one-time token for security. Once the initialization has been completed, the Manufacturer knows the IoT device DID, and the two have a permanent connection.

**2. IoT sends a self-generated
DID with the one-time token.**

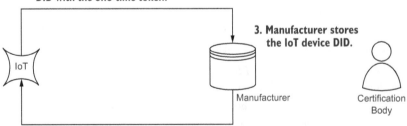

**3. Manufacturer stores
the IoT device DID.**

1. Manufacturer sends a one-time token.

**4. A DID document is stored in
the Verifiable Data Registry.**

Figure 19.1   The initialization process in which an IoT device generates a key pair, DID, and DID document and securely registers them with the Manufacturer

4 The Manufacturer creates its own DID and DID document and registers them in a verifiable data registry (VDR): a Layer 1 blockchain, distributed ledger technology (DLT), or other database.

In this first stage, the Certification Body is not yet involved.

Figure 19.2 shows the second stage, during which VCs are issued:

1 The Manufacturer connects to the Certification Body, which performs due diligence and then issues VC credential C to the Manufacturer as the holder. The Manufacturer's agent stores credential C in its wallet.

2 The Manufacturer generates a unique credential C2 linked to credential C and issues credential C2 to each of its IoT devices. The Manufacturer is now both an issuer and holder.

3 The manufacturer writes the DID and DID document of each device to the VDR.

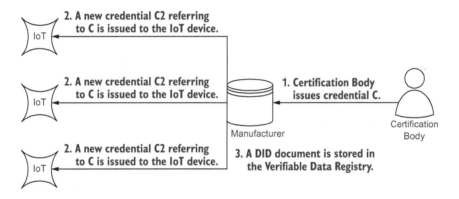

Figure 19.2 The Certification Body issues a quality credential.

If the Certification Body needs to revoke a certification credential in the future, it will update the *revocation registry* in the VDR (see chapter 7). The revocation registry allows a verifier to easily and quickly check the credential status without having to go back to the issuer.

Now let's expand the scenario by adding another actor: the Verifier. A verifier can be a human actor, another IoT device, or an organization. Figure 19.3 shows the scenario where the Verifier is the controller for an IoT network on which the Manufacturer wants to register a device:

1 The device requests to register on the IoT network, so the IoT network controller asks the IoT device for proof of a certified identity credential.

2 The IoT device responds with a verifiable presentation that includes a list of claims from the credential C2 and signed by the IoT device.

3 The IoT network controller first verifies the digital signatures by checking the VDR for the public keys associated with the DIDs of the Certification Body, the

Manufacturer, and the device. The IoT network controller next checks the revocation status of credential C2 against the VDR. Finally, the IoT network controller validates the claims from the C2 credential.

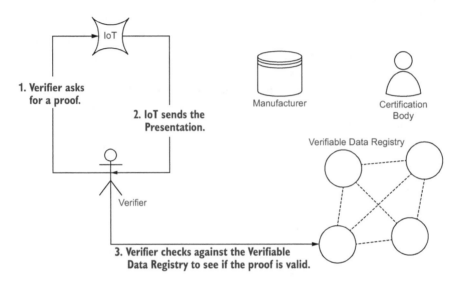

Figure 19.3   Verification process between the different parties

It is worth noting that neither the Certification Body nor the Manufacturer is needed for the actual verification process—only for the issuance of the original credentials. The IoT device can cryptographically prove its identity to the IoT network controller, and the VDR is the only service the IoT network controller needs to consult during verification.

Now let's look at an example to understand how this could be applied in real life.

19.5   *Tragic story: Bob's car hacked*

Imagine this not-so-fictional scenario:

> *Bob has just picked up his brand-new car. To celebrate, he and his partner Carol are going out for dinner. Bob parks his car in an unattended parking lot. While Bob and Carol are enjoying dinner, Evan breaks into Bob's new car and substitutes the integrated global positioning system (GPS) for an identical one, which reports back to Evan the current location of Bob's car. Now, Evan can know where Bob is at any time. After following Bob for a few months, Evan knows where he lives, which routes he drives, and where Carol lives. Evan is ready to execute his evil plan against Bob.*

Now let's apply the SSI IoT reference model to this scenario. This time, let's assume Bob's car's operating system includes SSI identity verification to ensure every component or subsystem in the car comes from a trusted source. When a new component is installed in the car, the initialization process requires the operating system (OS) to request proof of an identity credential from the component.

The component must reply with an acceptable proof. The OS checks the proof's cryptographic integrity and then uses an over-the-air (OTA) process to look up the manufacturer's DID in a VDR to get the public key required to verify the proof. If both of these verifications pass and the component's identity is confirmed, the OS then exchanges a peer DID with the component so subsequent communications can use a secure private channel known only to the two of them.

In this new version of the story, the rigged GPS component would fail at multiple layers. First, it would not have the original GPS's peer DID to re-establish the secure communication channel with the OS. Second, when the rigged GPS received the credential initialization request, it would have neither a DID nor the necessary credential from an approved manufacturer. Therefore the OS would not accept the rigged GPS—and it would warn Bob that someone was tampering with his car.

19.6 *The Austrian Power Grid*

While Bob's car might be a fanciful scenario, there is nothing fanciful about managing a power grid. It is a complex and serious business. The electric grid is made up of power producers, transmission operators, distribution operators, and consumers (residential and industrial). For example, the operator of the electric grid in Austria, the Austrian Power Grid (APG), is responsible for ensuring the reliable delivery of energy across all stakeholders. This means real-time management of power entering and leaving the grid while maintaining a stable frequency across the grid.

In early 2020, the APG and the Energy Web Foundation announced a proof of concept to enable the participation of small-scale distributed energy resources (DERs) in the APG [5]. Support for small-scale energy production (e.g., home-based solar energy) is part of a strategic goal to place Austria at the forefront of modern grid digitalization, increasing grid resilience and moving APG toward the goal of 100% renewable electricity by 2030.

Historically, the DER identification process would be conducted at every level of the grid, increasing financial costs to the DERs and grid operators and adding significant delays into the onboarding process. Thus there are strong incentives to create a high-assurance identity credential for a DER that can be trusted and shared across all stakeholders, eliminating a key barrier to grid decentralization.

Utilizing SSI, each DER can present its identity VC when interacting with the grid. When joining the grid, the VC for the DER can be cryptographically verified. The grid operator can then either accept or reject the DER with a much higher confidence level.

Once this SSI identity model has been set up, further improvements can be made, such as implementing reward models that give incentives to DERs to participate in the network. This reward system can also be implemented using blockchain technologies using the same SSI identity management scheme, using DIDs to identify the actors in the network and peer DID connections as secure private channels for transferring and redeeming rewards.

19.7   *SSI Scorecard for IoT*

Most people focus on the value of SSI for people and the organizations they deal with. However, the benefits of SSI apply equally to the entire IoT industry. In this chapter, we presented a story about how a replacement component could hijack a car's GPS system and how this could be prevented if manufacturers used an SSI high-assurance identity model for components. We then presented a generalized proposal for SSI-based IoT architecture and showed how it applies to real-world examples such as the Austrian Power Grid. In addition to much stronger security and privacy, we also believe SSI can also bring innovative new reward models for IoT actors and networks, helping grow their usage and the value they deliver.

For IoT, we evaluate that SSI will be transformative for business efficiencies and regulatory compliance, but it will also have clear positive effects for the bottom line and relationship management (table 19.1). The SSI Scorecard is color-coded as follows:

Transformative	Positive	Neutral	Negative

Table 19.1   SSI Scorecard: IoT

Category	Key benefits
Bottom Line	Right now, the security, privacy, and interoperability issues associated with IoT are holding back the market. Solving those problems can unlock an enormous amount of value for the manufacturers, owners, and users of IoT devices.
Business efficiencies	Decentralized authentication, authorization, and workflow management will offer substantial improvements for organizations managing IoT devices. It will significantly reduce the need for identity hubs for companies, generating more efficient and secure ecosystems. SSI is transformative for this scenario because it can redefine the verification processes. Furthermore, it can be a key element in creating a new *machine economy* among things, a topic already being discussed in academic fields.
User experience and convenience	The primary user experience benefits will be in security and device monitoring. When all IoT devices are identified and accountable for their actions, clearer signals can be sent to users, increasing their confidence in the system.
Relationship management	The DID-to-DID connections enabled by SSI architecture are ideal for building trust via mutual authentication and simplifying the management of IoT devices. The permanent connection also simplifies future IoT interactions and makes it easier to implement loyalty and rewards programs, further encouraging usage.
Regulatory compliance	Data identity, security, privacy, and protection are all needed in ecosystems containing IoT devices. Remote devices are particularly vulnerable to attackers. The situation is even more dangerous in critical infrastructures. Because such infrastructure tends to rely heavily on regulatory compliance, an SSI-based IoT approach is transformative in this sector.

> **SSI resources**
>
> To learn more about how the Internet of Things (IoT) impacts the world of SSI, check out https://ssimeetup.org/machine-identity-dids-verifiable-credentials-trust-interop erability-iot-webinar-25-mrinal-wadhwa.

References

1. Doffman, Zak. 2019. "Cyberattacks On IOT Devices Surge 300% In 2019, 'Measured In Billions', Report Claims." *Forbes*. https://www.forbes.com/sites/zakdoffman/2019/09/14/dangerous -cyberattacks-on-iot-devices-up-300-in-2019-now-rampant-report-claims/#461686625892.
2. JSOF. 2019. "Ripple20: 19 Zero-Day Vulnerabilities Amplified by the Supply Chain." https:// www.jsof-tech.com/ripple20.
3. i-SCOOP. n.d. "IoT 2019: Spending, Trends and Hindrances Across Industries." https://www .i-scoop.eu/internet-of-things-guide/iot-2019-spending-trends.
4. Fedrecheski, Geovane. 2020. "Self-Sovereign Identity for IoT Environments: A Perspective." https://arxiv.org/abs/2003.05106.
5. T&DWorld. 2020. "Austrian Power Grid, Energy Web Foundation Launch Proof of Concept to Use DERs for Frequency Regulation." https://www.tdworld.com/distributed-energy-resources/ article/21122056/austrian-power-grid-energy-web-foundation-launch-proof-of-concept-to-use -ders-for-frequency-regulation.

Animal care and guardianship just became crystal clear

Dr. Andrew Rowan, Chris Raczkowski, and Liwen Zhang

Transformative opportunities for SSI exist beyond the scope of identifiers and credentials for humans. The authors of this chapter are thought leaders for decentralized digital identity as applied to animals. Dr. Rowan has enjoyed a 40-year career dedicated to animal welfare, including long-term positions as the director of the Tufts Cummings School of Veterinary Medicine Center for Animals and Public Safety, CEO of Humane Society International, and chief scientific officer for the Humane Society of the United States. Liwen completed post-graduate studies at the University of Denver Graduate School of Social Work Institute for Human-Animal Connection and has helped start animal welfare not-for-profit organizations in China and Canada. Chris is a passionate entrepreneur with 20+ years of experience starting and leading companies focused on sustainable development in Asia, Europe, and North America, including SSI-oriented companies. All three authors are also dedicated guardians of a variety of pets! Their goal is to bring about a global paradigm shift where people and societies expect that animals with human or organizational guardians have legitimate digital identity credentials that acknowledge them as unique individuals with verifiable status in our digital society.

■ ■ ■

And it is true that the chances of the famous refugee are improved just as a dog with a name has a better chance to survive than a stray dog who is just a dog in general.

—Hannah Arendt, *The Origins of Totalitarianism* (Houghton Mifflin, 1951)

Humans have a deep need to assign names and identifiers to entities that are important and valuable to us. Conversely, we tend to overlook or disregard things for which we have not assigned, or cannot conveniently assign, formal identity. This book makes the connection between identity and value clear with regard to humans—for example, with refugees who have little chance of enjoying certain social status unless they have trusted, legally recognized identity credentials. But, the importance of legitimate identity extends far beyond the bounds of our human-centric bubble. We now have the opportunity—essentially for free—to attach trusted, legitimate identity to animals. By doing so, we can better recognize their status and inherent worth in human society and our shared world.

20.1 Enter Mei and Bailey

Mei (pronounced "May"), a capable, successful individual, was walking down the street one day and observed a man happily walking his dog through a park. It had been almost a year since her dog passed away, and she felt it was time to adopt a new furry family member. Next week she would go to an animal shelter and find a dog to be a new life companion.

As fate would have it, the previous week, a young man named Carlos found a homeless dog in the alley behind his apartment. Being a good-hearted person, he gently collected the scruffy little guy and took him to the local animal shelter. Thus began a collision of lives and happiness made possible by digital identity—for humans and animals!

20.1.1 Bailey gets a self-sovereign identity

After the scruffy dog arrived at the animal shelter, he was cleaned and started the admissions process. It was time for him to be registered as a proper member of society—meaning he would get his own digital identity credentials (chapter 7) and digital wallet (chapter 9). How could this happen for a dog? It was very easy and took just minutes. A shelter technician used an app on a tablet computer to take a few photos of the dog, add his new name (Bailey), and then issue a digital credential and upload it to a secure, cloud-based digital wallet.

Bailey was now somebody in society! His first digital identity credential used the same secure cryptographic technology as the digital credentials of the humans around him. Of course, being a dog, Bailey could not manage his own wallet—he didn't even have a smartphone to hold it! But that didn't matter—his new guardian, the shelter, could manage Bailey's wallet and credentials for him.

With this simple but important task completed, it was time for Bailey to gain additional cred. For Bailey to become an even more respectable member of society, he needed a few other credentials to demonstrate that he was an upstanding, legitimate individual. As Bailey completed the shelter's admissions processes, he went through vaccinations, a health check, neutering, RFID identification chip implant, and government registration. As shown in figure 20.1, technicians at the shelter added a digital credential to Bailey's wallet for each of these actions. With all of these credentials now in Bailey's digital wallet, he was ready for adoption!

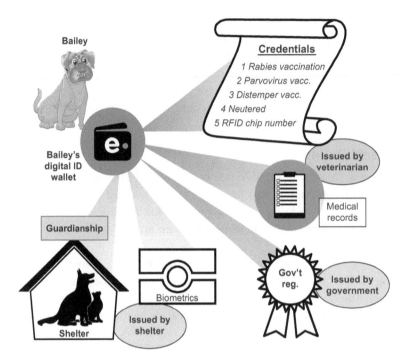

Figure 20.1   Bailey is issued digital identity credentials that are not owned by the shelter or any other agency. They are Bailey's credentials! Each one is cryptographically linked with his digital wallet.

20.1.2 Guardianship transfer

A few days after Bailey's admittance, Mei visited the shelter. It was love at first sight! At that moment, Mei and Bailey became family members. Now it was just a matter of completing a few digital credential transactions to formalize their relationship.

The shelter's staff carefully assessed Mei's suitability to be a good guardian for Bailey. Once she was approved, it took just a couple of minutes for the shelter staff to transfer guardianship of Bailey's digital wallet to Mei. This process is shown in figure 20.2.

Although Bailey's wallet and credentials remained his, Mei was now Bailey's new guardian. She has the authority and responsibility to manage his wallet and credentials. Bailey and Mei happily walked out of the shelter and into their new life together.

20.1.3 Vacation for Mei and Bailey

Many happy months passed for Mei and Bailey. One day, Mei decided to escape the big city for a weeklong holiday. She found a wonderful boarding home for Bailey, where she knew he would be comfortable for a week. Because both Mei and Bailey had verifiable digital credentials, the process of reserving a room at the boarding home was as easy as booking a hotel room for a human. As shown in figure 20.3, just a few clicks on her phone allowed Mei to share the credentials the boarding home required to prove Bailey's government registration and vaccinations. The boarding

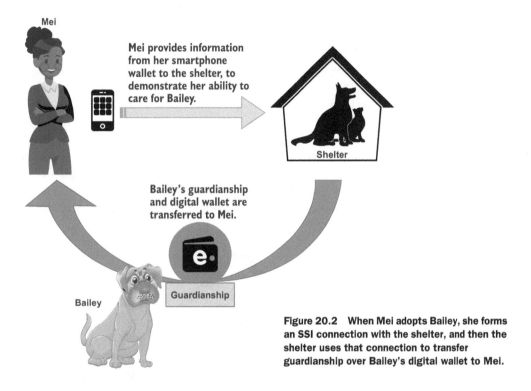

Mei provides information from her smartphone wallet to the shelter, to demonstrate her ability to care for Bailey.

Bailey's guardianship and digital wallet are transferred to Mei.

Figure 20.2 When Mei adopts Bailey, she forms an SSI connection with the shelter, and then the shelter uses that connection to transfer guardianship over Bailey's digital wallet to Mei.

home was then able to cryptographically verify those credentials in seconds (see chapters 7, 8, and 9 for details).

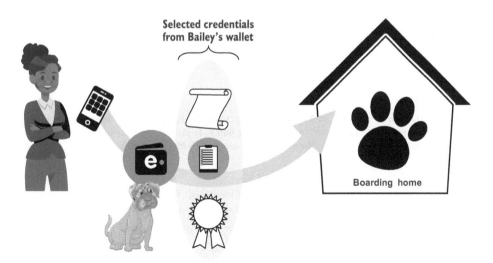

Selected credentials from Bailey's wallet

Figure 20.3 To prove to the boarding home that Bailey meets the check-in requirements, Mei shares proofs of Bailey's credentials from his wallet with the boarding home. In seconds, the boarding home can verify that credentials are digitally signed by the necessary issuing authorities.

When the day came for Bailey to check in to the boarding home, his digital credentials were once again central facilitators. Although the boarding home already knew Bailey carried the necessary credentials, how did they know this individual was actually Bailey? By doing a simple scan of Bailey's RFID chip and verifying against the photos taken by the shelter Bailey was admitted, it was easy to biometrically confirm that he was the same dog identified by the credentials in his wallet. The check-in process was effortlessly completed in under two minutes, and Mei was off to the airport.

As Mei settled into her airplane seat, she suddenly realized she had forgotten to give Bailey's prescription medicine to the boarding home. He had a minor ear infection that was easy to treat with the right medication. But without it, Bailey could be in trouble. Fortunately, as the guardian of Bailey's digital wallet, all Mei had to do was send a verification of the digital credential for Bailey's prescription to the boarding home, as shown in figure 20.4.

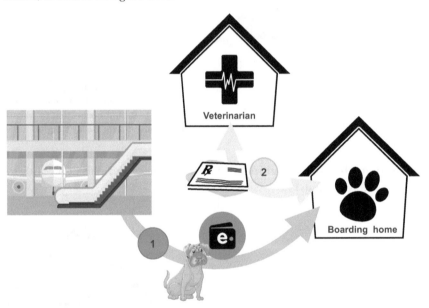

Figure 20.4   In step 1, Mei as Bailey's guardian, uses his digital wallet to send a proof of Bailey's medicine prescription credential to the boarding home. In step 2, the boarding home sends the prescription credential proof to the veterinarian along with Mei's authorization to get the medicine.

With the credential proof and Mei's digitally signed authorization, it was easy for the boarding home to purchase and administer the medicine. What could have been difficult without Bailey's digital credentials was now just a minor incident easily resolved in minutes.

20.1.4 *A storm and separation*

One weekend after her return from vacation, Mei let Bailey into her fenced backyard to play before going to her study to complete an urgent work project. While absorbed in her work, she didn't notice a sudden afternoon storm rapidly approaching. Bailey was very afraid of thunder; Mei always sat with him during such storms.

Suddenly, lightning struck just outside the backyard with a massive crash of thunder. Terrified, Bailey dashed toward the fence and jumped higher than he ever had before. In an instant, he was over the fence and racing down a storm-darkened alley.

Moments later, Mei rushed out to the back yard. Bailey was nowhere to be seen. Mei realized what had happened and jumped into her car. She spent the whole rain-splattered evening searching for her beloved family member.

As rain, lightning, and thunder crashed down around Bailey, he ran harder and harder. Exhausted after 10 minutes of racing through alleys and following strangely familiar smells, Bailey could run no more. He came to a stop under a small shelter by some smelly garbage bins and shivered.

At the same time, Carlos pulled his car out of the driving rain and into his garage. As he got out of his car, he spotted the small dog by his trash bins. Something about him looked familiar. Carlos beckoned him into the garage.

Bailey cocked his head to the side, looking curiously at this man. He recognized this human! Something told Bailey to trust him. When he saw a welcoming motion, he cautiously followed the man into his home.

20.1.5 Lost and found at your fingertips

Carlos was perplexed. This looked like the same dog he delivered to the shelter long ago, but he was clearly healthier and better kept. Although he did not have pets, Carlos remembered seeing a poster at the shelter where he dropped off Bailey, extolling the reasons to get your pet a digital identity. He recalled that it made it much easier to find the guardians of lost pets using a simple smartphone app. He went online to the shelter's website, found a link to a free app in an app store, and downloaded it to his smartphone. Following a few simple instructions, Carlos took several photos of Bailey and uploaded them.

This began the series of steps illustrated in figure 20.5. First, the app securely uploaded the photos to a cloud-based image-processing service available to pet guardians like Mei. There, clever AI image-recognition algorithms (like the ones used by Facebook and other internet giants) quickly linked these images with a specific pet guardian in the vicinity of Carlos' home. An instant later, Mei's smartphone chimed. Her heart stopped as she pulled over along a dark, rain-drenched street. She opened her digital wallet app and saw a message asking if she wanted to accept a notice of a lost dog that might be hers. With tears in her eyes, she punched Accept and saw her beloved Bailey.

Once again, the cryptographic magic of digital wallets and credentials made this interaction not only possible but also anonymous and almost effortless. Carlos was able to share images of a lost dog without revealing anything about himself to a stranger. Mei was able to receive images of a dog without revealing her identity. Once both parties consented, Mei was able to send an anonymous message to Carlos, saying she believed that this was her lost dog. Mei sent a proof of her government registration credential to

Carlos that included Bailey's photo, asking him to confirm if this appeared to be her dog. Carlos responded in the affirmative. All of this happened within minutes, with neither Carlos nor Mei needing to reveal any personal information about themselves.

Mei then sent Carlos a cryptographic proof that she was Bailey's guardian and asked where she could pick up Bailey. Until this point, neither Carlos nor Mei even knew each other's names, because their digital wallets were able to cryptographically protect their identities and share only proofs of the information each of them needed. Once his smartphone app verified Mei's guardianship credential, Carlos sent Mei his name and the address of a local café where he suggested they meet in 20 minutes.

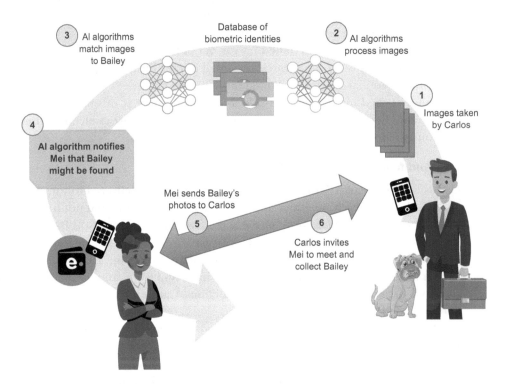

Figure 20.5   The steps in finding a lost dog: 1. Carlos uses a smartphone app to take photos of Bailey and upload them. 2. A cloud-based image analysis service compares them against a database of biometric pet identities. 3. A match is found for Bailey. 4. The system sends a notice to Mei as Bailey's guardian. 5. Mei can communicate securely but anonymously with Carlos to prove she is Bailey's guardian. 6. Carlos arranges a meeting with Mei to return Bailey to her.

Mei arrived at the café. Bailey spotted her as soon as she got out of her car, and there was a very happy and tearful reunion. Mei invited Carlos for tea to thank him for his act of kindness. They were amazed to learn how their lives were unknowingly linked by Bailey many months ago—and how they crossed paths again thanks to the power of digital credentials and digital guardianship.

20.2 *Digital identity unlocks opportunities for the well-being of animals and people*

Mei's story shows how digital ID credentials improved her life as well as Bailey's on a daily basis. But it is just the tip of the iceberg. Digital guardianship holds great promise for animals in many other situations. For example:

- With the mass adoption of biometric identification and digital credentials for pets, any lost animal will be just a few smartphone photos away from being reconnected with their guardian.

- Entire populations of endangered wild animals (e.g., rhinoceroses) can be assigned digital credentials, wallets, and guardians. Donors can contribute funds directly to the digital identity wallets of these animals so that the responsible guardian organization can help manage their well-being. Donors can receive secure, verifiable updates from the guardian and track how their funds are being used to support and protect those animals.

- Farmers with humane animal-management practices can create digital wallets and identities for their farm animals. Third-party inspectors can issue verifiable credentials into these wallets based on their inspections of the animal's living conditions. These credentials can follow the animal, or products from the animal, all the way down the supply chain, ultimately enabling a consumer to verify information about these farm animals—for example, that cheese came from sustainably and humanely farmed goats.

In all of these instances, accurately linking digital identity credentials to the physical animal is essential. For years there have been initiatives to identify wild, farmed, and companion animals with implanted RFID chips or other devices. But those initiatives have not been paired with easy, secure, privacy-respecting ways to use the value of those physical identification methods.

With SSI and cryptographically verifiable digital credentials—plus the additional software and governance frameworks (chapter 11) necessary to support digital guardianship—we can finally realize the full value of RFID and other identification technologies for animals of all kinds. And with digital wallets for those animals, we can store and share the credentials needed to protect those animals' health and well-being.

20.3 *SSI for animals reaffirms their inherent worth*

This chapter only begins to introduce the opportunity of digital identity for animals. Every situation where an animal is dependent on a human for guardianship can take advantage of the same SSI infrastructure developed for people who need guardianship (see the guardianship sections of chapters 9, 10, and 11). With trusted, private, and secure digital identity available for all, we have the potential to bring human societies one step closer to truly respecting the inherent worth and status of all individuals, including animals.

20.4 SSI Scorecard for pets and other animals

Table 20.1 evaluates the benefits of SSI and digital guardianship for pets and other animals. It is color-coded to show the following potential impacts:

Transformative	Positive	Neutral	Negative

Table 20.1 SSI Scorecard: animal identity

Category	Features/Benefits
Bottom line	Verifiable digital identity for animals will unlock tremendous benefits for both animals and humans. Standardized digital identity credentials issued to guardian wallets will legitimize the inherent worth of animals and improve their social status in society's eyes. Such credentials can also facilitate social connections and commerce between animal guardians and pet service organizations, resulting in new opportunities for the health and happiness of both animals and humans.
Business efficiencies	SSI for animals will simplify and improve many aspects of an animal's interaction with human society. Digital credentials will be especially transformative for animal-related services as they can largely replace many paper-based credentialing and manual verification processes. Entirely new business models become possible for animal ownership, sponsorship, care, and management.
User experience and convenience	The story of Mei and Bailey gives several examples of how the experience of animal ownership and guardianship will be transformed with various applications of digital credentials. They will enable frictionless interactions with pet service providers, make the transfer of ownership dramatically easier and safer, and simplify all aspects of complying with regulations.
Relationship management	SSI for animals does much more than create new commercial convenience and opportunity. It will inspire and empower a globally connected community of animal guardians and animal care organizations. When the world begins to accept that animals should have digital identities like humans, animals' social status will increase, which will improve the well-being of humans, animals, and our environment.
Regulatory compliance	SSI for animals employs exactly the same underlying technology and standards as for humans, so it can also produce the same regulatory benefits. Specifically, it will significantly simplify animal guardians' ability to register animals, maintain their vaccinations and health certificates, transfer ownership, and manage and share any other necessary records.

SSI resources

For more free content to learn about SSI, please go to IdentityBook.info and SSI Meetup.org/book.

Open democracy, voting, and SSI

21

Shannon Appelcline

Voting is a prime example of a system of collective choice that could be vastly improved by taking advantage of SSI to support making those collective choices over distance. Shannon Appelcline, the long-time editor-in-chief of the Rebooting the Web of Trust (RWOT) series of SSI conferences and a technical writer for Blockchain Commons, explores this topic in depth by outlining the problems with distance voting to date, considering the possibilities of true voter agency, and detailing how SSI fits into this new vision for open democracy.

The wonder of democracy is that members of a city, region, or country can vote to personally decide how their society is governed—through either direct or representative democracy. However, managing votes isn't as easy as it sounds, particularly in the ever-more-remote world of the twenty-first century.

In-person voting works relatively well because it's easy to block double voting when you can physically connect each individual person to a specific identity. When a state requires physical presence, it can verify identities by checking preauthenticated voter logs or comparing handwriting or signatures. Even if a state doesn't have sophisticated civic records, it can use other physical means to minimize double votes, such as inking thumbs with indelible ink. In-person voting also has other benefits, such as reducing coercion or undue influence that could otherwise corrupt democratic ideals.

Unfortunately, in-person voting offers strong security at the cost of accessibility: although a state can ensure that votes are proper, it also loses many possible voters.

There are cases when no one might be able to vote in person due to disasters of various sorts—as happened in various locales during the COVID-19 pandemic of 2020 [1, 2]. This directly contradicts the core desires and needs of a democracy, which is all about government by the people.

To expand our democracies by improving accessibility, we need to figure out how to authenticate identities as we move further away from a physical voting box. SSI can do this and, in the process, create new possibilities for voter agency that far exceed the capabilities of state-sponsored identities.

21.1   *The problems with postal voting*

For the past few decades, postal voting has been on the rise, allowing voters to assert their identities by mail. Once, it was solely the province of those who had an excuse to vote absentee, but today increasing numbers of people can vote by mail. In the United States, 28 states (and the District of Columbia) now allow early voting without an excuse, with Colorado, Washington, and Oregon voting entirely by mail [3]. As a result, postal voting in the United States has nearly tripled in recent decades, from 7.8% of votes cast in 1996 to 21% in 2016 [4]. Similarly, the UK enabled on-demand postal voting in 2001 [5] and saw 22% of their votes cast by mail in 2017 [6]. However, the rest of the world is only slowly edging toward this democratic innovation: many other countries still restrict postal voting to absentee and overseas voters.

Postal voting certainly improves the accessibility of democracy, as people can vote without leaving their homes. However, in taking the first step beyond in-person voting, it also loses some security benefits.

Although many claims of concern over voter fraud are politically motivated, *The Christian Science Monitor* [7] has illustrated several real cases of postal voting fraud in Florida and Texas, where attackers used the disconnect between the voter and the voting authority to introduce false or coerced ballots. Similar concerns regarding "undue influence," "personation," "bribery," and "treating" have been raised in the UK [8]. These examples are not isolated.

A particularly notable case occurred in 2018, in NC-9, the ninth congressional district for North Carolina in the United States. Here, statistical anomalies in the voting results revealed that an organization had been harvesting absentee ballots and altering them before their submission [9]. A high "unreturned" rate of postal ballots suggested that some may also have been discarded [10].

> **CONSIDER**   The problem in North Carolina resulted from centralization: the people who picked up the absentee ballots. Any centralized authority could similarly prove untrustworthy.

Together, these problems demonstrate how hard it is to reliably assert identity from afar, at least when using traditional identities. Even for this simple, well-understood method of distance voting, better solutions are needed than those supported by most of today's state-sponsored bureaucracies.

21.2   *The problems with e-voting*

Postal voting isn't the endgame for voting accessibility, as postal delivery itself is rapidly being left in the technological dust. In the modern world, the clear next step in voting accessibility is *e-voting*, where people will be able to vote using the internet. Unfortunately, e-voting is even more removed from in-person voting than postal voting and thus may be even more prone to security problems.

To date, e-voting has mostly been used by websites for ratings. Although online ratings are often useful, they also highlight significant problems with digital identities, which can be freely and anonymously created. Amazon has fought against both Sybil attacks [11] and paid reviews [12]. Similarly, Rotten Tomatoes has spent several years battling against the corruption of ratings for movies that have diverse leads—and was forced to entirely shut down the site's pre-release ratings as a result [13, 14].

> **CONSIDER**   To date, many problems with e-voting result from Sybils, which are multiple, fake accounts. How can you know that a digital person is "real"? That's one of the problems that SSI seeks to address.

An e-voting system that supported an open democracy would need to find solutions that worked much better than the bandages used so far on internet rating sites, as shown by Australia, France, and Spain, all of whom flirted with e-voting in recent years but ran into problems with security or misapplied results [15]. Although solutions may be difficult, there's a real need: after Hurricane Michael hit the Florida Panhandle in 2018, Bay County Supervisor of Elections Mark Andersen allowed about 150 people to vote by electronic methods, 11 of them via email [16]. Although this decision wasn't directly supported by U.S. law, it showed how electronic voting could support increased inclusivity. So how do we get there?

21.3   *Estonia: A case study*

As it happens, one state is already there: the Republic of Estonia. It has a mature e-voting system that depends on Estonia's national digital identity (https://e-estonia.com/solutions/e-identity). Although this is a state-issued identity, not an SSI-based identity, it offers a first look at using the internet to enable open democracy.

In Estonia's "i-voting," residents use their Estonian ID card and a computer to cast ballots during an early voting period and can change their votes up to the end of that period. This very accessible system also contains some thoughtful security. As explained in chapter 6, the system uses private keys for *authentication* and to generate digital signatures, which ensures *non-repudiability*. Other advantages include *privacy* and limited *mutability*. This has all paid off: when Estonia tested e-voting in local elections in 2005, fewer than 1,000 people used the system [17]. On the other hand, in 2019, almost 250,000 people voted via the internet, about 44% of the total voters (https://rk2019.valimised.ee/en/voting-result/voting-result-main.html).

However, there are issues with the Estonian i-voting system. A May 2014 "Independent Report on E-voting in Estonia" [18] raised serious concerns over whether votes or voting results might be changed. There have also been complaints about the limited publication of Estonia's e-voting code [19]. This dovetails poorly with societal trends, where voters have become increasingly suspicious of the systems used to manage their votes, even for in-person voting [20, 21].

Perhaps more importantly, the Estonian e-voting system *hasn't* actually shown an increase in the voting population: the 2011 and 2019 parliamentary elections each had about 63.5% voter turnout, despite a dramatic increase in e-voting in the same timeframe [22]. In the end, we must ask: is it enough simply to mirror in-person voting systems in these more distant scenarios? Or can we do something more? Or, to keep this on the topic of SSI: *could* we do more if we had a technological system that offered new possibilities?

21.4 *The three pillars of voting*

Although increased accessibility is a big win for open democracy, looking at voting systems solely through the lens of security and accessibility assesses them based on what they have been, rather than what they could be. If a democracy is truly about empowering the members of a state, then their ability to vote should be empowered, too. This can be done by improving the *voter's agency*—something that largely hasn't been considered in traditional systems.

These three pillars of security, accessibility, and agency can each be divided into more precise principles, which together outline both the needs and the possibilities of a fully open voting system.

21.4.1 *A state's bill of needs*

The state's bill of needs includes the following *principles of security*:

- *Authenticity*—A voter *must* be able to prove an identity. *We know each voter.*
- *Accreditation*—A voter *must* be able to prove that they have the right to vote via a means such as a verifiable credential (https://www.w3.org/TR/verifiable-claims-data-model). *We recognize each voter's authorization.*
- *Non-repudiability*—A voter *must not* be able to change or disclaim their vote after it's locked in. *We know each vote is unchanged by the voter.*
- *Immutability*—An attacker *must not* be able to change any vote. *We know each vote is unchanged by attackers.*
- *Auditability*—A state *must* be able to recount votes and verify their authenticity, accreditation, non-repudiability, and immutability. *We know that the voting results are accurate.*

21.4.2 *A voter's bill of rights*

The voter's bill of rights includes these *principles of accessibility*:

- *Openness*—A voter *must* be able to vote in a time, place, and manner that maximizes their likelihood of voting. *I can easily vote.*

- *Simplicity*—A voter *must* be able to vote without undue complexities or burdens. *I can simply vote.*

The voter's bill of rights also includes the following *principles of agency*:

- *Privacy*—A voter *must* be able to vote without others knowing how they voted. *I can keep my vote private.*
- *Assignability*—A voter *must* be able to proxy their vote on certain topics using delegation credentials, creating a delegative democracy [23]. *I can lend my vote to others.*
- *Mutability*—A voter *must* be able to change their vote up to the point where it is locked in, to support their agency and improve security by offsetting the possibilities of coercion and influence. *I can change my mind.*
- *Verifiability*—A voter *must* be able to verify that their vote has been accepted and tabulated. *I trust my vote was counted.*
- *Transparency*—A voter *must* be able to learn how the system works, so that they can verify its accuracy, as well. *I trust the outcome of the vote will be accurate.*
- *Provability*—A voter *must* be able to selectively disclose how they voted if they choose to, creating proofs that make this disclosure irrefutable. *I can choose to make my vote public.*
- *Permanence*—A voter *must not* be able to lose their right to vote, unless they do so in a well-understood way outlined by the transparent rules of the system. *I will always have my vote.*
- *Portability*—A voter *must* be able to use their identity and/or their credentials in a variety of different venues, as designated by their individual rules. *I can bring my voting record with me.*

21.5 The advantages of SSI

Though Estonia has been the most successful example of improving accessibility of voting without impinging on security, it didn't do much to increase the agency of its voters. It only meets two of the agency principles: *privacy*, assuming a voter trusts Estonia, and *mutability*. The more expansive possibilities for user agency are ignored, and that's in large part a failure of state-sponsored identities being used as the basis of e-voting systems. Truly empowering people requires that empowerment be built into the digital ecosystem from the beginning, starting with voters owning their own identities.

Enter (at last) SSI. It's not just a different technology, but also a different way of thinking. It changes identity from a passive system handed down by an all-powerful authority to something that each person individually controls. This makes each person their own agent in the system: they can decide how their identity is used. In other words, they have agency.

> **CONSIDER** Ground-breaking technologies are revolutionary. They don't just improve the efficiency of traditional tasks, they change how we think about them. Consider, for example, how the internet changed everything from looking up information to making purchases. SSI can be similarly revolutionary.

An e-voting system supporting agency begins with a voter who has personal control of their SSI credentials via their digital wallet (chapter 9) and decentralized identifiers (DIDs—chapter 8). This intrinsically supports three of the rights of agency: a DID can exist forever (*permanence*), interact with different systems (*portability*), and sign verifiable credentials (VCs) for delegates (*assignability*).

Although a state could restrict a person's ability to vote, it could never delete the DIDs or VCs associated with those votes, so the voter could continue to selectively reveal their votes in the future through consensual *provability*. Even better, a voter could use various VC-based methods of selective disclosure, including zero-knowledge proofs (ZKPs), to show a consistent voting record across city, regional, country, and even online voting realms.

This user-agency-focused e-voting system would exist as part of an ecosystem built on SSI ideals. The trustless consensus systems at the heart of such an ecosystem would engender more agency: the voting software would need to be *transparent*, with its code publicly available. This, in turn, would grant a voter *verifiability* because they could use the well-documented system to ensure that their vote was recorded. Finally, it would improve their *privacy* because the voter would no longer have to trust a state, just the trustless system.

The power of e-voting systems built on SSI infrastructure will only increase in the future, as those ecosystems become filled with smart contracts and enhanced personal agents. The possibilities of user agency multiply: a voter could use smart contracts to agree to make certain board-room votes based on corporate results, or they could use a personal agent to ensure that they were voting in a way that synchronized with their personal interests. And it all starts when a voting organization recognizes DIDs and verifiable credentials for e-voting.

For decades, we've been searching for ways to improve voting accessibility, with postal voting and now e-voting being the first steps along that route. And certainly, e-voting can revolutionize voting, creating a truly open democracy. But even there, we're not looking at larger possibilities. With SSI, we can change voters from simple inputs to integral members of the democratic process. We can give them agency in a way they've never had before and, in doing so, make democracy truly ours, perhaps for the first time.

21.5.1 *SSI Scorecard for voting*

The SSI Scorecard is color-coded as follows:

Transformative	Positive	Neutral	Negative

For voting, we evaluate that SSI will be the most transformative for user experience and convenience and regulatory compliance, but it will also have clear positive effects on the business-oriented bottom line and business efficiencies (table 21.1).

Table 21.1 SSI Scorecard: voting

Category	Features/Benefits
Bottom line	In an e-voting context, the bottom line is for the organizations (usually governments) collecting votes. These organizations aren't earning money from votes; instead, they try to get people to vote and do so at the lowest cost with the highest turnout and accuracy. Generally, the organizations will see positive improvements similar to those already resulting from the computerization of voter rolls, with reduced customer onboarding costs and reduced customer service costs occurring organically because this is integral to the SSI infrastructure. The security of SSI will also support some fraud reduction, although voter fraud is currently a small issue in general (despite its frequent politicization). The biggest bottom-line improvement will hopefully be improved voter turnout. There isn't strong evidence of this in postal or e-voting systems to date, but the improved accessibility of SSI e-voting offers the potential.
Business efficiencies	Benefits such as auto-authentication, auto-authorization, and workflow automation will offer incremental improvements for organizations staging votes. For vote casting, this will resolve problems with insufficient polling places and, thus, long lines, as well as curtailing some (minimal) voter fraud; for vote counting, it will improve inefficiencies in tabulation and collection.
User experience and convenience	The many benefits to users will be the most transformative, thanks to the user agency made possible by SSI-enabled voting. Auto-authentication and auto-authorization will be the prime drivers for improving accessibility: voters will find it easy to prove that they have the right to vote, without any chance of challenges denying those rights. Workflow automation will ensure that the carefully managed bureaucratic processes of physical voting effortlessly transfer to the e-voting world. However, delegation and guardianship offer the most transformative possibilities: today, we don't even consider the option of letting others vote for us in most governmental elections (although we do in business votes, where proxies rule); but in the future, it could become an integral part of our voting culture. This offers the possibility to reshape the republican form of government, where we elect representatives at a large scale, into something much more personal, where we each choose representatives for our own votes.
Relationship management	Minor benefits will be introduced to voting through improved relationship management, such as a voter knowing that they're talking to an actual voting organization through mutual authentication, a permanent connection improving the accessibility of future voting, or even a loyalty and rewards program encouraging it—but generally, these benefits aren't significant enough to make this area a major element of SSI-enabled voting.
Regulatory compliance	Voting tends to rely heavily on regulatory compliance, so even if these benefits aren't "sexy," they can still be transformational. Data security, data privacy, and data protection are all badly needed in a brave new world where foreign governments attack voting software. Meanwhile, data portability is another idea like delegation and guardianship that is so transformational to the whole voting process that it's impossible to fully see the repercussions: it grants a voter total agency over their voting record and the ability to move it and selectively disclose it as they see fit, for their benefit.

SSI resources

For more free content to learn about SSI, please go to IdentityBook.info and SSI Meetup.org/book.

References

1. Doubek, James. 2020. "Louisiana Postpones Presidential Primary Over Coronavirus Fears." NPR. https://www.npr.org/2020/03/13/815464629/louisiana-postpones-presidential-primary-over -coronavirus-fears.

2. Proctor, Kate. 2020. "Local Elections and London Mayoral Race Postponed for a Year." *The Guardian.* https://www.theguardian.com/world/2020/mar/13/local-london-mayoral-elections -postponed-year-coronavirus-uk.

3. National Conference of State Legislatures (NCSL). 2020. "Voting Outside the Polling Place: Absentee, All-Mail, and Other Voting at Home Options." http://www.ncsl.org/research/ elections-and-campaigns/absentee-and-early-voting.aspx.

4. File, Thom. 2018. "Characteristics of Voters in the Presidential Election of 2016." US Census Bureau. https://www.census.gov/content/dam/Census/library/publications/2018/demo/P20 -582.pdf.

5. Parliament of the United Kingdom. 2000. "Representation of the People Act 2000." The National Archives. http://www.legislation.gov.uk/ukpga/2000/2/contents.

6. Electoral Commission. 2017. "The Administration of the June 2017 UK General Election." https://www.electoralcommission.org.uk/sites/default/files/pdf_file/The-administration-of-the -June-2017-UK-general-election.pdf.

7. Richey, Warren. 2017. "Voting by Mail Grows in Popularity—But It is Reliable?" *The Christian Science Monitor.* https://www.csmonitor.com/USA/Politics/2017/1221/Voting-by-mail-grows-in -popularity-but-is-it-reliable.

8. White, Isobel. 2012. "Postal Voting and Electoral Fraud 2001–09." House of Commons Library. https://commonslibrary.parliament.uk/research-briefings/sn03667.

9. Blinder, Alan. 2019. "Inside a Fly-by-Night Operation to Harvest Ballots in North Carolina." *New York Times.* https://www.nytimes.com/2019/02/20/us/north-carolina-voter-fraud.html.

10. Gardella, Rich and Leigh Ann Caldwell. 2018. "Investigation into N.C. Election Fraud Focused on Unreturned Absentee Ballots." NBC News. https://www.nbcnews.com/politics/elections/ investigation-n-c-election-fraud-focused-unreturned-absentee-ballots-n948241.

11. Zheng, Haizhong, et al. 2017. "Smoke Screener or Straight Shooter: Detecting Elite Sybil Attacks in User-Review Social Networks." NDSS Symposium 2018. https://arxiv.org/pdf/1709.06916.pdf.

12. Kailath, Ryan. 2018. "Some Amazon Reviews Are Too Good to Be Believed. They're Paid For." All Things Considered. https://www.npr.org/2018/07/30/629800775/some-amazon-reviews -are-too-good-to-be-believed-theyre-paid-for.

13. RT Staff. 2019. "Hello, We're Making Some Changes." Rotten Tomatoes. https://editorial .rottentomatoes.com/article/making-some-changes.

14. Robertson, Adi. 2019. "How Movie Sites Are Dealing with Review-Bombing Trolls." *The Verge.* https://www.theverge.com/2019/3/7/18254548/film-review-sites-captain-marvel-bombing-chan ges-rotten-tomatoes-letterboxd.

15. Verified Voting Staff. 2019. "Internet Voting Outside the United States." https://web .archive.org/web/20200803084143/https://www.verifiedvoting.org/resources/internet-voting/ internet-voting-outside-the-united-states.

16. Koh, Elizabeth. 2018. "Hurricane-Ravaged Florida County Allowed Some 'Displaced' People to Vote by Email." *Tampa Bay Times.* https://www.tampabay.com/florida-politics/buzz/2018/11/ 12/hurricane-ravaged-florida-county-allowed-150-displaced-persons-to-vote-by-email.

17. Mardiste, David. 2007. "Estonia Set for World's First Internet Election." Reuters. https://www .reuters.com/article/us-estonia-election-web/estonia-set-for-world-first-internet-election-idUSL 213415120070221.

18. Halderman, J. Alex, et al. 2014. "Independent Report on E-Voting in Estonia." University of Michigan. https://estoniaevoting.org.

19. Ojasild, Heiki. 2013. "Open Letter on Freedom and Internet Voting to Estonia's National Electoral Committee." FSFE. https://fsfe.org/news/2013/news-20130730-01.en.html.

20. Tapper, Jake and Avery Miller. 2004. "Conspiracy Theories Abound After Bush Victory." ABC News. https://abcnews.go.com/WNT/story?id=239735.

21. Addley, Esther. 2014. "Scottish Referendum Vote-rigging Claims Spark Call for Recount." *The Guardian.* https://www.theguardian.com/politics/2014/sep/22/scottish-referendum-vote -rigging-claims-recount-petitions.

22. Vabariigi. n.d. "Statistics about Internet Voting in Estonia." https://web.archive.org/web/ 20120325012644/http://www.vvk.ee/voting-methods-in-estonia/engindex/statistics.

23. Ramos, Jose. January 2014. "Liquid Democracy: The App that Turns Everyone into a Politician". Shareable. http://www.shareable.net/blog/liquid-democracy-the-app-that-turns-everyone-into-a -politician.

Healthcare supply chain powered by SSI

Daniel Fritz and Marco Cuomo

For many industries, tracking and monitoring the movement of goods in global supply chains is a key priority—and sometimes a regulatory requirement. Daniel Fritz and Marco Cuomo, innovation leaders at the Swiss-based pharmaceutical company Novartis, outline how their industry's supply chain could be transformed—and how this can inspire other supply chain business leaders around the world to use SSI technologies.

■ ■ ■

Доверяй, но проверяй *(Trust, but verify)*

—Russian proverb adopted by President Ronald Reagan in
nuclear disarmament treaty negotiations with the Soviet Union

SSI will transform how supply chains operate—it is not a question of if, but when. A common, trusted, privacy-preserving approach for product and customer identification and transactions will reduce complexity, cost, and time. When broadly adopted, SSI will enable new business models for value-adding participants, resulting in benefits for local communities and the environment. Trusted end-to-end transparency for a supply chain is a good thing when considering a single industry. When SSI transforms several industries, the impact will not be just good—it can be a paradigm shift that can accelerate an industrial revolution.

What is a *supply chain*? It is "the global network used to deliver products and services from raw materials to end customers through an engineered flow of information, physical distribution, and cash" (www.apics.org/apics-for-individuals/publications-and-research/apics-dictionary). In this chapter, we examine some obvious impacts of SSI on the healthcare industry supply chain, which is subject to ever-increasing costs and regulatory compliance requirements. These examples can serve as a model for other industries and as inspiration for our readers because *everyone* is a patient, and the best ideas are not ours.

22.1 Emma's story

Our heroine, Emma, landed for a well-deserved two-week vacation at a kite-surfing mecca in South America. After checking in at her beach hotel, she realized, with no small degree of shock, that she had not packed her prescription medicine for hyper-thyroidism (an overactive thyroid gland). The prospect of finding an endocrinologist in a foreign country was worse than having her metabolism out of whack for the next two weeks. But Emma remembered she had the original prescription stored in her phone's digital wallet as a verifiable credential (VC) issued by her doctor. (In this context, a VC is the digital version of a prescription. VCs are introduced as a basic building block of SSI in chapter 2 and explained in great detail in chapter 7.) Her doctor had explained that electronic prescriptions and health records eliminated manual errors and streamlined all the processes—ultimately benefiting Emma's health. So with renewed confidence, Emma was off on her first vacation adventure—to the drug store!

The *farmácia* was conveniently just around the corner, and Emma was relieved that the friendly *farmacêutica*, who introduced herself as Clarisse, was eager to help a needy tourist, albeit with limited English. Clarisse asked Emma to verify her digital prescription with a scan of her patient identity. The result verified the doctor's DID and the authenticity of the prescription. (DIDs are another key building block of SSI, introduced in chapter 2 and explained in great detail in chapter 8.)

Clarisse brought out two different products. Emma didn't recognize the brands, and the packaging was in Portuguese. Clarisse tried to explain the products, but most of her explanation was lost in translation. A sinking feeling engulfed Emma before she remembered that she also had the Medicine Check app on her smartphone (see figure 22.1). She opened the app and scanned the first product's barcode. The app performed the check using a pseudonymous identifier that could not be traced back to her to protect her privacy. Who else needs to know about her health issues besides her doctor and the pharmacist?

Figure 22.1   The Medicine Check app. A user can select a specific supplier for additional information such as manufacturing location, sustainability policies, and licenses to do business.

The app immediately returned a confirmation of the package's authenticity—this was a real, registered product, not a counterfeit. Clarisse indicated that the barcode had a unique serial number embedded in it, which the manufacturer had also registered as a VC to the product. Emma could also access and read an electronic version of the patient package insert (the leaflet) in her own language. She could confirm that this was the right medicine for her. This *eLeaflet* clearly indicated that the dosage instructions were the same as her regular medicine. The app also indicated that the eLeaflet, issued as a VC to the product, was approved by a registered health authority. She was immediately relieved that her medicine was available, but was the other product better?

The second product was a little more expensive. The app confirmed its authenticity, but additional credentials were available, including the manufacturer's certification of its environmental and labor practices. There was also information on the manufacturer's suppliers, such as where the active drug ingredient was produced and who made it. The app also confirmed that the certifications were valid and not revoked.

Sustainability was important for Emma, and she appreciated the additional transparency. Feeling more informed, she opted for the second product. Clarisse processed the payment, which was automatically transacted through Emma's health insurance, as this was linked to the digital prescription.

Emma decided to register the medicine in her eWallet, which also served as her digital medicine cabinet. Emma could opt for standard notifications:

- Reminders to take the medicine according to her doctor's prescription
- Notifications if there was an update to the product information
- Alerts in the event of a recall impacting this specific batch of medicine
- Information on known drug interaction issues with other medicines in her cabinet
- Instructions on how to dispose of excess or expired product in an environmentally-friendly way

With the right medicine and the knowledge that her thyroid wasn't going to be an issue, Emma thanked Clarisse and left the store. The wind was starting to pick up—it was going to be a great vacation!

22.2   *Supply chain transparency and efficiency through SSI*

What drives buying decisions? Price, quality, brand recognition, and convenience (think of your favorite cola or the ease of Amazon). But consumers now want more information and proof about products, services, and suppliers: "Is this banana really organic? Who certified the farmer? Is it genetically modified? Was it shipped by air or sea?" The environmental, economic, and social sustainability of products and their supply chains increasingly influence buying decisions for both individuals and corporations.

Emma's buying decision was influenced by increased transparency and trust. That's a win-win for parties that add value to the product in a sustainable manner, not just Emma and the supplier. The supplier's employees, their families, their communities, and the environment can benefit. VCs will help meet increasing demand for transparency with digital, real-time, convenient, trusted information that will give people more confidence in the things they buy and the organizations they buy from.

> **CONSIDER**   Suppliers that voluntarily and automatically release their credentials to buyers add value to their products and services by increasing transparency and hence the trust of their buyers.

Fairtrade (https://www.fairtrade.net/about-fairtrade.html) is a good example of the value of increased transparency for products like coffee, honey, and bananas. The organization aims to benefit disadvantaged producers and increase consumer trust. Fairtrade audits its members to ensure sustainable business practices and uses a recognized label on its certified products. But how can an individual consumer trace back all the certifications? SSI-based VCs can enable Fairtrade's basic concept to rapidly scale across a broad spectrum of goods and services. It is as simple—and privacy-preserving—as the scan Emma performed on her two medicine choices. This can work for any product that can be labeled with a QR code or other scannable identifier.

Usually, you trust the person or company you buy from. Otherwise, you wouldn't give them your money. But it is not always that easy. Global supply chains extend across many organizations and geographies. In some industries, such as pharmaceuticals, onsite audits check suppliers' internal systems and policies to qualify them for doing business. That may assure a buyer about their direct suppliers, but whom are the suppliers buying from? Are the ingredients, materials, or services from their suppliers also produced sustainably?

SSI can create this required transparency in a way that scales to the full sourcing network and dynamically adapts to the continuous change that drives today's business environment. It can allow everyone in the supply chain to issue and verify credentials all along the value chain. Figure 22.2 depicts the buyer's dilemma when

Figure 22.2   Multi-tiered supplier networks: (left) without transparency of products and suppliers; (right) with full transparency. Which one would you prefer?

facing a supply chain decision. Will the buyer opt for limited supplier and product transparency from their direct supplier (tier 1)? Or will the buyer prefer to buy from a supplier whose own suppliers (tiers 2, 3, and on up the chain) voluntarily release information about their sustainable business practices?

22.3   *Industry ecosystem efficiency powered by SSI*

Emma's story can't happen overnight or without hard work and a change in mindset (a paradigm shift). Companies, consumers, and regulators have to work together toward this goal. Defining common data and protocol standards coupled with an effective governance model is a prerequisite to enable such transparency. This requires a common vision in the industry.

We can't have a Medicine Check app for every brand—it has to work globally for all brands. Suppliers need a common standard as well, like the Fairtrade requirements. But the benefits of such collaboration are clear for all parties. When manufacturers define and use common standards, apps can be developed across the industry, and there will be healthy competition between software developers for the best app for patients.

Think about a mobile app that can read and display eLeaflets from any brand or manufacturer. The patient will then decide which suits them best. Also, when all suppliers can present common credentials to prospective customers without the need to fill out new forms or conduct redundant audits, they all benefit. The necessary change is the industry's shared belief that supply chain transparency will increase a product's value to the consumer. That is an incentive worth competing for.

How would this approach work? Figure 22.3 provides an overview of such a verifiable supply chain ecosystem.

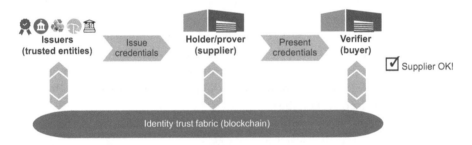

Figure 22.3   Improved transparency and trust in a supply chain ecosystem through VCs that facilitate the exchange of certificates, licenses, audit reports, and more

Product and supplier certifications or credentials can take the form of audit reports, government-issued licenses, agency certifications, or even reusable self-attestations. Basically, everything that needs an authoritative approval or stamp can be turned in a VC. Reusing these electronic credentials for multiple partners saves time, effort, and cost for all, because the whole process can be automated, and human interventions will be needed only for exceptions. Once this trusted relationship is established, frictionless transactions will result, improving supply chain efficiency.

Suppliers will be qualified for business more quickly, and they will also be rewarded for their transparency. This will be noticed and adopted by other suppliers up and down the line, especially those subject to expensive onsite audits that require significant preparation and resources.

The principle of SSI with VCs and DIDs puts the supplier in a position to ensure the confidentiality of sensitive information by strictly controlling its release. The supplier decides what proof it will provide for any request, again reducing effort and speeding up the process. In Emma's example, the drug supplier decided to automatically release proofs relating to the medicine's manufacture and the company's labor policies, updated in real time with the latest data.

Finally, the *concept of disintermediation* may remove some agents that specialize in bringing two parties together without any real transformation of a product's value. The analogy is a headhunter who screens candidates for a job opening on behalf of a hiring company. The hiring company could perform this task efficiently since it could standardize the requirements (degree, experience, work permit) and automate the process of checking a candidate's qualifications. Elimination of the non-value-adding middleman can only benefit the consumer in the end.

CONSIDER This core benefit of SSI and VCs applies to nearly any industry, workflow, or supply chain that brings together two interested parties.

22.4 *Future supply chain transformation across industries: The big picture*

In the supply chain definition, an *engineered flow of information* may sound quite organized and efficient. But that is rarely the case. Global import and export processes require a significant amount of documentation (paper!) that adds cost and complexity while keeping the end customer waiting for the product and the supplier waiting for cash.

Today's supply chain reality is a siloed separation where all partners maintain their own version of the truth in their systems. That information may include price, quantity, delivery date, product specification, handling instructions, location, supplier, and customer. Where there is collaboration and communication, it is usually set up in an inflexible peer-to-peer manner.

With SSI, everyone in the global network can have a single, trusted view of the truth, enabling increased coordination and collaboration. Trust relationships will facilitate order management and trade compliance. With globally traceable product identities, we can ameliorate problems like wasted and counterfeit products, releasing supply chain value that is currently locked up in siloes.

22.5 *Eliminating waste*

Perishable products sit and rot in storage due to a lack of efficient collaboration between supply chain partners. Customers end up paying for such process inefficiencies. One report estimates that 1.6 billion tons of the global food supply, valued at $1.2 trillion, go to waste annually [1]. The costs of this waste do not reflect the additional costs to the environment by harmful chemical fertilizers, subsidies, and additional transportation.

The unique and traceable identity of a product, coupled with other technologies, will go a long way to reducing waste. In the food industry, perishable products can be identified and accompanied by a sensor or Internet of Things (IoT) device (chapter 19), which is also holding a trusted identity, enabling real-time monitoring of location and temperature. Supply chain partners can reduce the duration of shipments and streamline processes to ensure direct delivery to the point of consumption. Substandard products can be replaced before they reach the consumer. This is especially important for life-saving products such as medicine and medical devices. A single source of truth across supply chains will also enable advanced analytical evaluation of the processes, accelerating the elimination of non-value-adding activities.

22.6   Authentication and quality

Counterfeits are rampant in many industries. In a report commissioned by the International Chamber of Commerce, they are estimated to compose as much as 2.5% of global trade [2]. The same report states that the economic impact of counterfeits continues to grow and will reach trillions of dollars, with millions of jobs lost due to criminal activities. The damage done by counterfeits extends beyond just an economic impact—*they also kill people.* The World Health Organization estimates that over 10% of medicinal products in low- to medium-income countries are fake and that hundreds of thousands of people die each year due to counterfeit drugs [3]. The Center for Disease Control and Prevention (CDC) estimates that counterfeits represent 9–41% of sales in developing countries (https://wwwnc.cdc.gov/travel/page/counterfeit -medicine).

> **CONSIDER**   Can consumers trust that the products they are buying (or ordering online) are authentic?

In a world of SSI, each participant in a supply chain, from raw material supplier to end customer, can either attest to or verify the product's authenticity. This is a game-changer, as it will put the power in the payer's hands to check suppliers and products before committing to a purchase. Authentication at point of purchase, through a quick scan from the phone, for example, can identify counterfeit products that follow illegal, hidden supply chains supported by bad actors. When consumers identify counterfeits before a purchase, the consumer is less likely to carry through on the purchase and more likely to purchase an authentic product. The consumer benefits from an authentic product, and the supplier benefits from more business. Another win-win deal (except for the counterfeiter!).

22.7   SSI Scorecard for the pharma supply chain

With SSI, we are on the verge of a new supply chain paradigm, where transparency of products, suppliers, consumers, and even "things" such as sensors and medical devices will enable new capabilities and rapidly disrupt supply chain setups, in all industries, for the better. In healthcare, incremental improvements are the subject of continuous debate at every level, from your doctor's office to the United Nations. But things have changed. Many people now realize that a digital transformation of the healthcare industry is priority #1. SSI will accelerate this change when it is broadly accepted and adopted by a critical mass of like-minded governments, enterprises, and organizations. Let's make it happen.

For the pharma supply chain, we evaluated all categories except Relationship Management as Transformative (table 22.1). We rated Relationship Management as Positive. The SSI Scorecard is color-coded as follows:

Transformative	Positive	Neutral	Negative

Table 22.1 SSI Scorecard: pharma supply chain

Category	Features/Benefits
Bottom line	Easy counterfeit identification (fraud reduction) could turn many buyers from fraudulent sellers to licensed pharmacies, resulting in the right medicine for patients with life-saving results. The trade and dispensation of prescription drugs is a regulated industry, legally enforced with required licenses and valid prescriptions and multi-million-dollar fines. SSI, along with standards and governance, can bring a common, scalable capability to validate the right to buy, sell, and dispense drugs (reduced onboarding time and costs). Personalized medicine is the future, and direct-to-patient models could replace online pharmacies (improved e-commerce sales).
Business efficiencies	Auto-authentication and auto-authorization will greatly streamline supply chain interactions, but workflow automation and payments will enable cross-functional and cross-enterprise business processes such as automatic replenishment, ordering, and invoicing. The potential to digitize supply chain documentation and streamline the order-to-cash process, trade documentation, and ultimately break down the silos between supply chain actors will greatly improve the current fragmentation and waste.
User experience and convenience	See Emma's story. The user experience for patients and healthcare providers will be truly transformational. Without logons and passwords, and with automated workflows and payments, a patient will not even have to leave home to see the (authenticated) doctor for a diagnosis and prescription, which will arrive by courier minutes after the online consultation. Additional services such as eLeaflets, digital recall, and dosage reminders will be trusted with SSI and will not require additional cost or effort.
Relationship management	Today, intermediaries connect parties through proprietary platforms or technologies. Interactions with third parties, whether suppliers, customers, distributors, regulators, or health care providers, are private, permanent, trusted, and verified through SSI. All parties benefit and are incentivized to engage because they can trust that their confidential information will be protected.
Regulatory compliance	Perhaps one of the most significant impacts of SSI will be on regulations. With the ability to easily identify the people, organizations, products, and devices in a healthcare supply chain scenario, regulators will be able to verify the integrity of the claims made for them. The release of a pharmaceutical batch to a market could be checked remotely by authorities (or even by algorithms) for data integrity, provenance, and compliance. This will truly be a game-changer for the healthcare industry.

SSI resources

For more free content to learn about SSI, please go to IdentityBook.info and SSI Meetup.org/book.

References

1. Hegnsholt, Esben, et al. 2018. "Tackling the 1.6-billion-ton Food Loss and Waste Crisis." BCG Henderson Institute. https://www.bcg.com/publications/2018/tackling-1.6-billion-ton-food-loss-and-waste-crisis.aspx.
2. International Chamber of Commerce. 2017. "Global Impacts of Counterfeiting and Piracy to Reach US$4.2 Trillion by 2022." https://iccwbo.org/media-wall/news-speeches/global-impacts-counterfeiting-piracy-reach-us4-2-trillion-2022.
3. World Health Organization. 2017. "1 in 10 Medical Products in Developing Countries Is Substandard or Falsified." https://www.who.int/news-room/detail/28-11-2017-1-in-10-medical-products-in-developing-countries-is-substandard-or-falsified.

Canada: Enabling self-sovereign identity

Tim Bouma and Dave Roberts

Identity is at the core of most government business processes and is the starting point for trust and confidence in interactions between people and their government. Tim Bouma and Dave Roberts, senior public servants with the Government of Canada, outline how traditional identity management within government is evolving to SSI.

This chapter provides an overview of how the elements of SSI are being adapted and developed to fit within the Canadian public sector context with the intention of effecting institutional change across different levels of government. This institutional change is about more than just adopting new technology; it requires putting in place the right policies, guidance, and frameworks that can drive change in a way that balances compliance, innovation, and agility.

The Government of Canada issued its first identity management policy in 2009, and for more than a decade, it has been working with provincial, territorial, and municipal jurisdictions to develop the Pan-Canadian Trust Framework (PCTF). The PCTF achieves several objectives: it supports policy requirements, enables the interoperability of many digital identity programs across different levels of government, and outlines how legacy identity technologies and SSI can coexist.

Being able to adopt emerging technology, such as SSI, is crucially important. The PCTF is being designed to take full advantage of the positive disruptive potential that the SSI model offers. With its unique governance structure and deep identity expertise, Canada is in a position to become a leader in digital identity. We hope that our experience and progress in SSI will inspire the governments of other countries to develop next-generation digital identity services.

23.1   The Canadian context

Canada is both a constitutional monarchy and a parliamentary democracy. The executive authority of the Government of Canada is vested formally in the Queen ("the Crown"). Although every act of government is carried out in the name of the Crown, the authority for those acts resides with the Canadian people, who are represented by democratically elected members of Parliament (the legislative authority). The Canadian Constitution divides the responsibilities of the Government into federal, provincial, and territorial jurisdiction and allows the provincial and territorial governments to delegate some of their responsibilities to municipal governments at their discretion.

The political, social, economic, and technological environment in Canada is far from static. Jurisdictions at all levels are rethinking how they will provide the next generation of digital services to Canadians. We are also embarking on a journey of reconciliation between Indigenous and non-Indigenous peoples. As recently as 1999, a new territory, Nunavut, was created as the outcome of the largest indigenous land claims agreement between the Government and the Inuit people.

This layered and dynamic governance environment has created an identity management ecosystem composed of multiple identity providers relying on authoritative source registries that span federal, provincial, and territorial jurisdiction. There is no appetite for a national identity system within Canada. Consequently, there is no single document or authority whose sole purpose is to identify an individual. Instead, many documents issued by different jurisdictions are in use. This decentralized approach has been effective in serving Canadians. However, it presents challenges in providing a consistent service experience across jurisdictions and in combating fraudulent activity.

Over time a federated identity model has evolved, known as the *Pan-Canadian Approach to Identity Management*. This federated identity model is seeing increasing adoption within the Canadian public sector. With the release in 2020 of the Pan-Canadian Trust Framework (https://github.com/canada-ca/PCTF-CCP), Canadian jurisdictions are now in a position to embrace the main elements of the SSI model.

23.2   The Canadian approach and policy framework

The adoption of the SSI model within the Canadian public sector is still being realized in 2021. It is too early to tell how it will change the technological or institutional infrastructure of Canadian public services. Terminology notwithstanding (many have issues with the term *self-sovereign*; see chapter 1 for an extensive discussion of its evolution), the model's core ideas are now being ingested and adapted for the Canadian public sector context. This has not been an overnight process but rather a deliberate, phased, and incremental approach over the past decade.

In its early days of defining identity management policy (c. 2005), the Government of Canada was primarily focused on ensuring the security and privacy of government programs using an enterprise approach. The secondary focus was delivering better services to Canadians. Over time, the focus has shifted from a program-centric approach to a user-centric model, which is better suited to adopting elements of the SSI model. Recognizing that technology evolves, sometimes in unpredictable ways, the Government of Canada has been careful in defining its identity management policies in a way that does not constrain implementations using established approaches yet allows for the adoption of new approaches and technologies.

> **NOTE** The Government of Canada Treasury Board policy instruments have been revised to reflect this new approach. The Directive on Identity Management, under the Policy on Government Security, was approved in 2019 and incorporated new definitions and requirements related to digital identities and trust frameworks. In April 2020, the Policy on Service and Digital went into effect. The Directive on Identity Management, reflecting its focus on the user-centric model, is now being transferred from the Policy on Government Security to the Policy on Service and Digital. Government of Canada Treasury Board policy instruments can be found at https://www.tbs-sct.gc.ca/pol/index-eng.aspx.

While emerging technologies such as SSI might be the better way, allowances need to be made for the coexistence of different identity models. Canadian jurisdictions currently employ centralized and federated identity models, which will continue to coexist for the foreseeable future.

The Government of Canada policy outcomes for identity management, developed long before the emergence of SSI, are general enough to enable SSI adoption. The first policy outcome is that government programs and services must ensure that they are interacting with the right person with confidence before providing a service to that person. The second policy outcome is that the Government of Canada can accept trusted digital identities originating from other jurisdictions once they meet the criteria of an approved trust framework. That approved trust framework is the Pan-Canadian Trust Framework, which is described in the following sections.

23.3 *The Pan-Canadian Trust Framework*

The *Pan-Canadian Trust Framework* (PCTF) is a model that consists of a set of agreed-on concepts, definitions, processes, and conformance criteria and an assessment approach. The PTCF standardizes how governments create, issue, and accept digital identities between jurisdictions and across different sectors within Canada and internationally.

While standardization is key, the PCTF itself is not a formal "standard" but, instead, is a framework that relates and applies existing standards, policies, guidelines, and practices—and where such standards and policies do not exist, specifies additional criteria. The role of the PCTF is to complement existing standards and policies, such as those concerned with security, privacy, and service delivery.

The PCTF is also not a formal governance framework. While it does map to Layer 4 of the Trust over IP stack (see section 23.8), it is first and foremost a tool to help assess a digital identity program in relation to the relevant legislation, policy, regulation, and agreements between parties.

The latest version of the PCTF is the outcome of over a decade of effort and collaboration between Canadian jurisdictions. Building on previous work undertaken by the Identity Management Subcommittee (IMSC, https://canada-ca.github.io/PCTF -CCP), work on the PCTF began in earnest in early 2015. After several iterations, consultations, and testing, the PCTF in February 2021 is at Version 1.2 and can be used to assess digital identity programs within the public sector. The PCTF has been developed to allow for a range of technologies, solution providers, and institutional arrangements without losing sight of the essential issue: how digital identity can be trusted such that government programs and services can use it.

The PCTF, in its 2021 version, supports the acceptance and mutual recognition of

- Digital identities of persons and organizations
- Digital relationships between persons, between organizations, and between persons and organizations

The PCTF is technology-agnostic and defined to encourage innovation and participation in the digital ecosystem. It allows for the interoperability of different platforms, services, architectures, and technologies. It will facilitate the transition from legacy identity technologies to SSI within the public sector. Furthermore, the PCTF is designed to use international digital identity frameworks, such as these:

- Electronic Identification, Authentication, and Trust Services (eIDAS) from the European Union (https://ssimeetup.org/eidas-regulation-anchoring-trust-self -sovereign-identity-systems-ignacio-alamillo-webinar-49)
- The Financial Action Task Force (FATF, https://www.fatf-gafi.org/publications/ fatfrecommendations/documents/digital-identity-guidance.html)
- The United Nations Commission on International Trade Law (UNCITRAL)

Figure 23.1 illustrates a high-level overview of the PCTF. As mentioned earlier, the goal of the PCTF is to enable trusted digital identities that can be accepted across levels of governments and jurisdictions.

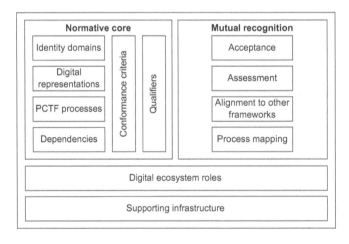

Figure 23.1   The main components of the PCTF used for the assessment and mutual recognition of digital identities

The PCTF model consists of four main components that we explain in the following sections:

- A *normative core* component that encapsulates the key concepts of the PCTF required for an assessment process
- A *mutual recognition* component that outlines the methodology used to assess and certify actors in the digital ecosystem
- A *digital ecosystem roles model* component that defines the roles and information flows within the digital ecosystem
- A *supporting infrastructure* component that describes the set of technical, operational, and policy enablers that serve as the underlying infrastructure of the PCTF

23.4 *The normative core*

The normative core encapsulates the key concepts of the PCTF that are required for a conformance-assessment process that can lead to mutual recognition between two or more jurisdictions that agree to recognize the conformance-assessment results. It has these subcomponents to further define what is required in the assessment and mutual recognition process: identity domains, digital representations, PCTF processes, dependencies, conformance criteria, and qualifiers.

The *identity domains* subcomponent specifies and distinguishes two types of identity:

- *Foundational identity* has been established or changed as a result of a foundational event (e.g., birth, person's legal name change, immigration, legal residency, naturalized citizenship, death, organization's legal name registration, organization's legal name change, or bankruptcy).
- *Contextual identity* is used for a specific purpose within a specific identity context (e.g., banking, health services, driver licensing, or social media). Depending on the identity context, a contextual identity may or may not be tied to a foundational identity.

NOTE In delivering programs and services, programs and service providers operate within a certain environment or set of circumstances, which in the domain of identity management is referred to as the *identity context*. The identity context is determined by factors such as mandate, target population (i.e., clients, customer base), and other responsibilities prescribed by legislation or agreements.

The *digital representations* subcomponent specifies digital representations as an electronic representation of any entity subject to legislation, policy, or regulations. Currently, two types of digital representations are defined:

- *Digital identity*—An electronic representation of a person or organization, used exclusively by that same person or organization to access valued services and carry out transactions with trust and confidence
- *Digital relationship*—An electronic representation of the relationship of one person to another person, one organization to another organization, or a person to an organization

As the PCTF evolves, these digital representations will be extended to include other entity types such as devices, digital assets, and smart contracts. It is also anticipated that in the future, the PCTF will be used to facilitate the mutual recognition of digital representations between countries.

The *PCTF processes* subcomponent specifies a set of atomic processes that can be separately assessed and certified to interoperate with one another in a digital ecosystem. An *atomic process* is a set of logically related activities that results in a state transition (The transformation of an object input state to an output state). Currently, 26 atomic processes are defined, including *identity resolution, identity verification, credential issuance,* and *formulate notice* (https://canada-ca.github.io/PCTF-CCP).

The *dependencies* subcomponent specifies two types of dependencies. First are dependencies that exist between atomic processes. Although each atomic process is functionally discrete, to produce an acceptable output, an atomic process may require the successful prior execution of another atomic process. Second are dependencies on external organizations for the provision of atomic process outputs. This type of dependency is identified and noted in the assessment process.

The *conformance criteria* define what is necessary to ensure the integrity of an atomic process. Conformance criteria are used to support an impartial, transparent, and evidence-based assessment and certification process. *Qualifiers* are applied to conformance criteria to further indicate a level of confidence, the stringency required, specific requirements in relation to another trust framework, an identity domain requirement, or a specific policy or regulatory requirement.

23.5 *Mutual recognition*

The subcomponents of the normative core are used in the *mutual recognition* component. The mutual recognition process begins with a *process mapping* exercise in which the program activities, business processes, and technical capabilities of the jurisdiction being assessed are mapped to the atomic processes defined in the PCTF. Once the existing business processes have been mapped to the atomic processes, an *assessment* is conducted, and a determination is made against each of the related atomic process conformance criteria. *Acceptance* is the process of formally approving the outcome of the assessment process. The acceptance process is dependent on the applicable governance, taking into account the respective mandates, legislation, regulations, and policies. Depending on the context, the mutual recognition may be formalized through the issuance of a letter of acceptance, or it may be part of a more formal arrangement or agreement. *Alignment to other frameworks* can assist in mutual recognition across international borders where other frameworks may be in use, such as the eIDAS regulation in the European Union.

23.6 *Digital ecosystem roles*

In developing the PCTF, it became apparent that the roles and responsibilities of the various digital ecosystem actors needed to be clarified. These actors consist of a wide range of government institutions, organizations, and individuals acting in various capacities. After analyzing existing models, including the W3C Verifiable Credentials model (https://www.w3.org/TR/vc-data-model), and working through several iterations, a generic conceptual model emerged, illustrated in figure 23.2.

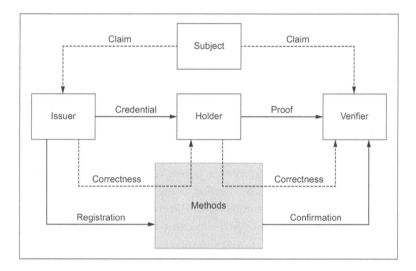

Figure 23.2 The Digital Ecosystem Roles Model defined in the PCTF can be used to adopt the SSI model with the Issuer, Holder, and Verifier roles.

You will recognize the Digital Ecosystems Roles Model as a more formal rendering of the verifiable credential trust triangle introduced in chapter 2 and examined in more detail in chapter 5. This more in-depth formulation consists of five roles and six information flows. The model has been made generic in the sense that anyone (government institution, organization, or individual) can assume any or several of these roles.

The *digital ecosystem roles* are the various roles an actor may assume:

- *Subject*—An entity about which *Claims* are made. (Note that a *digital representation* is an electronic representation of a Subject.)
- *Issuer*—An entity that asserts *Claims* about one or more *Subjects* creates a *Credential* from these Claims and transmits the Credential to a *Holder*.
- *Holder*—An entity that controls a *Credential* from which a *Proof* can be generated and presented to a *Verifier*. A Holder is usually, but not always, the *Subject* of a Credential.
- *Verifier*—An entity that consumes *Proofs* of *Claims* to deliver services or administer programs. A Verifier accepts a Proof from a *Holder*.
- *Method*—A generalized representation of various sets of rules and the entities that employ or administer those rules. Methods can encompass data models and related schemas, communications protocols, blockchains, centrally administered databases, and combinations of these and similar sets of rules. (Note the

parallel with the concept of DID methods in the W3C Decentralized Identifiers Specification, discussed at length in chapter 8.)

The *digital ecosystem information flows* between the actors in the system are as follows:

- *Claim*—An assertion made about a *Subject*.
- *Credential*—A set of one or more *Claims* made by an *Issuer*. The Claims in the Credential can be about more than one *Subject*.
- *Proof*—Information derived from one or more *Credentials* issued by one or more *Issuers* that is shared with a specific *Verifier*.
- *Correctness*—An assurance that a *Credential* or *Proof* conforms to particular *Methods*.
- *Registration*—A record created by an *Issuer*.
- *Confirmation*—A record confirmed by a *Verifier*.

This model does not assume any asymmetric power relationship between parties. Anyone can be *Subjects*, *Issuers*, *Holders*, and *Verifiers*, using many different *methods*. The digital ecosystem roles can be carried out by many different entities that perform specific roles under various labels. These specific roles can be categorized into the digital ecosystem roles, as shown in table 23.1. Given the variety of business, service, and technology models that exist within the digital ecosystem, roles may be performed by multiple different actors in a given context, or one actor may perform several roles.

Table 23.1 Mapping digital ecosystem roles to traditional roles in centralized and federated models.

Role	Examples
Issuer	Authoritative party, identity assurance provider, identity proofing service provider, identity provider, credential assurance provider, credential provider, authenticator provider, credential service provider, digital identity provider, delegated service provider
Subject	Person, organization, device
Holder	Digital identity owner
Verifier	Relying party, authentication service provider, digital identity consumer, delegated service provider
Methods	Infrastructure provider, network operator

23.7 *Supporting infrastructure*

The *supporting infrastructure* is the set of technical, operational, and policy enablers that serve as the underlying infrastructure of the PCTF. It is crucial to the PCTF; however, it is a separate component because many of the subcomponents already have established tools and processes (e.g., privacy impact assessment, security assessment, and authorization). The goal of the PCTF is to use as many of these tools and processes as possible while maintaining a focused set of PCTF-specific atomic processes and conformance criteria.

23.8 *Mapping the SSI stack to the PCTF model*

To enable SSI, the PCTF has been mapped to the ToIP stack (introduced in chapter 2 and discussed in greater detail in chapters 5 and 11); see figure 23.3. This mapping can help governments and industries better define how they can work together in developing a digital ecosystem that uses SSI.

Trust over IP stack	PCTF Model
Layer 4: Governance frameworks	Normative core
	Mutual recognition
Layer 3: Credential exchange	Digital ecosystem roles
Layer 2: DIDComm	Supporting infrastructure
Layer 1: DID registries	

Figure 23.3 The four layers of the Trust over IP stack corresponding to the main components of the PCTF model. This layer-correspondence model can assist in collaboration between the business/policy and technical communities.

Fortunately, the mapping is straightforward:

- *Layer 4*—The governance frameworks layer is mapped to the PCTF normative core and mutual recognition components. Although the PCTF is not a formal governance framework, it can be used as part of a broader governance framework to clearly link to policy, regulation, and legislation.
- *Layer 3*—The credential exchange layer is mapped to the digital ecosystem roles. These roles can be used to delineate who are *Issuers, Holders,* and *Verifiers* in the provision and exchange of verifiable credentials (VCs) and the sets of rules by which everyone needs to abide.
- *Layer 2—DIDComm* and *Layer 1 DID registries* are mapped to the supporting infrastructure. While enablers within the supporting infrastructure will be used to realize the SSI model, other enablers will continue to be used to ensure that existing centralized and federated models fit into the strategic picture.

23.9 *Using the Verifiable Credentials Model*

In developing the PCTF, the Canadian public sector has found itself in the midst of interesting developments in the areas of VCs. A sea change is happening in the public sector: a shift from program-centric information-sharing models to user-centric models in which individuals are empowered to present their own *digital proofs* or VCs.

To test the concept of VCs, the public sector is issuing innovative solution challenges to industry. These challenges are intended to determine the feasibility and characteristics of developing a national or global interoperable verification platform that can be used by a dynamic set of trusted issuers and a diverse population of users. One good example is aviation security, where many actors and authorities are operating across organizational and geographical boundaries. The goal is to prove that a decentralized, interoperable digital verification ecosystem can be built to be used by many independent issuers, operators, and—most importantly—users, using open source libraries and standards-based capabilities.

The Canadian public sector is now seeing the possibility that traditional intermediated services (such as centralized or federated login providers) may disappear. This may not happen in the near future, but the PCTF model is being adjusted to incorporate the more fundamental notion of VCs and generalize it to allow physical credentials (e.g., birth certificates and driver's licenses) to evolve digitally within the model.

The Canadian public sector is evaluating the implications of applying these technologies at the ecosystem-scale in both the public and private sectors. The PCTF may facilitate a migration to digital ecosystems using open standards-based VCs and independent verification systems.

23.10 *Enabling Self-Sovereign Identity*

Trust frameworks such as the PCTF and the SSI identity model are parts of a larger global picture. Domestically and internationally, there is a new and emerging global ecosystem incorporating a mixture of new technologies and legacy systems. It is anticipated that these technologies and approaches will coexist for the foreseeable future.

The PCTF can help focus on certain areas of the emerging ecosystem. In relation to SSI, as new concepts are tested and iterated, the PCTF can be used to relate these new concepts to existing business, policy, and legal frameworks and, when the time is right, drive institutional change.

Using the PCTF, the Government of Canada has assessed and accepted trusted digital identities from two provincial jurisdictions (Alberta and British Columbia). While the integration was achieved using traditional federated identity systems, early efforts have started to explore the use of the SSI model with the Alberta Credential Ecosystem (https://digitalcanada.io/ace-ssi/) and the British Columbia Verifiable Organizations Network (https://vonx.io).

23.11 *SSI Scorecard for the Pan-Canadian Trust Framework*

While the Government of Canada is actively pursuing SSI, it is still too early to predict the future. The PCTF is a tool to help understand SSI in the government context and drive institutional change to better serve Canadians. It will encourage new institutional relationships that can use SSI. If we approach SSI correctly, it will become pervasive and create a better digital ecosystem for everyone.

The benefits evaluation of widespread SSI adoption for Canada is color-coded, with the following potential impacts (table 23.2):

Transformative	Positive	Neutral	Negative

For this scenario, we consider the impact on relationship management to be positive. All other categories are evaluated as transformative.

Table 23.2   SSI Scorecard: Pan-Canadian Trust Framework

Category	Features/Benefits
Bottom line	SSI requires a new, externally focused perspective to help organizations recognize that they are members of a larger digital ecosystem. Without tools to help with institutional change management, the adoption of SSI will be piecemeal or fragmented at best.
	The PCTF helps with adopting new technologies that require institutional change management. It can be used to reconceptualize existing processes into the SSI model and increase understanding of how to fit in a larger digital ecosystem of standards-based issuers, holders, and verifiers. The possibility exists to create a verification capability that is as ubiquitous and globally accessible as the internet is today.
Business efficiencies	The potential efficiencies are far-ranging. No longer will there be a requirement for bespoke authentication apps that store personal information. With standards being developed to enable the SSI model, it will be possible to use digital wallets and VCs held within these wallets across a vast array of digital ecosystem services.
User experience and convenience	Much of the work that needs to be done is invisible to the user. What needs to be explicitly presented to the user and separately installed as applications will eventually disappear into the supporting hardware and verification protocols. The user will simply present who they are, knowing that they have full agency and a sense of security and safety with all of their digital interactions.
Relationship management	Using the PCTF and enabled by SSI, participants in the digital ecosystem can focus on developing and sustaining adaptable and flexible governance frameworks with the knowledge that vendors or technologies will not limit or constrain their relationships with each other.
Regulatory compliance	The PCTF can be used to map to existing legislation, policies, and regulations. The assessment and mutual recognition process can be formalized and aligned to full compliance requirements for Know Your Client (KYC) and Anti-Money Laundering (AML).

SSI resources

To learn more about how Canada and other countries will use SSI, check out https://ssimeetup.org/pan-canadian-trust-framework-pctf-ssi-tim-bouma-webinar-59.

From eIDAS to SSI
in the European Union

Dr. Ignacio Alamillo-Domingo

SSI has become a major technology theme for governments ranging from the United States, Canada, Korea, and Australia to New Zealand. In the previous chapter, two of the leading SSI pioneers in Canada explained how the Canadian government is approaching SSI. In this chapter, legal expert Dr. Ignacio Alamillo-Domingo shares the evolution of digital identity in the European Union to explain how all paths in Europe lead to SSI. Dr. Alamillo-Domingo is a legal expert in the European Blockchain Services Infrastructure project who is involved in standardization activities at ISO/TC307, CEN-CLC/JTC19, and ETSI TC ESI. He has a PhD in public law about the eIDAS.

Creating trust in internet transactions is one of the primary requirements for the proper functioning of the Information Society and—from the European Union (EU) perspective—of the internal European market. As chapter 1 explained, the initial internet architecture designed in the 1960s and 1970s did not prioritize security. Achieving an environment in which people feel safe and confident is necessary to promote the adoption of digital identity.

EU Regulation No 910/2014 of the European Parliament and the Council of July 23, 2014 on Electronic Identification, Authentication, and Trust Services (eIDAS) for the internal market was an important and transformative milestone in the legal regulation of the assurances of juridical traffic performed electronically [1].

NOTE In the EU, primary legislation is approved in a joint process involving the European Parliament (formed by representatives elected by European citizens) and the Council of the EU (formed by the Prime Ministries of the Member States of the Union). They are frequently referred to as *co-legislators.*

The eIDAS regulation constitutes the main trust framework in the EU and the European Economic Area (EEA) to support the *juridical acts* (expressions of will, intended to have legal consequences) performed electronically by natural and legal persons, typically on the internet. It is the historical result of two different approaches to identity management: *public key infrastructure* (PKI) and, later, *federated identity management* (FIM).

> **NOTE** You can read more about trust frameworks, also called governance frameworks, in chapter 11. We discuss PKI in chapter 6 and decentralized identifiers (DIDs) in chapter 8.

Before we can jump to how Europe is working toward SSI, we need to provide some background on how PKI and FIM evolved in Europe. This will allow us to understand the benefits of SSI in a European context.

24.1 PKI: The first regulated identity service facility in the EU

From a strictly chronological point of view, European legislation initially regulated information security mechanisms and services that were considered useful for conducting legal transactions on the internet. These included *digital signatures*: data appended to, or a cryptographic transformation of, a data unit that allows the recipient of the data unit to prove the source and integrity of the data unit and protect against forgery, e.g., by the recipient (ISO 7498-2).

Digital signature techniques ensure data origin authentication and data integrity and are used in non-repudiation services:

- *Data origin authentication* is corroboration that the source of data received is as claimed (ISO 7498-2).
- *Data integrity* is the property that data has not been altered or destroyed in an unauthorized manner (ISO/IEC 9797-1).
- A *non-repudiation service* generates, collects, maintains, makes available, and verifies evidence concerning a claimed event or action to resolve disputes about the occurrence or non-occurrence of the event or action (ISO/IEC 13888-1).

Thus, digital signatures were considered a potential substitute for handwritten signatures, especially when based on a PKI.

PKIs are formed by certification authorities (CA) that issue digital certificates binding a public key with an identified entity. They offer important levels of assurance (LOAs) concerning a person's identity or a system holding a public key. Thanks to the mathematical properties of the asymmetric cryptography underlying digital signatures (explained in chapter 6), digital certificates support the attribution of a signed document or message to a person identified in the certificate. In this sense, a digital certificate constitutes an identity service that can potentially be offered by private sector companies.

Nation-states realized that enacting laws for digital signatures based on CA activities could be an essential element for developing e-commerce. Another perceived benefit—and goal—was the possibility of harmonizing new laws for digital signatures within the United Nations framework—or at least establishing common principles in this field and providing an international infrastructure.

24.2   *The EU legal framework*

In the EU PKI, *certificates* are electronic documents issued by authorized entities that bind the name of a natural or legal person (and any other relevant identity attribute) to that person's public key. By following strict practices and controls, a certificate enables any party receiving a digital signature to have a high level of confidence in the signatory's identity.

Public key certificates are regulated as a specific trust service by the eIDAS Regulation. The regulation differentiates between three types of certificates according to their use: *natural person* certificates are used in connection with electronic signatures, *legal person* certificates are used in connection with *electronic seals*, and *website* certificates are used in connection with browsers and web servers.

The three types of certificates regulated in the EU legislation correspond to three uses of asymmetric (public key) cryptography:

- A digital signature created by a natural person is called an *electronic signature*, which can have the same legal effect as a handwritten signature.
- A digital signature created by a legal person, called an *electronic seal*, can have the same legal effect of ensuring the integrity of the data and correctness of the origin of the data to which the electronic seal is linked.
- A digital signature is used as an *authentication method implemented by a server* (e.g., using TLS 1.2). This is the kind of signature verified by your browser when you navigate to a website and see a green lock in the address bar.

In the eIDAS Regulation, the digital certificate is always treated as an electronic proof of identity, whether for a natural person or a legal entity and regardless of whether the certificate is used to support an electronic signature, an electronic seal, or the authentication of a website.

To underpin the confidence of relying parties, the eIDAS Regulation establishes a set of minimum standards for the content of each type of certificate and the minimum obligations of providers issuing them. These standards apply to all trust service providers (TSPs; in the EU, people or legal entities providing and preserving digital certificates to create and validate electronic signatures and to authenticate signatories as well as websites).

This raises the question of whether these certificates can be used in an entity-authentication service. Some Member States have admitted qualified certificates as a means of electronic ID at the national level. If a Member State decides to permit the use of electronic signature certificates or electronic seal certificates as an identification system for cross-border purposes, then this system will be part of the EU's Federation Identity Management scheme, explained later in this chapter.

Why should eIDAS-compliant PKI be considered an important first step toward SSI in the EU? There are several arguments for this:

- PKI legislation embodied in the eIDAS Regulation created *a legal statute concerning the subscriber of a public key certificate*. That means a TSP issuing a qualified certificate is subject to the strict rules of the eIDAS Regulation (and any national law complementing it), including the legal conditions for issuance and revocation of certificates. Because TSPs may only revoke a certificate when a legally recognized reason occurs, there is greater assurance in the certificate owner's autonomy. This at least partially aligns the EU PKI system with SSI principles.

- The eIDAS Regulation also defined the legal requirements for advanced electronic signatures and advanced electronic seals. These include ensuring that the signatory has control of the signature- or seal-creation data, thus *ensuring personal autonomy in managing their data* so third parties cannot seize it. In the case of natural persons, this control must be exclusive, which again is very aligned with the core assumptions of the SSI philosophy.

- The eIDAS Regulation also regulates the possibility of *delegated user key generation and management* with the delegating user maintaining control. This aligns with another important SSI principle supporting custodial cloud wallets and digital guardianship, as explained in chapters 9, 10, and 11.

- Practices, procedures, and legal knowledge developed for PKIs may serve as a baseline for SSI, specifically for the *verifiable credential* (VC) *management lifecycle*. This enables the SSI infrastructure to take advantage of more than 20 years of international standardization at organizations such as the ITU Telecommunication Standardization Sector (ITU-T), the Internet Engineering Task Force (IETF), and the European Telecommunications Standards Institute (ETSI).

While PKI is a valuable first step toward establishing a global identity metasystem for the internet, it cannot cover all the needs of such a system, even at the regional level. And PKI falls short on some SSI principles. For example, users are still dependent on a single TSP that could delete their identities for legitimate purposes, even if their activity is legally regulated and this deletion must respond to a reasonable cause. PKI also does not support segregating identifiers from other identity data.

Finally, PKI does not support *selective disclosure*: a data subject's ability to control disclosing only the exact data required by a verifier. Current digital certificate technology forces the user to share all the information contained within the certificate (which may infringe on EU data-protection regulations such as GDPR).

Due to this limitation, a certificate can contain only the minimum set of data required to support electronic signatures, electronic seals, and website authentication. Thus, paradoxically, in some European Member States, a certificate does not contain enough information to be used for unique identification purposes, at least at a European level.

These issues—and the fact that Member States and private businesses provide other authentication mechanisms such as strong multifactor authentication—have prevented PKI from becoming a global identity metasystem. The one exception may be TLS server certificates that comply with CA/Browser Forum policy requirements. The major internet browsers enforce these by including (or excluding) in the trust stores the root certificates for recognized CAs. There is a real danger that this practice could affect millions of users' certificates and identities if a CA is abruptly revoked due to a breach or industry pressure.

> **NOTE** Organized in 2005, the CA/Browser Forum (https://cabforum.org) is a voluntary group of CAs, vendors of internet browser software, and suppliers of other applications that use X.509 v.3 digital certificates for SSL/TLS and code signing.

This danger has helped drive interest in the SSI concept of a decentralized PKI (DPKI). This concept, first explained in chapter 1 and explored in more detail in chapters 5, 8, and 10, is a way of delivering the same core benefits that PKI supports today without the need to rely on centralized service providers (such as CAs) that are single points of failure. The attraction of DPKI meant a second step toward the identity metasystem occurred in the EU between 2000 and 2014: the construction of an EU identity federation and the further expansion of PKI.

24.3   *The EU identity federation*

Due to the identity-proofing limitations of the EU PKI regulations, and because the national electronic identification schemes of each Member State are not recognized by the other Member States, the EU created the eIDAS Regulation. It is an EU-wide identity federation that provides a mutual recognition system for any eID. In essence, it functions as a regional identity metasystem, although with some limitations.

24.3.1   *The legal concept of electronic identification (eID)*

To function as an identity metasystem, the eIDAS Regulation defined a specific vocabulary for comparing and evaluating national identity schemes and federating them at the EU level. Figure 24.1 illustrates the following concepts [2]:

- *Electronic identification*—The process of using person identification data in an electronic form uniquely representing either a natural or legal person, or a natural person representing a legal person (Article 3(1) of the eIDAS Regulation).
- *Person identification data*—A set of data enabling the identification of a natural or legal person, or a natural person representing a legal person, to be established (Article 3(3) of the eIDAS Regulation). Such a digital identity can be a name (one or two surnames) and a registration number assigned by the government. Given the existence of various sets of data that identify a person and the legal challenge of creating a unique identification aggregated with all possible identification data, the regulation generally refers to partial electronic

identities. In the case of the eIDAS, there is a minimum data set required to access public services.

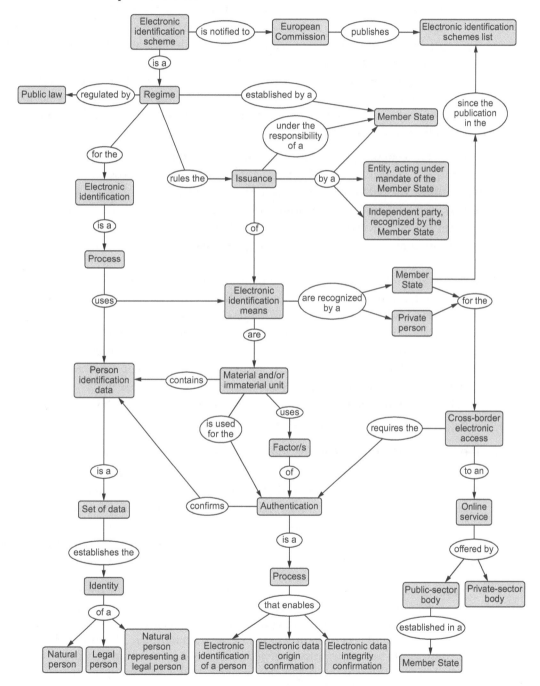

Figure 24.1 A conceptual map of electronic identification in the EU

- *Electronic identification scheme*—A system for electronic identification under which electronic identification means are issued to natural or legal persons, or natural persons representing legal persons (Article 3(4) of the eIDAS Regulation).
- *Electronic identification means*—A material and/or immaterial unit containing person identification data used for authentication for an online service (Article 3(2) of the eIDAS Regulation).
- *Authentication*—An electronic process that enables the electronic identification of a natural or legal person, or the origin and integrity of data in an electronic form to be confirmed (Article 3(5) of the eIDAS Regulation), referring to three well-known security services.

From an EU legal perspective, the concept of electronic identification is characterized by issuing *units that contain identification data* that serve for cross-border authentication, at least for public services. This legal abstraction supports many potential technology implementations, including digital certificates embedded in computer applications or on cryptographic cards, physical or logical devices that generate unique authentication codes (such as single-use passwords), and many others.

The sheer number and diversity of these different means of electronic identification—many of which were already being used in various Member States—created real security and interoperability challenges that hindered or prevented cross-border operations. This is why an EU-wide identity metasystem was needed and why pure entity authentication in cross-border transactions was the new regulation's core innovation. In addition, the eSign Directive covered authentication of data origin as well as data integrity—both of which are standard properties of advanced and qualified electronic signatures (and now also of advanced and qualified electronic seals).

This EU identity metasystem can support the core concepts of SSI because it is sufficiently neutral from a technological and organizational perspective.

24.3.2 *The scope of the eIDAS FIM Regulation and its relationship with national law*

As stipulated in Article 1(a), the eIDAS Regulation is limited to establishing "the conditions under which Member States recognize electronic identification means of natural and legal persons falling under a notified electronic identification scheme of another Member State." This means the core of the identity trust framework deals with the security and interoperability of electronic identification systems.

> **NOTE** From the perspective of the eIDAS Regulation, we can see that electronic identification is a collection of electronic public services, unlike trusted services—which can be offered as public or commercial services—that may be provided under direct or indirect management techniques. Electronic identification could also be a private service recognized by the Member State (see Article 7(a) of the eIDAS Regulation), always under its liability according to Article 11 of the eIDAS Regulation.

According to Article 6(1) of the eIDAS Regulation, for cross-border recognition of an electronic identification system to have a juridical effect, it must satisfy all three of the following conditions:

1 The electronic means of identification must have been issued under an electronic identification scheme included in a list published by the Commission in accordance with Article 9 of the eIDAS Regulation (which requires a Member State to provide advance notification of a new listing).

2 The electronic means of identification must use a substantial or high security level, and this must be equal to or higher than the level of security required for public sector bodies to access that service online in the first Member State.

3 The public sector body must use a substantial or high level of security in relation to accessing that service online. (Surprisingly, this provision precludes the possibility that a person with a better system than that requested by the public sector body can use it. For example, this will happen with a Spanish citizen who intends to use a Spanish National electronic ID to access a service in another Member State that only requires a low-quality password, due to the low-security sensitivity of the service.)

By establishing these requirements, the eIDAS Regulation focuses on enabling legally valid mutual recognition of digital identities issued by Member States within the territorial scope of application of the regulation, extending the right to use such systems to the rest of the EU Member States.

Although the legal effect of eIDAS is guaranteed only in relations between individuals and public sector bodies (in keeping with the EU's policies to enable the use of electronic means for public administration of Member States), EU FIM is designed to allow the use of electronic identification means notified by Member States under eIDAS for private sector purposes if so authorized by the identity provider's Member State.

There are several reasons eIDAS FIM may be considered a second critical step toward SSI adoption in the EU, especially in legally regulated environments:

- The eIDAS Regulation *is the primary electronic identification trust framework in the European Economic Area.*

- An eID is a *building block of the Digital Single Market,* allowing the establishment of cross-border electronic relationships in the e-Government field.

- eIDAS may be extended to include the *recognition of eIDs for private sector uses,* such as Anti-Money Laundering (AML) and Combating the Financing of Terrorism (CFT), online platforms, etc.

- The *technology-neutral approach* could easily allow the usage of SSI systems, constituting a real opportunity for their adoption.

- The eIDAS Regulation has a *strong influence in the international regulatory space,* thanks to the contributions of the United Nations Commission on International Trade Law (UNCITRAL).

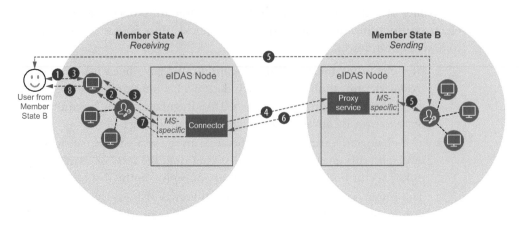

Figure 24.2   The eIDAS proxy node–to–proxy node scheme

At the time of publication, the EU identity metasystem has some potential limitations, especially in the proxy-to-proxy model shown in figure 24.2, which is more widely adopted than the proxy-to-middleware model.

The intervention of proxy nodes introduces some potential issues that can be better solved by adopting the SSI paradigm:

- *Social and legal issues*—The SSI model of distributed authentication can overcome the perceived lack of privacy with the centralized authentication required in the proxy-to-proxy model—an issue that could hold back the adoption of eIDAS. It will also allow the sharing of very sensitive data under conditions that will be acceptable from the EU GDPR perspective.
- *Technological and infrastructure capabilities of the identity provider* (resilience, continuity, capacity, security, and so on)—The SSI model will allow substituting a distributed ledger technology (DLT) for the centralized authentication node in the proxy-to-proxy model, which can both eliminate a single point of failure and offer better security guarantees.
- *Financial and liability aspects*—The public single-node model used in the proxy-to-proxy scheme makes it difficult to transfer costs to the trusting entities and overloads the issuer's liability, especially if it is a public authority. In contrast, with an SSI model using a DLT, the relying parties can bear the cost of authentication without the need to establish complex legal relationships. This approach can also reduce the potential liability of the issuer.

24.4   Summarizing the value of eIDAS for SSI adoption

As introduced in the previous sections, the eIDAS Regulation must be seen as the result of historical evolution, embodying two different identity trust frameworks:

- A *PKI-based trust framework* for qualified certificates that confirm the identity of a natural person, legal person, or website. Qualified certificates are usually used for identifying a person at the national level.

- A *FIM-based trust framework* covering any technology used for cross-border electronic identification and authentication purposes, including qualified certificates that comply with the minimum data set and security requirements.

The eIDAS Regulation may offer excellent support for legally valid SSI verifiable credentials. This is one reason Tim Bouma, co-author of chapter 23, coined the expression *legally enabled self-sovereign identity* (*LESS identity*) [3]. This term identifies a specific category of SSI VCs that meet legal requirements to differentiate from other SSI solutions that use different social trust mechanisms, such as reputation.

Legally valid SSI VCs would enjoy all of the advantages discussed in this book, such as full user control and portability, minimum disclosure, strong security and privacy, and broad interoperability. Given all of these advantages, how should eIDAS evolve in the future? Should it be adapted to include specific support for SSI?

This subject was addressed in a 2020 document called the *SSI eIDAS Legal Report* (https://joinup.ec.europa.eu/sites/default/files/document/2020-04/SSI_eIDAS_legal_report_final_0.pdf). It makes the point that a technologically neutral, broad interpretation of the eIDAS Regulation (more specifically, of the certificate definition) would support the use of a specific DID method (chapter 8) plus a specific type of VC (chapter 7) as a qualified certificate for both natural and legal persons.

Because qualified certificates confirm the subject's identity (signatory or seal creator), this specific combination of a DID method and a VC would have the same legal effect as for qualified certificates. It would also support advanced and qualified signatures and advanced qualified electronic seals in blockchain transactions. Moreover, this approach would facilitate a smooth transition from PKI to DPKI [4] and SSI systems while maintaining and even fostering a valuable market and reusing a convenient and proven supervisory and liability regime.

Although today electronic identification under the eIDAS Regulation is clearly aligned with classic FIM infrastructures such as those based on Security Assertion Markup Language (SAML) or OpenID, nothing in the eIDAS or its implementing acts should prevent the use of an SSI system as an end-to-end means of electronic identification.

Thus, the SSI eIDAS legal report considered a VC used for identification purposes *an eIDAS-compliant electronic means of identification* that could at the very least be used for transactions with public sector bodies and public administrations and—if so decided by issuers in the framework of the notified electronic identification scheme—with private sector entities for AML/CFT and other uses.

24.5   Scenarios for the adoption of SSI in the EU identity metasystem

Two different scenarios would help the adoption of SSI in the European identity metasystem. The first scenario (figure 24.3) would maintain the proxy nodes approach, as the SSI system would be used behind the currently existing node, ensuring immediate recognition and interoperable operation. While this is a transitional scenario, it would enable SSI to be integrated quickly, and it would not require any legal modifications to the eIDAS Regulation. It would not solve all the issues

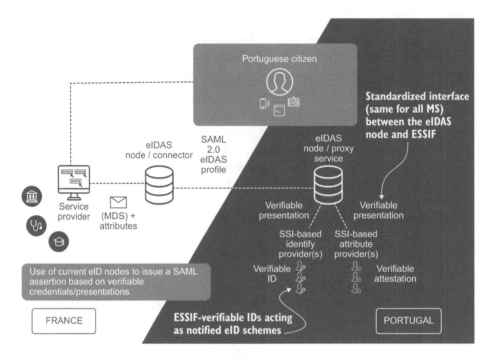

Figure 24.3 Adoption of SSI in the current EU identity metasystem

previously identified, but it would allow the incorporation of valuable SSI use cases already proven in private sector transactions, bridging trust between these two worlds.

The second scenario (figure 24.4) would evolve a middleware model, substituting SSI operational protocols and artifacts for the eIDAS proxy nodes. This opens many more potential uses.

As explained in section 10.1 of the SSI eIDAS legal report, eIDAS does not cover identity management in a broader sense, only electronic identification. Thus, it is not immediately applicable to issuing and sharing other VCs or presentations (European Blockchain Services Infrastructure [EBSI] and European SSI Framework [eSSIF] verifiable attestations) such as diplomas and employment credentials. This is understandable due to the legal standing of such credentials for proving identity. However, it makes it difficult to use such credentials in cross-border scenarios because of multiple sectoral regulations.

This second scenario could pave the way for the eIDAS Regulation to be extended to become a generalized framework for issuing and exchanging any type of VC. In other words, the real innovation SSI technology offers eIDAS is transforming the regulation to support legally valid, cross-border identity attestations of all kinds: age verification, diplomas, employment, and so on.

To be clear, the historical legal approach in the eIDAS Regulation is fully justified. It is concrete and detailed, containing precise legal definitions related to electronic

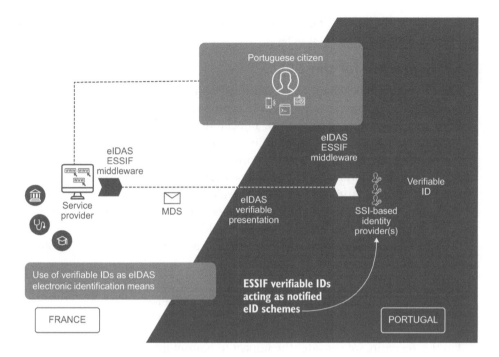

Figure 24.4   An SSI-enabled EU identity metasystem

identification (electronic identification scheme, electronic identification means, personal identification data), authentication, levels of assurance, interoperability, and governance rules. In short, it is a full legal trust framework for cross-border authentication, which is a vital part of identity management across a Union of Member States.

The proposal in this scenario would create a *parallel trust framework* for issuing and sharing other identity attributes. This objective cannot be accomplished in the same way as the current approach for electronic identification because the semantics and rules of these other identity attributes are quite different. While these other attributes could be used to identify a person (in a very general sense), they are not designed to be used for identification and authentication. However, the legal technique to support the juridical validity of these credentials would be the same; that is, the same notification procedure the eIDAS Regulation currently uses for registering new electronic means of identification would be used to register many other types of identity credentials as a way to ensure their quality, security, and interoperability.

The analysis of any sectoral framework regulating identity credentials (for example, diplomas in support of accreditation of professional qualifications, a use case included in the EBSI) shows the complexity of transforming the classical certifying documents normally issued by public administrations. To facilitate a quick transformation into verifiable attestations, a new equivalence rule could be proposed. This rule could authorize the use of a verifiable attestation according to the (new) eIDAS

Regulation whenever a legal norm required a document certifying an identity attribute for a natural or a legal person.

24.6 *SSI Scorecard for the EBSI*

The European Blockchain Services Infrastructure (EBSI) is a network of distributed nodes across Europe that will deliver cross-border public services as a result of the European Blockchain Partnership: a declaration signed by 27 Member States, Liechtenstein, and Norway to cooperate in the delivery of cross-border digital public services with the highest standards of security and privacy.

Europe, by building on its existing eIDAS infrastructure for electronic identification of individuals and legal entities, is well equipped to become a world leader in SSI adoption. This is fitting with Europe's democratic traditions and a significant opportunity to make Europe an example for the world.

The benefit evaluation of widespread SSI adoption for the EU is color-coded as follows:

Transformative	Positive	Neutral	Negative

For this scenario, we consider the impact to bottom line and regulatory compliance to be positive. All other categories are evaluated as transformative (table 24.1).

Table 24.1   SSI Scorecard: European Blockchain Services Infrastructure

Category	Features/Benefits
Bottom line	As proposed by the EBSI, a European SSI approach could fulfill the promises of the Digital Single Market while fostering and enhancing EU values. Using SSI for globally acceptable electronic identification and identity data sharing will allow EU citizens and companies to use their existing administrative identities and infrastructure to reduce fraud in e-commerce, have reliable access to new markets, and gain additional revenues by facilitating identity data exchanges.
Business efficiencies	EBSI SSI-enabled solutions will increase business efficiency thanks to owners self-managing their identity data, facilitating the onboarding of customers and business partners. This is particularly relevant to the adoption of decentralized business processes, where currently, identity silos hinder the benefits of digital transformation. This doesn't mean existing identity data sources disappear—especially those that are authoritative—but it does mean removing the significant barriers currently preventing global access and use of this trustworthy identity data.
User experience and convenience	EBSI SSI-enabled solutions will make it much easier for EU citizens to access and use their own identity data in any business or public administration context, especially in cross-border scenarios. This includes electronic identification that requires a substantial or high level of assurance to engage in legally binding actions. It will also enable easy selective sharing of pseudonymous data when needed, providing substantially more effective privacy.

Table 24.1   SSI Scorecard: European Blockchain Services Infrastructure *(continued)*

Category	Features/Benefits
Relationship management	Instead of needing to connect to multiple identity data sources in all Member States—and dealing with enormous technical, security, and interoperability complexity—businesses and public administrations will be able to establish and manage direct electronic relationships with their users. They will be able to accept existing credentials and issue their own credentials in this self-managed identity data ecosystem. Furthermore, since identity is characterized by relationships, EBSI SSI-enabled solutions will contribute to a self-managed, user-controlled social graph that can help unleash the potential value of the data without the intervention of centralized third parties.
Regulatory compliance	Due to its legal design, including an identity trust framework built on the eIDAS Regulation, EBSI SSI-enabled solutions can simplify and strengthen compliance with the legal and regulatory requirements applicable to business and administrative processes. This will help all companies operating in this new space with the appropriate guarantees.

SSI resources

To learn more about how the EU will benefit from SSI, check out https://ssi meetup.org/introducing-ssi-eidas-legal-report-ignacio-alamillo-webinar-55.

References

1. De Miguel-Asensio, P.A. 2015. *Derecho privado de Internet* (Quinta ed.). Cizur Menor, Navarra, España: Aranzadi.
2. Alamillo Domingo, I. 2019. *Identificación, firma y otras pruebas electrónicas. La regulación jurídico-administrativa de la acreditación de las transacciones electrónicas.* Cizur Menor, Navarra: Aranzadi.
3. Bouma, Tim. 2018. "Less Identity." https://trbouma.medium.com/less-identity-65f65d87f56b.
4. Reed, D., and G. Slepak. 2015. "DPKI's Answer to the Web's Trust Problems." White paper. Rebooting the Web of Trust.

appendix A
Additional
Livebook chapters

When we began reaching out to experts worldwide to share their perspectives about the impact of SSI in their specific industries and jurisdictions, we were overwhelmed by the number of responses we received. During the period when the book was delayed by the COVID-19 pandemic, word spread even further, resulting in the submission of even more outstanding chapters for part 4.

When it became clear that we had many more chapters than could fit within the length limit of the print book, the Manning editorial team offered to publish the rest of the submissions in the Livebook edition. In this appendix, we list the additional chapters that appear in the Livebook edition as of the time the book went to print. We hope to add more chapters on Livebook as other industry experts share their views about SSI, so keep checking the Livebook edition for updates.

Chapter 25: SSI, payments, and financial services
Amit Sharma

Traditional institutions, such as banks, credit unions, and government agencies involved in financial regulation, have been among the earliest potential adopters of SSI. But between 2.5 and 3.5 billion people and millions of organizations lack access to basic financial services. Banks often cite critical, expensive, and inefficient regulatory compliance requirements as the reasons they are forced to "de-risk" or exclude many individuals. SSI can pay dividends by helping enable financial access *and* protect financial system integrity at the same time by modernizing customer onboarding, fraud controls, and Know Your Customer (KYC), Anti-Money Laundering, and Counter-Terrorist Financing (AML/CFT) protections. Amit Sharma is the founder and CEO of FinClusive, a hybrid fin/reg-tech company that provides a full-stack financial crimes compliance (FCC) platform for individuals and companies that are underserved, excluded, and/or de-risked by traditional banking. He is also the chair of the Compliance and Inclusive Finance Working Group (CIFWG) at the Sovrin Foundation.

Chapter 26: Solving organizational identity with vLEIs

Stephan Wolf, Karla McKenna, and Christoph Schneider

Legal Entity Identifiers (LEIs) are an ISO standard for globally unique identifiers for any legal entity in any jurisdiction (corporation, partnership, sole proprietorship, nonprofit, and so on). The Global Legal Entity Identifier Foundation (GLEIF) was established in 2009 by the Financial Stability Board to provide a standard way to identify and track the financial dealings of a legal organization so it could not hide its identity and relationships under different registrations in different jurisdictions. With the emergence of SSI, GLEIF is expanding its focus to include the issuance of verifiable credentials for LEIs, called *vLEIs*. The vLEI system will enable instant and automated digital identity verification between counterparties operating across all industry sectors anywhere in the world. The chapter is authored by the GLEIF management team responsible for the vLEI program: Stephan Wolf (CEO), Karla McKenna (head of standards), and Christoph Schneider (head of IT development and operations).

Chapter 27: SSI and healthcare

Paul Knowles and Dr. Manreet Nijjar

Technological advances in portable medical device manufacturing have led to improved personal healthcare, but remote interactions between entities have resulted in fragmentation. With the convergence of technology and data propelling civil society into an era of artificial intelligence, the exponential rise in machine-generated data brings with it the need for a new paradigm in connectivity and handling personal data. In this chapter, Paul Knowles, co-founder of The Human Colossus Foundation, and Dr. Manreet Nijjar, consultant physician at Barts Health NHS Trust and co-founder of Truu, explain how trusted healthcare relationships can be maintained through SSI solutions in an increasingly decentralized healthcare industry.

Chapter 28: Enterprise identity and access management realized with SSI

André Kudra

As part 1 of this book explains, identity and access management (IAM) is already a well-established, multi-billion-dollar segment of the enterprise software market. SSI is the disruptive newcomer to this space. But that doesn't mean SSI needs to displace existing IAM systems so much as integrate with them. In this chapter, André Kudra, co-founder and CIO of esatus AG, one of Germany's leading enterprise security and IAM companies, explains the reality of how IAM is implemented in enterprises today, especially in large-scale organizations with complex application landscapes. Siloed data structures still predominate. In such environments, SSI technology can quickly find utility as a golden source for business facts. Furthermore, SSI can simplify and automate many IAM processes, particularly time-intensive onboarding processes or working across separate companies. André also walks through an entire start-to-finish retrofit scenario based on actual SSI integrations esatus has performed.

Chapter 29: Insurance reinvented with SSI

David Harney and Jamie Smith

In this chapter, David Harney, group CEO of Irish Life, and Jamie Smith, senior director for business development at Evernym, explain how SSI will transform how insurance is designed, operates, and is experienced. They explore how long-established insurance industry processes will change with individuals becoming the managers of their own digital identity and couriers of their own data. Insurance companies will be able to develop richer, longer-lasting relationships with customers; develop smarter insights to inform pricing and risk analyses; reduce fraud; lower costs; improve data compliance; and innovate with new insurance products and services—for example, around data integrity and authenticity. Individuals, too, will experience the impacts of SSI—not just cheaper, more personalized, smarter insurance products and services but also new products that help them understand their lives through data and decide what coverage they really need (and how much they actually need to pay).

Chapter 30: Enabling SSI in humanitarian contexts

Nathan Cooper and Amos Doornbos

Although SSI holds great promise in humanitarian contexts, implementing it is fraught with challenges—technical and non-technical. For example, humanitarian organizations operate in some of the most remote locations on Earth and work with some of the world's most vulnerable people. Most SSI infrastructure is web- and smartphone-based; most humanitarian contexts are not. Furthermore, in humanitarian contexts, it should be assumed the infrastructure is poor (networks, roads, power, health), connectivity is limited or non-existent, the environment is harsh (sandy, high temperatures, power surges, and so on), literacy rates are low (digital and linguistic), and the most common device is a feature phone at best. Nathan is senior advisor for innovation in disaster preparedness at the International Federation of Red Cross and Red Crescent Societies; Amos is disaster management strategy and systems director for World Vision International. Together, they know the realities of these challenges firsthand, so they speak from the heart when they explain what they believe will be necessary for SSI to help displaced and disadvantaged populations.

Chapter 31: Guardianship and other forms of Delegated Authority with Self-Sovereign Identity

Jack A. Najarian, Aamir S. Abdullah, Jeff Aresty, and Kaliya Young

As a term defined in the law, *guardianship* means something very specific. The term has subsequently been co-opted by technologists working on SSI infrastructure to describe certain relationships that involve entities holding verifiable credentials on behalf of people who cannot hold and present those credentials themselves. However, this does not necessarily fit within the legal definition of guardianship. It is important for policymakers and governance framework creators to understand this difference, because law and precedent matter greatly in the legal system. Acknowledging this difference will make it possible for lawmakers and technologists to develop appropriate governance frameworks for SSI technology that meet all their needs. Jack, Aamir, and Jeff are all attorneys with years of experience in internet law, and Kaliya "Identity Woman" Young is co-founder of the Internet Identity Workshop and co-author of chapter 16 on the evolution of the global SSI community.

Chapter 32: Design principles for SSI

Jasmin Huber and Johannes Seidlmeir

SSI has advanced considerably since its inception in 2016, but so far, there has not been a single definition of the essential principles of SSI. A widely referenced starting point is Christopher Allen's 10 principles of SSI (included in this book as appendix C). In this chapter, Jasmin and Johannes present an updated set of design principles to account for the continuing evolution and maturation of SSI. As researchers at the University of Bayreuth in Germany, they were motivated by the many misconceptions they found about the definition of SSI, both in academia and in practice. From their systematic study of the literature and a series of expert interviews, they derived this set of design principles that became the inspiration for the "Principles of SSI" published in 15 languages by the Sovrin Foundation in December 2020 (and included in this book as appendix E).

Chapter 33: SSI: Our dystopian nightmare

Philip Sheldrake

While much of this book paints a very bright picture of an SSI-enabled future, that future is far from assured. The answer to, "What could go wrong?" could fill an entire book. Philip Sheldrake of the AKASHA Foundation tries to condense that answer into one highly thought-provoking chapter about why SSI architecture can express only a small fraction of the richness of human identity and relationships—and why it may never be able to express the rest. He explains the very real dangers of how one-click identity could lead to a highly dystopian future and makes recommendations about how a new focus on *generative identity* can address these gaps. Philip is a technologist, chartered engineer, and web science researcher whose expertise spans digital innovation and analysis, process engineering, organizational design, marketing, and communications.

Chapter 34: Trust assurance in SSI ecosystems

Scott Perry

The trustworthiness of digital transactions is assured through a framework of governance constructs, accountability requirements, and skilled participants who play contributing roles for the benefit of all members of the ecosystem. This chapter will explore how digital trust is created and how the components of a trust assurance framework operate in an SSI ecosystem to achieve the appropriate risk mitigation for its stakeholders.

Chapter 35: The evolution of gaming with SSI

Sungjun (Calvin) Park and Jake Hostetler

The security of personal data and accounts is an issue across all industries and applications. However, the issue can be more critical and emotional for gamers because their account contains not only personal information, but proof of devoted time and purchased in-game assets—plus affinity for the gamer's virtual self. In this chapter, Sungjun (Calvin) Park, a product manager at a Korean blockchain company, and Jake Hostetler, a writer and SSI specialist at Metadium, explore how the gaming industry can be transformed with the implementation of SSI technologies.

appendix B
Landmark essays on SSI

As SSI has evolved since 2016 as a new approach to internet identity and decentralized digital trust, leaders in the SSI movement have published foundational essays examining critical aspects of this new paradigm—and the larger questions of digital, legal, organization, social, and cultural identity on which it is based. Since these essays are already widely referenced on the web, we offer this appendix as a guide to those that we have found particularly useful in the writing of this book. We apologize in advance for any others we may have left out—please contact us on the Manning Forum (https://livebook.manning.com/book/self-sovereign-identity/discussion) to nominate others.

"The Domains of Identity"

Kaliya "Identity Woman" Young

http://identitywoman.net/domains-of-identity

Written by the co-founder of the Internet Identity Workshop, this summary of the 16 distinct "domains" of identity was so clear and compelling that it later became the basis for a book on the topic. It is highly recommended as the place to start on any deeper exploration of digital identity in all its forms—simply because it clears up so many misconceptions just by framing the problem space properly. It is a wonderful complement to Kaliya's 2010 essay "The Identity Spectrum," which explains why identity is a spectrum and identifies six distinct "points" on this spectrum.

"New Hope for Digital Identity"

Doc Searls

https://www.linuxjournal.com/content/new-hope-digital-identity

This was written in late 2017 by Doc Searls, co-founder of the Internet Identity Workshop (and author of this book's foreword). It is one of the first essays to articulate why the infrastructure that was just beginning to be known as "self-sovereign identity" needed to be built into the heart of the internet—because the very future of how the internet works for individuals was at stake.

"The Architecture of Identity Systems"

Phil Windley

https://www.windley.com/archives/2020/09/the_architecture_of_identity_systems.shtml

Along with Kaliya and Doc, Phil is the third co-founder of the Internet Identity Workshop and author in 2005 of one of the first comprehensive books on digital identity. This essay is one of dozens that Phil has written about SSI on his blog during his tenure as the founding chairperson of the Sovrin Foundation. What makes it stand out is the comprehensive picture it paints of SSI architectures and how they can provide the internet's missing identity layer, finally giving us a way to enjoy life-like identity in our digital lives.

"Three Dimensions of Identity"

Jason Law and Daniel Hardman

https://medium.com/evernym/three-dimensions-of-identity-bc06ae4aec1c

This is another essay that goes to the very heart of the complexity of digital identity. It was written by two of the original creators of the open source codebase that became the basis for the Sovrin ledger (and that was contributed to the Linux Foundation to become the Hyperledger Indy ledger project). It explores the naive assertions that many have about what identity actually means: Is it authentication? Accounts and credentials? Personal data and metadata? Jason and Daniel argue that each of these perspectives simplifies too much. Identity manifests in several dimensions, and identity solutions (including SSI) must model all of these dimensions to be complete.

"Meta-Platforms and Cooperative Network-of-Network Effects"

Dr. Sam Smith

https://medium.com/selfrule/meta-platforms-and-cooperative-network-of-networks-effects-6e61eb1 5c586

The author of chapter 10 on decentralized key management, Sam is also the inventor of Key Event Receipt Infrastructure (KERI). In this groundbreaking essay (the equivalent of a full-length academic treatise), he lays out a very compelling argument that the network effects of meta-platforms—platforms of platforms—will always outperform individual platforms, much the way the internet outperformed (and eventually "ate") smaller networks. This is especially important for an SSI meta-platform (what Phil Windley calls an "identity metasystem" in his essay) because it could "provide both enough value and power to the participants to forever break the cycle of centralization."

"Verifiable Credentials Aren't Credentials. They're Containers."

Timothy Ruff

https://rufftimo.medium.com/verifiable-credentials-arent-credentials-they-re-con
tainers-fab5b3ae5c0

Timothy, co-founder of Evernym and now a principal at Digital Trust Ventures, was one of the most effective early evangelists of SSI. His essay "The Three Models of Digital Identity Relationships" is also cited in chapter 1 of this book. In this more recent essay, Timothy shares the insight that the term *verifiable credentials* is a misnomer. VCs are really containers—like shipping containers for data. He explains how VCs can contain other VCs, just like shipping containers contain other containers, and how the "seal" on a VC is like the seal on a shipping container—it verifies the integrity of the container but not the validity of the data payload inside. This is the first of a three-part series—we recommend all three.

"The Seven Deadly Sins of Customer Relationships"

Jamie Smith

http://evernym.com/seven-sins

Even as businesses everywhere race to collect more customer data, the relationship between brand and customer has become distant. Customer service has been replaced by faceless chatbots, privacy seems like a thing of the past, and our interactions feel disconnected across a growing number of touchpoints and systems. At the center of this divide are seven common but dangerous behaviors: the seven deadly sins of digital customer relationships. This series of essays from Jamie Smith, formerly lead consultant at personal data consultancy Ctrl-Shift in London, explores each of these behaviors and discusses how SSI can present an opportunity for businesses to not only offer better customer experiences but also rethink how they build trusted digital relationships from the ground up.

appendix C
The path to
self-sovereign identity

Christopher Allen

We originally planned to include this essay in the list of landmark essays in appendix B. However, it is central enough to the history of SSI that we wanted to include it directly in the body of the book. It was originally published by Christopher Allen on his website, Life with Alacrity, on April 25, 2016. The full version is available at http://www.lifewithalacrity.com/2016/04/the-path-to-self-sovereign-identity.html and includes footnotes and a glossary. Christopher is a pioneer in collaboration, security, and trust on the internet. In the late 1990s, he worked with Netscape to develop Secure Sockets Layer (SSL) and co-authored the IETF Transport Layer Security (TLS) standard that is at the heart of secure commerce on the web (it powers the lock on your browser address bar). Christopher is the founder of Blockchain Commons, a former co-chair of the W3C Credentials Community Group, and the founder of the semi-annual Rebooting the Web of Trust design workshops.

You can't spell "identity" without an "I"

Identity is a uniquely human concept. It is that ineffable "I" of self-consciousness, something that is understood worldwide by every person living in every culture. As René Descartes said, "Cogito ergo sum"—I think, therefore I am.

However, modern society has muddled this concept of identity. Today, nations and corporations conflate driver's licenses, Social Security cards, and other state-issued credentials with identity; this is problematic because it suggests a person can lose their very identity if a state revokes their credentials or even if they just cross state borders. *I think, but I am not.*

Identity in the digital world is even trickier. It suffers from the same problem of centralized control, but it's simultaneously very balkanized: identities are piecemeal, differing from one internet domain to another.

As the digital world becomes increasingly important to the physical world, it also presents a new opportunity; it offers the possibility of redefining modern concepts of identity. It might allow us to place identity back under our control—once more reuniting identity with the ineffable "I."

In recent years, this redefinition of identity has begun to have a new name: *self-sovereign identity*. However, to understand this term, we need to review some history of identity technology.

The evolution of identity

The models for online identity have advanced through four broad stages since the advent of the internet: centralized identity, federated identity, user-centric identity, and self-sovereign identity.

Phase one: Centralized identity (administrative control by a single authority or hierarchy)

In the internet's early days, centralized authorities became the issuers and authenticators of digital identity. Organizations like IANA (1988) determined the validity of IP addresses, and ICANN (1998) arbitrated domain names. Then, beginning in 1995, certificate authorities (CAs) stepped up to help internet commerce sites prove they were who they said they were.

Some of these organizations took a small step beyond centralization and created hierarchies. A root controller could anoint other organizations to each oversee its own hierarchy. However, the root still had the core power—it was just creating new, less-powerful centralizations beneath it.

Unfortunately, granting control of digital identity to centralized authorities of the online world suffers from the same problems caused by the state authorities of the physical world: users are locked in to a single authority that can deny their identity or even confirm a false identity. Centralization innately gives power to the centralized entities, not to the users.

As the internet grew, and as power accumulated across hierarchies, a further problem was revealed: identities were increasingly balkanized. They multiplied as websites did, forcing users to juggle dozens of identities on dozens of different sites—while having control over none of them.

To a large extent, identity on the internet today is still centralized—or at best, hierarchical. Digital identities are owned by CAs, domain registrars, and individual sites and then rented to users or revoked at any time. However, for the last two decades, there's also been a growing push to return identities to the people so that they actually could control them.

Interlude: Foreshadowing the future

Pretty Good Privacy (PGP, 1991) offered one of the first hints of what could become self-sovereign identity. It introduced the *Web of Trust*, which established trust for a digital identity by allowing peers to act as introducers and validators of public keys. Anyone could be a validator in the PGP model. The result was a powerful example of decentralized trust management, but it focused on email addresses, which meant that it still depended on centralized hierarchies. For a variety of reasons, PGP never became broadly adopted.

Other early thoughts appeared in "Establishing Identity without Certification Authority" (1996), a paper by Carl Ellison that examined how digital identity was created. He considered both authorities such as CAs and peer-to-peer systems like PGP options for defining digital identity. He then settled on a method for verifying online identity by exchanging shared secrets over a secure channel. This allowed users to control their own identity without depending on a managing authority.

Ellison was also at the heart of the simple public key infrastructure / simple distributed security infrastructure project (SPKI/SDSI, 1999). Its goal was to build a simpler public infrastructure for identity certificates that could replace the complicated X.509 system. Although centralized authorities were considered as an option, they were not the only option.

It was a beginning, but an even more revolutionary reconception of identity in the 21st century would be required to truly bring self-sovereignty to the forefront.

Phase two: Federated identity (administrative control by multiple, federated authorities)

The next major advancement for digital identity occurred at the turn of the century when a variety of commercial organizations moved beyond hierarchy to debalkanize online identity in a new manner.

Microsoft's Passport (1999) initiative was one of the first. It imagined federated identity, which allowed users to utilize the same identity on multiple sites. However, it put Microsoft at the center of the federation, which made it almost as centralized as traditional authorities.

In response, Sun Microsoft organized the Liberty Alliance (2001). It resisted the idea of centralized authority, instead creating a "true" federation, but the result was instead an oligarchy: the power of centralized authority was now divided among several powerful entities.

Federation improved on the problem of balkanization: users could wander from site to site under the system. However, each individual site remained an authority.

Phase three: User-centric identity (individual or administrative control across multiple authorities without requiring a federation)

The Augmented Social Network (ASN, 2000) laid the groundwork for a new sort of digital identity in its proposal to create a next-generation internet. In an extensive white paper, ASN suggested building "persistent online identity" into the very architecture of the internet. From the viewpoint of self-sovereign identity, its most important advance was "the assumption that every individual ought to have the right to control their or her own online identity." The ASN group felt that Passport and the Liberty Alliance could not meet these goals because the "business-based initiatives" put too much emphasis on the privatization of information and the modeling of users as consumers. These ASN ideas would become the foundation of much that followed.

The Identity Commons (2001–present) began to consolidate the new work on digital identity with a focus on decentralization. Its most important contribution may have been the creation, in association with the Identity Gang, of the Internet Identity Workshop (2005–present) working group. For the last 10 years, the IIW has advanced the idea of decentralized identity in a series of semi-yearly meetings.

The IIW community focused on a new term that countered the server-centric model of centralized authorities: *user-centric identity*. The term suggests that users are placed in the middle of the identity process. Initial discussions of the topic focused on creating a better user experience, which underlined the need to put users front and center in the quest for online identity. However, the definition of a user-centric identity soon expanded to include the desire for a user to have more control over their identity and for trust to be decentralized.

The work of the IIW has supported many new methods for creating digital identity, including OpenID (2005), OpenID 2.0 (2006), OpenID Connect (2014), OAuth (2010), and Fast IDenfication Online (FIDO, 2013). As implemented, user-centric methodologies tend to focus on two elements: user consent and interoperability. By adopting them, a user can decide to share an identity from one service to another and thus debalkanize their digital self.

The user-centric identity communities had even more ambitious visions; they intended to give users complete control of their digital identities. Unfortunately, powerful institutions co-opted their efforts and kept them from fully realizing their goals. Much as with the Liberty Alliance, final ownership of user-centric identities today remains with the entities that register them.

OpenID offers an example. A user can theoretically register their own OpenID, which they can then use autonomously. However, this takes some technical know-how, so the casual internet user is more likely to use an OpenID from one public website as a login for another. If the user selects a site that is long-lived and trustworthy, they can gain many of the advantages of a self-sovereign identity—but it could be taken away at any time by the registering entity!

Facebook Connect (2008) appeared a few years after OpenID, leveraging lessons learned, and thus was several times more successful largely due to a better user interface. Unfortunately, Facebook Connect veers even further from the original user-centric ideal of user control. To start with, there's no choice of provider; it's Facebook. Worse, Facebook has a history of arbitrarily closing accounts, as was seen in the recent real-name controversy. As a result, people who access other sites with their "user-centric" Facebook Connect identity may be even more vulnerable than OpenID users to losing that identity in multiple places at one time.

It's central authorities all over again. Worse, it's like state-controlled authentication of identity, except with a self-elected "rogue" state. In other words: being user-centric isn't enough.

Phase four: Self-sovereign identity (individual control across any number of authorities)

User-centric designs turned centralized identities into interoperable federated identities with centralized control while also respecting some level of user consent about how to share an identity (and with whom). It was an important step toward true user control of identity, but just a step. To take the next step required user autonomy.

This is the heart of *self-sovereign identity*, a term that's coming into increased use in the 2010s. Rather than just advocating that users be at the center of the identity process, self-sovereign identity requires that users be the rulers of their own identity.

One of the first references to identity sovereignty occurred in February 2012, when developer Moxie Marlinspike wrote about "Sovereign Source Authority." He said that individuals "have an established Right to an 'identity'" but that national registration destroys that sovereignty. Some ideas are in the air, so it's no surprise that almost simultaneously, in March 2012, Patrick Deegan began work on Open Mustard Seed, an open source framework that gives users control of their digital identity and their data in decentralized systems. It was one of several "personal cloud" initiatives that appeared around the same time.

Since then, the idea of self-sovereign identity has proliferated. Marlinspike has blogged about how the term has evolved. As a developer, he shows one way to address self-sovereign identity: as a mathematical policy, where cryptography is used to protect a user's autonomy and control. However, that's not the only model. Respect Network instead addresses self-sovereign identity as a legal policy; it defines contractual rules and principles that members of its network agree to follow. The Windhover Principles for Digital Identity, Trust, and Data and Evernym's Identity System Essentials offer some additional perspectives on the rapid advent of self-sovereign identity since 2012.

In the last year, self-sovereign identity has also entered the sphere of international policy. This has largely been driven by the refugee crisis that has beset Europe, which has resulted in many people lacking a recognized identity due to their flight from the state that issued their credentials. However, it's a longstanding international problem, as foreign workers have often been abused by the countries they work in due to the lack of state-issued credentials.

If self-sovereign identity was becoming relevant a few years ago, its importance has skyrocketed in light of current international crises. The time to move toward self-sovereign identity is now.

A definition of self-sovereign identity

With all that said, what is self-sovereign identity, exactly? The truth is that there's no consensus. As much as anything, this article is intended to begin a dialogue on that topic. However, I wish to offer a starting position.

Self-sovereign identity is the next step beyond user-centric identity, and that means it begins at the same place: the user must be central to the administration of identity. That requires not just the interoperability of a user's identity across multiple locations, with the user's consent, but also true user control of that digital identity, creating user autonomy. To accomplish this, a self-sovereign identity must be transportable; it can't be locked down to one site or locale.

A self-sovereign identity must also allow ordinary users to make claims, which could include personally identifying information or facts about personal capability or group membership. It can even contain information about the user that was asserted by other persons or groups.

In the creation of a self-sovereign identity, we must be careful to protect the individual. A self-sovereign identity must defend against financial and other losses, prevent human rights abuses by the powerful, and support the rights of the individual to be oneself and to freely associate.

However, there's a lot more to self-sovereign identity than just this brief summation. Any self-sovereign identity must also meet a series of guiding principles—and these principles provide a better, more comprehensive definition of what self-sovereign identity is. A proposal for them follows.

Ten principles of self-sovereign identity

A number of different people have written about the principles of identity. Kim Cameron wrote one of the earliest "Laws of Identity," while the aforementioned Respect Network policy and W3C Verifiable Claims Task Force FAQ offer additional perspectives on digital identity. This section draws on all of these ideas to create a group of principles specific to self-sovereign identity. As with the definition itself, consider these principles a departure point to provoke a discussion about what's truly important.

These principles attempt to ensure the user control that's at the heart of self-sovereign identity. However, they also recognize that identity can be a double-edged sword—usable for both beneficial and maleficent purposes. Thus, an identity system must balance transparency, fairness, and support of the commons with protection for the individual:

1. *Existence. Users must have an independent existence.* Any self-sovereign identity is ultimately based on the ineffable "I" that's at the heart of identity. It can never exist wholly in digital form. This must be the kernel of self that is upheld and supported. A self-sovereign identity simply makes public and accessible some limited aspects of the "I" that already exists.

2. *Control. Users must control their identities.* Subject to well-understood and secure algorithms that ensure the continued validity of an identity and its claims, the user is the ultimate authority on their identity. The user should always be able to refer to it, update it, or even hide it. The user must be able to choose levels of visibility, celebrity, or privacy, as they prefer. This doesn't mean that a user controls all of the claims on their identity: other users may make claims about a user, but they should not be central to the identity itself.

3   *Access. Users must have access to their own data.* A user must always be able to easily retrieve all the claims and other data within the user's identity. There must be no hidden data and no gatekeepers. This does not mean that a user can necessarily modify all the claims associated with the identity, but it does mean the user should be aware of them. It also does not mean that users have equal access to others' data, but to only their own.

4   *Transparency. Systems and algorithms must be transparent.* The systems used to administer and operate a network of identities must be open, both in how they function and in how they are managed and updated. The algorithms should be free, open-source, well-known, and as independent as possible of any particular architecture; anyone should be able to examine how they work.

5   *Persistence. Identities must be long-lived.* Preferably, identities should last forever, or at least for as long as the user wishes. Though private keys might need to be rotated and data might need to be changed, the identity remains. In the fast-moving world of the internet, this goal may not be entirely reasonable, so at the least, identities should last until they've been outdated by newer identity systems. This must not contradict a "right to be forgotten"; a user should be able to dispose of an identity if the user wishes, and claims should be modified or removed as appropriate over time. To do this requires a firm separation between an identity and its claims: they can't be tied forever.

6   *Portability. Information and services about identity must be transportable.* Identities must not be held by a singular third-party entity, even if it's a trusted entity that is expected to work in the best interest of the user. The problem is that entities can disappear—and on the internet, most eventually do. Regimes may change, users may move to different jurisdictions. Transportable identities ensure that users remain in control of their identity no matter what and can also improve an identity's persistence over time.

7   *Interoperability. Identities should be as widely usable as possible.* Identities are of little value if they work only in limited niches. The goal of a 21st-century digital identity system is to make identity information widely available, crossing international boundaries to create global identities without losing user control. Thanks to persistence and autonomy, these widely available identities can then become continually available.

8   *Consent. Users must agree to the use of their identity.* Any identity system is built around sharing that identity and its claims, and an interoperable system increases the amount of sharing that occurs. However, sharing of data must only occur with the consent of the user. Though other users such as an employer, a credit bureau, or a friend might present claims, the user must still offer consent for them to become valid. Note that this consent might not be interactive, but it must still be deliberate and well-understood.

9   *Minimalization. Disclosure of claims must be minimized.* When data is disclosed, that disclosure should involve the minimum amount of data necessary to accomplish

the task at hand. For example, if only a minimum age is called for, then the exact age should not be disclosed, and if only an age is requested, then the more precise date of birth should not be disclosed. This principle can be supported with selective disclosure, range proofs, and other zero-knowledge techniques, but non-correlatibility is still a very hard (perhaps impossible) task; the best we can do is to use minimalization to support privacy as best as possible.

10 *Protection. The rights of users must be protected.* When there is a conflict between the needs of the identity network and the rights of individual users, then the network should err on the side of preserving the freedoms and rights of the individuals over the needs of the network. To ensure this, identity authentication must occur through independent algorithms that are censorship-resistant and force-resilient and that are run in a decentralized manner.

Conclusion

The idea of digital identity has been evolving for a few decades now, from centralized identities to federated identities to user-centric identities to self-sovereign identities. However, even today exactly what a self-sovereign identity is, and what rules it should recognize, aren't well-known.

This article seeks to begin a dialogue on that topic, by offering up a definition and a set of principles as a starting point for this new form of user-controlled and persistent identity of the 21st century.

appendix D
Identity in the Ethereum blockchain ecosystem

Fabian Vogelsteller and Oliver Terbu

As chapter 1 explains, blockchain technology is the mother of SSI, pure and simple. The twin pillars of blockchain are Bitcoin and Ethereum, and while both communities have been active in SSI, Ethereum has been a particular hotbed due to the power and flexibility of smart contracts. Leading the charge has been Fabian Vogelsteller, who joined the Ethereum Foundation in July 2015 and has built some of its core applications, including the Ethereum Wallet and the Mist browser. His collaborator in this special appendix describing the evolution and standardization of SSI in the Ethereum ecosystem is Oliver Terbu, identity architect with Consen-Sys/uPort since 2018 and an active member of the W3C Credentials Community Group, the W3C Verifiable Claims Working Group, the Decentralized Identity Foundation, the Ethereum Enterprise Alliance, the OpenID Foundation, and others too numerous to mention.

Blockchains are consensus networks; they allow participants to view and modify the state of a distributed ledger using clear rules that are agreed upon by the network. There are many blockchains, and each has both its own rules and its own purpose: the Ethereum blockchain was built to create a distributed computing network.

Ethereum enables its distributed computing through *smart contracts*, which are simple programs that run in virtual machines: the Ethereum Virtual Machine (EVM) or Ethereum Flavored WebAssembly (eWASM). These smart contracts can be used to take specific actions, such as voting, or to transfer Ether, the native cryptocurrency of the Ethereum blockchain. They cost small transaction fees to run, paid with a unit called *gas*, which calculates fees in Ether.

Smart contracts can be quite complex: each one has different rules. They might be owned by individuals, by groups of people, or by no one at all. Most importantly, smart contracts can talk to each other, allowing one transaction to trigger a whole chain of actions on the network. This enables a variety of complex business logic, from simple wallets to proxy accounts and, yes, full-fledged identity systems.

But there isn't just one way to do something on Ethereum. Because it's a programmable blockchain, anyone can build anything using its Turing-complete smart contracts. The result is a rich and diverse ecosystem. In fact, the problem isn't finding exciting new things to do on the Ethereum blockchain but instead figuring out how to do them in organized and well-defined ways so that different systems can interoperate. That's where the ERCs (Ethereum Requests for Comment) come into play: each one defines a way to do something on the Ethereum network.

Two ERCs are of particular note for identity on the Ethereum blockchain: ERC 725 v2, the "Proxy Account," and ERC 1056, "Lightweight Identity." They help to ensure that self-sovereign identities on the Ethereum blockchain are interoperable, manageable, and verifiable.

Identity on the blockchain

Blockchains tend to offer specific advantages for identity systems, and Ethereum is no exception. Because blockchains are public databases that are accessible and verifiable by everyone, their identity data is public, too. Because self-sovereign identities on the blockchain are ultimately accounts that are manipulated by private keys, identities can be controlled by persons, companies, or objects; they can be traditional identities, simple profiles, blockchain access points, or avatars. Of course, the Ethereum blockchain moves beyond these traditional advantages because of its programmability. This means that Ethereum identities aren't just passive data but more complex computer programs.

There are also challenges to hosting identities on the blockchain. First, because blockchains are anonymous, there are issues when other systems need to recognize accounts, understand their relationships, or check attestations and claims.

Second, because blockchain data is visible to everyone, careful decisions have to be made about which personal data is stored on the blockchain ("on-chain") and which is instead stored elsewhere and linked to from the blockchain ("off-chain"). Each of these methodologies is supported by ERCs, which resolve some of the problems inherent in these schemes. They can each address the challenges of blockchain identity and do so in ways that are complementary, not exclusive.

Third, the keys for an identity need to be managed carefully. They need to be backed up, and provisions must be made to avoid losing identities when keys are lost. Although methods such as multi-signatures and key-recovery schemes such as Shamir's Secret Sharing exist to solve some key-management problems, nuance is required on Ethereum to support updating or replacing the permissions system associated with a smart contract without changing the identity itself, a topic that requires some additional discussion.

The keys to identity

Today, Ethereum decentralized applications (DApps) are all built around private keys, which are used to communicate with the smart contracts and move assets like Ether. This is both dangerous and limiting. On the one hand, if the private key is lost, then all access to the contract and assets is lost. This can be devastating because it means that the identity is effectively lost: there are no second chances in blockchain. In addition, it effectively restricts the number of people who can access the identity, which is not to the benefit of public identities such as avatars, personas, and company accounts, and also poses risks for key recovery. Any good blockchain identity system thus needs a complex identity-management scheme that goes beyond the simple use of private keys.

First, identity-management systems must solve the problem of updating permissions without changing the identity. One option is to create separate key-management and identity smart contracts. This way, the key management can be upgraded and evolve over time without needing to change the on-chain identifying address. This allows attached on-chain information such as claims, reputations, and other identifying information to stay unchanged even if the whole permission system is replaced. Another possibility is to integrate ownership change directly into the smart contract while ensuring that the account's identifying address does not change.

Second, identity-management systems should support robust features such as these:

- *Multiple access methods*—Could include signatures, multi-signatures, or even key-management smart contracts
- *Different key types*—Could exclusively support managing the contract, taking actions, or signing claims
- *Social recovery schemes*—Could allow private keys to be recovered by combining information from a variety of associations

Any of these key-management methodologies can apply to either on-chain or off-chain identity solutions, though each may approach the problem in a different way.

On-chain identity solutions

In an on-chain identity scheme, personal information is referenced from the blockchain identity: this could be public profile information or organizational data that is completely published on-chain, or it could be verifiable claims that don't reveal concrete personal identifying information. An on-chain identity scheme requires a smart contract that supports a key-value store so that both keys (such as "some claim" or "nickname") and values (such as "Person identified by ..." or "Superman") can be recorded—either self-issued or signed by the issuing party. This information can then be retrieved and verified automatically by other smart contracts, supporting interactions with ICOs or other gateway systems.

However, there's a notable drawback to this method: information stored on-chain is public and immutable. Although it may or may not be linked to a human, company, or other entity, it will live forever on the blockchain: even the *actions* associated with an identity will live forever!

Although immutable information of this sort can be beneficial for a number of *public* entities, maintaining *personal* data in such a public and immutable way can be much more problematic: most personal information is private and never needs to be seen by the public. Thus, careful decisions must be made when deciding which identities to host on-chain in this way.

ERC 725 v2: "Proxy Account"

ERC 725 v2: "Proxy Account" supports both identity-enabling key-value stores and a separate key-management methodology by creating a public blockchain profile that is a verifiable, manageable proxy account. Because of the standardization of the ERC, it can be integrated into user interfaces and easily verified by other smart contracts.

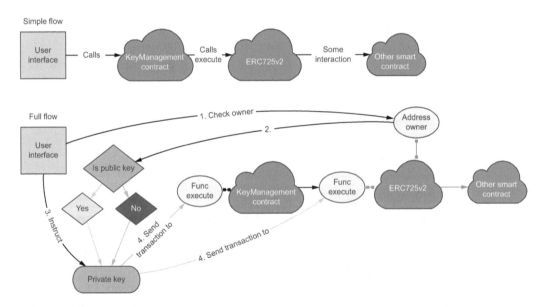

Figure D.1   Identity management using ERC 725 v2

The proxy account describes a simple smart contract that has an *owner* and a *key-value store*. In this methodology, the owner is the controller of the identity, and the key-value store encodes the attached information. The address of the smart contract then functions as the identifier for the digital identity.

The owner

Although ERC 725 v2 supports the typical DApp methodology of an owner being a simple private key, it also allows another smart contract to be an owner, and that contract could itself have specific rules for how it's controlled. This supports more complex key-management schemes such as multi-signatures and, more precisely, permissioned keys. Specific keys could even be restricted to only allow interactions with other specific smart contracts on a user-basis—or if the identity is an organization, on a staff-basis.

The controlling smart contract can also support submissions of transactions by third parties, provided that they contain a valid signature from one of the owner keys. This allows gas costs to be paid for by the application developer or by a third-party transaction relay service, without them having any control of the contract—which resolves a traditional problem where interacting on a blockchain otherwise requires all parties to have access to the blockchain's native cryptocurrency.

Because the owner of an ERC 725 v2 identity can be delegated, the owner of the smart contract can change. This permits the controlling smart contract to update and improve over time without changing the address of the smart contract, and therefore the identity's public identifier.

The key-value store

The key-value store of ERC 725 v2 allows arbitrary values to be set for 32-byte keys. This simple mechanics permits all sorts of information to be attached to the identity smart contract and proves that the information is permissioned, as only the owner can attach this information.

When this attached information is on-chain, it allows other smart contracts—such as ICOs, insurances, and decentralized exchanges—to automatically verify whether an account is allowed to take a certain action. The key-value store can also link to claim registries, reputation systems, zero-knowledge proofs, other smart contracts, or different types of on-chain identities. This all can occur without revealing anything about the person owning this account.

Although much of ERC 725 v2 is focused on on-chain solutions, its key-value store can additionally link to off-chain data through decentralized identifiers (DIDs) or Merkle root hashes. The flexibility of the ERC 725 v2 key-value store allows identities to record and link to a variety of information, creating an adaptable and thus future-proof identity system.

The public on-chain identity

The heart of the ERC 725 v2 digital identity is an Ethereum address owned by the smart contracts. Traditionally, these addresses were pure public keys, which are hard to manage and hard to verify; ERC 725 v2 is meant to create manageability and verifiability, laying the foundation for public on-chain identities.

These public identities may be quite different from the personal identities and their personally identifying information (PII), which are the heart of many self-sovereign identity systems. Instead, they're more likely to be public personas, digital avatars, and online influencers; corporations and institutions may also find this sort of public identity useful: they can use public on-chain identities to make their actions transparent, allowing for easy verification and supporting claims issuance. Because on-chain identities of this sort can list relevant information in a provable way, they can replace or supplement today's governmental registries for companies, professional profiles for workers, and information websites for public personas like stars or politicians.

Finally, on-chain public identities may be useful for some private individuals, such as traders and investors: they support automated on-chain interactions that require trusted and verified accounts—a use case that is currently hard to accommodate but that is now made transparent and safe.

These personal public identities can ultimately be as public or pseudonymous as a user requires. Although an on-chain identity *could* be linked to personally identifiable information, it *might* only be identified by specific claims: an on-chain identity for a professional driver could include claims that they have a driver's license and that they haven't had an accident or received a ticket in five years, but not include an actual name.

Personal semi-public identities may have even more uses in the future when blockchain pruning could introduce the right to be forgotten. But even absent that, there are clear needs for them in the modern day.

Off-chain identity solutions

In an off-chain identity scheme, identity information is kept in data storage such as hubs that are separate from the blockchain. The data can be linked from the blockchain by methods such as DIDs but is accessible only when specifically requested. This keeps off-chain data private and shareable on a peer-to-peer basis. It also supports strong controls over who can access the data and precise granularity for what data is shared.

Despite the clear privacy advantages of off-chain identity solutions, there are challenges here as well. First, interactions with a blockchain are more complicated; since accounts are just sets of links, they're essentially anonymous: owners, delegates, and accounts can be verified by smart contracts, but more intensive processes such as Know Your Customer (KYC) can't provide verification without breaking anonymity.

Second, off-chain identities can end up being less private than intended. If off-chain data is attached to transactions, then they ultimately end up linked to an on-chain account. This creates some of the same publicity dilemmas as on-chain identity solutions.

Third, transactions can bloat in size because of the need to sign data in transactions. And fourth, key management is once again complicated. Off-chain data is likely to be linked to specific keys rather than smart contracts; this means that losing a private key can still mean losing access to data, which can be devastating if it is a signed claim or attestation.

ERC 1056: "Lightweight Identity"

Much as with ERC 725 v2, ERC 1056, "Lightweight Identity," supports both on-chain and off-chain identity storage, but its lightweight registry is particularly useful for efficiently managing off-chain identity data by using the Ethereum network to increase the trustworthiness of that information. While identity data is managed off-chain, the ERC 1056 smart contract provides an on-chain anchor.

Although ERC 1056 is not specifically limited to public Ethereum networks and can be used with private and permissioned networks as well, it focuses on addressing common challenges of public Blockchains such as cost-efficiency, scalability, and, of course, key management. ERC 1056's primary use case is helping developers to onboard new users and to provide verifiable identity data.

The lightweight registry

ERC 1056's lightweight registry serves three major functions. First, it records the owner of an identity. Second, it records delegates that can act on the owner's behalf for a specified time. Third, it implements a decentralized public-key infrastructure (DPKI) with the ability to add keys and public attributes to the identity, creating a hub service endpoint

These elements enable the registry to secure off-chain identity data exchange, assuming that the identity data is associated with an identifier managed by the registry: another smart contract can authenticate and verify this off-chain data exchange by obtaining the cryptographic information linked to the data through the registry. In W3C verifiable credentials terminology, the holder includes an identifier contained in the registry in the data exchange and signs the presentation with the corresponding public key; a verifier then extracts the identifier and uses the registry to get the verification key of the holder to verify the signature of the presentation.

When keys or attributes are changed, these changes are not written to the ERC 1056 smart contract itself. Instead, Ethereum events are emitted and written to the Ethereum event log. Technically, they are included in transaction receipts, which are verified by Ethereum as the transaction receipt hashes are stored in blocks. The lightweight registry links these events with each other to allow a fast lookup of all relevant changes for an owner. This approach dramatically decreases the gas costs for identity management operations (IMOs). Any of these transactions can also be initiated by third parties as meta transactions. Although the owner still signs the operation, it can be submitted by the third party, who will pay the gas costs of the IMO. Figure D.2 illustrates how involved parties use ERC 1056 to manage or verify identity data.

Note that no personal data needs to be stored on Ethereum using ERC 1056. The DPKI can simply be used to link to hubs where the data is recorded. This may provide better compliance for regulations such as GDPR; there are still ongoing discussions on the topic, but if off-chain identity data is deleted, the on-chain information may no longer be considered personal data.

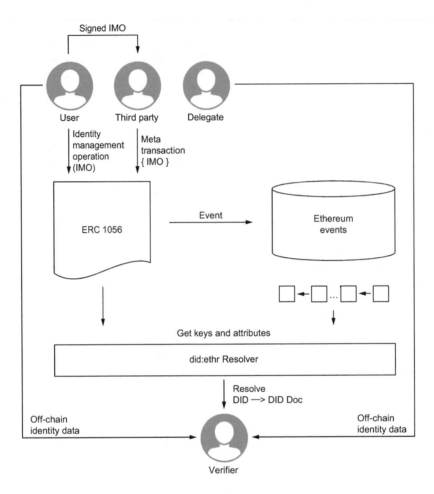

Figure D.2   Identity management using ERC 1056

Owner and delegates

ERC 1056 allows any Ethereum account to become the owner of an identity by the simple act of controlling its private keys: the owner of the identity is the same as the owner of the corresponding account. Because Ethereum accounts can be created off-chain, there's no need for an Ethereum transaction; there's also no need to deploy a new smart contract at this time, as a single ERC 1056 smart contract can track the owners of all identities for an application or a set of applications. These advantages largely eliminate gas costs at identity creation, which is crucial for use cases that need to create billions of identities, such as in the field of the Internet of Things.

Recording an owner on-chain is only required if the owner has changed. If the registry contains no entry about a particular identity, it is assumed that the owner has never changed and the public authentication and verification keys can be derived entirely off-chain by presenting the address of the Ethereum account.

It's still possible to use a proxy contract, such as a multi-signature contract, to become the owner of an ERC 1056 identity: the owner of the identity simply sets a new Ethereum account as the new owner in the smart contract, possibly using a meta transaction. This approach supports guardianships, enterprise-grade key management, social recovery, or more complex ownership relationships.

ERC 1056 identities can also have multiple delegates, which are Ethereum accounts that can act on behalf of the identity owner for a limited time, or until the owner revokes the delegate. This is useful when an identity owner wants to assign a representative or share the ownership of off-chain data with certain parties. For example, if the off-chain data is a credential used to unlock a smart lock, then the owner could add their partner as a delegate so that they can both access the protected goods.

Other ERCs

- ERC 725 v2 and ERC 1056 are the two most complete identity systems currently being standardized on Ethereum, but the diversity of the ecosystem ensures that there will be more. In fact, several proposals of smaller scope can already be found among the ERCs.
- ERC 734, "Key Manager" and ERC 735, "Claim Holder" work in combination with ERC 725 v2, providing more details on the key management and claims elements.
- ERC 780, "Ethereum Claims Registry," was in turn written by the author of ERC 1056 and provides standards for both self-issued claims and peer-to-peer claims.
- ERC 1812, "Ethereum Verifiable Claims," puts claims off-chain instead of on-chain, in part due to the pressure of new regulations such as the GDPR.

By the time you read this, there may be some fascinating new ERCs, approaching self-sovereign identity on the Ethereum blockchain in a new way.

Conclusion

ERC 725 and ERC 1056 are two different approaches to self-sovereign identity that function differently. ERC 725 focuses on making an Ethereum account into a public on-chain identity, which can have any amount of information attached. It is meant to live mainly on the blockchain and interact with other blockchain entities. ERC 1056, in contrast, keeps all of its identity information off-chain. The on-chain smart contract serves largely as a public key registry for that identity. And there will be more, because there's always another way to do things on Ethereum.

appendix E
The principles of SSI

In the fall of 2020, the Sovrin Foundation began stewarding an effort on behalf of the global SSI community to consolidate the various definitions of SSI into a single comprehensive set of principles. Over five months, through numerous meetings and doc-a-thons, including an Internet Identity Workshop session with over 80 participants, this list of principles was winnowed down to the following 12. In December 2020, these were translated into 15 languages by volunteers from around the world. All of these translations are published on behalf of the SSI community by the Sovrin Foundation at https://sovrin.org/principles-of-ssi. This is the English language version.

These foundational principles of SSI are intended for use by any digital identity ecosystem. Any organization is welcomed to incorporate these principles into its digital identity ecosystem governance framework provided they are included in their entirety. The principles of SSI shall be limited only by official laws and regulations that apply in a relevant jurisdiction.

1. REPRESENTATION
An SSI ecosystem shall provide the means for any entity—human, legal, natural, physical, or digital—to be represented by any number of digital identities.

2. INTEROPERABILITY
An SSI ecosystem shall enable digital identity data for an entity to be represented, exchanged, secured, protected, and verified interoperably using open, public, and royalty-free standards.

3. DECENTRALIZATION
An SSI ecosystem shall not require reliance on a centralized system to represent, control, or verify an entity's digital identity data.

4. CONTROL & AGENCY

An SSI ecosystem shall empower entities who have natural, human, or legal rights in relation to their identity ("identity rights holders") to control usage of their digital identity data and exert this control by employing and/or delegating to agents and guardians of their choice, including individuals, organizations, devices, and software.

5. PARTICIPATION

An SSI ecosystem shall not require an identity rights holder to participate.

6. EQUITY AND INCLUSION

An SSI ecosystem shall not exclude or discriminate against identity rights holders within its governance scope.

7. USABILITY, ACCESSIBILITY, AND CONSISTENCY

An SSI ecosystem shall maximize usability and accessibility of agents and other SSI components for identity rights holders, including consistency of user experience.

8. PORTABILITY

An SSI ecosystem shall not restrict the ability of identity rights holders to move or transfer a copy of their digital identity data to the agents or systems of their choice.

9. SECURITY

An SSI ecosystem shall empower identity rights holders to secure their digital identity data at rest and in motion, to control their own identifiers and encryption keys, and to employ end-to-end encryption for all interactions.

10. VERIFIABILITY AND AUTHENTICITY

An SSI ecosystem shall empower identity rights holders to provide verifiable proof of the authenticity of their digital identity data.

11. PRIVACY AND MINIMAL DISCLOSURE

An SSI ecosystem shall empower identity rights holders to protect the privacy of their digital identity data and to share the minimum digital identity data required for any particular interaction.

12. TRANSPARENCY

An SSI ecosystem shall empower identity rights holders and all other stakeholders to easily access and verify information necessary to understand the incentives, rules, policies, and algorithms under which agents and other components of SSI ecosystems operate.

contributing authors

AAMIR S. ABDULLAH (Livebook) is currently a law librarian in Colorado. He practiced law for five years in Texas, where he handled both state and federal cases. He is passionate about access to justice and the intersection of law and technology. He has been involved with Internetbar.org, Houston Legal Hackers, and the Sovrin Guardianship Task Force.

NACHO ALAMILLO (chapter 24) is a practicing European lawyer and managing partner at Astrea and CISO at Logalty. He also collaborates with the iDerTec Research group (University of Murcia) and serves as chief trust officer at Alastria Blockchain Ecosystem. He is involved in standardization activities including ETSI TC ESI, CEN-CLC/JTC19,ISO TC 307, and ISO/IEC-JTC1/SC27.

CHRISTOPHER ALLEN, @ChristopherA (appendix C), is an entrepreneur and technologist who specializes in collaboration, security, and trust. He worked with Netscape to develop SSL and co-authored the IETF TLS internet draft that is at the heart of secure commerce on the web. More recently, he was principal architect at Blockstream. Christopher is co-chair of the W3C Credentials CG, working on standards for decentralized identity, and founder of Blockchain Commons. He also founded and facilitates the semi-annual Rebooting the Web of Trust design workshops.

SHANNON APPELCLINE, @appelcline (chapter 21), is a technical writer with considerable experience in the blockchain ecosystem. He's worked for ECC cryptography innovator Certicom, Bitcoin leader Blockstream, and blockchain property-rights pioneer Bitmark. He's also the editor in chief for Rebooting the Web of Trust, where he's shepherded to publication over 40 papers on next-generation decentralized technologies.

JEFF ARESTY (Livebook) is an international business and e-commerce lawyer with over 40 years of experience in international business law, cyberlaw, and technology transfer. He is a leading expert in online dispute resolution and committed to promoting human rights through the use of technology and online justice systems. He founded Internetbar.org, Inc. (IBO) in April 2005 to create sustainable income opportunities for individuals from developing areas and conflict zones. By developing a harmonized legal framework for online interactions, IBO has been able to work with local partners worldwide, empowering their communities by using technology, communication, and innovative social and economic justice initiatives.

 TIM BOUMA, @trbouma (chapter 23), is a senior analyst for digital identity within the Cyber Security Division of the Office of Chief Information Officer, Government of Canada. He is the principal author of the Government of Canada Treasury Board policy instruments for identity management and the lead analyst for the development of the Pan-Canadian Trust Framework. He has authored or contributed to various policy and strategy papers, including the Pan-Canadian Assurance Model, the Pan-Canadian Approach to Trusting Identities, and Federating Identity Management in the Government of Canada.

 **DR. DANIEL BURNETT, @DanielCBurnett (chapter 7)**, has been at the forefront of key web and internet standards for two decades. He has been the chair or co-chair of multiple working groups in W3C and IETF and past chairman of the board of the VoiceXML Forum and is currently a director of the IEEE-ISTO. His career has taken him from Southwestern Bell and Nuance through Voxeo, Tropo, and now ConsenSys, in the PegaSys standards group. He is a co-editor of the Verifiable Credentials Data Model specification and a co-chair of the Verifiable Claims Working Group at W3C.

 **DAVID W. CHADWICK (chapter 7)** is a professor of information systems security at the University of Kent, UK. He has been working on distributed authorization systems for over 20 years and was the architect of the PERMIS authorization infrastructure, the first implementation of X.509 attribute certificates. He has contributed to international standards for over 30 years, has co-authored two internet RFCs, was the editor of X.518, wrote substantial portions of X.509 privilege management, and is currently an invited expert to the W3C Verifiable Credentials Working Group.

 NATHAN COOPER, @cooper_n_n (Livebook), is a senior advisor for innovation in disaster preparedness at the International Federation of Red Cross and Red Crescent Societies. During the last 20 years he has worked in varied international contexts preparing for and responding to humanitarian emergencies. Most recently, he pulled together a group of organizations to test blockchain as part of a cash-transfer system used to allocate aid to drought affected families in Kenya.

MARCO CUOMO (chapter 22) is a senior digital solutions architect responsible for exploring, engineering, and implementing new technologies such as blockchain, IoT, and API management. He has been with Novartis since 2005. Since 2016, his focus has been on blockchain and exploring various use cases in pharma. He has held various positions in software development, engineering, operations, service management, and solution design.

SANTIAGO DE DIEGO (chapter 19) is a mathematician and IT engineer from the University of Granada (UGR) with a background in pentesting and information security. He has participated in several national and international congresses related to programming and information security. He currently works as a cybersecurity researcher at Tecnalia Research & Innovation, where he does research about cybersecurity for critical infrastructures, distributed ledger technologies, and cryptography.

AMOS DOORNBOS, @AmosfromFaces (Livebook), is currently the disaster management strategy and systems director for World Vision International and a member of the Identity for All Council of the Sovrin Foundation. He has led the turnaround of last-mile digital registration systems for humanitarian organizations. Amos has over 15 years of experience working in and around humanitarian aid in over 25 countries.

RICHARD ESPLIN (chapter 12) is a product leader and technology evangelist. His diverse experience ranges from engineering to sales and marketing in both startups and global companies. He is focused on closing the digital divide by creating open source solutions for SSI at Evernym.

DANIEL FRITZ (chapter 22) is the supply chain domain architect at Novartis, responsible for the architecture vision and selection of emerging technologies that will transform the business. He has 25 years of leadership and supply chain IT experience in the US military, IT consulting, pharmaceutical manufacturing, and global supply chain organizations. He also is APICS CPIM and CSCP certified and has the SCOR-P endorsement.

DANIEL HARDMAN, @dhh1128 (chapters 3 and 5, Livebook), has been building software for several decades. He's led engineering teams at small startups, an incubator, and a continent-spanning business unit at a Fortune 500 company. Daniel has been involved in identity and privacy since his cybersecurity days, and in SSI and blockchain for the past several years, when he was chief architect at Evernym and then principle ecosystem engineer at SICPA. He participated in the initial launch of the Sovrin network and serves as secretary of the Sovrin Technical Governance Board.

DAVID HARNEY (Livebook) was appointed group CEO of Irish Life in July 2016 and has worked at Irish Life for over 30 years. He is a fellow of the Society of Actuaries in Ireland. David's focus is on transforming Ireland's health and financial well-being in the digital age.

JAKE HOSTETLER (Livebook) is an internationally minded writer focused on bringing awareness to the possibilities of blockchain, especially in the space of identity. As a member of team Metadium, he focuses on global partnerships with the goal of making "true" self-sovereign identity a reality. Jake grew up in the US and attended Dickinson College. After a few years in Philadelphia gaining experience in the pharmaceutical industry, he relocated to Aachen, Germany where he began writing and working in the software space. He relocated to Seoul, South Korea to support the team at Metadium.

JASMIN HUBER (Livebook) is a master's student at the Institute of Technology in Carlow, Ireland, majoring in supply chain management. During her bachelor studies in business administration at the University of Bayreuth in Germany, she specialized in the areas of operations management and information systems management. While focusing on business information systems, she became interested in the emerging topic of SSI and subsequently wrote her bachelor's thesis on it. Currently, she aims to combine the research fields of SSI and supply chain management in her master's thesis.

INFOMINER, @infominer33 (chapter 16), is an aspiring cypherpunk and a student of web-work, blockchain, and cryptosystems, with a focus on open source information exchange, decentralized identity, content-creation, and publishing. He is cataloging histories and information related to blockchain and cryptocurrency to make these complex topics more easily navigable. At the time of writing, decentralized identity and histories related to bitcoin are the most thoroughly covered subjects in that effort.

RIEKS JOOSTEN, @TNO_Research (chapter 2), is currently a senior scientist with TNO, where he is the scientific lead of the Self-Sovereign Identity group and the Networked Risk Management group. Since 2014, he has been a contributing expert member of the ISO/IEC JTC1/SC27 WG1 group that manages the 27000 series of IT security standards. He was responsible for architecting the world's fastest asymmetric crypto chip in the mid-1990s and was one of four individuals to create the operating system, system software, and software tools for the first handheld computers of Matsushita.

PAUL KNOWLES (Livebook) is head of the Advisory Council at The Human Colossus Foundation, a non-profit technological organization based in Geneva, Switzerland. He is a decentralized semantics expert whose 25-year career in pharmaceutical biometrics spans work with such companies as Roche, Novartis, GlaxoSmithKline, Amgen, and Pfizer. Paul is the

Inputs and Semantics working group lead at the Trust over IP Foundation, which is standardizing decentralized technologies including Overlays Capture Architecture (OCA) for harmonizing data semantics across data models and data representation formats. Paul is also an active contributor at IEEE, MyData Global, and the Kantara Initiative.

JASON LAW (appendix B) is co-founder and CTO at FixFake. A technologist, innovator, and entrepreneur, Jason's focus is on tools and tech that help us know what we see online is authentic. He was co-founder and CTO at Evernym and the lead architect of the open source distributed ledger technology that was contributed to the Sovrin Foundation to become the Sovrin ledger and then to the Linux Foundation to become the Hyperledger Indy project.

KARLA MCKENNA (Livebook) is head of standards and managing director for GLEIF Americas. An international standards specialist in the area of financial services, Karla is responsible for facilitating the development and implementation of standards at the Global Legal Entity Identifier Foundation (GLEIF). She chaired the International Organization for Standardization Technical Committee 68 (ISO/TC 68), Financial Services, from 2006 to 2018 and continues to work with the committee in the areas of standards interoperability, regulatory use, and best practices for financial services standards. Karla currently serves on the board of XBRL International and is a member of the inaugural board of the Eurofiling Foundation.

DR. ANDRÉ KUDRA (Livebook) is passionate about information security and SSI. He has a diploma plus a doctorate from European Business School (EBS) and a computer science bachelor's degree from James Madison University (USA). Since 2013, he has been CIO of esatus AG, a German tech company with a strong SSI vision. esatus is a Sovrin Founding Steward and a Trust over IP founding and steering member and contributes to the blockchain identity standardization efforts of ISO/TC 307. André is a Sovrin Trustee and a board member of TeleTrusT IT Security Association Germany, where he chairs the Blockchain and Secure Platform working groups.

JACK A. NAJARIAN (Livebook) is a corporate and real estate attorney who lives and practices in the Houston, Texas area. He primarily represents middle market companies and entrepreneurs and focuses on advising and representing clients in business transactions and structuring their businesses. In his free time, he enjoys volunteering and helping organizations like the Internet Bar Organization, of which he currently is a member, tackle large and important global legal issues such as digital identity.

DR. MANREET NIJJAR, @truu_id (Livebook), is a physician in infectious diseases and general internal medicine. He has worked for over a decade in frontline services for the National Health Service (NHS) in the UK. For the last four years, he has focused on the role of decentralized digital identity in healthcare ecosystems. He is a member of the project team evaluating the uses of distributed ledger technology in the NHS. He sits on an all-party Parliamentary subcommittee advisory group for blockchain and healthcare and co-chairs the IEEE pre-standards group for decentralized digital identity in healthcare.

DARRELL O'DONNELL, @darrello (chapter 9), is a technology entrepreneur, board member, and advisor for multiple investors, corporations, governments, and military clients. He is currently focused on decentralized identity and how it impacts finance, health care, and other industries. He actively volunteers in multiple technology and business communities and mentors young technologists.

DANIEL PARAMO (chapter 13) is the co-founder of swys and the founder of Echo Intelligent Solutions. In addition, he is an advisor for Xertify, a company that uses verifiable credentials, blockchain, and analytics to facilitate communication, issuance, and verification between students, workers, and institutions. He founded several startups associated with blockchain and the sharing economy and is a former account executive at Learning Machine and former business development and engineer at Bell Flight.

SUNGJUN (CALVIN) PARK (Livebook) focuses on developing new business to provide blockchain-bases services at Coinplug, Inc. He spent most of his young life in Toronto, where he studied computer science at the University of Waterloo. He later moved to Korea, his home country, and changed his field of studies to international business. His career began as a data scientist at Delivery Heros Korea, where he analyzed how different environmental factors and incentive models influence human behavior when purchasing goods and services. Sungjun currently leads multiple DID projects in South America and Southeast Asia, as well as other projects utilizing blockchain technology in South Korea.

SCOTT PERRY (Livebook) is the principal of Scott S. Perry CPA, PLLC, a licensed, nationally operated US CPA firm specializing in cybersecurity consulting and audit (and one of only a handful of CPA firms licensed to issue WebTrust opinion reports for certification authorities that issue digital certificates to websites). He has been an advisor and auditor in the US Federal PKI digital identity network since 2005. He is a contributor to the Sovrin Governance Framework and primary author of the Sovrin Trust Assurance Framework. He is a co-chair of the Trust Over IP Foundation Governance Stack Working Group.

JOHN PHILLIPS, @11dot2john (chapter 18), has over 20 years of international experience in sectors ranging from the space industry to finance and higher education. Powered by the 460degrees Expert Management Agency, he leads emerging technology and the work 460degrees performs with the education sector. John is currently a co-chair of the Sovrin Working Group on Guardianship and a member of the Working

Group on Credentialing for the National Blockchain Roadmap Steering Committee for the Australian Government's Department of Industry, Science, Energy, and Resources.

CHRIS RACZKOWSKI (chapter 20) has 25+ years of international professional experience with both large multinational corporations and startup companies, where he has helped to lead the development and commercialization of numerous technologies. His work responsibilities have included R&D, engineering, and executive business leadership roles. During the last three years he has helped to found and lead several companies, all of which are focused on SSI use cases, and he is the chairman of the Sovrin Foundation board of trustees.

DAVE ROBERTS (chapter 23) is a senior analyst for digital identity in the Office of the Chief Information Officer, Government of Canada. He has authored or contributed to various Government of Canada Treasury Board standards and specifications, including the Pan-Canadian Identity Management Validation Standard and the Pan-Canadian Identity Management Information Exchange Specification. Currently, Dave is the senior analyst for the development of the Public Sector Profile of the Pan-Canadian Trust Framework. He has over 35 years of experience working as an IT professional for the Government of Canada.

DR. ANDREW ROWAN (chapter 20) has more than 40 years of experience in animal welfare science and animal and environmental advocacy, including advocating the value of digital identities for animals to promote their welfare. He has served on many government and corporate consultative committees and numerous boards of national and international NGOs and most recently served as the CEO of Humane Society International along with the Board Chair of the Wildlife Land Trust of the HSUS.

TIMOTHY RUFF (appendix B) is a general partner of Digital Trust Ventures and currently CEO of Credential Master. He was the co-founder of Evernym and co-inventor of the Sovrin ledger. Timothy is the host of *Breaking Silos*, the first podcast dedicated to the business models made possible by SSI and verifiable credentials.

MARKUS SABADELLO, @peacekeeper (chapters 8 and 14), was an early participant in decentralization movements such as the Federated Social Web, Respect Network, and FreedomBox. He has worked as an analyst and consultant at the Harvard Berkman Center for Internet & Society, the MIT Media Lab's Human Dynamics Group, the World Economic Forum, and the Personal Data Ecosystem Consortium. In 2015, he founded Danube Tech, a consulting and development company that contributes to the Sovrin Foundation, the Decentralized Identity Foundation (DIF), and various SSI projects around the world. He is also a co-editor of the W3C DID Core 1.0 Specification.

CHRISTOPH SCHNEIDER (Livebook) is head of IT development and operations at the Global Legal Entity Identifier Foundation (GLEIF). In June 2017, Christoph joined the International Organization for Standardization (ISO) as co-leader of the Technical Committee 68 FinTech Technical Advisory Group (ISO TC 68 FinTech TAG) work stream dealing with digital identity. He has extensive experience in developing and implementing solutions in financial technology. He holds a MSc in business information systems from Technische Universität Darmstadt.

DOC SEARLS, @dsearls (foreword and appendix B), is one of four co-authors of The Cluetrain Manifesto, the book that single-handedly redefined how marketing would work on the Internet. He has been one of the world's leading advocates for the "voice of the customer." His 2012 book *The Intention Economy*, published by *Harvard Business Review*, described the transformation happening in business as customers finally take charge. The term *self-sovereign identity* was first coined on his Harvard Berkman mailing list on vendor relationship management (VRM). Doc is also one of the founders of the Internet Identity Workshop where the core tenets of SSI have been forged over the last 15 years.

JOHANNES SEDLMEIR (Livebook) is a researcher at Project Group Business & Information Systems Engineering at Fraunhofer FIT and pursues his PhD in information systems at the FIM Research Center, University of Bayreuth. His focus is on technical challenges and business implications of applying distributed ledger technologies (blockchains) in the public and private sectors, including scalability and performance challenges, energy consumption myths, and privacy and confidentiality issues. He received his MSc in theoretical and mathematical physics.

OSCAR LAGE SERRANO, @Oscar_Lage (chapter 19), is global head of cybersecurity at Tecnalia, a member of the advisory board of several companies, and leader of the first industrial blockchain laboratory in Europe. He is a member of the Enterprise Ethereum Alliance and Hyperledger, coordinator of the industrial node of the multisectorial Spanish Blockchain network (Alastria), a member of Blockchain Expert Policy Advisory Board at OECD, vice president of the blockchain committee of AMETIC, and a member of the main international forums of cybersecurity at the European Cyber Security Organization and the Center for Industrial Cybersecurity, among others.

AMIT SHARMA (Livebook) has engaged in a myriad of roles that intersect financial markets, risk management, regulatory compliance, and development. He is the founder and CEO of FinClusive, a hybrid fin-/reg-tech company dedicated to financial inclusion by providing a full-stack financial crimes compliance (FCC) platform with digital access to accounts and multi-form payments. Prior to FinClusive, Amit worked in both the public and private sectors, including with Empowerment Capital and Mitsubishi UFJ Securities and at the US Treasury Department; there, he was first at the inception of the Office of Terrorism and Financial Intelligence (TFI), where he drove strategies to combat transnational illicit finance threats, and later chief of staff to the deputy secretary and advisor to Treasury's senior team under Secretary Henry Paulson.

MICHAEL SHEA (chapter 19) has over 30 years of experience in the technology sector. He is currently the managing director of The Dingle Group, leads the Self-Sovereign Identity and IoT Task Force for the Sovrin Foundation, and is co-chair of the Trust and Identity Subgroup of the IEEE P2933 Clinical IoT Working Group. He has founded multiple businesses and is an Advisor to FootprintProject.org and eWINGZ.aero.

PHILIP SHELDRAKE (Livebook) is a researcher with the AKASHA Foundation. He is a chartered engineer with experience and expertise spanning digital innovation, process engineering, systems thinking, organizational design, marketing, and communications.

JAMIE SMITH (Livebook) is senior director, business development, at Evernym. With over 15 years of experience designing and delivering digital technologies and disruptive business models worldwide, he specializes in helping organizations embrace new SSI approaches and creating new digital ecosystems to drive growth.

SAMUEL M. SMITH PH.D. (chapter 10) works at the intersection of AI, blockchain, and decentralized identity systems as both an entrepreneur and strategic consultant. He has written and continues to write seminal white papers on decentralized identity, reputation AI, distributed computing, and machine learning and is active in shaping the underlying standards and driving their adoption. He was principal investigator on numerous federally funded research projects. He is the creator of KERI, and his early white papers provided inspiration for Sovrin and SSI.

OLIVER TERBU, @OliverTerbu (appendix D), has been an identity architect with ConsenSys/uPort since 2018. He is also an active member of standardization bodies and working groups such as the W3C Credentials Community Group, the W3C Verifiable Claims Working Group, and the Decentralized Identity Foundation working groups. He participates in the Ethereum Enterprise Alliance; the OpenID Foundation; ISO/IEC C307 WG2 Blockchain Privacy, Security, and Identity; and the CEN/CENELEC Focus Group on Blockchain and Distributed Ledger Technologies. Until 2018, he was a member of ISO/IEC JTC1/SC17 WG10 and coordinated the activities of online mobile driver license profiles.

DR. M. OSKAR VAN DEVENTER, @TNO_Research (chapter 2), is a senior scientist with TNO on blockchain networking and SSI. His focus is on public-private R&D partnerships, European collaborative R&D projects, and international standards. He is an active contributor to international standards bodies. Oskar is an assigned member of the Economic Advisory Council of Sovrin, the world-leading blockchain for SSI. He is also leading several projects on blockchain and SSI in the Techruption program.

FABIAN VOGELSTELLER, @feindura (appendix D), has built many open source projects, including an open source content management system (feindura.org). He joined the Ethereum Foundation in July 2015 and has built some of its core applications, such as the Ethereum wallet and the Mist browser. He worked on the RPC API and developer tools like web3.js—Ethereum's most-used JavaScript library. He also proposed the ERC 20 token standard and ERC 725 Proxy Account standard. He is currently building a blockchain called LUKSO for the fashion and design space.

PHIL WINDLEY, @windley (appendix B), is a principal engineer in the Office of Information Technology at Brigham Young University (BYU). He was the founding chair of the Sovrin Foundation, serving from 2016 to 2020. He is also the co-founder and organizer of the Internet Identity Workshop, serves as an adjunct professor of computer science at BYU, writes the popular *Technometria* blog, and is the author of the books *The Live Web* (2011) and *Digital Identity* (2005). Phil has been a computer science professor at BYU, founder and CTO of several internet technology companies, and served as CIO for the State of Utah. He holds a PhD in computer science from University of California, Davis.

STEPHAN WOLF (Livebook) is the CEO of the Global Legal Entity Identifier Foundation (GLEIF). Since January 2017, Stephan has been the co-convener of the International Organization for Standardization Technical Committee 68 FinTech Technical Advisory Group (ISO TC 68 FinTech TAG). In January 2017, he was named one of the Top 100 Leaders in Identity by One World Identity. He has extensive experience in establishing data operations and global implementation strategy. He co-founded IS Innovative Software GmbH in 1989 and served first as its managing director. He was later named spokesman of the executive board of its successor, IS.Teledata AG. This company ultimately became part of Interactive Data Corporation, where Stephan held the role of CTO.

KALIYA "IDENTITY WOMAN" YOUNG, @IdentityWoman (chapter 16 and Livebook), is the ecosystems director at the Covid Credentials Initiative. She co-founded the Internet Identity Workshop in 2005 with Doc Searls and Phil Windley. She is the author of *The Domains of Identity: A Framework for Understanding Identity Systems in Contemporary Society* (2020) and *A Comprehensive Guide to Self-Sovereign Identity* (2019). In 2012, she was named a

Young Global Leader by the World Economic Forum. In 2017, she received a MSc in identity management and security from UT Austin. She is a 2019 New America India-US Public Interest Technology Fellow. In January 2020, she was featured in *Wired UK*.

LIWEN ZHANG (chapter 20) has 10+ years of HR and operations management experience with international companies in Beijing, where she was a strategic business partner and project manager with a variety of global firms. Liwen is also an animal welfare advocate. As part of her advocacy, she co-founded the REAL animal welfare organization in China. She is also a co-founder and leader of the Canadian company ID Lynx Ltd. and the DignifID Animals Foundation, both of which are developing SSI use cases to support animal welfare.

SAJIDA ZOUARHI, @Saj_JZ (chapter 6), began her career as a research engineer at Orange Labs and the Computer Science Lab of Grenoble. In 2015, she co-founded the Kidner Project, a privacy-preserving distributed matching system for kidney transplants. She worked as a blockchain architect with leaders in the field such as ConsenSys, where she co-founded HellHound in 2018, a decentralized blind computation platform. In 2019 she became chief technology strategist of Nomadic Labs, a Tezos core R&D center. In 2020, she created Philea, a DAO-based platform using DeFi for sustainable social impact.

BRENT ZUNDEL (chapter 6) is a crypto engineer. He was an engineer for industrial control systems and wrote software for testing product quality before beginning work for Evernym, where he helps design privacy-preserving protocols for credential exchange. Brent also works closely with the Sovrin Foundation, a non-profit dedicated to providing a global public utility for identity, and with the W3C Verifiable Claims Working Group, who are designing an interoperable data model for verifiable credentials. Brent is also co-chair of the W3C Decentralized Identifiers (DIDs) Working Group.

index